LANDMARK CASES IN PRIVATE INTERNATIONAL LAW

This collection of essays contains in-depth analyses of 22 landmark cases in private international law, from *Penn v Lord Baltimore* in 1750 to *Brownlie v FS Cairo (Nile Plaza) LLC* in 2021. The contributors are experts drawn from academia and practice as well as from the bench.

Case law has been a central driver in the legal development of the English conflict of laws. Judge-made law does not just supply a source of law itself but also acts as the crucible in which other sources of law – legislation, international Treaty, European regulation, and ideas generated by jurists such as Joseph Story and Albert Venn Dicey – have been tested and applied.

This book sheds new light on the past and future evolution of private international law by focusing on the landmark cases which have fundamentally shaped the way that we think about this subject. The focus is on the English common law, but landmarks in Scotland, Australia and Canada are covered as well. Many of them concern disputes between commercial parties; others deal with issues such as marriage and domicile; and some arise from controversies in political, constitutional and international affairs.

The landmark cases tackled in this collection address significant issues in civil jurisdiction, governing law, foreign judgments and public policy. The essays place those landmarks in their historical context, explain their contemporary importance and consider their future relevance.

Landmark Cases in Private International Law

Edited by
William Day
and
Louise Merrett

•HART•

OXFORD • LONDON • NEW YORK • NEW DELHI • SYDNEY

HART PUBLISHING

Bloomsbury Publishing Plc

Kemp House, Chawley Park, Cumnor Hill, Oxford, OX2 9PH, UK

1385 Broadway, New York, NY 10018, USA

29 Earlsfort Terrace, Dublin 2, Ireland

HART PUBLISHING, the Hart/Stag logo, BLOOMSBURY and the Diana logo are trademarks of Bloomsbury Publishing Plc

First published in Great Britain 2023

A catalogue record for this book is available from the British Library.

A catalogue record for this book is available from the Library of Congress.

ISBN: HB: 978-1-50995-264-9
ePDF: 978-1-50995-266-3
ePub: 978-1-50995-265-6

Typeset by Compuscript Ltd, Shannon

Foreword

Both as a practising barrister and as a judge, many of the cases I have found most interesting involve private international law. Typically, they pose intricate and often difficult questions of law to be addressed against what is, or should be, a reasonably well-defined factual background. This provides the perfect setting for stimulating legal argument and challenging decision making, as is well illustrated by the twenty-two landmark cases which are described and analysed in this collection of essays. Each of these cases is of legal interest and significance but often their facts, or the wider factual context in which they arise, add to their interest, a feature vividly brought out in the book.

As the editors point out in their introduction, there was much debate over what makes a case a 'landmark' when the draft chapters for the book were presented and discussed at a conference in Cambridge. Having participated as a barrister (*Fiona Trust & Holding Corp v Privalov*) and as a judge (*Enka Insaat Ve Sanayi AS v OOO Insurance Company Chubb*) in two of the chosen cases, I can say that that they did not appear at the time to involve the laying of landmarks. Certainly, they were and are important, but only time will tell whether they are truly landmarks.

As the chosen cases show, the common law is a river which flows continually. What seemed to be a turning point at the time may prove not to be as the river flows elsewhere. Conversely, what seemed to be a mere meander may in fact prove to be a significant turning point. Collections of landmark cases such as this also highlight the vibrancy of the common law. While the main focus of the book is English common law, there are also chapters considering Australian, Canadian and Scottish cases.

A wide range of distinguished authors have contributed to this collection. Many have an academic background while others are serving judges, barristers and solicitors. Each author was allowed to choose his or her favoured landmark and the result is a wide tapestry. The cases chosen span the period from 1750 to 2021. As such, they provide an interesting historical perspective. It is noteworthy that the selection involves eight cases decided between 1865 and 1882 (*Peninsular and Oriental Steam Navigation Co v Shand* and *Lloyd v Guibert*; *Bell v Kennedy* and *Udny v Udny*; *Godard v Grey* and *Schibsby v Westenholz*; *Phillips v Eyre*; *Abouloff v Oppenheimer*) but only one (*AM Luther Co v James Sagor & Co*) decided in the 73 years between 1882 and 1955. There is then a flurry of cases towards the end of the twentieth century, including Lord Goff's seminal decisions in *Spiliada Maritime Corp v Cansulex Ltd (The Spiliada)* and *Societe Nationale Industrielle Aerospatiale v Lee Kui Jak*.

Looking to the future, as Andrew Dickinson does in the final chapter of the book, a significant recent landmark has been the end of what the editors describe as 'the UK's European adventure' on 31 December 2020. The reversion to common law rules of jurisdiction is undoubtedly going to lead to increased focus on and litigation over jurisdictional matters and it will be interesting to see how the experience of the European adventure influences future common law developments. Moreover, as Andrew Dickinson points out, the status of the Rome I and Rome II Regulations as retained EU law could lead to a 'choice of law revival' as the limited body of retained EU case law is distinctively developed by the UK courts. As this fascinating collection of landmark cases shows – time will tell.

The Rt Hon Lord Hamblen of Kersey
1 October 2022

Contents

List of Contributors

Ian Bergson is a barrister at Fountain Court Chambers, London.

Adrian Briggs KC (Hon) is Emeritus Professor of Private International Law and Emeritus Fellow of St Edmund Hall, University of Oxford.

Janeen Carruthers is Professor of Private Law, University of Glasgow.

Elizabeth Crawford is Professor Emeritus of Private International Law, University of Glasgow.

William Day is a barrister at 3 Verulam Buildings, London and Fellow of Downing College, University of Cambridge.

Andrew Dickinson is Professor of Law and Fellow of St Catherine's College, University of Oxford.

Joshua Folkard is a barrister at Twenty Essex, London, and Associate Lecturer (Teaching), University College London.

Sir David Foxton is a High Court Judge assigned to the King's Bench Division and Judge in Charge of the Commercial Court.

Uglješa Grušić is Associate Professor, University College London.

Trevor Hartley is Professor Emeritus of Law, London School of Economics.

David Joseph KC is a barrister at Essex Court Chambers, London.

Mary Keyes is Professor of Law, Griffith University.

Alexander Layton KC is a barrister at Twenty Essex, London and a Visiting Professor, King's College London.

Louise Merrett is Professor of International Commercial Law and Vice Master, Trinity College, University of Cambridge.

Alex Mills is Professor of Public and Private International Law, University College London.

Paul Mitchell is Professor of Laws, University College London.

Edwin Peel is Professor of Law and Fellow of Keble College, Oxford and a barrister at One Essex Court, London.

Benjamin Phelps is a barrister at 2 Temple Gardens, London.

Stephen GA Pitel is Professor of Law, Western University.

Pippa Rogerson is Professor of Private International Law and Master of Gonville and Caius College, University of Cambridge.

Máire Ní Shúilleabháin is Associate Professor, University College Dublin.

Sir Marcus Smith is a High Court Judge assigned to the Chancery Division and President of the Competition Appeal Tribunal.

Table of Cases

References are to page numbers

Table of UK Legislation

References are to page numbers

Statutes

Table of Overseas Legislation

References are to page numbers

AUSTRALIA

CANADA

UNITED STATES

Table of International Material

References are to page numbers

Introduction

WILLIAM DAY AND LOUISE MERRETT

IN 1858, THE barrister John Westlake published the first English treatise on private international law. His preface emphasised the importance of the case law to the subject:[1]

> … the duty [is to take] as groundwork the English decisions, and not the writings of foreign jurists, though using the latter freely for collateral and subordinate purposes. Such a course implies no disrespect to the great foreign lawyers who have created this portion of juristic science, but is made necessary by the binding authority of precedents among us, from the moment at least that enough of those precedents has accumulated to cover the field; and that this time has arrived is shown by the number of English cases here collected ….

It is hard not to see this as a rebuke to Joseph Story, the American academic and later Associate Justice of the Supreme Court of the United States, whose *Commentaries on the Conflict of Laws*, first published in 1834, lamented that:[2]

> Until a comparatively recent period, neither the English Lawyers, nor the English Judges seem to have their attention drawn towards [the conflict of laws], as a great branch of international jurisprudence, which they were required to administer. And, as far as their researches appear as yet to have gone, they are less profound and satisfactory, than their admirable expositions of municipal law … The subject has been discussed with much more fulness, learning, and ability by the foreign Jurists of continental Europe … I am not aware, that the works of these eminent Jurists have been cited at the English Bar; and I should draw the conclusion, that they are in great measure, if not altogether, unknown to the studies of Westminster Hall.

The landmark cases discussed in this collection of essays suggest – albeit with the benefit of hindsight – that Story rather than Westlake had the better understanding of the relative immaturity of English private international law in the mid nineteenth century. With one exception,[3] all of the cases in this book postdate Westlake's *Treatise*. In particular, as Lord Hamblen touches on in the foreword, it was a cluster of cases in the second half of the nineteenth century that established that parties could choose the law governing their contracts;[4]

[1] J Westlake, *A Treatise on Private International Law* (London, W Maxwell, 1858) vii.

[2] J Story, *Commentaries on the Conflict of Laws* (Boston, Hilliard Gray & Co, 1834) v–vi.

[3] *Penn v Lord Baltimore* (1750) 1 Ves Sen 444, 27 ER 1132, discussed in ch 1.

[4] *The Peninsula and Oriental Steam Navigation Co v Shand* [1865] 3 Moo NS 272, 16 ER 103 and *Lloyd v Guibert* (1865) LR 1 QB 115, discussed in ch 2.

that torts were to be governed by both English law and the law of the place where the wrong was committed;[5] that domicile of origin survived until another was acquired by choice, but original domicile could be revived once that choice had lapsed;[6] that foreign judgments could be recognised and enforced as a matter of obligation where the defendant either was within the territorial jurisdiction of the foreign court when the proceedings began or consensually participated in those proceedings;[7] and that such obligations arising from foreign judgments could be unravelled by fraud.[8]

These cases, which coincided with the first era of globalisation, established two principles which continue to animate modern English private international law: respect for not just the territorial sovereignty of other nations (the 'territoriality principle')[9] but also for party autonomy (the 'autonomy principle'). Yet it is also striking that none of these nineteenth century landmark cases were concerned with the law of civil jurisdiction. The landmarks in jurisdiction coincided with a later period of globalisation after the Second World War; most notably those associated with Henry Brandon in a line of cases on jurisdiction agreements including *The Eleftheria*;[10] and those associated with Robert Goff in his later decisions on the assertion or allocation of jurisdiction, including in *Spiliada* and *Aérospatiale*.[11] Today it remains jurisdiction rather than governing law or foreign judgments which generates most of the significant new cases in the conflict of laws, although a clean division between those branches of private international law is self-evidently impossible: for example, jurisdiction disputes also throw up issues of applicable law, as demonstrated by the recent Supreme Court decisions in *Enka v Chubb* and *Brownlie*.[12]

This book contains in-depth analyses of 22 landmark cases in private international law. The majority of the chapters were discussed as draft papers at a conference held by the Cambridge Private Law Centre at Downing College on 7 and 8 April 2022, coinciding (although this was not intentional on the part of the editors) with the centenary of the death of Albert Venn Dicey,[13] whose

[5] *Phillips v Eyre* (1870–71) LR 6 QB 1, discussed in ch 5.

[6] *Bell v Kennedy* (1868) 6 M (HL) 69 and *Udny v Udny* (1869) 7 M (HL) 89, discussed in ch 3.

[7] *Godard v Gray* (1870) LR 6 QB 139 and *Schibsby v Westenholz* (1870) LR 6 QB 155, discussed in ch 4.

[8] *Abouloff v Oppenheimer & Co* (1882) 10 QBD 295, discussed in ch 6.

[9] Also sometimes simply called 'comity', although that word (or that definition) is not free from controversy.

[10] *Owners of Cargo Lately Laden on Board the Eleftheria v Owners of the Eleftheria* [1970] P 94 (Ad), discussed in ch 10.

[11] *Spiliada Maritime Corporation v Cansulex Ltd* [1987] 1 AC 460 (HL) and *Société Nationale Industrielle Aérospatiale v Lee Kui Jak* [1987] AC 871 (HL), discussed in chs 11 and 12.

[12] *Enka Insaat Ve Sanayi AS v OOO Insurance Company Chubb* [2020] UKSC 38, [2020] 1 WLR 4117, *Four Seasons Holdings Inc v Brownlie* [2017] UKSC 80, [2018] 1 WLR 192, and *FS Cairo (Nile Plaza) LLC v Brownlie* [2021] UKSC 45, [2021] 3 WLR 1011, discussed in chs 17 and 18.

[13] We are grateful to Andrew Dickinson for bringing to our attention and assuming (rather generously!) that we were aware of and had deliberately chosen the dates on that basis.

1896 *Digest of the Law of England with reference to the Conflict of Laws* – which aimed to codify 'the principles adhered to by English judges when dealing with the conflict of laws'[14] – combined the best of Story's more theoretical and Westlake's more doctrinal analysis, and rapidly supplanted both of them as the principal textbook in the area. We cannot put it any better than Andrew Dickinson did at the conference: we could still have had a collection of essays on landmark cases in private international law if Dicey's *Digest* had never been written, but the list of cases (at least those after 1896) would likely have looked somewhat different.

While cases are an important driver for the development of private international law, of course they are far from being the only source. Not only is this an area where individual commentators such as Story and Dicey have had an outsized influence, the modern law has been increasingly shaped by legislation – not just the Victorian rules that created the structure for service out of the jurisdiction that remains recognisable today, but also in the tide of European instruments which came in during the Goffian revolution in the law of jurisdiction, and receded only recently. Nonetheless, the case law occupies a special place in private international law, since it does not just supply a source of law itself but also acts as the crucible in which these other sources of law are ultimately tested and applied. For those reasons, we suggest, scholarship focused on landmark cases in private international law is a worthwhile endeavour.

We hope the reader will find in these pages not just historical analyses of the conflict of laws, but also some explanation for why the modern law is as it is (an important function of any good history), as well as consideration of the direction in which the law might next go (for which Andrew Dickinson's 'scanning of the horizon' in chapter nineteen is essential reading). In a common law system, detailed examination of the case law remains the best way of distilling and understanding the underlying principles of private international law. While some Australian, Canadian and Scottish authority is considered in this collection,[15] the primary focus in this collection is on the English conflicts of laws. And, as matter of editorial policy, we have kept the focus within English law on the 'common law' conflicts of law, rather than the UK's European adventure between 1 January 1987 and 31 December 2020.[16]

The idea of scholarship focused on leading cases is, of course, well-established. The idea which animates the *Landmark Cases* series is that such cases can be characterised as historical events, a proper understanding of which requires looking at the context *beyond* just the law report.[17] That is true for a

[14] AV Dicey, *A Digest of the Law of England with reference to the Conflict of Laws* (London, Stevens & Sons, 1896) iv.

[15] See chs 3, 13 and 14.

[16] Although that is not to minimise the significant and long-lasting impact of those 34 years, especially for governing law, where the law has been domesticated essentially unchanged.

[17] See, eg, AWB Simpson, *Leading Cases in the Common Law* (Oxford, Clarendon Press, 1995) 10–12.

number of the landmark authorities considered in this addition to the series. Cases such as *Penn v Lord Baltimore*,[18] and *Phillips v Eyre*,[19] cannot be divorced from their wider colonial setting. Historical context similarly sheds new light on the Foreign Office's intervention in *Luther v James Sagor & Co*,[20] given the UK-Soviet treaty of 1921 was settled on the basis that it could be terminated if the appeal in those proceedings was not successful. The difficult common law marriage exception made in *Taczanowksa v Taczanowski* to the normal choice of law rules for the formal validity of marriage is perhaps best understood as a humane policy decision to avoid invalidating thousands of marriages after the Second World War; and no doubt the gendered and Christian-orientated formulation of that exception must itself be understood as reflecting the then-prevailing 1950s social attitudes.[21] The approach to jurisdiction clauses in *Fiona Trust* is in part explained by Lord Hoffmann's broader theories of contract law.[22] And the Canadian expansion of the test for enforcing foreign judgments in *Morguard Investments Ltd v De Savoye* can in large part be understood as belonging to an era where free trade ideals dominated.[23]

Inevitably, perhaps, for a gathering of private international lawyers, one pervading theme at the conference in Cambridge was characterisation. What makes a case a 'landmark'? The Oxford English Dictionary offers various definitions of an object described in such a way: '... set up to mark the boundary line'; '... which, by its conspicuousness, serves as a guide in the direction of one's course'; and '... which marks or is associated with some event or stage in a process; ... [especially] which marks a period or turning-point in the history of a thing'. When deployed to characterise a case, there is obviously some flexibility in the concept. A landmark can represent a starting or turning point (eg, choice of law in contract in *Lloyd v Guibert*,[24] now embodied as the 'cornerstone' of the Rome I Regulation),[25] or a milestone in the journey thereafter (such as *The Eleftheria*,[26] being neither the beginning nor the end of the development of the modern law on jurisdiction agreements), or the end point (probably the case for *Spiliada*).[27] But there are difficult cases at the borderline. Can House of Lords authorities on domicile – even though still good law – really be regarded as landmarks when they receive few modern citations?[28] Can *Godard v Gray* and

[18] *Penn v Lord Baltimore* (n 3). See ch 1.

[19] *Phillips v Eyre* (n 5). See ch 5.

[20] *Aksionairnoye Obschestvo Dlia Mechaniches-Koyi Obrabotky Diereva A M Luther (Company for Mechanical Woodworking A M Luther) v James Sagor and Company* [1921] 3 KB 532 (CA). See ch 7.

[21] *Taczanowksa v Taczanowski* [1957] P 301 (CA). See ch 9.

[22] *Fiona Trust & Holding Corp v Privalov* [2007] UKHL 40, [2007] 4 All ER 951. See ch 16.

[23] *Morguard Investments Ltd v De Savoye* [1990] 3 SCR 1077 (Can SC). See ch 13.

[24] *Lloyd v Guilbert* (n 4).

[25] Regulation (EC) No 593/3008 (Rome I).

[26] *The Eleftheria* (n 10).

[27] *Spiliada* (n 11).

[28] *Bell v Kennedy* (n 6) and *Udny v Udny* (n 6). See ch 3.

Schibsby v Westenholz still be landmarks when the obligation theory for foreign judgments struggles to explain large parts of the positive law?[29] On the other hand, is *Abouloff v Oppenheimer* now a stronger candidate for landmark status now that the law on re-opening domestic judgments has moved in the direction of its approach for re-opening foreign judgments?[30]

At the conference we adopted a thematic approach to the papers and, although in this book they appear chronologically, in the remainder of this introduction we will adopt a similar thematic approach. Beginning with jurisdiction, *Spiliada* – tackled by Edwin Peel in chapter eleven – is probably the case that most lawyers would immediately cite if asked to name a landmark case in private international law.[31] *Spilada* clarified and confirmed the analysis of the jurisdictional framework still used today by the courts, marking a decisive break with the governing principles from the earlier part of the twentieth century. Yet, as Pippa Rogerson pointed out at the conference, despite their continuing application in practice, the *Spiliada* line of cases also must be viewed a product of their time: while modern commercial life made cross border disputes increasingly common in the English courts in the 1970s and 1980s, those courts were still primarily operating in a paper-based system with witnesses generally only able to give evidence in an English trial by attending in person. In twenty-first century disputes, when identifying the natural forum at the first stage of the *forum conveniens* analysis, practical matters – such as the whereabouts of the parties and of factual and expert witnesses – surely now carry less weight given modern technology available to the parties, their witnesses, and the courts.

There was a broad consensus at the conference that Peel was right to suggest that the really difficult arguments in practice under the *Spiliada* framework now arise at the second stage, when it is alleged that there is a real risk that justice will not be achieved in the forum that otherwise would be the proper place for the resolution of the dispute.[32] There was some discussion at the conference about whether the House of Lords had been right in *Lubbe v Cape* to exclude public interest considerations not directly related to the interests of the parties.[33] For example, docketing considerations might be important to an under-resourced justice system: it might be said that foreign claimants should not be allowed to use the English courts where it would severely delay the just determination of disputes brought by domestic litigants whose taxes underwrite that system.

[29] *Godard v Gray* (n 7) and *Schibsby v Westenholz* (n 7). See ch 4.

[30] *Abouloff v Oppenheimer* (n 8). See ch 6.

[31] *Spiliada* (n 11).

[32] Of course, *Spiliada* itself was not really such a case: the claimant was saved (in circumstances where most factors pointed to another forum) at the first stage by a 'bootstraps' argument, relying on the resource which had already been invested in litigating in England to justify continuing to litigate in England. *Brownlie*, discussed in ch 18, is a modern equivalent: W Day, 'Pleading and Proving Foreign Law' (2022) 81 *Cambridge Law Journal* 24, 25.

[33] *Lubbe v Cape plc* [2000] 4 All ER 268 (HL) 281 (Lord Bingham) and 286–87 (Lord Hope).

Yet, even if it were right in principle to look beyond the interests of the parties, the picture is not clear cut; while the justice system tries to discourage the importation of certain disputes, such as defamation cases in the King's Bench Division, some specialist courts – most notably the Commercial Court – actively market themselves on the international field as appropriate fora for the resolution of cross-border disputes. The unconscious impact that such extra-curial activity may have on the determination of *forum conveniens* challenges remains unclear.

Chapter twelve by Trevor Hartley on *Aérospatiale*,[34] decided within a year of *Spiliada*, is in some senses *Spiliada*'s mirror image. The question can be put this way: if identification of the natural forum is central to the English court's analysis when exercising jurisdiction, should it also be central to the decision about whether to stop another court exercising jurisdiction? In answering that question in *Aérospatiale*, Lord Goff held that the *Spiliada* principles were relevant but not determinative; the overriding requirement remained whether an injunction was required in the interests of justice. Hartley criticises that as being too broad and uncertain a basis for the English court to interfere with other proceedings. While the anti-suit injunction in *Aérospatiale* was sought from the court which was said by the applicant also to be the natural forum for the dispute in the *Spiliada* sense, at the conference it was noted that an anti-suit injunction remained more problematic when neither sought in those circumstances nor to restrain a breach of a jurisdiction agreement. Nonetheless, the power to make such freestanding orders has been fortified by the Privy Council's recent decision in *Broad Idea v Convoy Collateral* that an injunction can be ordered even where there is no underlying cause of action.[35] Hartley's chapter suggests that the landmark status of *Aérospatiale* has been further enhanced given that the straightjacket on anti-suit injunctions in relation to other Member State courts has been removed by the UK departure from the EU, but also sounds a note of caution as to their efficacy given the capacity of EU Member State courts to issue counter-anti-suit injunctions.

Hartley also calls into question the reality of the claim that an anti-suit injunction does not interfere with the foreign court because it acts *in personam*; he considers this to be 'clearly nonsense'. There was considerable support for that view at the conference, but it does have some intellectual pedigree. Chapter one on *Penn v Lord Baltimore* – which Paul Mitchell has kindly permitted to be reproduced from *Landmark Cases in Equity* – is the most obvious example.[36] There, Lord Hardwicke LC's decision to intervene in the dispute as to the agreed borderline between two North American colonies was premised on the principle that the

[34] *Société Nationale Industrielle Aérospatiale v Lee Kui Jak* (n 11).
[35] *Broad Idea International Ltd v Convoy Collateral Ltd* [2021] UKPC 24, [2022] 2 WLR 703.
[36] *Penn v Lord Baltimore* (n 3). See C Mitchell and P Mitchell, *Landmark Cases in Equity* (Oxford, Hart Publishing, 2012) ch 4.

court 'cannot inforce their own decree *in rem*, in the present case: but that is not an objection against making a decree in the cause; for the strict primary decree in this court as a court of equity is *in personam*'.[37] Mitchell notes that the decision in *Penn v Lord Baltimore* has an uneasy relationship with the principle that the courts will not determine title to foreign land (another aspect of the territoriality principle), and that the context of Lord Hardwicke's decision had complexity and controversy lost in subsequent citation. A good example of the latter point is *The Earl of Portarlington v Soulby*,[38] where Lord Brougham LC was prepared to place substantial weight on a mere passing reference to *Penn v Lord Baltimore* for the *in personam* principle to justify the development of the anti-suit injunction:[39]

> ... nothing can be more unfounded than the doubts of the jurisdiction [in equity]. That is grounded, like all other jurisdiction of the Court, not upon any pretension to the exercise of judicial and administrative rights abroad, but on the circumstance of the person of the party on whom this order is made being within the power of the Court. If the Court can command him to bring home goods from abroad, or to assign chattel interests, or to convey real property locally situate abroad – if, for instance, as in *Penn v Lord Baltimore* ... it can decree the performance of an agreement touching the boundary of a province in North America ... in precisely the like manner it can restrain the party being within the limits of its jurisdiction from doing anything abroad, whether the thing forbidden be a conveyance or other act *in pais*, or the instituting or prosecution of an action in a foreign Court.

A perennial problem in jurisdiction challenges is the standard by which disputed matters need to be determined, at an interlocutory stage, especially where those same matters would also arise for determination at trial if jurisdiction were to be established. Only a move to determining jurisdiction alongside the merits at trial – something which, for example, can be directed in arbitration – would remove the complication of not being able to apply the usual standard of proof, ie the balance of probabilities.[40] In chapter fifteen, Pippa Rogerson traces the development of the *Canada Trust* gloss, requiring a claimant to have 'much the better of the argument' in a jurisdiction application.[41] Rogerson endorses the view that the courts take different approaches to the variety of disputed matters on a jurisdiction challenge:[42] more willing to reach a concluded view on matters of law, and on matters not in issue at trial, but (she suggests) still not willing enough to determine factual issues arising out of disputed evidence. The argument advanced in chapter fifteen is that the courts should not be afraid of making factual findings without the benefit of trial, and possibly in conflict with

[37] *Penn v Lord Baltimore* (n 3) 1139.

[38] *The Earl of Portarlington v Soulby* (1834) 3 My & K 104, 40 ER 40.

[39] ibid, 41–42.

[40] Which is not to say that arbitration proceedings that are not bifurcated do not have their own problems.

[41] *Canada Trust Co v Stolzenberg (No 2)* [1998] 1 WLR 547 (CA).

[42] See also I Bergson and J Folkard, 'Good Arguable Case' in W Day and S Worthington (eds), *Challenging Private Law: Lord Sumption on the Supreme Court* (Oxford, Hart, 2020).

the findings that would be made at trial, since that simply reflects the procedural context in which those findings have to be made; failing to grasp the nettle gives too much of an advantage to claimants who can exploit that uncertainty to insist that there is a triable issue that justifies the assertion of jurisdiction. There was some discussion at the conference as to what extent the recent reformulations of the *Canada Trust* gloss by the Supreme Court in the first *Brownlie* decision,[43] and Court of Appeal in *Kaefer*,[44] actually changed the law, rather than simply restating it and thus retaining the *Canada Trust* reticence to determine disputed factual matters. The debate on that point simply served to highlight the continuing uncertainty in this area.

The first and second *Brownlie* decisions are discussed further by Benjamin Phelps in chapter eighteen,[45] who appeared in the case as junior counsel for the defendants. He prefers (what he sees as) Lord Sumption's revised approach to the *Canada Trust* issue in the first *Brownlie* decision, as being 'distinctly practical and structured'. Whilst far too diplomatic openly to re-argue the gateway issue again, it is implicit in his chapter that Phelps also prefers the narrower approach adopted on the question of 'damage' by Lord Sumption and then Lord Leggatt on the two appeals:[46] the chapter explains the difficulties of Lord Lloyd-Jones's broader approach for economic loss, and the problems which arise in affording too great a role to *forum conveniens* in determining service out cases. While Phelps suggests that the second *Brownlie* decision qualifies as a landmark by settling the long-running debate over the scope of the tort gateway for service out of the jurisdiction, he also notes that Lord Leggatt's approach to the applicable law issues in that case opens up a potential new line of cases on the question of pleading and proving foreign law. There may therefore be a case for arguing that *Brownlie* qualifies as a landmark twice (or three times) over.

The approach to jurisdiction is somewhat different where the dispute falls within the scope of prior agreement between the parties that consensually allocates jurisdiction to a particular forum. But it was not always so. In chapter ten, William Day traces how English law changed the balance it struck between respect for territorial sovereignty on the one hand and party agreement on the other. The common law initially prioritised the former and so gave little, if any, weight to jurisdiction or arbitration agreements. This changed after statutory intervention by way of the Common Law Procedure Acts 1852 and 1854 and the Judicature Acts 1873 and 1875. However, it was not until 1944 that the Court of Appeal suggested in *obiter dicta* that there might be a common law power to stay

[43] *Four Seasons v Brownlie* (n 12) [4]–[7] (Lord Sumption).

[44] *Kaefer Aislamientos SA de CV v AMS Drilling Mexico SA de CV* [2019] EWCA Civ 10, [2019] 1 WLR 3514 [57]–[86] (Green LJ).

[45] *Four Seasons v Brownlie* (n 12) and *FS Cairo v Brownlie* (n 12).

[46] See too L Merrett 'Forum Conveniens' in W Day and S Worthington (eds), *Challenging Private Law: Lord Sumption on the Supreme Court* (Oxford, Hart, 2020).

English proceedings in favour of a chosen foreign court,[47] an idea subsequently taken up by Henry Brandon in a series of cases as counsel, Admiralty Judge, Lord Justice of Appeal and eventually Lord Ordinary of Appeal.[48] Focusing on Brandon J's well-known numbered propositions in *The Eleftheria*,[49] Day suggests that they have outlived their use. The better view is that the discretion to stay is now exercised by reference to a streamlined hierarchy: if there is no risk of an unjust determination of the dispute in the chosen jurisdiction, and also no (manufactured) injustice arising from irreconcilable judgments in parallel proceedings, only then should effect be given to the party choice of forum. Put another way, the jurisdiction agreement provides an answer at the first stage of the *Spiliada* framework, but it does not obviate the need to consider any injustices at the second stage.

While Brandon emphasised the presumptive strong effect of jurisdiction agreements at common law, he never formulated the issue as being governed or determined by contractual principles. On the Brandon view, jurisdiction agreements were given effect not because they are contracts but rather because, as a matter of policy, they are promises which ought normally to be respected. A contrast can therefore be drawn with the approach taken by Lord Hoffmann in *Fiona Trust*,[50] discussed by Sir Marcus Smith in chapter sixteen, where the effect of jurisdiction agreements was framed in purely contractual terms. Smith questions whether the 'one-stop-shop' presumption for construing jurisdiction agreements created by *Fiona Trust* – ie that rational businesspeople are presumed to have intended to settle all disputes in a single forum – is realistic and desirable. It works in straightforward cases where the parties have a single contract, and the dispute relates to something genuinely connected to that contract. But it does not work where (for example) the parties have entered into multiple choice of court (or arbitration) agreements across different contracts; it breaks down rapidly when third parties are involved (eg, an insurance broker in a dispute about cover between an insured and insurer), where courts have to face the problem of irreconcilable judgments in parallel proceedings; and it risks ignoring the fact that the dispute may not arise out of the relevant relationship created by the contract of which the jurisdiction agreement is part in the first place.[51] Commenting on the *Fiona Trust* paper at the conference, David Joseph KC noted

[47] *Racecourse Betting Control Board v Secretary of State for Air* [1944] Ch 114 (CA) 126 (MacKinnon LJ).

[48] *Cargo Lately Laden on Board the Fehmarn (Owners) v Fehmarn (Owners)* [1957] 1 WLR 815 (Ad) and [1958] 1 WLR 159 (CA); *The Eleftheria* (n 10); *Aratra Potato Co Ltd v Egyptian Navigation Co (The El Amria)* [1981] 2 Lloyd's Rep 119 (CA); *DSV Silo und Verwaltungsgesellschaft mbH v Owners of the Sennar (The Sennar) (No 2)* [1985] 1 WLR 490 (HL).

[49] *The Eleftheria* (n 10) 99–100.

[50] *Fiona Trust* (n 22).

[51] The same point can be put another way: the claim has to be properly characterised before the *Fiona Trust* presumption can sensibly be applied, but there is a risk in current practice that the presumption is used to answer the necessarily prior question of characterisation.

that, in public international law, investment treaty tribunals pay close attention to the particular treaty words conferring jurisdiction; he questioned why the same approach was not taken for jurisdiction clauses as a matter of private international law. Of course, to the extent that the relevance of the particular words is a question of contract law, the 'Supreme Court has begun to withdraw from the more advanced positions seized during the Hoffmann offensive',[52] and so the time may be ripe to revisit *Fiona Trust* and give its one-stop-shop presumption more nuanced effect.

Despite the papers on *The Eleftheria* and *Fiona Trust* not raising it directly, there was considerable discussion at the conference on the vexed question of damages for breach of jurisdiction agreements. Adrian Briggs persuasively argued, in the same vein as he has written, that:[53]

> If parties concluded a contract which provided that proceedings would not be brought by either of them before the courts of a foreign country, and then one party, in breach of this promise, brings such proceedings, he breaks his contract. It is the bringing of proceedings which constitutes the breach. No one forced him to do that; and a party to a contract who breaks his promise is liable in damages which are, at least when English law governs the contractual promise, a common law right. It took the courts a long time to acknowledge what now seems blindingly obvious, but there is no principled basis for complaining about such civil proceedings.

The fact that damages are available does not mean (contrary to what is perhaps implicitly assumed in *Fiona Trust*) that the jurisdiction agreement must always be contractual in its operation; it simply shows that the jurisdiction agreement can work on two planes, both at the level of private international law and also in domestic contract law. Further, beyond a broad consensus at the conference that damages should be available, there was real debate over the extent of such damages, and whether it should be limited to costs, or to allow recovery of some or all of the damages awarded in the non-chosen jurisdiction.[54] No doubt a landmark case will emerge on this point in due course. In the meantime, there is little prospect of contracting parties including a framework for liquidated damages or indemnities in their jurisdiction agreements because, as Simon James perceptively pointed out in discussion, that would risk undermining any application for the more potentially valuable remedy of an anti-suit injunction.

Whether framed in contractual or public policy terms, the key point introduced (or emphasised) by *The Eleftheria* was that there had to be an exceptionally strong countervailing factor to justify the court failing to respect the parties' forum selection. In Australia, by contrast, less weight is given to that

[52] Lord Sumption, 'A Question of Taste: The UK Supreme Court and the Interpretation of Contracts' in D Clarry (ed), *The UK Supreme Court Yearbook Volume 8* (2016–2017) (London, Appellate Press, 2018) 75.

[53] A Briggs, *The Conflict of Laws,* 4th edn (Oxford, OUP, 2020) 125.

[54] See, eg, *Union Discount Co Ltd v Zoller* [2001] EWCA Civ 1755, [2002] 1 WLR 1517.

factor. In chapter fourteen Mary Keyes discusses *Akai v The People's Insurance Company*,[55] the landmark decision on jurisdiction agreements in Australian law, where a bare majority of the High Court of Australia declined to enforce a jurisdiction agreement on public policy grounds. In that case, the majority considered that Australian insurance law – insofar as it had been modified by statute to produce a different result to English insurance law – supplied a basis in public policy for not enforcing a jurisdiction agreement in favour of the English courts. Keyes argues that, in not respecting the jurisdiction (and governing law) specifically negotiated by sophisticated parties, *Akai* demonstrated 'anti-internationalist and inequitable tendencies'. Keyes also points out that such an approach achieved little given the English court went on to issue an anti-suit injunction in support of the English proceedings brought in compliance with the jurisdiction agreement:[56] from the perspective of the English court, the parallel proceedings in Australia were not a good enough reason to ignore the jurisdiction agreement and stay the English proceedings or refuse the anti-suit injunction, since it would amount to rewarding the contract-breaker for their breach of contract. The different weight given to party autonomy in Australia after *Akai* thus provides an interesting and informative comparison to the approach established in England after *The Eleftheria*.

Turning to governing law, *Phillips v Eyre* is discussed by Uglješa Grušic and Alex Mills in chapter five.[57] This litigation arose out of colonial atrocity – the suppression by martial law of the Mourant Bay rebellion in Jamaica – where the plaintiff, Alexander Phillips, had been arrested and detained for 10 days without charge or trial, forced to witness the execution of 49 persons, and was given 100 lashes with a cat-o'-nine tails. The double actionability rule in tort law was used to shield the white English governor of Jamaica from a claim for trespass to the person from his political opponent, a black Jamaican. Undoubtedly liable as a matter of English law, the double actionability required the governor also to be liable in Jamaican law as the law of the place of the tort (*lex loci delicti*); which he was not, due to a self-serving 'Indemnity Act' which he had procured the Jamaican legislature to pass. At the conference in Cambridge, it was noted that there was a certain irony in the double actionability rule being used to shield human rights abuses in the nineteenth century, given the rule's residual role in modern English law is to protect human rights (particularly in defamation, where there can otherwise be freedom of expression issues from the application of foreign law) as well as its continuing application when seeking compensation for historic colonial wrongs.

In their chapter, Grušic and Mills seek to shed new light on *Phillips v Eyre* from a private international law perspective, by bringing into the analysis the constitutional, colonial and political background to the case, including the failed

[55] *Akai Pty Ltd v The People's Insurance Co Ltd* [1996] HCA 39, (1996) 188 CLR 418.
[56] *Akai Pty Ltd v The People's Insurance Co Ltd* [1998] 1 Lloyd's Rep 90 (Com Ct).
[57] *Phillips v Eyre* (n 5).

private criminal prosecution of Governor Eyre and the challenge under constitutional and colonial law to the Jamaican Indemnity Act. When that context is added, the difficult question then becomes why English law was applied *in addition* to Jamaican law. Grušic and Mills suggest that this was a product of *Phillips v Eyre* being a colonial dispute. The error in subsequent cases was to assume that there was a *lex fori* requirement for torts that did not arise in a similar colonial context. That error meant that the ability to sue for foreign torts was severely restrained by the double actionability rule, until the House of Lords and Privy Council began to introduce some flexibility to disapply one or other limb of the double actionability rule: first in *Boys v Chaplin* (where the House of Lords, or at least Lord Wilberforce, allowed some flexibility in not applying the *lex loci delicti*),[58] and then in *Red Sea Insurance Co v Bouygues* (where the Privy Council permitted the tort to be governed only by the *lex loci delicti*).[59] At the conference it was suggested by some attendees that *Bouygues* was the real landmark decision, which, over time, would have corrected the wrong course taken by the application of *Phillips v Eyre*, moving the English common law towards a general *lex loci delicti* rule (the destination now reached in Australian and Canadian law). As it was, a general *lex loci delicti* rule was introduced in statute months after *Bouygues* by the Private International Law (Miscellaneous Provisions) Act 1995, which in turn was later replaced by a rule in favour of the place of the damage in the Rome II Regulation.[60]

It is notable that the author of the leading judgment in *Phillips v Eyre*, Willes J, had also given judgment a few years earlier in the landmark case for choice of law in contract, *Lloyd v Guibert*.[61] As Adrian Briggs puts it in chapter two, his judgment in *Lloyd v Guibert* is a 'remarkable thing', which reset choice of law for contracts: by adopting a presumption that the law of the place in which the contract was made was the governing law, but only as being '*primâ facie* that which the parties intended, or ought to be presumed to have adopted as the footing upon which they dealt, and that such law ought therefore to prevail in the absence of circumstances indicating a different intention'.[62] *Lloyd v Guibert* is perhaps more of a landmark case than *Phillips v Eyre*: whereas the Rome II Regulation adopts an entirely different test for applicable law in tort, the Rome I Regulation still poses the same basic question for applicable law in contract as first posed in *Lloyd v Guibert* (ie what did the parties intend?); the only difference now lies in the presumptions used to infer or imply that choice in the absence of it being expressly communicated. Yet at the time it was decided, as Briggs explains, *Lloyd v Guibert* stood apart. A different approach had been taken to the law governing the substantive validity

[58] *Boys v Chaplin* [1971] AC 356 (HL).
[59] *Red Sea Insurance Co Ltd v Bouygues SA* [1995] 1 AC 190 (PC).
[60] Regulation (EC) No 864/2007 (Rome II).
[61] *Lloyd v Guibert* (n 4).
[62] ibid, 122.

of marriage vows in *Brook v Brook* in 1858, where the law of the parties' domicile was instead applied.[63] Nor was it followed by (or cited to) the Privy Council in *The Halley* in 1868,[64] a dispute arising out of the collision of two ships in Belgium waters, where the claim in negligence against the pilot might have been brought in contract or in tort. And, in his later judgment in *Phillip v Eyre*, Willes J appeared to change his characterisation of the rule, when he said that in both contract and tort the action should be governed by the law of the place that contract was made or the wrong committed, unless the parties intended some other law to apply; in that latter formulation, unlike *Lloyd v Guibert*, the law of the place was the general rule rather than supplying a presumption in the context of a different general rule based on party choice.[65] Put another way, in Willes J's later formulation, the territoriality principle appeared to be given greater weight than the autonomy principle in choice of law rules.

In the century after *Lloyd v Guibert*, the common law rule for choice of law in contract was refined into a two stage test: first, the court looked at the terms of the whole contract (applying English law as the law of the forum) to determine whether there was an express or implied choice of law; second, as a fallback, if there was no such choice on the terms of the contract, the system of law most closely connected to the agreement was applied. The continuing application of the Rome I Regulation means that there is little need in practice to revert to this common law test. Arbitration agreements are an exception, since they are excluded from the Regulation, but such agreements also cause conceptual problems because of the rule that they also should be treated as separate from the wider contracts of which they are part. In *Enka v Chubb*,[66] discussed in chapter seventeen, a majority of the Supreme Court held that, in the absence of choice of law in either the main contract or the arbitration agreement, the most closely connected law to the arbitration agreement should be that of the law of the seat. In this book, David Joseph KC, who appeared for the successful party in the Court of Appeal and the Supreme Court, prefers the approach adopted by the Court of Appeal, which adopted the law of the seat to apply to the arbitration agreement even where there was a choice of law in the main contract. Joseph argues in chapter seventeen that this gives best effect to the idea of arbitration as a 'single unified package'. At the conference there was some debate about whether conflict of laws in arbitration now represented a 'thing apart' from wider private international law applied by the English courts. Adrian Briggs tended towards that view, but some scepticism was expressed by Andrew Dickinson, who suggested that there may be no reason not to see jurisdiction agreements as involving a similar 'package deal'.

[63] *Brook v Brook* (1861) 9 HLC 193.
[64] *Liverpool, Brazil and River Plate Steam Navigation Co Ltd v Benham (The Halley)* (1867–69) LR 2 PC 193.
[65] *Phillips v Eyre* (n 5) 28.
[66] *Enka v Chubb* (n 12).

Moving away from commercial disputes, the first afternoon session of the conference at Downing saw discussion of governing law for marriage and domicile. *Taczanowksa v Taczanowski* created a common law exception to the usual rule that the formal requirements of the place at which marriage is celebrated must be observed for the marriage to be valid.[67] In chapter nine, Máire Ní Shúilleabháin criticises the opaqueness of the reasoning. She argues that, placed in its contemporaneous context, the decision was really a policy decision in solidarity of members and supporters of the allied forces who were understandably hostile to the authority of German and Italian marriage laws in the days immediately following the end of the Second World War. At the conference it was suggested that this kind of decision 'dispensing' with one part of the usual choice of law requirements has shades of the reasoning in *Boys v Chaplin*.[68] There was also a debate at the conference, prompted by the analysis in chapter nine, about whether a similar approach might be taken to validate same sex marriages in England which have been celebrated in intolerant jurisdictions; the problem with using *Taczanowksa* to pursue that reasoning is that a ban on same sex marriage is likely to be characterised as an issue of capacity rather than being about the formality of the celebrations. In any event, Ní Shúilleabháin suggests that the lack of subsequent citation of *Taczanowksa*, and the difficult legal reasoning within it, suggests that it may better be seen as a landmark of its time rather than a landmark in the modern conflict of laws.

A similar conclusion is reached by Elizabeth Crawford and Janeen Carruthers in chapter three when discussing the 'twin pillars' of domicile created by the House of Lords in the Scottish cases of *Bell v Kennedy* and *Udny v Udny*.[69] These cases together established the rules that the domicile of origin continues until another domicile is clearly chosen, and that, should such a choice lapse, the domicile of origin will revive. The first of these rules is perhaps intuitively attractive; the second more open to debate; and together they furnish yet another example of how the territoriality and autonomy principles can interact. But neither case receives much, if any, modern citation in the courts, and both have been 'very substantially eroded' by legislative developments, including the use in European instruments of 'habitual residence' rather than domicile and by a new (and – Crawford and Carruthers argue – difficult) statutory rule on domicile in Scotland. However, given the prevailing importance of domicile in issues of marriage, succession and other international family law matters, Crawford and Carruthers suggest that *Bell v Kennedy* and *Udny v Udny* deserve renewed attention. As with *forum conveniens* disputes, arguments over domicile can be immensely time consuming and expensive for the parties. There was some discussion at the conference as to whether there was any solution to this but,

[67] *Taczanowksa* (n 21).
[68] See text to n 58.
[69] *Bell v Kennedy* (n 6) and *Udny v Udny* (n 6).

beyond case management, no obvious candidate presented itself. The European concept of habitual residence was, of course, expected to cut through such arguments but has proved as open to sustained debate in practice as domicile.

Choice of law for property is represented in this collection by *Luther v Sagor*,[70] discussed by Sir David Foxton in chapter eight. Here, the territoriality principle overrides the autonomy principle: save where equity can act *in personam*,[71] the applicable law is that of the territory in which the property is situated. In *Luther v Sagor* the question was whether the English court would recognise the validity of the Soviet Government's confiscation of a factory and goods in the town of Staraya, around 180 miles south of St Petersburg. That in turn depended on whether the UK Government recognised the Soviet Government, in the place of the Russian Imperial Government, as the sovereign body in respect of that territory. The appeal was determined by correspondence from the Foreign Office confirming UK recognition the Soviet Government. Foxton discusses the decision's foundational status for the 'one voice' principle, by which the English courts will (where there is any dispute) follow the executive's instruction as to who to recognise as the legitimate government of any territory.[72] He also charts the troubled evolution of the act of state doctrine – distinct from a *lex situs* rule for property – out of Warrington LJ's judgment in *Luther v Sagor*, resulting in three different potential rules identified by the majority in *Belhaj v Straw*.[73] There was some discussion at the conference as to the correct characterisation of the act of state doctrine; whether it could act as a sword as well as a shield; and how the disapplication of the doctrine in *Kuwait Airways v Iraqi Airways* (in some senses, a decision comparable to *Taczanowksa*) could be sensibly applied in subsequent cases.[74] In his chapter, Foxton notes that the courts have 'heavily pruned' the doctrine over time in a way also seen in other aspects of public policy in private international law, such as the revenue rule.

The revenue rule itself is considered by Alexander Layton KC in chapter eight, through the prism of *Government of India v Taylor*.[75] The dispute arose from Delhi's first diesel power station, set up for the Durbar planned in 1903 by Edward VII and the city's principal source of electricity for decades thereafter. The power station company – incorporated in England – was placed into liquidation in 1949; the Indian Government sought to prove in the liquidation; the liquidator, Samuel Taylor, rejected the proof. The government then applied to the English court, supervising the insolvency proceedings, to challenge that decision. The principal early source for the revenue rule is Lord Mansfield's

[70] *Luther v Sagor* (n 20).

[71] See *Penn v Lord Baltimore* (n 3).

[72] Not always straightforward to interpret: see most recently *Maduro Board of the Central Bank of Venezuela v Guaido Board of the Central Bank of Venezuela* [2021] UKSC 57, [2022] 2 WLR 167.

[73] *Belhaj v Straw* [2017] UKSC 3, [2017] AC 964.

[74] *Kuwait Airways Corp v Iraqi Airways Co (Nos 4 and 5)* [2002] UKHL 19, [2002] AC 883.

[75] *Government of India v Taylor* [1955] AC 491 (HL).

dictum in *Holman v Johnson*, that 'no country ever takes notice of the revenue laws of another'.[76] The irony, as Layton points out, is that this was an observation about French law, not a remark about English law. But, as explained in chapter eight, that was the slender basis on which a line of cases developed, and Dicey's 'Rule 3' postulated, leading eventually to the House of Lords decision in *Government of India*, where the application was dismissed on that basis. Chapter eight also traces how *Government of India* has subsequently been narrowed by case law,[77] as well as by treaty and statutory provision. The continuing landmark status of the decision is therefore a matter of some debate.

Four landmark cases on foreign judgments are considered in this collection. Blackburn J's judgments in *Godard v Gray* and *Schibsby v Westenholz*,[78] both handed down on 10 December 1870, are considered by Joshua Folkard and Ian Bergson in chapter four. As Blackburn J summarised in *Schibsby*:[79]

> It is unnecessary to repeat again what we have already said in *Godard v Gray*. We think that, for the reasons there given, the true principle on which the judgments of foreign tribunals are enforced in England is … that the judgment of a court of competent jurisdiction over the defendant imposes a duty or obligation on the defendant to pay the sum for which judgment is given, which the courts in this country are bound to enforce; and consequently that anything which negatives that duty, or forms a legal excuse for not performing it, is a defence to the action.

At the conference, Folkard and Bergson provocatively questioned whether these cases deserved their landmark status given this obligation theory struggles to explain the current, positive law. In the final version of the chapter, while maintaining that criticism, they suggest that the cases nonetheless merit that recognition as landmarks given they 'set the direction of travel of English law'. The problem with the obligation theory, according to Folkard and Bergson, arises from it being contingent on an aspect of the territoriality principle, namely the idea of allegiance to a sovereign authority. If allegiance is what creates the obligation (or at least can create the obligation),[80] it is very difficult to understand why residence or citizenship are not grounds for competent jurisdiction. Indeed, Blackburn J considered they were grounds for competent jurisdiction;[81] the law only moved in a different direction in 1990 with the decision in *Adams v Cape*.[82] Folkard and Bergson also consider that 'fleeting'

[76] *Holman v Johnson* (1775) 1 Cowp 342, 343; 98 ER 1120, 1121.

[77] Most recently in *Skatteforvaltningen (Danish Customs and Tax Divisions) v Solo Capital Partners LLP (In Special Administration)* [2022] EWCA Civ 234, [2022] 2 All ER 563.

[78] *Godard v Gray* (n 7) and *Schibsby v Westenholz* (n 7).

[79] *Schibsby v Westenholz* (n 7) 159.

[80] In line with his published work, Adrian Briggs argued at the conference that party autonomy also (or instead) provided the basis for the obligation contained in a foreign judgment.

[81] *Schibsby v Westenholz* (n 7) 163.

[82] *Adams v Cape Industries plc* [1990] Ch 433 (CA).

presence as a basis competent jurisdiction poses challenges to the idea of allegiance, since a foreigner only fleetingly present in the jurisdiction will never be part of the relevant political community in a meaningful sense.

Folkard and Bergson also consider that the fraud defence to the recognition and enforcement of foreign judgments poses a challenge to the obligation theory because it means that, if there is any obligation at all, 'at best it must be a weak one'. Louise Merrett addresses the fraud defence in more detail in chapter six on *Abouloff v Oppenheimer*.[83] Although the rule from *Abouloff* has persisted without 'great enthusiasm', Merrett suggests that it could experience some form of rehabilitation given the Supreme Court's recent decision on fraud unravelling domestic judgments in *Takhar v Gracefield Developments*.[84] Merrett proposes a more nuanced approach to the fraud defence: there should be a difference in approach between collateral fraud (eg, bribery of the judge in the original court) and fraud on the merits (where the question should be left to the original court, absent special reasons). *Abouloff* was, of course, the latter case and the reason given by Lord Coleridge CJ as to why the English court could re-open the merits in those circumstances was technical, artificial and has since been rejected. The discussion of *Abouloff* at the conference focused on the abuse of process exceptions to the fraud defence created by *House of Spring Gardens v Waite*,[85] and *Owens Bank v Etoile Commerciale*,[86] which Merrett argues should be given wider scope. On the one hand, the open-textured and flexible nature of these exceptions are a cause for some uncertainty; on the other hand, it can be said that they reveal something about the proper target of the modern fraud defence, and limit the scope for challenges not based on new evidence as well as repeated attempts in different fora to impugn the judgment.

In chapter thirteen, Stephen Pitel considers the very different approach now taken to foreign judgments in Canada, as a result of the landmark decision in *Morguard v De Savoye*.[87] In *Morguard*, the Supreme Court of Canada shrugged off the narrow bases for competent jurisdiction in English law and recognised a broader category which applied where there was a 'real and substantial connection' between the forum and the dispute. While this has shades of the modern English approach to the court's own exercise of jurisdiction after the House of Lord's decision in *Spiliada*, *Morguard*'s approach to competent jurisdiction for the purposes of recognising and enforcing foreign judgments has since been rejected by the UK Supreme Court.[88] Pitel acknowledges the Canadian-specific constitutional and economic context for the decision in *Morguard* but argues that, in principle and in practice, the more liberal approach has much

[83] *Abouloff v Oppenheimer* (n 8).
[84] *Takhar v Gracefield Developments Ltd* [2019] UKSC 13, [2020] AC 450.
[85] *House of Spring Gardens v Waite* [1991] 1 QB 241 (CA).
[86] *Owens Bank Ltd v Etoile Commerciale SA* [1995] 1 WLR 44 (PC).
[87] *Morguard* (n 23).
[88] *Rubin v Eurofinance SA* [2012] UKSC 46, [2013] 1 AC 236 [109]–[110] (Lord Collins).

to commend it in other common law systems as well as in Canada. There were some sceptics amongst the English audience at the conference, who raised familiar objections that the test in *Morguard* lacked predictability (given the element of value judgement to the question of whether or not there was a real and substantial connection); opened Canadians up to being vulnerable to foreign litigation without achieving anything in return for Canadians; and should only be adopted if counter-balanced by a broader approach to defences to recognition and enforcement. Pitel has ready answers to all of these concerns in chapter thirteen, emphasising in particular that 'presumptive connecting factors' developed in Canada since *Morguard* supply a certain amount of predictability. Further, while the Supreme Court of Canada in *Beals v Saldanha* had shown openness to expanding the range of defences,[89] in the 30 years since *Morguard*, in practice there had been no need to do so. Irrespective of the range of views on the merit of *Morguard*, and whether it ought to be imported into English law, there is no denying its status as a landmark in the common law conflicts of law, and we are glad to see it covered in this collection.

We cannot conclude this introduction without emphasising how extremely grateful we are for the enthusiastic support of Clifford Chance for this project, without which it would not have been possible, and especially to Helen Carty, Anne Drakeford and Simon James, who also attended and chaired various sessions of the conference. We thank Lord Hamblen for providing the foreword. We are indebted to the contributors for the hard work which led to the excellent essays in this book. We also thank those who also contributed to the conference at Downing College in addition to those named above: Callum Caldwell, Niamh Davis, Richard Fentiman, Marie Louise Kinsler KC and Joanna Page. We are grateful to Isobel Williams for providing the cover art and to Kate Whetter and Rosie Mearns at Hart Publishing for their guidance and support throughout the project that was long in the making, having its origins as a 'lockdown project' during the COVID-19 pandemic. William would like to thank his wife Susie for allowing this project to eat into family time, although perhaps some parts of this book will be useful: Henry and Juliet (now three and one respectively) already demonstrate a knack for forum shopping as between parents, and have a deep sense as to which parent at any one time represents the real risk of injustice. Louise would also like to thank her husband both for his support generally and for contributing a chapter to the book, and notes that her children achieved landmarks of their own during this project (celebrating respectively 21st and 18th birthdays). Louise would finally like to pay special thanks to Will who was the inspiration and driving force behind this project, for his ideas, organisational skills and hard work, and also for being such a pleasure to work with.[90]

[89] *Beals v Saldanha* [2003] 3 SCR 416 (Can SC).

[90] As a final footnote to this introduction, the long awaited new (16th edn) edition of *Dicey, Morris and Collins on the Conflict of Laws* (London, Sweet & Maxwell, 2022) was published as this book was being prepared for publication. With a few exceptions, it has not been possible to update references from the 15th edn.

1

Penn v Lord Baltimore (1750)

PAUL MITCHELL*

I. INTRODUCTION

EQUITY ACTS *IN personam*. It has to. If it acted *in rem*, it would create a system of titles rivalling – and conflicting with – titles at common law. The result would be chaos. Thus, to take a simple example, when a court grants specific performance against a defaulting vendor of land, the decree does not transfer title to the land; it orders the vendor to do what is required to make such a transfer occur. At the same time, equity offers the vendor a powerful incentive to comply: failure to perform exposes him to fines or imprisonment for contempt of court. The rule that equity acts *in personam* is a restriction necessary for legal coherence.

But restrictions can be surprisingly liberating. Since equity is not concerned with the property itself, only with the person who has an obligation as regards that property, it does not matter if the property lies outside the court's jurisdiction. So long as the defendant is within the jurisdiction, an order can be made against him that requires him to deal with the property in a particular way. As Lindley LJ put it, in *Commissioners of Inland Revenue v G Angus & Co*,[1]

> a judgment for specific performance does not transfer the property to the purchaser. This is obvious enough if we consider the jurisdiction of the Court to decree the specific performance of an agreement for the purchase of land situate in a foreign country. Ever since *Penn v Lord Baltimore* the Court of Chancery has exercised that jurisdiction. But why? Because it did not affect or profess to affect by its decree the property itself; it acted only in personam and compelled the vendor to do whatever was necessary to be done, either in this country or abroad, to transfer the property to the purchaser.

In treating *Penn v Lord Baltimore*[2] as the foundation of equity's jurisdiction over foreign land, Lindley LJ was following established opinion. The case had been

* I would like to thank Joshua Getzler and CGJ Morse for their comments on an earlier draft.
[1] *Commissioners of Inland Revenue v G Angus & Co* (1889) 23 QBD 579, 596.
[2] *Penn v Lord Baltimore* (1750) 1 Ves Sen 444, 27 ER 1132.

(and continued to be) used to support that proposition in successive editions of White and Tudor's *Leading Cases in Equity*,[3] and six years earlier, in *Ewing v Orr Ewing*,[4] it had been cited by the House of Lords as an illustration of 'elementary principles'.[5] The case continues to be good law, although it has been subject to trenchant criticism. In particular, both judges and commentators have noted that the principle from *Penn v Lord Baltimore* has an uneasy relationship with the general principle of private international law that the courts will not determine title to foreign land.[6] As Lord Esher MR explained, for equity to order a defendant to effect a transfer of title to land abroad, was 'open to the strong objection, that the Court is doing indirectly what it dare not do directly'.[7] 'It seems to me,' he continued,

> that [*Penn v Lord Baltimore*] breaks the comity of national consent, because such a contract [concerning land abroad] deals with rights resulting from the ownership of land … by the consent of nations … a dispute as to such rights is among nations to be treated as a local action to be tried in the forum rei sitae.[8]

This essay shows that, whilst *Penn v Lord Baltimore*[9] undoubtedly does support the proposition that equity has jurisdiction affecting foreign land in certain circumstances, it is not a matter of 'elementary' principle. On the contrary, both the jurisdiction itself and the role of *Penn v Lord Baltimore* in establishing it are complex and controversial. The case we know as *Penn v Lord Baltimore*, decided in 1750, should really be known as *Penn v Lord Baltimore (No 2)*. *Penn v Lord Baltimore (No 1)*, decided five years earlier and reported by Ridgeway,[10] covers some of the same ground as the later case (including the jurisdiction point). In addition, there is a wealth of case law on equity's ability to affect foreign land (and foreign litigation), stretching back to the mid-seventeenth century. This case law offers a variety of reasons in support of the jurisdiction, and highlights the imperial political context in which the decisions were being made. The imperial context is in fact a strong theme in *Penn v Lord Baltimore (Nos 1 and 2)*, but lawyers' traditional habit of summarising and extracting pithy principles from complex texts has meant that, over time, the political nuance has been lost.

In short, this chapter argues that the principle for which *Penn v Lord Baltimore (No 2)* stands was shaped by the empire. It is a principle about the

[3] See, eg, F White and O Tudor, *A Selection of Leading Cases in Equity*, 2nd edn (London, Maxwell, 1858) 2.767; E Hewitt and J Richardson (eds), *White and Tudor's Leading Cases in Equity*, 9th edn (London, Maxwell, 1928) 1.638.

[4] *Ewing v Orr Ewing* (1883) 9 App Cas 34.

[5] ibid, 40 (Earl of Selborne LC).

[6] *British South Africa Company v Companhia de Moçambique* [1893] AC 602.

[7] *Companhia de Moçambique v British South Africa Company* [1892] 2 QB 358 (CA) 404–05.

[8] ibid, 405. See further L Collins (ed), *Dicey, Morris and Collins on the Conflict of Laws*, 14th edn (London, Sweet & Maxwell, 2006) para 23-050.

[9] *Penn* (n 2).

[10] *Pen v Lord Baltimore* (1745) Ridgeway Cases temp Hardwicke 332, 27 ER 847.

relationship between Britain and its colonies. Furthermore, the way in which the application of the principle developed was, similarly, responsive to imperial commercial needs. The imperial context also explains why the criticisms made of *Penn v Lord Baltimore* today did not feature in the eighteenth-century cases: there was, quite simply, no comity of nations issue in a question between Britain and one of her overseas possessions.

II. THE EVENTS

Lord Hardwicke LC's decision in *Penn v Lord Baltimore (No 2)* in 1750 was merely one stage of an ongoing dispute that had been simmering since the 1680s.[11] Lord Baltimore was the proprietor of Maryland, a colony created by a charter granted to the first Lord Baltimore in 1632. The colony's territory was extensive, but was limited in two ways that would later become troublesome. First, its northern boundary was 40°N latitude; second, it contained only '*hactenus terra inculta*', that is to say, land not cultivated by other Europeans. In 1680, William Penn petitioned Charles II for territory for a colony, and in 1681 Charles granted him a large area north of 40°N latitude. For the most part, the boundary with Maryland was to run along the line of 40°N; however, one section of the boundary was to take the form of part of a circle, radius 12 miles, drawn from the centre of the town of Newcastle. This unique boundary shape was dictated by the Duke of York, who had territory in Delaware. It probably looked quite neat on a map but, as we shall see, it proved challenging to mark out.

Penn seems initially to have been satisfied with the territory granted to him, but in 1682 he was dismayed to discover that the line of 40°N had been marked inaccurately. The true line was in fact further north. This was a problem, not so much on account of the reduction in area of the territory (which was still vast) but because it potentially deprived Penn's colony of access to the Delaware River.

Penn's solution was to obtain territory with direct sea access from the Duke of York. The Duke had been granted land on the Delaware peninsula, and in New Amsterdam, following his military successes against the Dutch in 1674. In 1682 Penn prevailed on the Duke to grant him those Delaware possessions. At this point, however, Lord Baltimore made his own claim to the Duke of York's territories in Delaware. The Dutch settlements there, he argued, had been seized by the Dutch in 1655 from a group of Swedes and Finns, who had established

[11] This section draws on the accounts in J Latrobe, *The History of Mason and Dixon's Line* (Philadelphia, Pa, Historical Society of Pennsylvania, 1855) and J Veech, *Mason and Dixon's Line: A History* (Pittsburgh, Pa, Haven, 1857), and on the chronology of events prepared by the Penns' counsel, William Murray, for the proceedings between the parties before the King in Council and later published in S Hazard (ed), *The Register of Pennsylvania* (Philadelphia, Pa, Geddes, 1828) vol 2, 200–03, 209–16.

themselves only in 1638. In 1632, when the Maryland charter was granted, that land had been uncultivated by Europeans, and was, therefore, part of Maryland.

Penn set to work in the hope of finding evidence of some European settlement prior to 1632 in the area. His agents managed to track down several elderly settlers, whose testimony showed a Dutch settlement as early as 1624, and a Dutch purchase of the area (from native Americans) in 1629. Baltimore, realising that his position was weakening, went to London to press for a hearing before the Lords of Trade and Plantations, before things got any worse. Penn followed him, but in such a panic that he left behind the crucial depositions.[12]

Their Lordships deferred the hearing. Once the documents had arrived, the case was heard. In November 1685 the Lords made their report, in which they rejected Baltimore's claim to the entirety of the Delaware peninsula and ruled that, for the avoidance of further dispute, the peninsula should be split down the middle – the western half going go Baltimore, the eastern half remaining with the Crown.[13] This result effectively confirmed Penn's position, for the Crown had granted the land to the Duke of York, who had, in turn, granted it to Penn.

Baltimore had lost the battle, but he was not about to concede the war. Charles II had died shortly before the Lords' decision, and had been succeeded by his brother, the Duke of York. Baltimore must have realised that he was unlikely to have much success through legal channels until there was a new monarch, and changed his strategy accordingly. Now he would simply use force to assert his claims on the ground, terrorising those settlers who refused to acknowledge his position. At the same time, he and his faction would adopt the most obstructive, uncooperative approach to litigation that they possibly could. The aim was to force a compromise on more generous terms than his strict charter rights allowed.

The Baltimore faction pursued this strategy successfully for nearly 50 years, combining legal time-wasting with strong-arm tactics. In the 1730s a new phase began, with the Baltimores showing some signs of wanting to negotiate final boundaries. Eventually, in 1732, an agreement was reached with the Penns. For our purposes, it had three key provisions. First, the Delaware peninsula would be divided as provided by the Lords in 1685. Second, the northern boundary of Maryland would no longer be 40°N latitude; instead, a line would be drawn by reference to various landmarks. Third, part of the boundary would still consist of a circle drawn 12 miles from Newcastle.

[12] N Wainwright, 'The Missing Evidence; *Penn v Baltimore*' (1956) 80 *Pennsylvania Magazine of History and Biography* 227; A Dunlap and C Weslager, 'More Missing Evidence: Two Depositions By Early Swedish Settlers' (1967) 91 *Pennsylvania Magazine of History and Biography* 35.

[13] The text of the Lords' decision is reproduced in 'Wm Penn and Lord Baltimore', Hazard (ed) (n 11) vol 2, 227.

If the Penns thought that the 1732 agreement signified a fundamental change of approach by the Baltimores, they were quickly disappointed. The agreement had provided for both sides to appoint commissioners, who would work together to mark out the boundaries. The Baltimore commissioners promptly started taking unmeritorious technical points, claiming, for instance, that the provision for a circle 12 miles from the centre of Newcastle meant that the *circumference* of such a circle should be 12 miles. A circle of that circumference would have a radius of about four miles. Progress stalled. Meanwhile, Marylanders, led by Thomas Cressap, were coercing and terrorising settlers into renouncing their allegiance to Pennsylvania. The Baltimores then opened a further line of attack, petitioning the King in Council in August 1734 for a confirmatory grant of all the lands in Maryland's original charter, *without restriction as to prior cultivation.* The Penns counter-petitioned. In May 1735, the King ordered that the matter should be adjourned until the end of Michaelmas Term, so as to give the Penns 'an opportunity to proceed in a Court of Equity, to obtain relief upon the said articles so insisted upon by them'.[14] Once that time had elapsed, either party was to be at liberty to apply to the Committee for Plantation Affairs.

The Penns promptly brought a Bill in Chancery for specific performance of the 1732 agreement. The Baltimore faction continued to force matters on the ground, leading the Penns to apply to the Lords for orders restraining violent disturbances. In 1737 the Lords agreed, and also prohibited the governors of either colony from granting land in the disputed area. A further order of 1738 reflected the terms of an agreed ceasefire, under which grants of vacant lands were to be permitted.

III. THE CHANCERY LITIGATION

The Penns' Bill for specific performance of the 1732 agreement made its first appearance in the law reports in relation to a hearing in 1745.[15] The defendant raised three points against it. First, the claimant lacked title to sue. Second, the court lacked jurisdiction. Third, the proper parties were not before the court. The first two points failed, but the third succeeded.

Dealing with the jurisdiction issue first, Lord Hardwicke LC held that the position of the parties as colonial proprietors was akin to that of feudatory lords, such as lords marchers, within England. A dispute between lords marchers was actionable in the Court of King's Bench, since that was where a writ of error lay from the court of the marches. A writ of error lay to the King in

[14] Hazard (ed) (n 11) vol 2, 211 (taken from the chronology prepared by the Penns' counsel, William Murray).

[15] *Pen* (n 10).

Council from courts in 'the provinces',[16] so it appeared at first sight that the claim should be determined by the King in Council. However, he continued, 'a court of equity-jurisdiction is *in personam*, and therefore can extend it wherever the parties persons are within its jurisdiction'.[17]

Lord Hardwicke LC disposed of the title to sue issue briefly, and then addressed the defendant's argument that the Attorney-General should have been made a party. He analysed the position as follows:[18]

> [T]he most material ground for making him a party is, that this agreement which is said to concern the proprietors of the said provinces only, will and must in the course and nature of it determine and affect the private properties of the subjects of those several provinces: For here are powers of government, jurisdiction, legislation, raising subsidies, together with all kinds of military powers granted by these deeds: If, in such case, proprietory Lords are to alter the bounds of their provinces, without the privity and consent of the crown, by whom alone such powers are vested, directed and disposed, consider the inconveniences that must follow; this is no less than transferring lands into different jurisdictions, legislations, &c you subject the people to different government, different assemblies, laws, courts, taxes, to which they never assented by their delegates.

The claimants were given liberty to amend their Bill.

Five years later the same case was back before the same judge. In *Penn v Lord Baltimore (No 2)*[19] the defendants now took four main points:

(a) the court had no jurisdiction – the jurisdiction was solely in the King in Council;
(b) the parties had no power to settle boundaries through their own acts – such an agreement amounted to an alienation, which was beyond the proprietors' powers;
(c) the court should not put the agreement into effect without the consent of the planters and tenants who would be affected by it;
(d) the agreement was not a proper one to enforce.

The fourth point had eight sub-headings:

(i) the agreement was merely voluntary;
(ii) the time for performance had lapsed;
(iii) the agreement effectively provided for a submission of differences to arbitration, which could not be supplied by the court;
(iv) the defendant had been imposed on, or surprised, by the terms of the agreement;

[16] ibid, 334, 847.
[17] ibid, 335, 847.
[18] ibid, 336–37, 848.
[19] *Penn* (n 2).

(v) the defendant had 'grossly'[20] mistaken his original rights; the terms of the agreement were too uncertain;
(vi) the claimant could not perform any covenant to convey territory on the Delaware peninsula, since that territory was the property of the Crown;
(vii) the court could not make an effective decree.

Lord Hardwicke began his judgment with the observation that the case was 'of a nature worthy the judicature of a Roman senate rather than of a single judge'.[21] However, he continued, the relief sought was 'the common and ordinary equity dispensed by this court', in the form of specific performance. The immediate effect of this opening passage was one of ambiguity: the case was both suitable and unsuitable for the Court of Chancery. This was a theme to which Lord Hardwicke would return at the conclusion of his judgment.

He then moved on to deal with the defendant's first point. As in *Pen v Lord Baltimore (No 1)*, Lord Hardwicke LC agreed that the original jurisdiction over colonial boundaries was with the King in Council. However, rather than asserting (as he had done in the earlier case) that equity's *in personam* jurisdiction allowed it to intervene when the defendant was within the jurisdiction, he took a more sophisticated approach. In this case, he explained, no original jurisdiction was necessary, because the court was being asked to enforce a contractual agreement made in England. The court could not have decreed the boundaries, but it could enforce the parties' agreement as to what those boundaries were. Rather than equity jurisdiction cutting across the jurisdiction of the King in Council, equity was now portrayed as assisting and complementing that jurisdiction.

The second point was disposed of on two alternative bases. On the first alternative, the settlement of boundaries by agreement did not amount to alienation at all, for 'the boundaries so settled are presumed to be the true and ancient limits'.[22] On the second alternative, assuming that there was alienation, such alienation was permissible under the colonial charters, provided that the colonies were not 'dismembered'. This was because the grants were in common socage, not *in capite* of the Crown.

The defendant's third objection also failed. The tenure of the planters would not be altered by the parties' agreement. In that sense, the situation was analogous to disputes between lords over the boundaries of a manor; in such cases the boundaries 'may be settled in suits between the lords of these manors without making the tenants parties'.[23] An additional reason why the planters did not need to be parties was that 'if there is no fraud or collusion, it must be presumed to be the true limits being made between parties in an adversary interest'.[24]

[20] ibid, 445, 1133.
[21] ibid, 446, 1134.
[22] ibid, 448, 1135.
[23] ibid, 449, 1136.
[24] ibid, 450, 1136.

Pausing here before we examine the defendant's multi-part fourth objection, three themes may be highlighted in the judge's analysis. First, the presumption that the parties' agreement was merely ascertaining the ancient boundaries was, on the facts of this case, unreal. The Baltimores' strategy over the course of the previous 70 years had been to force a compromise on terms more favourable to them than the original grant. Second, the legal concepts employed were strikingly feudal: tenure in socage, tenure *in capite*, disputes between lords of the manor. There is no sense that the colonial context was a new problem, to which such concepts were inapplicable. Third, the application of feudal analogies to the issue whether the planters should be parties concealed a deeper question. As Lord Hardwicke LC himself had highlighted, in *Pen v Lord Baltimore (No 1)*,[25] the interests of planters could not simply be disregarded. In the earlier case, those interests were protected by seeking the Attorney-General's approval, but the terms in which Lord Hardwicke LC analysed the position – particularly his reference to settlers being subjected to taxation without the agreement of their representatives – had more radical implications. Hardwicke's feudal analysis in the later case eliminated those revolutionary overtones, but, as with his suggestion that the agreement defined ancient boundaries, the law was closing its eyes to the political reality.

The defendant's fourth objection was also rejected. The agreement was not purely voluntary – consideration was provided by 'the settling boundaries, and peace and quiet'.[26] Lapse of time was not a problem either, particularly since the delay had not been caused by the party seeking specific performance. The agreement was not like an agreement to arbitrate, because it contained 'distinct, independent covenants',[27] and there was no evidence of imposition.

The mistake issue required closer analysis. Baltimore's charter had specified the northern boundary of Maryland at 40°N latitude. In theory, that should have been a fixed line, but advances in mathematics and surveying over the course of the previous century had revealed inaccuracies in earlier maps and geographical calculations. Over the course of time, the correct 40°N line was shown to be significantly further north than previously thought, but in 1750 it was still impossible to eliminate errors of two to three miles. The parties had, therefore, clearly been mistaken about the original location of Maryland's northern boundary – such a mistake was unavoidable – but, as Lord Hardwicke LC pointed out, such a mistake affected only the original boundaries, by making them doubtful. The newly-agreed boundaries were not defined by 40°N. In modern terms, we would say that the mistake as to the original boundaries was not fundamental.

The uncertainty issue, which had been much relied on by Lord Baltimore's commissioners, concerned the circular section of the boundary. The circle was

[25] *Pen* (n 10), text at n 18.
[26] *Penn* (n 2) 450, 1136.
[27] ibid.

to be drawn from the centre of Newcastle. But where, exactly, was that? A note of impatience can be detected in Lord Hardwicke's response: '[T]he middle of Newcastle, as near as can be computed must be found …'[28] Carrying out this terse instruction would not prove straightforward.

The defendant's penultimate point was that the claimant lacked the ability to perform his side of the agreement in relation to 'the lower counties'. This was the territory acquired from the Duke of York in 1682. In fact, the agreement did not call for the conveyance of any part of the lower counties, but Lord Hardwicke LC took the opportunity to assert that 'full and actual possession is sufficient title to maintain a suit for settling boundaries'.[29] 'In cases of this kind,' he continued,[30]

> of two great territories held of the crown, I will say once for all, that long possession and enjoyment, peopling and cultivating countries, is one of the best evidence of title to lands or districts of lands in America, that can be … for the great beneficial advantages, arising to the crown from settling, &c, is, that the navigation and the commerce of this country is thereby improved.

Finally, we reach the point for which *Penn v Lord Baltimore* is remembered today – that a decree concerning foreign land can be made. Lord Hardwicke LC set out the principle crisply: '[T]he court cannot inforce their own decree in rem, in the present case: but that is not an objection against making a decree in the cause; for the strict primary decree in this court as a court of equity is in personam …'[31] This was very much the same approach he had taken in *Pen v Lord Baltimore (No 1)*, but he now also referred to authorities supporting his position: *Richardson v Hamilton*, concerning a house in Philadelphia, and the case of Lord Anglesey, which concerned Irish estates.[32]

Each of the defendant's 11 objections had failed. But, despite this, the conclusion of Lord Hardwicke LC's judgment was rather ambivalent. The most that could be done against the defendant was to enforce the decree 'by process of contempt and sequestration'.[33] If the claimant wanted more, he would have to 'resort to another jurisdiction',[34] that is, the King in Council. Lord Hardwicke concluded by noting that the order of the Lords of Trade and Plantations, which had sent the case to Chancery in the first place, had envisaged such further proceedings. This classic equity case was not, it seems, really suitable for the Court of Chancery after all.

[28] ibid, 453, 1138.
[29] ibid.
[30] ibid, 454, 1138.
[31] ibid, 454, 1139.
[32] No report of the judgment in either case seems to have survived. Lord Anglesey's case in the Court of Chancery was probably ancillary to the House of Lords' decision in *Earl of Anglesey v Annesley* (1741) 1 Bro HL 289, 1 ER 573.
[33] *Penn* (n 2) 454, 1139.
[34] ibid.

When *Penn v Lord Baltimore (No 2)* is seen in its entirety, and in the context of both the earlier proceedings and the factual basis of the dispute, the case can be seen to be far more complex and sophisticated than previously appreciated. At its most fundamental level, *Penn v Lord Baltimore (No 2)* was about English law's ability to regulate a very specific kind of colonisation, which was characterised by the private enterprise of colonial proprietors exploiting territory distributed to them in London. The private status of those proprietors brought them within the jurisdiction of the ordinary courts, despite the fact that their powers and operations made them more akin to sovereigns.[35] The London-based distribution of territory, using maps, rulers and compasses, was bound to cause difficulty whenever the proprietors sought to delineate their territory.[36] The law's response, as seen in *Penn v Lord Baltimore (No 2)*, involved a sophisticated combination of analytical techniques. Some of those techniques involved analogies with existing categories. For instance, to the extent that an agreement to settle boundaries could be compared to a compromise agreement between private parties more generally, it was subject to orthodox contractual doctrines like consideration, certainty of terms, mistake, etc. To the extent that a dispute between colonial proprietors resembled a dispute between lords of manors, the colonists themselves needed to play no part. In other ways, however, Lord Hardwicke LC acknowledged that the situation was novel, and called for legal solutions driven by policy – thus, for instance, his assertion that 'long possession and enjoyment, peopling and cultivating countries, is one of the best evidence of title to lands or districts of lands in America'. The use of equity's *in personam* jurisdiction to affect foreign land lay somewhere between orthodoxy and outright novelty. The Court of Chancery had always needed to be mindful of trespassing into common law domains – hence its emphasis on the person – and equitable decrees concerning foreign land were not without precedent. On the other hand, as Lord Hardwicke LC realised, the decree *in personam* was a less than ideal remedy, since it could only provide a strong incentive to the defendant to perform his obligations. Furthermore, once the defendant was outside the jurisdiction, the equitable decree *in personam* could not reach him. This was particularly unsatisfactory where the security and prosperity of a large number of colonists depended on the defendant's compliance with the court's order. The facts of *Penn v Lord Baltimore (No 2)* provided a vivid illustration of the problem: the Baltimores' track record hardly suggested that they would be chastened by a judge 2,000 miles away delivering strictures about acting according to conscience.

[35] *Cf* the treatment of the East India Company in *Nabob of Arcot v East India Company* (1791) 3 Bro CC 292, 29 ER 544; (1792) 4 Bro CC 180, 29 ER 841.

[36] For a similar problem, concerning longitude, see *State of South Australia v State of Victoria* [1914] AC 283.

IV. PENN V LORD BALTIMORE 1750–62

The Baltimores responded to Lord Hardwicke's decree against them in their traditional fashion. Commissioners from Maryland and Pennsylvania were appointed to lay out the boundary together, and the Maryland commissioners were quickly taking technical points about both the radius and the centre of the circular section. They argued that the 12-mile radius had to be measured on the surface – that is, by laying the measuring chains flat on the ground. Where the terrain was undulating this would, of course, mean that the horizontal distance from the centre of the circle to its circumference was less than 12 miles. The Maryland commissioners claimed that several such surface measurements should be made, in different directions, and that an average should then be taken of the distances, measured horizontally, between the centre of the circle and the ends of those lines. That average figure should form the radius of the circle. The Pennsylvania commissioners' response to this nonsense was a model of dignity: '[T]he Words [of the decree are] so clear that in Our Opinions any endeavour to explain will rather serve to obscure than illustrate them.'[37] Nevertheless, the Maryland commissioners insisted, bringing the surveying work to a halt. Apparently the matter had to be referred back to Lord Hardwicke, who clarified that horizontal measurements were required.[38]

The dispute over the centre of Newcastle had elements of farce. John Watson, the Assistant Surveyor to the Pennsylvania Commissioners, reported in his diary for 17 September 1750 that 'after some Debate' it was agreed that the courthouse should be taken as the centre of Newcastle.[39] This uncharacteristically sensible solution was soon shown to have been based on a misunderstanding. The Maryland commissioners had handed the Pennsylvania commissioners a map with a pin-hole in it, which Watson had (naively) assumed marked the courthouse. In fact, Watson later reported, it was[40]

> since discovered to be intended for the Center of Gravity of the Town of New Castle, which it seems the Maryland Surveyors and Mathematicians attempted to find in this rediculous (sic) Manner Viz having made an exact plan of the Survey of the Town; upon a Piece of Paper, they carefully pared away the Edges by the Draught, untill no more than the Draught was left, when sticking a Pin thro it, they suspended it – thereby in different places untill they found a place whereby it might be suspended horizontally, wch Point or place they accepted as the Center of Gravity.

The death of Lord Baltimore prompted further litigation, with his son denying that he was bound by his father's agreement with the Penns. A very shortly-reported

[37] J Jordan, 'Penn versus Baltimore. Journal of John Watson, Assistant Surveyor to the Commissioners of the Province of Pennsylvania, 1750' (1914) 38 *Pennsylvania Magazine of History and Biography* 385, 399.
[38] Latrobe (n 11) 25.
[39] Jordan (n 37) 390.
[40] ibid, 401–02.

hearing in 1755 showed that the Baltimores were still trying to drag things out,[41] and there were further negotiations between the parties, which culminated in a new agreement in May 1761. It is tempting to infer some real feeling behind the formal language of the preamble to the agreement, which stated that the indenture 'witnesseth that for putting a final and perpetual end forever to all Disputes and Differences between the Parties', the boundaries had been agreed as set out.[42] Nearly 80 years after it had begun, the dispute was finally settled. The parties appointed two surveyors, Charles Mason and Jeremiah Dixon, to lay out what would later become known as the Mason-Dixon Line. They completed their work in 1762.

V. THE LAW OF THE COLONIES

By the time of the decisions in *Penn v Lord Baltimore (Nos 1 and 2)*, Britain was rich in colonial possessions, which had been acquired through a variety of methods, ranging from conquest to commerce. The acquisition of such possessions created (at least) two obvious legal problems, on which *Penn v Lord Baltimore* could shed light. First, what was the law governing those colonial possessions? Second, what role should English courts play in enforcing that law (whatever it was)?

Neither question was new when *Penn v Lord Baltimore* was decided. Unlike other colonial powers, such as Spain, the British governments of the seventeenth and eighteenth centuries did not systematically impose their own national law on the colonies.[43] The problem was left to the courts, and by 1750 the position seemed to be reasonably clear. In a crucial anonymous case from 1722, the Privy Council was reported as having set out three propositions:[44]

> 1st, That if there be a new and uninhabited country found out by English subjects, as the law is the birthright of every subject, so, wherever they go, they carry their laws with them, and therefore such new found country is to be governed by the laws of England; …
>
> 2dly, Where the King of England conquers a country … the conqueror, by saving the lives of the people conquered, gains a right and property in such people; in consequence of which he may impose upon them what laws he pleases. But,
>
> 3dly, Until such laws given by the conquering prince, the laws and customs of the conquered country shall hold place.

41 *Penn v Lord Baltimore* (1755) Dick 273, 21 ER 273.

42 C 12/17/2, 22 May 1761 (National Archive).

43 See generally B McPherson, 'The Mystery of Anonymous (1722)' (2001) 75 *Australian Law Journal* 169.

44 *Anonymous* 2 P Wms 75, 75–76; 24 ER 646, 646.

These carefully delineated categories drew a sharp distinction between newly-settled territory (where English law applied) and conquered territory (governed by the royal prerogative). Colonists strongly preferred to be governed by English law, not for merely patriotic reasons but because it offered some individual liberties and protection against abuse of power, which government by royal prerogative did not. In other words, the application of English law was not something resented by colonists, it was positively desired.[45]

The application of English law in the colonies, however, did not necessarily entail the jurisdiction of English courts over colonial disputes. A complex body of rules developed, with the position of equity being particularly problematic. One view, encapsulated in the submissions of counsel to the House of Lords in *Dutton v Howell*, was that the jurisdiction was extensive:[46]

> These Plantations are Parcel of the Realm, as Counties Palatine are: Their Rights and Interests are Every Day determined in Chancery here, only that for Necessity and Encouragement of Trade and Commerce, they make Plantation Lands as Assets in certain Cases to pay Debts; in all other Things they make Rules for them according to the common Course of English Equity: The Distance or the Contiguity of the Thing, makes no Alteration in the Case.

This passage would be reproduced in contemporary works of reference,[47] and may well have been a common assumption. Counsel also regarded jurisdiction over Irish matters as straightforward, observing that under the common law, a writ of error issued from Irish courts to England. Since Lord Hardwicke would rely on the Irish position in *Penn v Lord Baltimore*, it is important to investigate whether this assertion was correct.

A. Ireland

An examination of the equity cases concerning land in Ireland demonstrates that the position was nowhere near as clear as counsel in *Dutton v Howell* had suggested. Thus, in *Cartwright v Pettus*,[48] a Bill against joint tenants of lands in Ireland, asking for an account of profits and partition of the lands, was allowed as to the account but disallowed as to the partition. Lord Nottingham LC observed that the partition procedure would require the award of a commission into Ireland, which was beyond his powers. In *Comes Arglasse v Muschamp*,[49]

[45] McPherson (n 43) 179; B McPherson, 'How Equity Reached the Colonies' (2005) 5 *Queensland University of Technology Law and Justice Journal* 102, 102–03.

[46] *Dutton v Howell* (1693) Show 24, 33; 1 ER 17, 23.

[47] T Cunningham, *A New and Complete Law-Dictionary*, 3rd edn (London, JF & C Rivington, 1783) vol 1, 724 (under 'Foreign plantations'); C Viner, *A General Abridgment of Law and Equity*, 2nd edn (London, Robinson, Payne and Brook, 1793) vol 13, 411–12.

[48] *Cartwright v Pettus* (1675) 2 Ch Ca 214, 22 ER 916.

[49] *Comes Arglasse v Muschamp* (1682) 1 Vern 75, 23 ER 322.

by contrast, a Bill for relief against an annuity charged on Irish lands, which was alleged to have been obtained by fraud, was allowed. Lord Nottingham LC was clearly persuaded by counsel's emphasis on the role of the court being 'to relieve against frauds and cheats',[50] as he commented that '[t]his is surely only a jest put upon the jurisdiction of this court by the common lawyers'.[51] Lord Nottingham LC also referred to *Archer and Preston*, where, apparently, the Court of Chancery had assumed jurisdiction in a case concerning a contract for the sale of land in Ireland.

The report of *Comes Arglasse v Muschamp* suggested that the doctrine later relied on in *Penn v Lord Baltimore* was beginning to take shape. Counsel also highlighted an issue that the Lord Chancellor did not address but which highlighted a fundamental difficulty: if Irish law permitted the behaviour alleged to be fraudulent, he argued, 'this court had then the greater reason to retain this cause, and see justice done'.[52] As we shall see, the potential for equity's *in personam* jurisdiction to interpose obligations on claimants which would not be imposed by the law of the place where the property was situated, has continued to trouble the courts into the present century.[53]

Four years after *Comes Arglasse v Muschamp*, in *Earl of Kildare v Eustace*,[54] a very different approach to jurisdiction over Irish land was being espoused. Responding to a submission that Ireland was a conquered country, 'and a decree of this court may as well bind land in Ireland, as by every day's practice it doth lands that lie in foreign plantations',[55] and a further argument that 'the courts in England were proper expositors of the Irish laws; nay their judgment is to controul the opinion of the judges in Ireland, as upon writs of error',[56] the court assumed jurisdiction. The Lord Chancellor, Lord Beddingfield CJ and Lord Atkins CB held that 'the judges in England were proper expositors of the Irish laws'.[57] This was a jurisdiction based on political submission, not on the niceties of equitable principles.

The uneasy relationship between political reality and equitable doctrine was highlighted in *Sir John Fryer v Bernard*.[58] Here there was a motion for sequestration of the defendant's estate in Ireland for contempt of court. The Master of the Rolls, Sir Joseph Jekyll, refused the motion, holding that 'the process of this court could not affect any lands in Ireland'.[59] A more detailed report

[50] ibid, 76, 322.
[51] ibid, 77, 322.
[52] ibid, 76, 322.
[53] *R Griggs Group Ltd v Evans* [2004] EWHC 1088 (Ch), [2005] Ch 153. See further section VI.B below.
[54] *Earl of Kildare v Eustace* (1686) 1 Vern 419, 23 ER 559.
[55] ibid, 419, 559.
[56] ibid, 421, 560.
[57] ibid, 422, 561.
[58] *Sir John Fryar v Vernon* (1724) 9 Mod 124, 88 ER 355; Select Cases Temp King 5, 25 ER 191; *Sir John Fryer v Bernard* (1724) 2 P Wms 261, 24 ER 722.
[59] *Sir John Fryar v Vernon* (1724) 9 Mod 124, 124; 88 ER 355, 355.

reveals that the claimant sought to rely on a case concerning sequestration in North Carolina, where the Chancellor had said that that remedy might be available. Jekyll MR doubted that this could be correct: he recalled a Bill having been brought in Parliament to extend judgments to the plantations, and that Bill being rejected. The implication (it seems) was that judgments could not extend to the plantations under current law. He also hinted that such an extension would be politically problematic: '[A]s to the plantations, it is particularly odd as it affects the King's sovereignty in council over them …'.[60] This point – that the true jurisdiction was in the King in Council – would resurface in *Penn v Lord Baltimore*.

On appeal, Lord Macclesfield LC reversed the decision. A sequestration could be granted affecting land in Ireland, because English courts 'have a superintendent power over those in Ireland, and therefore writs of error lie in BR [Banco Regis – ie, the Court of King's Bench] in England to reverse judgments in BR in Ireland'.[61] For other plantations, such as North Carolina, the position was different: such sequestration 'should … be directed by the King in Council, where alone an appeal lies from decrees in the plantations'.[62] As in *Earl of Kildare v Eustace*, the focus was on political superiority, not equitable doctrine.

Thus it can be seen that when, in *Penn v Lord Baltimore (No 2)*, Lord Hardwicke LC invoked one of his own (unreported) decisions concerning estates in Ireland, it did not necessarily follow that a similar jurisdiction must exist for Pennsylvanian land. The most recent authority treated Ireland as a special case, with courts that were subject to writs of error in the King's Bench in London. Lord Hardwicke LC could hardly have been unaware of Ireland's unusual position, since one of his most important political speeches had argued that Ireland, as a conquered country, was automatically bound by parliamentary legislation.[63] No one had ever suggested that writs of error to the King's Bench in London lay from all colonial courts, so any general equitable power relating to land abroad could only be found in an elaboration of general principle derived from non-Irish situations.

B. General Principles of Jurisdiction

One significant, early development in the formulation of principles governing equity's jurisdiction over foreign land (outside Ireland) occurred in 1705, where the Court of Chancery assumed jurisdiction in a case brought by the mortgagee of the island of Sark against its owner.[64] 'The Court of Chancery,' it was said,

[60] *Sir John Fryar v Vernon* (1724) Select Cases Temp King 5, 6; 25 ER 191, 191.
[61] *Sir John Fryer v Bernard* (1724) 2 P Wms 261, 262; 24 ER 722, 723.
[62] ibid, 262, 723.
[63] P Thomas, 'Yorke, Philip', *Oxford Dictionary of National Biography* (online edition, 2011).
[64] *Toller v Carteret* (1705) 2 Vern 494, 23 ER 916.

'had … a jurisdiction, the defendant being served with the process here, *et aequitas agit in personam* …'.[65] This seems to have been the first time that equity's focus on the person (rather than the property) was expressly used to expand its jurisdiction. It was a powerful point, the full importance of which would only be fully developed by Lord Hardwicke in three cases that he decided before *Penn v Lord Baltimore (No 2)*. In *Angus v Angus*,[66] a Bill was brought for possession of land in Scotland, for discovery of rents and deeds, and for fraud in obtaining the deeds. The defendant pleaded that the court had no jurisdiction over lands in Scotland. Lord Hardwicke LC overruled the plea in relation to the fraud and discovery, since the court would 'act upon the person'.[67] As he explained, this principle had international implications – it would apply just as well to land in France as it did to land in Scotland. The part of the Bill claiming possession, however, was more problematic: all that the court could do was to order the defendant to transfer possession. A year later, in *Roberdeau v Rous*,[68] Lord Hardwicke LC was developing similar ideas in a case concerning possession of land at St Christopher's. Possession could not be granted because[69]

> this court has no jurisdiction so as to put persons into possession, in a place, where they have their own methods on such occasions, to which the party may have recourse; the present bill, therefore, is carrying the jurisdiction of this court further than it ever was before … Lands in the plantations are no more under the jurisdiction of this court, than lands in Scotland, for it only *agit in personam*.

However, that was not to say that the court was powerless: an injunction could be granted ordering the delivery of possession, just as the court could order specific performance of a sale of plantation estates.[70]

The final case, *Foster v Vassall*,[71] developed the ideas a stage further. The Bill was brought against executors, by the testator's son, praying for an account and payment. The defendant pleaded that both parties resided in Jamaica; the claimant had already sued him in the Jamaica Court of Chancery in 1745, where the defendant had put in an answer and account; furthermore, all relevant matters lay in Jamaica. Lord Hardwicke LC overruled the plea on the ground that it was technically defective, and acknowledged that, had the pleading been formally sound, it would have raised a 'considerable question'.[72] His description of the problem hinted at how he would have resolved it:[73]

> The different courts of equity are held under the same crown, though, in different dominions, and therefore, considering this [ie the Court of Chancery in Jamaica] as

[65] ibid, 495, 917.
[66] *Angus v Angus* (1737) West Temp Hardwicke 23, 25 ER 800.
[67] ibid, 23, 801.
[68] *Roberdeau v Rous* (1738) 1 Atk 543, 26 ER 342.
[69] ibid, 544, 342.
[70] ibid, 544, 342.
[71] *Foster v Vassall* (1747) 3 Atk 587, 26 ER 1138.
[72] ibid, 589, 1139.
[73] ibid.

> a court abroad, the point of jurisdiction is the same as if in *Ireland*; and it is certain where the provision is in *England*, let the cause of suit arise in *Ireland*, or the plantations, if the bill be brought in *England*, as the defendant is here, the courts do *agere in personam*, and may, by compulsion of the person, and process of the court, compel him to do justice.

Such an approach, he acknowledged, might well result in the 'inconvenience'[74] of two suits concerning the same matter. Lord Hardwicke LC did not elaborate further, but it is perhaps implicit in the passage quoted above that he did not envisage the two suits causing anything more than 'inconvenience': since both courts were applying the same equity, both should reach the same result. Lurking in the background was the question of what should happen if the laws of the country where the land was situated reached a conclusion different from English equity.

Some indication of how Lord Hardwicke LC would have answered this question may be gleaned from his decisions on the use of the writ *ne exeat regno* against foreigners. The writ prevented the defendant from leaving the jurisdiction of the court so as to evade Chancery process and deprive the claimant of his remedy.[75] In *Pearne v Lisle*,[76] the defendant was being sued for rent due for the hire of 14 slaves at Antigua, and for redelivery of the slaves. In discharging a previous order granting the writ, Lord Hardwicke LC commented that:[77]

> The person of the defendant is amenable, for he is a native of Antigua; he is going to Antigua: his effects, and likewise the Negroes, are there … It is a colony subject to England, and the plaintiff may have justice done him in the Courts there.

He elaborated on this further in *Robertson v Wilkie:*[78]

> It is a reason that generally prevails with me not to grant such writ, where one of the parties corresponding or dealing lives out of the kingdom, and the transactions are on the faith of having justice in the place where the parties respectively reside. And so it has been held where one lived in England, and the other in one of the plantations or settlements belonging to England, which are governed by the same laws, except some few peculiar to the place.

However, he continued, these reasons did not hold good where an action between two merchants would be held either at Gibraltar or Minorca if the defendant was allowed to leave England. In Gibraltar, 'the jurisdiction is not adapted to determining property and accounts between merchants'. In Minorca, the 'Spanish method of justice prevails'.[79]

[74] ibid, 589, 1140.
[75] See generally J Beames, *A Brief View of the Writ Ne Exeat Regno, as an Equitable Process*, 2nd edn (London, Pheney, Sweet, Maxwell & Stevens, 1824); on the application of the writ to foreigners, see 64–68.
[76] *Pearne v Lisle* (1749) Amb 75, 27 ER 47.
[77] ibid, 77, 48.
[78] *Robertson v Wilkie* (1753) Amb 177, 177; 27 ER 119, 119.
[79] ibid, 177, 119.

Lord Hardwicke's reasoning in *Robertson v Wilkie* was later doubted by Lord Thurlow LC: 'justice,' he observed, 'would be equally certain',[80] whether at Gibraltar or Minorca. That criticism, however, seems to miss Lord Hardwicke's point. For Hardwicke, the certainty of justice somewhere, under some legal system or other, was not sufficient for the Court of Chancery to relinquish its hold over the defendant. What was needed, as in *Pearne v Lisle*, was ready access to justice according to English law. If that was not available, the Court of Chancery would step in.

C. Pennsylvania

As it happened, Lord Hardwicke had recently acted on the understanding that the Court of Chancery would intervene if justice according to English law was unavailable, when, in *Penn v Lord Baltimore*, he ordered specific performance that had to take place in Pennsylvania. At that time Pennsylvania had no courts of equity, it only had courts of common law.[81] Those common law courts would later incorporate various aspects of equity, but the first reported case to begin that process of incorporation did not occur until 1768.[82] Even when large parts of equity had been accepted by the Pennsylvania courts, they were still unable to devise a common law replicant of specific performance: the closest equivalent was an award of conditional damages, which overvalued the property in question in the hope that the defendant would be persuaded to return the property rather than overpay for it.[83]

It is important to emphasise that Pennsylvania's lack of an equity court was not an accident, nor an oversight. Penn's charter had granted him the right to set up such a court, but he had decided not to, apparently being struck by the happy position of the native Americans, who were not 'perplexed by Chancery suits'.[84] Penn's decision was also probably influenced by Chancery's reputation for arbitrariness. Lord Nottingham's attempts to place equity on a more principled basis would improve its reputation in time, but in the early 1680s, when Penn's decision was being made, Nottingham's judgments had hardly been reported at all.[85]

[80] *Atkinson v Leonard* (1791) 3 Bro CC 218, 223; 29 ER 499, 502.

[81] See generally S Fisher, 'The Administration of Equity Through Common Law Forms' (1885) 1 *Law Quarterly Review* 455; S Liverant and W Hitchler, 'A History of Equity in Pennsylvania' (1932–1933) 37 *Dickinson Law Review* 156.

[82] *Swift v Hawkins* (1768) 1 Dallas 17.

[83] Fisher (n 81) 461–62. The conditional damages technique closely resembles the classical Roman solution to the same problem: B Nicholas, *An Introduction to Roman Law* (Oxford, Clarendon Press, 1975) 101–02; D Johnston, *Roman Law in Context* (Cambridge, CUP, 1999) 117–18.

[84] Fisher (n 81) 455; Liverant and Hitchler (n 81) 158. Penn also envied their freedom from bills of lading.

[85] B McPherson, 'How Equity Reached the Colonies' (2005) 5 *Queensland University of Technology Law and Justice Journal* 102, 105; D Yale, 'Finch, Heneage', *Oxford Dictionary of National Biography* (n 63).

The General Assembly of Pennsylvania seems to have taken a more optimistic view of equity, and made several attempts to create equity jurisdictions. All of these attempts, however, were repealed by the British Parliament, until, in 1720, a Court of Equity was finally created. The Court sat for 16 years, but was then effectively abolished by the colonists. The reasons for the abolition are striking: the objection was not to the content of equity doctrine in itself but to the method of administering it. As was typical of equity in the colonies,[86] it was not administered by specialist Chancery judges, steeped in equity principles; it was administered by the Governor, either alone or in Council. The governors claimed this right on the basis that, like the Lord Chancellor in England, they held the great seal for their respective provinces.[87] Whilst that might make the Governor's administration of equity technically defensible, the reality of the King's representative sitting as a judge with special responsibility for property was unacceptable to many colonists. It was exactly the kind of arbitrary royal power that they had travelled halfway round the world to escape.

The pressure began to build in Pennsylvania from 1726, with the colonists arguing that the Court of Chancery was contrary to the guarantee in Pennsylvania's *Charter of Privileges* that no one could be required to answer a complaint relating to property before the Governor or Council.[88] Meanwhile, events in the neighbouring province of New York highlighted the potential for abuse of the Governor's Chancery powers,[89] which seem to have spurred on the Pennsylvania Assembly, in 1735, to pass a resolution that the Court of Equity was, indeed, contrary to the *Charter of Privileges*. The Attorney-General and Solicitor-General in England were asked for their view, and replied that the Court was not contrary to the *Charter*. The Assembly responded by introducing a Bill to remove all Chancery powers from the Governor, but in the meantime the Governor had died, and his successor made no attempt to exercise any Chancery powers.

The history of equity in eighteenth-century Pennsylvania casts light on *Penn v Lord Baltimore* in two ways. First, it shows that the authority which Lord Hardwicke referred to in support of equity's jurisdiction over land in Pennsylvania – *Richardson v Hamilton* (1733) – was decided under conditions very different from those in *Penn v Lord Baltimore*. In *Richardson* specific performance was theoretically available from the Pennsylvania Court of Equity; by the time of the decision in *Penn* it was not. So, whilst *Richardson* could be interpreted as an English court applying the same equity that applied in Pennsylvania, *Penn* could not be justified on that basis. However, although

[86] McPherson (n 85) 106–09.

[87] ibid, 106. See further J Smith and L Hershkowitz, 'Courts of Equity in the Province of New York: The Cosby Controversy, 1732–1736' (1972) 16 *American Journal of Legal History* 1, 9–11.

[88] Liverant and Hitchler (n 81) 163–64.

[89] Smith and Hershkowitz (n 87).

no record of a judgment in *Richardson v Hamilton* has survived, it seems to have been a more complicated case than Lord Hardwicke's brief reference to it suggested. The case was concerned with confiscation of property under a private act of the Pennsylvania Assembly, which had subsequently been disallowed by an Order in Council.[90] The claimants failed to regain possession in Pennsylvania, but were granted an order for delivery of possession in the Court of Chancery in England. It is not entirely clear why the claimants had not previously applied to the Court of Equity in Pennsylvania, especially since the Governor (who would have sat in the case) had some sympathy with the claimants' complaints. Part of the explanation may well have been that the Richardsons realised that any equity suit in Pennsylvania was likely to be ineffective. By 1733 the Governor's Chancery powers were being questioned, and for him (effectively) to overrule the Pennsylvania Assembly would have almost certainly precipitated a crisis. Certainly the Richardsons' adversary, Alexander Hamilton, could have been relied upon to make political capital out of any such decree by the Governor, and indeed to have made a point of disobeying it: his republican sympathies were well known, and he would soon be demonstrating his formidable combination of political and legal abilities in New York, in the trial of the radical printer, Peter Zenger.[91] The Richardsons may well have chosen London as the venue for their Chancery claim in an attempt to exert pressure on Hamilton, whilst simultaneously limiting his opportunity to score political points. Unfortunately, there seems to be no record of the judgment of Lord King LC, so we have no way of knowing whether he gave any consideration to the fact that the claimants were not availing themselves of a theoretically available, but practically unattractive, local equitable remedy.

The second way in which the Pennsylvania position casts light on *Penn v Lord Baltimore* is by showing the strikingly political dimension of the court's decision to grant specific performance. The Pennsylvania colonists had decided to do away with their court of equity, because it smacked of remote royal interference; yet here was a judge, thousands of miles away, giving orders for the demarcation of their territory. Chancery doctrines were being invoked to justify central control over colonial land, despite the colonists' emphatic local rejection of those doctrines. The irony may not have been lost on William Penn's descendants, that they were having to rely on an institution that Penn himself had decided they were better off without.

[90] J Smith, *Appeals to the Privy Council from the American Plantations* (New York, Columbia University Press, 1950) 628–31. Additional background on the case may be found in P Wilson Coldham, 'Clarke, Curtis, and Richardson, of Barbados, Delaware and Philadelphia' (1973) 61 *National Genealogical Society Quarterly* 3.

[91] Smith and Hershkowitz (n 87) 41.

VI. THE APPLICATION OF PENN v LORD BALTIMORE

A. Expansion

In the 50 years or so after the decision in *Penn v Lord Baltimore*, the doctrine that equity acted *in personam* and could, therefore, affect property outside the jurisdiction, took root to such an extent that Lord Eldon LC, in 1804, could assert that '[t]here is no doubt of the jurisdiction upon contracts as to land in the West Indies, if the persons are here'.[92] As in *Penn v Lord Baltimore* itself, the primary focus was on colonial land; as the colonies expanded, so did the practical importance of the principle itself. Colonial expansion also brought the principle to bear on legal regimes where it was not quite so easy to distinguish between *in rem* and *in personam* effect. Thus, for instance, six eminent counsels' advice was sought by the East India Company as to whether Lord Clive could sue in Chancery to enforce a *jaghire* of Indian land.[93] Lord Hardwicke's son, Charles Yorke, emphasised the *in personam* principle, but seems to have been in a minority in concluding that the *jaghire* was like a claim for rent, which raised no issue of title.[94] Thurlow, who gave the most elaborate opinion the other way, took the view that[95]

> if the contract were concerning a real subject, always extant in a foreign independant [sic] country, always in the actual disposition of their justice, I should think the English court of chancery ought not to interpose in it ... [T]he court of chancery here cannot strip a rent of that relation which in point of title it bears to the land, so far as to decree upon it, any more than an action could be maintained here for the use and occupation of lands in France.

The *in personam* principle also opened the way for injunctions restraining proceedings in other jurisdictions.[96] The possibility of such injunctions had initially been denied, despite the bar's opinion to the contrary,[97] but by the early nineteenth century there were signs that judicial attitudes were changing. Thus, in *Harrison v Gurney*[98] Lord Eldon LC granted an injunction restraining proceedings by trustees in Ireland, although the precise basis for doing so was not discussed. Three years earlier, in *Kennedy v Earl of Cassillis*,[99] the same judge had refused an injunction sought against the Court of Session, on the basis that such an injunction could never be enforced[100] – clearly an injunction addressed

[92] *Jackson v Petrie* (1804) 10 Ves Jun 164, 165; 32 ER 807, 807.

[93] A *jaghire* was (typically) a short-term grant of land by an Indian ruler to a successful military commander, made in recognition of military service.

[94] F Hargrave, *Collectanea Juridica* (London, W Clarke, 1810) vol 1, 247–48.

[95] ibid, 254–55. *Cf St Pierre v South American Stores (Gath and Chaves) Limited* [1936] 1 KB 382.

[96] D Altaras, 'The Anti-Suit Injunction: Historical Overview' (2009) 75(3) *Arbitration* 327.

[97] *Love v Baker* (1665) 1 Ch Ca 67, 22 ER 698.

[98] *Harrison v Gurney* (1821) 2 Jac & W 563, 37 ER 743.

[99] *Kennedy v Earl of Cassillis* (1818) 2 Swan 313, 36 ER 635.

[100] ibid, 322, 638.

to the court itself was not the solution. The principled basis for an injunction restraining proceedings else-where was finally articulated by Lord Brougham LC in *Lord Portarlington v Soulby*.[101] There, relying expressly on *Penn v Lord Baltimore*, Lord Brougham LC explained that the jurisdiction was[102]

> grounded, like all other jurisdiction of the Court, not upon any pretension to the exercise of judicial and administrative rights abroad, but on the circumstance of the person of the party on whom this order is being made being within the power of this Court.

The most significant application of *Penn v Lord Baltimore* concerned situations where the law of the place where the land was situated was different from English law. As we have seen in the previous section, the decision in *Penn v Lord Baltimore* itself could only be justified on the assumption that the Court of Chancery in London could give a remedy despite no similar remedy being available in the place where the land was situated. However, the point had not been expressly considered, and in *Pike v Hoare*,[103] decided 13 years after *Penn v Lord Baltimore*, a very different approach was taken. The claim was, essentially, a challenge to the validity of a will made by the claimant's brother; all the land affected by the will lay in Pennsylvania. Lord Northington LC regarded the latter fact as crucial:[104]

> I build my opinion materially on the fact of the lands lying in *Pennsylvania*, for a will of lands lying in any of the colonies is not triable in *Westminster Hall*; if it were, it would be introductive of great confusion, and be very detrimental to the colonies. We have colonies and factories in the four quarters of the world, and each colony and factory have distinct laws of their own. Judges in *Westminster Hall* are not acquainted with the laws of the several colonies and factories; they are local. In *Penn v Lord Baltimore*, Lord Hardwicke made the distinction, and said, it was the contract that gave the court jurisdiction in that case; the principles of equity being the same in all places.

The Bill was refused.

Although Lord Northington LC claimed to be acting on the principles set out in *Penn v Lord Baltimore*, his reasoning could not be supported by that case. The principles of equity were not the same in Pennsylvania and England – Pennsylvania provided no specific remedies, England did. But Lord Northington LC was not mistaken in attributing the idea that equity was the same in all places to Lord Hardwicke: Hardwicke had said almost exactly that in *Foster v Vassall*.[105] Lord Northington LC was, perhaps, trying to return the law to the

[101] *Lord Portarlington v Soulby* (1834) 3 My & K 104, 40 ER 40.
[102] ibid, 108, 41–42.
[103] *Pike v Hoare* (1763) 2 Eden 182, 28 ER 867; Amb 428, 27 ER 286.
[104] (1763) 2 Eden 183–84, 28 ER 867.
[105] (1747) 3 Atk 587, 26 ER 1138. Discussed above, text at n 73.

narrower position that Hardwicke had espoused before *Penn v Lord Baltimore*. That earlier position certainly had the advantage of eliminating clashes between the courts of different jurisdictions, but it would have effectively limited the *Penn v Lord Baltimore* principle to British colonies where equity had not been modified. Had Lord Northington LC's view prevailed, we would hear little of *Penn v Lord Baltimore* today.

However, Lord Northington's view did not prevail. In *Lord Cranstown v Johnston*,[106] Arden MR explicitly established the crucial principle that even if the law of the place where the land was situated would refuse a remedy, equity could intervene – relying on the *in personam* jurisdiction – to prevent fraud. Thus, where a creditor had forced a judicial sale of the debtor's estate in St Christopher's (in the West Indies), and had acquired that estate at an undervalue, an equitable remedy was available, despite the fact that, under the statute law of St Christopher's, the sale was unimpeachable. Arden MR's analysis was forthright:[107]

> [W]ith regard to any contract made or equity in this country respecting lands in a foreign country, particularly the British dominions, this Court will hold the same jurisdiction, as if they were situated in England ... [The creditor] has gained an advantage, which neither the law of this country nor of any other country would permit. I will lay down the rule as broad as this: this Court will not permit him to avail himself of the law of any other country to do what would be gross injustice.

This emphasis on English law concepts of fraud and contract would be reaffirmed by Cottenham LC in *In re Courtney, ex parte Pollard*,[108] with a significant caveat:[109]

> If indeed the law of the country where the land is situate should not permit or not enable the defendant to do what the court might otherwise think it right to decree, it would be useless and unjust to direct him to do the act; but when there is no such impediment, the courts of this country, in the exercise of their jurisdiction over contracts made here, or in administering equities between parties residing here, act upon their own rules, and are not influenced by any consideration of what the effect of such contracts might be in the country where the lands are situate, or of the manner in which the courts of such countries might deal with such equities.

As the editors of Dicey, Morris and Collins point out, it is not entirely clear how stringent a prohibition is needed,[110] but from the facts of *Lord Cranstown v Johnston* (which Lord Cottenham LC cited), it is clearly insufficient to prevent a Chancery decree to show that the foreign law makes no provision for fraud.

[106] *Lord Cranstown v Johnston* (1796) 3 Ves Jun 170, 30 ER 952.
[107] ibid, 182–83, 959.
[108] *In re Courtney, ex parte Pollard* (1840) Mont & Ch 239.
[109] ibid, 250–51.
[110] L Collins (ed), *Dicey, Morris and Collins on the Conflict of Laws*, 14th edn (London, Sweet & Maxwell, 2006) para 23.045.

Similarly, the facts of *In re Courtney, ex parte Pollard* concerned an equitable mortgage of land in Scotland; Scots law did not recognise equitable mortgages, but that did not prevent the English Court of Chancery making an *in personam* order to enforce one.

The disregard for foreign law shown in *Lord Cranstown v Johnston* and *In re Courtney, ex parte Pollard* troubled Joseph Story, who observed that[111]

> the doctrine of the English Courts of Chancery, on this head of jurisdiction, seems carried to an extent, which may perhaps, in some cases, not find a perfect warrant in the general principles of international public law; and, therefore, it must have a very uncertain basis, as to its recognition in foreign countries, so far as it may be supposed to be founded on the comity of nations.

The *Lord Cranstown* case, he felt, could only be justified by the fact that all the parties were British subjects, and the original judgment was on a British island.[112]

Such caution, however, did not prevail, and during the course of the nineteenth and twentieth centuries, the doctrine from *Penn v Lord Baltimore* was applied to property all over the world, from Scottish cottages,[113] to Shanghai houses[114] and Brazilian sugar plantations.[115] As Francis Palmer was quick to recognise, and the courts later acknowledged,[116] the *in personam* principle had a valuable commercial aspect: it allowed owners of land abroad to raise finance, without having to go to the trouble and expense of having to satisfy local legal requirements; and it also made loans secured on foreign land more attractive to lenders, who were not obliged to enforce their rights in foreign courts. Thus, in the fourth edition of his *Company Precedents*, Palmer stated that[117]

> land situate abroad, but belonging to a company registered here, can in most cases be effectually charged in favour of debenture holders or their trustees, without regard to the formalities required by the local law in relation to transfers or mortgages. For it was settled long since that the Court of Chancery, by virtue of its jurisdiction *in personam*, would, as between persons resident here, enforce equities in regard to foreign land. *Penn v Lord Baltimore* …

Palmer also recognised that the equitable interest of the creditor was not perfectly protected, in the sense that it might be displaced by other charges satisfying the relevant foreign law. 'But,' he continued, 'this is a risk which in may cases the parties are contented to run; the principal object being to give the debenture holders a preference over general creditors of the company, and

[111] J Story, *Commentaries on the Conflict of Laws*, 5th edn (Boston, Mass, Little, Brown and Company, 1857) 888.
[112] ibid, 889.
[113] *Coote v Jecks* (1872) 13 LR Eq 597.
[114] *Ex parte Holthausen* (1874) LR 9 Ch App 722.
[115] *Duder v Amsterdamsch Trustees Kantoor* [1902] 2 Ch 132.
[116] *In re The Anchor Line (Henderson Brothers) Limited* [1937] 1 Ch 483.
[117] F Palmer, *Company Precedents*, 4th edn (London, Stevens & Sons, 1888) 378.

not to fetter the company in dealing with its property.'[118] Palmer obviously had in mind British companies raising finance from British lenders, secured against overseas assets. For such companies, the *Penn v Lord Baltimore* principle meant that commerce and conscience walked hand in hand.

B. Third Parties

Although the dominant theme in the development of the principle from *Penn v Lord Baltimore* was one of broadening and generalising, one significant limitation emerged relating to third parties. Whilst equity would intervene to enforce contracts, and to prevent fraud as between the perpetrator and victim, it would not protect equitable rights against third parties. Thus, for instance, in the leading case of *Norris v Chambres*,[119] the director of a company had advanced £40,000 of his own funds for the purchase by the company of a mine in Prussia. The purchase fell through, but the vendor retained the part-payment. The mine was later sold to another (related) company, with the vendor giving credit for £40,000 already received. The court held that no declaration of lien over the mine in favour of the director's estate could be made. Sir John Romilly MR made it clear that he had reservations about the *Penn v Lord Baltimore* principle generally, and was certainly not prepared to extend it.[120] The decision was affirmed by Lord Campbell LC, who observed that the principle from *Penn v Lord Baltimore* 'was founded on any contract or privity' between the parties.[121] A similar approach was taken later in *Deschamps v Miller*.[122]

This limitation on the principle has troubled judges and commentators. As Peter Prescott QC pointed out in *R Griggs Group Ltd v Evans*,[123] third party purchasers of land with notice of the claimant's interest would, prima facie, be regarded as fraudulent, using that word in its broad equitable sense. It therefore seems to be a contradiction in terms to state that the *Penn v Lord Baltimore* principle is used to restrain fraud, but does not apply to third party purchasers with notice. Peter Prescott QC took the view that *Norris v Chambres*[124] and *Deschamps v Miller*[125] have now been overtaken by more modern developments in private international law. Today, he explained, such cases would not

[118] ibid, 379. *Cf* the more cautious approach taken by Palmer's later editors: eg, A Topham (ed), *Palmer's Company Law: A Practical Handbook for Lawyers and Business Men*, 10th edn (London, Stevens, 1916) 274.
[119] *Norris v Chambres* (1861) 29 Beav 246, 54 ER 621; (1861) 3 De GF & J 583, 45 ER 1004.
[120] (1861) 29 Beav 246, 253–55; 54 ER 621, 624–25.
[121] (1861) 3 De GF & J 583, 584; 45 ER 1004, 1005.
[122] *Deschamps v Miller* [1908] 1 Ch 856.
[123] *R Griggs Group Ltd v Evans* [2004] EWHC 1088 (Ch), [2005] Ch 153.
[124] *Norris v Chambres* (n 119).
[125] *Deschamps v Miller* (n 122).

be seen as raising a question of jurisdiction, but as raising a question of choice of law.[126]

Assuming that the approach of Peter Prescott QC is adopted by the appellate courts, the third-party issue no longer causes practical difficulties today. However, the reasons why the courts found the issue so difficult illustrate a fundamental feature of the *Penn v Lord Baltimore* principle. At a broad level, the theme running through the speeches in *Norris v Chambres*[127] and *Deschamps v Miller*[128] was that it could not be right simply to apply English equitable rules without reference to foreign law. Unfortunately there was strong authority – in the form of the decisions in *Lord Cranstown v Johnston*[129] and *In re Courtney, ex parte Pollard*[130] – that no such reference could be made. Rather than proceeding in a manner that they were convinced would be incorrect, the courts chose to limit the application of the *Penn v Lord Baltimore* principle so as to exclude third party cases.

In fact, what cases like *Norris v Chambres* and *Deschamps v Miller* illustrated was that the assessment of fraud without reference to foreign law was fundamentally flawed. The point was demonstrated by *Hicks v Powell*,[131] a decision of Lord Hatherley LC. There, a house in Madras had been conveyed to the claimant by the vendor, but the conveyance had not been registered. A year later, the vendor purported to mortgage the same house to the defendant, who had notice of the earlier conveyance but relied on the fact that the prior conveyance was not registered. The mortgage deed was registered. Under the Indian Registration Act 1864, all deeds of conveyance were required to be registered within 12 months of conveyance taking place; any deeds not so registered could not be produced in evidence.

Lord Hatherley LC refused the claimant's application for a declaration of priority, commenting:[132]

> There is great difficulty in understanding how, in the case of a covenant which could not be enforced if the parties were in India, a right to sue can arise from the circumstance of the person sought to be charged changing his residence before the institution of the suit.

'It would be very strange …' he added, 'if the claimant could obtain rights over land in India through an action in England, which could not have been obtained in the Indian courts …'.[133]

[126] *Griggs* (n 123) [90]–[110].
[127] *Norris v Chambres* (n 119).
[128] *Deschamps v Miller* (n 122).
[129] *Lord Cranstown* (n 106).
[130] *Courtney* (n 108).
[131] *Hicks v Powell* (1869) LR 4 Ch App 741.
[132] ibid, 745.
[133] ibid, 746.

Although he did not quite put it in this way, the problem that Lord Hatherley LC had identified was that equitable fraud was relative, not absolute. What might be fraud in one system need not be fraud in another. Thus where, as in India, the system of registration provided that unregistered transfers were to be of no effect, it was not fraudulent for a third party with notice of such a transaction to rely on his strict legal rights; where no registration scheme was in place, the third party with notice was likely to be fraudulent. The real problem in *Norris v Chambres* and *Deschamps v Miller* was not that the defendants were third parties with notice; it was that the courts could not make any sensible decision about fraud without information about the foreign legal system.[134] In essence, the problem went back to the unqualified assertions in *Lord Cranstown v Johnston* and *In re Courtney, ex parte Pollard* that foreign law should be disregarded.

VII. CONCLUSION

Penn v Lord Baltimore is a landmark case for more reasons than are traditionally recognised. It provides an invaluable insight into the legal machinery of colonialism, demonstrating how a wide range of legal concepts from sources as diverse as feudalism and compromise agreements could be harnessed to solve essentially novel problems. It also highlights the peculiar, private-enterprise nature of early colonial ventures, and the way that the law responded by resolving disputes within a private law framework. At the level of general equity doctrine, its landmark status derives not from having created the *in personam* doctrine, but from having facilitated a particular approach to it, whereby English courts were given licence to supplement foreign law. As this chapter has shown, this licence to give remedies where they were not available abroad gave English courts extensive powers over colonial land, and allowed land abroad to be readily used as security for loans. In short, *Penn v Lord Baltimore* had both political and commercial significance, in addition to its undoubted importance as a landmark case in private international law.

[134] This point is perhaps hinted at by Jessel MR in *Norton v Florence Land and Public Works Company* (1877) 7 Ch D 332, 336.

2

Peninsular and Oriental Steam Navigation Company v Shand and *Lloyd v Guibert* (1865)

ADRIAN BRIGGS

How should a court identify the law that governs a contract? Or, perhaps more precisely, how should a court identify the law which tells it, and tells the parties, whether there is a contract by which they are bound to each other, and if there is, what are the obligations it creates? What role, if any, should be allocated to or reserved by the law of the forum? Such questions have, no doubt, been asked for centuries, but the evolution of the answer yielded by the common law reminds us of the great work done and not done by the conflicts lawyers of the nineteenth century.

I. BACKGROUND

For English authority the scene was set, a century before Dicey, by *Male v Roberts*.[1] A young member of the Royal Circus, then performing in Edinburgh, had been supplied with alcohol by Mr Cockburn.[2] Cockburn demanded payment, and arrested[3] his customer when cash was not forthcoming. Another member of the circus settled the debt, and in due course brought proceedings against the drinker in England, though whether on a contract of loan or for money paid to the defendant's use the reporter[4] does not make it clear. The ungrateful defendant pled his infancy as a defence to the claim. Lord Eldon, briefly Chief Justice of the Common Pleas, wasted no words: 'It appears from

[1] *Malev Roberts* (1800) 3 Esp 163, 170 ER 574.

[2] Cockburn of Leith was, then as now, an Edinburgh wine merchant, who went on to found the eponymous port house.

[3] On a warrant of *meditatio fugae*.

[4] Espinasse, alas.

the evidence in this cause that the cause of action arose in Scotland; the contract must be therefore governed by the law of that country where the contract arises. Would infancy be a good defence by the law of Scotland, had the action been commenced there?' The question went unanswered; but we may still observe that the law of the place of contracting governed the obligation, and that capacity to contract was taken to be governed by the *lex contractus*. The fact that there was no sufficient evidence of Scots law before the court evidently meant that it was the claimant, rather than the defendant, who lost: the reasoning appears to be that the claimant had failed to prove that his claim was good in Scots law, rather than that the defendant, who had raised the plea of infancy, had failed to make good his defence. Lord Eldon specifically denied that any shortcoming in the evidence of Scots law could be filled by a presumption that foreign law was the same as English law: a proposition whose application was still tormenting the courts two centuries later.[5] The report of the case may leave a little to be desired, but it makes it clear that the law governing the contract was the law of the place where it was made.

Thirty years later, Story expanded on the point. He entertained no doubt as to the state of the common law: the validity of a contract, and much else about it, had to be governed by the law of the place where it was made.[6] Insofar as there was need to justify recourse to the law of the place of contracting, he asserted: 'if valid there, it is by the general law of nations, *jure gentium*, held valid everywhere by tacit or implied consent'. He went on to warn that if this approach were not adopted, 'the nation which should refuse to recognise the common principles would soon find its whole commercial intercourse reduced to a state like that in which it now exists with savage tribes, with the barbarous nations of Sumatra, and with other portions of Asia washed by the Pacific'. That seems rather pungent, even for a conflicts lawyer.[7] In fact, Story's preference for the law of the place of making the contract was, it seems, being contrasted with the law of the place where it was to be performed, the unexposed template for this analysis appearing to be that of a contract made between people in a relatively developed common law jurisdiction but calling for acts by way of performance in faraway places with strange-sounding names. Given those parameters, it was unsurprising that adherence to the law of the place of contracting held the greater attraction.

[5] See *FS Cairo (Nile Plaza) LLC v Brownlie* [2021] UKSC 45, [2021] 3 WLR 1011, discussed in ch 18 in this volume.

[6] J Story, *Commentaries on the Conflict of Laws* (Boston, Hilliard Gray & Co, 1834) para 242. The quotations are from that one paragraph.

[7] That said, in *Lloyd v Guibert* (1865) LR 1 QB 115, Willes J argued against the application of the law of the place of contracting by observing (at 128) that there were 'not a few half-savage places in Africa and Asia, with neither ships nor maritime laws …' which would make the application of the place of contracting an awkward one. He obviously had a different paradigm in mind.

Thirty more years on, and the winds of change were starting to blow. In England, the thinking through was being done in the courts in the brilliant 1860s, still 30 years before Dicey set about organising the law on the grand scale. Shortly before he elaborated definitive choice of law rules for torts, Willes J charted the course for the private international law of contracts to be prised free of the iron grip of the law of the place where the contract was made. The decision of the Court of Exchequer Chamber in *Lloyd v Guibert* is the foundation on which the private international law of contract is built, and Willes J is its architect. It is the work of a judge at the very height of his power.[8] However, it was preceded by, and we must start with, a striking decision of the Privy Council, the practical importance of which may lie in the manner in which Willes J used or abused it to buttress his decision.

II. PENINSULAR AND ORIENTAL STEAM NAVIGATION COMPANY v SHAND

Charles Farquhar Shand was born in 1812 into an Aberdeenshire family which had interests, as is no longer fashionable to boast, in the sugar industry in the West Indies and Mauritius. He was appointed to serve as the sixth Chief Justice of Mauritius, a colony which had been acquired from France in 1814. Family business interests apart, the office was one for which a Scots lawyer was intellectually well suited, the legal system of Mauritius being, then as now, civilian rather than common law. More surprising, perhaps, was the fact that as he departed for the tropics, the incoming Chief Justice packed a trunk of 'cloaks, an over-coat, and plaids': not so well suited, one may think. This hairy and uncongenial wardrobe was lost in transit, to the evident distress of its owner. In litigation before the Supreme Court of Mauritius, if you please, the Chief Justice obtained an order that compensation be paid to him by the Peninsular and Oriental Steam Navigation Company, with whom he had contracted for his passage from Southampton to Mauritius. He prevailed as claimant in the Court of which he was Chief Justice in spite of an exclusion clause in the contract which had provided that 'the Company do not hold themselves liable for damage to or detention of passenger's baggage'. P&O might not have held themselves liable, but the Supreme Court of Mauritius did, on the apparent basis that as a matter of French law the contractual exclusion of liability was ineffective. The Supreme Court's reasoning is not dwelt on in the judgment of the Privy Council, but unless it was based on an improbably early form of consumer protection

[8] In *Roles v Nathan* [1963] 1 WLR 1117 (CA) 1122, Lord Denning MR cited the observation and hope of the draughtsman of the Occupiers' Liability Act 1957, that 'the Act would replace a principle of the common law with a new principle of the common law; instead of having the Judgment of Mr Justice Willes construed as if it were a statute, one is to have a statute which can be construed as if it were a Judgment of Mr Justice Willes'.

law, it is almost inexplicable.[9] Still, it would have taken a notably sturdy court to dismiss the claim raised by its Chief Justice in respect of his collection of vanishing tweeds.

On appeal to the Privy Council,[10] P&O contended that the issue in the case, namely the legal validity of the exclusion clause in the contract, should not be referred to or determined by the laws of Mauritius. The Privy Council agreed: the Mauritius Court should have applied English law, and had it done so the exclusion clause would have absolved P&O of liability. The legal basis for its conclusion as to the applicable law was somewhat blurred by the judgment, which appeared to be driven in part by the law of merits. The contract had been made in England between a British subject and an English company. The law of the place where the contract was made was said to be the law to which the parties were understood to submit and agreed to impose upon their contract; the judgment observes, almost casually, that this 'seems perfectly clear as to the actual intention of the contracting parties'.[11] And after a review of the circumstances of the contract it said a little more: 'The actual intention of the parties therefore must be taken clearly to have been to treat this as an English contract, to be interpreted according to the rules of English law.'[12]

Those circumstances were that the contract was made in England between British subjects; the first leg of the journey was to be on an English ship; that the journey would involve travelling through places where something might go wrong, as it did at Suez; that the company had drafted the exclusion clause by which it proposed to limit its liability; and that the passenger had signed his agreement to it. The idea that any passenger – let alone the Chief Justice of Mauritius – should say that although he signed the company's document and well understood its intentions, he intended the contract to be governed by a law which would render the clause a nullity, would be an affront to the conscience of the court: had he been unhappy with the terms of the offer he, of all people, could have refused to sign. The result was that the contract was governed by English law, as this was to be found to be the actual, and the only legitimate, intention of the parties when they made it.

As said, it is not hard to detect some distaste for the position seemingly taken by the Chief Justice: at this distance the whole thing looks pretty shabby. One may then ask why the Court did not simply rely on the proposition that a contract would generally be presumed to be governed by the laws of the place where it was made. That would have given a clear basis for the application of English law. But would that have been desirable? The Court will have been aware

[9] And, for what it is worth, it stands in curious contrast to French law on the limitation of liability by a ship-owner and sea carrier, which led to the decision in *Lloyd v Guibert*. The judgment of the Supreme Court gives off a fish-like smell.

[10] *Peninsular And Oriental Steam Navigation Company v Shand* (1865) 3 Moo PC NS 272, 16 ER 103 (PC).

[11] ibid, 291, 110.

[12] ibid, 292, 111.

that trade in and across what was then a sprawling empire will involve contracts made in a great variety of places, many of which may be no more significant than the place from which materials, raw or manufactured, are boxed up and carried away: profits à prendre in a rather direct sense, perhaps. Not all contracts were made in England; a place of contracting rule would very quickly generate problems for which another solution would be needed. Indeed, part of the journey from Southampton to Mauritius involved carriage of goods by sand, from Alexandria to Suez, the canal being incomplete when the contract was made. Had that part of the journey been made under a contract made in Egypt, which was not inconceivable, the idea that Egyptian law would have been held to govern would, surely, have been preposterous. Intention, at least if the Court had control of the idea by conducting the search for a presumed or legitimate intention, allowed an acceptable outcome for respectable reasons.

One may be struck by the origin of the idea that the Court will identify a *lex contractus* under which the contract, or the most material term of the contract, will be valid. The exclusion clause was taken to be valid as a matter of English law, but void under French law. Did the company intend to stipulate for a nullity? Of course it did not; the Court deduced that that reflection got it closer to the proposition than English, not French, law governed the clause and the contract. The presumption in favour of validity has had something of a chequered history,[13] but it was, at best, a rhetorical point, not a legal one. The task of the Court was to identify the law which the parties should be presumed to have intended to govern the contract. Of course, as it knew in advance the consequences of each possible answer, the process of reasoning was hardly disinterested; but the outcome was clear enough.

III. LLOYD v GUIBERT

The stage was set for Willes J to clear the decks. His judgment in the Exchequer Chamber, in *Lloyd v Guibert* is a remarkable thing. It dismisses the appeal without examining the grounds on which the court below (which is to say, Blackburn J)[14] had arrived at the same conclusion. It cited and relied on, with evident confidence, a wide range of French doctrinal writings, as well as provisions of the German and Spanish codes. He referred to Shand's case only as authority for the proposition that the law at the port of discharge was not, as such, the *lex contractus*. That, he felt, left him free to determine, without limit or constraint, how to identify the law which governed the contract, or which, as we shall see, governed the ground of exemption from liability relied on by the defendant.

[13] Its most recent contribution to the common law was in *Enka Insaat ve Sanayi AS v OOO Insurance Company Chubb* [2020] UKSC 38, [2020] 1 WLR 4117 which, at [95], ascribed it to *Coke upon Littleton* (1628).

[14] *Lloyd v Guibert* (1864) 33 LJ (QB) 241.

Lloyd was a British subject based at St Thomas in the Danish West Indies.[15] He chartered the *Olivier*, a French ship in French ownership for a voyage from St Marc in Haiti to Le Havre, Liverpool or London at his option: one immediately sees how the law of the place of performance would have been pretty useless to serve as *lex contractus*. The charterparty was entered by the master of the *Olivier* pursuant to his general authority as such. Lloyd shipped a cargo of 'divers goods and merchandizes', to the value of £3,000, at St Marc, for Liverpool. The *Olivier* was damaged by an Atlantic storm and put into Fayal, in the Azores, for repair. The master, without funds or credit, raised what was needed for repair upon bottomry of ship, freight and cargo and, when the repair was effected, proceeded to Liverpool where the cargo was discharged. The bondholder sued on his bond in the Admiralty Court, but the value of ship and freight fell short of the debt. Liability for the shortfall therefore fell upon Lloyd, as cargo owner, who had to pay up to secure its release. Lloyd then sued Guibert for indemnity in respect of that sum, on the basis of a promise implied,[16] as he said, into the contract made at St Thomas.

It was pretty clear that the success or otherwise of that contention would depend on the law that governed the contract. As a matter of English law, as well as Danish, Haitian, and Portuguese law, as the Court accepted, the shipowner's liability was personal and unlimited, not restricted to the value of ship and freight. It would follow that Lloyd had paid in respect of Guibert's liability, and would be entitled to be reimbursed for it. But according to French law, a shipowner said to be liable for obligations undertaken by the master could abandon ship and freight to the shippers, and by doing so be absolved from further liability. This, apparently, was what Guibert had done; and as a matter of French law, as the Court accepted, this satisfied and extinguished Lloyd's claim against him.

The broad question before the Court was whether the answer was to be given by the law of Denmark (as *lex loci contractus*, the law of the place where the contract between Lloyd and Guibert was made), or the law of Portugal (the Azores being the place of making the bottomry bond to which the principle *locus regit actum* might point); or the law of England (as a sort of *lex loci solutionis*, the law of what became the place of contractual performance); or by the general maritime law, whatever that might mean; or by French law, for which there existed a variety of possible justifications. The only common ground was that the law of Haiti (a place at which part of the contracted-for performance was due and made) was not the answer. It did not

[15] Later purchased by the United States, which re-named the territory the United States Virgin Islands.

[16] Today such a claim might be analysed as one of unjust enrichment, the debt of the shipowner to the bondholder having been discharged by the cargo owner; something similar might also be said of *Male v Roberts*. But in the absence of a recognisable conflicts rule for such cases, the claim proceeded as a contractual one.

appear to be doubted that once the applicable law had been identified, the answer it gave was not liable to be qualified or displaced by any contradictory rule of English law or principle of English public policy.

There were four parts to the answer: to locate the issue for decision within a legal category for which a conflicts rule existed (characterisation, long before anyone used the word); to specify the range of systems from which the law governing the contract was to be selected; to identify the English rule of the conflict of laws applicable to that category; and to apply the relevant rule of the legal system so identified. Of these, the final one was easy and was not a matter of dispute. The third addressed the question which had also been before the Privy Council in *P&O v Shand*, and we will come to it shortly: it is the point for which the case is principally known.

The first part of the analysis, though, was remarkable; Willes J evidently saw it as plain and obvious. With a clarity of expression which may startle those who forget their history, Willes J explained why the task for the Court was to identify the law governing the contract between Lloyd and Guibert and to apply it:[17]

> It often happens, however, that disputes arise, not as to the terms of the contract, but as to their application to unforeseen questions, which arise incidentally or accidentally in the course of performance, and which the contract does not answer in terms, yet are within the sphere of the relation established thereby, and cannot be decided as between strangers.

There was no suggestion that it was open to a contracting party to pretend to sidestep the contract and to sue (or defend) on the basis of a distinct legal relationship such as tort or bailment, as might, or as could equally, exist between strangers. If the facts and matters complained of arose 'within the sphere of the relation established thereby'[18] the contract, the *lex contractus* applied to it: not to the contract, but the relationship established by the contract.

The idea took hold quickly. In *The Gaetano and Maria*,[19] another case involving the effect as against the cargo owner of a bottomry bond executed at Fayal, although the charterparty was concluded in London, the shipper was English, and the cargo was to be carried to England, the ship was Italian and the contract between the parties, and hence the authority of the master, was therefore governed by Italian law. In *The August*,[20] a cargo of pepper was to be shipped from Singapore to London on a German ship. Heavy weather caused the ship's master to seek shelter in Table Bay, after which he, being unable to obtain timely instructions, sold off in Cape Town that part of the cargo that was feared to be weather-damaged. In proceedings for breach of contract and for conversion, the High Court applied the law that governed the contract for sea carriage,

[17] *Lloyd v Guibert* (n 7) 120.
[18] ibid.
[19] *The Gaetano and Maria* (1882) LR 7 PD 137 (CA).
[20] *The August* [1891] P 328.

which it found to be German law, the law of the flag of the ship. No suggestion that the alleged conversion might be governed by a different law appears to have been judicially countenanced. The law that governed the relationship created by the contract appeared to apply to it and to all of it.

The clarity of this statement of the common law conflict of laws came to be obscured,[21] not only by the mists of time, but also by a principle of domestic law, which permitted a claimant to allege, pick, and choose between[22] concurrent obligations. This became transposed into the conflict of laws, allowing the claimant a degree of power to manipulate the identification of the law which the Court would apply.[23] It is arresting, however, to see how closely the approach of Willes J resembles what was, until recently, the settled jurisprudence of the European Court on special jurisdiction under the Brussels Convention and Regulation; *sub sole nihil novi est*.

As to the second point, Willes J proceeded on the footing that the real issue was to identify the law that governed the contract between Lloyd and Guibert; he rejected the contention that the real issue was that the liability of a ship-owner for the acts of the master, and that this was to be referred to the 'general maritime law'.[24] It was necessary to identify the issue that the Court had to decide. No doubt one could frame a question of authority (of the master to commit the principal) or perhaps of the effect of a bond on non-party whose cargo was hypothecated,[25] but Willes J did not see that as the issue calling for a decision by the Court: there was a relationship between Lloyd and Guibert which had been voluntarily entered into, and that provided the framework within which the obligations of the parties to each other in general, and the obligation to reimburse the cargo-owner, had to be addressed.

Just as important was that there was no such thing as the general maritime law, unless this was a reference to those parts of English law routinely administered by the Court of Admiralty and the Privy Council on appeal therefrom; and if that is what it was, it was no more than an opaque reference to English law. As Willes J said:[26]

> In truth, any general, much more any universal, maritime law binding on all nations using the highway of the sea in time of peace, except when limited as administered in some court, is easier longed for than found.

When he went on to ask what the general content of such law might be, there was no answer to be given; when directed to the more specific question, whether ship-owners should be absolutely answerable for the acts of their master, there was even less. Questions of that kind found their answer in terms of national

[21] In the writer's opinion, most regrettably.
[22] In the peculiar sense of not having to choose between.
[23] *Coupland v Arabian Gulf Oil Co* [1983] 1 WLR 1136 (CA).
[24] *Lloyd v Guibert* (n 7) 123–26.
[25] This was how the issue was framed by Blackburn J in the court below: *Lloyd v Guibert* (n 14).
[26] *Lloyd v Guibert* (n 7) 124–25.

policy and economy. The French doctrinal writers referred to by Willes J disagreed on the point, which was probably enough to debunk the idea that there might nevertheless be found a universal maritime law capable of answering the questions thrown up by commercial litigation.

The approach of Willes J also explains why other attempts to allow a non-national system of 'rules' to serve as *lex contractus* will fail, at least at common law. One may accept that there may be contracts made by members of an informal community or interest group, for whom or which special rules might be proposed: the *lex maritima* for contracts concerned with the sea, or *lex mercatoria* for mercantile engagements, or even the magical teachings of a cult or religion for those subscribed to it. The idea that any of these could serve in a court as a *lex contractus* was as fanciful then as it is now. Granted, the custom of the trade, or the expectations of the market, may have a cameo role as data for the application of whatever the *lex contractus* is: one may call to mind the manner in which recoverable damage for breach of a charterparty by late redelivery may be assessed with half an eye on the common assumption of those having business in the market.[27] But the only law capable of governing a contract was the law of a state. The question was how it was to be found.

We turn to the third point, which was to decide what was the system of municipal law that governed the contract between Lloyd and Guibert. The Privy Council in *P&O v Shand* had placed significant weight on the fact that the contract was made in England, though over the course of the judgment the significance of the place of contracting was partially eclipsed by the concurrent observation that the parties to the contract were to be taken to have intended that English law govern it. As both factors led to English law, it was unsurprising that the judgment made approving reference to them both. Had the facts been otherwise, and the arrangements made to traverse the sands of Suez been made separately in Egypt, it is easy to predict that the hold of the *lex loci contractus* would have been fatally weakened.

But in *Lloyd v Guibert*, the hold of the law of the place of contracting was plainly weaker. Neither party really belonged to the Danish West Indies where the contract was made, although both had been[28] present there for the purpose of trade: the nature of trade within empires meant that contracts will often have been made in places from which materials were to be shipped or carted back home. Those places may not all have conformed to the disobliging description offered by Story, but some will have; and the idea that the law of that place might – on any basis – be the proper law of the contract for sea carriage will not have been remotely attractive. No doubt being able to see into the future and to guard against it, Willes J redirected the law's attention. He relegated the law of the place of contracting to be, but to be no more than, a starting point: it would be

[27] *Transfield Shipping Inc v Mercator Shipping Inc, The Achilleas* [2008] UKHL 48, [2009] 1 AC 61.
[28] The length and nature of their presence there is not recorded.

the law which, prima facie, parties intended or may be presumed to have used as the basis for their engagement, but if there were circumstances to indicate a different intention, that different intention would indicate the *lex contractus* and displace the presumption. It is assumed, though was not said, that the relevant intention could be a positive one directed to a different law, as well as a simply negative one, to not subject the contract to the laws of the place of its making.

The place of performance was rejected as *lex contractus*, as it was surely bound to be. It is true that Savigny was in favour of treating the place of fulfilment, which appears, if not precisely, then to approximate to the place of performance, as the 'forum of the obligation'. Such analysis had little practical attraction. After all, the contract in *Lloyd v Guibert* was to be performed in the Danish West Indies, and in Haiti, and on the high seas, and at the port of discharge, the identity of which was not determined when the contract was made. And in any event, Savigny was bound to qualify this idea by inquiring 'at what place the fulfilment may be thought of and expected by the parties'.[29] That degree of uncertainty was never going to appeal to an English court. Willes J observed that the application of the law of the place of final performance – a floating choice of law, if ever one was – had been rejected by the Privy Council and would hardly work in the case before him, and said no more about it. Portuguese law, equally unascertainable at the point of contracting, may have governed the contract created by the bottomry bond, but that did no more than provide data for the contractual dispute which arose in relation to the charterparty.

The statement of principle was framed as follows. The Court's approach to the question would:[30]

> … endeavour to be guided in its solution by a steady application of the general principle already stated, *viz*, that the rights of the parties to a contract are to be judged of by that law which they intended, or rather by which they may justly be presumed to have bound themselves.

All others having been rejected, French law was the law identified by the Court as the law governing the contract. It was the law 'which they intended, or rather by which Lloyd and Guibert may justly be presumed to have bound themselves'. Why? The answer seems to have been as much negative – all the alternatives were liable to generate erratic outcomes – as positive: the ship was French, and was in some sense a floating piece of French territory, under French jurisdiction. It was neither inconvenient, nor should it have been surprising, that French law should apply to contractual obligations arising from its use. The fact that the claimant knew little about French law did not impress the judge, who tartly observed that many Englishmen making contracts in England are pretty ignorant of English law.[31] The law of the state to which the ship belonged

[29] FC von Savigny, *Private International Law, A Treatise on the Conflict of Laws*, trans W Guthrie (London, Stevens & Sons, 1869) 156.
[30] *Lloyd v Guibert* (n 7) 123.
[31] ibid, 129.

should govern, because this was a world in which ships of the merchant marine were proud to fly their home flag and there were no 'flags of convenience'[32] or other shabby rags. The law of the flag was most likely to have been the assumption of the parties (it is unclear whether they were ever asked), as well as being consistent and intelligible as the answer in the generality of such cases.

IV. THE EFFECT OF LLOYD v GUIBERT WITHIN THE LAW OF CONTRACT

So far as the private international law of contract is concerned, the primary importance of *Lloyd v Guibert* is that it did more than any case to break the hold of the law of the place where the contract was made as *lex contractus*. That is to say, it started the process by which English lawyers analysed the question of what law governed a contract and how that law should be identified. The law of the place of its making ceased to be the proper law of the contract; and the law taken to have been intended by the parties governed the contractual obligation or (in some cases) the supposed contractual obligation. That is not to say that the moment the ink was dry on the judgment no judge or other lawyer would be heard to say that a contract was governed by the law of the place where it was made, but the law is a conservative profession, and it takes time to learn new lessons. It may be argued that what, in fact, the case did was to replace one fixed rule with another – the law of the place of contracting with the law of the flag – but that was not *Lloyd v Guibert*'s doing, and if subsequent cases on sea carriage found an easy route to a clear solution, that just goes to show how persuasive the reasoning of Willes J was. And in any event, the suggestion that the law of the flag was applicable independently of any reference to the presumed intentions of the actual parties was quickly countered.[33] That left the test as one of intention and only intention, however that may be particularised. Three principal points may now be made.

First, and most importantly, the fairest reading of the judgment of Willes J is that he identified the *lex contractus* as the law which the parties *may be presumed* to have intended: the telling 'or rather'[34] in the passage quoted above rather gives the game away. Finding the law thus identified appears neither to depend on showing that the parties did in fact have such an intention, nor to be defeated by a showing that either or both did not have it: it would appear to

[32] That did not last: in *Chartered Mercantile Bank of India London & China v Netherlands India Steam Navigation Co Ltd* (1883) 10 QBD 521 (CA) it appeared that the ship was registered in the name of a Dutch trustee in order to allow it to trade at Java, which was a Dutch possession. The law of the flag was, therefore, not the law intended to govern the bill of lading issued by the master. *Lloyd v Guibert* was held to be plainly distinguishable per Lindley LJ at 540.

[33] *Chartered Mercantile Bank of India London & China v Netherlands India Steam Navigation Co Ltd* (n 32).

[34] See text to n 30.

be objectively ascertained from the bench, and not subjectively ascertained by the self-serving assertions of the parties themselves: a managed intention, perhaps. Of course, if the parties were to declare their intentions it would be hard to do other than treat that as objectively decisive; but where they did not, the solution offered is clear, simple, direct, and reliable.

It is reasonable to suppose that Willes J framed the rule as he did so as to maintain a level of judicial control, but also to head off the argument, uncomfortably well founded in fact and experience, that the parties probably had no relevant intentions as to governing law to call their own. The Court had already disposed of the objection that the charterer was ignorant of French law by observing that most Englishmen were ignorant in respect of English law; but it is hard to see how the parties can have intended something which had never crossed their mind: for many the issue of a contract's governing law will be an unknown unknown: the rules of the conflict of laws do not leap to every mind, even today. A deemed or presumed intention is less perturbed by such human frailties or legal objections.

Even so, the side effect of placing the focus on a presumed intention is bound to prompt the question whether the rule should really be recast to identify the law as to which the parties actually, subjectively, had a common intention, assuming that such a thing could be demonstrated. And if the question is what the parties intended, is a declaration of that intention, in the form of a choice, decisive (or, to put it another way, is the expression of a choice the only reliable demonstration of an actual intention)? And if the parties cannot be shown to have had an actual common intention, does it really make sense to presume them to have had an intention as to the *lex contractus* (and if it does not, how should the default rule be formulated)? And if the parties are free to choose the law which will govern their contract, are they also free to make enforceable promises to each other as to the law which will be applied to a dispute arising from their contract (and if not, why not)? The theory and practice of party autonomy in the private international law of contract starts with this decision, and asks all these questions. It is still answering them.

The second point is smaller but more awkward to deal with. The intention of which we have been speaking is intention as to governing law. Of course, had greater significance been attached to *P&O v Shand*, one might also have expected the common law to attach greater significance to a presumption, at least, that a contract was intended to be governed, and therefore was governed, by a law under which it or its principal terms would have been valid. For if one asks whether a contracting party might have intended the contract to be void of material effect, only one answer is really tenable. The intention that the contract was valid was, one supposes, an intention held by both parties. The Privy Council had been considerably exercised by the possibility that the Chief Justice, of all people, party to a contract which contained an exclusion clause, might argue that he intended the contract to be governed by a law which would compromise or deny its validity and effectiveness. One possible response might be to elevate the presumption of contractual validity to the point where it might itself identify the *lex contractus*.

It is arguable that this view commended itself to the majority of the Supreme Court in *Enka v Chubb*,[35] when it was seeking to ascertain the law governing (and hence governing the interpretation of) an arbitration agreement. The alternative, of lower profile, would be to take a decisively-objective view of the matter and to consider that the contract was governed by the law which, in the opinion of the court, the parties must be taken to have intended to govern it, and to accept that one aspect of governing is deciding whether the relationship entered into imposes obligations or not. That would allow the court to decide for itself the law which was taken to have been intended, and to allow the court to take account of this strand of intention to the extent it considers appropriate.

For Willes J, though, it was expedient to treat *Shand* as a case which denied the supremacy of the law of the place of performance, and to leave it at that. It follows that the contention that, whatever else they may or may not have intended, the parties intended the contract to be valid and binding, and therefore intended whatever it took to bring that intention into being, remains an awkward element in the formulation of an intention-to-be-governed-by test.

The third point is rather different, in that it does not focus on the issue of whether to apply the law of the place of contracting or the law to which the parties directed themselves; it is remarkable and important. Willes J evidently had no qualms about ignoring the rule of English domestic law, on the unlimited liability of ship-owners, which contrasted so sharply with the position of French law.

There was much to be applauded in Willes J's rejection of any suggestion that the rule of French law, in favour of the defendant, could be refused application in an English court by reason of its variance from the corresponding rule of English law. The result in *Lloyd v Guibert* was that the rule of French law, allowing a ship-owner to limit his liability by surrender of the ship and freight, leaving the cargo-owner exposed, was applied by the English court: to the clear disadvantage of an English claimant, and in spite of the fact that the plain rule of English domestic law was to the opposite. There was no suggestion that the English rule was inherently superior, or that there was a problem for a court in giving judgment which sharply contradicted English domestic law.[36] This conclusion could not be based on the proposition that there was no connection to England, given the intended destination of the goods. It was adopted without the need to justify it. And in this respect *Lloyd v Guibert* was something of a false dawn.

[35] *Enka v Chubb* (n 13), discussed in ch 17 in this volume.

[36] It also suggests that the idea of a pan-national 'maritime law' would be very hard to ascertain or to defend.

V. THE INEFFECTIVENESS OF LLOYD v GUIBERT OUTSIDE THE LAW OF CONTRACT (AND A DISASTER AVERTED)

At this point we should take a step back and sideways, and observe that all this was taking place within a broader debate about the role of the law of the place, the *lex loci actus*, in conflicts thinking. As we have mentioned, Story had been a strong advocate for its application, and as the only institutional writer of any fame his views were persuasive. But they were not unquestioned. In a rather different context, only a few years earlier the House of Lords had considered the marvellously Yorkshire case of one William Brook.[37] He had married Charlotte in 1840; she died in 1847. In 1850 he married her sister Emily, this time in Denmark.[38] Five years later, in Germany, they succumbed to cholera,[39] and the question of inheritance came before the English courts. As a matter of Danish law there had been no impediment to the marriage of a deceased wife's sister; as a matter of English statute law such a marriage was prohibited.

It was argued for the children of the second marriage that the law of the place of its contracting determined the validity of this (marriage) contract as well, this with the emphatic support of Story; but the Vice Chancellor, and then the House of Lords, disagreed. They all rejected the simple proposition that the validity of a contract of marriage was determined by the law of the place where it was made, though the reasons are a real stew. The Vice-Chancellor put it nicely: England was 'the country with a view to which, and in which, the marriage was to have its permanent effect':[40] a pattern of reasoning which reflects the approach in *Lloyd v Guibert*, or which serves as a forerunner for the law of the intended matrimonial home as the law governing the capacity of parties to marry.[41] But in the House of Lords it appears that neither the *lex loci actus* nor the law to which the parties looked was acceptable. The laws of the place might govern the formalities, but on the question of validity the law of the domicile governed. There was a difference between marriage and other civil contracts. The English statute overrode whatever answer the conflict of laws might have provided; it applied to English spouses marrying in Denmark or anywhere else; it could not be right that English law could be side-stepped by making a short sea crossing; the marriage might have been described as incestuous or revolting;[42] and the rule in the statute was also God's law (or that of Henry VIII,[43] which is evidently the same thing). Whichever of these one took,

[37] *Brook v Brook* (1861) 9 HLC 193.

[38] Neither sister is known to have been a novelist, alas.

[39] It makes a change from tuberculosis.

[40] *Brook v Brook* (1858) 3 Sm & Giff 481, 532 (Stuart VC). This does seem rather hard to reconcile with the reported facts, but never mind.

[41] This had been the proposal of Professor Cheshire, but in spite of the glancing reference to it in *Brook v Brook*, and occasionally thereafter, its home remained in *doctrine* rather than *jurisprudence*.

[42] These preposterous adjectives splatter the judgments in a most disagreeable way.

[43] *Sottomayor v De Barros (No 2)* (1879–80) LR 5 PD 94, 105, referring to Marriage Act 1540.

the proposition that the law of the place of contracting told one all the law one needed to know was plainly rejected. But just as clearly rejected, at least implicitly, was any suggestion that the essential validity of a marriage should be governed by the law to which the parties may be presumed to have submitted themselves in respect of it; so also any suggestion that the selection of applicable law should reflect a presumption of validity. Whether one can explain any or all of this by saying that status is a thing apart is debatable.

Returning to the narrative, and to the third point made above, about the exclusion of English domestic law. For in this respect *Lloyd v Guibert* stands in sharp contrast to another decision of the Privy Council, on appeal from the Court of Admiralty, in *The Halley*,[44] and to its long survival in the law. The essence of the question in *The Halley* was whether a ship-owner was liable for damage resulting from the negligence of a pilot to whose control (or lack of) the ship had been surrendered when in Belgian waters as required by Belgian law. The ship was in Belgian waters as a matter of choice, meaning that the obligation to use the services of the Belgian pilot was voluntary but inescapable; if one had asked which was the law to which the parties must be presumed to have been looking to ascertain any liability which they might face if things went awry, it would obviously have been Belgian law. Belgian law on liability for unexpected accidents differed from English law in a way not dissimilar from that in which French and English were shown to disagree in *Lloyd v Guibert*; the parallel between the cases is not hard to spot. Yet soon after Willes J had been willing to apply the relevant French rule on liability in contradiction of English domestic law, the Privy Council in *The Halley* had done the opposite with the relevant rule of Belgian law on liability for damage done by an incompetent pilot: the answer given by Belgian law contradicted English law, and it would not, therefore, be the answer given by the court.

The Halley, of course, had gone to the Privy Council rather than the Exchequer Chamber, just as *P&O v Shand* had done. And it may be that it took a while for the new approach to contracts to be appreciated by the Privy Council.[45] In *The Halley* that Court had admitted that in a contract case an English court would 'inquire into and act upon' the law of a foreign country if the contract was made there and the foreign law is incorporated into the contract so that it becomes necessary to the construction of the contract. That was not what Willes J had said, neither was it what he meant, but a hankering for the old faith can sometimes linger on after a revolution. However, it might have been

[44] *Liverpool Brazil and River Plate Steam Navigation Co v Benham (The Halley)* (1867–69) LR 2 PC 193 (PC), reversing the decision of Sir Robert Phillimore (1867) 2 Adm & Ecc 3. See on this M Hancock 'Torts in the Conflict of Laws: The First Rule in *Phillips v Eyre*' (1940) 3 *University of Toronto Law Journal* 400.

[45] One may also note that it did take time for *Lloyd v Guibert* to sink in, at least in the Chancery Division: as late as 1880, Fry J could still say, in *Rousillon v Rousillon* (1880) 14 Ch D 351 (Ch) 369, that the contract was governed by French law because it was made in France.

hoped that Willes J, when *Phillips v Eyre* presented him with the opportunity to deal with choice of law for oversea torts, would have felt free to examine and narrow or weaken the basis on which *The Halley* had been decided.

As explored in more detail in chapter five, the facts of *Phillips v Eyre* were gruesome, and the judgment, alas, is horrible.[46] So far as concerned the application – by way of exoneration of the homicidal Governor Eyre – of an Act of the colonial legislature, Willes J was at pains to justify its legitimacy by reference to Jamaican law, and it led him to say the following:[47]

> A right of action, whether it arise from contract governed by the law of the place or wrong, is equally the creature of the law of the place and subordinate thereto. The terms of the contract or the character of the subject-matter may shew that the parties intended their bargain to be governed by some other law; but, primâ facie, it falls under the law of the place where it was made. And in like manner the civil liability arising out of a wrong derives its birth from the law of the place, and its character is determined by that law.

This does not quite undo the good work which had been done six years earlier, but it does it no favours. It seems to offer no distinct role to the presumed intentions of the parties, even though it would have been easy enough to do so and to come to the same conclusion about the application of Jamaican law.

It then got worse. As to the proposition that, if the obligation is governed by foreign law, there is no reason to look to, still less apply, the law of the forum – which had appeared to be an essential part of the reasoning in *Lloyd v Guibert* – Willes J seems to have had something completely different in mind. He held that the claim in tort could not succeed unless it would also have succeeded under English domestic law. He regarded *The Halley* as correctly decided.[48] This is a puzzle and a problem, for it seems to say for torts what had been clearly and precisely denied for contracts.

The judgment in *Phillips v Eyre* may suggest that *Lloyd v Guibert* had been decided as it was because the claim was bad as a matter of French law, opening and leaving open the question how it would have been dealt with if the claim for reimbursement had been good by French law as *lex contractus*, but would have been bad if the contract or claim had been governed by English law. Would Willes J have been so clear that the claimant could recover by reference to the *lex contractus* when the *lex fori* would have given the defendant a good defence, as it did in *The Halley*? We do not know, and cannot tell.[49]

[46] *Phillips v Eyre* (1870–71) LR 6 QB 1 (Ex Ch).

[47] ibid, 28.

[48] It is doubtful whether he was distracted by the problem that common law courts did not originally have jurisdiction over foreign torts: a problem which was solved by the fiction that the foreign place was, in fact, in London (for example, 'in the city of Paris in France, to wit, in the parish of St Mary le Bow in the Ward of Cheap': try finding that on Google maps) which would have opened up the equally mad possibility that English law was the *lex loci delicti commissi*.

[49] Though the Privy Council in *Shand's* case suggested, by its approval of an 1864 decision of the French Supreme Court, that the claim would be good if good under the *lex contractus* even though it would have been bad under the *lex fori*: *P&O v Shand* (n 10) 292, 111.

It is therefore difficult to say how close we came to sustaining a rule of double actionability in the private international law of contract. It may just be sufficient to say that it does not appear to have occurred to anyone to argue that a contract claim, good by the *lex contractus*, would fail if it would not have been sustainable were the same contract to have governed by English law: this may have been more the result of luck than judgment, but there it is.[50] But for good or ill – and it is undoubtedly for good – the common law of contract was formulated and survived as a rule of single reference, and the ill wind, too close to which the private international law of contract may have sailed in 1870, suddenly changed direction and did a century's worth of damage to the private international law of tort instead.

VI. CONCLUSION

Based on the foregoing, it seems that, so far as the common law is concerned, the proposition that the parties' obligations to each other should be governed 'by that law which they intended, or rather by which they may justly be presumed to have bound themselves' is good and sufficient in contract. It is not good enough in tort; and it is not even part of the debate in marriage.

This, it is submitted, is the real lesson of *Lloyd v Guibert* and of the cases which colour the broader background. The fundamental questions for the common law conflict of laws were: (i) whether the parties to a transaction, a relationship, or an accident, had to take the applicable law as given, or could point to intentions or legitimate expectations, objectively or subjectively ascertained, as to the law that governed it; and (ii) whether the rules of English domestic law would could be rendered redundant by the rules for choice of law.

The answers were settled, in the 1860s, as follows: for contract, the parties may choose or intend the law to be applied, and English domestic law is thereby excluded. For torts, the parties cannot choose or intend the law to be applied, and the role of English domestic law is to be universally or indiscriminately applicable; it took a century to break the pernicious stranglehold of English domestic law on oversea torts. For marriage, the parties cannot choose or intend the law to be applied: the law that governs their ability to marry is in their blood, and it cannot be escaped even by travelling to the ends of the earth. These answers then prevailed in the English common law, with little or no judicial interrogation, for a century.

This diversity in treatment may seem puzzling to academic writers, but does not seem to have perturbed the judges. One may ask why. For if one considers contracts and torts as members of the same family of civil obligations, as

[50] One may also compare the actual reasoning in *Brook v Brook* (n 37) with what might have been framed as a rule of double reference: that the marriage is not valid unless it is valid under the law of the place where celebrated and would have been valid if celebrated in England.

modern legal thinking seems to do, the dissimilarity of treatment in the conflicts rules is very striking indeed. If one considers contracts and marriages to be cousins which are related by the consensual nature of the relationship and the manifestation of free will on which each depends, the difference in respect for individual autonomy is still surprising. It does not seem that anyone was particularly concerned to ask about or explain the coherence or incoherence of the work product of the1860s and by the time anyone might have got round to it, the law might as well have been set in stone.

Some will see in that stability and predictability and the strength of the common law. Others will see creativity followed by ossification: both may be right, but the latter is far closer to the honest truth.[51] The result is a series of rules of the conflict of laws, conceived and developed in seeming isolation from each other, and practically immutable once they had been articulated. It is of course true that courts spent some time fine-tuning or fiddling around with the details: asking whether the doctrine of the proper law of the contract comprised two rules or three, whether the law was properly expressed in terms of choice or intention, whether there were any limits on what law might be chosen or intended, and so forth. But nowhere did a court seriously ask, still less explain, why the structural model identified for contracts was so unsuitable for use outside that context. It is in this lack of curiosity, perhaps, that one sees the true common law method of the conflict of laws.

[51] Of course, if one reformulates some of the relevant law as governing capacity to effect the transaction one may say that the distinction between contract and marriage is not quite so sharp, but Lord Eldon would not have seen the point. And there was, of course, sometimes an opportunity for English public policy to intervene, but that was only ever to remove an objectionable foreign law from application, never to disconnect English domestic law from an issue to which it otherwise applied: see *Rousillon v Rousillon* (n 45) (contract in restraint of trade); *Sottomayor v De Barros (No 2)* (n 43) (marriage to first cousin without permission of the Bishop of Rome).

3

Bell v Kennedy (1868) and *Udny v Udny* (1869)

ELIZABETH CRAWFORD AND JANEEN CARRUTHERS

I. CONSTRUCTION OF THE PILLARS

THE STRUCTURE WHICH constitutes the rules of ascription of domicile long used by English and Scots courts rests upon the twin pillars of *Bell v Kennedy* and *Udny v Udny*.[1] These are House of Lords Scottish cases – significant decisions handed down on appeal from the Inner House of the Court of Session and twin not only in the equally important role that each plays in the fabric of the rules, but also notably close in date (the decision in *Bell* having been delivered on 14 May 1868, and that in *Udny* on 3 June 1869). *Bell* lays down the rule of survival of domicile of origin (no matter that the *propositus* has left it in a final manner) until clearly displaced, ie until such time as it is clearly established, on the balance of probabilities, that the *propositus* has acquired a domicile of choice *animo et facto*. *Udny* supplies the rule of revival of the domicile of origin of a *propositus* should there be a gap in their domicile narrative.

A. *Bell v Kennedy*

The litigation in *Bell* was protracted. Cairns LC noted with regret that its history began in the Court of Session in 1858 and that in the course of proceedings to the House of Lords no fewer than 16 interlocutors had been pronounced. The case concerns a claim of inheritance, namely, the claim of a daughter (Mrs Mary Anne Bell or Kennedy) of John Bell and the late Mrs Mary Ann Bell (née Hosack) to a share in the estate of Mary Ann *sub nom* a share of the goods held in communion between John and Mary Ann during their marriage

[1] *Bell v Kennedy* (1868) 6 M (HL) 69 and *Udny v Udny* (1869) 7 M (HL) 89.

and due to issue, on the death of the predeceasing spouse, under a vestigial form of community of property between spouses, which existed in Scots law until removed by statute in 1855. The claim could succeed only if the deceased died domiciled in Scotland. There had even been delay in making the claim, for the death in childbirth of Mary Ann had occurred on 28 September 1838, which date is the *tempus inspiciendum*. The connecting factor in this problem of succession being the ultimate domicile of Mary Ann, the crux of the matter was the domicile of John Bell on 28 September 1838, since the domicile of a wife *ex lege* (until 1974)[2] followed that of her husband.

John Bell was born in Jamaica, of parents of Scottish stock but Jamaican domicile. As a legitimate child, Bell's domicile of origin followed that which his father had at the date of Bell's birth, namely, Jamaican. On the death of his mother when he was aged two, Bell was sent to Scotland for his care and education. After continental travels, Bell returned to Jamaica aged 21, and assumed responsibility for the family's 'Woodstock' estate, his father having died. Bell prospered in Jamaica, became a respected resident, and married Mary Ann Hosack there in 1828. They had three children in Jamaica, but Bell, for health reasons and having ceased to be enamoured of the island,[3] resolved to leave and return to Britain. He sold the Woodstock estate and left Jamaica in 1837 'for good'. Immediately thereafter, the family lived in Edinburgh under the roof of Bell's mother-in-law, where they remained until 1 June 1838. The Edinburgh house being too small for the family's needs, Bell took a year's lease of the estate of Trochraigue in Ayrshire, in the south of Scotland. Although the family favoured settling in Scotland, it could not be said that at the *tempus inspiciendum* Bell was sufficiently firm in his resolve to justify their Lordships finding adequate *animus* for Scotland. The ultimate decision whether or not to remain in Scotland depended upon the contingency of Bell finding a satisfactory property there. Though commentators may seek to keep separate the two factors of *factum* and *animus*, frequently they bear upon each other.

Cairns LC took the view that, at the crucial date, Bell was undecided and had not resolved to live in Scotland.[4] He would have been equally likely to buy an estate in England and settle there. It is rare in domicile cases pertaining to the law of succession (but not in other legal contexts, discussed below) for the court to hear the evidence of one of the main parties to the drama as to his thoughts and intentions.[5] It is for the court to determine the weight to be

[2] Domicile and Matrimonial Proceedings Act 1973, s 1.

[3] The Jamaican law regulating slavery was changed in 1834, to introduce, in the first instance, a 'system of apprenticeship', and ultimately, in 1838, to provide for 'complete emancipation'. The case report discloses that Bell disapproved of the changes: *Bell* (n 1) 70 (Lord Cairns LC).

[4] Compare ibid, 78 Lord Westbury.

[5] ibid, 70 (Lord Cairns LC). Another example is *Flynn v Flynn (No 1)* [1968] 1 All ER 49 (Ch). See also *Udny* (n 1) 93 (Lord Hatherley LC).

given to such evidence.[6] In correspondence, Bell complained of the weather and of the price of land, and expressed dissatisfaction with the country pursuits available; in a letter dated 26 September 1837, to his brother-in-law in Jamaica, he disclosed that he would 'go to Canada, Jamaica, or Australia, without hesitation' and declared that he had lost 'his land-buying mania' in Britain.[7]

Writing again on 27 December 1837, he was no more enamoured with Scotland ('As to the country, I like none of it … [I] have had a fishing-rod in my hands only for two hours, and caught nothing, I bought a horse, and might as well have bought a bear, … he bites so'), or with the prospect of acquiring property in Scotland ('I have not purchased an estate, and am not likely to do so').[8] He envisaged a trip to the South of France to ascertain if the climate there was more agreeable to him for the purpose of permanent residence.[9] The Lord Chancellor concluded that the respondents, Mrs Mary Anne Bell or Kennedy and her husband, had entirely failed to discharge the onus which lay upon them to persuade the court that her father, at the relevant date, had acquired a 'Scotch' domicile. After his wife's death, John Bell bought the estate of Enterkine in Ayrshire and the court accepted that his domicile, at the point of litigation, was Scots. But there is no admission anywhere in the speeches that the court might seek enlightenment on the state of mind of the *propositus* at 28 September 1838 by having regard to events occurring *after* the *punctum temporis*.

The House of Lords held that the Lord Ordinary had been wrong to hold that Bell had acquired a Scots domicile immediately on arrival at his mother-in-law's house in Edinburgh. Nor could the Lord Chancellor concur with the finding of Lord Cowan in the Inner House of the Court of Session, that Bell acquired Scots domicile on taking the lease of Trochraigue; it was merely a temporary place of sojourn while a decision on residence (which would bear upon domicile) was pondered – Bell's purpose was in suspense.[10] In contrast, if *animus* can be established, something as temporary as living in a hotel would have been accepted as constituting residence.[11] The House of Lords was unanimous in its view that 'the domicile of origin adheres until a new domicile is acquired'.[12] This was sufficient for determination of the case. Bell's domicile as at the date of his wife's death and, therefore, the *lex successionis* to govern the distribution of Mrs Bell's estate, was Jamaican, ruling out the claim of the respondents under Scots law.

Thus was one of the twin domicile pillars constructed. Domicile of origin endures unless and until set in abeyance by acquisition of a domicile of choice

[6] *Bell* (n 1) 72 (Lord Cairns LC).
[7] ibid, 73.
[8] ibid.
[9] ibid, 74 (Lord Cairns LC).
[10] ibid, 80. Lord Colonsay found the case to be more nicely balanced but did not dissent.
[11] ibid, 76 (Lord Cranworth) and 77 (Lord Chelmsford).
[12] Ibid, 78 (Lord Westbury).

animo et facto. The concept of *animus* gives to the court a flexible tool to generate a result which, in broad terms, the court deems desirable. The court must be taken to be aware of the consequences of its finding as to intention and therefore as to domicile.[13] The burden of proof of establishing acquisition of domicile of choice lies upon the party in whose interests it is to aver a change of domicile; no burden lies on the other party to explain, or justify, long residence in another legal system.[14]

The words 'placed in abeyance' lead the gaze to the prospect of the other pillar, which is constituted by the decision of the House of Lords, given very shortly thereafter, in the case of *Udny*.

B. *Udny v Udny*

The advantage which application of Scots law offered in *Udny* was the change of status of the respondent, John Henry Udny, from illegitimate to legitimated *per subsequens matrimonium*, which, if bestowed, would have entitled him to succeed to the estate of Udny, Aberdeenshire. By English law then, John Henry would have been subject to the doctrine of indelibility of bastardy and ineligible to succeed.

By Scots applicable law rules, for legitimation to occur, a father need have legal capacity so to legitimate his child by his personal law only at the (later) date of marriage, and not at the (anterior) date of the birth. The applicable law rule of English law prior to 1926 was stricter, requiring capacity so to legitimate by the domiciliary law of the father both at the date of birth and of subsequent marriage. Section 1 of the Legitimacy Act 1926 introduced into English law 'legitimation by subsequent marriage of parents'. Section 8 brought the English applicable law rule into line with the Scots rule. Were the *propositus* in *Udny* to have been of English domicile at the date of birth of John Henry Udny, but of Scots domicile at the later date of marriage, there would have been a bar to the recognition in England of his change of status to 'legitimated'.[15]

John Udny, the respondent's grandfather, was of Scots domicile of origin. Born in 1727 in Aberdeen, he travelled in adulthood to Venice, engaged in business there and was appointed British consul at Leghorn (Livorno), a position he held until his death in 1800 in London, when on a temporary visit there.

[13] See J Fawcett, 'Result Selection in Domicile Cases' (1985) 5 *Oxford Journal of Legal Studies* 378, 379. Fawcett notes, at 380, that domicile litigation (as at 1985) arises mainly in the areas of succession, divorce jurisdiction and taxation, and observes that 'There is evidence that in each of these areas the courts wish to achieve certain policy objectives.' The policy objectives he identifies (380–81) are honouring a testator's expectation; exercising divorce jurisdiction where possible; and protecting 'foreigners' from the application of domestic UK tax laws.

[14] *In re Capdevielle* (1864) 2 Hurl & C 985, 159 ER 408; *Jopp v Wood* (1865) 2 De G.J. & S. 323, 46 ER 400; *Winans v Attorney General (No 1)* [1904] AC 287 (HL); *Liverpool Royal Infirmary v Ramsay* [1930] AC 588 (HL); *Inland Revenue Commissioners v Bullock* [1976] 3 All ER 35 (CA).

[15] *Udny* (n 1) 94–95 (Lord Hatherley LC).

John Udny married in 1777 and with his wife had two children, born at Leghorn, one being John Robert Udny, the respondent's father. In 1794, John Udny became heir of entail to the estate of Udny, his elder brother having no sons.

The case is concerned with the life of John Robert Udny.[16] Having returned with his mother from Italy to London, he was sent in 1794 to study at Edinburgh University. In 1796, on a visit to Aberdeen, the freedom of the city was conferred on him. He entered the army in 1797. In 1802, John Robert Udny succeeded to the estate of Udny. There was no mansion house on the estate; the *propositus* contemplated restoring Udny Castle but did not have the means to do so. He remained in the army until 1812, when he sold his commission and retired with the rank of Colonel to concentrate on horse racing. That year, Colonel Udny married an Englishwoman[17] and lived with her in a rented house in Grosvenor Street, London until 1845; this was his sole residence in those years.

During this long period, in which he had no gainful employment, the Colonel, as Laird of Udny, took an interest in the estate, visiting yearly, staying with friends or in hotels. He found living in England congenial partly because of his fondness for horse racing. In 1845, to escape creditors (horse racing debts) he went to live in Boulogne, France, having disposed of the London lease and house contents. The *propositus*'s wife joined him in Boulogne but soon returned to England and died there in 1846.

Colonel Udny then formed a relationship with Ann Allat who lived with him thereafter in Boulogne. In the next nine years, he generally avoided visiting England, but made occasional visits to Scotland. Ann gave birth to John Henry Udny, the respondent, on 9 May 1853, at Camberwell, London. In November 1853, Colonel Udny and Ann left Boulogne for Scotland, and were married in East Lothian on 2 January 1854. Thereafter Colonel Udny lived in Scotland until his death in Edinburgh in 1861. Having taken legal advice, he was conscious of the benefits of having a Scots domicile with regard to the status and in turn, the inheritance prospects, of his son, John Henry Udny.

There arose a competition to succeed to the estate of Udny, between George Udny, substitute heir of entail (the appellant in the House of Lords) and John Henry Udny. George, a London barrister who conducted his own case, sought declarator of bastardy in respect of John Henry. The central question was whether or not Colonel Udny was domiciled in Scotland at the date of his marriage to Ann on 2 January 1854.

[16] As in *Bell v Kennedy*, so too in *Udny*, a party with an apparent cameo role – in *Udny*, the respondent's grandfather and father in a case concerning the respondent's status; and in *Bell v Kennedy*, Mary Anne Bell's father, John Bell, in a claim in her mother's estate – became the principal player. The length and detail of the family narrative, as presented at first instance and on appeal in the Court of Session, and then in the House of Lords, and reproduced in outline here, confirms a prominent feature of the rules of domicile, namely the careful and expensive delving into family history which a reasoned domicile opinion may demand.

[17] The marriage produced a son, John Augustus, who would have succeeded to the estate of Udny had he not predeceased his father in the 1850s.

The Lord Ordinary found that John Udny (the respondent's grandfather), throughout his years of residence and employment in Italy, retained his Scots domicile of origin, which domicile accordingly was conferred at birth on his son John Robert (later Colonel) Udny; and that Colonel Udny was of Scots domicile at the date of his marriage to Ann in 1854. The Second Division of the Inner House of the Court of Session confirmed the decision that Colonel Udny was of Scots domicile throughout his life, and, in particular, that he was of Scots domicile at the date of birth of the respondent *and* at his marriage to Ann six months later. On appeal to the House of Lords, their Lordships held that Colonel Udny never lost his Scots domicile of origin; but that, even if he had acquired an English domicile of choice during his 33 years' residence in England, he would have lost that domicile on leaving England in 1845, at which point his Scots domicile of origin would have revived. While domicile of origin subsists until overtaken, a domicile of choice is lost upon physical departure from the legal system of choice *animo non revertendi.*

Lord Chancellor Hatherley, though less convinced than his Scottish brethren of the continuance of Scottish domicile during the London years (1812–1845), held that on Colonel Udny's breaking up of his London home and departure from England, his Scots domicile of origin revived.[18] His Lordship has the task of distinguishing certain early cases,[19] and the benefit of relying on others,[20] in order to lay down the principle that a man should not be held to a domicile of choice 'resolutely forsaken'. He took the view that it was natural in a period of uncertainty that the *propositus* should fall back upon the domicile of origin. By contrast, 'The character that is gained by residence ceases by residence.'[21] This neat form of words is intended to distinguish between the differing natures of domiciles of origin and of choice (which lie at the root of the revival rule), but it has to be made clear that, in order to effect loss of domicile of choice, the physical quitting of that legal system must be accompanied by mental abandonment thereof.[22]

While domicile of choice depends on a person's will and act, domicile of origin is a creature of law, and it would be inconsistent with principle to suppose that, by mere act of the party, it can be entirely extinguished. Hence, whenever there is no other domicile, domicile of origin does not require to be reconstituted *animo et facto* in the manner necessary for acquisition of a domicile of choice.[23]

[18] There was no suggestion that his involuntary departure from England precluded his loss of English domicile of choice; motive is not a bar to the acquisition of domicile of choice (*Carswell v Carswell* (1881) 8 R 901; *Stavert v Stavert* (1882) 9 R 519), nor seemingly to the loss thereof. There was no suggestion of acquisition of French domicile of choice.

[19] *Munroe v Douglas* (1820) 5 Madd 379, 56 ER 940.

[20] *Munro v Munro* (184) 7 Cl & Fin 842, 7 ER 1288; J Story, *Commentaries on the Conflict of Laws* (Boston, Hilliard Gray & Co, 1834), sec 47. See *Udny* (n 1) 96 (Lord Hatherley LC).

[21] *The Indian Chief* (1801) 3 C Robb 12, 165 ER 367. See *Udny* (n 1) 96 (Lord Hatherley LC).

[22] One can debate whether the requisite *animus* should be *animo non revertendi* or *sine animo revertendi*. See, eg, *Flynn v Flynn* (n 5) and *Morgan v Cilento* [2004] EWHC 188 (Ch).

[23] *Udny* (n 1) 99 (Lord Westbury).

Referring to Story,[24] Lord Chelmsford opined that the doctrine of revival appears to be founded on principle, if not upon direct authority. Thus was put in place the second domicile pillar.

Other legal systems may take a different view in relation to the revival doctrine.[25] In 1985, proposals were made to reform the law of domicile in the UK.[26] In 1987, after consultation, the Law Commission and Scottish Law Commission produced recommendations contained in *Private International Law: The Law of Domicile*,[27] including in relation to 'revival of domicile received at birth'.[28] The effect in some circumstances of the revival rule may be seen to be inappropriate; but the effect of a continuance rule of domicile of choice equally or more so, the *propositus ex hypothesi* having rejected for the future the domicile previously adopted. Ultimately, the Law Commissions recommended that the doctrine of revival of the domicile received at birth should be abolished and that an adult's domicile should continue until he obtains another domicile.[29] These changes were never implemented, and the revival rule established in *Udny* remains.

II. EMBELLISHMENTS

In the century and a half following *Bell v Kennedy* and *Udny*, the pediment has been set across the twin pillars, and case law and legislation over the intervening years have adorned the stonework.[30]

A. Lawfulness of Residence

One of the foundation stones – the definition of *factum* – arose as the central issue in *Puttick v Attorney-General*,[31] in which the position was accepted by

[24] Story (n 20) sec 48; *Udny* (n 1) 97 (Lord Chelmsford).

[25] See, eg, *Re Jones Estate* (1921) 182 NW 227 (Supreme Court of Iowa).

[26] Law Commission and Scottish Law Commission, *Private International Law: The Law of Domicile* (Law Com Working Paper No 88 and Scot Law Com Memo No 63). There had been earlier attempts to reform the rules. The report of the Wynn-Parry Committee (Cm No 9068, 1954) had recommended abolition of domicile of origin, introduction of a continuance rule, independent domicile for judicially separated wives, and the dependence of a child's domicile upon that of the party having custody. Domicile Bills were introduced in 1958 and 1959, but each was withdrawn. Further recommendations on domicile, not acted on, were contained in the Private International Law Committee, *Seventh Report of the Lord Chancellor's Private International Law Committee* (Cm 1955, 1963).

[27] Law Commission and Scottish Law Commission, *Private International Law: The Law of Domicile* (Law Com No 168 and Scot Law Com No107, 1987) para 8.7.

[28] ibid, paras 5.23–5.25.

[29] ibid, para 5.25.

[30] *Lord Advocate v Brown's Trustees* 1907 SC 333, 338 (Lord McLaren).

[31] *Puttick v Attorney General* [1980] Fam 1 (Fam).

Sir George Baker, President of the Family Division, that acquisition of domicile of choice in a country cannot be founded upon residence which is illegal by the law of that country. This statement was qualified by the unanimous decision of the House of Lords in *Mark v Mark*,[32] a divorce jurisdiction case, involving Nigerian nationals. The wife issued a divorce petition in England, relying initially for jurisdiction solely upon her habitual residence there over the previous 12 months, but her petition later was amended to include the claim that she had acquired an English domicile of choice. Having first admitted that the English court had jurisdiction, the husband later changed his mind on the point, and applied for a stay of the English proceedings, on the basis that he had commenced proceedings already in Nigeria. He argued that the habitual residence of the wife in England for 12 months prior to the petition could not clothe the court with jurisdiction because her presence there was unlawful. She was classed as an 'overstayer', ie a person whose leave to remain in the UK had expired. The judge at first instance held that while the wife could not be regarded as habitually resident in England, by reason of the unlawfulness of her presence, she could rely upon her presence there as a basis for the acquisition of a domicile of choice. The Court of Appeal dismissed the husband's appeal, finding that the wife not only had acquired an English domicile of choice by the time of litigation, but also had been habitually resident in England for the previous 12 months. In the House of Lords, on the question of domicile,[33] Baroness Hale found that until *Puttick* there was little English case authority on the point of 'lawfulness', though sources drew on authorities from other Commonwealth jurisdictions.[34] Treating the matter as one of principle and having regard to the object of the rules of domicile – which, in her Ladyship's view, is to discover the system of law with which the *propositus* is most closely connected for a range of purposes[35] – she stated that 'Sometimes that connection will be an advantage to him. Sometimes it will not.'[36] Her Ladyship did not view the conferring of English domicile as a necessary benefit, or the withholding of it as a necessary punishment. Taking a purposive approach, the House of Lords concluded that there was no reason in principle why a person whose presence in England is unlawful cannot acquire a domicile of choice there. Recognising the appropriateness of England as a divorce forum in the instant case did not offend any general principle that a person cannot be allowed to benefit from their own criminal conduct. Baroness Hale took the view that in the circumstances presented, the state had no particular interest, one way or another.[37] As a matter of fact, the

[32] *Mark v Mark* [2006] 1 AC 98 (HL).
[33] On the residence point, Baroness Hale held that for the purpose of the 1973 Act, s 5(2) (but not necessarily for other statutory provisions), the residence of the petitioner need not be lawful residence.
[34] *Mark v Mark* (n 32) [38].
[35] ibid, [44].
[36] ibid.
[37] ibid, [44]. Contrast peerage claims: *Re Barony of Moynihan* [2000] 1 FLR 113 (HL).

wife's position was precarious, and comparable to the situations of the petitioner in each of *Boldrini*[38] and *Cruh*,[39] but that did not preclude her acquisition of English domicile of choice.

In view of the unanimous decision in *Mark*, previously held views based upon *Puttick* must be regarded with caution, part of its strength having been diminished. Much will depend on subject-matter context.

B. Domicile of Married Women

Belatedly, and advisedly, the legislative chisel was taken to one of the domicile cornerstones by means of the Domicile and Matrimonial Proceedings Act 1973. At common law, as demonstrated by *Bell v Kennedy*, there was unity of domicile between husband and wife, a wife taking her husband's domicile as a matter of law at the point of marriage.[40] This rule still affects questions relating to the domicile of women married before 1 January 1974. By section 1 of the 1973 Act the position now is as follows:

> (1) Subject to subsection (2) below, the domicile of a married woman as at any time after the coming into force of this section shall, instead of being the same as her husband's by virtue only of marriage, be ascertained by reference to the same factors as in the case of any other individual capable of having an independent domicile.
>
> (2) Where immediately before this section came into force a woman was married and then had her husband's domicile by dependence, she is to be treated as retaining that domicile (as a domicile of choice,[41] if it is not also her domicile of origin) unless and until it is changed by acquisition or revival of another domicile, either on or after the coming into force of this section.

This statutory change, expected to be the last word on the matter, proved not to be so. Where a woman was married before 1 January 1974, her domicile would change, on the interpretation of section 1(2) given in *Inland Revenue Commissioners v Duchess of Portland*,[42] only in accordance with the usual rules for loss of domicile of choice. There was to be no more lenient rule.[43] Hence, in the case of the Duchess, while it was always clear that her intention was to

[38] *Boldrini v Boldrini* [1932] P 9 (CA) (regarding an illegal alien).

[39] *Cruh v Cruh* [1945] 2 All ER 545 (where a party is subject to a deportation order, the intention to remain so long as the host state permits was sufficient to constitute *animus*).

[40] *Re Cooke's Trustees* (1887) 56 LT 737; *Low v Low* (1891) 19 R 115; *Le Mesurier v Le Mesurier* [1895] AC 517 (PC); *Re Mackenzie* [1911] 1 Ch 578 (Ch); *Mackinnon's Trustees v Lord Advocate* [1921] 1 AC 146 (HL); *Attorney General for Alberta v Cook* [1926] AC 444 (PC); *Dunne v Saban* [1955] P 178; *Re Scullard* [1957] Ch 107 (Ch); and *Faye v Inland Revenue Commissioners* (1961) 40 TC 103 (Ch).

[41] Known as a 'deemed domicile of choice'.

[42] *Inland Revenue Commissioners v Duchess of Portland* [1982] Ch 314 (Ch).

[43] ibid, 318 (Nourse J).

return ultimately to Canada, her practice of taking long holidays in Quebec did not mean, after 1 January 1974 upon a proper construction of the Act, that she had ceased to reside in England. Her English domicile of dependence (ie deemed domicile of choice) remained. The alternative statutory intervention would have been to reactivate the wife's domicile of origin, if different, on analogy with *Udny*, but retaining the domicile of the husband as a deemed domicile of choice was consonant with the rule on retention of domicile of choice by residence alone.

III. WEATHERING AND EROSION

There has also been some weathering and erosion of the domicile construction, with parts of the stonework being gradually worn, if not entirely whittled away, by modern developments.

A. Family Law (Scotland) Act 2006

In Scots law, the twin pillars have been very substantially eroded by legislative intervention, namely, by section 22 of the Family Law (Scotland) Act 2006. An aim of the Act was to complete the process of removal from Scots law of the status of illegitimacy[44] and, in turn, to remove the 'link between a child's domicile and that of his parent's marital status in relation to both the domicile of origin and dependant [sic] domicile'.[45]

The express purpose of section 22 ('Domicile of persons under 16') is to effect the ascription of domicile of persons under 16, according to the following rules:

> A child shall be domiciled in the same country as his parents[46] where:
>
> (a) his parents are domiciled in the same country as each other; and
> (b) he has a home with a parent or a home (or homes) with both of them.
>
> Where these conditions are not satisfied (section 22(3)), the child shall be domiciled in the country with which he has for the time being the closest connection.

Reliance is placed on the test 'having a home with', suggesting perhaps an emotional tie, rather than, or in addition to, a purely factual tie based on ordinary residence. One would assume that where a child is sent from his parents' home to another country for education, or for reasons of safety, his 'home' (notional) must yet be held to be with his parents.[47]

[44] Effected by s 21.

[45] Explanatory notes to Family Law (Scotland) Bill, para 30.

[46] The 2006 Act does not provide a special rule for adopted children; nor does the Act make it clear whether or not the word 'parent' includes adoptive parent.

[47] Compare *Williams, Petitioner*, 1977 SLT (Notes) 2.

More fundamentally, the Act makes no reference to the terms 'domicile of origin' and 'domicile of choice'. It is naïve and regrettable that full consideration was not given to the implications of this ad hoc statutory incursion into the framework of the domicile rules. Silence about the name of the under-16 domicile, and its place in the general scheme, is damaging to the coherence of the domicile rules. The domicile of origin acted, and acts still in English law, as the 'anchor' domicile, providing certainty at times of uncertainty. Legislating under the heading 'Domicile of persons under 16', without appreciating its repercussions on the ascertainment of domicile at subsequent points in an individual's life, was ill-advised. The Law Commissions' 1987 proposals, whatever view one takes of their desirability, contained a suggested corpus of rules on domicile, including the abolition of domicile of origin,[48] whereas that which is contained in the 2006 Act purports to be restricted to the alteration of particular rules, without appreciating the domino effect.

Drafting transitional provisions is notoriously difficult, perhaps especially in domicile.[49] The Act does not make plain the time at which the section 22 rule is to take effect. One might have hoped that it would take effect from its date of commencement (4 May 2006) forward,[50] to regulate the domiciles of those who, at the date of coming into force of the Act, were under 16 and those at that date not yet born – the difficulty of establishing, at the time of death of a nonagenarian, for the purpose, say, of distribution of his estate, his 'under-16' domicile does not seem to have been appreciated.[51] The point is still untested.

Since the domicile of origin rules cannot co-exist with section 22, the continuing applicability of the ratio of *Bell v Kennedy* in Scotland must be doubted. Moreover, the question arises whether or not the principle of revival of domicile of origin has survived for use by a Scots court. If a person having a Scottish 'under-16' domicile acquires a 'post-16' domicile in New South Wales, and then departs that place in a final manner, and meets his death shortly thereafter on a visit to Tasmania, the question would be whether he died domiciled in Scotland (with his 'under-16' domicile intact) or in New South Wales (on the basis of a continuance rule). The 2006 Act is silent as to the solution.

Revival of the 'under-16' domicile would not be without complication. Domicile of origin is a fixed connecting factor, but 'under-16' domicile might vary

[48] Law Com and Scot Law Com (n 27) para 4.24.

[49] ibid, para.8.7 and cl 1(2), 2(3). It was suggested that changes in the rules of domicile should apply to determine the domicile of a person as at any time *after* the legislation should come into force; and that the 'new' rules should apply also to times *before* the legislation should come into force, but only for the purpose of determining where, at a time *after* the legislation should come into force, a person is domiciled.

[50] Though this is by no means borne out by the Family Law (Scotland) Act 2006 (Commencement, Transitional Provisions and Savings) Order 2006, which in Art 4 merely enacts that the provisions of s 22, inter alia, shall not apply in relation to any proceedings which commenced before 4 May 2006.

[51] Compare *Cyganik v Agulian* [2006] EWCA Civ 129 [46] (Mummery LJ), quoting Kierkegaard: 'Life must be lived forwards, but can only be understood backwards.'

during the years from infancy to 16; which 'under-16' domicile would revive – that which was ascribed at birth, or the one latest held? The doubt which attends this conjecture demonstrates the inadequacies of incomplete drafting. But the absence of reported case law suggests that this and related problems of interpretation have not presented to any significant extent in practice.

B. Increased Use of the Connecting Factor of Habitual Residence

The Europeanisation of private international law rules[52] has led to increased use, and significance, of the connecting factor of habitual residence in UK courts.[53] When first employed, habitual residence appeared, seductively, to be a 'simple, non-technical' connecting factor,[54] but age and use have revealed that impression to be misleading. This is not the place in which to carry out a full comparison and contrast of domicile and habitual residence, but it suffices to say that, as the meaning of habitual residence has become increasingly elaborate and less convincingly a straightforward matter of fact, so too it has become more difficult to distinguish, on the one hand, the criteria relevant to acquisition of domicile of choice and, on the other, the indicia for establishing habitual residence. The cross-over in terms of physical residence has long been recognised,[55] and in the context of case law on international child abduction, the intention of the *propositus* has become a relevant factor in the ascertainment of habitual residence.

In *In re LC (Children)*,[56] the UK Supreme Court stated expressly that the acquisition of habitual residence is not a matter of intention: '… one does not acquire a habitual residence merely by intending to do so; nor does one fail to acquire one merely by not intending to do so'.[57] But by introducing a novel mental dimension into the determination of a petition for return of a child under the 1980 Hague Convention on the Civil Aspects of International Child Abduction, the Court made explicit the link between integration in a social and family environment – which is key to establishing a child's habitual residence in a particular country[58] – and intention.[59]

[52] See, eg, Regulation (EC) No 1347/2000 (Brussels II Regulation) and Regulation (EC) 2201/2003 (Brussels II *bis* Regulation).

[53] For background, see JM Carruthers, 'Discerning the Meaning of 'Habitual Residence of The Child' in UK Courts: A Case for the Oracle of Delphi' (2019–2020) 21 *Yearbook of Private International Law* 1.

[54] EM Clive, 'The Concept of Habitual Residence' (1997) 6 *Juridical Review* 137.

[55] P Rogerson, 'Habitual Residence: The New Domicile?' (2000) 49 *International & Comparative Law Quarterly* 86, 100.

[56] *In re LC (Children)* [2014] UKSC 1, [2014] AC 1038.

[57] ibid, [59] (Baroness Hale).

[58] Case C-523/07 *Proceedings brought by A* [2010] Fam 42.

[59] *In re LC (Children)* (n 56) [37] (Lord Wilson).

Widening the role traditionally afforded under the 1980 Hague Convention to a child's state of mind (namely, the ability to voice objection in terms of Article 13), the Supreme Court consigned to history the notion previously adhered to in UK courts,[60] that evidence of state of mind was never relevant to the determination of an individual's habitual residence. Thus, the assertions and insights of an adolescent child regarding their state of mind during a period of residence in a country now are relevant to the determination whether or not the residence there was habitual. 'Integration' is not to be viewed solely through the lens of physical settlement, but also may entail consideration of the state of mind of the young person in question. Therefore, it is clear that the state of mind of an adolescent *propositus* may be relevant in determining not only their domicile, but also their habitual residence. It is likely that this approach will influence courts in assessing habitual residence in other legal contexts.

Habitual residence is still distinguishable from domicile inasmuch as the twin pillars of *Bell v Kennedy* and *Udny* represent clear and unequivocal rules such as do not typically apply in relation to habitual residence. It will be interesting to monitor, in light of the UK's withdrawal from the EU, the extent to which the legal systems of the UK continue to uphold domicile as a preferred connecting factor for personal law matters or whether, increasingly, habitual residence is adopted (as the sole or alternative connecting factor, eg as in parental order applications discussed below) – and in that eventuality, to observe the extent to which further interpretative gloss may be added by way of a continually developing body of case law. From an EU perspective, it is noteworthy that Brussels II *bis* Recast,[61] Article 3(b), conferring jurisdiction in matrimonial matters on the courts of the Member State of the nationality of both spouses, makes no patent reference to the use of domicile as a connecting factor.[62] However, Article 2(3) provides that for the purposes of the instrument,[63] the concept of 'domicile' replaces the concept of 'nationality' for Ireland and has the same meaning as it has under that legal system.[64]

IV. TESTING THE STRENGTH OF THE TWIN PILLARS

Modern legislative instances of use of domicile as a connecting factor afford opportunities to stress-test the strength of the twin pillars. Three statutory instances will be considered: matrimonial jurisdiction, inheritance, and surrogacy.

[60] See, eg, *R v Barnet LBC Ex p Shah* [1983] 2 AC 309 (HL) 344 (Lord Scarman).
[61] Regulation (EU) No 2019/1111 (Brussels II *bis* Recast Regulation).
[62] Contrast Brussels II *bis*, Art 3.1(b).
[63] Brussels II *bis* Recast, Arts 3, 6, 10, 12, 13, 51, 59, 75, 94 and 102.
[64] Compare Brussels II *bis*, Art 3.2.

A. Jurisdiction in Matrimonial Proceedings

The use of domicile in the context of matrimonial jurisdiction has a long history.[65] The concept of matrimonial domicile was rendered redundant by the UK Privy Council in *Le Mesurier v Le Mesurier*.[66] The modern starting point is the Domicile and Matrimonial Proceedings Act 1973.[67] The 1973 Act, in Parts II (Jurisdiction in Matrimonial Proceedings (England and Wales)), III (Scotland) and IV (Northern Ireland), laid down rules of jurisdiction in divorce on the basis of either party's domicile or one year's habitual residence in the legal system in question, tempered by a system of obligatory,[68] mandatory,[69] and discretionary[70] stays/sists.

Although the Europeanisation of private international law rules increased in UK courts the significance of the connecting factor of habitual residence, domicile continued to play an important part.[71] With effect from 1 January 2021, on account of the UK's withdrawal from the EU, the shape and content of the matrimonial jurisdiction rules applicable in UK courts has reverted to being a matter of UK domestic law. While the post-Brexit approach to matrimonial jurisdiction in England and Wales essentially replicates for courts in England and Wales the basic structure of Brussels II *bis*, Article 3[72] (albeit adding a supplementary ground of jurisdiction, namely, the domicile in England and Wales of either party to the marriage),[73] the post-Brexit rules of matrimonial jurisdiction in Scotland evidence a retreat to the simpler, 'pre-Brussels' position.[74] Notably, however, domicile continues to feature as a primary connecting factor in both sets of rules, and can be fiercely contested.[75]

[65] JM Carruthers, 'Your Place or Mine? Jurisdiction in Matrimonial and Related Proceedings – A Scottish Perspective' in JM Velasco Retamosa and MV Cuartero Rubio (eds), *La Vida Familiar Internacional En Una Europa Compleja: Cuestiones Abiertas Y Problemas De La Práctica* (Tirant lo Blanch, 2022).

[66] *Le Mesurier v Le Mesurier* [1895] AC 517 (PC).

[67] For background, see Scottish Law Commission, Family Law: Report on the Jurisdiction in Consistorial Causes affecting Matrimonial Status (Scot Law Com No 25, 1972). See also, in England and Wales, Law Commission, Report on Jurisdiction in Matrimonial Causes (Law Com No 48, 1972).

[68] Sch 1, para 8 (England and Wales).

[69] Sch 3, para 8 (Scotland).

[70] Sch 1, para 9 (England and Wales); sch 3, para 9 (Scotland).

[71] Brussels II *bis*, Art 3(b).

[72] Jurisdiction and Judgments (Family) (Amendment etc.) (EU Exit) Regulations 2019.

[73] Sch 1, rule 7(g).

[74] The Jurisdiction and Judgments (Family, Civil Partnership and Marriage (Same Sex Couples) (EU Exit) (Scotland) (Amendment etc.) Regulations 2019.

[75] See, eg, *Pierburg v Pierburg* [2019] EWFC 24, [2019] 1 WLR 4335; *U v J (Domicile: Habitual Residence)* [2017] EWHC 449 (Fam); *Chai v Peng* [2014] EWHC 1519 (Fam); *Sekhri v Ray* [2014] EWCA Civ 119; *Divall v Divall* [2014] EWHC 95 (Fam); *O v O* [2010] EWHC 3539 (Fam); *M v M (Divorce: Domicile)* [2010] EWHC 982 (Fam); *A v L* [2009] EWHC 1448 (Fam); *Williamson v Williamson* 2009 Fam LR 44; *Munro v Munro* [2007] EWHC 3315 (Fam); *Re N (Jurisdiction)* [2007] EWHC 1274 (Fam); *R v R (Divorce: Jurisdiction: Domicile)* [2006] 1 F.L.R. 389; *Breuning v Breuning* [2002] EWHC 236 (Fam); *M v M (Divorce: Jurisdiction: Validity of Marriage)* [2001] 2 FLR 6 (Fam); and *Spence v Spence* 1995 SLT 335.

A typical modern example is *KMM v NAM (Jurisdiction)*,[76] in which is seen the 'tactical jockeying'[77] that can be so characteristic of domicile disputes. The purpose of the English proceedings was to determine whether the husband (H) was domiciled in England and Wales for the purposes of matrimonial and related parental responsibility proceedings. Having argued, initially, for the purposes of bringing the divorce petition, that he was domiciled in England, H subsequently changed position to argue that he was domiciled in Scotland (his legal system of origin), seeking, by that time, to have his petition dismissed for want of jurisdiction. Equally self-serving, the wife (W) initially argued that H was domiciled in Scotland or in the UAE (where the family had moved temporarily from England) but changed her position to say that at all material times H, like W, was domiciled in England and Wales. The court concluded that H was domiciled in England and Wales at the time he filed his domicile petition,[78] but there is no reference to *Bell v Kennedy* or to the rule of survival of domicile of origin.[79]

Notably, the court did not properly 'anchor' the petitioner by identifying, explicitly, what was his domicile of origin. Reference is made to place of birth (Scotland) and upbringing there (by a Scottish mother and an English father),[80] and to departure from Scotland many years later, including the absence thereafter of any physical home in Scotland,[81] but the court at no point ascertains the *propositus*'s domicile of origin, nor refers expressly to the survival rule. Rather, the focus is on H's attitude towards England, and then Dubai. Acquisition (and continuation) of English domicile of choice ultimately is established, but without properly starting at the beginning of the legal narrative. Nor is there any reference to the revival rule in *Udny*, even in the consideration of whether or not, pursuant to acquisition of English domicile of choice, H subsequently lost that domicile upon moving to live in Dubai.[82]

Despite the centrality of domicile to the determination of the case, not atypically there was no reference to the twin pillars and therefore they cannot be said to play any explicit role in supporting the decision. Nor can the decision be said to support them.

B. Inheritance and Family Dependants Act 1975

In the English canon, a certain number of domicile cases present as claims of inheritance, on intestacy or against the will, by disappointed relatives of the

[76] *KMM v NAM (Jurisdiction)* [2021] EWHC 2300 (Fam), [2022] 2 FCR 180.
[77] ibid, [20] (Sir Jonathan Cohen).
[78] ibid, [44] (Sir Jonathan Cohen).
[79] Nor, correctly, to the changes introduced into Scots law by the Family Law (Scotland) Act 2006, s 22. The forum must apply its own rules of domicile: *In re Annesley* [1926] Ch 692 (Ch).
[80] *KMM v NAM* (n 76) [7]–[9] (Sir Jonathan Cohen).
[81] ibid, [13] and [40] (Sir Jonathan Cohen).
[82] ibid, [41] (Sir Jonathan Cohen).

deceased in terms of the Inheritance and Family Dependants Act 1975. The deceased's domicile in England and Wales is a pre-condition of such claims: the so-called 'domicile gateway'.[83] A review of the relevant case law reveals a solid bank of careful decisions,[84] but no mention of *Bell v Kennedy* and some evidence of departure from the traditional approach to onus.

An analogous right, with corresponding domicile gateway, exists in Scots law. The Family Law (Scotland) Act 2006, by section 29, confers upon a surviving cohabitant a right to seek payment of a capital sum and/or a transfer of property out of the deceased cohabitant's intestate estate, provided that the deceased immediately before death was domiciled in Scotland.[85]

More generally, domicile remains the pre-eminent tool to adjudge cross-border problems arising in succession. In UK legal systems, the ultimate domicile governs all substantive questions of succession, testate or intestate, to the moveable estate of the deceased, but it may also govern important subsidiary or anterior questions including the interpretation of a testamentary instrument. Such a case is *Clarke-Sullivan v Clarke-Sullivan (A Child)*,[86] in which the English High Court considered the law applicable to the interpretation of a will made, whilst living in Dubai, by Katherine Clarke Sullivan, a New Zealand national. She later lived in London until her premature death. The Court was required to construe a clause in the will by which the testatrix bequeathed her residuary estate to a trust which, by the time of her death, no longer existed, and to decide if the clause could be read as intending to create a trust on the terms of the previous trust deed. The case concerned not the material or essential validity of the will (or the clause),[87] but rather an issue of interpretation, bringing into play the choice of law rule that questions of construction or interpretation are governed by the system of law intended by the testator, which is presumed to be the law of her domicile at the time when the will is made,[88] unless a contrary intention appears from the will. This is a weak rule; there are instances where the court prefers to apply the domicile at death.[89]

The task of ascertaining Katherine's domicile at the time of the making of her will was a delicate one. The Court established that she had a domicile

[83] Inheritance (Provision for Family and Dependants) Act 1975, s 1(1). See EB Crawford and JM Carruthers, 'The Law of Unintended Consequences: The Inheritance and Trustees' Powers Bill' (2014) 18 *Edinburgh Law Review* 133.

[84] See, eg, *Re Harmsworth (Deceased)* [1982] 3 WLUK 168; *Bheekhun v Williams* [1999] 2 FLR 229, [1999] Fam Law 379; *Wilson v Jones (Preliminary Issue)* (Unreported, Chancery Division, 8 June 2000); *Morgan v Cilento* (n 22); *Cyganik v Agulian* [2006] EWCA Civ 129; *Holliday v Musa* [2010] EWCA Civ 335; *Peters v Pinder* [2009] SGHC 90, [2011] WTLR 1399; *Sylvester v Sylvester* [2014] WTLR 127 (Ch); *Kebbeh v Farmer* [2015] EWHC 3827 (Ch); and *Re Kohli (Deceased)* [2019] EWHC 193 (Ch); *Kohli v Proles* [2018] EWHC 767 (Ch) (citing *Udny*).

[85] A test not satisfied in *Chebotareva v Khandro (King's Executrix)* 2008 Fam LR 66.

[86] *Clarke-Sullivan v Clarke-Sullivan (A Child)* [2021] EWHC 4 (Ch).

[87] ibid, [36] (Master Clark).

[88] ibid, [37]–[40] (Master Clark).

[89] See, eg, *Re Cunnington* [1924] 1 Ch 68 (Ch).

of origin in New Zealand. After her marriage to a New Zealand citizen, the couple lived in London and Dubai. Master Clark had no difficulty in dismissing Dubai as a possible domicile of choice. The question was whether Katherine had acquired a domicile of choice in England. Inasmuch as the Master identified as the nub of the issue whether she had formed sufficient *animus* for England – and concluded that she had not – the reasoning is consistent with *Bell v Kennedy*, but it is notable that the case was not cited in argument. Instead of examination of early decisions of high standing, modern domicile cases, from whatever area of law, reveal a tendency to eschew such study and to rely upon quotation *ad longum* from secondary sources.[90]

C. Cross-border Surrogacy

Domicile plays a significant part in cases concerning cross-border surrogacy. Such cases as presently come before UK courts typically present as applications under sections 54 and 54A of the Human Fertilisation and Embryology Act 2008 for a 'parental order', namely, one which provides for a child to be treated in law as the child of the applicant(s). It is a prerequisite of granting such an order that, in the case of an application made by two people, at the time of the application and the making of the order either or both of the applicants must be domiciled 'in the UK' or in the Channel Islands or the Isle of Man.[91] This domicile requirement is one of jurisdiction, the aim being to vest jurisdiction in a forum which can be shown to have a suitably strong connection with the parties or one of them.[92]

If a parental order is granted by a UK forum, the child will be treated as the child of the applicants. The effect is transformative. As always with domicile, if the applicant(s) satisfy(ies) the court as to 'UK domicile' at the date of application and at the date of the grant of order, there is nothing to stop them leaving 'for good' the next day.

[90] *Clarke-Sullivan* (n 86) [43]. Compare *Barlow Clowes International Ltd v Henwood* [2008] EWCA Civ 577 [8]–[21] (Arden LJ).

[91] S 54(4)(b). Compare in the case of an application made by one person, s 54A(3)(b). By way of illustration, see *A v B* [2021] EWFC 103; *Re Z (Parental Order: Child's Home)* [2021] EWHC 29 (Fam); *Y v W* [2017] EWFC 60; *AB v GH* [2016] EWHC 63 (Fam); *JV v AR* [2015] EWHC 4756 (Fam); *Re G (Parental Orders)* [2014] EWHC 1561 (Fam); *Re Q (A Child) (Parental Order: Domicile)* [2014] EWHC 1307 (Fam); *Re B-G (A Child) (Parental Orders: Domicile)* [2014] EWHC 444 (Fam); *Re A (Parental Order: Domicile)* [2013] EWHC 426 (Fam); *Z v C (Parental Order: Domicile)* [2011] EWHC 3181 (Fam); and *Re G (Surrogacy: Foreign Domicile)* [2007] EWHC 2814 (Fam).

[92] The Law Commission and Scottish Law Commission have consulted, inter alia, on whether or not to introduce an additional, alternative eligibility requirement of habitual residence to assist those unable to meet the domicile criterion: Law Commission and Scottish Law Commission, *Building families through surrogacy: a new law; a joint consultation paper* (Law Com CP No 244 and Scottish Law Com DP No 167) (para 12.15).

An examination of relevant case law reveals the facilitative character of the judgments – not only in relation to satisfaction of the domicile criterion, but also in relation to other statutory conditions.[93] Case law shows that it will normally be in a child's best interests for a court to grant the section 54 application,[94] and applications for parental orders regularly are granted.

Even where domicile is in issue, rarely does an application fail for lack of jurisdiction on domicile grounds. However, in *Re G*,[95] a case in the English High Court before McFarlane J (now Sir Andrew McFarlane, President of the Family Division, and Head of Family Justice), the commissioning spouses were both Turkish nationals and domiciliaries who had used a British surrogacy agency to assist them in procuring a daughter. The parents had spent only a very short time in the UK and could not possibly be said to have acquired English domicile.[96] While a solution might be found through the Intercountry Adoption Convention, no parental order could be made.

In very different circumstances, in *Y v Z* and *W v X*,[97] Theis J narrates a complex tale of conflicting divorce, adoption and surrogacy proceedings taking place concurrently in Florida, New York and England respectively. The relationship of the married, homosexual commissioning parents had broken down and when the section 54 application came before the English court it was clear that only one of the parties, Z, wished to proceed; the other, Y, had withdrawn from the action and opposed the grant of the order. A child had been conceived with the help of a Missouri-resident mother, using genetic material of Y. Both Y and Z had strong connections to Florida, but Z sought to argue, for the purposes of the English surrogacy action – but not for the purposes of the Florida divorce proceedings which he had initiated – that he had acquired English domicile of choice through moving in 2004 to London for work, buying property there, entering there into a civil partnership with Y (later converted into a marriage), being granted British citizenship, and explaining his visits to Florida as being of a compassionate nature, to visit his mother. But Theis J found the pull of Florida to be for Z magnetic and she did not accept Z's argument in favour of acquisition of English domicile. Had the applicants been at one in their wish to obtain a parental order, and the circumstances propitious for the family

[93] Such as to free and unconditional consent of the surrogate mother (s 54(6), eg, *Re D (Minors) (Surrogacy)* [2012] EWHC 2631 (Fam)); payment of money or other benefit (s 54(8), eg, *Re L (A Child) (Parental Order: Foreign Surrogacy)* [2010] EWHC 3146 (Fam); *Re X (Children) (Parental Order: Retrospective Authorisation of Payments)* [2011] EWHC 3147; *J v G (Parental Orders)* [2013] EWHC 1432 (Fam); and *Re G (Parental Orders)* [2014] EWHC 1561 (Fam)); and timeous submission of application (s 54(3), eg, *Re X (A Child) (Surrogacy: Time Limit)* [2014] EWHC 3135).

[94] See, eg, *Re C (A Child) (Parental Order)* [2013] EWHC 2413 (Fam); [2014] 1 FLR 654. Compare *C v S* 1996 SLT 1387.

[95] *Re G (Surrogacy: Foreign Domicile)* [2007] EWHC 2814 (Fam).

[96] ibid, [15] (McFarlane J).

[97] *Y v Z* and *W v X* [2017] EWFC 60.

rather than disastrous, Theis J might easily have reached a different domicile conclusion – for the trend in these surrogacy cases is to find the jurisdiction requirement of domicile 'in the UK' satisfied. However, argument often is short and perfunctory, and citation of authority sparse, reference usually being made to decisions from this narrow area,[98] raising the suspicion of the creation of a genre within the legal concept of domicile which hitherto has been regarded as unitary (apart from statutory specialties in tax law).

There is seldom any explanation in these surrogacy cases of how domicile of origin is bestowed. Likewise, it is rarely made clear that domicile of origin is deemed to continue unless/until displaced *animo et facto* by a domicile of choice. The heresy, often repeated, is that the applicant has 'abandoned' their domicile of origin. A stronger significance than is customarily accorded in domicile cases seems to be laid upon the acquisition of citizenship.[99] A feature special to these cases and often augmenting the argument in favour of *animus* for England, is the fact that a more liberal view of same sex unions and families created by surrogacy obtains in the UK than in the erstwhile 'home' legal system of the applicants. By reason of the nature of the process, much reliance is placed on the written and oral testimony of applicants, whereas in other areas where a decision on domicile is required, the views of the *propositus* may only rarely be available and will be viewed with circumspection.[100]

Surrogacy is a very particular area of law. Applications usually are unopposed and there exists no party in whose interest it is to dispute domicile.[101] Following introduction of the Adoption and Children Act 2002 into section 54,[102] the welfare of the child is no longer the first but the paramount consideration.[103] If a good outcome can be achieved for the child, a lengthy assessment of *animus*, as demonstrated by Scarman J in *Fuld*,[104] may be inappropriate.

V. CONCLUSION

The province of domicile remains wide, encompassing status, especially relating to marriage, matrimonial jurisdiction, applicable law in annulment, wills and succession, and innominate and unusual cases,[105] and has been enlarged through

[98] *AB v GH* [2016] EWHC 63 (Fam).

[99] *Wahl v Attorney General* (1932) 147 LT 382; *Ross v Ross* [1930] AC 1 (HL); and *In re Fuld (Deceased) (No 3)* [1968] P 675.

[100] *Ross v Ross* (n 99) 6 (Lord Buckmaster).

[101] In this statutory context, where domicile serves a gateway purpose, the court is acutely aware of the implications of its finding on domicile. Compare Fawcett (n 13).

[102] Human Fertilisation and Embryology (Parental Orders) Regulations 2010.

[103] Re Human Fertilisation and Embryology (Parental Orders) Regulations 2010 (SI 2010/985); *Re L (A Child) (Parental Order: Foreign Surrogacy)* [2010] EWHC 3146 (Fam) [9] (Hedley J).

[104] *Fuld* (n 99).

[105] See, eg, *Re S (Hospital Patient: Foreign Curator)* [1995] 4 All ER 30 (Fam).

statute, as in relation to applications for parental orders. However, the cost of domicile litigation is well known. In *KMM v NAM (Jurisdiction)*, Sir Jonathan Cohen expressed horror that the parties had spent some 20 per cent of their wealth in proceedings that were still at a preliminary stage.[106] By contrast, if neither party to litigation raises the issue of domicile in a situation where identity of the personal law may be significant, there will be no battle at all,[107] and the only 'loser' is the development of the subject.

At the outset of this chapter, we stated that the structure which constitutes the rules of ascription of domicile long used by English and Scots courts rests upon the twin pillars of *Bell v Kennedy* and *Udny v Udny*. A Westlaw search (as at 12 July 2022) of all cases citing *Bell v Kennedy* reveals that it has been cited in only 13 cases[108] and of those, the preponderance of use is in Scots cases. The equivalent search in respect of *Udny v Udny* reveals greater volume of citation,[109] but few modern instances. The more frequent reference to *Udny* than to *Bell* is surprising inasmuch as the principle of *Udny*, namely revival of domicile of origin, is not universally supported.

Although the principle of continuance of domicile of origin laid down in *Bell* is less frequently enunciated in case law, it is generally honoured in the unchallenged expectation that the burden of proof of change of domicile lies on the party averring change – although the incidence of use in pleading and in judgments of the phrases 'abandonment of domicile of origin' and 'relinquishing of domicile of origin', potentially skewing the evidential onus, is observable.[110] Likewise, the insistence in *Bell v Kennedy* on strictly limiting the

[106] *KMM v NAM* (n 76) [50].

[107] See, eg, *Mahmood v Mahmood* 1993 SLT 589 and *Mahmud v Mahmud* 1994 SLT 599.

[108] *Brown v Brown (Husband and wife: Jurisdiction)*1967 SLT (Notes) 44; *Chebotareva v Khandro* (n 85); *Corbidge v Somerville* 1914 1 SLT 304; *Crumpton's Judicial Factor v Finch-Noyes* 1918 SC 378; *Henwood v Barlow Clowes International Ltd (In Liquidation)* [2007] EWHC 1579 (Ch); *Holden v Holden* [1968] 1 WLUK 214; *Marchant v Marchant (Divorce: Jurisdiction)* 1948 SLT 143; *Ramsay v Liverpool Royal Infirmary* (n 13); *Reddington v Riach's Executor* 2002 SLT 537; *Ross v Ross* (n 99); *Spence v Spence* (n 75); *Walter v Campbell* (1907) 15 SLT 412; and *Williamson v Williamson* (n 75).

[109] *Austin v Mitchell* [2020] EWHC 3486 (Ch); *Beaman v Beaman* (1967) 53 MPR 205; *Blair v Kay's Trustees* 1940 SLT 464; *Bosville v Lord Macdonald* 1910 SC 597; *Brown v Brown* (n 108); *Chebotareva v Khandro* (n 85); *Corbidge v Somerville* (n 108); *Crumpton's Judicial Factor v Finch-Noyes* (n 108); *Elmquist v Elmquist* 1961 SLT (Notes) 71; *Re Evans (Deceased)* [1947] Ch 695; *Re Flynn (No 1)* (n 5); *Forbes v Forbes* (1910) 2 SLT 425; *Gaines-Cooper v Revenue and Customs Commissioners* [2007] EWHC 2617 (Ch); *Gould v Gould (No 2)* 1968 SLT 98; *Henwood v Barlow Clowes International* (n 90); *Marchant v Marchant* (n 108); *Marchioness of Huntly v Gaskell* (1902) 4 F 1014; *Marsh v Marsh* 2002 SLT 87; *Morgan v Cilento* (n 22); *Ramsay v Liverpool Royal Infirmary* (n 13); *Rankin v Rankin* 1960 SLT 308; *Re Kohli* (n 84); *Reddington* (n 108); *Russell v Russell and Roebuck* [1957] P 375; *Spence v Spence* (n 75); *Sylvester v Sylvester* (n 84); *Thomson, Petitioner* 1980 SLT (Notes) 29; *Williamson v Williamson* (n 75); *Willar v Willar* 1954 SLT 267; *Walter v Campbell* (n 108).

[110] See, eg, *Wilson v Jones (Preliminary Issue)* [2000] 6 WLUK 135 (Unreported, Chancery Division, 8 June 2000); and *Puttick* (n 31) 18 (Sir George Baker). In *Kebbeh v Farmer* [2015] EWHC 3827 (Ch), the deceased was found to have an English domicile of origin, but to be of Gambian domicile of choice at death: the court held that the links with England were insufficient to override the strong evidence that Gambia was the deceased's home; this is a strange way of expressing the matter of onus.

judicial view to facts established at the *tempus inspiciendum* may be in danger of being overborne.[111] These incursions may be seen as chipping away at the twin pillars – though with regard to Scots law, the legislative damage to the pillars is fundamental.

Despite domicile being a unitary concept, the rigour of argument in litigation varies, often according to the nature of the case and the existence or not of competing financial or other interests; a tax liability dispute is likely to be argued with more intensity than an application for a parental order in a cross-border surrogacy case. Modern life and the cost of litigation cannot afford the luxury of extensive pleading and lengthy judicial deliberation on domicile; this economic reality chimes with the mobility of individuals and the more tenuous link that individuals often have to their legal system of origin.

[111] See, eg, *Gaines-Cooper* (n 109).

4

Godard v Gray and *Schibsby v Westenholz* (1870)

JOSHUA FOLKARD AND IAN BERGSON*

THIS CHAPTER CONSIDERS the recognition and enforcement of foreign judgments, and specifically the 'obligation theory' underpinning the common law rules which clearly emerged in the nineteenth century in the twin cases of *Godard v Gray* and *Schibsby v Westenholz*.[1] The chapter is structured as follows: (I) we first address the decisions in *Godard* and *Schibsby* and the obligation theory itself; (II) we then put the domestic common law in context and consider developments in other jurisdictions (including most notably Canada), which have diverged from the English approach; (III) we argue that the obligation theory struggles to explain the current positive law of England and Wales; and (IV) we draw the threads together by way of conclusion and draw on our survey of the foreign jurisprudence to reinforce our conclusions on *Godard* and *Schibsby*.

I. GODARD, SCHIBSBY AND THE OBLIGATION THEORY

In the mid-nineteenth century, two merchants with French citizenship[2] or residence[3] concluded contracts with English[4] or English-resident[5] merchants. The first French merchant was Mr Charles Godard, who in September 1865 chartered the steamer *Como* from the English Messrs Gray Brothers to transport coal from Cardiff to St Nazaire.[6] The second merchant is believed to have

* We would like to thank the participants at the conference for their illuminating comments on a previous draft of this chapter. We would also like to thank Stephen Lacey of Linklaters for his comments on an earlier draft. All errors are our own.

[1] *Godard v Gray* (1870–71) LR 6 QB 139 (QB) and *Schibsby v Westenholz* (1879–71) LR 6 QB 155 (QB).
[2] *Godard* (n 1) 147.
[3] *Schibsby* (n 1) 157.
[4] *Godard* (n 1) 147.
[5] *Schibsby* (n 1) 157.
[6] *Godard* (n 1) 140 and 147.

been Mr Peter-Michelson Schibsby, a Dane resident at Caen in Normandy.[7] Mr Schibsby concluded an FOB contract for the shipment of Swedish oats to Caen with Westenholz Brothers, a firm of London merchants.[8] Disputes arose in relation to both contracts.

Mr Godard[9] and Mr Schibsby[10] both obtained judgments in their favour from the French courts. As for Mr Godard, his charterparty had included the term: 'Penalty for non-performance of this agreement, estimated amount of freight.'[11] The first-instance French court awarded him damages in the amount of freight on two voyages, subsequently reduced by the Imperial Court of Rennes to the estimated freight for one voyage (8,921 French francs).[12] Messrs Gray Brothers had appeared unsuccessfully before both the French first-instance and superior courts.[13] Mr Schibsby was awarded 11,537 French francs by the Tribunal of Commerce at Caen for short delivery.[14] Although Westenholz Brothers were served with a copy of proceedings by the French consulate in London, they made no appearance in the French proceedings.[15] Despite the English jury's subsequent conclusion that they had sufficient notice and knowledge of the summons and the pendency of the French proceedings to have appeared,[16] that decision turned out to have been a good one. Both Mr Godard and Mr Schibsby sought (in modern terminology) to have the French judgments recognised and enforced in England.

Mr Schibsby's trial came on during Hilary Term 1870.[17] The hearing appeared to have gone well for him, with Blackburn J expressing the (qualified) opinion that he was entitled to a verdict in his favour.[18] Unfortunately for Mr Schibsby, however, Blackburn J (also with Hannen and Mellor JJ) heard argument in Mr Godard's case on 6 May 1870.[19] Blackburn J held that he 'had consequently occasion to consider the whole subject of the law of England as to enforcing foreign judgments', and had therefore 'changed' his opinion on Mr Schibsby's case.[20] Judgments in both *Godard* and *Schibsby* were handed down on 10 December 1870. The judgment was given in *Godard* by: (i) Blackburn and Mellor JJ (albeit delivered by Blackburn J); and (ii) Hannen J. In *Schibsby*,

[7] A Dickinson, '*Schibsby v Westenholz* and the recognition and enforcement of judgments in England' (2018) 134 *Law Quarterly Review* 426, 426 and n 5.
[8] ibid, 426 and n 6.
[9] *Godard* (n 1) 147.
[10] *Schibsby* (n 1) 158.
[11] *Godard* (n 1) 147.
[12] ibid, 139, 142–43 and 147.
[13] ibid, 141–42.
[14] *Schibsby* (n 1) 155 and 158.
[15] ibid, 155 and 158.
[16] ibid, 158.
[17] ibid, 155.
[18] ibid, 158.
[19] *Godard* (n 1) 144.
[20] *Schibsby* (n 1) 158.

Blackburn J gave the judgment of the entire Court (Blackburn, Mellor, Hannen and Lush JJ). His Lordship stated that although Lush J had not been party to the discussions in *Godard*, he had nevertheless 'perused' and 'approved' the judgment in that case.[21]

Ultimately, in *Schibsby* Westenholz Brothers' application for a non-suit was successful. In modern terms, Mr Schibsby was unable to obtain recognition or enforcement of his French judgment. This result was reached on the basis that 'there existed nothing in the present case imposing on [Westenholz Brothers] any duty to obey the judgment of a French tribunal'.[22] Mr Godard had more luck. His judgment against Messrs Gray Brothers was recognised and enforced on the basis of the principle (per Blackburn and Mellor JJ) that '[w]here a court of competent jurisdiction has adjudicated a certain sum to be due from one person to another, a legal obligation arises to pay that sum, on which an action of debt to enforce the judgment may be maintained'.[23] That was despite Blackburn J's conclusion that the French courts had erred in English law by concluding that the clause cited above operated to fix a contract-breaker's liability.[24] This rationale has become known as the obligation theory.

Before turning to the Commonwealth and other modern authorities, it is useful to distinguish the obligation theory from other potential explanations which were rejected in *Godard* and *Schibsby*. First, Blackburn J in *Godard* contrasted the English approach to the enforcement of judgments at common law with those of continental nations (including France) which 'do not enforce the judgments of other countries, unless there are reciprocal treaties to that effect'. Since the touchstone for recognition and enforcement at common law was the obligation theory, this did not require reciprocity.[25] Second, Blackburn J also contrasted the obligation-based approach of the common law with an approach that would enforce foreign judgments 'out of politeness and courtesy to the tribunals of other countries', ie which was founded on comity-based considerations.[26] Third, consistent with the obligation theory, the foreign judgment was not merely to be considered 'evidence of the original cause of action' which could be met by 'any counter evidence negativing the existence of that

[21] ibid, 159.

[22] ibid, 163.

[23] *Godard* (n 1) 148, citing the earlier judgment of Parke B in *Williams v Jones* (1845) 13 M & W 628, 633 (which concerned a domestic judgment from the county court).

[24] *Godard* (n 1) 147.

[25] ibid, 148. For a modern case recognising that reciprocity is not relevant outside the sphere of matrimonial proceedings at common law, see *Rubin v Eurofinance SA* [2012] UKSC 46, [2013] 1 AC 236 [127] (Lord Collins).

[26] *Godard* (n 1) 152. See also *Schibsby* (n 1) 159: 'if the principle on which foreign judgments were enforced was that which is loosely called 'comity', we could hardly decline to enforce a foreign judgment given in France against a resident in Great Britain under circumstances hardly, if at all, distinguishable from those under which we, mutatis mutandis, might give judgment against a resident in France; but it is quite different if the principle be that which we have just laid down [ie the obligation theory]'.

original cause of action'.[27] As noted above, the Court held that the obligation to obey the judgment was not affected by the fact the foreign court made an error of law which appears on the face of the judgment.[28]

II. COMMONWEALTH AND OTHER COMMON LAW AUTHORITIES

Godard and *Schibsby* are 'landmark'[29] cases, in the sense that they set the direction of travel of English law and the recognition and enforcement of judgments for more than a century, and firmly embedded the obligation theory in English jurisprudence. Those cases are, however, 'landmarks' in a broader sense, namely by virtue of the influence they have had on the development of rules concerning the recognition and enforcement of judgments in the Commonwealth and other jurisdictions.

The jurisprudence elsewhere in the common law world adopts to a greater or lesser extent divergent approaches to the enforcement of foreign judgments. Canada has gone the furthest in developing an alternative approach, which is more permissive than the English cases such as *Godard* and *Schibsby* underpinned by the obligation theory. The obligation theory has also been the subject of recent criticism by the Court of Appeal of Singapore, which appeared receptive to the Canadian approach. By contrast, the Supreme Court of Ireland has declined to follow the Canadian authorities and has maintained the approach set out in *Dicey, Morris & Collins*.

This section will first examine the Canadian developments, before turning to consider how they have been received elsewhere. We will consider in turn Ireland, Hong Kong, Singapore, New Zealand and Australia.

A. Canada[30]

In *Morguard Investments Ltd v De Savoye*,[31] the Supreme Court of Canada applied a modified approach to the enforcement of judgments between different Canadian provinces. The claimant sought to enforce a judgment obtained

[27] *Godard* (n 1) 150.

[28] ibid, 151. This remains good law today: L Collins (ed), *Dicey, Morris & Collins on the Conflict of Laws*, 15th edn (London, Sweet & Maxwell, 2012) para 14R-118, rule 48 (concerning the inability to impeach a foreign judgment for an error of fact or law).

[29] We are grateful to Stephen Pitel and Andrew Dickinson for their very helpful comments on an earlier draft of this chapter at the conference, concerning the various possible meanings of the term 'landmark'.

[30] We are grateful to Stephen Pitel for a very helpful and illuminating discussion on the Canadian law position at the conference.

[31] *Morguard Investments Ltd v De Savoye* [1990] 3 SCR 1077 (SCC). This case and the Canadian jurisprudence is discussed in detail in ch 13 in this volume.

in Alberta for mortgage arrears after foreclosure where the mortgagor, Mr De Savoye (although residing in Alberta at the time of the mortgage) had subsequently moved to British Columbia. He was accordingly not present in Alberta at the time of the commencement of the action for the purposes of the traditional common law rules. The Supreme Court of Canada held the Albertan judgment was enforceable in British Columbia nonetheless.

La Forest J, giving the judgment of the Court, noted that the common law regarding the recognition and enforcement of foreign judgments was firmly anchored in the principle of territoriality as interpreted and applied by the English courts in the nineteenth century. This had been 'unthinkingly adopted' by the Canadian courts, even in relation to judgments given in sister-provinces.[32] The Court held that the world had changed since the English rules were developed, including in light of modern means of travel and communication, and the rules on judgment enforcement appeared ripe for reappraisal. A broader conception of comity was appropriate in this context, which was not based simply on respect for decisions of a foreign sovereign but convenience and necessity given the division of legal authority among sovereign states. In any case, there was no comparison between modern interprovincial relationships and those between foreign countries in the nineteenth century and it was inappropriate to apply the English rules within the single country of Canada.[33] Where a defendant is outside the province of the court exercising jurisdiction, La Forest J suggested there would need to be a 'real and substantial connection with the action' before that province's judgment would be enforceable in another province (which he held was plainly satisfied in respect of Alberta on the facts of the case at issue).[34] Prior to the Canadian Supreme Court's judgment (in an article published in 1987), Professor Briggs had advocated a similar approach be adopted in England. Specifically, Professor Briggs contended that – in light of recent developments to the English law of *forum non conveniens* in the jurisdiction context and the House of Lords' seminal decision in *Spiliada*[35] – foreign judgments given by the natural forum for the action should now be recognised in England.[36]

In *Beals v Saldanha*,[37] the Supreme Court of Canada took the analysis in *Morguard* a stage further and applied the 'real and substantial connection' test established for interprovincial judgments to foreign judgments. It held that a Florida judgment in relation to the sale of land in Florida for US$8,000 (which in the event was for over US$200,000 in compensatory damages and US$50,000

[32] ibid, 1095 and see also 1087 and 1091–92.

[33] ibid, 1095–03.

[34] ibid, 1108 and see also 1104.

[35] *Spiliada Maritime Corp v Cansulex Ltd* [1987] AC 460 (HL) which is addressed in detail in ch 11 in this volume.

[36] A Briggs, 'Which Foreign Judgments Should We Recognise Today?' (1987) 36 *International & Comparative Law Quarterly* 240.

[37] *Beals v Saldanha* [2003] 3 SCR 416 (SCC).

in punitive damages) was enforceable in Canada against two Ontario residents. Major J, giving the judgment for the majority, held that there were compelling reasons for applying the approach in *Morguard* in this context and no principled reason to decline to do so.[38] He opined that the notions of comity and reciprocity considered in *Morguard* were equally applicable to judgments made by courts outside Canada and '[i]n the absence of a different statutory approach, it is reasonable that a domestic court recognize and enforce a foreign judgment where the foreign court assumed jurisdiction on the same basis as the domestic court would, for example, on the basis of a 'real and substantial connection' test'.[39] A 'real and substantial' connection was now to be regarded as the 'overriding factor in the determination of jurisdiction', albeit subject to the caveat that the presence of the 'traditional indicia of jurisdiction' would serve to bolster the real and substantial connection to the action or parties.[40]

Consistent with Professor Briggs' 1987 article, he initially welcomed the approach to international jurisdiction in *Morguard*[41] and *Beals*,[42] observing that in the latter case the Supreme Court of Canada was 'right to do as it did in widening the grounds of acceptable international jurisdictional competence', albeit it was necessary to consider how the defences allowed by Canadian common law needed to respond to the change.[43] More recently, Professor Briggs has been more circumspect, criticising the decision in *Beals* on both principled and practical grounds, including because of the uncertainty and consequent difficulties it can create for a defendant in deciding whether to defend a claim brought in the foreign forum.[44] By contrast, Professor Dickinson has advocated that *Schibsby* be put to one side and the English court should adopt a more flexible approach to questions of recognition and enforcement by reference to natural justice questions and in a manner broadly consistent with the underlying principles in *Beals*.[45]

Subsequently, in the context of determining the jurisdictional requirements to bring an action in Canada to enforce a foreign judgment, the Supreme Court of Canada held in *Chevron Corporation v Yaiguaje* that there is no need to show a real and substantial connection between the enforcing forum – ie Canada – and the judgment debtor or dispute.[46] It observed that the foreign court needs to

[38] ibid, [19].
[39] ibid, [29] and [27]–[28].
[40] ibid, [37]. Major J described these indicia as 'attornment [ie submission to the jurisdiction], agreement to submit, residence and presence in the foreign jurisdiction'. The logic of this approach was questioned by LeBel J ([207]: who dissented on natural justice grounds). See also [23] (requiring a 'real and substantial connection with either the subject matter of the action or the defendant …').
[41] A Briggs, 'Foreign Judgments: More Surprises' (1992) 108 *Law Quarterly Review* 549.
[42] A Briggs, 'Crossing the River by Feeling the Stones: Rethinking the Law on Foreign Judgments' (2004) 8 *Singapore Year Book of International Law* 1.
[43] ibid, 22.
[44] A Briggs, 'Recognition of Foreign Judgments: A Matter of Obligation' (2013) 129 *Law Quarterly Review* 87, 95.
[45] Dickinson (n 7) 448–49.
[46] *Chevron Corporation v Yaiguaje* [2015] 3 SCR 69 (SCC).

have a 'real and substantial connection' with the litigants or the subject matter of the dispute or the traditional bases of jurisdiction may be satisfied as the prerequisite to enforcing a foreign judgment in Canada.[47]

The effect of the above authorities is to produce a more permissive, flexible and 'soft-edged' regime to the enforcement of foreign judgments in Canada.

B. Ireland

The Irish Supreme Court declined to follow the Supreme Court of Canada's approach in *Beals* in *Re Flightlease (Ireland) Ltd.*[48] The liquidators of an Irish company sought directions ex ante from the Irish courts as to whether any judgment in a claim brought against the company by a Swiss counterparty in the Swiss courts would be recognised and enforced in Ireland.

Finnegan J's leading judgment upheld the trial judge's reasons for refusing to follow the Canadian jurisprudence. They can broadly be divided into four categories. First, the absence of other common law authority following the Canadian approach and the lack of consensus in the common law world as to the reasons for the change. Second, certain academic commentary cautioning against the Canadian approach. This included commentary from Professor Briggs that the approach in *Beals* 'does not focus on whether the party to be bound has assumed an obligation, but on whether the Canadian court should impose one for reasons of its own' which represents a 'fundamental reorientation of the law of foreign judgments …'.[49] Third, the prospect of injustice if a person made a decision as to whether to participate in foreign proceedings on the basis of a view as to what the common law was, and this is later changed. Fourth, that the change would in reality amount to legislation, as opposed to an orderly evolution of common law principles.

O'Donnell J gave a short concurring judgment joining in the result, but with nuances to his reasoning.[50] He indicated that he did so with no particular enthusiasm for an outcome where (what is now) *Dicey*'s rule 43 applied to determine the enforceability of a foreign judgment in Ireland, which had 'little to recommend it at the level of legal theory'.[51] He opined that the principal merit of the Dicey rule was its 'certainty and therefore predictability', but the 'real and substantial connection' test offered substantially more in terms of inherent merit, albeit with a 'much heavier price in terms of uncertainty

[47] ibid, [27].
[48] *Re Flightlease (Ireland) Ltd* [2012] IESC 12, [2012] 1 IR 722.
[49] ibid, [55].
[50] For academic support for O'Donnell J's concurring judgment, see D Kenny, 'Re Flightlease: The 'Real and Substantial Connection' Test for Recognition and Enforcement of Foreign Judgments Failure to Take Flight in Ireland' [2014] *International & Comparative Law Quarterly* 197.
[51] *Re Flightlease* (n 48) [74].

and unpredictability'.[52] O'Donnell J ultimately concluded that the adoption of the Canadian approach would not produce any measurable improvement in Irish law, even if it could be achieved by judicial decision alone (which he doubted).[53]

The Irish Supreme Court's decision has subsequently been referred to with apparent approval by the UK Supreme Court in *Rubin v Eurofinance SA*,[54] when declining to adopt more liberal rules to the enforcement of foreign judgments in the insolvency context in the absence of legislation.[55]

C. Hong Kong

There is first instance authority in Hong Kong declining to follow *Beals* for the purposes of an interlocutory application.[56] The deputy judge saw force in the submission that 'in the absence of exceptional justification, the Hong Kong court should and would not see fit to even start considering the application of the Canadian approach in place of the well-established approach [ie that set out in *Dicey*]'.[57] The consequence was that an English default judgment given against certain defendants who were served out of the jurisdiction with the English court's permission was not enforceable in Hong Kong such as to provide the claimant with a good arguable case to continue a Hong Kong freezing order.

D. Singapore

In *Merck Sharp & Dohme Corp v Merck KGaA*, Singapore's highest court, the Court of Appeal of Singapore, expressed real doubt about the utility of the obligation theory at common law.[58] The Court's observations were made in the context of a different but related issue, namely the operation of issue estoppel in Singapore from foreign judgments. The Court cited Blackburn J's

[52] ibid, [83].
[53] ibid, [90].
[54] *Rubin* (n 25).
[55] No challenge on the appeal was made to the general *Dicey* rule, only its application to foreign insolvency orders: *Rubin* (n 25) [113]. The Privy Council has also remarked on the differing paths taken now taken by English and Canadian law: *Vizcaya Partners Ltd v Picard* [2016] UKPC 5, [2016] 3 All ER 181 [54] n 1.
[56] *Islamic Republic of Iran Shipping Lines v Phiniqia International Shipping LLC* [2014] HKCU 1697 [26]–[35]. See also the first instance decision in *Fabiano Hotels Ltd v Profitmax Holdings Inc* [2017] HKCU 2354 [17], citing amongst others *Godard* and *Schibsby* and observing that 'Recognition and enforcement of a foreign judgment is founded on the doctrine of obligation …'.
[57] *Phiniqia* (n 56) [34]–[35].
[58] *Merck Sharp & Dohme Corp v Merck KGaA* [2021] SGCA 14.

explanation of the obligation theory in *Schibsby* and observed that the doctrine has been 'criticised for presupposing what it is supposed to explain, and for being unable to account for the recognition of foreign judgments that impose no obligations but instead make declarations of status'.[59] It referred with apparent approval to the Supreme Court of Canada's analysis of comity in *Beals* and the extension of the 'jurisdictional bases of recognising foreign judgments beyond presence, residence and submission, to the foreign court having a "real and substantial connection" to the action or to the parties to the litigation'. It concluded that considerations of 'transnational comity and reciprocal respect among courts of independent jurisdictions have come to undergird the recognition of foreign judgments at common law and by extension, the doctrine of transnational issue estoppel'.[60] Consistent with these observations (and in contrast to the traditional English approach based on the obligation theory), the Court of Appeal of Singapore specifically left open for consideration in a future case whether reciprocity should be a precondition to the recognition of foreign judgments at common law.[61] Although the implications of *Merck* remain to be seen, academic commentary recognises that it signals possible fundamental changes to Singapore common law on foreign judgments.[62]

E. New Zealand

The New Zealand Court of Appeal has recently re-affirmed, in *Almarzooqi v Salih*, the general proposition that judgments are not enforced at common law in New Zealand on the basis of reciprocity, but because of an obligation to comply with the judgment owing to the foreign court having international jurisdiction in accordance with New Zealand's private international law rules,[63] which approves the UK Supreme Court's decision in *Rubin*.[64] The case concerned an attempt by a wife following divorce to seek a marriage dowry from the husband in the New Zealand courts inter alia by enforcing a Dubai judgment in the wife's favour at common law.[65] On the wife's further application for leave to appeal to

[59] ibid, [30].

[60] ibid, [31] and [33]; compare the earlier consideration of comity and the obligation theory in *Hong Pian Tee v Les Placements Germain Gauthier Inc* [2002] SGCA 18 [31].

[61] *Merck* (n 58) [39].

[62] Y Ming, 'The Changing Global Landscape for Foreign Judgments', Yong Pung How Professorship of Law Lecture 2021 (6 May 2021).

[63] *Almarzooqi v Salih* [2021] NZCA 330, [2021] NZFLR 501 [31]–[36].

[64] ibid, n 26: as the Court noted, the position is otherwise for New Zealand statutory regimes such as the Reciprocal Enforcement of Judgments Act 1934. For earlier recognition of the obligation theory in New Zealand, see also *Von Wyl v Engeler* [1998] 3 NZLR 416 (CA) 420.

[65] The Court of Appeal also rejected a further argument that the principle of reciprocity could apply given the matrimonial context: *Almarzooqi* (n 63) [39]–[59].

New Zealand's highest court (the Supreme Court of New Zealand), the wife invited it to re-consider the conditions under which New Zealand enforces the judgments of foreign courts, on the basis it is inflexible and inconsistent with access to justice considerations.[66] She asked the Court to follow the lead of the Supreme Court of Canada in *Beals* and adopt the 'real and substantial' connection test. This was resisted by the husband on the basis that the Canadian approach is an outlier (citing *Flightlease*). The Supreme Court refused to grant leave, observing that on its facts the proposed appeal was not a good vehicle to address *Beals* and that the current law in New Zealand is 'clear'. The Court also observed that 'at least as matters stand, it is preferable for any development of the New Zealand position to be by international agreement rather than by this Court'.[67]

F. Australia

The Australian common law has not departed from the traditional English approach to determining a foreign court's international jurisdiction by adopting the Canadian jurisprudence.[68] A leading Australian text on conflict of laws opines that it is 'unlikely that Australian courts will be bold enough to adopt [the Canadian] 'real and substantial test' for recognition and enforcement of foreign judgments …'. It generally summarises the position in terms consonant with the English commentaries.[69]

III. SOUND THEORETICAL BASIS FOR THE MODERN LAW?

This section will argue that, despite the status of *Schibsby* and *Godard* as 'landmark' cases in the sense outlined above, the obligation theory which clearly emerged from those cases struggles to explain the current, positive law on the recognition and enforcement of judgments at common law in England and Wales.

The methodology adopted in this section will be two-fold. First, it will be considered that any theory seeking to explain the basis for recognition and enforcement of judgments must explain the current law in a normative, rather than a merely doctrinal, sense. The obligation theory posits that the making

[66] *Almarzooqi v Salih* [2021] NZSC 161 [9]–[10].

[67] ibid, [11], which also refers to the Hague Judgments Convention 2019 (which has not yet entered into force, as to which see below).

[68] Briggs (n 42) 12 and see, eg, *Martyn v Graham* [2003] QDC 447 [21]–[26]; *Maleski v Hampson* [2013] NSWSC 1794 [4]–[8]; and *Macquarie Bank Ltd v Juno Holdings S.a.r.l.* [2015] NSWSC 1260 [23]–[26].

[69] M Davies, A Bell, P Brereton and M Douglas, *Nygh's Conflict of Laws in Australia* 10th edn (Melbourne, Lexis Nexis Australia, 2019) para 40.9. See also paras 40.2–40.3, 40.44 and 40.46.

of a foreign judgment creates an obligation on the party against whom that judgment is given, independent of the substantive obligations or cause(s) of action which gave rise to that judgment.[70] In order to provide a satisfactory explanation of the current law, though, any such theory must explain *why* that secondary, independent obligation arises.[71] In *Rubin v Eurofinance SA*, Lord Collins referred to the obligation theory as 'a purely theoretical and historical basis for the enforcement of foreign judgments at common law'.[72] If that is all the obligation theory amounts to, it is submitted that this is insufficient to provide a sound basis for the current rules on the recognition and enforcement of judgments. Equally, a conclusory statement that in certain circumstances a defendant will be taken to have accepted the foreign court's jurisdiction is, without more, insufficient.

Second, in terms of methodology this section will assess the obligation theory by reference not only to the question of whether the foreign court is held to have had 'international jurisdiction' over the English defendant or respondent, but also to what is generally termed the 'defences' to recognition and enforcement.[73] Traditionally the analysis as to whether a foreign judgment should be recognised and enforced has been divided into two steps, in the terminology of *Dicey*'s rules: first, whether the foreign judgment has been given 'by the court of a foreign country with jurisdiction to give that judgment' (ie international jurisdiction);[74] and, second, whether that judgment can be 'impeached',[75] including whether it is 'impeachable for fraud'.[76] This dichotomy derives to an extent from *Godard* and *Schibsby* themselves. In *Godard*, Blackburn J stated that 'We enforce a legal obligation, and we admit any defence which shews that there is no legal obligation or a legal excuse for not fulfilling.'[77] His Lordship stated similarly in *Schibsby* that:

> the true principle on which the judgments of foreign tribunals are enforced in England is that … the judgment of a court of competent jurisdiction over the defendant imposes a duty or obligation on the defendant to pay the sum for which judgment is given, which the courts in this country are bound to enforce; and consequently that anything which negatives that duty, or forms a legal excuse for not performing it, is a defence to the action.

[70] P Rogerson, *Collier's Conflict of Laws*, 4th edn (Cambridge, CUP, 2013) 219–21.

[71] Ho expresses this point by dismissing theories which cannot explain why judgments are enforced as 'question begging': Ho, 'Policies Underlying the Enforcement of Foreign Commercial Judgments' (1997) 46 *International & Comparative Law Quarterly* 443, 445.

[72] *Rubin* (n 25) [9]. A position criticised in Briggs (n 44) 100.

[73] See, eg, *Collier* (n 70) 253.

[74] *Dicey, Morris & Collins*, 15th edn (n 28) para 14R-020, rule 42.

[75] ibid, para 14R-128, rule 49.

[76] ibid, para 14R-137, rule 50. See, to similar effect: *Collier* (n 70) 237 and 253 and A Briggs, *Civil Jurisdiction and Judgments*, 7th edn (London, Routledge, 2021) para 34.02.

[77] *Godard* (n 1) 158. See also 148–49: 'it seems to follow that anything which negatives the existence of that legal obligation, or excuses the defendant from the performance of it, must form a good defence to the action'.

It has increasingly been recognised by academics, however, that in assessing the recognition and enforcement of judgments it is important to have regard to both 'stages' of the traditional analysis. As Professor Briggs stated in commenting on the Supreme Court of Canada's decision in *Beals v Saldanha*,[78] 'Jurisdiction and defence are, in this corner of the law, indissociable. It cannot be right to make radical changes to one while supposing that this has no impact on the other. The recognition of foreign judgments is a machine. It is not a box of unconnected bits and pieces.'[79]

As for definitions, the obligation theory is often said to be normatively justified by concepts of 'sovereignty' and allegiance to a 'sovereign'.[80] Whilst disputed concepts, this section will adopt Ho's two-dimensional definition of 'sovereignty'.[81] The first, 'internal' dimension connotes being a 'supreme authority within a political community'.[82] The second, 'external' dimension means 'in the context of relations between States' 'independence ... freedom from unwanted external intervention, including interference by a foreign judicial authority'.[83] It is submitted that it is the first, internal dimension which is most relevant to this discussion (as explained further below).

Against that methodology and definition, there are several difficulties in trying to use the obligation theory to explain the current, positive law on the recognition and enforcement of judgments at common law.[84] This section will focus on three: (1) residence or citizenship not constituting a central, or general, ground of international jurisdiction; (2) fleeting presence being held sufficient to found international jurisdiction; and (3) the tension between the fraud exception and the obligation theory. Each of these will be considered in turn.

A. Residence or Citizenship not Central/General Ground of International Jurisdiction

As Dickinson has convincingly argued,[85] if allegiance to the sovereign authority pursuant to which the foreign judgment was promulgated were the normative basis for recognition and enforcement of judgments, one would expect a defendant or respondent's citizenship or residence in relation to that foreign state to be

[78] *Beals* (n 37).
[79] Briggs (n 42) 22.
[80] See, eg, Briggs (n 44) 93.
[81] Ho (n 71) 447–48.
[82] ibid 447.
[83] ibid 447–48.
[84] Other significant difficulties highlighted in the literature include the principle that a cause of action does not, at common law, merge in the foreign judgment (reversed by statute in the UK by s 34 of the Civil Jurisdiction and Judgments Act 1982) and explaining why foreign judgments on status are recognised notwithstanding that they do not impose obligations: see Ho (n 71) 445.
[85] Dickinson (n 7) 437.

a central, or general, ground of international jurisdiction. If a foreign judgment gives rise to secondary, independent obligation(s) by virtue of the fact that they are promulgated under the 'supreme authority within a political community',[86] surely the defendant or respondent's citizenship of, or residence in, that community would be the 'focal meaning', or 'ideal type'[87] of such allegiance?

Consistently, although somewhat ironically given that *Schibsby* is seen as (at least one of the) foundations of the modern law, this appeared to be what Blackburn J thought in that case. When listing the circumstances in which international jurisdiction would be held to be established, his Lordship stated that:[88]

> If [Westenholz and others] had been at the time of the judgment subjects of the country whose judgment is sought to be enforced against them, we think that its laws would have bound them. Again, if [Westenholz and others] had been at the time when the suit was commenced resident in the country, so as to have the benefit of its laws protecting them, or, as it is sometimes expressed, owing temporary allegiance to that country, we think that its laws would have bound them.

This imprint was still evident in the Edwardian Court of Appeal's frequently cited decision in *Emanuel v Symon*, in which Buckley LJ held that:[89]

> In actions in personam there are five cases in which the Courts of this country will enforce a foreign judgment: (1.) Where the defendant is a subject of the foreign country in which the judgment has been obtained; (2.) where he was resident in the foreign country when the action began; (3.) where the defendant in the character of plaintiff has selected the forum in which he is afterwards sued; (4.) where he has voluntarily appeared; and (5.) where he has contracted to submit himself to the forum in which the judgment was obtained.

The residence-based part of this approach was fossilised in two inter-war statutory regimes relating to the recognition and enforcement of judgments, both of which were intended to reflect what was then (understood to be) the common law position.[90] Section 9(2) of the Administration of Justice Act 1920 barred registration of a foreign judgment if 'the judgment debtor, being a person who was neither carrying on business nor ordinarily resident within the jurisdiction of the original court, did not voluntarily appear or otherwise submit or agree to submit to the jurisdiction of that court'. To similar effect, section 4(2) of the

[86] Ho (n 71) 447.

[87] For a record of the origin of these terms, see J Finnis, *Natural Law & Natural Rights*, 2nd edn (Oxford, OUP, 2011) 9–10.

[88] *Schibsby* (n 1) 163.

[89] *Emanuel v Symon* [1908] 1 KB 302 (CA) 309–10. See, to similar effect, Lord Alverstone CJ at 309 and Kennedy LJ, at 313. See also the subsequent approval of *Emanuel v Symon* in *In re Trepca Mines Ltd* [1960] 1 WLR 1273 (CA) 1281–82, rejecting an earlier dictum of Denning LJ suggesting the English court should recognise a foreign judgment where it is exercising a jurisdiction that corresponds to the English rules on service out.

[90] Briggs (n 76) para 35.01.

Foreign Judgments (Reciprocal Enforcement) Act 1933 provided that 'the courts of the country of the original court shall … be deemed to have had jurisdiction' where (inter alia) 'the judgment debtor, being a defendant in the original court, was at the time when the proceedings were instituted resident in, or being a body corporate had its principal place of business in, the country of that court'.

As late as 1 January 1987, what was then *Dicey*'s rule 37, First Case was framed in terms of residence, stating that:[91]

> … a court of a foreign country outside the United Kingdom has jurisdiction to give a judgment in personam capable of enforcement or recognition in the following cases … If the judgment debtor was, at the time the proceedings were instituted, resident (or, perhaps, present) in the foreign country.

In 1990, however, 120 years of logical consistency was called into question with the decision in *Adams v Cape Industries plc*.[92] In that case, the Court of Appeal turned the historic case law on its head, confirming that the mere presence of a defendant or respondent would suffice and leaving open the question of whether residence without presence was sufficient.[93] Slade LJ, giving the judgment of the Court, concluded as follows after consideration of three authorities:[94]

> in the absence of any form of submission to the foreign court, such competence [ie international jurisdiction] depends on the physical presence of the defendant in the country concerned at the time of suit. (We leave open the question whether residence without presence will suffice.)

Commentators are divided as to how the question left open by the Court of Appeal in *Adams v Cape* would be resolved in a decided case. *Dicey*'s rule 43, First Case has been amended to refer only to presence.[95] *Collier's Conflict of Laws* states that citizenship has been 'discredited' and residence 'replaced with presence'.[96] Briggs states that 'notwithstanding abstract arguments to the contrary' 'The nationality or domicile of the parties is quite irrelevant.'[97] *Cheshire, North & Fawcett* appears to keep the flame alive, relying on the passage of *Schibsby* cited above for the proposition that, although no English authority contains an 'actual decision' that 'Political nationality' would be sufficient to found international jurisdiction 'the suggestion that this is enough has been affirmed *obiter* in several cases'.[98]

[91] L Collins, *Dicey and Morris on The Conflict of Laws*, 11th edn (London, Stevens & Sons, 1987) 436.

[92] *Adams v Cape Industries plc* [1990] 1 Ch 433 (CA).

[93] ibid, 518.

[94] ibid, 517–18. Namely (in reverse chronological order): *Employers Liability Assurance Corp Ltd v Sedgwick Collins & Co Ltd* [1927] AC 95 (HL); *Carrick v Hancock* (1895) 12 TLR 59 (HL); and *Singh v Rajah of Faridkote* [1894] AC 670 (PC).

[95] *Dicey, Morris & Collins*, 15th edn (n 28) para 14R-057, rule 43.

[96] *Collier* (n 70) 237–38.

[97] Briggs (n 76) para 34.18.

[98] P Torremans et al, *Cheshire, North & Fawcett: Private International Law*, 15th edn (Oxford, OUP, 2017) 540.

It is true[99] that in *Rubin* Lord Collins (with whom Lords Walker and Sumption agreed) noted – perhaps unsurprisingly – without dissent that following *Adams v Cape* he had amended what is now *Dicey*'s rule 43 to 'substantially its present form'.[100] However this question would ultimately be decided as a matter of *ratio*, though, it is clear that neither citizenship nor residence are the 'focal meaning' or 'ideal type' of the allegiance to sovereign authority said to give rise to international jurisdiction. We return to the significance of this below.

B. Fleeting Presence

The flip-side of the point made above is the (to some, notorious) acceptance by the modern law of international jurisdiction established by fleeting presence of the defendant or respondent in the foreign jurisdiction. This head of international jurisdiction is sometimes referred to as 'tag' jurisdiction.[101] As noted above, *Schibsby* spoke in terms of the defendant or respondent being 'subjects of the country whose judgment is sought to be enforced against them' and 'resident in the country', as opposed to being present (and, certainly not, fleetingly present).[102]

Whilst it is often said that this acceptance mostly (or only) affects individuals, that is not necessarily the case. Although not a recognition/enforcement of foreign judgments case, *Dunlop Pneumatic Tyre Co Ltd v AG Cudwell & Co* provides a good example.[103] In that case, two representatives of a German company worked a 'stand' at the National Cycle Show at Crystal Palace for nine days.[104] On the seventh day, the company's junior representative was served at the show with a writ. Lord Collins MR held that the German company had been conducting its own business at some fixed place within the jurisdiction for a sufficient period of time, noting that in 'the case of an exhibition … as much business in the kind of goods exhibited might probably be done in nine days as in as many months in an ordinary town'.[105]

Many commentators have criticised the 'fleeting presence' rule on the basis that it is 'overinclusive'.[106] In the very recent edition of his book *Civil Jurisdiction & Judgments*, Professor Briggs has, however, maintained a staunch defence of 'tag' jurisdiction on two bases: one from principle; the other from practicality.[107]

[99] As pointed out in Briggs (n 76) para 34.05.
[100] *Rubin* (n 25) [8] (Lord Collins)
[101] See, eg, Briggs (n 76) para 34.05 and 34.19, n 132.
[102] *Schibsby* (n 1) 163.
[103] *Dunlop Pneumatic Tyre Co Ltd v AG Cudwell & Co* [1902] 1 KB 342 (CA).
[104] ibid, 348 (Collins MR).
[105] ibid, 347.
[106] Kenny (n 50) 200.
[107] Briggs (n 76) para 34.05.

Whilst there is much to be said for his practical arguments we are here concerned with the former, namely that:[108]

> In terms of principle, the doctrine of comity, according to which the rules of private international law respect and give effect to exercises of sovereignty, easily accepts that if a person is present within the territorial jurisdiction of a foreign sovereign, exercises of that authority over him should be respected and, within limits, given effect afterwards: what is true for things is also true for persons.

It is submitted that there are two difficulties with this justification. First, it focuses on what Ho and this section has termed the 'external' dimension of sovereignty. It does not, however, provide any reason why the act of service on a foreigner fleetingly present makes them part, in any meaningful sense, of the 'political community' over which sovereign authority is exercised (ie the 'internal' dimension of sovereignty referred to above).

Second, it is suggested that the justification proves too much. Although caveated by the term 'within limits', it would seem to apply notwithstanding the lack of any voluntarily assumed allegiance to a sovereign. The literature discusses circumstances such as where 'the judgment debtor had been tricked or kidnapped into setting foot on that territory'.[109] Whilst it is obviously correct that such conduct would not found international jurisdiction, it is unclear why any involuntary presence,[110] or presence intended for limited purposes such as a connecting flight,[111] or even a holiday[112] could provide any normative basis for secondary, independent obligation(s) on the defendant or respondent to obey judgments which arise as a result of that presence. As noted by the Court of Appeal in *Adams v Cape* (apparently referring to the facts of *Dunlop Pneumatic v AG Cudwell*), 'the idea that … a foreign company of manufacturers, present in the United Kingdom for a few days only through having set up a stall at an exhibition, thereby incurred a duty of fealty to the King-Emperor is surely fanciful'.[113]

Schibsby advanced both a normative foundation for, and grounds of, international jurisdiction which were logically reconcilable with one another. As outlined above in respect of both residence/citizenship and fleeting presence, those grounds have since changed but the foundation is said to have stayed the same the same. It is submitted that the foundation no longer fits the grounds.

[108] ibid.

[109] *Collier's* (n 70) 239.

[110] Dickinson (n 7) 436 gives the example of a defendant or respondent 'flying over the Isle of Wight'.

[111] ibid 436.

[112] See the personal anecdote recorded at *Collier's* (n 70) 239.

[113] *Adams* (n 92) 553.

C. The Fraud Exception

In addition to the above, in assessing the obligation theory this chapter also as a matter of methodology considers what are often considered 'defences' to the recognition and the enforcement of judgments, in particular the fraud exception. It is necessary at the outset, however, to be clear as to the scope of the fraud exception, also known as the '*Abouloff v Oppenheimer* rule'.[114] *Collier's Conflict of Laws* sub-categorises the fraud exception as follows:[115]

> A judgment which has been obtained by tricking the foreign court, for example, by perjury or bribing a witness, is not recognisable due to fraud ('a fraud on the court'). Nor is the judgment recognisable or enforceable if the foreign court itself acted fraudulently, for example, if the judge was biased ('a fraud by the court'). However, fraud goes further than these clear examples. If the substantive case in the foreign court raises an allegation of fraud, a judgment on that matter may not be recognised or enforced ('fraud on the merits'). A foreign judgment will not be recognised or enforced if the judgment debtor was coerced or threatened with violence in the course of the case ('collateral fraud'). In any of these cases, it does not generally matter that the foreign court investigated the possibility of fraud and rejected it.

Thus, *Collier's Conflict of Laws* appears to suggest that there is a (sub-)category of fraud separate to 'a fraud on the court', and aside from the general caveat that 'it does not generally matter that the foreign court investigated the possibility of fraud and rejected it'.[116] This is described as a situation in which 'the substantive case in the foreign court raises an allegation of fraud'.[117] If correct, this would give the fraud exception a very wide scope because it would apply whenever the proceedings giving rise to the foreign judgment involved any allegation of fraud. Such a broad interpretation of the fraud exception does not appear to be accepted by other private international law textbooks. *Dicey* states that a foreign judgment is 'impeachable by fraud' 'if obtained by fraud'.[118] *Briggs* refers to the situation where 'a judgment has been obtained by fraud'.[119] *Cheshire* says that 'a foreign judgment is impeachable for fraud in the sense that upon proof of operative … fraud without which the judgment would not have been obtained to a high degree of probability by the person alleging it the judgment cannot be given effect'.[120]

The only authority cited by *Collier's Conflict of Laws* for the apparently freestanding 'fraud on the merits' category is *Vadala v Lawes*.[121] The allegations

[114] After the decision in *Abouloff v Oppenheimer & Co* (1882) 10 QBD 295 which is addressed in detail in ch 6 in this volume.
[115] *Collier's* (n 70) 254–45.
[116] ibid, 255.
[117] ibid, 254.
[118] *Dicey, Morris & Collins*, 15th edn (n 28) paras 14R-137, rule 50, and 14-138.
[119] Briggs (n 76) para 34.28.
[120] *Cheshire* (n 98) 569.
[121] *Vadala v Lawes* [1890] 25 QBD 310 (CA).

made in *Vadala v Lawes*, however, appear to have been that 'the judgment of the Italian Court was obtained by fraud'.[122] In particular, the defendant or respondent alleged: 'a shuffling of bills ... in the Italian Courts, a substitution of some genuine ones for some forged ones', such that 'by that shuffle and fraud the Italian Courts were imposed upon';[123] and 'the plaintiff in Italy fraudulently represent[ing] these bills as commercial bills when he knew they were not', 'thereby impos[ing] on the Courts and obtain[ing] his judgment'.[124] It therefore appears that *Vadala v Lawes* was (in the *Collier's* terminology) 'a fraud on the court' case. Moreover, the reasoning in *Vadala v Lawes* does not seem to support a broader rendering of the exception. Lindley LJ's rationale was that: 'I cannot read the judgments [in *Abouloff v Oppenheimer*] without seeing that they amount to this: that if the fraud upon the foreign Court consists in the fact that the plaintiff has induced that Court by fraud to come to a wrong conclusion, you can re-open the whole case ....'[125] His Lordship was not saying that any substantive fraud case can be re-opened.

What *Vadala v Lawes* did decide, however, is that the fraud exception can apply even where the fraud alleged by the defendant or respondent was raised before, but rejected by, the foreign court.[126] Despite appellate challenges to this proposition over the years,[127] this remains the position.[128] In *AK Investment v Kyrgyz Mobil Tel Ltd*, the Privy Council confirmed specifically that 'a foreign judgment may be impeached for fraud even though no newly discovered evidence is produced and even though the fraud might have been produced, or even was produced and rejected, in the foreign court'.[129]

There appear only to be two relevant limitations on the fraud exception. First, there must be prima facie evidence of fraud,[130] failing which it would amount to an abuse of process to relitigate the matter: *Owens Bank Ltd v Étoile Commerciale S.A.*[131] Second, where the issue of fraud has already been

[122] ibid, 314–15.
[123] ibid.
[124] ibid, 315.
[125] ibid, 317.
[126] ibid.
[127] For example, *Owens Bank Ltd v Bracco* [1992] 2 AC 443 (CA and HL), which ended unsuccessfully with Lord Bridge stating (at 489) that 'if the law is now in need of reform, it is for the legislature, not the judiciary, to effect it'.
[128] See, by contrast, the public policy exception where it is alleged that a judgment enforces a contract which furthers an act to be performed where it is illegal under the law of the place where it is to be performed. In such a case, fresh evidence of the illegality must be adduced: *Collier's* (n 70) 253.
[129] *AK Investment CJSC v Kyrgyz Mobil Tel Ltd* [2011] UKPC 7, [2012] 1 WLR 1804 [109] (Lord Collins).
[130] It is unclear whether this threshold is consistent with that Blackburn J suggested in *Godard* (n 1). In that case the Court held (at 149) that 'Probably the defendant may shew that the judgment was obtained by the fraud of the plaintiff, for that would shew that the defendant was excused from the performance of an obligation thus obtained.'
[131] *Owens Bank Ltd v Etoile Commerciale SA* [1995] 1 WLR 44 (PC). Lord Templeman stated (at 51) that: 'Where allegations of fraud have been made and determined abroad, summary judgment or striking out in subsequent proceedings are appropriate remedies in the absence of plausible

(re-)litigated for a second time in the foreign court (for example, on a subsequent application to set aside the original judgment), the losing party is not entitled to mount a third challenge in England and Wales: *House of Spring Gardens Ltd v Waite*.[132] The decision by a foreign court that a judgment from the courts of that country was (or was not) obtained by fraud can create an estoppel in the English proceedings.

Standing back, what the fraud exception means practically is that whenever: (1) Party A in foreign proceedings denies any allegation made against them which must have been within their own knowledge; (2) the foreign court accepts that denial; (3) the other party (Party B) can adduce prima facie evidence that Party A knew their denial was wrong (despite the foreign court accepting it) the foreign court's judgment can be reviewed *de novo*. Empirically, this is a common factual situation. It is in once sense wider than *Collier's* proposed 'fraud on the merits' category, since it extends to every cause of action or substantive allegation (and not just allegations of fraud).

It has been noted by many commentators that the fraud exception constitutes a significant in-road into the principle of the finality of judgments.[133] It is submitted here, however, that there is at least a significant tension between the low bar for the fraud exception and the obligation theory. If there is an obligation at all in such cases, at best it must be a very weak one. Where prima facie evidence is adduced, there is not even any meaningful obligation because the English court will embark on a *de novo* review of the foreign judgment. Supporters of the obligation theory argue that there is a prima facie obligation which is overridden by a counter-veiling policy to prevent fraud.[134] Where international jurisdiction is founded on voluntary submission to the jurisdiction (whether by contract or appearance), the normative basis for denial of any free-standing obligation to comply with the foreign judgment is not hard to seek: the fraud undermines any such consent.[135] It is more difficult to explain the position, though, where international jurisdiction is established by mere presence.[136]

In terms of the possible future development of the law, the Privy Council has stated that 'a nuanced approach might be required' to the fraud exception 'depending on the reliability of the foreign legal system, the scope for challenge in the foreign court and the type of fraud alleged'.[137] If this is the future

evidence disclosing at least a *prima facie* case of fraud. No strict rule can be laid down; in every case the court must decide whether justice requires the further investigation of alleged fraud or requires that the plaintiff, having obtained a foreign judgment, shall no longer be frustrated in enforcing that judgment.'

[132] *House of Spring Gardens Ltd v Waite* [1991] 1 QB 241 (CA).

[133] *Collier's* (n 70) 255.

[134] Briggs (n 76) para 34.28.

[135] Briggs (n 44) 97.

[136] ibid, 97.

[137] *AK Investment* (n 129) [116] (Lord Collins).

direction of travel, it is doubtful that such a 'nuanced approach' is consistent with the notion that all judgments create secondary, independent obligations for the defendant or respondent to comply with them.

IV. CONCLUSION

There are several senses in which two cases from 1870 could be said to be 'landmarks'. In one sense, a theory of the recognition and enforcement of judgments clearly emerged from *Godard* and *Schibsby* which has since been adopted in numerous Commonwealth and common law countries, in particular Ireland, Hong Kong, Australia and New Zealand.

However, it is apparent from an analysis of the fit between the obligation theory and English law and modern appellate authorities (such as the United Kingdom Supreme Court decision in *Rubin* or the recent Court of Appeal of Singapore decision in *Merck*) that the obligation theory espoused in *Godard* and *Schibsby* does not meaningfully assist in explaining the current, positive law on the recognition and enforcement of foreign judgments. The obligation theory has become de-tethered over time from the positive law it is supposed to justify. This can be illustrated by the English Court of Appeal's decision in *Adams v Cape*. This pushed the grounds of international jurisdiction in England set out in *Godard* and *Schibsby* from residence to presence, but nevertheless purported to uphold the obligation theory as the foundation for the recognition and enforcement of judgments. Merely stating that a person is under an obligation to obey a foreign judgment does not explain *why* they are under that obligation, or provide a justification for the criteria that the common law uses in a particular jurisdiction to determine when such an obligation arises.

The divergent approaches to the enforcement of foreign judgments now emerging across the common law world give rise to a familiar tension between the advantages of hard-edged but more inflexible rules on the one hand, and an approach relying on a more holistic, multi-factorial assessment on the other.[138] Even for jurisdictions such as Ireland which have rejected the Canadian 'real and substantial connection' approach, reservations were expressed by O'Donnell J in *Flightlease* about the intrinsic merit of the traditional rules. It is submitted that in this context, there is much to be said in policy terms for an approach that prioritises certainty, given the difficulties a 'soft-edged' approach may create in determining ex ante whether a foreign judgment will be enforced in England. Naturally, this is of particular importance for a defendant who needs to decide in short order whether to defend a claim brought against them abroad, but it is important too for a claimant in being advised at the outset on jurisdiction and

[138] See, eg, in the context of illegality, *Patel v Mirza* [2016] UKSC 42, [2017] AC 467 [81]–[83] (Lord Toulson).

the prospect of enforcing a judgment from the jurisdiction where the claimant intends to issue proceedings in the defendant's home jurisdiction, or where they have assets.

There is a separate issue exemplified by the contrasting decisions in *Beals* and *Flightlease* as regards how far appellate courts can and should go in making substantial changes to the common law rules on the enforcement of foreign judgments, or how far any reform is now a matter for legislation (for example, through the development of multi-lateral instruments to supplement the common law rules where that is thought necessary).[139] As regards the latter, prior to the UK's departure from the European Union much of the ground on the recognition and enforcement of foreign judgments was covered by the Brussels and Lugano jurisdictional regimes. This regime is based on reciprocity rather than the obligation theory espoused in *Godard* and *Schibsby*. As matters stand, these European regimes no longer apply following the end of the Brexit transition/implementation period but there are other multi-lateral instruments either in force or on the horizon. In particular, the UK has acceded in own right to the Hague Convention of 30 June 2005 on Choice of Court Agreements, albeit that its material scope (focussed on exclusive choice of court agreements concluded in civil and commercial matters after its entry into force) and geographic scope[140] remain relatively limited. There is also the Hague Convention of 2 July 2019 on the Recognition and Enforcement of Foreign Judgments in Civil or Commercial Matters, with a much broader ambit and scope. It has not yet entered into force, but the Council of the European Union recently decided to accede. Whatever the future may bring, for the time being at least travellers from an increased number of jurisdictions are finding *Godard* and *Schibsby* in seeking their way.

[139] See, eg, *Rubin* (n 25) [129] (Lord Collins).

[140] As matters stand, save for the UK only the European Union (on behalf of all its Member States other than Denmark), Denmark, Mexico, Montenegro and Singapore have ratified the Choice of Court Convention. The US and China are among the countries who have signed but not ratified it.

5

Phillips v Eyre (1870)

UGLJEŠA GRUŠIĆ AND ALEX MILLS

I. INTRODUCTION

THE JUDGMENT OF the Court of Exchequer Chamber in *Phillips v Eyre* is widely known among conflicts lawyers as the origin of the double-actionability rule.[1] For over a century, this rule was used in England and many other common law countries to deal with foreign torts, and it continues to be applied in England to historical wrongs and defamation claims. It is also widely known that *Phillips v Eyre* concerned a dispute between Alexander Phillips, a native Jamaican, and Edward John Eyre, a famous Australian explorer and former governor of Jamaica, concerning the arrest and torture of Phillips during the suppression of the 1865 Morant Bay uprising under martial law.

This suffices to regard *Phillips v Eyre* as a landmark case.[2] But there are other reasons for giving *Phillips v Eyre* this status. The Court of Exchequer Chamber's judgment ended the efforts of the co-called Jamaica Committee to use English law and courts to hold Eyre legally responsible for the ruthless suppression of the Morant Bay uprising, and particularly for the execution of George William Gordon, Governor Eyre's leading political opponent. In its core, therefore, *Phillips v Eyre* was a case about the nature and scope of martial law, executive power and civil liberties of British subjects in times of emergency, and the rule of law in a sprawling empire. Although the criminal prosecution and civil proceedings against Eyre were ultimately unsuccessful, Dicey, a supporter of the Jamaica Committee, cited *Phillips v Eyre* as authority for the proposition that 'In England the idea of legal equality, or of the universal subjection of all classes, to one law administered by the ordinary Courts, has been pushed to its utmost limit.'[3] Many of the broader issues raised by the 'Governor Eyre Controversy'

[1] *Phillips v Eyre* (1870–71) LR 6 QB 1 (Ex Ch).

[2] See also P Hantford, 'Edward John Eyre and the Conflict of Laws' (2008) 32 *Melbourne University Law Review* 822.

[3] AV Dicey, *Introduction to the Study of the Law of the Constitution* (London, Macmillan and Co, 1889) 181.

are of contemporary relevance, as shown by the recent litigation in England concerning historical wrongs in former colonies. The double actionability-rule continues to be applied in England to defamation claims, at least in part because it is claimed to protect the right of free speech necessary for the functioning of the UK as a modern democracy. The double-actionability rule is still applied to determine the law applicable to foreign torts in general in some common law countries.[4]

This chapter has two aims. First, it recounts the history and contemporary relevance of the double-actionability rule. It explores the origin and nature of the rule, problems surrounding its application, its almost complete abolition in the UK, its abolition in Australia and Canada, and its continuing application in England to historical wrongs and defamation claims. Second, this chapter places *Phillips v Eyre* in a broader historical, political, and legal context. It outlines the history of the Governor Eyre Controversy and the constitutional issues which it raised, and notes the contemporary relevance in England of some of these issues.

This chapter is divided in six sections. Following this introduction, the second section describes the Governor Eyre Controversy and the place of *Phillips v Eyre* therein. The third section explores the origin of the rule in *Phillips v Eyre*. The fourth section traces the subsequent development of the rule, in particular problems surrounding its application, the large case law to which it led, its almost complete abolition in the UK, and its abolition in Australia and Canada. It also considers the very limited influence of the decision on the development of choice of law in tort in the US. The fifth section notes the contexts in which the rule in *Phillips v Eyre* has continuing contemporary relevance in England, before the sixth concludes.

II. GOVERNOR EYRE CONTROVERSY[5]

The story of Jamaica as a British colony began in 1655, when Oliver Cromwell's fleet drove the Spanish out of the island. Although acquired by conquest,

[4] British Virgin Islands: *Livingston Properties Equities Inc v JSC MCC Eurochem* (Eastern Caribbean Supreme Court, 18 September 2018); Ghana: *Wachter v Harlley* [1968] GLR 1069; Hong Kong: *Kwok Yu Keung v Yeung Pang Cheung* [2005] HKCFI 779; India: *Kotah Transport Ltd v The Jhalawar Transport Service Ltd* AIR 1960 Raj 224 (Rajasthan High Court); Kenya: *Rage Mohammed Ali v Abdullahim Maasai* [2005] eKLR(High Court, 28 October 2002); Nigeria: *Herb v Devimco International BV* [2001] 52 WRN 19 (Court of Appeal); Singapore: *Parno v SC Marine Pte Ltd* [1999] 4 SLR 579 (Court of Appeal). Also in Japan: Art 22 of the Act on General Rules for Application of Laws; J Yokoyama, *Private International Law in Japan,* 2nd edn (Alphen aan den Rijn, Wolters Kluwer, 2019) 84.

[5] This section is based on G Heuman, *'The Killing Time': The Morant Bay Rebellion in Jamaica* (London, Macmillan, 1994); RW Kostal, *A Jurisprudence of Power: Victorian Empire and the Rule of Law* (Oxford, OUP, 2008); B Semmel, *The Governor Eyre Controversy* (London, MacGibbon & Kee, 1962); E Williams, *From Columbus to Castro: The History of the Caribbean* (London, Vintage Books, 1970). See also G Dutton, *In Search of Edward John Eyre* (London, Macmillan, 1982).

Jamaica was treated as a settled, not as a conquered or ceded, colony.[6] This is because Jamaica was acquired in what was, from the point of view of the restored monarchy, illegal warfare and because the Spanish fled the island, leaving no settlement or administrative structure behind.[7] Consequently, English law applied in Jamaica and English settlers had all the rights and liberties of English subjects.[8] This was confirmed by the royal proclamation of 1661, which declared that all children of natural born subjects of England to be born in Jamaica would be 'free denizens of England' with the same privileges as free born subjects of England. From the early days, however, the population of Jamaica also consisted of slaves who were brought to work on sugar plantations, and who had few rights. Following the establishment of a civilian government in Jamaica, the 1662 royal commission and instructions to the governor provided for the creation of 'representative' government. Among the early enactments of the Jamaican legislature were a 1664 statute declaring that the laws and statutes of England should be the law of Jamaica and, in 1681, the first of an unbroken chain of statutes permitting the governor and the council to declare martial law.

A. Morant Bay Uprising and Suppression

The conditions in Jamaica on the eve of the Morant Bay uprising were characterised by economic decline and political tension. Sugar had been the backbone of the Jamaican economy since the sixteenth century and had decisively influenced all aspects of life on the island. The loss of competitiveness of the Jamaican sugar industry led to economic decline that commenced at the end of the eighteenth and the beginning of the nineteenth century. The economic crisis was compounded by other factors. Slavery was generally abolished throughout the British Empire in 1838. Many former slaves withdrew their labour from sugar plantations and established freeholds or moved to towns. Free trade policies, which gradually led to the equalisation of the import duties on imperial and foreign sugar, were adopted in 1846. This removed a preferential treatment for Jamaican sugar in Britain, its main export market. This had a profound economic impact in Jamaica: the sugar market collapsed, unemployment rose, and the wages on plantations decreased. At the same time, planters obtained a concession from colonial and imperial governments in the form of encouragement of Asian immigration as a means of ensuring a steady supply of cheap labour. In the 1860s, natural disasters, including droughts, fires and epidemics, and the 1861–65 United States Civil War increased the

[6] *Campbell v Hall* (1774) 1 Cowp 204, 212; 98 ER 1045, 1049 (Lord Mansfield); R Codlin, *Historical Foundations of Jamaican Law* (Kingston, Jamaica, Canoe Press, 2003) ch 1.
[7] LG Barnet, *The Constitutional Law of Jamaica* (Oxford, OUP, 1977) 1.
[8] K Roberts-Wray, *Commonwealth and Colonial Law* (London, Stevens & Co, 1966) 540–42.

scarcity and inflation of the prices of food and essential goods. Sugar had also decisively influenced Jamaican demographics. Following the establishment of the colony, the number of white planters, officials and labourers was quickly dwarfed by the number of slaves brought from Africa. According to the census of 1861, Jamaica had a population of 441,255, only 13,816 (3.13 per cent) of whom were white. Only about 2,000 people (0.004 per cent), mainly whites, had the right to vote. This was fertile ground for political tension, which arose mainly over land access, labour issues, taxation, unfairness of the judicial system, suffrage, and Asian immigration. While key offices were held by the white population, there were some non-white officials and religious leaders who represented the interests of the black population. George William Gordon, a mixed-race merchant, landowner, planter, newspaper publisher, magistrate, member of the Jamaica Assembly and a lay Baptist preacher, led the political opposition to Governor Eyre. The demands that the black population made of the colonial and imperial governments fell on deaf ears. Previous Jamaican disturbances and events in other colonies, such as the 1791–1804 Haitian Revolution and the 1857 Indian Mutiny, kept the white population of Jamaica in constant fear of rebellion.

The uprising started on 11 October 1865, when a crowd of black men and women, led by the Baptist preacher Paul Bogle, attacked and burned the courthouse at the town of Morant Bay and killed 18 people, local officials and militiamen. Two days later, Governor Eyre and the council declared martial law in the county of Surrey, except for Kingston. The martial law lasted 30 days, although the uprising was put down within a week with virtually no resistance. Many black Jamaicans were tortured or killed, either after courts-martial or summarily, and many houses were burned. A key moment of the suppression was Gordon's arrest and execution. He was arrested in Kingston, an area under civilian law, and transferred to Morant Bay, an area under martial law. Following a flawed court-martial, he was convicted and sentenced to death. Since it was unclear whether the common law of martial law entailed comprehensive legal immunity for the exercise of the discretion of military commanders in the field, the Jamaican legislature, under the influence of Governor Eyre, enacted an indemnity law following the termination of martial law in November 1865. The Indemnity Act provided that 'all persons, whosoever in good faith and of loyal resolve have acted for the crushing of this rebellious outbreak, should be indemnified and kept harmless for such their acts of loyalty'. The validity of this statute ultimately depended on the British Government, which had the prerogative power to disallow provisions of colonial statutes.

B. Reaction in Britain

The ruthless suppression of the uprising, and in particular the execution of Governor Eyre's leading political opponent, sharply divided opinions in Britain.

Many were shocked by the actions of soldiers and militiamen and wanted Eyre held legally responsible for his personal involvement in, and supervision of, the allegedly illegal use of force. Eyre's critics in Britain included a mix of Christian non-conformists and evangelicals, anti-slavery activists, social reformers advocating electoral reform and labour rights, and radical politicians. They coalesced as the Jamaica Committee on 19 December 1965. The principal aim of this committee was to persuade the British Government to institute an investigation of the events in Jamaica, influence the investigation, and engage lawyers to prosecute Eyre and senior military officers in England. On the other hand, many regarded Eyre as a hero who kept the colony of Jamaica within the empire and saved its white population. Once it became obvious that the Jamaica Committee was serious about prosecuting Eyre, his supporters formed the Eyre Committee on 30 August 1866. Both committees were run and supported by prominent people. For example, the Jamaica Committee was for most of the time chaired by John Stuart Mill; it was supported by John Bright, Charles Buxton, Charles Darwin, Albert Venn Dicey, Thomas Hughes, Thomas Huxley, Charles Lyell, and Herbert Spencer. The Eyre Committee was for a while chaired by Thomas Carlyle; it was supported by Charles Dickens, Joseph Hooker, Charles Kingsley, Roderick Murchison, John Ruskin, Alfred Tennyson, and John Tyndall. Although its immediate concern was the ruthless suppression of the Morant Bay uprising, the real issues in the Governor Eyre Controversy were much closer to home. The members and supporters of the Jamaica Committee were concerned with the protection of civil liberties under the British constitution and the accountability of military and civilian officers under British law, and were worried that Eyre's impunity could motivate the British Government to use brutal force under martial law to suppress the movements for the extension of the suffrage and improvement of labour rights in Britain. The members and supporters of the Eyre Committee were motivated by the preservation of order and security in the empire and fear of Fenian violence.

Eyre's critics quickly won their first victory. In December 1865 the British Government decided to suspend Governor Eyre from his duties and to send a royal commission of inquiry to Jamaica to undertake an investigation of the uprising and its suppression. The commission completed its report in April 1866. It concluded that the declaration of martial law was valid. But the implementation of martial law was problematic because the punishments inflicted were excessive and the martial law was unnecessarily long. The commission found that Crown forces killed 439 and tortured about 600 non-white Jamaicans and burned about 1,000 houses, while no soldier or militiaman had been injured. The commission also indicated that Gordon's court-martial was defective. The commission recommended that Governor Eyre be relieved of duty. The British Government acted on this advice, but refused to commence criminal proceedings against Eyre or senior military officers in England. The Crown assented to the Indemnity Act in June 1866. However, the British Government did instruct Jamaican authorities to prosecute those who committed serious crimes when they fomented or suppressed the uprising. But Jamaican grand juries found there was insufficient evidence to justify trials of militia officers. Similarly, two soldiers tried by courts-martial in Jamaica were acquitted. The only legal avenues open to holding Eyre and senior military officers responsible was to commence private criminal prosecution or civil proceedings in England. Some of the most distinguished members of the Victorian bar participated in these proceedings. The Jamaica Committee retained Sir James Fitzjames Stephen for the criminal prosecutions. Lead counsel in *Phillips v Eyre* was John Richard Quain, a fellow of University College in London. The Eyre Committee had its own heavyweights, the most prominent of which was Hardinge Giffard, later Earl of Halsbury.

C. Prosecutions

The Jamaica Committee commenced two private criminal prosecutions in England for the alleged murder of Gordon and one private criminal prosecution for crimes under the Colonial Governors Act 1700. The first prosecution for murder was commenced in London on 6 February 1867 against the naval officer Abercrombie Nelson and the army officer Herbert Brand, who were instrumental in Gordon's court-martial and execution. Eyre was not prosecuted on this occasion because he had moved to Shropshire after his return to England and was thus outside the jurisdiction of the London court. The second prosecution for murder was commenced against Eyre in the Shropshire town of Market Drayton on 25 March 1867. Both prosecutions were unsuccessful. On 12 April 1867 the grand jury dismissed the indictment in the first prosecution. On 27 March 1867 the magistrates found that there was no contestable issue to put to a trial judge and jury in the second prosecution. The prosecution for crimes under the Colonial Governors Act was commenced against Eyre in London on 20 April 1868. This prosecution was also unsuccessful because the grand jury dismissed the indictment on 2 June 1868. The importance of these prosecutions lies in the authoritative judicial pronouncements on the powers of the Crown and its agents in British colonies and on the British law of martial law by Lord Chief Justice Cockburn in the grand jury charge in *The Queen v Nelson and Brand* and by Justice Blackburn in a separate jury charge in *The Queen v Eyre*. The two judges disagreed on the nature and scope of martial law. Conflicts lawyers have so far ignored this material. But that is a mistake. As discussed in more detail below in section III, the claim in *Phillips v Eyre* depended on the existence and extent of the Crown's prerogative to suspend the common law rights of British subjects in case of rebellion by declaring martial law. Cockburn CJ and Blackburn J offered two competing views on the existence and scope of the Crown's prerogative power. But they agreed that the general law, that is English common law, governed the existence and extent of this prerogative power in Jamaica. This, in turn, allows us to advance a novel explanation for the first limb of the rule in *Phillips v Eyre* in section III that is based on the constitutional background of this case.

According to Cockburn CJ,[9] the power of a colonial governor to declare martial law could be derived from the commission he received from the Crown or from imperial or local legislation. Such legal authority ultimately depended on the terms of the commission, on whether the Crown had the prerogative to proclaim martial law, and on whether the colonial legislature acted within its jurisdiction. If a colonial governor did not have the power to declare martial law, the governor, as well as those taking part in it, could be exposed to criminal and civil responsibility. Since Jamaica was a settled colony, its inhabitants had all the rights and liberties of British subjects, including all the rights and liberties enjoyed against the prerogatives of the Crown in England. The 'great constitutional question' at the heart of the case was whether the Sovereign has, 'by virtue of the prerogative of the Crown, in the event of rebellion, the power of establishing and exercising martial law within the realm of England?'[10] Whilst the Crown was entitled to use all necessary force to repel an armed invasion or rebellion, it had no prerogative to declare or enforce martial law against civilians. The Jamaican statute under which Governor Eyre declared martial law also did not and could not have given him and the military the power to arrest, try, and execute civilians outside the ordinary courts of law. 'Martial law' was nothing else than ordinary military law.

Blackburn J was of a different view.[11] Governor Eyre's legal duty and responsibility depended on the power he had 'either by the general law or by particular statutes referring to his particular case'.[12] The powers of a colonial governor were more extensive than those of a lord-lieutenant of an English county or a mayor of an English borough. Governor Eyre's powers were, therefore, governed by Jamaican law, which consisted of the general law (English common law as it stood at the time of Charles II) and imperial and local legislation. The Jamaican legislature could, within the limits of the Colonial Laws Validity Act 1865 and subject to the Crown's right to disallow colonial legislation, alter English law within the colony in the same way as the UK Parliament could alter English law within the UK. In Jamaica, common law 'has been completely altered by the Jamaica Statutes … and very greatly extended power is given to the Governor of Jamaica more than ever was possessed by the Crown in this country, or by the officers of the Crown in this country'.[13] Under Jamaican statutes, governors had 'very arbitrary and great power' 'to supersede the ordinary process of law, the

[9] F Cockburn (ed), *Charge of the Lord Chief Justice of England to the Grand Jury at the Central Criminal Court in the Case of The Queen against Nelson and Brand* (London, William Ridgway, 1867).

[10] ibid, 20.

[11] WF Finlason (ed), *Report of the Case of the Queen v Eyre Containing the Charge of Mr Justice Blackburn* (London, Chapman and Hall and Stevens & Son, 1868).

[12] ibid, 55.

[13] ibid, 75.

ordinary common law, and to try all manner of things by this summary process' upon a declaration of martial law.[14]

Following the grand jury's dismissal of the indictment against Eyre, the only legal avenue still open to holding Eyre responsible was civil proceedings in England. Alexander Phillips, a black Jamaican, was a self-described 'gentleman' freeholder. He was a political opponent of Governor Eyre before the uprising. He was, like Gordon, arrested in an area under civilian law and transferred to Morant Bay, where he was detained for ten days without charge or trial, forced to witness the execution of 49 persons and was given 100 lashes with a cat-o'-nine tails. After the termination of martial law, Phillips was charged with conspiracy to commit treason, but eventually acquitted. Supporters of the Jamaica Committee subsequently paid for his travel to, and maintenance in, England, as well as legal costs. Phillips brought a civil claim again Eyre for damages for trespass to the person on 7 November 1867.

III. ORIGIN OF THE RULE IN PHILLIPS v EYRE

English law gives everyone the right to be free of unjustifiable trespass to the person and to sue, even officials, for damages for the infringement of that right. The Governor Eyre controversy pitted these rights against the need to preserve order and security in a sprawling empire, using brutal force if (thought) necessary. The civil proceedings in *Phillips v Eyre* were the last attempt to hold Eyre legally responsible for the ruthless suppression of the Morant Bay uprising, and thereby to procure a decision by an English court that martial law was unconstitutional, and that the common law protected the civil liberties of British subjects even in the face of a declaration of martial law. This section outlines the arguments advanced by the parties before the Court of Queen's Bench and the Court of Exchequer Chamber, presents the two courts' judgments on the conflict of laws issues that arose, and explores the origin of the rule in *Phillips v Eyre*.

The procedural history of the civil proceedings in *Phillips v Eyre* is well-documented.[15] A key feature of this case is that it was not decided on the merits, but following a preliminary hearing on Phillips' demurrer. Essentially, Phillips admitted the material facts alleged in Eyre's pleadings, but objected to the legal validity of Eyre's plea that the Indemnity Act of the Jamaican legislature provided him with a complete defence. Given the importance of the case, Cockburn CJ presided over a panel of three judges of the Court of Queen's Bench, Lush and Hayes JJ being the other two members. In his pleadings, Phillips set forth seven separate allegations of torts. His main arguments were that he acquired a vested right of action in England the moment the torts were committed, and that the Jamaican legislature had no power to divest him,

[14] ibid, 78.
[15] Kostal (n 5) 'Epilogue'.

a British subject, of that right. Phillips relied on an old precedent to support these arguments. In *Mostyn v Fabrigas*,[16] the Court of King's Bench ordered a former governor of a British colony to pay damages for torts committed in the colony under colour of his office. In his defence, Eyre relied on the principles of parliamentary sovereignty and devolved governmental power in the empire. He argued that imperial law gave the Jamaican legislature the power to discharge a right of action accrued within the colony, and that the English courts had to recognise an exercise of this power. Cockburn CJ, who gave the judgment of the Court, accepted Eyre's defence.[17] For present purposes, the most important aspect of Cockburn CJ's judgment was the way in which he supported his conclusion that the Jamaican legislature validly discharged Phillip's right of action in England. Cockburn CJ applied the *lex loci delicti*. He justified the application of Jamaican law by invoking the ideas of comity and legitimate expectations of the parties,[18] and relied on two precedents where the *lex loci delicti* was applied to provide a defence in proceedings in England.[19] He also noted that, in *Scott v Lord Seymour*,[20] the question was left open as to whether, to found an action for damages in England, an act must be unlawful and actionable under both the *lex loci delicti* and English law.[21]

Phillips appealed against this judgment. His arguments on the constitutional issue became more refined. He argued that, since it was created by the Crown, not Parliament, the Jamaican legislature did not have the power to pass valid acts of indemnity. He also argued that the Indemnity Act was repugnant to English law and imperial statutes, that it could not deprive him of a vested right of action in England, and that comity did not extend to foreign *ex post facto* legislation rendering acts legal that were previously illegal. Eyre repeated the arguments advanced in the lower court. He further argued that the Privy Council opinion in *The Halley* required double-actionability for foreign torts, and that comity required recognition of the Indemnity Act.[22] Willes J gave the judgment of the Court of Exchequer Chamber (Kelly CB, Martin, Channell, Pigott and Cleasby BB, Willes and Brett JJ) dismissing the appeal.[23] He clarified that the Court was dealing only with the narrow question of the validity and effect of the Indemnity Act.[24] As is well known, Willes J set out the following rule in his judgment:

> As a general rule, in order to found a suit in England for a wrong alleged to have been committed abroad, two conditions must be fulfilled. First, the wrong must be

[16] *Mostyn v Fabrigas* (1774) 1 Cowp 161, 98 ER 1021.

[17] *Phillips v Eyre* (1869) LR 4 QB 225.

[18] ibid, 239, 241–42.

[19] ibid, 240–41, referring to *R v Lesley* (1860) Bell CC 220, 169 ER 1236; *Dobree v Napier* (1836) 2 Bing NC 781, 132 ER 301.

[20] *Scott v Lord Seymour* (1862) 1 Hurl & C 219, 158 ER 865.

[21] *Phillips v Eyre* (n 17) 239–40, 242.

[22] *Liverpool Brazil and River Plate Steam Navigation Co v Benham (The Halley)* (1867–69) LR 2 PC 193 (PC).

[23] *Phillips v Eyre* (n 1).

[24] ibid, 14.

> of such a character that it would have been actionable if committed in England … Secondly, the act must not have been justifiable by the law of the place where it was done.[25]

Interestingly, less than five years earlier Willes J had given the judgment of the Court of Exchequer Chamber (Erle CJ, Pollock CB, Martin B, Willes and Keating JJ and Pigott B) in *Lloyd v Guibert*,[26] discussed by Adrian Briggs in chapter two, in which he adopted the sole application of the *lex contractus* as the law applicable to contracts. As Briggs observes, *Phillips v Eyre* thus created a curious rift in the English choice of law rules for obligations that lasted for over century. What led Willes J to adopt a fundamentally different choice of law rule for tort? To answer this question, we need to examine the origin and nature of the two limbs of the rule in *Phillips v Eyre*.

A. The First Limb of the Rule

Willes J derived the first limb of the rule in *Phillips v Eyre* from the Privy Council's opinion in *The Halley*.[27] This case concerned a collision between a British and a foreign vessel in Belgium. The British vessel was under the control of a compulsory pilot. The British defendant would have been delictually liable under Belgian law. There was no liability under English law. Sir Robert Phillimore in the High Court classified the issue at hand as one of substance, applied Belgian law as the *lex loci delicti*, and held that the application of Belgian law was not contrary to English public policy.[28] The Privy Council allowed the appeal, holding that it was 'contrary to principle and to authority to hold, that an English Court of Justice will enforce a Foreign Municipal law, and will give a remedy in the shape of damages in respect of an act which, according to its own principles, imposes no liability on the person from whom the damages are claimed'.[29] To find the origin of the first limb of the rule in *Phillips v Eyre*, one must, therefore, look at the reasons behind the Privy Council's opinion in *The Halley*.

[25] ibid, 28–9.

[26] *Lloyd v Guibert* (1865–66) LR 1 QB 115. The Privy Council had held in *Peninsular and Oriental Steam Navigation Co v Shand* (1865) 3 Moo PC NS 272, 16 ER 103 (PC) that the *lex contractus* applied to a contract less than 6 months before the Court of Exchequer Chamber's judgment in *Lloyd v Guibert*. *Peninsular and Oriental Steam Navigation Co v Shand* was not cited in *Lloyd v Guibert*.

[27] *The Halley* (n 22).

[28] *Liverpool Brazil and River Plate Steam Navigation Co v Benham (The Halley)* (1867–69) LR 2 A & E 3.

[29] *The Halley* (n 22) 204. But see earlier cases in which the English courts imposed liability which would not have existed if English municipal law had applied: *Nostra Signora de Los Dolores* (1813) 1 Dods 290, 165 ER; *Madrazo v Willes* (1820) 3 B & Ald 353, 106 ER 692; *The Zollverein* (1856) Sw 96, 166 ER 1038.

Four explanations have been advanced for the first limb of the rule in *Phillips v Eyre* in conflicts scholarship. One explanation, whose main proponent is Yntema, is that the first limb of the rule in *Phillips v Eyre* referred to the jurisdictional requirements that had to be met before an English court could hear a claim for a foreign tort under the *lex loci delicti*.[30] This explanation is based on the fact that Willes J derived the term 'actionable' from a passage in *The Halley* in which the Privy Council cited the note to *Mostyn v Fabrigas* in *Smith's Leading Cases*[31] as key authority for the proposition that 'there seems to be no reason why aliens should not sue in England for personal injuries done to them by other aliens abroad, when such injuries are actionable both by the law of England and also by that of the country where they are committed'.[32] According to Yntema, Willes J used the term 'actionable' 'in its natural sense as "cognisable" or "triable," not as referring to substantive "liability"'.[33] Yntema found support for this argument in the fact that Willes J, who was a co-editor of *Smith's Leading Cases* at the time of the *Phillips v Eyre* litigation, assisted the editors of two subsequent editions of *Smith's Leading Cases* in which the note to *Phillips v Eyre* asserted that 'a "right of action", whether for contract or for wrong, and the corresponding "civil liability", is "the creature of the law of the place", while the two rules latterly supposed to contain the quintessence of English conflicts law respecting torts are not mentioned!'[34] Although the 'jurisdictional' approach to the rule in *Phillips v Eyre* was later accepted by some courts in England, Australia and Canada, it was eventually firmly rejected by the House of Lords in *Boys v Chaplin*.[35]

The other explanations for the first limb of the rule in *Phillips v Eyre* that have been advanced in conflicts scholarship regard all aspects of the rule in *Phillips v Eyre* as choice of law rules. One explanation is that, in the early period of English private international law, the English courts could not assume jurisdiction over a transitory action concerning an act abroad unless the claimant pleaded by way of fiction that the act had taken place in England. 'Having thus naturalized the foreign act, it seems that English law applied as a matter of course.'[36] Another explanation is that English law was applied in *The Halley* for

[30] HE Yntema, 'Review of Falconbridge's *Essays on the Conflict of Laws*' (1949) 27 *Canadian Bar Review* 116, 117–20 and 'Dicey: An American Commentary' (1951) 4 *International & Comparative Law Quarterly* 1, 7–9. See also P Gerber, 'Tort Liability in the Conflict of Laws' (1966) 40 *Australian Law Journal* 44, 49–50 and DB Spence, 'Conflict of Laws in Automobile Negligence Cases' (1949) 27 *Canadian Bar Review* 661.

[31] HS Keating and JS Willes, *Smith's Selection of Leading Cases on Various Branches of the Law: With Notes*, vol 1 (London, T&J W Johnson, 1852) 656.

[32] *The Halley* (n 22) 203–04. However, both parties in *Mostyn v Fabrigas* were British subjects.

[33] Yntema, 'Dicey: An American Commentary' (n 30) 8.

[34] Yntema, 'Review of Falconbridge's *Essays on the Conflict of Laws*' (n 30) 119.

[35] *Boys v Chaplin* [1971] AC 356 (HL) 385 (Lord Wilberforce). See further section IV below.

[36] K Lipstein, '*Phillips v Eyre*, A Re-Interpretation' in E von Caemmerer, S Mentschikoff and K Zweigert (eds), *Ius Privatum Gentium*, vol 1 (Tuebingen, JCB Mohr (Paul Siebeck) 1969) 411, 413. See also Hantford (n 2) 853–4; CGJ Morse, *Torts in Private International Law* (Amsterdam, North-Holland Publishing Company, 1978) 9–10.

reasons of public policy.[37] This explanation is based on the idea that tort law is a private system of deterrence, punishment and moral condemnation and thus an expression of important public policies. Foreign tort laws imposing liability for behaviour that English law considered innocent was an unacceptable intrusion of foreign public policies which English courts would not enforce. A third explanation is that the Privy Council in *The Halley* was influenced by the ideas of Savigny and Wächter.[38] Even though the Privy Council did not refer to these authors in its opinion, it was aware of Savigny's ideas because the defendant had cited Savigny in argument,[39] and the High Court had discussed Savigny's ideas in its judgment.[40] Savigny, in turn, was influenced by Wächter.[41] The two scholars regarded tort law as performing primarily a public function of deterring and punishing the commission of wrongdoing, considered laws relating to delicts as analogous to penal laws, and thus thought that delicts should be governed by the *lex fori*.[42]

There is, however, one more explanation for the first limb of the rule in *Phillips v Eyre*, which lies in the constitutional background of this case and the eighteenth century case of *Mostyn v Fabrigas*.[43] As mentioned above, in *Phillips v Eyre* the Court of Exchequer's Chamber was decisively influenced by the Privy Council opinion in *The Halley*, and the Privy Council in this case was decisively influenced by the note to *Mostyn v Fabrigas* in *Smith's Leading Cases*. The facts of *Mostyn v Fabrigas* were strikingly similar to those of *Phillips v Eyre*. The governor of Minorca, a British colony at the time, was sued for damages for trespass to the person allegedly committed in the colony in purported exercise of his powers. The powers of a colonial governor were derived from three sources: royal commission and instructions, imperial legislation, and local law. The Crown could only confer on a colonial governor the powers that it itself possessed. A governor acting within his powers could

[37] DJ Bederman, 'Compulsory Pilotage, Public Policy, and the Early Private International Law of Torts' (1990) 64 *Tulane Law Review* 1033; Dicey (n 3) 32, 35–6, 661; M Hancock, 'Torts in the Conflict of Laws: The First Rule in *Phillips v Eyre*' (1940) 3 *University of Toronto Law Journal* 400, 405; *Torts in the Conflict of Laws* (Ann Arbor, The University of Michigan Press, 1942) 11, 14; 'Torts Problems in the Conflict of Laws Resolved by Statutory Construction: *The Halley* and Other Older Cases Revisited' (1968) 18 *University of Toronto Law Journal* 331, 341–47; Otto Kahn-Freund, 'Reflections on Public Policy in the English Conflict of Laws' (1953) 39 *Transactions of the Grotius Society* 39, 45–6, 48–53. See also *The Halley* (n 28) 13–7 and (n 22) 203.

[38] O Kahn-Freund, 'Delictual Liability and the Conflict of Laws' (1968–II) 124 *Recueil des Cours* 1, 12–4; Kahn-Freund (n 37) 51–53; S Peari, *The Foundation of Choice of Law: Choice and Equality* (Oxford, OUP, 2018) 266–68; HE Yntema, 'The Historic Bases of Private International Law' (1953) 2 *American Journal of Comparative Law* 297, 311.

[39] *The Halley* (n 22) 195.

[40] *The Halley* (n 28) 17–8.

[41] FC von Savigny, *Private International Law, A Treatise on the Conflict of Laws*, trans W Guthrie (London, Stevens & Sons, 1869) 203, fn (x).

[42] ibid, 203, 205–7; CG von Wächter, *Über die Collision der Privatrechtsgesetze verschiedener Staaten* (Frankfurt, Vico, 1841) 425.

[43] *Mostyn v Fabrigas* (n 16).

not be liable in tort.[44] In cases like *Phillips v Eyre* and *Mostyn v Fabrigas*, therefore, the tortious liability of a governor for purporting to exercise his powers depended on the scope of the Crown's prerogative and the terms of his commission and instructions. And these, in turn, were governed by the general law, that is English common law.

In *Mostyn v Fabrigas*, Lord Mansfield, after deciding that the Court had jurisdiction, stated that 'the governor must be tried in England, to see whether he has exercised the authority delegated to him by the letters patent legally and properly; or whether he has abused it in violation of the *laws of England*, and the trust so reposed in him'.[45] This was derived from the principle of colonial law that those born in the King's overseas dominions were British subjects, with all the rights and liberties which that status entailed.[46]

The case for the application of English law in *Phillips v Eyre* was even stronger. Jamaica was treated as a settled colony in which English law applied. Cockburn CJ and Blackburn J had agreed, in their grand jury charges in *The Queen v Nelson and Brand* and *The Queen v Eyre*, that English common law governed the existence and extent of the Crown's prerogative to suspend the common law rights of British subjects in case of rebellion by declaring martial law. Cockburn CJ and Blackburn J, however, disagreed on whether a declaration of martial law had any effect at common law and, if so, whether the actions of a colonial governor done for the purpose of suppressing a rebellion under martial law were shielded from tortious liability at common law. Since the actions of Governor Eyre were justified under the Indemnity Act, the Court did not have to decide on the extent of the rights and liberties of British subjects in a colony and on the powers of a colonial governor at common law. But if it had been necessary to decide these issues, they could have been decided only by reference to common law. The Court of Exchequer Chamber recognised this in the last paragraph of its judgment:[47]

> We have thus discussed the validity of the defence upon the only question argued by counsel, touching the effect of the colonial Act, but *we are not to be understood as thereby intimating any opinion that the plea might not be sustained upon more general grounds as shewing that the acts complained of were incident to the enforcement of martial law*. It is, however, unnecessary to discuss this further question, because we are of opinion with the Court below that the colonial Act of Indemnity, even upon the assumption that the acts complained of were originally actionable, furnishes an answer to the action.

The justifications for the first limb of the rule in *Phillips v Eyre* may, therefore, be found not only in private international law precedent, principle or theory,

[44] *Musgrave v Pulido* (1879) 5 App Cas 102 (PC) 111. See also *Cameron v Kyte* (1835) 3 Kn 332, 12 ER 678; *Hill v Bigge* (1841) 3 Moo PC 465, 13 ER 189; opinion of De Grey CJ in *Fabrigas v Mostyn*, when that case was before the Common Pleas (1774) 1 Cowp 161, 169; 98 ER 1021, 1026.

[45] *Mostyn v Fabrigas* (n 16) 173, 1028 (emphasis added).

[46] BH McPherson, *The Reception of English Law Abroad* (Brisbane, Supreme Court of Queensland Library, 2007) 13–4, 86–7, ch 6.

[47] *Phillips v Eyre* (n 17) 31 (emphasis added).

but also in the particular colonial context which was before the Court, which raised questions of great consequence for the legal constitution of the British Empire. It may not always have been sufficiently appreciated, by subsequent judges and scholars alike, that this was not merely a case about a tort committed by a private citizen in a foreign country, but about the sources of authority of a colonial governor appointed as a public representative of the Crown.

B. The Second Limb of the Rule

The second limb of the rule in *Phillips v Eyre*, namely that 'the act must not have been justifiable by the law of the place where it was done',[48] was founded upon two ideas. The first was that private rights had a territorial origin, which meant that the *lex loci delicti* governed the issue of basis of liability. A civil or legal obligation and the corresponding accessory right of action that arose out of a wrong were said to be 'the creature[s] of the law of the place and subordinate thereto'; 'the civil liability arising out of a wrong derives its birth from the law of the place, and its character is determined by that law'.[49] This is not surprising. The territorial origin of English private international law is well known.[50] In the Middle Ages, when jury members were still witnesses, a trial of a cause of action in tort could only be held in the *locus delicti*.[51] When the needs of international commerce and intercourse in the seventeenth century forced the common law courts to assert jurisdiction over transitory actions and develop choice of law rules, they 'managed to combine their own territorial tradition with a respect for similar territorial claims on the part of neighbouring legal systems'.[52] With respect to torts, the old territorial rules on venue became the rule that the *lex loci delicti* could provide justification to a foreign tort.[53] The second idea on which the second limb of the rule in *Phillips v Eyre* was founded was comity.[54] This also explains Willes J' reliance on cases on what is now called the foreign act of state doctrine.[55] The comity doctrine, developed by Ulrich Huber, had

[48] ibid, 29.
[49] ibid, 28.
[50] PE Nygh, 'The Territorial Origin of English Private International Law' (1964–1967) 2 *University of Tasmania Law Review* 28; AN Sack, 'Conflicts of Laws in the History of the English Law' in *Law: A Century of Progress 1835–1935*, vol 3 (New York, New York University Press, 1937) 342.
[51] Nygh (n 50) 29.
[52] ibid, 28.
[53] *Blad v Bamfield* (1673) 3 Swans 603, 604; 36 ER 991, 992; *Dutton v Howell* (1693) Show Parl Cas 24, 30–1; 1 ER 17, 21; *Wey v Rally* (1704) 6 Mod 195; 87 ER 948; *Mostyn v Fabrigas* (n 16) 175, 1029; *Rafael v Verelst* (1776) 2 Wm Bl 1055, 1058; 96 ER 621, 622–23; *Collett v Lord Keith* (1802) 2 East 260; 102 ER 368.
[54] *Phillips v Eyre* (n 1) 30–1.
[55] *Blad v Bamfield* (n 53); *Dobree v Napier* (n 19); *R v Lesley* (n 19). At the time, the foreign act of state doctrine was regarded as being derived from the doctrine of comity: *Hatch v Baez* (1876) 7 Hun 596, 599.

a considerable influence on English private international law.[56] Huber conception of comity was built on a territorialist theory of state sovereignty: respect for a foreign state meant giving territorial effect to its laws. Hubers's ideas appealed to English conflicts lawyers because they provided a rational basis for the English choice of law principles and rules, which the English courts had developed autonomously by adopting the idea of territoriality.[57] This also served as a basis for the adoption of the vested rights theory by Dicey.[58] It, therefore, comes as no surprise that Willes J stated in *Phillips v Eyre* that 'an act committed abroad, if valid and unquestionable by the law of the place, cannot, so far as civil liability is concerned, be drawn in question elsewhere'.[59]

IV. THE COMMON LAW LEGACY OF PHILLIPS v EYRE

This section examines the legacy of the rule in *Phillips v Eyre*, considering its subsequent interpretation and reform in the UK (including by the Privy Council), Australia, and Canada, and its influence (or rather lack of influence) in the US. Although *Phillips v Eyre* has had a significant and enduring impact, this legacy does not, on the whole, reflect very favourably on the decision, for three reasons. First, because of the variety of interpretations of the rule which have been adopted in subsequent case law, reflecting a significant uncertainty regarding the precise requirements of the rule and its motivation. Second, because the rule was subject to significant modification by the courts, due to concerns that it could lead to inappropriate or unjust outcomes. Third, because the rule has largely been rejected through statutory or judicial reform in each of the states examined, aside from the US where the rule was never adopted. It is true that the rule, as subsequently modified, retains some influence as part of English law, in the context of historical wrongs and defamation claims, as discussed in section V below. The common law legacy of *Phillips v Eyre* is largely, however, a story of courts struggling to interpret and apply the decision in a way which sits comfortably with their evolving understanding of the policy objectives which should be achieved by choice of law rules in tort.

[56] AE Anton, 'The Introduction into English Practice of Continental Theories on the Conflict of Laws' (1956) 5 *International & Comparative Law Quarterly* 534; DJ Llewelyn Davies, 'The Influence of Huber's *De Conflictu Legum* on English Private International Law' (1937) 18 *British Yearbook of International Law* 49.

[57] EG Lorenzen, 'Huber's *De Conflictu Legum*' (1918–1919) 13 *Illinois Law Review* 375, 394; Nygh (n 50) 39–40.

[58] See, eg, AV Dicey, *A Digest of the Law of England with reference to the Conflict of Laws* (London, Stevens & Sons, 1896) 9–10.

[59] *Phillips v Eyre* (n 1) 28.

A. United Kingdom

An early occasion for considering the rule in *Phillips v Eyre* arose only a few years later, in *The M Moxham*.[60] Suit was brought by the English owners of a Spanish pier against the English owners of a ship which had collided with it. By English law the shipowner might be liable, but by Spanish law, which the shipowner argued to be applicable, it would not. Although *Phillips v Eyre* was raised in argument, at first instance Sir Robert Phillimore considered the issue to be 'whether the law of Spain or the law of England is to be applied to the circumstances of the case', rejecting the relevance of *Phillips v Eyre* as 'in great measure dependent upon peculiar circumstances and upon the powers of a colonial legislature as recognised by the law of the empire'.[61] English law was held to be applicable, at least to the key issue of whether the owner of an English registered ship would be responsible for the acts of its master. On appeal, the Court drew on *Phillips v Eyre* as authority, but held that liability would be excluded because the case would be governed by Spanish law.[62] Although there was some recognition of the rule in *Phillips v Eyre*, one judge expressly held that 'by applying the principles enunciated in *Phillips v Eyre*, we are able to arrive at the conclusion, in the present case, that the law of Spain, and not the law of England, applies'.[63] This reasoning is very difficult to square with *Phillips v Eyre*, but to the extent that it can be reconciled *The M Moxham* appears to be authority for the idea that the rule in *Phillips v Eyre* requires at least applying the law of the place of the tort.

A decade later, a distinctive set of facts arose for consideration in *Machado v Fontes*,[64] leading to a different but equally questionable interpretation and application of *Phillips v Eyre*. The claimant brought proceedings for an alleged libel arising from a pamphlet alleged to have been published in Brazil. The evidence presented was that Brazilian law would not allow civil recovery of damages for libel, although libel could potentially be subject to criminal prosecution. The Court of Appeal considered *Phillips v Eyre* to have established, and *The M Moxham* to have confirmed, that an action could lie in England, implicitly under English law, as long as the conduct concerned was 'wrongful' or not 'innocent', 'authorized', or 'excusable', under the law of the place of the act.[65] Once again, this decision is very difficult to reconcile with *Phillips v Eyre*, or indeed *The M Moxham*. One of the reasons given for giving effect to the law of the place of the tort in *Phillips v Eyre* was that 'the civil liability arising out of a wrong derives its birth from the law of the place, and its character

[60] *The M Moxham* (1875) 1 PD 43.
[61] ibid, 50.
[62] *The M Moxham* (1876) 1 PD 107 (CA) 111, 114–15.
[63] ibid, 115.
[64] *Machado v Fontes* [1897] 2 QB 231 (CA).
[65] ibid, 233–34, 236.

is determined by that law',[66] but in *Machado v Fontes* there was no such civil liability at all. Where *The M Moxham* suggested that the applicable law was the law of the place of the tort, perhaps even solely the law of that place, *Machado v Fontes* applied exclusively the law of the forum and considered actionability under the civil law of the place of the tort unnecessary so long as the relevant conduct was criminalised.[67] The combination of these two decisions arguably left the rule in *Phillips v Eyre* even less clear than it was when adopted.

It is not claimed that the confusion thereby created made the rule in *Phillips v Eyre* difficult to apply in every case. In the 1901 case of *Carr v Fracis Times & Co*,[68] for example, property was seised in the territory of Muscat, with the authority of the Sultan, the sovereign ruler. Although it was not disputed that the act would have been wrongful under English law if carried out in England, the House of Lords held that no action could lie because the act was lawful under the law of the place of the tort. In 1923 two Privy Council decisions on appeal from the Canadian courts similarly refused to allow claims in tort on the basis that no damages were recoverable under the law of the place of injury.[69] Nevertheless, the difficulties experienced by other courts in applying *Phillips v Eyre*, particularly those in Australia (discussed below), were also reflected in recurring academic criticism, which addressed not merely the interpretation of the rule but also its policy basis.[70] On the one hand, the rule appears too strict, in precluding liability under foreign law merely because English law is different – essentially making all rules of English tort law rules of public policy with which foreign law must be compatible. On the other hand, the rule appears too broad, in allowing for liability even if the conduct giving rise to the claim in tort was not civilly actionable under the law of the place where the person acted – suggesting, it seems, either that English law imposed liability without any jurisdictional justification, or that the defendant's subsequent arrival in England retrospectively gave rise to liability. The decision of the Scottish Court of Session in *McElroy v McAllister*,[71] dealing with a fatal accident involving Scottish parties in England, raised a further concern. Although the facts were complex, essentially English law and Scots law might each provide a cause of action for a widow in such circumstances, but on different grounds and subject to different limitations. The effect of the rule in *Phillips v Eyre* was however

[66] *Phillips v Eyre* (n 1) 28.

[67] This also gives rise to an incidental concern as to whether the English courts would, contrary to the usual prohibition, be indirectly enforcing rules of foreign criminal law in these circumstances.

[68] *Carr v Fracis Times & Co* [1902] AC 176 (HL).

[69] *Walpole v Canadian Northern Railway Co* [1923] AC 113 (PC); *McMillan v Canadian Northern Railway Co* [1923] AC 120 (PC).

[70] For early criticism see, eg, EG Lorenzen, 'Tort Liability and the Conflict of Laws' (1931) 47 *Law Quarterly Review* 483; JG Foster, 'Some Defects in the English Rules of Conflict of Laws' (1935) 16 *British Yearbook of International Law* 84; AH Robertson, 'The Choice of Law for Tort Liability in the Conflict of Laws' (1940) 4 *Modern Law Review* 27.

[71] *McElroy v McAllister* [1949] SC 110.

that no claim was available unless actionable in both systems, and thus substantive liability was generally excluded (with the exception of a small amount that could be recovered in both systems for funeral costs). The decision illustrates the danger that a strict application of the rule in *Phillips v Eyre* risks undermining the policies of both legal systems, and it prompted prominent calls for greater flexibility in choice of law in tort.[72]

Despite this widespread dissatisfaction, the House of Lords did not have occasion to revisit the rule until the late 1960s. In *Boys v Chaplin*,[73] the Court heard a claim arising out of a car accident in Malta between two English parties. Under Maltese law, damages would not be available for pain and suffering or loss of amenities, whereas under English law these could be claimed and would indeed form the bulk of the recoverable loss. The case raised two uncertainties regarding the operation of the rule in *Phillips v Eyre*. First, whether the rule applied in relation to causes of action or categories of damage – that is, whether it was only necessary to show double-actionability for the cause of action, or double-recoverability for each type of damage claimed. Second, whether the rule might allow for an exception to be adopted in favour of the exclusive application of the law of the forum. Before the case reached the House of Lords, however, the Court of Appeal[74] had multiplied the existing uncertainties, as the three judges variously held that the rule in *Phillips v Eyre* was either a rule of jurisdiction, a rule of public policy, or a complex choice of law rule, and that the claim should consequently be governed by either the law of the forum (Upjohn LJ), the law of the place of the tort (Diplock LJ), or the 'proper law of the tort' (Lord Denning MR) (adjudged to be English law).

In the House of Lords, Lord Wilberforce observed of *Phillips v Eyre* that 'Like many judgments given at a time when the relevant part of the law was in course of formation, it is not without its ambiguities, or, as a century of experience perhaps permits us to say, its contradictions.'[75] The judgment of the House of Lords in *Boys v Chaplin*, however, was not without its own ambiguities or contradictions. Although not strictly arising on the facts, the Lords (by clear majority) did take the opportunity to set aside the decision in *Machado v Fontes*, finding that only civil actionability (and not criminality) under the law of the place of the tort would be a relevant consideration. The characterisation of the rule in *Phillips v Eyre* as a jurisdictional rule (as apparently contemplated by the Court of Appeal) was also firmly rejected.[76] Beyond this, the Lords concluded that English law should apply, but for various reasons. One theory was that double-actionability required only the claim to be actionable under the

[72] See particularly JHC Morris, 'Torts in the Conflict of Laws' (1949) 12 *Modern Law Review* 228; 'The Proper Law of a Tort' (1951) 64 *Harvard Law Review* 881.

[73] *Boys v Chaplin* (n 35).

[74] *Boys v Chaplin* [1968] 2 QB 1 (CA).

[75] *Boys v Chaplin* (n 35) 384.

[76] ibid, 385 (Lord Wilberforce).

law of the place of the tort, leaving the types (and quantification) of damages for English law.[77] Another was that double-actionability generally required that the type of damages be recoverable under both the law of the place of the tort and the law of the forum, but that the rule should be subject to a flexible exception which would allow for the exclusive application of English law. This was justified either because of 'the identity and circumstances of the parties … [as] British subjects temporarily serving in Malta',[78] or more broadly because of the need for 'flexibility in the interest of individual justice',[79] taking into account the interests of the affected states,[80] or by identifying the law with 'the most significant relationship to the occurrence and the parties'.[81] The Privy Council was later to observe that the reasons given in *Boys v Chaplin* 'varied to such an extent that both academic writers and judges in other cases have expressed doubt as to whether there can be extracted from the speeches one binding ratio decidendi'.[82] However, subsequent decisions have generally preferred to follow (certain aspects of) the judgment of Lord Wilberforce, applying English law to any claim in tort in the English courts (as if the relevant events had taken place in England), subject to the condition that the claim is civilly actionable under the law of the place of the tort, and subject to a further flexible exception which allows the general rule to be departed from in the interests of justice.[83]

A further issue was addressed in *Metall und Rohstoff AG v Donaldson Lufkin & Jenrette Inc*.[84] The complex facts of this case may, for present purposes, be summarised as involving a cross-border tort where certain acts were carried out in New York and others in England, with damage also suffered in England. The Court of Appeal clarified the application of the double-actionability rule in the context of cross-border torts ('double locality cases'), an issue which had not arisen in *Phillips v Eyre* or *Boys v Chaplin*. The relevant test, borrowed from the jurisdictional context, was where 'as a matter of substance' the torts were committed. On the facts, this was held to be in England, and in such a case no question of double-actionability arose – the claim was exclusively governed by English law.

The final stage in the development of the common law rule came in the decision of *Red Sea Insurance Co Ltd v Bouygues SA*.[85] The Privy Council held that

[77] This appears to be the best explanation for the judgments of Lord Guest, Lord Donovan and Lord Pearson.

[78] ibid, 380 (Lord Hodson).

[79] ibid, 389 (Lord Wilberforce).

[80] ibid, 392 (Lord Wilberforce).

[81] ibid, 391 (Lord Wilberforce).

[82] *Red Sea Insurance Co Ltd v Bouygues SA* [1995] 1 AC 190 (PC) 198 (Lord Slynn).

[83] See, eg, *Church of Scientology of California v Commissioner of Police of the Metropolis* (1976) 120 SJ 690 (CA); *Coupland v Arabian Gulf Oil Co* [1983] 1 WLR 1136 (CA); *Johnson v Coventry Churchill International Ltd* [1992] 3 All ER 14 (QB) (applying the exception in favour of English law).

[84] *Metall und Rohstoff AG v Donaldson Lufkin & Jenrette Inc* [1990] 1 QB 391 (CA).

[85] *Red Sea v Bouygues* (n 82).

a claim in tort brought before the courts of Hong Kong (against a company incorporated in Hong Kong, but with its head office in Saudi Arabia) arising out of problems with construction work in Saudi Arabia could be governed exclusively by the law of Saudi Arabia. In so doing, the Court clarified the scope of the flexible exception to the double-actionability rule. In previous cases (including *Boys v Chaplin*) the exception had led to the application of the law of the forum, and so could be interpreted as allowing the Court to disapply the requirement of actionability under the law of the place of the tort (actionability under the law of the place of the tort could thus be understood as a – dispensable – condition for an action to proceed, but not as forming part of the applicable law). Here, the Court disapplied the double-actionability rule (so understood) in its entirety, replacing it with the exclusive application of the law of the place of the tort – the *lex loci delicti* became the applicable law, not just relevant in a determination of an 'actionability' condition.[86] In addition, the Court clarified that the exception could operate to a claim in its entirety, and not just in relation to certain issues – *Boys v Chaplin* had allowed the exception to apply selectively, but had not thereby excluded a more wholesale application. However, some further uncertainty was perhaps introduced in the explanation offered as to how the exception should operate. The Court suggested at certain points that it should be based on whether the law of the place of the tort had the 'most significant relationship' with the claim.[87] Although the justification for this rule was meeting the 'interests of justice', this account of the rule appears to require evaluation of objective connecting factors rather than the more flexible justice-based test which had been proposed in *Boys v Chaplin*.

Less than four months after the decision in *Red Sea*, the rule in *Phillips v Eyre* was substantially rejected through the adoption of the Private International Law (Miscellaneous Provisions) Act 1995.[88] The legislation was not, however, a reaction to the decision in *Red Sea*, but rather the result of a Law Commission reform proposal which was initiated in 1979 as a response to (abandoned) proposals for European regulation in the field,[89] and which led to a Report

[86] The exception was also applied in favour of the law of the place of the tort in *Pearce v Ove Arup Partnership Ltd* [2000] Ch 403 (CA), although arguably unnecessarily, as the Court appeared to ask itself whether the acts complained of were actionable in England (they were not, because English copyright law did not apply extraterritorially), rather than whether the claim would have been actionable under English law *had the relevant acts taken place in England* (the correct test from earlier cases).

[87] *Red Sea v Bouygues* (n 82) 206.

[88] In New Zealand, the rule in *Phillips v Eyre* was similarly applied until the Private International Law (Choice of Law in Tort) Act 2017 was adopted (see, eg, *The Seven Pioneer* [2001] 2 Lloyd's Rep 57 (NZHC)). The Act is closely modelled on the UK Act, although with some significant points of difference – including the fact that the New Zealand legislation does not exclude defamation from its scope, as discussed in section V below.

[89] The initial proposal for EU choice of law rules in respect of contractual and non-contractual obligations was narrowed to deal exclusively with contractual obligations, in the 1980 Rome Convention on the law applicable to contractual obligations: [1998] OJ C 27 (consolidated version).

proposing reform in 1990.[90] The Report noted that 'The exceptional role given to the substantive domestic law of the forum in the law of tort, apart from being almost unknown in the private international law of any other country, is parochial in appearance', and also contrary to the general principle that 'the introduction of a foreign element may make it just to apply a foreign law to determine a dispute, even though the substantive provisions of that foreign law might be different from our own'.[91] The Act essentially established a two stage test for determining the law applicable to a tort. Section 11(1) established the general rule, 'that the applicable law is the law of the country in which the events constituting the tort or delict in question occur', offering further guidance in section 11(2) on how that law should be determined where 'elements of those events occur in different countries'. Essentially, the basic rule adopted here was a *lex loci delicti* rule – the law of the place of the tort. The second stage of the test, set out in section 12, provided for a flexible exception, under which a different law may be applied if this appears substantially more appropriate on the basis of a comparison of the connecting factors between the tort and different countries. The Act thereby abandoned the mandatory role for the law of the forum which had been adopted in *Phillips v Eyre* (although later subject to a flexible exception), except through a general recognition of the ubiquitous public policy safety net (section 14(3)(a)(i)) – it thereby brought choice of law in tort in line with the general principles underlying other choice of law rules. Importantly, however, the Act excluded defamation claims from its scope, preserving the double-actionability rule in that field, as discussed in section V below.

The rules governing choice of law in tort in the UK were further developed through the EU's adoption of the Rome II Regulation on the law applicable to non-contractual obligations,[92] which was enacted in 2007 and came into force in 2009. Defamation was, however, excluded from the scope of the Rome II Regulation, under Article 1(2)(g), alongside violations of privacy.[93] The general rule for torts in the Rome II Regulation, like that in the 1995 Act, includes a basic rule in favour of the law of the place of the tort[94] and a flexible exception where another law is manifestly more closely connected.[95] It departs from the 1995 Act in some important respects, however, including through the adoption of specialised choice of law rules for particular torts,[96] the adoption of the law of the common habitual residence of the parties as an

[90] Law Commission and Scottish Law Commission, *Private International Law: Choice of Law in Tort and Delict* (Law Com No 193 and Scot Law Com No 129, 1990).

[91] ibid, para 2.7.

[92] Regulation (EC) No 864/2007 (Rome II).

[93] Claims in 'privacy' are not excluded from the 1995 Act, and thus remain subject to that Act.

[94] Rome II, Art 4(1).

[95] ibid, Art 4(3).

[96] ibid, Arts 5–9, see also Arts 10–13 dealing with other non-contractual claims.

alternative general rule (overriding the law of the place of the tort),[97] the identification of the place of the tort as the place of the direct damage (in cases of cross-border torts),[98] and in providing a limited direct role for party autonomy in choice of law in tort.[99] Despite these innovations, it may generally be viewed as consistent with the ethos of the 1995 Act, in rejecting the special role of the law of the forum which was characteristic of the rule in *Phillips v Eyre*. Notwithstanding Brexit, the Rome II Regulation has been retained as part of UK law[100] and thus for most torts now provides the relevant choice of law rules – exceptions are discussed in section V below.

B. Australia and Canada

The common law in Australia and Canada inherited the decision in *Phillips v Eyre*, and the double-actionability rule formed the applicable choice of law rule in tort for most of the twentieth century. As in the UK, however, significant uncertainties arose in relation to its application. In *Koop v Bebb*,[101] for example, the High Court of Australia questioned[102] the authority of *Machado v Fontes*, anticipating the later rejection of that rule by the House of Lords in *Boys v Chaplin*. On the other hand, however, the Court expressly rejected a vested rights approach (which had appeared to be part of the reasoning in *Phillips v Eyre*, and inconsistent with *Machado v Fontes*), and therefore rejected the idea that the cause of action was based on the law of the place of the tort.[103] Instead, the Court appeared to suggest (although not clearly) that it was the law of the forum which exclusively applied, subject to the condition of civil actionability under the law of the place of the tort.[104]

The High Court of Australia returned to these questions in *Anderson v Eric Anderson Radio & TV Pty Ltd*,[105] in a case which further complicated the analysis as it involved both Australian federal and state jurisdiction, and also raised a question of whether a claim for which a complete defence was available (because of contributory negligence) was nevertheless still 'actionable'. For present purposes, it is enough to note that some judges of the Court grappled directly with the ambiguities in the earlier Australian and English authorities. Kitto J, for example, although acknowledging criticism of *Phillips v Eyre* and

[97] ibid, Art 4(2).
[98] ibid, Art 4(1); recitals 16–17.
[99] ibid, Art 14.
[100] Law Applicable to Contractual Obligations and Non-Contractual Obligations (Amendment etc.) (EU Exit) Regulations 2019.
[101] *Koop v Bebb* [1951] HCA 77.
[102] ibid, [11].
[103] ibid, [11] (citing *Phillips v Eyre*), but see the separate opinion of McTiernan J suggesting to the contrary that the law of the place of the tort governed (also citing *Phillips v Eyre*).
[104] ibid, [12].
[105] *Anderson v Eric Anderson Radio & TV Pty Ltd* [1965] HCA 61.

suggesting that 'The whole subject may perhaps need to be re-examined some day'[106] nevertheless felt constrained to apply the double-actionability rule, defeating a claim for which there was a complete defence under the law of the forum (New South Wales) but only a partial defence under the law of the place of the tort (the Australian Capital Territory, a federal territory). Windeyer J, more controversially, considered the double-actionability rule as a rule 'concerning the jurisdiction of English courts in cases concerning foreign torts',[107] asking 'But when the two conditions are fulfilled – when the act is wrongful by the law of the forum and in the place where it occurred – what then?' He concluded that the law of the forum ought to apply exclusively. This 'jurisdictional' approach to the rule in *Phillips v Eyre*, which anticipated the approach of at least one Court of Appeal judge in *Boys v Chaplin*, was applied by some Australian courts – for example, the Supreme Court of the Australian Capital Territory in *Hartley v Venn*.[108] It was also applied in some Canadian decisions, such as *Gagnon v Lecavalier*.[109] In other Australian courts, however, such as the New South Wales Court of Appeal in *Kolsky v Mayne Nickless Ltd*,[110] decided shortly after the House of Lords decision in *Boys v Chaplin*, the Court expressly rejected the idea that the double-actionability rule involved a question of jurisdiction at all, describing it as a doctrine of 'substantive law'.[111] Nevertheless, the Court only applied the law of the forum – it was irrelevant that the law of the place of the tort (but not the law of the forum) would provide a partial defence, because forum law applied once it was established that the claim was actionable under both laws.[112]

It is notable that all of these disputes involved tort claims across the borders of Australian states or Canadian provinces, rather than international claims, and in many of these cases the courts grappled with the question of whether analysis of the choice of law issues should be affected by the relevant federal system.

The idea that the Australian Constitution or federal structure might provide a basis on which to reject the rule in *Phillips v Eyre* was explored by the High Court in *Breavington* v *Godleman*,[113] although without a clear majority. Wilson and Gaudron JJ argued that the Constitution created territorial limits on the

[106] ibid, [4].

[107] ibid, [1].

[108] *Hartley v Venn* (1967) 10 FLR 151.

[109] *Gagnon v Lecavalier* [1967] 63 DLR (2d) 12.

[110] *Kolsky v Mayne Nickless Ltd* (1970) 72 SR (NSW) 437. See also, eg, *Kemp v Piper* [1971] SASR 25.

[111] *Kolsky* (n 110) 444.

[112] The flexibility added to English law by the House of Lords in *Boys v Chaplin* was acknowledged, but not adopted by the Court, in part because of uncertainty as to how this flexibility ought to operate: ibid, 448. It was, however, applied by other Australian courts: see, eg, *Warren v Warren* [1972] Qd R 386; *Corcoran v Corcoran* [1974] VR 164.

[113] *Breavington v Godleman* (1988) 169 CLR 41 (HCA).

sovereignty of each of the states,[114] and that this limited the choice of law rules each state could adopt. Mason J rejected a specific role for the Constitution in developing private international law, but held with Wilson and Gaudron JJ that the federal context had an effect on choice of law rules, concluding that it required the application of a *lex loci delicti* rule in inter-state torts. Deane J argued that the territorial limitation of each state sovereign and the fundamentally unitary system of law established by the Constitution meant that the common law rules of private international law were inapplicable. Instead, he argued, a new federal standard 'sufficient relevant nexus' test ought to be applied.[115] Although four out of the seven judges rejected the existing common law approach, they thus did so in three separate judgments for a variety of different reasons, which limited the impact of their decisions. The idea of a constitutional limit on inter-state choice of law rules was indeed subsequently rejected in *McKain v RW Miller & Co (SA) Pty Ltd*,[116] and *Stevens v Head*,[117] which held that the choice of law rules formulated by Brennan J in *Breavington v Godleman*, a restatement of the *Phillips v Eyre* test, continued to apply (unless modified by state legislation).

However, the Canadian Supreme Court took up the baton with the decision of *Tolofson v Jensen*.[118] Although the case concerned an inter-provincial tort, the Court addressed the choice of law rules to be applied in both internal and international disputes. In respect of inter-provincial torts, the Court drew on the idea that the sovereign power of the Canadian provinces is subject to territorial limitation. As a result, and drawing on the reasoning of some members of the Australian High Court in *Breavington v Godleman*,[119] the Court held that the character of the constitutional system mandated the application of a *lex loci delicti* rule for inter-provincial torts. In respect of international torts, the Court reasoned that 'it is to the underlying reality of the international legal order … that we must turn if we are to structure a rational and workable system of private international law',[120] and that 'on the international plane, the relevant underlying reality is the territorial limits of law under the international legal order'.[121] Thus, the *lex loci delicti* rule was held to be equally applicable in international tort disputes, although (for international cases only) subject to a discretion to apply the law of the forum.

[114] ibid, [42]; see also Deane J at, eg, [15] and [25].
[115] ibid, [27].
[116] *McKain v RW Miller & Co (SA) Pty Ltd* (1992) 174 CLR 1.
[117] *Stevens v Head* (1993) 176 CLR 433.
[118] *Tolofson v Jensen* [1994] 3 SCR 1022 (SCC).
[119] ibid, 1063. The Court suggested (at 1052) that Australia had established a *lex loci delicti* rule, which was actually not the case at the time, given its rejection in *McKain v Miller* (n 116) and *Stevens v Head* (n 117).
[120] *Tolofson v Jensen* (n 118) 1047–48.
[121] ibid, 1047.

In turn, under the influence of *Tolofson v Jensen*,[122] the Australian High Court finally accepted a constitutional effect on choice of law rules in *John Pfeiffer Pty Ltd v Rogerson*.[123] The Court held that the constitutional idea of a unitary federal system with territorially limited state sovereigns implied a *lex loci delicti* rule for choice of law in Australian inter-state tort disputes, with no equivalent to the flexible exception under the traditional common law approach. Only a mechanical territorial choice of law rule, it was held, would satisfy the constitutional requirement for a clear territorial division of the sovereign competencies of the states. Kirby J perhaps went furthest, rejecting the legacy of *Phillips v Eyre* under the headings 'An inappropriate borrowing from English law' and 'A confusion of related but different concepts' (particularly the confusion of jurisdictional and choice of law requirements), and noting the statutory rejection of *Phillips v Eyre* in the UK.

In *Regie National des Usines Renault SA v Zhang*,[124] the *lex loci delicti* rule was extended to international torts. Given that the constitutional arguments from *John Pfeiffer Pty Ltd v Rogerson* were inapplicable to international torts, this required new justification. The extension of the new approach beyond the inter-state context was largely based on a general preference for the predictability and territoriality of the *lex loci delicti* rule, and the pragmatic basis that it is better to have a consistent single approach for both internal and international choice of law disputes.[125] Unlike the approach adopted in Canada,[126] the Australian High Court extended the inflexibility of the *lex loci delicti* rule to the international sphere, rejecting the idea that in the international context the Court should reserve the right to apply the *lex fori* or another more closely connected law.[127]

C. United States

The decision in *Phillips v Eyre* had a curious influence (or perhaps absence of influence) in the US. In *Leonard v Columbia Steam Navigation Co*,[128] the New York Court of Appeals developed its own doctrine, under which claims in tort were to be governed by the law of the place of the tort, subject to the condition that the law of the place of the tort was 'similar' to the law of

[122] See, eg, *John Pfeiffer Pty Ltd v Rogerson* (2000) 203 CLR 503 [87], [111ff] (Kirby J).

[123] ibid.

[124] *Regie National des Usines Renault SA v Zhang* (2002) 210 CLR 491.

[125] ibid, [125ff] (Kirby J).

[126] *Tolofson v Jensen* (n 118).

[127] For the difficulties thereby created, see *Neilson* v *Overseas Projects Corporation of Victoria Ltd* [2005] HCA 54, discussed in A Mills, 'Renvoi and the Proof of Foreign Law in Australia' (2006) 65 *Cambridge Law Journal* 37.

[128] *Leonard v Columbia Steam Navigation* Co 84 NY 48 (1881).

the forum. The following month this decision was endorsed by the US Supreme Court, in *Dennick v Railroad Co*,[129] and the doctrine was formally adopted by the Supreme Court in *Texas & Pacific Railway Co v Cox*.[130] Although expressed in terms which perhaps suggest something like double-actionability, it was clear that the rule thus adopted was nothing more than the application of the *lex loci delicti*, subject to a public policy exception where the law of the forum was too dissimilar to foreign law.[131] Indeed, in the official report of *Dennick v Railroad Co*, the decision in *Phillips v Eyre* was cited for the proposition that under 'the principle of comity, the foreign law, if not contrary to the public policy of the country where the suit is brought, nor to abstract justice or pure morals, will be recognized and enforced'.[132] In *Huntington v Attrill*,[133] the decision in *Phillips v Eyre* was (more accurately) cited as authority for the double-actionability rule under English law, but only in the context of observing that 'such is not the law of this court'.[134] Although based on somewhat dubious authority, this approach was also supported by the development of the vested rights or obligation theory, which supported the territorial approach to choice of law which dominated thinking in the US in the late nineteenth and early twentieth century. This was exemplified in the First Restatement on Conflict of Laws in 1934, which adopted at section 382 the *lex loci delicti* as the choice of law rule in tort, and in judgments like *Slater v Mexican National R Co*,[135] in which the US Supreme Court famously held that:[136]

> The theory of the foreign suit is that, although the act complained of was subject to no law having force in the forum, it gave rise to an obligation, an obligatio, which, like other obligations, follows the person, and may be enforced wherever the person may be found. But as the only source of this obligation is the law of the place of the act, it follows that that law determines not merely the existence of the obligation, but equally determines its extent.

This theory would, of course, be later challenged by the US conflict of laws 'revolution', in which choice of law in tort was particularly contested – but those developments were a rejection of a more straightforward territorial choice of law rule, not of the double-actionability rule, which never played a part in US law.

[129] *Dennick v Railroad Co* 103 US 11 (1881).

[130] *Texas & Pacific Railway Co v Cox* 145 US 593 (1892).

[131] ibid, 605.

[132] *Dennick v Railroad Co* (n 129) 14.

[133] *Huntington v Attrill* 146 US 657 (1892).

[134] ibid, 670. The doctrine was, nevertheless, occasionally applied. See, eg, *The Brantford City* 29 F 373 (1886) and *The Lamington* 87 F 752 (1898), each citing with approval *Phillips v Eyre* as authority for the double-actionability rule.

[135] *Slater v Mexican National R Co* 194 US 120 (1908).

[136] ibid, 126 (citations omitted). See similarly *Loucks v Standard Oil Co of New York* 120 NE 198 (1918), rejecting *Phillips v Eyre*, and also rejecting the similarity doctrine, in favour of a simple application of the law of the place of the tort.

V. THE CONTEMPORARY RELEVANCE OF THE DOUBLE-ACTIONABILITY RULE IN ENGLAND

As explained above, the double-actionability rule has largely been rejected, including in the UK through the 1995 Act, later in turn largely replaced by the Rome II Regulation. It is, however, more than of just historical interest, as it remains a part of the law in two important respects.

The first is that, exceptionally, a claim in tort may arise from events prior to the date of entry into force of the 1995 Act, and therefore outside its temporal scope. This arose in *Sophocleous v Secretary of State for Foreign and Commonwealth Affairs*,[137] a case concerning torts allegedly committed in Cyprus in the 1950s by the UK and its colonial agents. In order to determine the applicable law, including the relevant limitation periods, the Court of Appeal applied the double-actionability rule (citing to *Phillips v Eyre*). In so doing, the Court rejected the decision at first instance that a flexible exception should be adopted in favour of the exclusive application of English law. The double-actionability rule thus continues to be applicable to the kinds of cases in which it originated, namely to claims arising from atrocities committed during the suppression of independence movements in former colonies.

The second context for continued application of the rule in *Phillips v Eyre* is in disputes which fall outside the subject matter scope of the 1995 Act, in particular claims for defamation. The Law Commission report which led to the adoption of the 1995 Act considered that defamation raised particular concerns 'given the public interest in free speech and in the proper functioning of public institutions', arguing that 'it is not desirable that those who make statements in this country should have their freedom of expression circumscribed by the application of foreign law',[138] although did not propose the exclusion of defamation but rather its regulation by a specialised rule. This suggestion was not adopted, but the public interest considerations led to the exclusion of defamation from the 1995 Act altogether.[139] Defamation was equally excluded from the scope of the Rome II Regulation, under Article 1(2)(g), alongside violations of privacy.[140] This exclusion is intended to be temporary, although despite prompting from the European Parliament the European Commission has not yet taken any further steps in the matter. The continued application of the double-actionability rule to defamation claims is therefore not so much a matter of policy design, but rather a failure to adopt reforms. However, one

[137] *Sophocleous v Secretary of State for Foreign and Commonwealth Affairs* [2018] EWCA Civ 2167, [2019] 2 WLR 956.

[138] *Private International Law: Choice of Law in Tort and Delict* (n 90) para 3.31.

[139] Although it is of interest that the Private International Law (Choice of Law in Tort) Act 2017 in New Zealand, which is in very similar terms to the 1995 Act, does not exclude defamation from its scope.

[140] Claims in 'privacy' are not excluded from the 1995 Act, and thus remain subject to that Act.

of the reasons why general choice of law rules in tort have not been considered suitable for defamation is that treating defamation purely as a matter of private law does not seem entirely satisfactory, because of the important public interests involved in free speech protection in a democracy. Although the double-actionability rule is not consistent with the general principles underlying choice of law rules, it certainly does recognise an English public interest in regulating free speech, in the particular role it gives to the law of the forum – English media organisations sued in England, for example, at least ordinarily benefit from any defences to defamation claims under English law, regardless of where in the world their publications are received and read. It is no coincidence that the media were, indeed, vocal in supporting the exclusion of defamation claims from these modern attempts to reform choice of law in tort.[141] In parliamentary debates on what became the 1995 Act, Lord Lester of Herne Hill (a former barrister) had similarly observed:[142]

> I believe that there is an important point of principle here. Freedom of expression and freedom of the press are vital civil rights and liberties which … are restricted under English law only where necessary in a democratic society in accordance with the common law and Article 10 of the European Convention on Human Rights. Surely, in this age of global communications, it would be quite wrong for the freedom of the press in this country and elsewhere to be chilled or restricted by applying in English courts the laws of foreign countries which are far more repressive of freedom of expression.

It may, however, certainly be questioned whether this insistence on English free speech protections regardless of the location or targeting of the relevant communication is always appropriate – the effect of *Phillips v Eyre* in this context is arguably to give mandatory effect to English tort law in a way which might not always seem consistent with general principle. Nevertheless, it is undoubtedly difficult to design a rule which balances the competing interests involved, particularly in a cross-border context engaging more than one state's conception of the appropriate balance between the protection of free speech and reputation.

This difficulty is indeed amply demonstrated by experience subsequent to the passage of the 1995 Act. Although the continued application of the double-actionability rule in the context of defamation was at least partly motivated by the idea that English defamation law would protect English free speech against the lower standards of foreign law, a quite different and more significant practical concern has arisen as a consequence of two factors. First, technological developments mean that communications very readily cross borders, and thus material produced by a foreign publisher may frequently be considered to be

[141] The role of media representatives in formulating the Bill was noted by Lord Wilberforce: Hansard, HL Deb 2 May 1995, vol 563, col 1362.

[142] Hansard, HL Deb 6 December 1994, vol 559, col 839.

published in England (as well as numerous other locations) for jurisdictional and choice of law purposes.[143] Second, English law is in fact *less* protective of free speech than some foreign systems, particularly US law. In combination, these factors have allowed and encouraged defamation claimants to bring claims against foreign (particularly US) defendants in the English courts, raising concerns that private international law assists in suppressing rather than protecting free speech in this context, only partially addressed by statutory reform.[144] These issues are not unique to England,[145] and are not a product of the double-actionability rule itself but rather the rule that torts located in England are governed exclusively by English law (and establish a basis of jurisdiction for the English courts), as well as the chilling effect of the expense (particularly in England) of defending defamation proceedings. They nevertheless further illustrate the complexity of the modern interaction between private international law and defamation law which has thus far led to defamation claims being excluded from reforms and remaining subject to otherwise outmoded choice of law rules.

VI. CONCLUSION

In certain respects, the decision in *Phillips v Eyre*, although undoubtedly a landmark, gives the impression of belonging to a pre-modern era. It does not reflect the principles or values of modern private international law, but rather seems a product of its colonial context, and/or of outmoded thinking regarding tort law's public function. Since the decision was made it has been misinterpreted, misapplied, criticised, qualified, and even ignored by other courts, and ultimately rejected either by statutory or judicial reform in many common law countries. In many respects, its lasting influence is not as a ruling, but as a provocation – a challenge ultimately taken up by courts and legislators, to think more deeply about choice of law in tort, and to bring the principles of private international law to bear in designing a choice of law rule in tort which better reflects the range of competing policy interests involved. But *Phillips v Eyre* is more than a fossil – it is rather what biologists refer to as a living fossil, a species which exists in both fossil record and alive in the modern world, because of its continuing role in England in relation to defamation claims. Encountering *Phillips v Eyre* is also a bit like catching a coelacanth,

[143] See generally A Mills, 'The Law Applicable to Cross-border Defamation on Social Media: Whose Law Governs Free Speech in "Facebookistan"?' (2015) 7 *Journal of Media Law* 1; T Hartley, 'Libel Tourism and Conflict of Laws' (2010) 59 *International & Comparative Law Quarterly* 25.

[144] The Defamation Act 2013 was an initial response; the UK Ministry of Justice is presently considering legislation in response to a further public consultation on Strategic Lawsuits Against Public Participation ('SLAPPs'), which closed on 19 May 2022.

[145] The European Commission has also proposed a Directive to address SLAPPs. See Commission Proposal COM(2022) 177 (27 April 2022).

or stumbling over a Wollemi Pine – discovering that the choice of law rule in defamation in England, including even for defamation claims on the internet, derives from a case excusing a nineteenth century colonial atrocity. The deficiencies of the double-actionability rule are well recognised, but in England the provocation of *Phillips v Eyre* remains unanswered as no rule has been found to replace it in the context of defamation, a tort imbued with public interest and not just private right. The story of *Phillips v Eyre* therefore has an ending almost as curious as its beginning – it endures not as a reflection of any inherent wisdom in its decision, but as the legacy of a colonial wrong which is now relied on (rightly or wrongly) to protect the rights of free speech necessary for the functioning of a modern democracy.

6

Abouloff v Oppenheimer (1882)

LOUISE MERRETT

I. INTRODUCTION

As Lord Briggs colourfully put it, in *Takhar v Gracefield Developments Ltd*,[1] the extent to which fraud should be a defence to the enforcement of a judgment

> turns on the outcome of a bare-knuckle fight between two important and long-established principles of public policy. The first is that fraud unravels all. The second is that there must come an end to litigation.

The first of these principles is that fraud is a thing apart and that once proved vitiates judgments, contracts and all transactions whatsoever.[2] However, there are occasions when the desire to undo an otherwise binding act or decision because of fraud, appears to be in direct contradiction to the second important principle, namely the principle of finality. Any determination may be imperfect but at some point the law must close the book and in the interests of peace, certainty and security prevent further inquiry.[3]

The Supreme Court in *Takhar* was considering the conflict between these two important principles in the context of an English judgment. But the same issue, or at least an analogous question, arises in relation to fraud as a defence the enforcement of a foreign judgment and it was this issue which was famously raised by the case of *Abouloff v Oppenheimer & Co*.[4]

II. THE DECISION IN ABOULOFF v OPPENHEIMER

On 9 March 1877, the District Court of Tiflis, in the empire of Russia, ordered the defendants to return certain goods of the plaintiff, or in default their value.

[1] *Takhar v Gracefield Developments Ltd* [2019] UKSC 13, [2020] AC 450 [68].

[2] ibid, [43] (Lord Kerr) referring to this statement of the general principle in *HIH Casualty and General Insurance Ltd v Chase Manhattan Bank* [2003] UKHL 6, [2003] 1 All ER (Comm) 349 [15] (Lord Bingham).

[3] *Takhar* (n 1) [44] (Lord Kerr) citing *The Ampthill Peerage* [1977] AC 547 (HL) 569 (Lord Wilberforce).

[4] *Abouloff v Oppenheimer & Co* (1882) 10 QBD 295.

The defendants appealed against the judgment to the High Court of Tiflis. The judgment was confirmed and defendants were ordered to pay further costs and expenses. The plaintiff claimed these sums in the High Court in England, relying on the judgments as giving her good causes of action.

As explored in chapter four, by the time *Aboulof*f was decided in 1882, it had been established in *Godard v Gray* and *Schibsby v Westenholz* that English courts can and should enforce obligations created by foreign judgments.[5] As Lord Coleridge CJ said in *Abouloff*,

> I do not think it necessary to inquire for the present purpose what is the strictly accurate mode of stating the principle, on which the courts of this country enforce the obligation created by foreign judgments … it is enough for me to say that the English courts do enforce obligations created by judgments ….[6]

However, in defence of the action to enforce the Russian judgments, the defendants alleged that the judgments were obtained by gross fraud of the plaintiff and her husband in fraudulently representing that the goods in question were not in their possession whereas they were.[7] In reply, the plaintiff argued that the defence was bad, principally on the ground that the allegations of fraud were before the courts at Tiflis; that those courts had jurisdiction to examine the defence and did examine it, and came to a conclusion against the defendants; and therefore that, whether this conclusion was right or wrong on the matters of fact, the question of the plaintiff's alleged fraud could not now be tried or litigated in the courts of England.

Thus arose the conflict referred to by Lord Briggs at the beginning of this chapter. The principle of finality and comity on which the enforcement of foreign judgments rests suggested that a final judgment having been reached in Russia, that judgment should be enforced without the English courts reconsidering the merits of the dispute. On the other hand, did the fact that the defence relied on constituted fraud trump the otherwise final judgment?

Lord Coleridge CJ[8] began by noting the broad proposition that where a judgment has been obtained by the fraud of a party to a suit in a foreign country, he cannot prevent the question of fraud from being litigated in the courts of this country, when he seeks to enforce the judgment so obtained. The justice of that proposition, he said, was obvious: if it were not so, the court would have to disregard a well-established rule of law that no man shall take advantage of his own wrong. As this formulation of the principle makes clear, the proposition is not

[5] *Godard v Gray* (1870–71) LR 6 QB 139 (QB) and *Schibsby v Westenholz* (1879–71) LR 6 QB 155 (QB).

[6] *Abouloff v Oppenheimer* (n 4) 300.

[7] Except in relation to those of the goods that the plaintiff had from time to time secretly and fraudulently disposed of.

[8] Baggallay LJ agreed that the appeal should be dismissed but his judgment dealt with a narrow hypothetical point concerning the foreign court's role in deceit.

simply that 'fraud unravels all', rather, the principle rests on the doctrine of *ex turpi causa*: no one should benefit from their own wrong. This point was further emphasised by Brett LJ, stressing that the fraud in question was the fraud of the plaintiff herself. It was not permissible to question the judgment of the foreign court on the basis of a wrong appreciation of facts or law or 'frauds perpetrated on the courts by witnesses other than the plaintiff and her husband'.[9]

However, the Court also recognised that this principle might be said to conflict with another equally clear proposition, namely, that the courts of this country in dealing with a foreign judgment will not inquire whether the foreign court pronounced a judgment correct in point of law, or right and accurate in point of fact, and that inasmuch as the defence now relied on might have been, and perhaps was, brought before the foreign court which decided against the allegation of fraud, the foreign court was mistaken and not misled. Rather than directly dealing with these contradictory principles, the Court first sought to avoid this apparent conflict by relying on what has been described as a technical argument.[10] The Court reasoned that the 'same' issue had not in fact been decided by the Russian courts, thus the finality issue did not arise:

> We are to decide whether the courts at Tiflis have been misled by the fraud of the plaintiff; but the question whether they were misled, never could have been submitted to them, never could have been in issue before them, and therefore never could have been decided by them. The English courts are not either re-trying or even re-discussing any question which was or could have been submitted to the determination of the Russian courts.[11]

> It has been contended that the same issue ought not to be tried in an English court which was tried in the Russian courts, but I agree that the question whether the Russian courts were deceived, never could be an issue in the action tried before them.[12]

The argument is not only technical, but artificial. The Russian court made a factual finding that the goods were not in the possession of the plaintiff. The argument was that this was not the issue before the English court; the English court had to decide whether the Russian court was misled into finding that the goods were not in the possession of the plaintiff. But it must be implicit in the factual finding that the court believed the evidence and the case put before it.

This technical argument has been criticised and indeed ultimately rejected in later cases. For example, in *Owens Bank Ltd v Bracco*, this part of the Court's reasoning in *Abouloff* was considered unconvincing. In the Court of Appeal, Parker LJ noted that any court, in considering whether a claim is honest or fraudulent, having regard to the evidence on both sides, must be considering

[9] *Abouloff v Oppenheimer* (n 4) 307.

[10] In *Vadala v Lawes* (1890) 25 QBD 310 (CA) 317 the court referred to this as the 'meeting of a technical argument by technical answer'.

[11] *Abouloff v Oppenheimer* (n 4) 302 (Lord Coleridge CJ).

[12] ibid, 306 (Brett LJ).

and deciding whether the claimant is trying to mislead the court.[13] Similarly, the Court in *Westacre Investments Inc v Jugoimport SDPR Holding Co Ltd* held that this argument 'does not bear logical analysis'.[14] If the court was required to determine an issue of fact, it was required to determine the truth of the evidence adduced in support of that fact: and there was no substantial difference between the two issues. The argument can also be distinguished from that which succeeded in *Yukos Capital Sarl v OJSC Rosneft Oil Co*.[15] In that case, the issue for the Dutch court was whether the recognition of a Russian judgment annulling an arbitration award would be contrary to Dutch public policy. When the same award was sought to be enforced in England the question was whether enforcement was contrary to English public policy, which was or might be different from Dutch public policy which was in substance a different question.

Leaving aside that 'technical' response, and going back to the fundamental conflict between finality and fraud, the substantive decision in *Abouloff* was that the fraud defence should prevail:[16]

> I think, therefore, on the broad ground that no man can take advantage of his own wrong, and that it is a principle of law that no action can be maintained on the judgment of a court either in this country or in any other, which has been obtained by the fraud of the person seeking to enforce it, that the defence is good.

The generality of the *Abouloff* principle was established in *Vadala v Lawes*.[17] The plaintiff in *Vadala* sought to argue that *Abouloff* must be read with reference to the special circumstances of the case, and that fraud can only be set up where it is as to a matter extraneous to the questions decided in the foreign court. The Court noted that there were two rules at play: (1) a party to an action can impeach a judgment if it is procured by fraud: whether that is a judgment of an English court or a foreign court; and (2) when you bring an action on a foreign judgment, you cannot go into the merits which have been tried in the foreign court. The question was what happened when these two rules were combined or in conflict; which is to prevail?

This, according to the Court in *Vadala*, was the issue raised directly in *Abouloff* and decided: if the fraud upon the foreign court consisted in the fact that the plaintiff had induced that court by fraud to come to a wrong conclusion, the whole of the case could be reopened by the enforcing court in England although the court would have to go into the very facts which were investigated and which were in issue in the foreign court. Accordingly, as discussed further below, in contrast to the position in relation to a domestic judgment, the Court

[13] *Owens Bank Ltd v Bracco* [1992] 2 AC 443 (CA and HL) 466.

[14] *Westacre Investments Inc v Jugoimport SDPR Holding Co Ltd* [1999] QB 740 (Com Ct) 782 (Colman J).

[15] *Yukos Capital Sarl v OJSC Rosneft Oil Co* [2012] EWCA Civ 855, [2014] QB 458.

[16] *Abouloff v Oppenheimer* (n 4) 303 (Lord Coleridge CJ).

[17] *Vadala v Lawes* (n 10).

implied that the judgment can be reopened even if the issue had already been determined and even if there is no new evidence of fraud.

Thus the *Abouloff* principle was established. In the context of recognition and enforcement of foreign judgments at common law, a foreign judgment may be impeached for fraud even though no newly discovered evidence is produced and even though the evidence of fraud might have been produced, or even was produced and rejected, in the foreign court.[18]

III. CRITICISMS OF THE ABOULOFF PRINCIPLE

Although the *Abouloff* principle has been approved on a number of occasions, this has not always been with great enthusiasm.

It has been pointed out that it is a very old decision, and that the law, particularly relating to the regard to be paid to foreign courts, may well have moved on. For example, in *House of Spring Gardens Ltd v Waite*,[19] the court noted that *Abouloff* has been considerably criticised over the years and was decided at a time when English courts paid scant regard to the jurisprudence of other countries. In *Owens Bank Ltd v Bracco*,[20] the House of Lords commented that it appreciated the force of the argument that it might be time to reassess the rule, and that if the issue were governed only by the common law that they would have considered the basis for the rule in detail, but the judgment at issue was one covered by a statutory regime, namely the Administration of Justice Act 1920.[21] The 1920 Act was intended to reflect the rule in *Abouloff* so any review would have to be by Parliament:[22]

> I recognise that, as a matter of policy, there may be a very strong case to be made in the 1990s in favour of according to overseas judgments the same finality as the courts accord to English judgments. But enforcement of overseas judgments is now primarily governed by the statutory codes of 1920 and 1933. Since these cannot be altered except by further legislation, it seems to me out of the question to alter the common law rule by overruling *Abouloff* and *Vadala v Lawes*. To do so would produce the absurd result that an overseas judgment creditor, denied statutory enforcement on the ground that he had obtained his judgment by fraud, could succeed in a common law action to enforce his judgment because the evidence on which the judgment debtor relied did not satisfy the English rule. Accordingly the whole field is effectively governed by statute and, if the law is now in need of reform, it is for the legislature, not the judiciary, to effect it.

[18] This was how the principle was summarised by Lord Collins in *AK Investment CJSC v Kyrgyz Mobil Tel Ltd* [2011] UKPC 7, [2012] 1 WLR 1804 [109].

[19] *House of Spring Gardens Ltd v Waite* [1991] 1 QB 241 (CA) 251 (Stuart-Smith LJ).

[20] *Owens Bank v Bracco* (n 13).

[21] The Administration of Justice Act 1920 provides for the registration and reciprocal enforcement of judgments from certain countries. The substantive rules for enforcement mirror those which applied at common law.

[22] *Owens Bank v Bracco* (n 13) 489 (Lord Bridge).

The Privy Council in *AK Investment CJSC v Kyrgyz Mobil Tel Ltd* carried out a more extensive review of the *Abouloff* principle.[23] The case involved proceedings to enforce a *Kyrgyz* judgment in the Isle of Man High Court. The defendants resisted enforcement on a number of grounds including that the judgment of the Kyrgyz court had been procured by fraud. In challenging this defence, the correctness of the decision of *Abouloff* was raised as well as whether it should be applied by the Isle of Man courts. The Privy Council noted that the rule in *Abouloff* had received considerable criticism.[24] They summarised the following arguments which were relied on against the rule:

(a) The *Abouloff* principle ignores the doctrines of cause of action and issue estoppel and the nature of the doctrine of obligation, and is wrong in principle. However, the court in *Abouloff* itself accepted that the finality principle was engaged and the force of that principle; the question was whether it is right that as a matter of policy and principle the fraud principle should prevail where the two come into conflict.
(b) That the policy underlying *Abouloff* is objectionable and wrong, and is inconsistent with judicial comity. A policy which requires a Manx court to appropriate for itself the responsibility of deciding whether a foreign court was deceived, especially where the foreign court has its own procedure for setting aside judgments obtained in such circumstances, is anomalous and unjustifiable. This argument raises the issue of exhaustion of local remedies which will be considered further in section V.D below.
(c) Finally, and most importantly, the most consistent criticism of the *Abouloff* principle is that the rule should be the same as that applied to setting aside English judgments.[25] The Privy Council noted that 'the appellants submit that the rule in *Abouloff* should not be applied in the Isle of Man because … the courts should apply the same rules in relation to foreign judgments as they apply at common law to the setting aside of a domestic judgment'.[26]

The scope of the defence of fraud in relation to English judgments was recently considered by the Supreme Court in *Takhar* and the implications of this

[23] *AK Investment* (n 18).

[24] ibid, [112], referring to the literature cited in L Collins (ed), *Dicey, Morris and Collins on the Conflict of Laws,* 14th edn (London, Sweet & Maxwell, 2006) para 14-129. The rule has also been repudiated by the Supreme Court of Canada in *Beals v Saldanha* [2003] 3 SCR 416 1.

[25] See, eg, *Interdesco SA v Nullifire Ltd* [1992] 1 Lloyd's Rep 180 (Com Ct), a case about the Brussels Convention, where, in adopting a stricter approach to European cases, Phillips J commented that generally, the Court should not normally entertain a challenge to a Convention judgment in circumstances where it would not permit a challenge to an English judgment.

[26] *AK Investment* (n 18) [115]. This argument was also raised in *Owens Bank Ltd v Bracco* (n 13) 489 in the passage referred to above, and in *Dicey, Morris & Collins*, 14th edn (n 24) para 14-139, where it is stated that the main criticism is that it 'stands in square opposition to the principle of conclusiveness and also to the principle that English judgments can only be impeached for fraud if new evidence of a decisive character has since been discovered'.

decision on the position for foreign judgments is considered further in section V below. Ultimately, having considered all these arguments, the Privy Council concluded:[27]

> These are powerful arguments, but the present case shows that, even if the rule in *Aboulo*ff were no longer to represent the law, simply to apply the English rules to foreign judgments might lead to real injustice. To decide, on an application to set aside service, an issue which requires 'detailed argument and mature considerations' (*American Cyanamid Co v Ethicon Ltd…*) would be an inappropriate application of the 'bound to fail' / 'serious issue to be tried' tests. Extremely important issues of policy would be involved in deciding whether to change a rule which has stood for almost 120 years. In particular the facts of this case shows that a nuanced approach might be required, depending on the reliability of the foreign legal system, the scope for challenge in the foreign court and the type of fraud alleged.

IV. EXTENT OF THE ABOULOFF PRINCIPLE

Even though the decision in *Aboulo*ff has never been overruled, it has been distinguished and/or has not been adopted in other jurisdictions or in different contexts. Furthermore, the English courts have established two exceptions to the rule.

A. The *Aboulo*ff Principle in Different Contexts

The *Aboulo*ff principle does not apply to the enforcement of foreign arbitration awards. In *Westacre*,[28] Colman J considered an application to enforce a Swiss arbitration award. It was alleged that a number of witnesses had given perjured evidence, and that therefore the award had been obtained by fraud. The defendant relied on *Aboulo*ff in interpreting the public policy exception to enforcement of arbitration awards under the New York Convention.

Colman J noted that there was the 'strongest conceivable public policy' against re-opening of an issue of fact determined by arbitration.[29] If the public policy defence in the New York Convention allowed parties to relitigate on the basis of alleged perjury, a major inroad would be made into the finality of Convention awards. Furthermore, the same public policy applies as to English awards. The introduction of fresh evidence in order to disturb an English award is subject to requirements similar to those relating to the introduction of fresh evidence to challenge an English judgment. In particular, the fresh evidence must be of sufficient cogency and weight to be likely to have influenced the

[27] *AK Investment* (n 18) [116].
[28] *Westacre* (n 14).
[29] ibid, 782.

arbitrator's conclusion and the evidence must not have been available or reasonably obtainable at the time of the hearing.[30] The authorities do not suggest that any different rule applies to foreign arbitrations. Indeed, if anything, the approach to fraud being raised should be stricter in the case of foreign awards because the defence could and should have been raised by the supervisory court as a ground for setting aside the award.[31]

Accordingly, where a party to a foreign New York Convention arbitration award alleges at the enforcement stage that it has been obtained by perjured evidence that party will not normally be permitted to adduce additional evidence in the English courts to make good that allegation unless it is established that: (i) the evidence sought to be adduced is of sufficient cogency and weight to be likely to have materially influenced the arbitrators' conclusion had it been advanced at the hearing; and (ii) the evidence was not available or reasonably obtainable either (a) at the time of the hearing of the arbitration; or (b) at such time as would have enabled the party concerned to have adduced it in the court of supervisory jurisdiction to support an application to reverse the arbitrators' award if such procedure were available. Where the additional evidence has already been deployed before the court of supervisory jurisdiction for the purpose of an application for the setting aside or remission of the award but the application has failed, the public policy of finality would normally require that the English courts should not permit that further evidence to be adduced at the stage of enforcement.[32]

The *Abouloff* principle has also been rejected in Scotland. In *Clarke v Fennoscandia*,[33] the Court of Session (Outer House) held that in Scotland, a party seeking to challenge a judgment on the basis that it had been fraudulently obtained, was required to aver fraud extrinsic to the proceedings. Averments of perjury were not enough. Although averments of subornation of perjury would be. Further, it is required to be proved that fraud was not known at the relevant time and could not have been discovered.[34]

[30] See section V below for discussion of the decision of the Supreme Court in *Takhar* where the position in relation to English judgments was reviewed.

[31] *Westacre* (n 14) 782.

[32] See further *Eastern European Engineering Limited v Vijay Construction (Pty) Ltd* [2018] EWHC 2713 (Comm).

[33] *Clarke v Fennoscandia (No 3)* 2004 SC 197.

[34] The Court noted that it appeared that less stringent tests were applied at common law in England (ie the *Abouloff* principle) but that there was no reason to suppose the position was the same in Scotland. The Court also noted that it was now accepted that the position was different in Canada and Australia. In *Union of India v Bumper Development Corp* [1995] 4 WLUK 233, the Court of Queen's Bench (Alberta) was asked to enforce an English judgment and the defendant relied on fraud. There was no argument that there were new facts, the defence rested on *Abouloff*. The Court noted that Canadian courts only recognised extrinsic fraud, ie, fraud of a type which deprives a person of an adequate opportunity to present their case not intrinsic to allegations going to the existence and substance of the cause of action. Further, estoppel cannot be disturbed except upon allegation and proof of new facts.

B. Exceptions to the *Abouloff* Principle

In *House of Spring Gardens Ltd v Waite*,[35] a judgment had been given in proceedings in Ireland. Following the dismissal of an appeal by the Supreme Court, two of the defendants brought a further action to set aside the judgment, alleging that it was obtained by fraud. The action was dismissed. When the plaintiff sought to enforce the judgment in England, the defendants attempted to raise fraud again, relying on *Abouloff*. The court refused to allow the defence, holding that the scope of the decision in *Abouloff* should not be extended, and was clearly distinguishable.[36] In none of the cases where that principle had been applied was the question whether the judgment was obtained by fraud litigated in a separate and second action in the foreign jurisdiction. Unless the second action was itself impeached for fraud, it was conclusive of the matter thereby adjudicated on and created an estoppel. It would also have been an abuse of process to relitigate the very same issues in England, not least because the defendants themselves chose the foreign forum, which was the natural forum in which to challenge the original judgment. Accordingly, the principle in *Abouloff* will not apply where fraud has been raised in separate proceedings. A decision by a foreign court (whether or not a court of the country from which the judgment originates) that a foreign judgment was (or was not) obtained by fraud can create an estoppel in English proceedings although it will always be necessary to be cautious in the particular case.

In *Owens Bank Ltd v Etoile Commerciale SA*,[37] the Commercial Court in Paris had given judgment on a guarantee. On appeal, the defendant's allegations of fraud were rejected and the appeal dismissed. The defendant then commenced proceedings in St Vincent and the Grenadines claiming damages for fraud and alleging that the claimant had produced a forged guarantee to the French court. The proceedings were struck out. When the plaintiff sought to enforce the French judgment in St Vincent the defendant sought to rely on the same alleged fraud. The judge declined to allow summary judgment, but that decision was overturned by the Court of Appeal on the ground that it would be an abuse of process of the court to permit the fraud defence to be raised given the history of the litigation. The defendant appealed to the Privy Council. The plaintiff argued first that the judgment in St Vincent and the judgment of the Court of Appeal in Paris created an issue estoppel (relying on the decision in *House of Spring Gardens Ltd v Waite*). Second, the plaintiff argued that the court should reconsider the *Abouloff* rule. The Privy Council, while noting that these were interesting and important arguments, held that ultimately it was not necessary to deal with them because there was a much shorter answer to the appeal.[38]

[35] *House of Spring Gardens* (n 19).
[36] ibid, 251.
[37] *Owens Bank Ltd v Etoile Commerciale SA* [1995] 1 WLR 44 (PC).
[38] ibid, 51.

Every court has an inherent power to prevent misuse of its process, whether by a plaintiff or a defendant. There was nothing in the authorities which precluded a party from obtaining summary judgment or an order striking out a pleading on the grounds of abuse of process where a fraud was alleged. It was axiomatic that where fraud was alleged full particulars should be given. Where allegations of fraud had been made and determined abroad, summary judgment or striking out in subsequent proceedings were appropriate remedies in the absence of plausible evidence disclosing at least a prima facie case of fraud. No strict rule could be laid down; in every case the court must decide whether justice required the further investigation of alleged fraud or required that the plaintiff, having obtained a foreign judgment, should no longer be frustrated in enforcing that judgment.

House of Spring Gardens is a relatively narrow exception as it depends on fraud having been considered in separate proceedings. However, *Etoile* is potentially a much more significant inroad into the *Abouloff* principle. On the facts of a particular case, it can be an abuse of process to raise fraud again. For example, as discussed further in section V.B below, if fraud has been raised before, and there is no new evidence, in certain circumstances, it could be held to be an abuse to raise fraud again in enforcement proceedings.

V. FRAUD AS A DEFENCE TO AN ENGLISH JUDGMENT

A consistent criticism of the *Abouloff* principle has been that it is said to be at odds with the approach taken to the fraud defence in the context of domestic English judgments. Before turning to consider the approach to English judgments, as clarified in *Takhar*, it is important to note that there are reasons why a different approach might be appropriate in the context of foreign judgments, although courts have not always been clear and consistent in articulating what and why that might be.

For example, in *Westacre*,[39] in the context of a foreign arbitration award, the court said that if anything the rule should be stricter for re-opening a foreign award than in relation to an English award because the defence should have been raised before the supervisory court as a ground for setting aside the award. This is linked to the question of whether a defendant must exhaust local appeal remedies before fraud can be raised as a defence to enforcement which is considered in subsection D below.

Dicey, Morris & Collins makes the point that the result of holding that a judgment is invalid for fraud is more limited in the case of a foreign judgment than in relation to an English judgment.[40] A finding of fraud in relation to a

[39] *Westacre* (n 14) 782.
[40] *Dicey, Morris & Collins*, 14th edn (n 24) para 14-139.

foreign judgment only affects enforcement in England and does not destroy the judgment entirely thus: 'it is not difficult to argue that the nature of the evidence required to justify these two discrete results need not be identical in quality'. Here the opposite seems to be being suggested, that is, that it should be easier to raise on fraud in the case of a foreign judgment because the consequences are less severe.

The Privy Council in *AK Investments* made a slightly different point, that is, that judgments from different jurisdictions might need to be considered separately, depending on the reliability of the foreign legal system, the scope for challenge in the foreign court and the type of fraud alleged.[41]

In any event, the fundamental premise that the *Abouloff* principle should be modified to mirror the position in relation to English judgments may need to be re-evaluated following the decision of the Supreme Court in *Takhar v Gracefield Development Ltd* where the Court re-considered the position in relation to domestic judgments.

A. The Decision of the Supreme Court in *Takhar*

The Court of Appeal in *Takhar*, overturning the judgment of Newey J, had held that for an English judgment to be set aside on the basis of fraud, a party had to establish that there was evidence of fraud which was not available at the time of trial and could not have been discovered with reasonable diligence. In other words, the fact that fraud was alleged, did not affect the normal reasonable diligence requirement for relying on new evidence. The Court of Appeal had relied on two statements of what was said to be the rule in relation to English judgments in two of the foreign judgment cases discussed above. In *Owens Bank v Etoile*, Lord Templeman in the Privy Council stated:[42]

> An English judgment is impeachable in an English court on the ground that the first judgment was obtained by fraud but only by the production and establishment of evidence newly discovered since the trial and not reasonably discoverable before the trial ....

Lord Bridge, in the House of Lords in *Owens Bank v Bracco*, suggested that the common law rule was:[43]

> that the unsuccessful party who has been sued to judgment is not permitted to challenge that judgment on the ground that it was obtained by fraud unless he is able to prove that fraud by fresh evidence which was not available to him and could not have been discovered with reasonable diligence before the judgment was delivered.

[41] *AK Investment* (n 18) [116].
[42] *Owens Bank v Etoile* (n 37) 48.
[43] *Owens Bank v Bracco* (n 13) 483.

The Supreme Court overturned the decision of the Court of Appeal. Lord Kerr distinguished, and if necessary, disapproved the descriptions of the position in relation to English judgments; principally on the basis that in both cases there was a proposed re-litigation of the issue of fraud which had been determined in the earlier litigation (which was not the case on the facts in *Takhar*).[44] The alleged fraud in *Takhar* (an allegation that a signature had been forged) had not been raised in the proceedings below. The Supreme Court held that where it could be shown that a judgment had been obtained by fraud, and where no allegation of fraud had been raised at the trial, a requirement of reasonable diligence should not be imposed on the party seeking to set aside the judgment on the basis of new evidence.

The Supreme Court considered the foreign judgment cases, particularly *Etoille* and *Bracco* referred to above. However, the Court held that read properly those cases concerned the position where the fraud defence had actually been raised in the foreign proceedings. Furthermore, and in any event, if they went further than that they should not be followed:[45]

> In my view, it ought now to be recognised that where it can be shown that a judgment has been obtained by fraud, and where no allegation of fraud had been raised at the trial which led to that judgment, a requirement of reasonable diligence should not be imposed on the party seeking to set aside the judgment.

Essentially, where fraud is involved, questions of finality are sometimes trumped by the fact that fraud, potentially at least, unravels all:[46]

> The idea that a fraudulent individual should profit from passivity or lack of reasonable diligence on the part of his or her opponent seems antithetical to any notion of justice. Quite apart from this, the defrauder, in obtaining a judgment, has perpetrated a deception not only on their opponent and the court but on the rule of law.

Lord Sumption similarly commented that the due diligence requirement is based on something which the law would expect a reasonable person to do in his own interest and in that of the efficient conduct of litigation. However, the basis on which the law unmakes transactions, including judgments, which have been procured by fraud is that a reasonable person is entitled to assume honesty in those with whom he deals:[47]

> He is not expected to conduct himself or his affairs on the footing that other persons are dishonest unless he knows that they are. It follows that unless on the earlier

[44] *Takhar* (n 1) [42] (Lord Kerr, with whom Lords Hodge, Lloyd-Jones and Kitchen concurred).

[45] ibid, [54] (Lord Kerr).

[46] ibid, [52] (Lord Kerr) referring to the judgment of Newey J himself referring to the reasoning in the Australian and Canadian cases.

[47] ibid, [43] (Lord Sumption, with whom Lords Hodge, Lloyd-Jones and Kitchen also concurred). Lord Briggs agreed on the result but would have preferred a more flexible approach to deciding whether or not it is an abuse of process to raise fraud taking into account all the circumstances and under which the court can apply a fact-intensive evaluative approach to the question of whether lack of diligence in pursuing a case in fraud during the first proceedings ought to render a particular claim to set aside the judgment in those proceedings for fraud an abuse of process.

> occasion the claimant deliberately decided not to investigate a suspected fraud or rely on a known one, it cannot be said that he 'should' have raised it.

The Supreme Court has therefore clarified the position in relation to English judgments: a judgment can be challenged for fraud on the basis of new evidence, even if the evidence of fraud might have been discovered earlier and specifically there is no due diligence requirement. It seems very likely that the part of the *Abouloff* principle which encompasses this principle will be reinforced by the decision in *Takhar*. Criticism of the *Abouloff* principle based on its apparent inconsistency with the rules applied to English judgments will, in this respect, no longer be maintainable. Furthermore, the reasoning relied on by the Supreme Court, that is, that because parties are entitled to assume honesty they cannot be prevented from raising fraud by an allegation of a lack of diligence, seems to apply in the same way to foreign judgments. However, as described above, the *Abouloff* principle goes further in that it applies even when fraud has already been raised and there is no new evidence. The impact, if any, of *Takhar* on the more extreme parts of the *Abouloff* principle is less clear. Indeed, the Supreme Court left open two issues where the facts could be distinguished from those in *Takhar.*

B. Fraud Raised and Rejected in Earlier Proceedings

The Supreme Court in *Takhar* distinguished the situation where fraud had actually been raised and rejected in earlier proceedings. Lord Kerr said:[48]

> Where fraud has been raised at the original trial and new evidence as to the existence of the fraud is prayed in aid to advance a case for setting aside the judgment, it seems to me that it can be argued that the court having to deal with that application should have a discretion as to whether to entertain the application. Since that question does not arise in the present appeal, I do not express any final view on it.

Lord Sumption said:[49]

> I would leave open the question whether the position as I have summarised it is any different where the fraud was raised in the earlier proceedings but unsuccessfully. My provisional view is that the position is the same, for the same reasons. If decisive new evidence is deployed to establish the fraud, an action to set aside the judgment will lie irrespective of whether it could reasonably have been deployed on the earlier occasion unless a deliberate decision was then taken not to investigate or rely on the material.

Although ultimately leaving the issue open, both Lords Kerr and Sumption seemed to prefer the view that if decisive new evidence is relied on, it may not matter that fraud has already been raised and determined in the earlier proceedings.

[48] ibid, [55].
[49] ibid, [66].

This again provides some support or at least a counter argument for criticism of this aspect of the rule in *Abouloff*. However, it also highlights an important difference in relation to the approach to foreign judgments. As is apparent from the decision in *Abouloff* itself, in the case of foreign judgments fraud can be raised again even without there being decisive new evidence. In other words, in many cases the due diligence requirement is academic in foreign judgment cases because no new evidence is being relied on.

In an English judgment case, if the issue of fraud has already been decided by an English court, there is no reason to re-open that decision unless there is new evidence. That is not necessarily the case in foreign judgment cases. According to the *Abouloff* principle, the view of the foreign court is not binding in the case of fraud, so that the defence can be raised again before the English court even on the same evidence. In *Jet Holdings Inc v Patel*,[50] for example, an action was brought in England to enforce a Californian judgment and the defence that the judgment was obtained by fraud was raised. The court pointed out that where the objection to enforcement is based on jurisdiction it is plain that the foreign court's decision on its own jurisdiction is neither conclusive nor relevant. The foreign court cannot haul itself up by its own bootstraps. The court then commented that the same reasoning must apply where enforcement is resisted on the ground of fraud.

In other words, the foreign court's decision as to fraud cannot be decisive. The foreign court's view on fraud is neither conclusive nor relevant whether the fraud is said to go directly to the cause of action or collateral fraud. In this respect, the rule reflects the view that comity does not require the decision of a foreign court always to be given the same deference as a decision of an English court. The decision in *Takhar* provides no support for this aspect of the *Abouloff* principle. However, as discussed below, it may be supportable on practical grounds. The stage has yet to be reached where the English court would be happy to be bound by a decision on fraud from every possible court in the world and the *Abouloff* principle stops the court from having to make potentially invidious comparisons of different courts, judges or systems.

C. Deliberate Decision Not to Investigate the Fraud

The second issue which was left open by the Supreme Court in *Takhar* was whether the position might be different if the defendant had deliberately not investigated the fraud at an earlier stage. Lord Kerr said:

> The second [qualification] relates to the possibility that, in some circumstances, a deliberate decision may have been taken not to investigate the possibility of fraud in advance of the first trial, even if that had been suspected. If that could be established,

[50] *Jet Holdings Inc v Patel* [1990] 1 QB 335 (CA).

again, I believe that a discretion whether to allow an application to set aside the judgment would be appropriate but, once more, I express no final view on the question.

Lord Sumption, in the passage set out above,[51] also refers to a possible exception where a deliberate decision was taken not to investigate or rely on the material. This can again be contrasted with the position in relation to foreign judgments. As described above, the application of the *Abouloff* principle does not depend on there being new evidence. For example, in *Syal v Heyward*,[52] the court held that if a prima facie case of fraud was established, it was not essential that the facts supporting the allegation of fraud should have been discovered since the date of the foreign judgment. By contrast, it was said, under section 4 of the Foreign Judgments (Reciprocal Enforcement) Act 1933,[53] the question is not one of fraud on the plaintiff, but of fraud on the court. In that context it is established that if the defendant shows a prima facie case that the court was deceived, he is entitled to have that issue tried even though the court may have to go into defences which could have been raised at the first trial.[54]

D. Exhaustion of Local Remedies

A final issue which arises specifically in the case of foreign judgments is whether there is or should be a requirement that the defendant exhaust local remedies (for example, an appeal or application to set aside the judgment) in the jurisdiction where the judgment was granted, either instead of or before raising fraud as a defence to enforcement. This issue does not arise directly in relation to English judgments.

There is authority to suggest that, where fraud is alleged, a defendant is not required to exhaust local remedies before applying to the English court to impeach the judgment. For example, in *Agbara v Shell Petroleum Development Co of Nigeria Ltd*,[55] the court held that a subsequent appellate process in Nigeria did not militate against the conclusion of breach of natural justice, relying, by analogy, on the approach used for judgments obtained by fraud. The court applied *Adams v Cape Industries plc* where Slade LJ stated:[56]

> It is at least clear that our law does not oblige a defendant who can show that a foreign judgment has been obtained by fraud to have used any available remedy in the foreign court with reference to that fraud if he is successfully to impeach that judgment in our courts: see *Abouloff v Oppenheimer* … and *Jet Holdings* ….

[51] ibid, 344–45 (Staughton LJ).
[52] *Syal v Heyward* [1948] 2 KB 443 (CA).
[53] Which, like the 1920 Act, sets out a reciprocal regime for enforcement of judgments from certain countries.
[54] *Syal v Heyward* (n 52) 448.
[55] *Agbara v Shell Petroleum Development Co of Nigeria Ltd* [2019] EWHC 3340 (QB).
[56] *Adams v Cape Industries plc* [1990] Ch 433 (CA) 569.

If the *Abouloff* principle is retained, bolstered at least in part by the decision in *Takhar*, this element may need to be reconsidered. In cases governed by the Brussels regime,[57] there was a clear requirement to exhaust the remedies in the judgment granting jurisdiction. *Interdesco v Nullifire* concerned the enforcement of a French judgment under the Brussels Convention. It was common ground that the public policy defence in the Convention could cover fraud. The question was whether the *Abouloff* approach to fraud applied in Convention cases. Philips J said not.[58] In Convention cases, the principle that there can be no review on the merits prevails where the foreign court has ruled on precisely the matter. That meant that the *Abouloff* principle could not be applied, at least in its most extreme formulation. Even in situations where the defendant sought to raise a fresh case of fraud, the judge adopted a stricter approach. The court should consider first whether a remedy lies in the foreign jurisdiction in question. On the facts, the defence should have been left to the French court. Cases governed by the Brussels regime involve judgments from the courts of other EU countries. The European rules apply in the context of a system of trust and confidence between European courts. In that context, it may be understandable that a judgment debtor is required to appeal or challenge the judgment in the country where it was granted (which will necessarily be another EU state). However, the time may not yet have arrived when the English court would be prepared to treat every legal system in the world in the same way. Accordingly, it is unlikely that the enforcing court would apply a rule that in every case local remedies must have been exhausted.[59]

VI. CONCLUSION

The decision in *Takhar* has to some extent rehabilitated the principle in *Abouloff* and cemented its landmark status. However, in contrast to the position explained in *Takhar*, in order to challenge a foreign judgment, there is no need to adduce new evidence. This remains a fundamental way in which foreign judgments are not accorded binding status.

Any change to the *Abouloff* principle may well require a more nuanced rule. First, it may be necessary to treat collateral fraud differently from fraud on the merits. If the process of the foreign court is directly impugned, for example, because it is alleged that the judge was bribed, then it is right that that allegation

[57] The Convention (and its successor Regulations), prior to the UK leaving the EU, governed jurisdiction and the enforcement of judgments in European cases.

[58] *Interdesco* (n 25) 189.

[59] This decision was approved and followed by the Court of Appeal in *SISRO v Ampersand Software BV* [1994] ILPr 55 (CA): the defendant sought to challenge the registration of a French judgment on the basis that the judgment had been obtained by fraudulent means even though an appeal on this ground had failed in France. Means of redress were available in France, which meant there was no breach of public policy by registering the judgment in England.

should be capable of being raised as of right before an enforcing court. There is reason to suppose that the decision-making process itself was rendered unreliable by fraud. But in a case like *Aboulof* or *Takhar*, where the fraud is of the party in presenting evidence, sometimes referred to as fraud on the merits, there is no direct reason to impugn the decision-making process of the foreign court. In such a case, has the time come to accord respect to the process of that court, for example, in deciding which witness to believe, unless there is new evidence?

In a system based on mutual trust and confidence between different courts, such as that between EU countries, that position has been reached. However, outside such a reciprocal system, the problem is, as the Privy Council recognised in *AK Investments*, it remains the case that there are foreign courts and foreign courts for these purposes. One answer is to treat all courts as reliable and accept that any issues with the quality of justice or procedures in those courts should properly and only be dealt with by the separate natural justice defence (and/or breach of the right to a fair trial guaranteed by Article 6 of ECHR). Alternatively, if the courts are not ready for that step, and in order to avoid invidious judgments about the reliability of the courts in individual cases, the *Aboulof* principle gives the English court the chance to review the fraud defence for itself. Furthermore, greater use of the abuse of process jurisdiction could limit abuse of the *Aboulof* principle. In cases where there is no new evidence or fraud, which has already been raised and determined, and perhaps where the defendant took a deliberate decision not to raise fraud, the enforcing court should be alive to the possibility that it may be an abuse of process to raise the fraud defence again.

7

AM Luther Co v James Sagor & Co (1921)

SIR DAVID FOXTON*

On 10 February 1920, the Prime Minister David Lloyd George informed the House of Commons that 'trade, in my opinion, will bring an end to the ferocity, the rapine, and the crudities of Bolshevism surer than any other method'.[1] For a country which had committed land and sea forces in support of the Whites in the civil war until October 1919, a trading relationship with the new regime represented a challenging policy shift which did not find universal support in Lloyd George's Cabinet.[2] It faced the further challenge that if Anglo-Soviet trade was to be practicable, the Soviets had to be able to deliver their exports, and the gold necessary to pay for their imports, into this country free from the claims of those asserting title under the pre-Soviet legal order. This, in turn, depended on whether the English courts would recognise the Soviet legal system and the validity of the acts of confiscation on which Soviet title depended. These questions fell to be resolved by the Court of Appeal in *Luther v Sagor*.[3] The Court provided one clear answer: the courts were required to follow the executive's recognition of the Soviet regime. It also offered support for a principle that English courts would not adjudicate on the legality or validity of the acts of foreign governments taking effect within their territory – the

* I would like to thank Dapo Akande for his assistance.

[1] HC Deb 10 February 1920, vol 125, col 46.

[2] Winston Churchill, the Secretary of State for War, was strongly opposed, heading the anti-Bolshevik group in Cabinet. At one stage he contemplated resigning if the Trade Agreement went ahead: MV Glenny, 'The Anglo-Soviet Trade Agreement, March 1921' (1970) 5 *Journal of Contemporary History* 63, 72, 74–76.

[3] *Aksionairnoye Obschestvo Dlia Mechaniches-Koyi Obrabotky Diereva A M Luther (Company for Mechanical Woodworking A M Luther) v James Sagor and Company* [1921] 3 KB 532 (CA). Sir Frederick Pollock, editor of the Law Reports, inserted 'sic' after the title, stating 'in the Record; the Transliteration Is Not Quite Correct or Consistent'. The case is likely to have been of interest to Pollock, whose son had 'narrowly escaped with his life from the Bolsheviks' in 1919, when Chief Commissioner to Poland for the Galicia Fund under the Russian Red Cross: (1920) 36 *Law Quarterly Review* 334, 337.

foreign act of state doctrine. This chapter considers the background to the case; how the Court of Appeal resolved the issues before it, and how the principles relating to recognition of regimes and foreign acts of state have fared over the ensuing century.

I. THE BACKGROUND TO THE DECISION

A. The Political Background

Lloyd George began moves to normalise trading relations with the Soviet regime from the start of 1920.[4] Initially, trade was permitted only with Russian co-operative societies, in the hope that the issue of recognition of the new government could thereby be avoided,[5] but from April onwards the British moved steadily towards a policy of de facto recognition. The Foreign Office, under Earl Curzon of Kedleston, might have been expected to have been at the vanguard of such a major change in strategic direction. However, Curzon was strongly anti-Bolshevik, and less inclined towards a policy which saw Britain acting independently of its wartime allies, and he was cut out of this aspect of government policy in what has been described as a 'blatant snub'.[6] Lloyd George sought to reconcile the decision to pursue trade negotiations with the Soviet Government with the reluctance of the Foreign Office to recognise the new regime by asserting that these were distinct and independent questions. However, as one Foreign Office mandarin noted, 'the resumption of commerce between England and Russia would in the course of a short time involve virtual de facto recognition of the Soviet Government', albeit 'we are anxious that trade should be resumed without recognition'.[7] Mindful of the direction in which trade might lead, the Foreign Office sought to discourage British businesses from dealing with the Soviets whenever possible,[8] and was particularly concerned that the resumption of trade would eliminate one of the bargaining chips which could be used to combat Soviet expansionism.[9]

[4] On this issue see CA White, *British and American Commercial Relations with Soviet Russia, 1918–1924* (Chapel Hill, University of North Carolina Press, 1992) ch 5.

[5] EL Woodward and R Butler (eds), *Documents on British Foreign Policy 1919–1939* series 1, vol 2 (London, HMSO, 1947) No 74, 'Notes of a Meeting of the Heads of Delegations of the American, British, French, and Italian Governments', 16 January 1920. The Allied Supreme Council pronounced that the arrangements did 'not involve any modification of the Allied policy with regard to the Soviet Government'.

[6] White (n 4) 118.

[7] Owen O'Malley to Joseph Gregory of the Foreign Office Russian Department, 'Memorandum Submitted to San Remo Conference Drawing Attention to Salient Points in the Question of the Resumption of Russian Trade', 12 April 1920, FO/371/4304.

[8] White (n 4) 123–24.

[9] ibid 130.

In May 1920, the Soviet delegation under Leonard Krassin arrived in England and began negotiations with English manufacturers, placing orders worth £1,788,500.[10] Talks with the UK Government began on 31 May 1920, Curzon having achieved a consensus within Cabinet on 28 May that there would no agreement on trade 'unless a general agreement on the political questions at issue with the Soviet government were arrived at'.[11] Little progress had been made by the time Krassin and his deputy returned to Russia on 2 July, albeit not long after his departure the Foreign Office certified that Krassin was an 'authorised representative of the Soviet Government' who should be exempt from the processes of the English courts.[12] Negotiations resumed on Krassin's return to London on 1 August 1920.[13] On the British side, the negotiations involved a 'three-sided tug of war' within the Cabinet between Lloyd George, keen to sign a deal as quickly as possible, Curzon who felt the British should hold out until the Soviets had conceded ground on other issues, and Churchill, who hoped to kill the proposal off altogether. As a result, the British did not present the Soviets with a proposal until 29 November. Given the tensions between Downing Street and Carlton Gardens, when negotiations resumed Lloyd George entrusted the task to Sir Robert Horne, President of the Board of Trade.[14]

B. The Legal Background

Support for a principle that the English courts will not enquire into the legality or validity of foreign governmental acts can be found in cases going back to the seventeenth century, with many commentators pointing to the early manifestation of such a rule in *Blad v Bamfield*.[15] In *Blad*, the English court refused to entertain proceedings brought to challenge the validity of Danish letters patent which had been relied upon to seize the applicant's goods in Danish territory. In *Duke of Brunswick v King of Hanover*,[16] Lord Cottenham LC held that '[a] foreign Sovereign coming into this country cannot be made responsible here for

[10] Glenny (n 2) 63 and White (n 4) 129. RH Ullman, *The Anglo-Soviet Accord* (Princeton, Princeton University Press, 1972) 89 notes that 'Krasin is the correct transliteration from the Russian; he himself, however, signed his name Krassin when writing in German or English'. For a brief summary of Krassin's remarkable career see Glenny (n 2) n 6.

[11] 'Conclusions of a Conference of Ministers … on Friday 28 May 1921', CAB 23/21.4.

[12] Letter of 28 July 1920. The issue was eventually tested when an attempt was made to serve Krassin with court process. The Court of Appeal held that, while Earl Curzon's letter might have had the effect of rendering him immune from service of suit when the letter was written, this was no longer the position once his status in Britain became that of Russia's agent under the Trade Agreement, which conferred no such immunity: *Fenton Textile Association Limited v Krassin* (1921) 9 Lloyd's Rep 466 (CA).

[13] Glenny (n 2) 72.

[14] White (n 4) 12.

[15] *Blad v Bamfield* (1674) 3 Swans 604, 607; 36 ER 992, 993.

[16] *Duke of Brunswick v King of Hanover* (1848) 2 HL Cas 1, 17–18; 9 ER 993, 998–99 (HL).

an act done in his sovereign character in his own country' because 'the Courts of this country cannot sit in judgment upon an act of a Sovereign, effected by virtue of his Sovereign authority abroad'. However, the conceptual basis of these, and other decisions,[17] and whether they reflected an independent act of state doctrine, the application of the lex situs to the place of the tort or the assertion of sovereign immunity by the respondent was unclear.[18] A foreign act of state doctrine had, however, been recognised in a number of US cases,[19] and received support from a reasonably clear statement in the High Court of Australia.[20]

So far as recognition is concerned, by 1921 it was already clearly established that a statement by the executive as to the status of a foreign sovereign was decisive before the courts.[21] However, English authority as to the effect of recognition on acts taking place before the date of recognition was decidedly thin. Once again, there was a substantial body of relevant US authority: *Williams v Bruffy*,[22] *Underhill v Hernandez*,[23] and *Oetjen v Central Leisure Leather Co*.[24] Sir Thomas Scrutton, one of the judges in *Luther*, was later to suggest that the US owed the advanced state of its jurisprudence on this subject to the fact that it was 'situate in the neighbourhood of South and Central American Republics, where the life of any Government is precarious and its death rarely by natural causes',[25] although, more recently, the precarious nature of political life in that region has contributed to the development of English jurisprudence as well.

The Treasury took the view that property confiscated by the Soviets – be it goods or gold – and brought to England would be treated as stolen property, but that view was strongly disputed by the Law Officers at a meeting of 3 June 1920, on the basis that the very act of dealing with Krassin would amount to de facto recognition of the Soviet regime.[26] In an impressively bullish opinion, the Law Officers advised that:[27]

> Assuming that the Soviet Government is to be considered as the de facto Government of Russia, and that the gold or goods in question have been nationalised, requisitioned

[17] *Gladstone v Ottoman Bank* (1883) 1 H&M 505, 71 ER 221, KB and *Carr v Fracis Times & Co* [1902] AC 176, (HL).

[18] For proponents of the view that the case did not establish an act of state doctrine see D Lloyd-Jones, 'Act of Foreign State in English Law: The Ghost Goes East' (1981–82) 22 *Virginia Journal of International Law* 432, 444 and M Zander, 'The Act of State Doctrine' (1959) *American Journal of International Law* 826, 837.

[19] In particular *Underhill v Hernandez* (1897) 168 US 250, 252.

[20] *Potter v Broken Hill Pty Ltd* (1906) 3 CLR 479 (HCA) 506.

[21] *Mighell v Sultan of Johore* [1894] 1 QB 149, CA, an action for breach of promise brought by Jenny Mighell against 'the Sultan of the State and Territory of Johore, otherwise known as Albert Baker'.

[22] *Williams v Bruffy* (1877) 96 US 176.

[23] *Underhill v Hernandez* (1897) 168 US 250, 252.

[24] *Oetjen v Central Leisure Leather Co* (1917) 246 US 297.

[25] *Princess Paley Olga v Weisz* [1929] 1 KB 718 (CA) 724.

[26] Ullman (n 10) 101.

[27] FO/371/5434, 'Question for Law Officers, from the Inter-Departmental Russian Trade Committee' of 31 May 1920 and 'Opinion of the Law Officers of the Crown, Gordon Hewart and Ernest M Pollock, Law Officers' Department, to EE Wise for the Prime Minister, 4 June 1920'.

> or confiscated by or under [the] authority of the government, we are of the opinion that a British subject could not successfully initiate litigation to obtain possession of gold or goods sent to this country ... The validity or propriety of the possession of the gold or goods, being the executive act of a de facto foreign government, is not a matter into which the Courts of this country would, in our opinion, have jurisdiction to enquire. The remedy, if any, of persons aggrieved is, we think, exclusively diplomatic and not legal.

A great deal rested on that opinion. The four drafts of the Trade Treaty exchanged between August 1920 and March 1921 all included a provision by which the British Government undertook to take no steps itself to seize Soviet gold or commodities. No such undertaking was offered in relation to actions brought by private interests, and the Soviets had a right of termination if such claims were upheld by the English courts.[28]

II. LUTHER v SAGOR

A. The First Instance Hearing and its Aftermath

Luther was formed in 1898, under the laws of the Empire of Russia, and carried on business until a decree of the Soviet Government of 20 June 1918 declared that all mechanical sawmills of certain kinds were henceforth the property of the Russian Federal Republic. Luther had manufactured timber for the British company Venesta Ltd, which it had stamped with Venesta's trademark. In 1919, agents of the Soviet Government confiscated Luther's mill and stock, and on 14 August 1920, while he was in Britain conducting the trade negotiations, Krassin entered into a contract to sell the Venesta-stamped timber to Sagor & Co, who, with notable *hutzpah*, immediately offered it for sale to Venesta Ltd. Luther became aware of the sale, and made its intention to assert title to the timber apparent. In response, Sagor obtained a letter from the Foreign Office on 5 October 1920 which stated that 'His Majesty's Government assent to the claim of the [Russian Commercial] Delegation to represent in this country a State Government of Russia.' The letter was written during the *quietus* in the trade negotiations, when Curzon was still holding out for better terms, and it may have reflected his ambivalence, or at least his belief that it would be possible to trade with the Soviet regime without recognising it.[29] For whatever reason, the letter stopped notably short of confirming recognition of the Soviet regime, and the weakness of that response may have encouraged Luther to engage in its own

[28] Ullman (n 10) 421–23.

[29] As seen, for example in his letter purporting to refute the assertion of the French diplomat Jules Cambon that the trade negotiations involved 'however you may disguise it, some sort of recognition of the Soviet Government': R Butler and JPT Bury (eds), *Documents on British Foreign Policy 1919–1939* series 1, vol 12 (London, HMSO, 1962) No 709.

correspondence with the Foreign Office. When it did so, it elicited a response from Lord Curzon on 27 November stating that:

> For a certain limited purpose His Majesty's Government has regarded M. Krassin as exempt from the process of the Courts, and also for the like limited purpose His Majesty's Government has assented to the claim that that which M. Krassin represents in this country is a State Government of Russia, but that beyond these propositions the Foreign Office has not gone, nor moreover do these expressions of opinion purport to decide difficult and it may be very special questions of law upon which it may become necessary for the Courts to pronounce. I am to add that His Majesty's Government have never officially recognised the Soviet Government in any way.

The hearing of Luther's claim came before Roche J on 29 November 1920, and Mr Muller of the Soviet trade delegation gave evidence.[30] Judgment was delivered on 21 December 1920.[31] Roche J held that to make good its title, Sagor had to establish the validity of the 1918 Decree. He accepted, on the authority of *Mighell*, that 'the proper source of information as to a foreign power, its status and sovereignty, is the Sovereign of this country through the Government'.[32] However, he found the information provided by the Foreign Office 'guarded', and his own efforts to procure something more definitive were unavailing, the Secretary of State having said 'that he had no further information which he desired to place before me'. On that basis, he was not satisfied that His Majesty's Government had recognised the Soviet Government as the government of a Russian Federative Republic. He did not find it necessary to consider Luther's alternative argument that the 1918 Decree should not be recognised because its content was 'not conformable to the usage of nations', but he rejected Sagor's argument that Luther (whose head office was in territory which now formed part of Estonia, albeit the site of its mill was in Russia) should be treated as an Estonian company and thereby precluded by the Estonian–Russian peace treaty of 2 February 1920 from bringing its claim.

On the very day Roche J handed down judgment, Lenin gave a speech in Moscow in favour of the Trade Agreement, while in London, Lloyd George, Bonar Law and Horne were seeking to iron out the outstanding issues with Krassin.[33] The decision caused immediate consternation among the Soviet trade delegation. That evening, Krassin asked Lloyd George to overturn the decision by legislation if necessary, but Lloyd George was unwilling to pay the high political cost of trying to push such legislation through Parliament.[34] Either Lloyd George was (characteristically) unclear as to his position, or Krassin heard what

[30] The proceedings are reported at (1920) 5 Lloyd's Rep 287.
[31] *Luther v Sagor* [1921] 1 KB 456 (KB).
[32] ibid, 476.
[33] Glenny (n 2) 79–80.
[34] Ullman (n 10) 431.

he wanted to hear. The 'Monthly Review of Revolutionary Movements in British Dominions Overseas and Foreign Countries'[35] for December 1920 noted that on his departure from the UK, Mr Krassin had identified as one of the three obstacles to the successful negotiation of a trade agreement 'the question of the immunity of the gold or goods sold which the Soviet authorities might send to this country in the course of trade'. The report continued:

> M Krassin stated that he was given to understand that something would be done if the courts gave judgment against them. It does not appear, however, that even M Krassin has completely understood the position of the British Government in respect of the courts of law, which he apparently believes to be in some way amenable to Government pressure. M Krassim was clearly of the opinion that in the *Sagor* judgment strings had been pulled against the Soviet authorities. Clever engineer and able politician as he is, his knowledge of the theory of the British Constitution is somewhat to seek.

When regard is had to the rather lacklustre engagement of the Foreign Office during the first instance hearing, Krassin's comments may not have been wholly wide of the mark, even if the strings had been pulled via a different mechanism to that which Krassin may have supposed. The *Sagor* judgment remained an ongoing obstacle to Anglo–Soviet negotiations, with the Soviets halting further shipments of plywood.[36] Georgy Chicherin, First People's Commissar of Foreign Affairs, informed the British that 'confirmation of this [the *Sagor*] decision by a higher court, or similar judgements with respect to Russian gold or goods, would render the trade agreement unworkable, and would therefore be a lawful ground for its immediate automatic termination'.[37] Article XIII of the Trade Agreement signed on 16 March 1921 stated:[38]

> Provided also that if as the result of any action in the Courts of the United Kingdom with the attachment or arrest of any gold, funds, securities, property or commodities not being [i]dentifiable as the exclusive property of a British subject, consigned to the United Kingdom by the Russian Soviet Government or its representatives judgment is delivered by the Court under which such gold, funds, securities, property or commodities are held to be validly attached on account of obligations incurred by the Russian Soviet Government or by any previous Russian Government before the date of the signature of this Agreement, the Russian Soviet Government shall have the right to terminate the Agreement forthwith.

[35] December 1920, CAB 24-118-94, 31.

[36] The 'Monthly Review of Revolutionary Movements in British Dominions Overseas and Foreign Countries' for January 1921', CAB 24-120-15, 34–5.

[37] 'Foreign Countries Report' of 9 February 1921, CAB 24-154-36, 8. See also 'Monthly Review of Revolutionary Movements in British Dominions Overseas and Foreign Countries' for February 1921, CAB 24-120-66, 37.

[38] Anglo-Soviet Trade Agreement 1921: wwi.lib.byu.edu/index.php/Anglo-Soviet_Trade_Agreement (accessed 22 July 2022).

B. The Hearing in the Court of Appeal

Following the signing of the Trade Agreement, Sagor set about bolstering its case for the appeal, writing to the Foreign Office on 12 April 1921 to ask for a certificate confirming that His Majesty's Government had recognised the Soviet Government as the de facto government of Russia. The following day, Mr Gregory, Head of the Foreign Office Russian Section, sought the advice of the Law Officers as to the effect of the Trade Agreement, to be advised that 'it would be correct [to say] that His Majesty's Government recognise the Soviet Government as the de facto Government of Russia' and that 'it necessarily follows that direct diplomatic relations can be established between representatives of the Soviet Government and the Secretary of State for Foreign Affairs'.[39] On 20 April 1921, the Foreign Office wrote providing the requested confirmation, and two days later, the Foreign Office confirmed that the Provisional Government had been recognised as the Government of Russia on coming into power on 14 March 1917, and that it remained in power until 13 December 1917 when it was 'dispersed by the Soviet authorities'.

With the benefit of these clear statements, the Court allowed the appeal, readily concluding that the Soviet Government had now been recognised as the de facto Government of Russia, and that this had happened in April 1921. That brought the two further questions into play: whether de facto as opposed to de jure recognition extended back to June 1918, when the first of the acts relied upon by Sagor in establishing its title occurred, and whether the Court was willing to consider the validity and legality of the Soviet seizures. On the first issue, the Court held that the effect of the Foreign Office correspondence was that the Soviet Government had clearly established itself before the 1918 Decree, although whether that correspondence was preclusive in its effect, or simply the best evidence before the Court, was the subject of differing views.[40]

So far as the second issue is concerned, the judgment of Bankes LJ appears to do no more than apply the lex situs rule in determining title to movables,[41]

[39] JD Gregory to the Law Offices of the Crown, No 66, 13 April 1921 and 'Report of the Law Officers' of 18 April 1921, FO 418/55.

[40] Bankes LJ can be read as supporting both approaches: *Luther v Sagor* (n 3) 542–43; Warrington and Scrutton LJJ the preclusive analysis at 548–49 and 555–57 respectively (but with the Court having to determine the issue in the absence of a statement by the government).

[41] ibid, 545–46. Some commentators have interpreted *Luther* in this way: eg, K Lipstein, 'Recognition of Governments and the Application of Foreign Laws' (1950) 36 *Transactions of the Grotius Society* 157, 159 and Zander (n 18) 835. The Court of Appeal later suggested that the decisions in *Luther* and *Princess Olga* 'may now be subject to some reinterpretation. In those cases there was no attempt to deflect recognition of the Russian decrees by reference to English public policy. In such circumstances it may not have mattered much whether the courts gave effect to those decrees under the more limited doctrine of the territorial act of state principle or the wider principle of non-justiciability': *Kuwait Airways Corpn v Iraqi Airways Co (Nos 4 and 5)* [2002] 2 AC 883 (CA) [322] (Brooke LJ).

but Warrington LJ – making the most of his appearance as a substitute in *the* Court of Appeal by producing the most notable judgment – appeared to support a rule of immunity ratione materiae in relation to certain acts of foreign states, holding that 'it is well settled that the validity of the acts of an independent sovereign government in relation to property and persons within its jurisdiction cannot be questioned in the Courts of this country'.[42] Scrutton LJ referred to the doctrine of sovereign immunity (which only applies when a sovereign is directly impleaded) and reasoned, wholly impermissibly, that it followed from the Soviet Government's immunity in proceedings brought to challenge its title to the goods in England that there could be no 'indirect' challenge premised on that government's inability to transfer good title to the defendant.[43] However, he also lent some support to the nascent act of state doctrine, referring to the Soviet legislation as 'acts of a sovereign state the validity of which cannot be questioned by the Courts of this country, unless it is possible to do so for the second reason argued before us, incompatibility with the moral and political policy of the United Kingdom'.[44] As to the latter suggestion, he noted that 'it appears a serious breach of international comity, if a state is recognized as a sovereign independent state, to postulate that its legislation is "contrary to essential principles of justice and morality"'.[45] In a memorable swipe at the post-war fiscal burden, he continued:

> Individuals must contribute to the welfare of the state, and at present British citizens who may contribute to the state more than half their income in income tax and super tax, and a large proportion of their capital in death duties, can hardly declare a foreign state immoral which considers (though we may think wrongly) that to vest individual property in the state as representing all the citizens is the best form of proprietary right.

That nascent doctrine of foreign act of state received unequivocal support in *Princess Paley Olga v Weisz*, Russell LJ holding that 'this court will not inquire into the legality of acts done by a foreign government against its own subjects in respect of property situate in its own territory'.[46] In that case, there was a finding that the taking of the property in issue was valid under Soviet law, but the Court made it clear that the act of state doctrine would have answered the Princess' claim even if this had not been the case.[47] As FA Mann noted, 'the very feature of the doctrine of the foreign act of State' is to 'foreclose any inquiry into the validity of the act'.[48]

[42] *Luther v Sagor* (n 3) 548–49.
[43] As Lipstein noted (n 41) 159 'an independent, and it is believed indefensible, train of thought'.
[44] *Luther v Sagor* (n 3) 556.
[45] ibid, 558–59.
[46] *Olga v Weisz* (n 25) 736. See also 728 (Sankey LJ) and 724–25 (Scrutton LJ).
[47] ibid, 723–25 (Scrutton LJ), 728–30 (Sankey LJ) and 736 (Russell LJ).
[48] FA Mann, *Foreign Affairs in English Courts* (Oxford, OUP, 1986) 168.

C. The Immediate Aftermath

Luther appealed to the House of Lords,[49] but the case was compromised before argument. The Court of Appeal had, therefore, settled the status of goods sold into this jurisdiction under the Trade Agreement.[50] However the status of confiscated bullion brought into this jurisdiction, and whether it could be attached by those holding sovereign debt of the ancien regimes, remained unresolved. This had been a particular concern of the Soviets throughout the negotiations, and remained a sufficiently sensitive issue after the Court of Appeal decision for Krassin and Horne to agree that a small quantity of confiscated gold would be shipped to England to be the subject of a test case. Horne noted that the gold would have to be 'subject to such order as the Courts of the United Kingdom may pronounce in accordance with the usual judicial procedure'. If a final decision of a court of first instance was in favour of Soviet title, then the British Government would put in place a regime for the use of the gold to pay for British exports and/or to its re-export to other countries as appropriate.[51] If it was adverse, the Soviet Government had the right to cancel the Trade Agreement. Horne's confidence in a successful outcome, and in the fact that the case would not progress beyond first instance, is noticeable – as White noted, he was 'clearly anticipating no problem in establishing the Soviet title'.[52] That test case was brought on in the Chancery Division, in *AG Marshall v Mary Grinbaum*.[53] The Bank of England participated in the case, obtaining expert evidence from Dr VR Idelson that, as a matter of Russian law, Soviet gold roubles were not attachable in respect of obligations of the previous Tsarist and Provisional governments.[54] Peterson J accepted Dr Idelson's evidence 'on the basis of a rather dubious tsarist law that denied state bondholders any legal claim to the state gold reserves',[55] and on that narrow basis held that the gold could not be attached in respect of debts due from previous Russian governments.

Christine White has stated that 'the outcome of the two cases in the British courts … had the effect of transforming the [Trade A]greement from a primarily academic instrument into one that provided the Soviets with the ability to trade direct with Britain'.[56] There was an immediate increase in timber, grain

[49] Papers relating to the appeal appear in the Parliamentary Archive: HL/PO/JO/10/10/720A/24 and HL/PO/JO/10/10/701/669.

[50] A further challenge to the Krassin-Sagor timber contract failed in *Bragoseo Ltd v J Sagor & Co* (1921) 8 Lloyd's Rep 388.

[51] The so-called 'Gold Letter' from Horne to Krassin of 11 January 1921 which was attached to, but not formally part of, the Trade Agreement: *DBFP* (n 29), series 1, vol 12, No 828.

[52] White (n 4) 173.

[53] *AG Marshall v Mary Grinbaum* (1921) 8 Lloyd's Rep 342.

[54] On Dr Idelson see VV Veeder, 'The Lena Goldfields Arbitration: The Historical Roots of Three Ideas' (1998) 47 *International & Comparative Law Quarterly* 747, n 61. At n 62, Veeder notes that Dr Idelson was paid 100 guineas by the Bank of England's solicitors, Freshfields & Leese, for his work.

[55] White (n 4) 173.

[56] ibid 171.

and petroleum imports from Russia, and some increase in British exports,[57] the court decisions and the Trade Agreement combining to confer 'legitimacy' on what had previously been seen as an outlaw state.[58] However, the trade balance was always in the Soviet's favour,[59] and after the ARCOS raid, and the resultant revelations of acts of espionage and agitprop by the Soviet representatives, the British broke off diplomatic relations and renounced the Trade Agreement in 1927.[60]

III. SUBSEQUENT LEGAL DEVELOPMENTS

As Popplewell LJ has noted, *Luther v Sagor* addressed two 'separate and distinct steps … whether the Court is bound to treat a body as a sovereign government … [and] … whether, in the light of the answer to the first question, issues dependent upon the acts of such a government are justiciable'.[61] *Luther* addressed both issues in fewer than 5,000 words. The Supreme Court's decision on recognition and aspects of the foreign act of state doctrine in *Maduro Board of the Central Bank of Venezuela v Guaidó Board of the Central Bank of Venezuela* exceeds 30,000 words,[62] and the Supreme Court's treatment of the foreign act of state doctrine in *Belhaj v Straw* is over twice that length.[63] The contrast is not simply a consequence of the lost art of the judicial laconic, but reflects the extent to which *Luther* opened up scope for argument on these issues – and in particular the foreign act of state doctrine – but did relatively little to resolve them. In Karl Lipstein's memorable phrase, act of state as it emerged from that decision was a 'slogan and not a rule'.[64] The remainder of this chapter considers the subsequent development of the principles so economically sketched out in *Luther*.

IV. RECOGNITION OF FOREIGN GOVERNMENTS

A. The 'One Voice' Principal

Recognition serves to determine not simply title to property or rights vested in a sovereign state, but also which body of law comprises the law of the state

[57] Imports were £882,863 in 1921 and £2,765,061 the following year. The export figures were £2,181,007 and £3,678,525: HC Deb 17 July 1923, vol 166, col 219.

[58] White (n 4) 175.

[59] Glenny (n 2) 66.

[60] H Flory, 'The Arcos Raid and the Rupture of Anglo-Soviet Relations, 1927' [1977] *Journal of Contemporary History* 707.

[61] *Mohamed v Breish & Ors* [2020] EWCA Civ 637, [2020] 1 CLC 858, [69].

[62] *Maduro Board of the Central Bank of Venezuela v Guaidó Board of the Central Bank of Venezuela* [2021] UKSC 57, [2022] 2 WLR 167.

[63] *Belhaj v Straw* [2017] UKSC 3, [2017] AC 964.

[64] Lipstein (n 41) 158.

in question, and which adjudications represent decisions of the courts of that state. Should such a significant issue be one which the court determines itself on the evidence before it, or should a statement by the UK Government as to its position be conclusive? The majority in *Luther* supported the latter view, and while there have been periodic attempts by judges to make their own determination of this issue, or at least to ensure that the position as certified by the executive corresponds with reality,[65] the conclusiveness of such an executive statement is now firmly established.[66] This rule reflects the fact that foreign relations are entrusted to the executive branch of government. For that reason, the issue of which body should be recognised as the government of a sovereign state is one on which the judicial branch of government should defer to the executive branch under the 'one voice' principle,[67] rather than offering its own (possibly competing) view.

The UK Government announced in 1980 that it would no longer formally recognise governments following an unconstitutional regime change,[68] and that the UK Government's attitude to the new regime should 'be inferred from the nature of the dealings, if any, which we may have with it'.[69] This restatement of policy notwithstanding, there have continued to be (rare) occasions on which the government has either recognised, or formally declined to recognise, a new regime.[70] In the absence of such statements, the issue of whether a particular body is the government of a foreign state falls to be determined by the court as a matter of fact.[71]

B. Interpreting the Executive Voice

Difficulties have continued to arise when (as in *Luther*) the executive has spoken in an equivocal voice, or where the executive's words appear to be inconsistent with either its own actions or an obvious and undeniable state of affairs 'on the ground'.[72]

[65] For the development of the position see *Maduro* (n 62) [70]–[77].

[66] *Duff Development Co Ltd v Government of Kelantan* [1942] AC 797 (HL) and *Maduro* (n 62) [78].

[67] *Government of the Republic of Spain v SS Arantzazu Mendi (The Arantzazu Mendi)* [1939] AC 25 (HL) 264.

[68] HC Deb 25 April 1980 vol 983 col 277 (Statement of the Lord Privy Seal) and HL Deb 28 April 1980 vol 408 cols 1121–1122 (Statement of the Secretary of State for Foreign and Commonwealth Affairs).

[69] HC Deb 23 May 1980 vol 985 col 385.

[70] *Maduro* (n 62) [68].

[71] *Republic of Somalia v Woodhouse Drake & Carey (Suisse) SA* [1993] QB 4 (QB); *Kuwait Airways Corpn v Iraqi Airways Co (No 5)* [1999] CLC 31 (Com Ct) 65.

[72] See, eg, Lord Denning's attempt in *Hesperides Hotel Ltd & anr v Aegean Holidays Limited & anr* [1978] QB 205, (CA) to recognise the laws of the Turkish Republic of Northern Cyprus on the basis of the regime's de facto control, even though the UK Government had withheld such recognition.

In *Carl Zeiss Stiftung v Rayner and Keeler Limited*,[73] an issue arose as to the status of legislation of the government of the German Democratic Republic (GDR). The Foreign Office certified that the Government of the GDR was not recognised de jure or de facto, but that the Soviet Union was entitled de jure to exercise sovereign authority over eastern Germany. The House of Lords was able to reconcile the terms of the Foreign Office certificate with the practical reality of the East German regime by treating the enactments of the GDR Government as those of a subsidiary body of the Soviet Union, even though the Soviet Union had itself disclaimed such sovereign authority. Lord Wilberforce[74] hinted that if this route had not been open, there might have been some scope for limited judicial recognition of GDR legislation concerning matters of private rights or acts of ordinary administration.

A similar pragmatism can be seen in *Gur Corp v Trust Bank of Africa Ltd*,[75] in which a three-way dispute arose between the 'Ciskei Public Body of Works', its contractor and the contractor's guarantor. The Foreign Office informed the Court that the so-called independent homeland was not recognised, either de jure or de facto, as an independent sovereign state, but failed to answer its enquiry as to which state was recognised as exercising sovereign authority within the territory of Ciskei. Once again, the Court was able to overcome any difficulties by treating the legislative enactments of Ciskei as delegated legislation by a subordinate body of the Republic of South Africa Government. However, Sir John Donaldson saw 'great force' in Lord Wilberforce suggestion that there was room for a limited enclave of judicial de facto recognition in some cases, 'since it is one thing to treat a state or government as being "without the law" but quite another to treat the inhabitants of its territory as "outlaws" who cannot effectively marry, beget legitimate children, purchase goods on credit or undertake countless day-to-day activities having legal consequences'.[76]

More recently, two decisions of the Court of Appeal held that if the effect of an executive certificate is ambiguous, the court is entitled to look more widely at the dealings which the UK Government has had with the new regime for the purpose of interpreting the certificate. The first, *Mohamed v Breish and others*,[77] concerned the status of the Government of National Accord of Libya, which the Foreign and Commonwealth Office (FCO) confirmed was 'the legitimate executive authorit[y] of Libya', in a certificate which did not use the word recognition. The second, *Maduro Board of the Central Bank of Venezuela v*

[73] *Carl Zeiss Stiftung v Rayner and Keeler Limited* [1967] 1 AC 853 (HL). In the *Maduro* case in the Court of Appeal [2020] EWCA Civ 1249, [2021] QB 455, Males LJ noted at [118] that this represented 'the solution to the problem, while remaining loyal to the "one voice" principle'.

[74] *Carl Zeiss Stiftung v Rayner* (n 73) 954–55.

[75] *Gur Corp v Trust Bank of Africa Ltd* [1987] QB 599 (CA).

[76] ibid, 622. See also *MM v NA (Declaration of Marital Status: Unrecognised State)* [2020] EWHC 93 Fam [66] (Roberts J).

[77] *Mohamed v Breish* [2020] EWCA Civ 637, [2020] 1 CLC 858 (CA).

Guaidó Board of the Central Bank of Venezuela,[78] involved a dispute between two bodies each claiming to be the validly appointed board of the Central Bank of Venezuela. In *Maduro*, the terms of the FCO certificates – stating that 'the United Kingdom now recognises Juna Guaidó as the constitutional interim President of Venezuela' – might be thought to have been clear enough, but as any contract lawyer well knows, once the interpretative exercise ceases to be confined to the four corners of the document under consideration, the scope for identifying potential ambiguities is correspondingly enlarged. Males LJ noted that executive statements 'may be incomplete or ambiguous, either deliberately, for example, in a case of particular sensitivity, or through inadvertence'.[79] In that case, while informing the Court of its recognition of Mr Guaidó, the UK Government still maintained diplomatic relations with the Maduro regime, had denied that status to Guaidó officials, and might be said to be speaking with two voices itself. In these circumstances, the Court of Appeal held that it was perfectly possible for the UK Government to recognise Mr Guaidó as the de jure President (the person *entitled* to be President), and Mr Maduro as the de facto President, and that looking at the 'ambiguous, or at any rate less than unequivocal'[80] statement in the context of the government's other actions, further enquiry was necessary.

However, this approach was firmly rejected by the Supreme Court when hearing the *Maduro* appeal. The Court was not permitted to 'look beyond the terms of the certificate' for the purpose of identifying any ambiguity in its effect,[81] and if there was an ambiguity on its face, the only permissible course was to seek clarification from the FCO.[82] The distinction between recognition of a government de jure and de facto, which the Court of Appeal had relied upon when identifying an ambiguity in circumstances in which the government's actions might appear to bely its words, was also criticised. Lord Lloyd-Jones observed that 'great caution is necessary in employing these concepts as they are not precise terms of art and their meaning may vary according to context'.[83] In short, in those cases where the government issued an express statement of recognition or non-recognition, it was a case of 'do as I say, whatever I do'.

It is now clear, therefore, that if the executive chooses to issue a statement as to recognition, then the statement and any further clarification of it by the executive exclusively occupy the field. If the executive chooses not to make such a statement, then the court must identify the government or head of state by making its own findings of fact. These are mutually exclusive approaches.

[78] *Maduro* (n 73).
[79] ibid, [107]. See also *Duff Development v Kelantan* [1924] AC 797 (HL) 82–25 (Lord Sumner).
[80] *Maduro* (n 73) [123].
[81] *Maduro* (n 62) [93].
[82] ibid, [96].
[83] ibid, [84]–[86], [99].

V. FOREIGN ACTS OF STATE

The decision in *Luther* briefly sketched out the basis for a foreign act of state doctrine, but the task of filling in that outline was left to subsequent decisions. Where does the doctrine stand now that the highest court has had the opportunity critically to examine it on three occasions?[84] It is convenient to examine the current state of doctrine by reference to the three potential rules identified by the majority[85] in the most extended consideration by the highest court, *Belhaj v Straw*: (i) a rule of private international law that a foreign state's legislation or other laws would normally be recognised and treated as valid in relation to acts within its territorial jurisdiction (rule 1);[86] (ii) a rule that a domestic court will recognise, and not question, foreign executive acts which take place or take effect within its territory (rule 2);[87] and (iii) a rule that the courts will not adjudicate on matters which involve a challenge to the lawfulness of the act of a foreign state of such a nature that a municipal judge cannot or ought not rule on it (rule 3).

A. The Territorial Limitation

Rules 1 and 2 both reflect the formulation of the foreign act of state doctrine in *Luther* as one limited to the effect of foreign legislation or executive acts *within the territory of the foreign state*. For that reason, in *The Jupiter (No 3)*,[88] Hill J refused to give effect to decrees of the Russian Socialist Federative Soviet Republic purporting to dissolve a ship-owning company and take ownership of its ships, there being no evidence that the ship in issue had ever been within the Republic's territory. This outcome can be rationalised on private international law grounds, as an application of the lex situs rule, or on the basis that the recognition of the sovereignty of foreign states only extends as far as the territorial limits of that sovereignty.[89] Despite occasional suggestions to the contrary,[90] it is now clear

[84] *Kuwait Airways* (n 41), *Belhaj v Straw* (n 63) and *Maduro* (n 62).

[85] *Belhaj v Straw* (n 63). Lord Neuberger, with whom Lord Wilson, Baroness Hale and Lord Clarke agreed, although Lord Wilson stated that he was not expressing any view on those issues which it was not necessary for the Court to decide. The first and third rules identified by Lord Mance at [11] are in broadly similar terms, but his version of the second rule differs in important respects. As Lord Lloyd-Jones noted in *Maduro* (n 62) [112], 'the judgments … reveal widely differing views on a number of aspects of the topic'.

[86] *Belhaj v Straw* (n 63) [121].

[87] ibid, [122].

[88] *The Jupiter (No 3)* [1927] P 122 (Ad) 145. See also *In re Russian Bank for Foreign Trade* [1933] 1 Ch 745 (Ch) 766–67. See also *Peer International Corp v Termidor Music Publishers (No 1)* [2004] Ch 212 (CA) (Cuban legislation expropriating intellectual property not given effect in respect of UK copyright).

[89] *Kuwait Airways* (n 41) [318].

[90] See, eg, *Olga v Weisz* (n 25) 736; *Anglo-Iranian Oil v Jaffrate (The Rose Mary)* [1953] 1 WLR 247 (SC of Aden) 258.

that, within those territorial limits, no distinction is drawn between acts of the foreign state affecting its own nationals, and those affecting foreign nationals.[91] Equally, the fact that acts taking effect within the foreign sovereign's territory may reverberate outside that territory – for example where appointments made to a state body determine who is then able to give instruction as to the disposition of assets abroad – does not preclude the application of the doctrine.[92]

However, rule 3 is not so confined.[93] The principle now reflected in this rule first emerged as a result of the extraordinary facts of *Buttes Gas & Oil Co v Hammer (No 3)*,[94] a libel claim in which it was alleged that the Ruler of Sharjah had colluded with Buttes Gas to backdate a decree extending Sharjah's territorial waters. In the House of Lords, after referring to the foreign act of state doctrine, Lord Wilberforce identified a 'more general principle that the courts will not adjudicate on the transactions of sovereign States'.[95] That principle was engaged because adjudicating on the *Buttes* dispute would have required a municipal court to determine contentious issues of international law such as the maritime boundaries between three states, and whether these states had breached their obligations under international law.[96] The principle was subsequently applied in cases raising disputes of international law between sovereign states, in *JH Rayner (Mincing Lane) Ltd v Department of Trade and Industry*,[97] and *Westland Helicopters v Arab Organisation for Industrialisation*.[98]

In *Belhaj*, rule 3 was described as encompassing a number of different, but connected, rules of judicial abstention: the court, as a municipal court, would not decide on 'dealings between sovereign states', 'the legality of acts of a foreign government in the conduct of foreign affairs' and 'international treaties and conventions, which have not become incorporated into domestic law by the legislature'.[99] It was suggested in *Belhaj* that judges should 'not be enthusiastic in declining to determine a claim under the third rule',[100] and that in some cases

[91] *In re Claim by Helbert Wagg & Co* [1956] 1 Ch 323 (Ch) 348–49; *Yukos Capital v OJSC Rosneft Oil* [2014] QB 458 (CA) [42].

[92] *Maduro Board* (n 62) [147]–[150].

[93] *Belhaj v Straw* (n 63) [123]. See also *Yukos Capital* (n 91) which suggested that the principle formulated by Lord Wilberforce was 'not so much a separate principle, but a more general and fundamental principle of non-justiciability' ([48]) which in 'special, and perhaps, exceptional circumstances' applied extra-territorially ([66]).

[94] *Buttes Gas & Oil Co v Hammer (No 3)* [1982] AC 888 (HL) in which, as Lloyd-Jones noted, 'the House of Lords acknowledges unequivocally for the first time a principal of judicial restraint or abstention rendering certain sovereign acts of foreign states non-justiciable': 'Act of Foreign State in English Law: The Ghost Goes East' (n 18) 434.

[95] *Buttes Gas* (n 94) 931.

[96] ibid, 937.

[97] *JH Rayner (Mincing Lane) Ltd v Department of Trade and Industry* [1990] 2 AC 418 (HL).

[98] *Westland Helicopters Ltd v Arab Organisation for Industrialisation* [1994] 2 Lloyd's Rep 608 (Com Ct).

[99] *Belhaj v Straw* (n 63) [128].

[100] ibid, [140].

where it might otherwise apply, the rule might be ousted by public policy or international law considerations.[101]

B. The Types of Governmental Acts which Engage the Doctrine

Rules 1 and 2 broadly concern acts of the legislative and executive branches of government.[102] The majority of the Supreme Court in *Belhaj* formulated the rules applicable to acts of those two branches of government in different terms. In particular, the Court was willing to contemplate the application of rule 1[103] and rule 3[104] to acts of the foreign state inflicting personal injury, but not rule 2,[105] which was discussed exclusively by reference to acts interfering with property. In *Maduro*, the Supreme Court rejected the argument that rule 2 was *confined* to acts interfering with property, holding that it applied (at least) to the acts of appointment to a public body in issue in that case.[106] In places, Lord Lloyd-Jones appears to leave open the possibility that rule 2 was no narrower than rule 1 in this respect.[107] A possible rationalisation is that all three rules are *capable* of applying to such acts, but that the scope of the application of public policy or international law exceptions to the rule in such a context is greater for executive than legislative acts.

What of acts by the third branch of government, the judiciary? *Luther* did not touch on this issue, and there are separate rules which determine whether foreign judgments have preclusive effect or can be the subject of enforcement proceedings under English law. In particular, there is a requirement that the jurisdiction of the foreign court is established on a basis recognised at common law. Like the foreign act of state doctrine, these are essentially territorial – 'all jurisdiction is territorial and *extra territorium jusdicenti, impune non paretur*', as Lord Selborne noted in *Sirdar Gurdyal Singh v Rajah of Faridkote*.[108] This is certainly true of jurisdiction based on presence, and the other forms of jurisdiction based on submission or voluntary participation all involve some nexus between the defendant and the actions of the foreign court within its own

[101] ibid, [157].

[102] Broadly because not all laws of a state may derive from acts of legislation, for example the common law.

[103] *Belhaj v Straw* (n 63) [159]. As would Lord Sumption in his 'municipal act of state' category: [229], [232]. Lord Mance limited the first category to actions against property: [11(iii)(b)].

[104] *Belhaj v Straw* (n 63) [123] referring to *R (Khan) v Secretary of State for Foreign and Commonwealth Affairs* [2014] EWCA Civ 24, [2014] 1 WLR 872) and [160(iv].

[105] *Belhaj v Straw* (n 63) [160].

[106] *Maduro Board* (n 62) [139]–[146].

[107] ibid, [139]–[140], [181].

[108] *Sirdar Gurdyal Singh v Rajah of Faridkote* [1894] AC 670 (PC) 683–84. See also *Adams v Cape Industries Plc* [1990] Ch 433 (CA) 517–518.

territory.[109] Where the territorial requirement is satisfied, the English court will not re-open the foreign judgment on its merits,[110] subject to certain long-standing exceptions of judgments procured by fraud, judgments which are contrary to public policy or where the defendant was denied due process.[111]

The argument that judicial decisions of a foreign state benefit from the act of state doctrine in its full rigour was rejected by the Privy Council in *Altimo Holdings and Investment Ltd v Kyrgyz Mobil Tel Ltd*,[112] so far as prospective decisions of a foreign legal system are concerned, and in relation to past decisions in *Yukos Capital SARL v Rosneft Oil Co (No 2)*,[113] albeit both cases make it clear that assessments of actual or the risk of prospective misconduct by a foreign court should only be made on cogent evidence.[114] That difference in approach was justified because 'sovereigns act on their own plane: they are responsible to their own peoples, but internationally they are responsible only in accordance with international law and internationally recognised norms'. Courts, in contrast, 'are always responsible for their acts, both domestically and internationally'.

This conclusion can be justified on other grounds. Foreign court decisions are essentially adjudicative – purporting to apply a pre-existing body of legal principle to pre-existing facts as found by the court. Where the requirements for recognising a foreign judgment are satisfied, the determination by that court of any issues will ordinarily be decisive as between the parties in litigation in this jurisdiction. If the foreign court's adjudication is not preclusive, because it does not meet the requirements for recognition under English law, it will remain open to the judgment creditor to seek to establish its case de novo in England, if the English courts have jurisdiction and the law applied by the foreign court is applicable under English choice of law principles (just as it remained open to Rosneft in the *Yukos* case to rely on the allegations which had featured in the Russian set-aside judgment to the extent that they gave rise to a public policy defence to enforcement under English law).

C. Challenges to the Validity of Foreign Acts of State under Foreign Law

Formulations of the foreign act of state doctrine have often framed it as a doctrine which prevents the courts from adjudicating on the *validity* of such acts. Scrutton LJ referred in *Luther* to 'acts of a sovereign state the validity of

[109] L Collins, *Dicey, Morris & Collins on the Conflict of Laws*, 16th edn (London, Sweet & Maxwell, 2018) rr 43 (para 14R-05) and 47 (para 14R-108).
[110] ibid r 58 (para 14R-118).
[111] ibid r 50 (para 14R-137); r 51 (para 14R-152) and r 52 (para 14R-162).
[112] *AK Investment CJSC v Kyrgyz Mobil Tel Ltd* [2011] UKPC 7, [2012] 1 WLR 1804 [101].
[113] *Yukos Capital* (n 91) [73].
[114] ibid, [86]–[87].

which cannot be questioned by the Courts of this country',[115] and Warrington LJ similarly described the question before the court as whether it was entitled to investigate the validity of the proceedings by which the Soviet Government had vested itself with title.[116] It has subsequently been noted that the doctrine only applies when the court is being asked to determine the *legal* effectiveness of a foreign act of state, rather than its existence as a matter of fact. As Rix LJ noted in *Yukos*, it is this which distinguishes cases raising the act of state doctrine from routine references to foreign legislation applicable under English choice of law rules.[117]

It is possible to find decisions permitting challenges before the English court to the constitutionality of foreign executive acts under the foreign constitution. The Court of Appeal in *Al-Jedda v Secretary of State for Defence*[118] was willing to consider the constitutionality of executive acts taking place in Iraq under the Iraqi Constitution. The majority in *Belhaj* were unwilling to formulate rule 2 in terms which would ordinarily apply to *unlawful* executive acts, Lord Neuberger observing that if an executive act was unlawful according to the law of the territory concerned, he was not convinced as a matter of principle that it should not be treated as unlawful by a court of the UK. For this reason. Lord Neuberger formulated rule 2 as a principle which applied to executive acts which were lawful, or at least not unlawful, under the law of the territory where they took effect. He was willing to contemplate that the effect of unlawful acts relating to property and property rights might be recognised, to provide clarity and certainty, but he left the point open. Lord Mance would have confined the application of rule 2 to unlawful acts undertaken in conditions of unrest or civil emergency,[119] but as Lord Sumption noted, limiting the doctrine to 'cases involving a general breakdown of civil society or states without law' would involve 'formidable definitional problems'.[120]

It might have been possible to confine the application of rule 2 to unlawful acts of particular kinds. A distinction is drawn for the purposes of the Crown act of state doctrine between 'high acts of policy'[121] and 'any ordinary governmental act'.[122] A similar distinction, between executive or administrative acts intended to be subject to ordinary laws and more fundamental exercises of sovereign power, was drawn by Rix LJ in *Yukos*.[123] He distinguished between executive

[115] *Luther v Sagor* (n 3) 557.
[116] ibid, 546.
[117] *Yukos Capital* (n 91) [110].
[118] *Al-Jedda v Secretary of State for Defence* [2010] EWCA Civ 758, [2011] QB 773 [74] (Arden LJ) and [189] (Elias LJ).
[119] *Belhaj v Straw* (n 63) [11(b)] and [38].
[120] ibid, [232].
[121] *Nissan v Attorney-General* [1970] AC 179 (HL) 211–12 (Lord Reid).
[122] Although contrast the observation in Lloyd-Jones 'Act of Foreign State in English Law' (n 18) 436 that 'no purpose is served by seeking to draw analogies between these different principles'.
[123] *Yukos Capital* (n 91) [133].

and administrative taxes imposed pursuant to a code which was 'designed to operate according to law and to be subject to legal and indeed judicial rulings', and 'legislation or decrees or the acts of commanders in the field'. It could have been argued that unlawful executive acts should only attract the benefits of rule 2 in cases in which the executive acknowledged at the time of the act that it was one of 'high policy' involving the application of core sovereign powers (with whatever opprobrium that might entail), rather than attempting to 'operat[e] under the colour' of the ordinary legal system. However, rule 2 has not been so confined, the Supreme Court in *Maduro* confirming its application to unlawful executive acts within the territory of the foreign state. Lord Lloyd-Jones referred to 'a substantial line of authority'[124] in support of such a principle including Warrington and Scrutton LJJ in *Luther*,[125] and all the members of the court in *Princess Paley Olga*.[126] The application of rule 2 to unlawful acts was 'founded on the respect due to the sovereignty and independence of foreign states' and was 'intended to promote comity in inter-state relations'.

What of rule 1? There are cases in which an English court has investigated the validity of acts or decrees of a foreign state under the foreign constitution, but the cases were concerned with the extra-territorial consequences of the foreign legislation in issue.[127] In *Buck v Attorney-General*,[128] Diplock LJ held that issues raised as to the validity of the Sierra Leone Constitution itself were not justiciable. In *Belhaj*, Lord Mance appeared to contemplate the court hearing 'any legal challenge permissible under the foreign legal system'[129] including, in the case of laws, their constitutionality.[130] However, following *Maduro*, it is now clear that such a challenge falls foul of rule 1, not just in cases in which the challenge to the legislation involved politically contentious issues, such as alleged corruption in the legislative process or the expropriatory or discriminatory nature of the legislation,[131] but also where it is said that there has been some formal or procedural deficiency, such as the failure to publish the legislation in the official gazette.[132] Disputes as to the proper interpretation of foreign legislation do not engage rule 1,[133] but what of the position where the consequence of one interpretation would be to withdraw the legal basis for delegated legislation or the

[124] *Maduro Board* (n 62) [135].
[125] *Luther v Sagor* (n 3) 548, 558–59.
[126] *Olga v Weisz* (n 25) 729–30, 736.
[127] *In Re Amand* [1941] 2 KB 239 (KB); [1942] 1 KB 445 (CA) (in which the Court determined that a Dutch decree was unconstitutional, albeit the decree in question purported to have effect in England); *A/S Tallinna Laevauhisus v Tallinna Shipping Co* (1947) 80 Lloyd's Rep 99 (CA) (the constitutionality of an Estonian statute so far as it effected funds in England).
[128] *Buck v Attorney-General* [1965] Ch 745 (CA) 770.
[129] *Belhaj v Straw* (n 63) [65].
[130] ibid, [73(iii)].
[131] Examples given by Rix LJ in *Yukos Capital* (n 91) [110].
[132] *Maduro Board* (n 62) [177]–[178].
[133] ibid, [179].

administrative acts or decisions of executive bodies? The effect of *Maduro* is that these subordinate decrees or decisions engage rules 1 or 2 in their own right. It was for that reason that the validity of the Transitional Statute in that case was ultimately irrelevant to the status of the appointments made by the recognised Government of Venezuela before the English courts.[134]

D. The Intersection of Foreign Legislative or Executive Acts and Foreign Court Decisions

The application of the foreign act of state doctrine can give rise to particular complexities in those cases in which the acts said to constitute the foreign act of state have themselves been the subject of, or are said to involve, decisions of that state's courts.

In *Maduro* the intersection arose because the foreign acts of state in issue – legislative and executive – had been held to be *invalid* as a matter of Venezuelan law by the highest court of Venezuela. As the Supreme Court noted,[135] the result was that there were two bodies with sovereign power in Venezuela (the executive, as recognised by the UK Government, and the judiciary), each of which had taken a relevant act (the former in making the appointments, the latter in declaring them invalid as a matter of Venezuelan law). This raised the potential for a conflict between rule 1 and rule 2 (as applicable to unlawful executive acts) first identified by Lord Neuberger in *Belhaj*.[136] In *Maduro*, Lord Lloyd-Jones rejected the argument that, in these circumstances, the foreign act of state doctrine required the English court to defer to the acts of the executive, notwithstanding the decision of the judicial branch of government that the acts were invalid. He held that the foreign act of state doctrine was premised on the objectional nature of the courts of one state intruding in the internal affairs of another,[137] and observed:[138]

> This rationale can have no application, however, where courts in this jurisdiction merely give effect to a judicial decision whereby the courts of the foreign state concerned, acting within their proper constitutional sphere, have previously declared the executive acts to be unlawful and nullities. If a UK court were to give effect to such a foreign judgment, it would not itself be sitting in judgment on the executive act but giving effect to the view of it taken by the judicial branch of government within the foreign state. Lord Neuberger's Rule 2 could therefore have no application to such a situation.

[134] ibid, [179]–[180].
[135] ibid, [154]–[155].
[136] *Belhaj v Straw* (n 63) [137], [142] and see also Lord Mance at [65].
[137] *Maduro Board* (n 62) [165].
[138] ibid, [169].

The decision whether or not to give effect to such a judgment would itself be subject to the less-deferential test applicable to the recognition of foreign judgments, and the judgment would not be recognised to the extent that it was premised on the appointing body not being the government of Venezuela in circumstances in which the UK Government had taken the contrary position.[139] This was the position both where a judgment of a foreign court held that legislation was invalid and where the court found that an executive act was unlawful under local law.[140]

In *Yukos Capital v OJSC Rosneft Oil*,[141] the claimant alleged that as part of an ongoing campaign unlawfully to expropriate its assets, the foreign state had interfered in its domestic court process to procure the set-aside decision. The issue arose as to whether this contention triggered the application of the foreign act of state doctrine in its full rigour, or only the less onerous standards of judicial comity applicable to decisions as to the recognition and enforcement of foreign judgment. In *Yukos*, the ultimate question for the English court was whether to recognise the foreign court's annulment decision, and in these circumstances the English court was naturally reluctant to distinguish between those parts of the campaign of expropriation which bore directly on the judicial decision, and those which formed part of the run up to it. Rix LJ held that the tax assessments, although executive rather than judicial acts, were 'unlike legislation or decrees or the acts of commanders in the field, which are the familiar terrain of the act of state jurisprudence' because they functioned 'within a tax code which is designed to operate according to law and to be subject to legal and indeed judicial rulings'.[142] He concluded:[143]

> Ultimately, and looking at the arguments in this case more broadly, the question is whether in the modern world the English court can be asked to recognise judicial decisions which a party to those decisions alleges have been brought about by judicially corrupt means. In a world which increasingly speaks about the rule of law, it should not in principle be open to another party to those decisions to claim an immunity from adjudication on the ground that an investigation into those allegations is protected by deference due to the legislative or executive acts of a foreign sovereign.

E. The Role of Public Policy and International Law

Luther rejected the argument that the Soviet legislation in that case was so immoral that the English court should refuse to recognise it. However, it is now

[139] ibid, [170].
[140] ibid, [176]–[177].
[141] *Yukos Capital* (n 91).
[142] ibid, [133].
[143] ibid, [135].

clear that there are some foreign acts of state which will be denied recognition on normative grounds. The argument that the court should refuse to recognise foreign legislation which is contrary to international law received support in *The Rose Mary*,[144] a case concerned with Iranian legislation nationalising an oil concession. However, Upjohn J appeared to regard public policy as a less unruly horse for the purposes of a similar argument in *In re claim by Helbert Wagg*.[145]

It was also on that basis that the non-recognition argument succeeded in respect of Nazi legislation discriminating against Jews in *Oppenheimer v Cattermole*,[146] albeit the decision recognised that international law might inform the public policy determination. There is an important distinction between the two approaches. A municipal court refusing to recognise a foreign act of state on public policy grounds is applying municipal law, whereas the court could refuse to recognise foreign legislation which was contrary to international law even though it would have been obliged to give effect to municipal legislation which was similarly non-compliant.[147]

In *Kuwait Airways Corpn v Iraqi Airways Co (Nos 4 and 5)*,[148] the House of Lords relied on a breach of international law as a basis for refusing to give effect to a foreign act of state, while emphasising both the distinct planes on which international and municipal law operate, and the fact that municipal courts are not competent to determine the legality of the conduct of states on the international plane.[149] The necessary balance between these competing policies was achieved in that case by requiring a breach of a fundamental and well-established rule of international law,[150] and, as Lord Hope stressed, where the fact of the breach was sufficiently clear and flagrant (in that case it had been established by the United Nations).[151]

VI. CONCLUSION

Luther involved the attempted transplantation of two transatlantic judicial kernels addressing the relationship of the judicial and executive branches

[144] *The Rose Mary* (n 90). A case in which the Supreme Court of Aden accepted arguments to this effect from Sir Hartley Shawcross and Elihu Lauterpacht.

[145] *Helbert Wagg* (n 91) 352–53 (German statute of 1933 discharging a foreign currency debt).

[146] *Oppenheimer v Cattermole (Inspector of Taxes)* [1976] AC 249 (HL).

[147] *Cf* Zander (n 18) 842: 'the fact that a municipal court is bound to apply its own law, even if it be in direct conflict with international law, appears to be no reason why it should approach foreign law in the same way'.

[148] *Kuwait Airways* (n 41).

[149] For recognition of this rule of judicial inhibition a century ago, see *Johnstone v Peddlar* [1921] 2 AC 262 (HL) 290 (Lord Sumner).

[150] *Kuwait Airways* (n 41) [29].

[151] ibid, [149].

of government.[152] The first – dealing with the recognition of foreign government – rapidly prospered, and now clearly requires the courts to defer to the executive on those occasions when the executive chooses to speak on the issue of recognition, however it chooses to act. The act of state doctrine, by contrast, took longer to flourish. Francis Mann, writing in 1986, described it as 'one of the most difficult and most perplexing topics which, in the field of foreign affairs, may face the municipal judge in England'[153] and suggested that 'the doctrine of the foreign act of State displays in every respect such uncertainty and confusion and rests on so slippery a basis that its application becomes a matter of speculation'. As well as uncertainty as to the types of sovereign act to which the doctrine applied, Mann was concerned the English courts might prove to be 'more timid than the executive' if unwilling to adjudicate on the validity of the acts of foreign governments under their own law, or international law.[154] In his conclusion, he observed that 'the House [of Lords] has never had the opportunity of being squarely confronted with the question whether English law includes a rule to the effect that that the validity of the foreign act of state (either under its own law or under English law or under international law) cannot be questioned'.[155]

Now that the highest court has had three opportunities to engage with the doctrine, its scope of application has been heavily pruned, and Dr Mann would no doubt have been gratified that the courts have been provided with a number of tools with which to keep future growth in check. To that extent, it has followed the same trajectory as the 'Revenue Rule', in which an earlier and more absolute formulation of the principle has been significantly qualified over time – although in this case, so as to reduce the deference accorded to the acts of a sovereign within its territory, as opposed to a greater readiness to give effect to such acts in this jurisdiction.[156] However, the effect of the Supreme Court's decision in *Maduro* is that the doctrine has survived the 'withering on the vine' which the *Belhaj* case appeared to pre-figure, and 'the consummation devoutly wished by that great scholar'[157] – the abolition of the doctrine – has not come to pass. One hundred years on, the legacy of *Luther v Sagor* remains very much alive, its status as a great case in the conflict of laws secure.

[152] Or perhaps re-transplantation: see Lloyd-Jones, 'Act of Foreign State in English Law' (n 18) 439: 'the seeds sown in *Duke of Brunswick* were soon to grow to maturity in the fertile legal soil of the New World'.
[153] FA Mann, *Foreign Affairs in English Courts* (Oxford, OUP, 1986) 164.
[154] ibid 177–81.
[155] ibid 181.
[156] See ch 8 in this volume.
[157] *Belhaj v Straw* (n 63) [247] (Lord Sumption).

8

Government of India v Taylor (1955)

ALEXANDER LAYTON KC

I. INTRODUCTION: THE 'REVENUE RULE'

If the decision of the House of Lords in January 1955 in *Government of India v Taylor* is a landmark,[1] it marks land that had been well-known, if sparely mapped, since the late eighteenth century. But the land is marginal land, occupying space of uncertain scope between public and private law and between the interests of differing states. It is not well-reasoned nor, despite engaging with grand expressions of state interests, is it founded securely on a bedrock of principle. Today, it can provide an attractive refuge for crooks and smugglers, which is doubtless why parts of it have since been extensively undermined.[2]

The land marked by the decision is the so-called 'revenue rule', which is the subject of the first limb of *Dicey*'s rule 3:[3]

> English courts have no jurisdiction to entertain an action: (1) for the enforcement, either directly or indirectly, of a [penal,] revenue [or other public] law of a foreign state; or (2) founded upon an act of state.

Shortly after this chapter was finalised for publication, the new edition of *Dicey* was published, wherein rule 3 has become rule 20, but the substance of the rule has not changed, and references to rule 3 in this chapter should be understood accordingly.

This chapter will aim to trace the development of the rule as it applies to foreign revenue laws and consider its current status. Like its sibling, the rule against recognising or enforcing other public laws, the revenue rule is closely associated with and grew out of the rule against enforcing foreign penal laws; but consideration of those rules and the cases that mark out the land that they occupy is beyond the scope of this chapter.

[1] *Government of India v Taylor* [1955] AC 491 (HL).

[2] See B Mallinak, 'The Revenue Rule: A Common Law Doctrine for the Twenty-First Century' (2006) 16 *Duke Journal of Comparative and International Law* 79.

[3] L Collins, *Dicey, Morris & Collins on the Conflict of Laws*, 15th edn (London, Sweet & Maxwell, 2018) para 5R-019.

II. ORIGINS OF THE RULE

The origins of the rule are obscure. In a rudimentary form, it seems to have been taken as axiomatic from at least the first half of the eighteenth century that English courts would not give effect to at least some aspects of foreign law. One of the earliest examples involves the Court of Exchequer in *Attorney-General v Lutwydge*,[4] treating the question as one of jurisdiction. Soon after the Union of England and Scotland, the issue arose whether the court had what today would be called subject-matter jurisdiction in respect of a bond given for the payment of duties on tobacco imported into Scotland. Lord Chief Baron Pengelly observed that 'Before the union this court had no jurisdiction of the revenues in Scotland' and so the question, which was adjourned for consideration by the Exchequer Chamber, was whether the statute had conferred on it a jurisdiction which hitherto it had not had.

The Responsibility of Shipowners Act 1733 made shipowners liable for goods taken in by their vessels' masters even without the privity of the shipowner. In *Boucher v Lawson*,[5] the issue arose whether, before that Act, a plaintiff could recover from a shipowner for the loss of goods taken on board by the master. The case concerned a quantity of Portuguese gold, in circumstances where it had been taken on board by the master, Fletcher, for delivery to the plaintiff, Boucher, in London. But on demand the gold had not been delivered and the action was raised against the owner. Earlier cases had held the owner liable, but on the ground that the owner was entitled to the freight. In this case, a complicating factor was a special verdict by which the jury had held that by a custom of the trade in Portuguese gold, the freight was due solely to the master and not to the owner. This feature eventually carried the day for the defendant. But one of the issues which arose was whether the fact that, by the law of Portugal, the trade in gold was unlawful meant that the case was to be distinguished from the earlier decisions. The point was dismissed by Lord Hardwicke CJ succinctly: 'I think the unlawfulness of the trade makes no difference, for it is not material to us what the law of Portugal is, but what the law of England is, and here in England it is not only a lawful trade, but very much encouraged.'[6]

By the 1770s, however, the point seemed to have become more refined, as it was then clear that not every aspect of foreign law was to be ignored by English courts. The issue arose in *Holman v Johnson* whether a claim for the price of tea sold and delivered in France pursuant to a French law contract by a French resident was recoverable in England in circumstances where the defendant

[4] *Attorney-General v Lutwydge* (1729) Bunbury 280; 145 ER 674.
[5] *Boucher v Lawson* (1735) 1 Cases T Hard 194; 95 ER 125.
[6] ibid, 198; 127.

intended, to the plaintiff's knowledge, to smuggle the tea into England in breach of English customs laws. Lord Mansfield started his judgment by saying that:[7]

> There can be no doubt, but that every action tried here must be tried by the law of England; but the law of England says, that in a variety of circumstances, with regard to contracts legally made abroad, the laws of the country where the cause of action arose shall govern. – There are a great many cases which every country says shall be determined by the laws of foreign countries where they arise.

Pausing there, that observation is notable to contemporary eyes both for the recognition that conflict of laws rules form part of domestic law, and for the suggestion that such rules have a universal quality. He then continues:[8]

> But I do not see how the principles on which that doctrine obtains are applicable to the present case. *For no country ever takes notice of the revenue laws of another.*

That last sentence is taken as the principal early source for what is now the first limb of *Dicey*'s rule, although the irony is that the facts were such that it must have been an observation about French law, by which the legality of the contract was being judged, rather than English law. The judgment goes on to reject an argument that the claim should fail as being founded on an illegal or immoral act: 'An immoral contract it certainly is not; for the revenue laws themselves, as well as the offences against them, are all positive juris.' Having concluded that the contract was lawful by French law and not contrary to English revenue laws, Lord Mansfield cited Huber,[9] to the effect that a contract for the sale of goods which is unlawful at the place where it is concluded is null, but if sold and delivered at a place where it is not prohibited, the contract is valid. 'The doctrine Huberus lays down, is founded in good sense and upon general principles of justice. I entirely agree with him'.[10]

The dictum was repeated by Lord Mansfield four years later in *Planché v Fletcher*,[11] in which insurers sought to avoid a claim on their policy. Goods had been shipped from Gravesend, ostensibly bound for Ostend, but actually intended for France. This practice, which was found to be notorious, was designed to minimise the duties payable in France, which were lower on goods shipped from Ostend than those shipped from England. Following the declaration of the War of 1778 between England and France, the goods were seized

[7] *Holman v Johnson* (1775) 1 Cowp 342, 343; 98 ER 1120, 1121.

[8] ibid.

[9] ibid, 344; 1121. Huber's work's full title is *De Conflictu Legum Diversarum in Diversis Imperiis*, which constitutes a part of title 3, part 2, book 1, of Huber's *Praelectionum juris civilis, tomi tres*: see EG Lorenzen, 'Huber's *De Conflictu Legum*' (1918–1919) 13 *Illinois Law Review* 375, where the influence of Huber and other Dutch theorists on the eighteenth century development of English and American conflict of laws principles is discussed and the full Latin text of *De Conflictu Legum*, with an English translation, is set out.

[10] ibid, Lorenzen, 344; 1121.

[11] *Planché v Fletcher* (1779) 1 Dougl. 251; 99 ER 164.

by British customs officers in the Channel and the plaintiffs claimed on their insurance policy. The insurers' defence asserted that they had been a victim of a fraud on the basis that it had been represented to them that the goods were bound for Ostend; but the court held that there had been no fraud and rejected that defence.

It is striking that Lord Mansfield's dictum was obiter in both *Holman* and *Planché* and it was not until 1908 that any reported case (at least in England) had been decided on the basis of the rule. *Sydney Municipal Council v Bull* was an action in the King's Bench Division seeking to recover from Sir Frederick Cook sums said to be due from him as a statutory debt due in respect of property he owned in Sydney.[12] The sums were imposed by a New South Wales statute, the Moore Street Improvement Act of 1890, as rates or contributions payable by the owners of property in Moore Street in order to fund improvements by the plaintiff corporation.[13] Henry Bull, who had covenanted to indemnify Cook, was named as a third party and given leave to defend the action. Grantham J, however, seems to have had no doubt about the matter and, without citing authority, said:[14]

> The action is in the nature of an action for a penalty or to recover a tax; it is analogous to an action brought in one country to enforce the revenue laws of another. In such cases it is always been held that an action will not lie outside the confines of the last-mentioned State.

Following this decision, the wording of *Dicey*'s rule was amended from, 'The court has no jurisdiction to entertain an action for the enforcement, either directly or indirectly, of a penal law of a foreign country' by the addition of the words 'or revenue' after 'penal', thereby lending extra weight to the assumption that the law was as Lord Mansfield's obiter dictum had stated it to be.

Notwithstanding that no less an authority than remarks of Scrutton LJ in a judgment of 1920 suggested that the point was not definitively decided and required reconsideration,[15] the assumption that English courts would not

[12] *Sydney Municipal Council v Bull* [1909] 1 KB 7 (KB).

[13] The Act was problematic. Sydney's City Solicitor, GC Waldron, who had taken the opinion of Sir Julian Salomons QC, recorded in a memorandum of 18 October 1898 'six deficiencies' in the Act, stating, 'Generally I may say the Act is very badly drafted and proceedings thereunder are in many cases impracticable': www.archives.cityofsydney.nsw.gov.au/nodes/view/1571343#idx1929714 (accessed 23 August 2022). Salomons was himself a major, if controversial, figure in the New South Wales legal world of his day: www.adb.anu.edu.au/biography/salomons-sir-julian-emanuel-4532 (accessed 23 August 2022).

[14] *Sydney Municipal Council v Bull* (n 12) 12 That was one of two *ratione decidendi*, the other (perhaps less convincingly) being that the action was a mixed action, containing elements of both a personal and a real action, and as such, citing Joseph Story, it was properly referable to the *forum rei sitae*. The contention of the plaintiffs would amount to this, that a foreign legislature, by imposing a personal liability on its own subjects for its own municipal purposes can thereby impose upon the courts of this country the duty of adjudicating upon questions which by the law of England are not properly cognisable by these courts.

[15] *Ralli Brothers v Compañia Naviera Sota Y Aznar* [1920] 2 KB 287 (CA). The issue was whether part of freight payable under a charterparty in Spain, was recoverable in circumstances where

enforce foreign revenue laws gained further momentum in the 1920s, first in *King of the Hellenes v Brostrom*,[16] and then in *Re Visser*.[17] The first of these was a claim by the Greek monarch for the money representing a cargo of currants and sultanas which had been shipped to England on bills of lading that, in breach of Greek laws, were not issued in the name of certain banks approved by the Greek authorities. The purpose of the Greek law was to enable the Greek Government to control the rate of foreign exchange and, it seems, to recover a proportion of the price. What was fatal to the claim was that the Greek law did not invalidate the bills of lading. Rather it provided the Greek Government with, in effect, a lien over the goods. Rowlatt J characterised the claim as being based on what English law treated as a revenue law. He said this:[18]

> It is perfectly elementary that a foreign government cannot come here – nor will the Courts of other countries allow our Government to go there – and sue a person found in that jurisdiction for taxes levied and which he is declared to be liable to by the country to which he belongs; and if you cannot do it against a person I can see no reason at all why such process should be allowed against goods. It seems to me to be a simple case of enforcing in the directest possible way the revenue provisions of a foreign State.

The claim in *Re Visser* was made by the Dutch monarch against Dutch citizens for a debt owed by them under Dutch law. The defendants were executors and heirs of one David Visser and the debt was for succession duty on Visser's estate. The motion before the court was for the statement of claim to be struck out as disclosing no reasonable cause of action. It was argued that the previous decisions, with one exception, were all obiter and that no case actually established that the courts would not recognise and enforce a foreign revenue law. The exception was *Municipal Council of Sydney v Bull*,[19] which the plaintiff sought to distinguish on the basis that it concerned the law of a foreign municipality rather than of a foreign state. But Tomlin J rejected that distinction and held that it was his duty to follow it, but went on to state his own opinion of the matter in these terms:[20]

> My own opinion is that there is a well recognized rule, which has been enforced for at least 200 years or thereabouts, under which these Courts will not collect the taxes of

Spanish law capped the price payable for freight. Scrutton LJ said, at 300: 'In my opinion the law is correctly stated by Professor Dicey in *The Conflict of Laws* … where he says: 'A contract … is, in general, invalid in so far as … the performance of it is unlawful by the law of the country where the contract is to be performed' – and I reserve liberty to consider whether it is any longer an exception to this proposition that this country will not consider the fact that the contract is obnoxious only to the revenue laws of the foreign country where it is to be performed as an obstacle to enforcing it in the English Courts. The early authorities on this point require reconsideration, in view of the obligations of international comity as now understood.'

[16] *King of the Hellenes v Brostrom* (1923) 16 Lloyd Law's Rep 190 (KB).

[17] *Re Visser* [1928] Ch 877 (Ch).

[18] *King of the Hellenes v Brostrom* (n 16) 193.

[19] *Sydney Municipal Council v Bull* (n 12).

[20] *Re Visser* (n 17) 883.

> foreign States for the benefit of the sovereigns of those foreign States; and this is one of those actions which these Courts will not entertain.

By 1928, therefore, at least at first instance and despite doubts being expressed in the Court of Appeal, the revenue rule had become established law. Remarkably, that had happened without any convincing explanation having been given for the rule in the cases.

The first policy explanation in a case seems to have come in 1929 from the US in the form of a concurring judgment in *Moore v Mitchell* given by the great judge Learned Hand, sitting in the Court of Appeals for the Second Circuit, who founded his reasoning on the principle of comity.[21] The claim was by the County Treasurer of Grant County, Illinois, against the executors of the will of Richard Edwards Breed for local property taxes for which the deceased had been assessed to be liable following his death. The property was outwith the state of Illinois and the executors were administering the estate in New York. Among other problems faced by the claim were, as Judge Manton put it, the 'settled principles of private international law, which preclude one state from acting as a collector of taxes for a sister state, and from enforcing its penal or revenue laws as such. The revenue laws of one state have no force in another.' Judge Learned Hand delivered a judgment concurring in the result:[22]

> We must … decide whether a tax lawfully imposed in a foreign state can be collected by suit in a federal court sitting in another state. … Generally it is, of course, true that a liability arising under the law of a foreign state will be recognized by the courts of another, and it is not here relevant whether foreign liability is enforced, or another, precisely similar, raised by the law of the forum. A recognized exception is in the case of criminal and penal liabilities.

He then cited a number of authorities, including *Huntington v Attrill*,[23] and *Municipal Council of Sydney v Bull*,[24] but said that the point concerning revenue laws had never been decided by a federal court. He continued:[25]

> While the origin of the exception in the case of penal liabilities does not appear in the books, a sound basis for it exists, in my judgment, which includes liabilities for taxes as well. Even in the case of ordinary municipal liabilities, a court will not recognize those arising in a foreign state, if they run counter to the 'settled public policy' of its own. Thus a scrutiny of the liability is necessarily always in reserve, and the possibility that it will be found not to accord with the policy of the domestic state. This is not a troublesome or delicate inquiry when the question arises between private persons, but it takes on quite another face when it concerns the relations between the foreign state and its own citizens or even those who may be temporarily within

[21] *Moore v Mitchell* (1929) 30 F 2d 600.
[22] ibid, 603.
[23] *Huntington v Attrill* [1893] AC 150 (PC); *Huntington* (1892) 146 US 657. The case in both jurisdictions is authority for the proposition that a state will not enforce the penal laws of another.
[24] *Sydney Municipal Council v Bull* (n 12).
[25] *Moore v Mitchell* (n 21) 604.

> its borders. To pass upon the provisions for the public order of another state is, or at any rate should be, beyond the powers of a court; it involves the relations between the states themselves, with which courts are incompetent to deal, and which are intrusted to other authorities. It may commit the domestic state to a position which would seriously embarrass its neighbor. Revenue laws fall within the same reasoning; they affect a state in matters as vital to its existence as its criminal laws. No court ought to undertake an inquiry which it cannot prosecute without determining whether those laws are consonant with its own notions of what is proper.

Judge Hand's rationale for the rule was cited and adopted by Kingsmill Moore J in 1950 in the High Court of Justice of Ireland, approved the following year on appeal to the Supreme Court of Ireland, in *Peter Buchanan Ltd and Marchag v McVey*.[26] But it was not until 1953 that the matter again came for decision before the English court in our landmark case.

III. GOVERNMENT OF INDIA v TAYLOR

A. Facts

When he came to the throne in 1902, Edward VII intended to visit India the following year for a 'Durbar' at which he would be crowned Emperor of India. In the event, the King did not attend, but the Durbar went ahead anyway, the Viceroy, Lord Curzon, making sure that the occasion amounted to a magnificent show of power and wealth.[27] Although Calcutta was the capital of British India, the Durbar took place at Delhi. Huge preparations were required and prompted frantic economic activity, including the development of electricity supplies. The first officially recorded diesel power station in Delhi was set up by a John Fleming who established his diesel power station near the Lahori Gate. Fleming obtained a licence for it in 1905 under the Indian Electricity Act 1903, although it seems likely that it had been in operation for a time before then. The company was formed in 1908 as the Delhi Electric Supply and Traction Company and in 1911 expanded its generating capacity with a steam generation station. In 1916, it was incorporated as an English company. It seems that it became Delhi's principal source of domestic electricity until, in March 1947 following Indian independence, its business and assets were taken over for Rs8,211,580 by the Delhi Central Electricity Power Authority, which exercised an option that had been contained in the original licence to Fleming. The proceeds were remitted to England.

It is what happened next that forms the basis of the decision. Indian legislation passed in April 1947 gave rise to a liability in India to pay tax on 'any profits

[26] *Peter Buchanan Ltd and Marchag v McVey* [1955] AC 516 (Note) 529.

[27] A Hashmi, 'Overhead Wires in Delhi – A Brief History of the Unholy Mess' (*The Wire*, 16 March 2019) www.thewire.in/urban/delhi-the-wires-overhead (accessed 6 August 2022).

or gains arising from the sale, exchange or transfer of capital assets effected after March 31 1946'. In May 1949, the company went into voluntary liquidation, the respondent Samuel Henry Taylor, along with a co-director being appointed joint liquidators. In March 1951, the liquidators placed a notice in the Gazette of India calling on all creditors of the company to prove their debts or claims and in October 1951 the (Indian) Commissioner of Income Tax served a demand. There were disputes about the amount of tax due and although some payment was made out of assets in India, it was clear that there was some further sum by way of Indian capital gains tax that remained outstanding.

In May 1953, Taylor (by then, the sole liquidator) rejected the Indian Government's claims stating that no part of the company's assets (all of which were then in England) could properly be applied in payment of any claim for taxes by a foreign government. Was Taylor right to reject the claim on that basis? That was the issue that led to the decision in this case.

B. Companies Court and Court of Appeal

Thereupon, India applied to the High Court in England under section 307 of the Companies Act 1948, 'for an order that Samuel Henry Taylor the liquidator of the above-named company in the voluntary winding-up thereof rejecting the claim of the Indian Government may be reversed and the said claim may be allowed in full'. The application was heard by Vaisey J who made an order on 30 July 1953 that, 'the court doth not think fit to make any order on the said application'.[28]

The Indian Government appealed to the Court of Appeal, which heard the appeal over five days in November 1953.[29] Counsel for the Indian Government argued that the revenue rule had never been applied to the winding up of a company, and that there was no general rule that the courts will never enforce the revenue laws of another country. They said that the decision in *Re Visser* was merely that no action could be brought, and that it was concerned with penal laws not revenue laws generally (a bit of a stretch, given that the case concerned succession taxes). It had not decided that the courts of England would never enforce the revenue law of a foreign country. They also argued that the rule did not apply to Commonwealth countries. Counsel for the liquidator argued that the authorities supported the proposition that the courts of England could not be used to collect foreign taxes, and cited the rule as stated in *Dicey*. There was also a point about whether the proceedings concerned a 'liability' for the purposes of the Companies Act.

[28] *In re Delhi Electric Supply and Traction Co Ltd.* (Chancery Division, *The Times*, 31 July 1953).
[29] *India v Taylor* [1954] Ch 131 (CA).

The lead judgment was given by Sir Raymond Evershed MR. He noted that:[30]

> The existence of the so-called rule in regard to collecting taxes claimed by foreign countries has undoubtedly been assumed for very many years ... [but] it is only rarely and recently that its validity has been directly tested in cases which are at all comparable to the present and it has never been directly tested in this court in such a case.

He therefore undertook a rather full review of the earlier cases and concluded:[31]

> Having looked at these cases, I think they show that a general rule in the form stated by Lord Mansfield (whatever may be its exact scope) was treated by lawyers in this country in the eighteenth century as well established. I think that it is equally clear that the rule has continued thenceforward to be accepted. As I have already said, its origin may well have had to do with questions of freedom of trade and the direct application to that problem of customs duties imposed by foreign countries. But that is no more than the accident of its birth, and does not affect the existence of the principle and its applicability to other forms of revenue which may from time to time emerge. I think, then, that these cases show that, though the full import of the words, "no country ever takes notice of the revenue laws of another," may require explanation or even qualification, the true rule, which was then regarded and should be now regarded as well established, is that claims by representatives of a sovereign foreign State to recover penalties or the revenues of that State will not be enforceable in these courts.

He went on to consider *Municipal Council of Sydney v Bull*,[32] and *Re Visser*,[33] approving both judgments, and pointed out that Parliament had recognised or enacted the rule in section 1(2) of the Foreign Judgments (Reciprocal Enforcement) Act 1933, which provided that one of the conditions for enforcement of judgments to which it applied was that 'there is payable under it a sum of money, not being a sum payable in respect of taxes or other charges of a like nature or in respect of a fine or other penalty'. He considered and rejected arguments based on currency exchange cases and rejected India's arguments about the 'liability' point and the suggested non-application to Commonwealth countries. Jenkins LJ and Morris LJ each delivered a concurring judgment, although Morris LJ was plainly unhappy that the result was that the company was able to avoid paying its taxes.

C. House of Lords

India appealed further to the House of Lords, which heard the appeal over 4 days in November 1954, delivering their judgments in January 1955.[34] On this

[30] ibid, 144.
[31] ibid, 151 (citation omitted).
[32] *Sydney Municipal Council v Bull* (n 12).
[33] *Re Visser* (n 17).
[34] *India v Taylor* [1955] AC 491 (HL).

occasion, the appellants widened their criticism of the revenue rule, arguing that, although widely assumed, there was no actual reported case of a foreign government recovering taxes in England, nor vice versa. They argued that Lord Mansfield's dictum applied to cases where there was no question of enforcement of foreign tax law, and rather the issue was whether the English courts would enforce a contract illegal in its place of performance. They argued that there were no adequate reasons for imposition of the rule, which anyway only applied to penalties imposed by a foreign state for breach of its laws. Turning to arguments which had been advanced in favour of the rule, they contended that it could not be right to say that recognising foreign tax laws would be derogatory to sovereignty or cause political embarrassment, because the courts never refuse to enforce foreign laws to which comparable objections could be raised. Nor could the rule be contrary to public policy unless confiscatory. Taxes are not penal, they said, and the rule could not be based on the difficulty of enforcing foreign tax law as the courts never refuse to investigate foreign law on that ground. They argued that it was desirable in the interests of comity that this country should be able to enforce its own tax laws abroad and that it was highly undesirable that this country should become a haven for foreign tax-dodgers.

The liquidator's counsel relied on the proposition that it was elementary that English courts could not be used to enforce foreign revenue law and said that a foreign sovereign could not sue here on a right that was entirely dependent on his own prerogative or made by virtue of his power to make laws. Rather more convincingly, perhaps, they argued that the right to sue in a foreign country was a matter of private international law, which was concerned with private rights, whereas penal, revenue and confiscatory laws dealt with public claims by a sovereign, not private rights.

Viscount Simonds's was the first judgment.[35] Unpromisingly for the appellant, he started by saying that he had no doubt that the lower courts were right and he was 'greatly surprised to hear it suggested that the courts of this country would and should entertain a suit by a foreign State to recover a tax', and went on to quote the dicta of Lord Mansfield and recite the position taken in the early cases. He acknowledged that Lord Mansfield:[36]

> was not directly concerned with the case of a foreign power suing in an English court to recover revenue, but with the validity of a contract made abroad where the seller was not implicated in smuggling operations which contravened the revenue laws of this country or with the rights of insurers where a ship which had cleared for Ostend went direct to Nantes thereby affecting the customs dues payable abroad. But in each case he could not have reached his conclusion but for the fact that he applied the rule that no country ever takes notice of the revenue laws of another.

[35] *India v Taylor* (n 1) 503–09.
[36] ibid, 503–04.

He did, however, recognise that, 'the history and origin of the rule, if it be a rule, are not easy to ascertain and there is on the whole remarkably little authority upon the subject'. He also accepted that the words 'take notice of' should not be applied too widely, as there were cases in which, although not enforcing foreign revenue laws, the courts were bound to recognise some of the effects of those laws. He also pointed to the Foreign Judgments (Reciprocal Enforcement) Act 1933, section 1(2)(b) where the rule appeared to have been recognised by Parliament.[37] What Viscount Simonds did not do was to provide any independent policy justification for the rule.

Lord Morton agreed with Viscount Simmonds,[38] and Lord Reid,[39] concurred, thus constituting a majority for Viscount Simmonds' reasoning (such as it was). But the remaining two Law Lords, agreeing in the result, provided much more cogent (and somewhat different) reasoning.

Lord Keith started by agreeing with Viscount Simonds, but then referred to the decision of Kingsmill Moore J in the Irish High Court in the case of *Peter Buchanan Ltd* which was, at that time, unreported.[40] As we have seen, that judgment quoted the reasoning of Judge Learned Hand in *Moore v Mitchell*.[41] Lord Keith distilled the Irish judgment as illustrating two propositions, namely, '(1) that there are circumstances in which the courts will have regard to the revenue laws of another country; and (2) that in no circumstances will the courts directly or indirectly enforce the revenue laws of another country'.[42] He pointed out that the House was not concerned with the first proposition or with the limits to be placed on it. He went on to identify a principled basis for the rule in the notion of sovereignty:[43]

> One explanation of the rule … may be thought to be that enforcement of a claim for taxes is but an extension of the sovereign power which imposed the taxes, and that an assertion of sovereign authority by one State within the territory of another, as distinct from a patrimonial claim by a foreign sovereign, is (treaty or convention apart) contrary to all concepts of independent sovereignties.

But he pointed out that another explanation was given by Judge Learned Hand, in *Moore v Mitchell*, which he went on to quote,[44] namely the difficulty of reviewing public provisions of another state. The first of these passages has frequently been quoted in the case law and, even though none of the other Lords expressly endorsed it, it probably today forms the acknowledged basis of the rule in English law.

[37] ibid, 506.
[38] ibid, 509.
[39] ibid.
[40] *Peter Buchanan* (n 26).
[41] *Moore v Mitchell* (n 21).
[42] *India v Taylor* (n 1) 510.
[43] ibid, 511.
[44] *Moore v Mitchell* (n 21).

Lord Somervell said that Lord Mansfield's dictum was directed to a different problem, namely in considering illegality under a foreign *lex loci contractus* and then proceeded to consider illegality under English law. He referred to Scrutton LJ's reservation of the issue of whether English courts would enforce a contract to break the revenue laws of a foreign state and made clear he was not considering that issue. He then went on to consider other legal policy arguments, stating that the matter must be decided on principle. He suggested that comity was not an adequate ground on which to enforce foreign revenue laws:[45]

> If one State could collect its taxes through the courts of another, it would have arisen through what is described, vaguely perhaps, as comity or the general practice of nations inter se. The appellant was therefore in a difficulty from the outset in that after considerable research no case of any country could be found in which taxes due to State A had been enforced in the courts of State B.

In a passage which is heartening to those who favour a comparative law approach, Lord Somervell included a quotation in French:[46]

> The following passage from Pillet's Traité de Droit International Privé, 1924, paragraph 674, confirms the negative result of counsel's researches in respect of French law: 'Les jugements rendus en matiére [sic] criminelle ne sont pas les seuls qui soient soumis à la loi de la territorialité absolue. Les jugements rendus en matière fiscale ne sont eux non plus susceptible d'aucune execution à l'étranger, et l'on n'a même jamais songé à la possibilité de faire exécuter sur le territoire de l'un d'eux une sentence relative aux droits fiscaux de l'Etat qui aurait été rendue sur le territoire d'un autre'.

Translated:

> Judgments on criminal matters are not the only ones limited by the law of absolute territoriality. Judgments rendered on tax matters also cannot be enforced abroad, and no one has contemplated the possibility of enforcing an award on the territory of one state that concerns tax which ought to have been rendered in the territory of another state.

He was equally unimpressed by the idea that administrative convenience might provide a rationale for enforcing foreign revenue laws:[47]

> Tax gathering is an administrative act, though in settling the quantum as well as in the final act of collection judicial process may be involved. Our courts will apply foreign law if it is the proper law of a contract, the subject of a suit. Tax gathering is not a matter of contract but of authority and administration as between the State and those within its jurisdiction. If one considers the initial stages of the process, which may, as the records of your Lordships' House show, be intricate and prolonged, it would be remarkable comity if State B allowed the time of its courts to be expended

[45] *India v Taylor* (n 1) 514.
[46] ibid, 515.
[47] ibid, 514–15.

> in assisting in this regard the tax gatherers of State A. Once a judgment has been obtained and it is a question only of its enforcement the factor of time and expense will normally have disappeared. The principle remains the claim is one for a tax.
>
> That fact, I think, itself justifies what has been clearly the practice of States. They have not in the past thought it appropriate to seek to use legal process abroad against debtor taxpayers. They assumed, rightly, that the courts would object to being so used.

Each of the main judgments also considered and dismissed arguments on the 'liability' point under the Companies Act.

Of the five judgments in the House of Lords, therefore, only Lord Keith's provides positive reasons for the rule, while Lord Somervell rejected policy arguments to the contrary. What none of them consider, at least in any structured way, is the question of whether the rule extends beyond direct enforcement to cover also indirect enforcement. The closest they get to that point is noting that the court will recognise some effects of foreign revenue laws, including the effects of foreign illegality under the law applicable to contracts.[48]

All that can be said with certainty in the light of *India v Taylor* is that Lord Mansfield's dictum in *Holman v Johnson*, that 'no country ever takes notice of the revenue laws of another', in some form and to some extent forms part of English common law. The parameters of the rule and qualifications to it, if any, remained unclear in light of that decision.

IV. SUBSEQUENT DEVELOPMENTS

It would be beyond the scope of this chapter to undertake a detailed review of how the English case law has developed since 1955. However, before coming to the latest examination of the rule by the Court of Appeal, a handful of cases can be mentioned which illustrate the propositions in *India v Taylor* being applied (or distinguished).

In *Rossano v Manufacturers' Life Ins Co*,[49] McNair J[50] relied on *India v Taylor* in refusing to recognise Egyptian garnishee orders against the defendant insurers as a defence to a claim for payment under life insurance policies, where the orders had been served on the defendant by the Egyptian revenue authorities in respect of tax alleged to be due by the plaintiff.

Williams & Humbert Ltd v W&H Trade Marks (Jersey) Ltd concerned the effect on certain trademarks of Spanish expropriation decrees.[51] The defendants

[48] *Ralli Brothers* (n 16).

[49] *Rossano v Manufacturers' Life Ins Co* [1963] 2 QB 352 (QB).

[50] Sir William McNair, not to be confused with his distinguished older brother Arnold who was a judge of the International Court and later the first president of the European Court of Human rights.

[51] *Williams & Humbert Ltd v W&H Trade Marks (Jersey) Ltd* [1986] AC 368 (HL).

argued that those decrees were penal in nature and should not be recognised in England. The House of Lords held that the action did not constitute an attempt to enforce the decrees and the principle that a country could not collect its taxes outside its territories could not be used to contradict the English recognition of foreign expropriation laws. In his speech, Lord Mackay (with whom three of the other Lords agreed) considered the extent to which to which the *India v Taylor* decision applied to indirect enforcement. In a passage which has since taken on a critical importance, he said:[52]

> No countenance was given in *Government of India v Taylor* … [nor in other cases] to the suggestion that an action in this country could be properly described as the indirect enforcement of a penal or revenue law in another country when no claim under that law remained unsatisfied. The existence of such unsatisfied claim to the satisfaction of which the proceeds of the action will be applied appears to me to be an essential feature of the principle enunciated in the Buchanan case … for refusing to allow the action to succeed.

In *United States of America v Inkley*,[53] Lord Keith's explanation in *India v Taylor* for the revenue rule as being based on resisting an excess of sovereign power was relied on by the Court of Appeal to reject a claim by the US to enforce a bail bond which, although civil in form, nonetheless constituted part of the foreign penal law.

In *State of Norway's Application (Nos 1 & 2)*,[54] the House of Lords held that the revenue rule did not extend to seeking assistance in obtaining evidence to be used in the enforcement of Norwegian tax laws. Lord Goff said that it was important to observe that the rule in *India v Taylor* 'is limited to cases of direct or indirect enforcement in this country of the revenue laws of a foreign state'. He cited *Dicey* as saying that indirect enforcement occurs when the foreign state (or its nominee) in form seeks a remedy which in substance is designed to give the foreign law extraterritorial effect, or where a private party raises a defence based on the foreign law in order to vindicate or assert the right of the foreign state, and said that he had been unable to discover any case of indirect enforcement that went beyond those two propositions.[55] He also pointed out that while *Dicey*'s rule stated that the Court had 'no jurisdiction' to entertain an action for the enforcement of a foreign revenue law, he inclined to the view, suggested by Lord Keith in *India v Taylor*, that the true basis of the rule was that English law would not give effect to the extra-territorial assertion of the sovereign power of the foreign state which would be involved in enforcing its revenue laws.[56]

[52] ibid, 440–41.
[53] *United States of America v Inkley* [1989] QB 255 (CA).
[54] *State of Norway's Application (Nos 1 & 2)* [1990] 1 AC 723 (HL).
[55] ibid, 809.
[56] ibid, 807.

V. SKAT

Skatteforvaltningen ('SKAT') is the Danish tax authority. It brought proceedings in England against Solo Capital Partners LLP and 113 other defendants seeking to recover sums which had been paid by way of refunds of Danish withholding tax in circumstances where the refunds were alleged to have been induced by fraud.[57] The case is a paradigm example of the importance of characterisation in a private international law analysis. A preliminary issue was tried as to whether the claims for refunds were to be characterised as claims for the indirect enforcement of Danish revenue law. As both the Commercial Court Judge, Andrew Baker J, and the Court of Appeal emphasised (and as was common ground) that was a question for English law and not for Danish law.

Andrew Baker J decided that the claims were indeed to be regarded as the indirect enforcement of foreign revenue law and dismissed the claim. His reliance on the authorities drew particularly on the Irish *Peter Buchanan* decision,[58] and on *Mbasogo v Logo Ltd*,[59] a case involving the property and interests of Equatorial Guinea in which, following close analysis of the authorities, the Court of Appeal had dismissed claims based on the exercise of sovereign authority in a foreign state. It had held:[60]

> The critical question is whether in bringing a claim, a claimant is doing an act which is of a sovereign character or which is done by virtue of sovereign authority; and whether the claim involves the exercise or assertion of a sovereign right. If so, then the court will not determine or enforce the claim. On the other hand, if in bringing the claim the claimant is not doing an act which is of a sovereign character or by virtue of sovereign authority and the claim does not involve the exercise or assertion of a sovereign right and the claim does not seek to vindicate a sovereign act or acts, then the court will both determine and enforce it.

On his analysis of the authorities, Andrew Baker J held that it was necessary to look past the form of the claim and consider the substance of the claim which (and this is the critical point):[61]

> … is determined by the central interest, in bringing the claim, of the sovereign by whom it is brought or whose interests, directly or indirectly, it is brought.

SKAT appealed successfully against that ruling, the Court of Appeal ruling that the claims were not, either in form or substance, claims to enforce either Danish revenue law or Denmark's other sovereign rights, but were claims to recover sums which had been paid out from SKAT's general funds as a result of

[57] *Skatteforvaltningen v Solo Capital Partners LLP (in Special Administration)* [2021] EWHC 974 (Comm), [2021] 1 WLR 4237 and on appeal [2022] EWCA Civ 234, [2022] 3 WLR 397.
[58] *Peter Buchanan* (n 26).
[59] *Mbasogo v Logo Ltd* [2006] EWCA Civ 1370, [2007] QB 846.
[60] ibid, [50].
[61] *SKAT (HC)* (n 57) [75(iv)].

fraudulent misrepresentations. The judgment of Sir Julian Flaux C, with which the other members of the Court agreed, considered and appears to have rejected the 'central interest' analysis which had informed the judge's characterisation of the claim. He acknowledged that the Court must consider the substance and not just the form of the claim, but said that the critical starting point of the analysis was to focus on the scope of *Dicey's* rule:[62]

> What it renders inadmissible (whether under the narrower revenue rule or the wider sovereign powers rule) is an action, that is a claim, to enforce directly or indirectly a foreign revenue, penal or other public law. In its narrower form, the revenue rule, what it prohibits is enforcement of a direct or indirect claim for tax which is due but unpaid …
>
> In my judgment, this claim against the SKAT defendants is not a claim to unpaid tax or a claim to recover tax at all. It is a claim to recover monies which had been abstracted from SKAT's general funds by fraud. The alleged fraud defendants' submission that the claim to the refund is still a claim to tax is simply wrong as a matter of analysis and the judge fell into error in accepting that submission. Furthermore, because there is no unsatisfied claim to tax, the "essential feature" of the revenue rule as Lord Mackay described it in Williams & Humbert is absent. There is no qualification in his judgment of that essential feature where the claimant is the sovereign foreign state itself …. Rather he expresses the limitation on the revenue rule in quite categorical terms. Accordingly, there being no unsatisfied claim to tax in the present case, the revenue rule does not apply, even though SKAT may be an emanation of the Danish state.

Looking at the landscape marked by *India v Taylor* at this point, the picture emerges of a landscape which has been uneven, but where the overall lie of the land shows a narrowing understanding of the breadth of the exclusion of foreign revenue law in cases of indirect enforcement. It is clear now from the *SKAT* case, if it was not clear already, that the existence of an unsatisfied claim to the satisfaction of which the proceeds of the action will be applied is essential to the operation of the revenue rule in English law.

VI. TREATIES AND STATUTORY PROVISIONS

If, a century or more ago, a foreign sovereign wished to pursue a claim for tax in this country, it might have tried to have recourse to the courts to pursue its claim, but would, since the eighteenth century, have run into the difficulties posed by the exclusion of foreign revenue law in English common law. But more recently, and in particular in the two-thirds of a century since *India v Taylor*, that problem has been much reduced by the growth of international treaties to which the UK is a party. For example, since 2008, the UK has been a state party to the

[62] *SKAT (CA)* (n 57) [126] and [128]. The Supreme Court has since given permission to appeal in *SKAT*.

OECD's Convention on Mutual Administrative Assistance in Tax Matters, in which 146 jurisdictions worldwide participate.[63] Article 11 of that Convention provides, subject to certain conditions, for the requested state to take the necessary steps to recover tax claims of the applicant state 'as if they were its own tax claims'. In addition the UK has double taxation agreements with around 130 foreign countries, making it one of the largest networks globally.[64] Many such treaties contain a provision requiring the contracting states to lend assistance to each other in the collection of revenue claims.[65] Such agreements are given the force of domestic law by section 173 of the Finance Act 2005 and they take precedence over the revenue rule.[66] A further statutory inroad into the revenue rule was made in respect of insolvency proceedings by the UNCITRAL Model Law on Cross-Border Insolvency of 30 May 1997, given effect by the Cross-Border Insolvency Regulations 2006, made pursuant to section 14 of the Insolvency Act 2000. Article 13(3) of the Model Law provides that in proceedings to which the Model Law applies, 'A claim may not be challenged solely on the grounds that it is a claim by a foreign tax or social security authority but such a claim may be challenged – (a) on the ground that it is in whole or in part a penalty, or (b) on any other ground that a claim might be rejected in a proceeding under British insolvency law.'

VII. CONCLUSION

Does the House of Lords' decision in *India v Taylor* merit the accolade of being regarded as a landmark case? Its status as a landmark case arguably derives from that fact that it re-affirmed a long-held view of the law, but that view was more than a little vague at its margins. Only the dicta of Lord Keith and to a lesser extent of Lord Somervelle moved that understanding forward, and it is noticeable that they did not endorse each other's views and that those dicta, in turn, were not endorsed by other members of the House.[67] The second rationale given by Lord Keith for the rule, borrowed in turn from Judge Learned Hand

[63] Convention on Mutual Administrative Assistance in Tax Matters: www.oecd.org/ctp/exchange-of-tax-information/convention-on-mutual-administrative-assistance-in-tax-matters.htm (accessed 26 August 2022).

[64] Institute of Chartered Accountants of England & Wales: www.icaew.com/library/guide-to-services/how-can-i-find-a-double-tax-treaty (accessed 26 August 2022).

[65] See, eg, Art 24A of the Convention Between the Government of the United Kingdom of Great Britain and Northern Ireland and the Government of Canada for the avoidance of double taxation and the prevention of fiscal evasion with respect to taxes on income and capital gains of 21 July 2014.

[66] *Ben Nevis (Holdings) Ltd & Anor v Commissioners for HM Revenue & Customs* [2013] EWCA Civ 578 [6] and [53] (Lloyd-Jones LJ).

[67] Well, almost. Viscount Simonds does mention (*India v Taylor* (n 1) 508) that he had been told by Lord Keith that the latter had discovered an Irish case that confirmed the view that he had expressed, but he does not say that he had even looked at it!

via the judgment of the Irish High Court in *Peter Buchanan*, was the difficulty of reviewing the public provisions of another state. Whatever the current status of that rationale, it is now clear that the English revenue rule is founded on the first of Lord Keith's alternative rationales, namely respect for the sovereignty of foreign states and for the limits of that sovereignty. The use of that sovereignty by states entering into treaties with each other providing for the enforcement of foreign revenue laws, along with the trend in the common law narrowing the scope of the revenue rule in cases of indirect enforcement to cases based on unsatisfied tax claims, means that to a large extent the practical importance of the revenue rule is now greatly diminished.

9

Taczanowska v Taczanowski (1957)

MÁIRE NÍ SHÚILLEABHÁIN

I. INTRODUCTION

TACZANOKWSKA V TACZANOWSKI,[1] a judgment of the English Court of Appeal of 1957, is concerned with the common law choice of law rules for determining the formal validity of marriage. With formal validity, the question is how a marriage ought to be constituted – with different countries having different views as to the necessity for (or adequacy of) a civil or religious ceremony and as to the need for physical presence, witnesses, publicity, registration, notice periods and the words to be spoken at the ceremony. Some states are accepting of informality,[2] while others (like England since Lord Hardwicke's Act 1753[3]) insist on adherence to highly technical requirements within the domestic legal order.[4] Such formalities are intended to avoid clandestine marriages, to safeguard against bigamy and non-consensual marriage, and to allow for a straightforward determination of marital status.[5]

The long-standing view of English private international law (and the common law) was that formal validity is governed by the law of the place of celebration (the *lex loci celebrationis*).[6] This *lex loci* principle was described by the Privy Council in 1929 as 'one question better settled than any other in international law' (*Berthiaume v Dastous*).[7] The *lex loci* rule was subject to a number

[1] *Taczanowska (orse Roth) v Taczanowski* [1957] P 301 (CA).

[2] See, eg, in legal systems based on Islamic law, see P Shah, 'Inconvenient Marriages, or What Happens When Ethnic Minorities Marry Trans-jurisdictionally' (2010) 6 *Utrecht Law Review* 17, 24.

[3] See JA Andrews, 'The Common Law Marriage' (1959) 22 *Modern Law Review* 396; S Cretney, *Family Law in the Twentieth Century: A History* (Oxford, OUP, 2003) 5.

[4] Currently the Marriage Act 1949.

[5] Cretney (n 3) 5, 9; also the UN Convention on Consent to Marriage, Minimum Age for Marriage and Registration of Marriages 1962.

[6] *Scrimshire v Scrimshire* (1752) 2 Hag Con 395, discussed by D Mendes da Costa, 'The Formalities of Marriage in the Conflict of Laws' (1958) 7 *International & Comparative Law Quarterly* 217, 218.

[7] *Berthiaume v Dastous* [1930] AC 79 (PC) 83. The *lex loci* principle had also received strong support from the House of Lords in *Starkowski (otherwise Urbanski) v Attorney-General* [1954] AC 155 (HL), decided only 4 years before *Taczanowska*.

of exceptions but prior to the *Taczanowska* case, such exceptions were thought to be relatively narrow in scope. Non-compliance with foreign formalities could be forgiven if compliance was impossible[8] – and, in that event, British subjects were permitted to marry overseas *per verba de praesenti*, by a simple exchange of vows, as per the canon law which had applied in England up until 1753.[9] This form of marriage (which was also sanctioned for British subjects marrying in British colonies in the nineteenth and early twentieth centuries[10]) became known as 'common law marriage'. There were also tentative suggestions in the early case-law that members of the British armed forces could contract 'common law marriage' when they were stationed overseas[11] – but this common law development was overtaken by statute in 1823[12] when legislation made express provision for the celebration of marriages of members of the British forces serving abroad.[13] This legislation also allowed for overseas British consular marriages of UK nationals – and such forces and consular marriages would be formally valid in the eyes of English law without any consideration of compliance with the *lex loci celebrationis*.[14]

Taczanowska v Taczanowski shattered this orderly consensus in giving new (indeterminate) life to the 'common law marriage' exception to the *lex loci* rule and in extending its application to couples without any British nationality or English domicile. As will be seen, the Court of Appeal in *Taczanowska* was rather vague on the circumstances in which this exception might come into play and there were some suggestions that the *lex loci* 'rule' was merely a rebuttable presumption which depended on voluntary submission.[15]

In the subsequent English case-law of the 1950s and early 1960s, *Taczanowska* was labelled 'a highly important decision',[16] and, to this day, it commands detailed discussion in some of the main English textbooks on private

[8] Mendes da Costa (n 6) 238; also *Ruding v Smith* (1821) 2 Hag Con 371; *Kent v Burgess* (1840) 11 Sim 361.

[9] Mendes da Costa (n 6) 239. Lord Stowell in *Ruding* emphasised the 'Britishness' of the parties.

[10] In such circumstances, however, the common law marriage doctrine did not operate as an exception to the *lex loci* – but as part of the *lex loci* – because English law was considered to be the governing law in such territories: see *Maclean v Cristall* (1849) 7 Notes of Cases, Supp 17; *Wolfenden v Wolfenden* [1946] P 61; *Penhas v Tan Soo Eng* [1953] AC 304; Mendes da Costa (n 6) 236–37. This distinction is acknowledged in *Taczanowska* (n 1) 328–29.

[11] *Burn v Farrar* (1819) 2 Hag Con 369; *Ruding v Smith* (n 8).

[12] 4 Geo 4 c 91.

[13] The 1823 Act was subsequently superseded by the Foreign Marriage Act 1892. More recently, the Marriage (Same Sex Couples) Act 2013, s 13 provided for the repeal of the 1892 Act and for its replacement with a broadly similar scheme set out in Sch 6 to the 2013 Act. For a detailed discussion of these statutory exceptions, see JJ Fawcett, M Ní Shuilleabháin and S Shah, *Human Rights and Private International Law* (Oxford, OUP, 2016) 625–31.

[14] See n 40 below: there was also support in the literature for the view that validity under a foreign personal law might suffice if there was a difficulty in complying with the *lex loci*.

[15] *Taczanowska* (n 1) 325, 330, 332.

[16] *Kochanski v Kochanska* [1958] P 147, 151.

international law.[17] It is often described as a 'leading' case.[18] *Taczanowska* was widely debated in the learned journals of the time, including in a journal article written by the judge who gave the leading judgment in the case.[19] The case was reported in the national press and was perceived as a 'test case' which would determine the fate of thousands of other marriages which were similarly celebrated across Europe in the chaotic aftermath of the Second World War.[20] The judgment has however been criticised as 'wrongly decided … not supported by authority'[21] and as 'judicial legislation'.[22] Commentators also highlighted the 'drastic' revision of the common law marriage exception[23] and the 'startling'[24] and 'remarkable'[25] nature of the proposition of law laid down in *Taczanowska*.

Taczanowska is probably best seen as a humane policy decision[26] and as an expression of solidarity with members (and supporters) of the allied forces who were understandably hostile to the authority of German and Italian marriage laws in the days immediately following the end of the war. In the face of rather unconvincing legal reasoning,[27] the overriding impression is one of 'result selection'[28] and of a court determined to deploy the common law to regularise and support the multitudes of European marriages celebrated amid the confusion of the post-war era.[29] The judges in *Taczanowska* may also have been anxious to protect the children of these marriages from the social and legal disadvantages then attaching to the status of 'illegitimacy'.[30]

[17] P Torremans (ed), *Cheshire, North & Fawcett Private International Law*, 15th edn (Oxford, OUP, 2017) 905–07; L Collins (ed), *Dicey, Morris & Collins on the Conflict of Laws*, 15th edn (London, Sweet & Maxwell, 2012) 929–30; J Hill and M Ní Shúilleabháin, *Clarkson & Hill's Conflict of Laws*, 5th edn (Oxford, OUP, 2016) 362– 63; D McClean and V Ruiz Abou-Nigm, *Morris: The Conflict of Laws*, 9th edn (London, Sweet & Maxwell, 2016) 275–76.

[18] *Cheshire, North & Fawcett* (n 17) 905; McClean and Ruiz Abou-Nigm (n 17) 275.

[19] C Hodson, 'Common Law Marriage' (1958) 7 *International & Comparative Law Quarterly* 205; Andrews (n 3); Mendes da Costa (n 6); I Brownlie and PRH Webb, 'Belligerent Occupation and Common-Law Marriages' (1963) 39 *British Yearbook of International Law* 457; P Carter, 'Formal Validity of Marriage' (1957) 33 *British Yearbook of International Law* 332; K Lipstein, 'Marriage – Foreigner in Armed Forces Abroad – Common Law Marriage – Under British Command' (1957) 15 *Cambridge Law Journal* 126, OM Stone, 'Uncommon Law' (1957) 20 *Modern Law Review* 505; LJ Blom-Cooper, 'Uncommon Law Revisited' (1957) 20 *MLR* 641; PRH Webb, 'More Uncommon Law' (1958) 21 *Modern Law Review* 90.

[20] Mendes da Costa (n 6) 225; *Cheshire, North and Fawcett* (n 17) 905–906; McClean and Ruiz Abou-Nigm (n 17) 275.

[21] Mendes da Costa (n 6) 226.

[22] ibid, 245.

[23] Carter (n 19) 333.

[24] EJ Cohn, 'The External Effects of the *Travers v Holley* Doctrine' (1958) 7 *International & Comparative Law Quarterly* 637, 647.

[25] JC Hall, 'Common Law Marriage' (1987) 46 *Cambridge Law Journal* 106, 107.

[26] Mendes da Costa (n 6) 225; A Briggs, *Private International Law in English Courts* (Oxford, OUP, 2014) 900.

[27] See the reasoning discussed in section VII below.

[28] See JJ Fawcett, 'Result Selection in Domicile Cases' (1985) 5 *Oxford Journal of Legal Studies* 378 making a similar argument in a different context.

[29] *Cheshire, North & Fawcett* (n 17) 905–06; Blom-Cooper (n 19) 641.

[30] Cretney (n 3) 545.

The longer-term implications of the case are difficult to gauge. Citations have tailed off – and, as will be seen, *Taczanowska* has met with a lacklustre response in other common law jurisdictions. Nonetheless, the judgment has opened a door which will be difficult to close and it is possible that its expansive interpretation of common law marriage will be leveraged in new directions, for example, in facilitating the recognition of same-sex marriages celebrated in an overseas jurisdiction which does not facilitate this form of marriage.[31]

As indicated above, the *Taczanowska* decision is easily understood as an act of judicial mercy and an illustration of *favor matrimonii* in 'extraordinary times'[32] and from that perspective is perhaps justified. Nonetheless, it must also be criticised for its disregard of core concerns of the conflict of laws (certainty and universality, avoidance of limping marriage) and for undermining the policy interests pursued by formalities of marriage (proof of marriage, ease of administration, consent to marriage). These matters are discussed further below.

II. BACKGROUND

The *Taczanowksa* case concerned the formal validity of a marriage celebrated in a Roman Catholic church in Rome in 1946. The spouses were both Polish and domiciled in Poland, the husband a member of the occupying Polish army and the wife a Polish civilian, and the officiating priest was a Polish army chaplain. Italian marriage laws required the reading of certain passages of the Italian civil code and for subsequent registration, and so the marriage was invalid as a matter of Italian domestic law insofar as these requirements were not met. Italian law also allowed for celebration of marriage in accordance with the law of the nationality, but insofar as contemporary Polish laws required a secular civil ceremony, this renvoi could not validate the marriage. While the marriage was therefore formally defective from the perspective of Italian and Polish law, it was accepted that the parties fully intended to contract a valid marriage and that the officiating priest was likely assuming an authority under Polish law, which had only recently been removed. The couple moved to England in 1947 where a child was born to them. Subsequently, in 1955, at a time when relations had soured, the wife petitioned the English courts for a decree of nullity, on the (previously uncontentious) basis that the marriage was formally defective under the law of the place of celebration.

[31] Briggs (n 26) 900; Fawcett, Ní Shúilleabháin and Shah (n 13) 636.

[32] Briggs (n 26) 900. It is important to note that while the judgment validated and supported the many irregular marriages concluded in the post-war years; it was, for the immediate petitioner at hand, a harsh decision which denied her the decree of nullity to which she would have been entitled on a conventional application of the *lex loci* rule.

III. ORTHODOX ADHERENCE TO THE LEX LOCI RULE IN THE HIGH COURT

The decree of nullity was granted by the English High Court in an orthodox application of the *lex loci* rule. The husband and the Queen's Proctor had raised a number of arguments in favour of validity, but all were rejected by Karminski J 'with very considerable reluctance'.[33] The 1892 Foreign Marriage Act (legislation providing for validation of British forces marriages) was inapplicable insofar as the Polish chaplains in Italy were not under direct British command.[34] The Queen's Proctor had suggested recognition as a common law marriage highlighting the previous authorities which exempted the 'conqueror' from the 'laws of the conquered' and which allowed for validation of marriage in the face of impossibility in complying with the *lex loci*.[35] Karminski J accepted that the marriage of a member of an occupying force might require 'special consideration' but noting the emphasis of Britishness and Englishness in the earlier authorities, he felt he could not extend them to 'foreigners' with a Polish personal law.[36] The judge also acknowledged the possibility of common law marriage in the face of 'insuperable difficulty' in complying with the *lex loci* but found that there was no such difficulty here 'indeed no difficulty of any kind, in the celebration at that time and place of a marriage valid by Italian law'.[37]

IV. REVOLUTION IN THE COURT OF APPEAL

A unanimous Court of Appeal reversed the decision of Karminski J and found the marriage to be valid and entitled to recognition as a common law marriage. Hodson LJ gave the leading judgment of the Court, with Parker and Ormerod LJJ giving separate (shorter) concurring judgments. While the decision was unanimous, much of the reasoning of the Court of Appeal is rather opaque and it is very difficult to identify the ratio decidendi. Nonetheless, there was relative clarity on some points of law. First, it was strongly suggested in the judgments of Hodson and Parker LJJ that the personal law should have no role in determining the formal validity of foreign marriages unless the law of the place of celebration allowed for validation under the personal law.[38] Thus, it was envisaged that 'partial' or 'single' renvoi would extend to formalities of marriage under the English conflict of laws – and the application of the law of the place of celebration would include the application of its conflicts rules insofar as they allowed

[33] *Taczanowska* (n 1) 314.
[34] Karminski J also found that the 1892 Act required one of the spouses to be British but this interpretation was rejected on appeal: ibid, 310–11; see also 319–20 (CA).
[35] ibid, 311–12.
[36] ibid.
[37] ibid, 313.
[38] ibid, 318–19, 326 (Hodson LJ); 331 (Parker LJ).

for celebration in accordance with the personal law (whether that be based on the *lex domicilii* or the *lex patriae*). *Taczanowska* was thus noted for its support of renvoi in a domain where it had hitherto played no significant role.[39] In rejecting any direct reference to the personal law, however, *Taczanowska* had moved away from a widely-held view that the personal law (*lex domicilii*) could potentially supply validity in the event that the domestic formalities of the place of celebration could not easily be met.[40] Hodson LJ was also clear in his view that the presence of an episcopally ordained clergyman was a core ingredient of a common law marriage[41] (a proposition which is contested in the literature).[42]

What was most unclear was the precise legal basis for invoking the common law marriage doctrine. Citing earlier cases such as *Ruding v Smith*,[43] *Scrimshire v Scrimshire*,[44] and *Burn v Farrar*,[45] Hodson LJ emphasised the belligerent occupation of Italy by the Polish forces[46] alongside the idea that conquerors are free to disregard the laws of the conquered.[47] He also stressed the lack of submission to Italian law on the facts at hand[48] – and the legitimacy of applying English common law where the forum is English.[49] He recognised that while the earlier cases on common law marriage had involved British subjects, 'the common law conception of marriage knows no distinction of race or nationality'.[50]

Hodson LJ also drew support from a (then) recent Australian case, *Savenis v Savenis*,[51] which had recognised as a common law marriage an irregular marriage between two Lithuanians in Germany in 1945. Hodson LJ acknowledged that the *Savenis* case was founded on an 'insuperable difficulty' in complying with

[39] *Dicey, Morris & Collins*, 15th edn (n 17) 922; Carter (n 19) 333; Mendes de Costa (n 6) 261.

[40] JG Fleming, 'Common Law Marriage' (1951) 4 *The International Law Quarterly* 500, 502; Carter (n 19) 334, 336; Mendes da Costa (n 6) 248–249. One might wonder whether the court's reluctance to subject the parties' Roman Catholic marriage to the law of the domicile might have been influenced by the friction between the Roman Catholic church in Poland and the newly established (communist) Lublin Government: if the parties were hostile to the application of Italian law, might they also have been hostile to the new Polish law which had recently removed the right to contract a valid civil marriage through a Roman Catholic ceremony? See further GH Janczewski, 'The Origin of the Lublin Government' (1972) 50 *The Slavonic and East European Review* 140; R Monticone, 'The Catholic Church in Poland, 1945–1966' (1966) *The Polish Review* 75; also *Taczanowska* (n 1) 306–07.

[41] *Taczanowska* (n 1) 326.

[42] Rejecting the need for such a clergyman, see Carter (n 19) 334; *Dicey, Morris & Collins*, 15th edn (n 17) 926. But see also Mendes da Costa (n 6) 239–242 who is in agreement with Hodson LJ on this point.

[43] *Ruding v Smith* (n 8).

[44] *Scrimshire v Scrimshire* (n 6).

[45] *Burn v Farrar* (n 11).

[46] *Taczanowska* (n 1) 321.

[47] ibid, 322–23, 325–26.

[48] ibid, 321, 325–26. See Mendes da Costa (n 6) 227 criticising the reliance on *Scrimshire* for this proposition of law.

[49] *Taczanowska* (n 1) 326

[50] ibid, 326.

[51] *Savenis v Savenis and Szmeck* [1950] SASR 309.

German law in the absence of available registrars, and accepted that there had been no such impossibility in the case at hand.[52] Nonetheless *Savenis* provided support for the extension of common law marriage to couples with a nationality and domicile wholly unconnected to the common law. Unfortunately, Hodson LJ appeared to be unaware of subsequent Australian case-law which had sought to limit the authority of *Savenis* and which had rejected the use of the common law marriage exception in validating the marriages of foreigners with no personal connection to the common law.[53]

Echoing Hodson LJ, Parker LJ also emphasised the legitimacy of having recourse to the *lex fori*[54] and he conceptualised the *lex loci* rule as one based on voluntary submission to local marriage laws.[55] He also referenced the 'law of nations' and its special treatment of military forces in belligerent occupation.[56] Ormerod LJ took a slightly different approach, inferring a lack of submission in circumstances 'where the husband is in Italy not from choice but under the orders of his military superiors'.[57] Thus, Ormerod LJ gave emphasis to the absence of free will and suggested an enhanced role for common law marriage in circumstances where a couple's (or spouse's) presence on a particular territory is involuntary.

V. SUBSEQUENT DEVELOPMENT IN THE ENGLISH COURTS

In *Kochanski v Kochanska*,[58] decided only a few weeks after the Court of Appeal's ruling in *Taczanowska*, the English High Court adopted a notably liberal interpretation of *Taczanowska*, and recognised as a common law marriage the religious marriage of two Poles in Germany in 1945 at a time when they were living in a displaced persons camp (and neither was in Germany in a military capacity as part of an army in belligerent occupation). Sachs J opined that the common law marriage doctrine was applicable in circumstances beyond those of insuperable difficulty and belligerent occupation, and he ruled that the presumption of subjection to German law was rebutted in the circumstances at hand where the parties had lived in a context of deliberate separation from German society and German law.[59] While the marriage here had not complied with the *lex loci* (German law which required a secular civil ceremony), it had

[52] *Taczanowska* (n 1) 324–25, 327.
[53] *Maksymec v Maksymec* (1956) 72 WN (NSW) 522 discussed by Blom-Cooper (n 19) 642; Andrews (n 3) 402.
[54] *Taczanowska* (n 1) 329.
[55] ibid, 330.
[56] ibid, 330–31.
[57] ibid, 332.
[58] *Kochanski v Kochanska* [1958] P 147.
[59] ibid, 152–53.

complied with the law of the domicile (Polish law) and Sachs J queried as to whether – in the interests of comity and consistency – it might be better to apply the personal law in lieu of the common law, in circumstances where it was not reasonable to insist on adherence to the *lex loci*.[60]

Subsequent English cases highlighted the uncertain scope of the common law marriage doctrine as conceived in *Taczanowska* and attempts were made to rein in and restrict this line of authority. Phillimore J struck a critical tone in *Lazarewicz v Lazarewicz*,[61] refusing to recognise a marriage celebrated in Italy in circumstances which were mostly very similar to those in *Taczanowska*, although the wife here had Italian (and Polish) heritage and the officiating (Polish) priest was not an army chaplain. Phillimore J expressed the view that it would be 'anomalous' if a marriage invalid under Polish and Italian law, were held valid in English law.[62] In *Merker v Merker*[63] the English High Court rejected any assumption that *Taczanowska* allowed any person marrying abroad 'to elect whether they should be married by the local law or in some other way', and to demand recognition as a common law marriage in the latter case.[64] Sir Jocelyn Simon opined that such an interpretation of *Taczanowska* would 'leave the rule in *Berthiaume v Dastous* in tatters' and would 'introduce anarchy in a field where order and comity are particularly required'.[65]

The matter came back before the English Court of Appeal in *Preston v Preston*.[66] The facts of *Preston* were on all-fours with the facts of *Kochanski* and the Court recognised the marriage as a common law marriage.[67] Nonetheless the language of the Court was much more restrained – and Ormerod LJ (who had also sat in the *Taczanowska* case) expressed the view that the basis for the *Taczanowska* judgment 'was that, although parties who marry in a foreign country must be considered to have submitted to the laws of that country so far at least as the form of marriage is concerned, such a rule did not apply in the case of a soldier serving in a force of belligerent occupation'.[68] Noting the demands of 'international comity', Ormerod LJ also observed that 'the courts should be reluctant to extend the instances where compliance with the lex loci is unnecessary to constitute a valid marriage'.[69] While not attempting an exhaustive

[60] ibid, 154–55.

[61] *Lazarewicz (orse Fadanelli) v Lazarewicz* [1962] P 171.

[62] ibid, 177.

[63] *Merker v Merker* [1963] P 283.

[64] ibid, 295.

[65] ibid, 295. In *Merker* a German court decree was considered determinative and the irregular German marriage was found to be invalid (although the English court conceded that it would have been validated by *Taczanowska* had there been no German decree).

[66] *Preston (orse Putynski) v Preston (orse Putynska) (orse Basinska)* [1963] P 411.

[67] *Preston* concerned the religious marriage of two Poles who had been residing at the same camp as the couple in *Kochanski* although the court characterised the camp somewhat differently in *Preston*. The officiating priest was the same in both cases.

[68] *Preston* (n 66) 426.

[69] ibid, 427.

statement of when common law marriage might be sanctioned, Ormerod LJ said that 'it is not enough for the parties to say or to show by their actions that they do not intend to submit' to the *lex loci*.[70] In accepting that the marriage at hand could be recognised as a common law marriage, Ormerod LJ emphasised the husband's previous service in the Polish army and the camp's existence as part of the 'hostile occupation of Germany'.[71]

VI. IMPACT OF TACZANOWSKA

Notwithstanding the subsequent attempts to refine and distinguish *Taczanowska*, the scope of application of the common law marriage exception remains highly uncertain. Even if it is accepted (as is often suggested[72]) that the doctrine is confined to the two situations of insuperable difficulty and belligerent occupation, many details of its applicability have yet to be resolved. Andrews raises the pertinent question as to whether British nationals are debarred from availing of the common law marriage exception if they had the option of marrying in accordance with the statutory scheme for services or consular marriages.[73] The extension of common law marriage might seem unnecessarily generous in those circumstances, but equally it would be odd to deny common law marriage to British nationals in circumstances where it would be sanctioned for others. It is also unclear as to whether those who were nationals of, or domiciled in, the place of celebration can plead the common law marriage exception, or whether it is restricted to 'outsiders'.[74] *Lazarewics* lends support to such a restriction – in suggesting that there could be no common law marriage for a woman with Italian nationality marrying in Italy.[75] Ormerod LJ had suggested in *Taczanowska* that the doctrine might only avail outsiders whose presence is involuntary, but he appeared to have retreated from this position in *Preston v Preston* in sanctioning common law marriage for a couple in circumstances where it was unclear as to why they were in Germany and where there was no evidence of any compulsion to remain there.[76] Another question is whether the doctrine will only extend to 'sympathetic' army personnel, or whether it applies equally to those armies whose activities are condemned by the British Government. Dicey suggests that logically it must,[77] but as Briggs points out this is an unattractive proposition.[78]

[70] ibid.
[71] ibid, 424, 427.
[72] *Dicey, Morris & Collins*, 15th edn (n 17) 917–18.
[73] Andrews (n 3) 406.
[74] ibid 407.
[75] *Lazarewicz* (n 61) 180.
[76] *Preston* (n 66) 424.
[77] *Dicey, Morris & Collins*, 15th edn (n 17) 929.
[78] Briggs (n 26) 900.

There is also some doubt as to whether the *lex loci* doctrine retains its primacy in cases of belligerent occupation – in other words, whether the common law marriage test should only be considered in the event of non-compliance with the *lex loci*, or whether compliance with the *lex loci* should be ignored if it was clear that there was no intention to comply with the *lex loci*. A related question is whether there must be (non-)submission by both spouses, or whether only the intentions of the spouse in belligerent occupation are relevant.

While English judges have made some efforts to confine the scope of *Taczanowska* to situations of insuperable difficulty and belligerent occupation, the facts of *Preston* and (in particular) *Kochanski* tend to extend the common law marriage exception beyond those narrow circumstances. There are also numerous dicta which may support a much broader interpretation of the doctrine – for example, both in *Kochanski* and in *Taczanowska* it is suggested that common law marriage may come into play where conformity with the *lex loci* would be 'contrary to the conscience'.[79] These dicta could be used to press for exemption from the *lex loci* simply because its content is in some way objectionable to the spouses.[80] Alive to these possibilities for an expansive interpretation, commentators have suggested that common law marriage should not be available to those who are merely on holiday and that perhaps (in view of the ease of modern travel) there should be some requirement of urgency, or of the absence of alternative options.[81]

As has been seen, Hodson LJ in *Taczanowska* had insisted that common law marriage must be celebrated before an 'episcopally ordained clergyman' (considering himself to be bound by the House of Lords decision in *R v Millis* on this point).[82] However, Russell LJ expressed doubt as to such a requirement in *Preston*,[83] and in the modern era, such a requirement must surely be untenable in view of the English courts' obligations under section 6 of the Human Rights Act 1998. Any prioritisation of religious marriage ceremonies would constitute a discriminatory interference with the right to freedom of religion under Article 9 ECHR, as indeed would any preferential treatment of adherents to certain religions (eg, Roman Catholics, Anglicans where the priests are episcopally ordained) over others where they are not (eg, Presbyterians).[84] Further,

[79] *Kochanski* (n 58) 152; *Taczanowska* (n 1) 332 (Ormerod LJ referring to the judgment of Karminski J).

[80] See the decision of the Family Court of Australia in *Nygh v Kasey* [2010] FamCA 145 discussed in section X below.

[81] McClean and Ruiz Abou-Nigm (n 17) 274; Briggs (n 26) 899–900; Clarkson & Hill (n 17) 359–60.

[82] *Taczanowska* (n 1) 326 referring to *R v Millis* (1844) 10 Cl & Fin 534 (HL). Writing extra-judicially, Hodson (n 19) 208–09 was critical of *Millis* and of the requirement for the presence of an episcopally-ordained clergyman.

[83] *Preston* (n 66) 436.

[84] Fawcett, Ní Shúilleabháin and Shah (n 13) 632, 687. *Negrepontis-Giannisis v Greece* App No 56759/08 3 May 2011 suggests that where personal status is concerned, private international law rules based on anachronistic canon law norms are very likely to be incompatible with the ECHR.

even if the involvement of clergy could reasonably be mandated, any insistence that the officiating minister must be male would be objectionable as gender-discrimination in the exercise of the right to respect for family life (Article 14 taken with article 8 ECHR).

There is also another (more significant) gender bias in *Taczanowska* and its successor cases insofar as the focus is almost exclusively on the husband and his affiliations and intentions while the wives remain mostly invisible. This tendency is, for example, in evidence in the judgment of Ormerod LJ in *Preston* where it is observed that 'there is little or no evidence of the status of the wife, but … this does not seem to be material'.[85] This side-lining of women is also reflected in his later reference to *Ruding v Smith*: he notes that '[a]part from the fact that the wife was born in India and came to the Cape in 1796, nothing seems to be known about her'.[86] While it is legitimate to suggest that only one spouse needs to be in belligerent occupation – or experiencing insuperable difficulty – the modern law cannot continue this pattern of a very gendered scrutiny of the facts.[87]

VII. CRITICAL ANALYSIS OF TACZANOWSKA'S COMMON LAW MARRIAGE DOCTRINE

Taczanowska is a decision with weak foundations in the common law and the charge of 'judicial legislation'[88] is perhaps justified. There is much reliance on *Burn v Farrar*[89] and *Ruding v Smith*[90] but these cases concerned the overseas marriages of British army personnel and neither judgment sought to establish any new principle of law. No final decision was reached in *Burn v Farrar*[91] and Lord Stowell in *Ruding v Smith* expressed his 'desire to be understood as not extending this decision beyond cases including nearly the same circumstances'[92] (and indeed the 'guarded and limited nature' of the judgment is acknowledged by Hodson LJ in *Taczanowska*[93]). As already noted, the Australian *Savenis* case,[94]

[85] *Preston* (n 66) 424.
[86] ibid, 425.
[87] UN Convention on the Elimination of All Forms of Discrimination Against Women ('CEDAW'), Art 16(1)(a) requires 'equality of men and women' in regulating entry into marriage.
[88] Mendes da Costa (n 6) 245.
[89] *Burn v Farrar* (n 11): see *Taczanowska* (n 1) 321–22, 330.
[90] *Ruding v Smith* (n 8): see *Taczanowska* (n 1) 322–24, 331–32.
[91] *Burn v Farrar* (n 11) 370; *Taczanowska* (n 1) 322 ('I shall give no decided opinion on that point at present'). As is noted by Parker LJ (at 331), the nullity question in *Burn v Farrar* never came to trial.
[92] *Ruding v Smith* (n 8) 394; *Taczanowska* (n 1) 324.
[93] *Taczanowska* (n 1) 324 (also at 331, per Parker LJ). Hodson LJ further acknowledges (at 324) that *Ruding v Smith* is 'only to be taken as authority for the particular case' and (at 325) that 'there is no authority which goes the whole length of the submissions of the Queen's Proctor in this case'. He also accepts (at 324) that *Ruding* was based in part on insuperable difficulty in complying with the *lex loci*.
[94] *Savenis v Savenis* (n 51).

also invoked in support of the Court of Appeal's reasoning,[95] had already been doubted in subsequent Australian case-law.[96] Furthermore, in the *Starkowski v Attorney-General* case,[97] decided only four years prior to *Taczanowska*, the House of Lords had not given any consideration to the possibility of 'common law marriage' in determining the validity of a Roman Catholic marriage of Polish civilians in Austria in 1945 (in contravention of the contemporary Austrian requirement for celebration at a civil registry). The marriage in *Starkowski* was upheld but only on the basis of its retrospective approval under Austrian law. If the principles laid down in *Taczanowska* and *Kochanski* were well-founded in the common law, then this marriage would arguably have been valid even without retrospective approval by the Austrian authority, and one would have expected the House of Lords to be alert to this possibility.[98]

The Court of Appeal's transposition of principles of public international law is also questionable. As Brownlie and Webb point out,[99] the Court of Appeal appears to rely on the concept of 'belligerent occupation',[100] a technical category of public international law, but also on the 'anachronistic' idea of non-submission of conquerors to the laws of the conquered.[101] In public international law, the idea of 'belligerent occupation' was a rejection of the theory of 'conquest' (which had survived up until the mid-late nineteenth century but had been discredited by the early twentieth century).[102] Therefore the Court of Appeal's simultaneous use of ideas of 'conquest' and 'belligerent occupation' is unsound from the perspective of public international law. Also, while the belligerent occupier is not necessarily bound by the laws of the occupied,[103] and may adopt new laws where required,[104] it is unclear as to how, as a matter of public international law, the Polish occupier may be considered to be subject to the English common law.

From a private international law perspective, *Taczanowska* has been criticised for its use of the *lex fori* in a domain where universality is necessary to

[95] *Taczanowska* (n 1) 327–28, 331.

[96] See section IV above. Also, insofar as Hodson and Parker LJJ sought to rely on *Scrimshire v Scrimshire* (n 6) in justification of their reliance on voluntary submission (at 325–326, 330), Mendes da Costa (n 6) 227 argues that *Scrimshire* does not really provide authority for this proposition of law.

[97] *Starkowski (otherwise Urbanski) v Attorney-General* (n 7).

[98] See Andrews (n 3) 405; also the submissions of the Queen's Proctor in *Lazarewicz* (n 61) 173–74. Of course, this would depend on common law marriage being available to Polish civilians but this is at least arguable based on *Kochanski* (n 58).

[99] Brownlie and Webb (n 19) 458–60.

[100] See *Taczanowska* (n 1) 321, 330.

[101] ibid, 322–23, 325–26, 331.

[102] E Benvenisti, 'The Origins of the Concept of Belligerent Occupation' (2008) 26 *Law and History Review* 621, 627.

[103] ibid 632.

[104] See A McNair, 'Municipal Effects of Belligerent Occupation' (1941) 57 *Law Quarterly Review* 33, 47; Y Dinstein, *The International Law of Belligerent Occupation* (Boston, CUP, 2009) 108.

avoid limping marriages[105] and where there is a broad international consensus in favour of the application of the *lex loci celebrationis*.[106] In other domains of choice-of-law, international instruments suggest a flexible attitude towards formalities and a willingness to allow any one of an array of connected laws to supply formal validity,[107] but in the domain of marriage, no such pattern has emerged, and the *lex loci* rule has retained its global primacy. It is arguable that in facilitating recognition of marriages which are invalid under both the *lex loci* and the personal law, English law is pursuing an isolationist policy which deviates sharply from private international law norms, and which is inimical to consistency in personal status.[108] In private international law literature, *Taczanowska* is also criticised for applying English law to those who have no connection with England at the time of marriage, and can have no expectation that its laws will be brought to bear.[109] This criticism would be very well-justified if the technicalities of the Marriage Act 1949 were being imposed on foreign marriages of foreign domiciliaries – but it is perhaps fair to say that the imposition of the common law marriage test is really only demanding marriage in its most basic form, stripped to its bare essentials.[110] Also, as some of the English judges have pointed out, this test reflects the traditional canon law throughout Europe and not some peculiarly English conception of marriage.[111]

There is strong support in the literature for the use of the personal law in default of the *lex loci* being available (as the law of second resort),[112] and it is suggested that since the dual domicile test works for essential validity or capacity, it can also work for formal validity.[113] However, in the view of this author, there is merit in Hodson and Parker LJJs' concerns respecting cases of diverging domiciles.[114] The reality is that capacity requirements will only ever impact on a small minority of couples (at least in the case of different-sex couples) and for the vast majority of spouses (assuming they are unrelated adults of sound mind at the time of marrying), compliance with capacity requirements is a given – even under divergent domiciliary laws.[115] Compliance with formality

[105] Stone (n 19) 505–506; Mendes da Costa (n 6) 234–235; Andrews (n 3) 404.

[106] D Coester-Waltjen, 'Marriage' in J Basedow (ed), *Encyclopaedia of Private International Law* (Cheltenham, Edward Elgar, 2017) 1228–29.

[107] See, eg, Art 11 of the Regulation (EC) No 593/2008 (Rome I) and the Hague Form of Wills Convention 1961.

[108] Cohn (n 24) 647–648.

[109] See Andrews (n 3) 406.

[110] *Dicey, Morris & Collins* (n 17) 930; Briggs (n 26) 899. This perspective assumes that the required involvement of an episcopally-ordained clergyman is no longer good law (if it ever was).

[111] Russell LJ in *Preston* (n 66) 416; Phillimore J in *Lazarewicz* (n 61) 177.

[112] D Fine, 'The Formal Sufficiency of Foreign Marriage' (1976) 7 *Federal Law Review* 49, 60–63; Carter (n 19) 336; Mendes da Costa (n 6) 249–250; *Dicey, Morris & Collins* (n 17) 928.

[113] Carter (n 19) 336; Andrews (n 3) 405.

[114] *Taczanowska* (n 1) 326, 331.

[115] Incapacity is a much more pressing concern for same-sex couples and the dual domicile test is much more likely to have an invalidating effect on same-sex marriages: see M Ní Shúilleabháin, 'Same-Sex Marriage and the Conflict of Laws – the Unresolved Cross-Border Dimension' (2019) 135 *Law Quarterly Review* 374.

rules cannot however be assumed in the same way and the likelihood of a single ceremony aligning with the technicalities of two different sets of domestic formality laws is in reality rather slim.

Taczanowska's support for partial renvoi is to be (cautiously) welcomed.[116] Where both the *lex loci* and the personal law allow for formal validity of marriage, it makes no sense for other countries to insist on invalidity simply because there was non-compliance with the internal domestic rules of the *lex loci*. (Indeed, those local forms may not have been available to the parties and they may have been directed to the use of their national law by way of consular marriage for example.) If, in such circumstances, validity under the personal law satisfies the *lex loci*, it should also suffice elsewhere. This invocation of renvoi promotes consistency and the avoidance of limping marriages, and while there are practical and conceptual difficulties associated with the use of renvoi, its application is probably justified in this policy context where the law favours validity (*favor matrimonii*).[117] Of course, there may be circumstances where a marriage has been celebrated in compliance with the domestic rules of the *lex loci*, where the conflicts rules of that place of celebration demand compliance with the law of the nationality (for example) – with the result that a partial renvoi will lead to invalidity. Nonetheless, it seems that on balance the use of partial renvoi is defensible – even in the latter case where it leads to invalidity.

VIII. TACZANOWSKA AND THE RIGHT OF MARRIAGE

Taczanowska has a complex interaction with human rights law. The case was decided at a time when human rights law was in its infancy, and as has been seen, some aspects of the common law marriage doctrine, as articulated in the late 1950s and early 1960s, are clearly incompatible with contemporary standards on gender and religious discrimination. Nonetheless, the common law marriage exception can also be seen as a vehicle for the protection of human rights interests, and particularly for the realisation of the right of marriage[118] (protected under Article 12 ECHR and under many other human rights instruments)[119] and of the right to respect for family life (Article 8 ECHR).[120] ECHR contracting states owe particular obligations to ensure the enjoyment of these rights by army personnel[121] – and so the extension of a special mode of marriage for those in

[116] Mendes da Costa (n 6) 261.
[117] On the universality of *favor matrimonii*, see Coester-Waltjen (n 106) 1227.
[118] Fawcett, Ní Shúilleabháin and Shah (n 13) 634–35.
[119] ibid, 592.
[120] ibid, 582.
[121] Council of Europe Committee of Ministers, *Human Rights of Members of the Armed Forces* Recommendation CM/Rec (2010) 4, 15; Council of Europe Parliamentary Assembly, *Human Rights of Members of the Armed Forces*, Recommendation 1742 (2006).

belligerent occupation may be justified on human rights grounds. Human rights law also insists on strict scrutiny of restrictions on the right to marry,[122] and in that context, a mechanism for overcoming insuperable difficulty is consistent with the ethos of Article 12 ECHR. However, human rights law is also strongly supportive of the use of formalities[123] and does not require recognition of self-devised marriage ceremonies.[124] It is accepted that it is reasonable for national laws to require a 'public undertaking' so that marriage is amenable to 'objective verification'.[125] The 1962 UN Convention on Consent to Marriage requires national marriage laws to insist on publicity and party presence and registration in order to safeguard against non-consensual marriage and to protect human rights in that context.[126] It follows that any very broad construction of *Taczanowska* which tends to provide a general opt-out from the formalities of the *lex loci*[127] would not be supported by human rights law.[128]

A difficult question is whether human rights law would support the invocation of the common law exception whenever the relevant foreign formalities are incompatible with human rights norms[129] – for example, where the relevant foreign form entails a degree of gender discrimination, or where the place of celebration does not facilitate the formalisation of same-sex relationships in any way. In such circumstances, much may depend on whether the parties had alternative options or a subsequent opportunity for regularisation of their status.[130]

IX. THE INFLUENCE OF TACZANOWSKA ON OTHER COMMON LAW JURISDICTIONS

Taczanowska v Taczanowski appears to have had a relatively limited impact on the law in other common law jurisdictions. *Taczanowska* is cited and discussed in the leading Irish textbook on conflict of laws[131] and in a report of the Irish Law Reform Commission.[132] However, in *Hassan v Minister for Justice, Equality and Law Reform*, Fennelly J expressed doubt as to whether the common law marriage exception could validate a foreign marriage where neither the ceremony nor the parties had any connection with a common law jurisdiction.[133]

[122] See, eg, *O'Donoghue v UK* (2011) 53 EHRR 1; *B and L v UK* (2006) 42 EHRR 11.
[123] *Muñoz Díaz v Spain* (2010) 50 EHRR 49.
[124] *Hopic v Netherlands* App No 13158/87 4 July 1991; *X v Germany* App No 6167/73 18 December 1974.
[125] *Van der Heijden v Netherlands* (2013) 57 EHRR 13 [68]–[69].
[126] See the preamble to the Convention.
[127] See Webb (n 19) 94.
[128] Fawcett, Ní Shúilleabháin and Shah (n 13) 634–36.
[129] ibid, 634.
[130] *Muñoz Díaz v Spain* (n 123).
[131] W Binchy, *Irish Conflict of Laws* (London, Butterworth, 1988) 229.
[132] Law Reform Commission, *Report on Private International Law Aspects of Capacity to Marry and Choice of Law in Proceedings for Nullity of Marriage* (LRC 19, 1985) 34–36.
[133] *Hassan v Minister for Justice, Equality and Law Reform* [2013] IESC 8 [47].

Taczanowska has been widely cited and discussed in Australian case-law[134] and literature,[135] and the common law marriage exception to the *lex loci* rule is well-established under Australian law.[136] However, as has been seen,[137] this development in the Australian common law preceded *Taczanowska*, and cannot be directly attributed to the influence of the judgment of the English Court of Appeal in *Taczanowska*. In practice, the Australian courts tend to cite *Taczanowska* alongside the (many) indigenous cases on common law marriage and it is not treated as the decisive authority.[138] Also, while there may have been some exceptions, most notably the recent case of *Nygh & Kasey*,[139] discussed below, in general the Australian jurisprudence has been relatively restrained and has exhibited a strong commitment to the *lex loci* rule.[140]

In Canada, as in Ireland, *Taczanowska* appears to have had relatively little impact. The case is discussed in some journal articles[141] and is mentioned in textbooks,[142] but the CanLII database reveals only two case citations[143] (and *Taczanowska* was not directly on point in either case but only cited in passing). The *Taczanowska* case is briefly mentioned in Hook and Wass on *The Conflict of Laws in New Zealand* but there is no suggestion that the case has exerted any significant influence on the law in New Zealand.[144] Crawford and Carruthers report that in Scotland the *lex loci* rule is enshrined in section 38(1) of the Family Law (Scotland) Act 2006.[145] Referring to *Taczanowska* in the context of the English common law, the authors indicate that while such an exception

[134] *X and X* [1983] Fam CA 4 [20]–[21]; *Kuklycz v Kuklycz* [1972] VR 50, 51; *Katavic v Katavic* [1977] Fam CA 73; *Milder v Milder* [1959] VR 95.

[135] See, eg, Fine (n 112); A Hiller, 'Formalities of Marriage Where Compliance with the *Lex Loci Celebrationis* is Impossible' (1958) 2 *Sydney Law Review* 592; J Hanlon, 'Milder v Milder' (1959) 2 *Melbourne University Law Review* 257; M Tilbury, G Davis and B Opeskin, *Conflict of Laws in Australia* (Melbourne, OUP, 2002) 605–606.

[136] Tilbury, Davis and Opeskin (n 135) 601.

[137] See section IV above discussing *Savenis v Savenis* (n 51).

[138] See, eg, the discussion of previous authorities in *X and X* (n 134) and *Katavic v Katavic* (n 134). Indeed, *Taczanowska* is not cited at all in the two most recent Australian cases on the common law marriage exception: *Nygh & Kasey* (n 80) and *Lin & Nicoll* [2016] Fam CA 401 (although *Kochanski* is cited in *Nygh v Kasey*).

[139] *Nygh v Kasey* (n 80) [85]. For a critical view of *Nygh v Kasey*, see S Harder, 'Recent Judicial Aberrations in Australian Private International Law' (2012) 19 *Australian International Law Journal* 161.

[140] See, eg, *X and X* (n 134); *Katavic v Katavic* (n 134); *Milder v Milder* (n 134) defining 'insuperable difficulty' narrowly and refusing to sanction the use of the common law marriage exception.

[141] P Maddaugh, 'Validity of Marriage and the Conflict of Laws: A Critique of the Present Anglo-American Position' (1973) 23 *University of Toronto Law Journal* 117, 141–42; A Swan, 'A New Approach to Marriage and Divorce in the Conflict of Laws' (1974) 24 *University of Toronto Law Journal* 17.

[142] See, eg, S Pitel and N Rafferty, *Conflict of Laws*, 2nd edn (Toronto, Irwin, 2016) 403, 406.

[143] *Keddie v Currie* [1991] CanLII 5731; *Re Lin* [1992] CanLII 6225.

[144] M Hook and J Wass, *The Conflict of Laws in New Zealand* (Wellington, LexisNexis, 2020) 628.

[145] E Crawford and J Carruthers, *International Private Law: A Scots Perspective*, 4th edn (Edinburgh, W Green, 2015) 332.

'may have existed in Scots common law' prior to the coming into force of section 38(1), it is now unlikely that any such exception could apply.[146]

X. THE FUTURE OF TACZANOWSKA'S COMMON LAW MARRIAGE DOCTRINE

As has been seen, *Taczanowska* led a stream of English cases in the late 1950s and early 1960s, but there have been very few citations by the English courts since then.[147] The question then arises as to whether the case is likely to have any further impact on English law. In this regard two possibilities present themselves.

First, the development of human rights law may give a new lease of life to the common law marriage exception as developed by *Taczanowska*. A recent Australian authority, *Nygh & Kasey*,[148] sanctioned the use of the exception where the laws of the place of celebration (Thailand) were perceived to be gender-discriminatory, and where as a consequence the spouses refused to complete a mandatory procedural step. This case is controversial because the spouses, who lived in Australia, were only on a short trip to Thailand at the time of the marriage ceremony – and had ready access to a form of marriage which did not so discriminate.[149] Nonetheless, it is possible that the English courts may also be asked to deploy the common law marriage exception in circumstances where the non-compliance with the *lex loci* is arguably justified by human rights interests.

Second, it is possible that the common law marriage doctrine may be invoked by same-sex couples as a remedy for the lack of formalisation options in many (if not most) foreign legal orders. European human rights law would provide some level of support for such a strategy: while the Strasbourg Court has not yet guaranteed a right of marriage for same-sex couples,[150] it has recognised that Article 8 ECHR is violated where contracting states fail to allow for any mode of formalisation of same-sex relationships.[151] Of course, the ECHR is not binding on third countries, but it may be argued that contracting states owe a positive obligation to recognise a self-devised ceremony where this was the only option available to the same-sex partners in the third-country legal order in which they found themselves. This argument will be significantly strengthened if the European Court of Human Rights moves to guarantee a right of same-sex

[146] Crawford and Carruthers (n 145) 335–36.

[147] The 'precedent map' on the Westlaw UK database suggests that there has been only 1 citation since the early 1960s, in *Collett (otherwise Sakazova) v Collett* [1968] P 482.

[148] *Nygh & Kasey* (n 80).

[149] See Harder (n 139) 178 arguing that it was 'patently absurd' to excuse the non-compliance with the *lex loci* in these circumstances.

[150] *Schalk and Kopf v Austria* (2011) 53 EHRR 20.

[151] *Oliari v Italy* Apps Nos 18766/11 and 36030/11 21 July 2015; *Fedotova v Russia* App No 40792/10 13 July 2021.

marriage under Article 12 ECHR. Restrictions on Article 12 rights are subject to much stricter scrutiny,[152] and a litigant could rely by analogy on the case-law demanding the positive facilitation of marriage by prisoners whose right of marriage was curtailed by their physical circumstances.[153]

Even without recourse to human rights law, same-sex partners could invoke the 'insuperable difficulty' presented by the laws of a country which does not permit of marriage or registered partnership for them, and demand recognition based on the traditional common law marriage exception. It is, however, possible that the exception might be considered inapplicable insofar as the inability to marry is attributable to an incapacity and not to a formal deficiency as such.[154] Also, insofar as a same-sex couple, living in a country which does not offer same-sex marriage or registered partnership, would be able to travel to another country which does, it might be argued that recourse to the common law marriage doctrine is excessive, and that a self-devised ceremony could only be recognised in an exceptional cases where there was truly no alternative (for example, in circumstances of illness or impecuniosity[155]).

XI. CONCLUSION

Writing extra-judicially about *Taczanowska*, Hodson LJ opined that 'it is not for me to say whether the Court of Appeal has gone too far in recognition of a common law marriage'.[156] He preferred to wait for 'the verdict of the legal historians of the future' to determine whether the Court of Appeal fell into error.[157] This chapter attempts to provide an answer to this difficult question and to assess the 'landmark' status of the *Taczanowska* ruling.

It is suggested that the Court of Appeal did 'go too far' and did 'fall into error'. In the view of this author, it is entirely legitimate for lawmakers to create some limited exceptions to the *lex loci* rule – to cater for situations where compliance with the *lex loci* could not reasonably be expected – however, any such exception needs to be clearly and precisely formulated to ensure legal certainty for affected spouses and to avoid any significant weakening of the *lex loci* rule. The opaqueness of the reasoning in *Taczanowska*, and the emphasis of voluntary submission, created a common law marriage exception with

[152] Fawcett, Ní Shúilleabháin and Shah (n 13) 592.

[153] ibid 597.

[154] See Briggs (n 26) 900. If, however, a foreign incapacity to marry a person of the same sex offends public policy in the eyes of the recognising state (as is arguably the case in England), then there is no longer any problem of essential invalidity – the only barrier is the lack of any available form, and thus the only question is one of formal validity.

[155] See *O'Donoghue v UK* (n 122); *B and L v UK* (n 122): financial barriers to a right of marriage may engage Art 12 ECHR.

[156] Hodson (n 19) 216.

[157] ibid 216.

very fuzzy boundaries, and parties to irregular overseas marriages were left in a state of uncertainty regarding their English marital status. The vagueness of the doctrine also allowed for somewhat arbitrary differentiation between couples who had married in very similar circumstances.[158]

Given the revolutionary nature of the judgment, and the judgment's status as a test case affecting thousands of couples, *Taczanowska* certainly qualified as a landmark judgment of private international law in the late 1950s and early 1960s. Whether it retains that status is debatable. While it is possible that the common law marriage doctrine (and the authority of *Taczanowska*) may experience a revival – as a new mechanism for securing compliance with human rights norms and/or protection for same-sex couples – it is equally possible that it will soon fade away into obscurity as a curiosity of legal history.

[158] For example, as between the couple in *Taczanowska* (n 1) and the couple in *Lazarewicz* (n 61).

10

The Eleftheria (1970)

WILLIAM DAY*

I. INTRODUCTION

THE JURISDICTIONAL EFFECT of an exclusive choice of court agreement at common law is relatively easy to summarise in principle, even if often not straightforward to apply in practice.[1] Where the dispute falls within the scope of a clause choosing the English court, and a claim is served on a defendant in England, an application for a stay is most unlikely to succeed. Such a clause used to provide a gateway for permission to serve out of the jurisdiction,[2] but instead now provides a basis to serve out without permission;[3] and it also weighs heavily against any argument that the court should declare that it has no jurisdiction because it is not the proper place in which to bring the claim.[4] Conversely, where a dispute falls within the scope of a clause choosing a foreign court as the exclusive forum, an application to stay English proceedings served in the jurisdiction is very likely to be successful, and an application for permission to serve out of the jurisdiction should normally fail.

This treatment of jurisdiction agreements – giving them very significant influence but not a determinative voice – is often attributed to the decision of Brandon J in *The Eleftheria*.[5] That was a case which concerned an application to continue proceedings as of right in England in the face of a foreign jurisdiction

* I am very grateful to Niamh Davis for her research assistance, and for thoughts from Alex Mills on an earlier draft, in addition to the helpful discussion of the paper at the conference.

[1] For the purposes of this chapter, non-exclusive jurisdiction agreements, arbitration agreements and international instruments, such as the Regulation (EU) No 1215/2012 and the Hague Convention on Choice of Court Agreements 2005, are largely put to one side. Likewise, the controversial question of damages for breach of a jurisdiction agreement is not addressed.

[2] PD 6B, para 3.1(6)(d), removed on 6 April 2021.

[3] CPR 6.33(2B)(b), added on 6 April 2021.

[4] CPR 6.37(3).

[5] *Owners of Cargo Lately Laden on Board the Eleftheria v Owners of the Eleftheria* [1970] P 94 (Ad).

clause. The detail of the case is considered later but it is helpful to quote the famous numbered propositions set down by Brandon J at the outset:[6]

> (1) Where plaintiffs sue in England in breach of an agreement to refer disputes to a foreign court, and the defendants apply for a stay, the English court, assuming the claim to be otherwise within its jurisdiction, is not bound to grant a stay but has a discretion whether to do so or not.
> (2) The discretion should be exercised by granting a stay unless strong cause for not doing so is shown.
> (3) The burden of proving such strong cause is on the plaintiffs.
> (4) In exercising its discretion the court should take into account all the circumstances of the particular case.
> (5) In particular, but without prejudice to (4), the following matters, where they arise, may properly be regarded:
>
> (a) In what country the evidence on the issues of fact is situated, or more readily available, and the effect of that on the relative convenience and expense of trial as between the English and foreign courts.
> (b) Whether the law of the foreign court applies and, if so, whether it differs from English law in any material respects.
> (c) With what country either party is connected, and how closely.
> (d) Whether the defendants genuinely desire trial in the foreign country, or are only seeking procedural advantages.
> (e) Whether the plaintiffs would be prejudiced by having to sue in the foreign court because they would:
>
> (i) be deprived of security for their claim;
> (ii) be unable to enforce any judgment obtained;
> (iii) be faced with a time-bar not applicable in England; or
> (iv) for political, racial, religious or other reasons be unlikely to get a fair trial.

The Eleftheria is normally seen as a 'starting point'[7] in the modern law on the enforcement of jurisdiction agreements. As Adrian Briggs puts it,[8] *The Eleftheria* is the first of a 'trio of decisions which paved the way' for the modern leading decision on anti-suit injunctions by the House of Lords in *Donohue v Armco Inc.*[9] The impact of *The Eleftheria* has not been limited to England. It was rapidly exported to other common law systems, and has been favourably cited and applied by (*inter alios*) the Supreme Court of the United States of America in *M/S Bremen v Zapata Off-Shore Co*,[10] the High Court of Australia

[6] ibid, 99–100, reformatted for ease of review.
[7] See, eg, D Joseph, *Jurisdiction and Arbitration Agreements and their Enforcement,* 3rd edn (London, Sweet & Maxwell, 2015) para 10.07.
[8] A Briggs, *Civil Jurisdiction and Judgments,* 7th edn (London, Informa Law, 2021) 473.
[9] *Donohue v Armco Inc* [2001] UKHL 64, [2002] 1 All ER 749.
[10] *M/S Bremen v Zapata Off-Shore Co* [1972] 92 S Ct 1907, 1913 (Burger CJ).

in *Akai Pty Ltd v People's Insurance Co Ltd* (considered by Mary Keyes later in this collection),[11] the New Zealand Court of Appeal in *Society of Lloyd's and Oxford Members' Agency Ltd v Hyslop*,[12] the Supreme Court of Canada in *Ecu-Line NV v ZI Pompey Industrie* and more recently in *Douez v Facebook Inc*,[13] and by the Court of Appeal of Singapore in *Vinmar Overseas (Singapore) Pte Ltd v PTT International Trading Pte Ltd*[14] – all of which are important, if not landmark, cases in their own right within their respective private international legal systems.

The purpose of this chapter is to show that *The Eleftheria* is not the start of this story. Brandon J's numbered propositions can be seen as a distillation of what had gone before, rather than themselves laying the foundation for the decisions in *Donohue* in England and the equivalent modern landmarks in other common law jurisdictions. Nor is *The Eleftheria* the end of the story: the numbered propositions set out above are no longer an accurate summary of the modern law. Understood in this way, *The Eleftheria* remains a landmark, but more as a milestone on the journey, rather than where that journey began or finished. This chapter therefore begins by considering what preceded *The Eleftheria*, before tackling the case itself, and then tracing the subsequent development of the law, and the issues of principle which remain unanswered.

II. BEFORE THE ELEFTHERIA

Today it is possible to make the case, confidently, that private international law can be divided into the part which turns on party agreement, and that which

[11] *Akai Pty Ltd v People's Insurance Co Ltd* [1996] HCA 39, (1996) 188 CLR 418, 428–29 (Dawson and McHugh JJ, dissenting) and 445 (Toohey, Gaudron and Gummow JJ, in the majority, albeit not expressly referring to *The Eleftheria*). See further ch 14 in this volume. For the wider impact of *The Eleftheria* on Australian jurisprudence, see M Keyes 'Jurisdiction under the Hague Choice of Courts Convention: Its likely impact on Australian practice' (2009) 5 *Journal of Private International Law* 181, 200–04.

[12] *Society of Lloyd's and Oxford Members' Agency Ltd v Hyslop* [1993] 3 NZLR 135 (NZCA) 142–43 (Richardson J) and 154 (McKay J). *The Eleftheria* appears to have been adopted as the leading authority at High Court level in the 1980s: see M Ong, 'Rethinking Jurisdiction Clauses in New Zealand: The Hague Convention and Beyond' (2013) 19 *Auckland University Law Review* 219, 228.

[13] *Ecu-Line NV v ZI Pompey Industrie* 2003 SCC 27, [2003] 1 SCR 450, [19]–[21], [39] (Bastarache J); *Douez v Facebook Inc* 2017 SCC 33, [2017] 1 SCR 751, [29]–[30], [36], [67], [73] (Karakatsanis, Wagner and Gascon JJ) [89], [93] (Abella J) and [149], [153], [155], [172] (McLachlin CJ and Côté J, dissenting). The first application of *The Eleftheria* in Canada was much earlier, probably *M/V Sea Pearl v Seven Seas Dry Cargo Shipping Corporation* (1982) 139 DLR (3d) 669.

[14] *Vinmar Overseas (Singapore) Pte Ltd v PTT International Trading Pte Ltd* [2018] SGCA 65, [2018] 2 SLR 1271, [71]–[73], [113] (Steven Chong JA). The influence of *The Eleftheria* in Singapore probably begins with *Amerco Timbers Pte Ltd v Chatsworth Timber Corporation* [1977] 2 MLJ 181 (Sing CA), although it was not expressly cited there by the Court of Appeal: see TK Sing 'Stay of Actions Based on Exclusive Jurisdiction Clauses under English and Singapore Law (Part I)' [1991] *Singapore Journal of Legal Studies* 103, 106.

does not.[15] But in the eighteenth and early nineteenth centuries the questions of who should administer justice and by what rules were seen primarily in terms of the principles of state sovereignty, territorial power, and allegiance of subjects to their relevant polities. As Story put it in 1834, in the first edition of his *Commentaries on the Conflict of Laws*, 'jurisdiction, to be rightfully exercised, must be founded either upon the person being within the territory, or the thing being in the territory; for, otherwise, there can be no sovereignty exercised', adding that for persons or things within the territory 'the jurisdiction of the sovereign is complete and irresistible'.[16] On these principles, there was little (or no) place for private parties either to contract out of the English court system ('derogation agreements') or to agree to extend its jurisdiction beyond its territorial frontiers ('prorogation agreements').

The role for party autonomy in the modern law of jurisdiction starts with the Common Law Procedure Acts 1852 and 1854, which – despite the prevailing influence of Story at the time – contained some important departures from those principles. But before we address those statutes, it is as well to say something about the position at common law before the mid nineteenth century.[17]

A. Derogation Agreements before the 1852 and 1854 Acts

While commercial parties trading in England have long been attracted to the idea of choosing their forum – be it an arbitral tribunal, or a particular court – the judiciary's initial reception of that idea was decidedly chilly, especially as regards derogation agreements.[18] The brief law report of *Kill v Hollister* from 1749, for example, shows that judgment was given following trial, despite an insurance policy providing that any dispute between the policyholder and the insurer should be referred to arbitration. That was said to be because 'the agreement of the parties cannot oust this Court'.[19] The same sentiment can be found in the decision of *Gienar v Meyer*, in 1796.[20] Kenyon LCJ declared that 'no

[15] See, eg, A Briggs, *Agreements on Jurisdiction and Choice of Law* (Oxford, OUP, 2007); A Mills, *Party Autonomy in Private International Law* (Cambridge, CUP, 2018).

[16] J Story, *Commentaries on the Conflict of Laws,* 1st edn (Boston, Hilliard, Gray & Co, 1834) 450 and 451.

[17] See further, eg, M Pryles 'The Basis of Adjudicatory Competence in Private International Law' (1972) 21 *International & Comparative Law Quarterly* 61, 67–69; A Dickinson, 'Keeping Up Appearances: The Development of the Adjudicatory Jurisdiction in the English Courts' (2017) 86 *British Yearbook of International Law* 6, 10–24.

[18] At least insofar as an *irrevocable* choice was purportedly made to arbitrate; it seems that a revocable arbitration agreement was acceptable to the English courts: see further S Brekoulakis, 'The Historical Treatment of Arbitration under English Law and the Development of the Policy Favouring Arbitration' (2019) 39 *Oxford Journal of Legal Studies* 124.

[19] *Kill v Hollister* (1764) 1 Wilson KB 129, 95 ER 532.

[20] *Gienar v Meyer* (1796) 2 Black (H) 603, 126 ER 728. See also *Johnson v Machielsne* (1811) 3 Camp 1811, 170 ER 1300.

persons in this country can by an agreement between themselves exclude themselves from the jurisdiction of the king's courts'.[21]

Importantly, however, on the facts of *Gienar* the Lord Chief Justice was prepared to make an exception. The plaintiff was a Dutch seaman employed on a ship carrying the Dutch flag, for a journey from Rotterdam to Barcelona and back again. In his articles of employment, he had agreed not to sue the ship's master anywhere other than in the Netherlands. On the return journey, however, the vessel was detained by the Royal Navy and eventually returned to Rotterdam some two years after it had first left. In light of that diversion, the ship's master sought to pay only 18 months wages for the two-year voyage. The seaman sued for the balance in the Court of Common Pleas in London. Because both parties were Dutch, Kenyon LCJ reasoned that the Court could 'look into the contract' and consider whether it would lead to a result that would be either 'unjust or contrary to the laws' or the chosen jurisdiction.[22] In an early forerunner of the type of analysis now regularly adopted by English judges, the Court concluded that the choice of court agreement in the articles of employment ought to be upheld. Not only was it reasonable for parties in Holland to stipulate that only the Dutch court should hear a dispute relating to a voyage that began and finished in Holland, since litigating elsewhere could place a real hardship on one or other party, but it was also sensible as a matter of policy in the maritime context, because it created an 'additional tie' on the crew to complete the voyage and return to the home port.

Gienar v Meyer thus demonstrates not only the importance placed on territorial sovereignty, and allegiance of subjects to their sovereigns, but also an early judicial instinct to give effect to party agreement where reconcilable with the former considerations.[23] In *Giener* itself, it seems that it was permissible to formulate an exception because neither party was a subject of the King. As Story put it (albeit without reference to *Gienar v Meyer*), one exception to the general rule linking sovereignty over persons to their presence in the sovereign's territory was that: 'Every nation has hitherto assumed it as clear, that it possesses the right to regulate and govern its own native born subjects everywhere; and consequently, that its laws extend to, and bind, such subjects at all times and in all places.'[24]

English law's nascent (albeit qualified) instinct in favour of party autonomy shown in *Gienar* became stronger with the passage of time. Mills has noted that in the early nineteenth century the courts developed the principle of jurisdiction

[21] *Gienar* (n 20) 730.

[22] ibid, 731.

[23] Lord Kenyon was not alone in having such an instinct. His predecessor in office, Lord Mansfield, had similarly emphasised the value of commercial parties being able to exercise autonomy in their forum choices: see, eg, *Hawkins v Colclough* (1757) 1 Burr 274, 277; 97 ER 311, 312. See too Brekoulakis (n 18) 140 and Mills (n 15) 33–34.

[24] Story (n 16) 22.

by submission, reflecting 'a shift in focus in the principles of private international law jurisdiction – away from concerns of international law and inter-state power, and towards concerns of fairness to individual defendants'.[25] This can be seen, for example, in Savigny's treatise on private international law, which appeared to recognise a substantial role in the law of jurisdiction for some form of party autonomy.[26] Nor was private international law alone in moving towards giving greater weight to party autonomy. Pothier's *Traité des Obligations* was translated into English in 1806 and 'first gave expression to the notion that a contract is primarily an agreement based on the intention of the parties, and that it is their will which creates the legal obligation'.[27] As Atiyah put it,[28] one characteristic of the will theory as adopted by the judiciary by the mid-nineteenth century 'was the tendency to attribute all the consequences of a contract to the will of those who made it … The somewhat mystical idea had gained acceptance that an obligation could be created by a communion of wills, an act of joint, if purely mental procreation'.[29] Once contractual obligations were understood by judges as the product of party autonomy, it was more difficult as a matter of principle to deny those same parties to the ability to stipulate the forum to determine any disputes as to the obligations they had created.

This tension between ideas of state and individual sovereignty was apparent in the famous *Scott v Avery* litigation, which reached the House of Lords in 1856.[30] There, maritime insurance policies provided that the insurers had to settle the relevant allocation of loss before the insurers' committee first, and then (if not agreed) by arbitration, and only then (if still disputed) could an insurer bring a claim before the English court. In breach of this condition precedent, litigation was commenced before any arbitration award was obtained. The Court of Exchequer gave judgment to the plaintiff, which was then reversed by the Court of Exchequer Chamber. Eleven puisne judges were then assembled to hear *en banc* the argument before the House of Lords,[31] and give their advice to the Lords of Appeal in Ordinary before the latter determined the final appeal. Argument was heard on 25 June 1855, and the Court then adjourned. On 9 July 1855, clearly struggling with how to resolve the conflicting principles, the puisne judges requested yet further time.

Eventually, proceedings re-convened on 19 May 1856, with the lower judges split in their advice on whether to construe the multi-tiered dispute resolution

[25] Mills (n 15) 34.

[26] FC von Savigny, *Private International Law, A Treatise on the Conflict of Laws*, trans W Guthrie (London, Stevens & Sons, 1869) 152–53. *Cf* Mills (n 15) 35.

[27] P Atiyah, *The Rise and Fall of Freedom of Contract* (Oxford, Clarendon Press, 1979) 399–400.

[28] Perhaps over-strongly, but the basic point is still a good one.

[29] Atiyah (n 27) 405 and 407.

[30] *Scott v Avery* (1856) 5 HL Case 811, 10 ER 1121.

[31] Parke B, Alderson B, Coleridge J, Maule J, Cresswell J, Wightman J, Erle J, Williams J, Martin J, Crompton J, and Crowder J.

clause as an illegitimate and invalid ouster of the Court,[32] or a legitimate and valid condition precedent for the accrual of a cause of action.[33] On 10 July 1856, the Lord Chancellor (Lord Cranworth) and Lord Campbell (the third judge, Lord Brougham, agreeing with both of them) gave judgment. Despite its artificiality,[34] they came down in favour of the latter construction in order to give effect to party autonomy and the arbitration agreement. But, at the same time, the Law Lords expressly approved *Kill v Hollister* and emphasised that 'there is no doubt of the general principle … parties cannot by contract oust the ordinary Courts of their jurisdiction'.[35] *Scott v Avery* therefore did nothing to relieve the tension within the common law between territorial and party autonomy conceptions of civil jurisdiction.

B. Prorogation Agreements after the 1852 Act

At this point it is convenient to move from derogation agreements to prorogation agreements. Shortly before *Scott v Avery*, the Common Law Procedure Act 1852 received Royal Assent. The 1852 Act applied to the common law courts at Westminster and, in broad terms, drew a distinction between service of a writ (ie a claim) as of right within the inherent, territorial jurisdiction of those courts[36] and service on British subjects or foreigners outside the jurisdiction in certain (very limited) circumstances prescribed by statute, and only then could the proceedings continue with the permission of the court.[37] The ability to serve a writ out of England marked a significant, albeit narrow, departure from Story's prevailing territorial approach to the law of jurisdiction. The Judicature Act 1873, which implemented the administrative fusion of the courts of common law and equity, preserved this distinction between territorial service and service out of the jurisdiction for the new English High Court, but with some modifications. Under the rules at Schedule 1 to the Act, a writ could be served 'in the manner in which personal service is now made' in England.[38] Service out of the jurisdiction could take place when 'it appears fit' to the Court and either 'the cause of action has arisen within the jurisdiction, or is properly cognizable against a defendant within the jurisdiction'.[39]

[32] The view expressed by Martin B, Crompton J and Alderson B.

[33] The view expressed by Crowder J, Wrightman J, Cresswell J and Coleridge J.

[34] Atiyah (n 27) 387.

[35] *Scott* (n 30) 1135 (Lord Cranworth). See too 1138: 'Where an action is indispensable, you cannot oust the Court of its jurisdiction over the subject, because justice cannot be done without the exercise of that jurisdiction. That is all, and there is no doubt about that' (Lord Campbell).

[36] Common Law Procedure Acts 1852, s 2.

[37] ibid, ss 18–19.

[38] Supreme Court of Judicature Act 1873, Sch 1, rule 5.

[39] ibid, Sch 1, rule 6.

The 1873 Act appeared to envisage a much broader exception to territorial jurisdiction than that under the 1852 Act.[40] The Judicature Act 1875 consolidated that wider exception. Under the 1875 Act, Order II ('Writ of summons and procedure'), rule 4 provided that no writ 'for service out of the jurisdiction, or of which notice is to be given out of the jurisdiction, shall be issued without the leave of a Court or Judge'. For the purposes of obtaining leave, Order XI ('Service out of the jurisdiction') contained jurisdictional 'gateways'[41] in rule 1 for service out based on property, contract, and acts and damage in the jurisdiction. These gateways appear to have been understood initially as a codification of when a cause of action would be treated as having 'arisen' within the jurisdiction,[42] and therefore cemented the approach in the 1873 Act. The application for leave of the Court had to be supported by evidence identifying where the defendant was to be found and whether the defendant was a British subject.[43] It was only where a claim was shown on the evidence to pass through a gateway that the Court would have discretion to give permission for service out of the jurisdiction.

The Rules of the Supreme Court 1883 completed the 'jurisdictional Holy Trinity',[44] refining the gateways (although they have been the subject of regular adjustment ever since), and requiring the supporting evidence to demonstrate that there was a 'good' cause of action and that the case was a 'proper one' for service out.[45] The cases gradually disclosed a framework for answering that third question (which we would now call *forum non conveniens*) with the basic idea of 'balance of convenience' emerging early on:[46] the courts considered matters such as the location of the parties and witnesses,[47] whether the case was sufficiently strong to justify 'the great difficulty and annoyance' to a defendant overseas having to litigate in England,[48] and whether the claim was properly

[40] '... the Common Law Procedure Act ... was rather stricter than is the rule under the Judicature Act as to service out of the jurisdiction': *Fowler v Barstow* (1881) 20 Ch D 240 (CA) 243 (Jessel MR).

[41] To use the modern terminology; the language of 'gateways' did not exist at the time. These previously had been contained in 'General Orders'.

[42] See, eg, *Great Australian Gold Mining Company v Martin* (1877) 5 Ch D 1 (CA) 11 (James LJ) and 15–17 (Bramwell JA). *Cf* D Foxton, 'The Jurisdictional Gateways – Some (very) Modest Proposals' [2022] *Lloyd's Maritime and Commercial Law Quarterly* 70, 75.

[43] 1875 Rules, Order XI, rule 3.

[44] Foxton (n 42) 70.

[45] 1883 Rules, Order XI, rule 4.

[46] *Harris v Fleming* (1879) 13 Ch D 208 (Ch) 213 (Hall VC); *Robey & Co v The Snaefell Mining Co Ltd* (1887) 20 QBD 152 (QBD) 154 (Stephen J).

[47] See, eg, *Harris* (n 46) 213 (Hall VC); *Robey* (n 46) 154 (Stephen J).

[48] The earliest example is probably *Great Australian Gold Mining Company* (n 42) 11 (James LJ). Bramwell JA put it rather more bluntly at 16: '... it is certainly an inordinate thing that without good cause a man should be dragged from the antipodes to answer a claim ...'. The more cited example is *Société Générale de Paris v Dreyfus Brothers* (1884) 29 Ch D 239 (Ch) 243–44 (Pearson J) noting the question was 'whether this Court ought to put a foreigner, who owes no allegiance here, to the inconvenience and annoyance of being brought to contest his rights in this country', such that 'I do intend, to a certain extent at all events, to ascertain, as far as I can, whether there are any merits on the Plaintiffs' side which would justify me in allowing this service to stand.' This was overturned

limited to an action which had accrued in England.[49] Jurisdiction agreements came to assume some significance when considering the 'balance of convenience', at least by 1926.[50]

In contrast, jurisdiction agreements had no role to play at the earlier stage of identifying a jurisdictional gateway. There was originally no gateway for jurisdiction agreements. In particular, the original 1875 contract gateway simply provided:[51]

> … whenever the contract which is sought to be enforced or rescinded, dissolved, annulled, or otherwise affected in any such action, or for the breach whereof damages or other relief are or is demanded in such action, was made or entered into within the jurisdiction ….

As amended in 1883, the contract ground was in fact narrowed:[52]

> The Court has jurisdiction whenever the action is founded on any breach, or alleged breach, in England, or any contract, wherever made, which, according to the terms thereof, ought to be performed in England ….

The omission of jurisdiction agreements is entirely unsurprising. The gateways at this time were intended to capture when a *cause of action* had arisen in the jurisdiction, such that it would be appropriate for the English court to allow service on a defendant out of the jurisdiction; a prorogation agreement said nothing about where a cause of action accrued, but only where it was to be litigated. The argument that a prorogation agreement could act as a substitute for a gateway for jurisdiction itself would thus face the obstacle, in Lord Esher MR's words, of the 'well-known rule … that the consent of parties cannot give the Court a jurisdiction which it does not otherwise possess'.[53] The gateways were 'exhaustive'[54] of the circumstances in which an exception would be made to the territorial limitations that otherwise applied to its jurisdiction.

In his first edition of the *Conflict of Laws*,[55] in 1896, Professor Dicey displayed some confusion on this point. Although jurisdiction agreements

on appeal ((1887) 37 Ch D 215 (CA)) but this basic approach was not criticised, and indeed was subsequently quoted with approval on many occasions including in *The Hagen* [1908] P 189 (CA) 201 (Farwell LJ) and *Spiliada Maritime Corp v Cansulex Ltd* (1987) AC 460 (HL) 481 (Lord Goff).

[49] See, eg, *Thomas v The Duchess Dowager of Hamilton* (1886) 17 QBD 592 (CA).

[50] *Re Schintz* [1926] 710 (CA) 720 (Lord Hanworth MR) and 724–25 (Warrington LJ); *cf Ellinger v Guinness, Mahon & Co Frankfurter Bank AG* [1939] 4 All ER 16 (Ch) 23 (Morton J).

[51] 1875 Rules, Order XI, rule 1.

[52] 1883 Rules, Order XI, rule 1(e).

[53] *Re Alymer* (1887) 20 QBD 258 (CA) 262 (Lord Esher MR).

[54] *Re Eager* (1882) 22 Ch D 86 (CA) 87 (Jessel MR). See also *Preston v Lamont* (1876) 1 Ex D 361, 363 (Bramwell B) and 364 (Amphlett B); *Cresswell v Parker* (1879) 11 Ch D 601 (CA) 603 (James LJ); *In Re Busfield* (1886) 32 Ch D 123 (Ch) 127 (Chitty J, upheld on appeal); *Western National Bank of the City of New York v Perez, Triana & Co* (1891) 1 QB 304 (CA) 311 (Lord Esher MR); *Tassell v Hallen* [1892] 1 QB 321 (QBD) 323 (Lord Coleridge LCJ); *Re Cliff* (1895) 2 Ch 21 (Ch) 23 (North J, upheld on appeal).

[55] AV Dicey, *A Digest of the Law of England with reference to the Conflict of Laws,* 1st edn (London, Stevens & Sons, 1896).

occupied no special place in his general principles and rules on the conflict of laws, they make brief appearance within his 'principle of submission', which was primarily concerned with parties who voluntarily appeared in proceedings. Dicey posited that:[56]

> So, again, does a person [fall into the Court's jurisdiction] who, *though he would not be otherwise liable to the Court's jurisdiction*, has made it part of a contract that questions arising under the contract shall be decided by the Court.

Yet, at the same time, Dicey also argued that his principle of submission did not confer jurisdiction where none otherwise would exist, but instead 'remov[ed] objections thereto' where jurisdiction did otherwise exist.[57] The apparent contradiction between these two propositions was not explained. In any event, the first proposition was clearly wrong. In *British Wagon Co Ltd v Gray*,[58] also decided in 1896 (in time for Dicey to make passing reference to it, but apparently not to grapple with its implications),[59] the plaintiffs let coal wagons to the defendant; the latter were in Yorkshire, the former in Scotland. The contract provided:

> This agreement shall in all respects be construed and carried into effect according to the law of England, and for the purposes thereof the tenant hereby submits to the jurisdiction of the High Court of Justice in England.

Mathew J refused leave to serve out and, on appeal, the matter came before Lord Esher MR who (unsurprisingly, given the terms of his earlier judgment)[60] agreed: 'The Court is forbidden to exercise the jurisdiction which it is now asked to exercise, and cannot regard the contract of the parties as to the extent of its jurisdiction.'[61]

It was, however, different where the parties had contracted to enable service of the writ within the inherent, territorial jurisdiction. So, for example, in *Tharsis Sulphur & Copper Co v Société des Metaux*,[62] a contract for the export of copper from England to France named a third party in London as agent for the French buyer 'on whom any writ or other legal process arising out of the contract might be served'. In an action for the price, the seller was validly served by service on that agent. However fine the distinction between *Tharsis* and *British Wagon* was, it was enough for well-advised commercial parties to begin drafting their prorogation clauses in a way which could be effective, ie by stipulating a place for service rather than the forum for litigation.[63]

[56] ibid, 224, emphasis added. See too 42 and 370.

[57] ibid, 224.

[58] *British Wagon Co Ltd v Gray* [1896] 1 QB 35 (CA).

[59] Dicey (n 55) 225 and 337.

[60] See n 53.

[61] *British Wagon* (n 61) 37.

[62] *Tharsis Sulphur & Copper Co v Société des Metaux* (1889) LT 924 (QB).

[63] See, eg, *Montgomery, Jones & Co v Liebenthal & Co* [1989] 1 QB 487 (CA), where service could take place on either party at the offices of the London Corn Trade Association. The distinction is

Further intervention by the Rules Committee was required to remove the need to dance like angels on a pinhead. In 1920, rule 2A was introduced into Order XI, which provided:[64]

> Notwithstanding anything contained in rule 1 of this Order, the parties to any contract may agree (a) that the High Court of Justice shall have jurisdiction to entertain any action in respect of such contract, and, moreover or in the alternative, (b) that service of any writ of summons in any such action may be effected at any place within or out of the jurisdiction on any party or on any person on behalf of any party or in any manner specified or indicated in such contract ....

As observed in the third edition of Dicey's *Conflict of Laws*, the 'net effect' of rule 2A was to 'extend the jurisdiction of the Court to any case in which the parties have either expressly or implicitly agreed to accept such jurisdiction', which Dicey saw as being 'in accordance with' the principle of submission articulated in his first edition.[65] Part (a) of rule 2A overturned *British Wagon* and part (b) codified and extended *Tharsis*. Although in 1987 part (a) would be folded into the contract gateway in rule 1, until then it continued to be framed as an *exception* to the gateways. That exceptional status made sense on the original conception of the gateways as examples of when a cause of action accrued in the jurisdiction;[66] it made less sense as the gateway developed in the twentieth century, becoming instead a rag-bag collection of rules to legitimate the taking of extra-territorial jurisdiction.[67] By that stage, far from constituting an exception to the later iterations of the gateways, prorogation agreements were seen as supplying one such connection to the jurisdiction, and a strong one at that.[68]

C. Derogation Agreements after the 1854 Act

It is unsurprising that the Rules Committee chose, in effect, to override *British Wagon* in 1920, because the treatment of prorogation agreements looked anomalous compared with the position reached by that stage in respect of derogation agreements.

still relevant today in that it means that the claim will either be served in the jurisdiction or out of it; the real absurdity in the late 1800s was that one form of the clause was effective and the other ineffective, despite having the same substantive purpose.

[64] *Kenneth Allison Ltd v AE Limehouse & Co* [1992] 1 AC 105 (HL) (HL) 117 (Lord Bridge); *NML Capital Ltd v Republic of Argentina* [2011] UKSC 31, [2011] 2 AC 495 [125] (Lord Collins).

[65] AV Dicey and A Berriedale Keith, *A Digest of the Law of England with reference to the Conflict of Laws*, 3rd edn (London, Stevens & Sons, 1922).

[66] Text to n 42.

[67] Foxton (n 42).

[68] The modern law has now come full circle: a jurisdiction agreement in favour of the English courts now again operates as an exception to the gateways; the existence of such a prorogation clause now exempts a party from having to seek permission to serve out: see text to n 3.

Although the dispute in *Scott v Avery* itself had come slightly too early to benefit from it, section 11 of the Common Law Procedure Act 1854 relevantly provided:

> Whenever the Parties to any Deed or Instrument in Writing to be hereafter made or executed, or any of them, shall agree that any then existing or future Differences between them or any of them shall be referred to Arbitration … it shall be lawful for the Court in which Action or Suit is brought … to make a Rule or Order staying all Proceedings in such Action or Suit.

Statutory permission gave the courts the legitimacy they needed to exercise a discretion not to hear a dispute on the basis that another forum had been chosen. And it was not long before judges began to adopt the fiction that 'Arbitration' in the 1854 Act should be read as going beyond true arbitration to include litigation before a nominated foreign court, and exercising their discretion accordingly – thereby establishing, in effect, proposition (1) in *The Eleftheria*.[69]

That important step was taken in 1878 by the Court of Appeal in *Law v Garrett*.[70] A partnership agreement made in Russia and governed by Russian law between three men (British subjects – unlike in *Gienar v Meyer*) contained an agreement to refer all disputes to the St Petersburg Commercial Court. One of them sued in England complaining about steps taken in Russia by the other two to wind up the partnership; the latter two sought a stay of proceedings in London and a reference to the St Petersburg Commercial Court. At first instance, Bacon VC asserted without much analysis that the words of section 11 were 'wide enough to comprehend' a reference to a foreign court.[71] On appeal, Baggallay LJ agreed.[72] The English proceedings were stayed without hesitation.

No reference was made at first instance or on appeal to the pre-1854 case law. Section 11 appears to have acted as a convenient *tabula rasa*, allowing these judges to give (what they saw as) proper effect to party autonomy. While the construction of the statute is surprising, the fact that these judges were willing to be creative to achieve this objective is not. This was high noon for party autonomy.[73] Sir George Jessel MR had only three years earlier identified freedom of contract as a 'paramount public policy' with which the courts should not lightly interfere.[74] And as explored elsewhere in this collection,[75] by this time the courts had begun to recognise that parties to a contract could choose the law that governed it.[76] If parties could now choose a contract's law, the objection

[69] Text to n 6.

[70] *Law v Garrett* (1878) 8 ChD 26 (CA).

[71] ibid, 30.

[72] ibid, 37.

[73] Atiyah (n 27) 387.

[74] *Printing and Numerical Registering Co v Sampson* (1874–75) LR 19 Eq 462 (CA) 465. See too *Bennet v Bennet* (1876) 43 LT 264 (CA) 247 (Jessel MR).

[75] See ch 2 in this volume.

[76] *Lloyd v Guibert* (1865) (1865–1866) LR 1 QB 115; *Peninsular and Oriental Steam Navigation Co v Shand* (1865) 3 Moo PC NS 272 (PC). See also, shortly after *Law v Garrett*, *Chartered Mercantile*

to them choosing the forum in which to litigate about it was difficult to sustain, especially where (as in *Law v Garrett* itself) the choice of forum was consistent with the chosen law.

However, the significance of *Law v Garrett* may not have been appreciated at the time. Not only did Dicey's *The Conflict of Laws* not cite *Gienar v Meyer* or *Scott v Avery* at all, it made only passing reference to *Law v Garrett*.[77] Dicey's view, rather oddly, was that *Law v Garrett* did 'not directly raise the question of jurisdiction': although he accepted that the judgment 'implies that the agreement gave jurisdiction to the Russian court', he seemed to miss the jurisdictional implication for the English court of the stay of the English proceedings.[78] Nonetheless, *Law v Garrett* was repeatedly upheld in the years which followed. That purposive interpretation was continued when section 11 of the Common Law Procedure Act 1854 was repealed in favour of section 4 of the Arbitration Act 1889, which preserved the discretion to stay in favour of arbitration but was worded somewhat differently.[79] And, by 1908, the 'general rule' was that the court should give effect to a foreign jurisdiction agreement unless 'unless for some good cause there is reason to think that the matter ought to be determined otherwise than by the tribunal to which the parties have deliberately agreed to submit their differences'[80] – an early iteration of proposition (2) in *The Eleftheria*.[81]

However, it took well over half a century after *Law v Garrett* for the courts finally to have the courage to abandon the comfort of the arbitration fiction, and give direct jurisdictional effect to party agreement in favour of a foreign jurisdiction. The first step was taken in *Racecourse Betting Control Board v Secretary for Air*, which actually had nothing to do with private international law. It involved a challenge to a decision of the General Claims Tribunal regarding compensation for buildings acquired by the government using emergency powers in the Second World War, and a (bad) analogy was made in submission between arbitration and a body like the Tribunal.[82] In *obiter dicta*, MacKinnon LJ criticised *Law v Garrett* and the cases which followed it:

> In each of those [cases] the contract of the parties provided for the decision of any dispute by a foreign court, in each one of the parties brought an action in breach of

Bank of India v Netherlands India Steam Navigation Co Ltd (1883) 10 QBD 521 (CA) and *Jacobs Marcus & Co v Crédit Lyonnais* (1884) 12 QBD 589 (CA).

[77] Dicey (n 55) 377–78.

[78] ibid 378.

[79] *Austrian Lloyd Steamship Co v Gresham Life Assurance Society Ltd* [1903] 1 KB 249 (CA). *The Athénée* [1922] 11 Lloyd's Law Rep 6 (CA); *The Vestris* [1932] 43 Lloyd's Law Rep 86 (Ad). In the first case the proceedings were stayed; in the second and third, they were not.

[80] *Kirchner & Co v Gruban* [1909] 1 Ch 413 (Ch) 418 (Eve J). See also *The Cap Blanco* [1913] P 130 (CA) 136 (Sir Samuel Evans). In both cases the stay was granted.

[81] Text to n 6.

[82] *Racecourse Betting Control Board v Secretary for Air* [1944] Ch 114 (CA).

> his agreement, and in each his action was stayed. It is, I think, rather unfortunate that the power and duty of the court to stay the action was said to be under section 4 of the Arbitration Act 1889. In truth, that power and duty arose under a wider general principle, namely, that the court makes people abide by their contracts, and, therefore, will restrain a plaintiff from bringing an action which he is doing in breach of his agreement with the defendant that any dispute between them shall be otherwise determined. Section 4 of the Arbitration Act 1889 only applies this principle to one type of such an agreement. The three cases cited really apply it to another type, and it would have been, I think, more logical to say, not that the plaintiff could be restrained under section 4 of the Act, but that he could be restrained under the principle of which that section is a particular example.

Here, for the first time, the court was openly contemplating that the discretion to stay was triggered not by statutory instruction but rather by judicial respect for *pacta sunt servanda*.

Two years after the decision of the Court of Appeal in *Racecourse*, in 1946, Henry Brandon was called to the bar by the Inner Temple. He started practice at 7 King's Bench Walk in probate, divorce and admiralty and later moved to 3 Essex Court to focus on commercial work. It was there that he appeared as counsel in *The Fehmarn* before Willmer J.[83] *The Fehmarn* concerned a claim for damage to goods delivered in England where the bill of lading provided that 'All claims and disputes arising under and in connection with this bill of lading shall be judged in the USSR.' The claim began as of right in England rather than under Order XI. Brandon, as counsel for the claimant, invited the court to not to give effect to derogation agreement in favour of the USSR. Willmer J noted MacKinnon J's analysis in *Racecourse* but declined to express a view on it, in a passage worth setting out *in extenso*:[84]

> It is not, I think, necessary, for me to express any opinion of my own as to whether the Court, in a case of this character, has an inherent jurisdiction to be exercised on wide general principles, or whether it merely proceeds by way of analogy to cases where there is a submission under the Arbitration Act. Whichever be the correct view, it is well established that, where there is a provision in a contract providing that disputes are to be referred to a foreign tribunal, then, *prima facie*, this Court will stay proceedings instituted in this country in breach of such agreement, and will only allow them to proceed when satisfied that it is just and proper to do so. I think that fairly states the principle to be applied, and it is right to mention that Mr Brandon, in arguing the case for the plaintiffs, frankly admitted that the burden of proof was upon him to displace the *prima facie* right of the defendants to have these proceedings stayed and to have the case tried by the chosen foreign tribunal ....

He added:

> ... it requires a strong case to satisfy the Court that that agreement should be overridden and that proceedings in this country should be allowed to continue. But, in the

[83] *Cargo Lately Laden on Board the Fehmarn (Owners) v Fehmarn (Owners)* [1957] 1 WLR 815 (Ad).

[84] ibid, 820–21.

> end, it is, and must necessarily be, a matter for the discretion of the Court, having regard to all the circumstances of the particular case. That being so, I do not think it would be profitable to refer in detail to the numerous cases which were cited to me, where the principle as I have tried to state it has been stated over and over again, but the discretion of the Court was exercised one way or other having regard to the circumstances of the particular case.

The importance of these passages cannot be overstated. Brandon's concession as counsel as to the burden of proof as to strong cause appears to be first expression of what became proposition (3) in his own judgment in *The Eleftheria*; Willmer J's substitution of 'good cause' for 'strong case' in *The Fehmarn* also found a central place in propositions (2) and (3) in the later case; and Willmer J's emphasis on the need to have regard to all the circumstances of the case became *The Eleftheria*'s proposition (4).[85] On the facts, Willmer J considered that the burden of proof had been satisfied on the facts before him, because he was concerned that forcing the parties to go to the USSR might deprive the plaintiffs 'of any remedy at all', or at least proceedings or a judgment that would be of value (including for the purposes of arresting the ship), as well as there being a considerable increase in cost to the parties and inconvenience to witnesses in having to go to Soviet Russia.[86]

The Fehmarn went on appeal;[87] Brandon, now led by Sir George Honeyman QC, successfully appeared for the respondent. Lord Denning MR gave the leading judgment, with short concurring judgments from Morris and Hodson LJJ, who confirmed on the point of principle that MacKinnon LJ's analysis in *Racecourse* was to be preferred to the earlier fiction of arbitration.[88] However, the Master of the Rolls framed the analysis in a strikingly different way to Willmer J at first instance. Lord Denning said that the relevant question was 'Is this dispute a matter which properly belongs to the Courts of this country?', and answered in the positive on the basis that 'the dispute is more closely connected with England than Russia': the goods had been surveyed and allegedly been discovered damaged on delivery in England, English proceedings conferred the advantage of arrest for securing the claim (which was seen as the true motivation behind the defendants' attempts to stay the English proceedings), none of the parties were Russian, and the fact that the bill of lading was governed by Russian law was not seen as 'decisive'.[89] The fact of the derogation agreement appeared to carry much less weight with Lord Denning on appeal than with Willmer J at first instance.

[85] Text to n 6.

[86] *The Fehmarn (Ad)* (n 83) 821–22.

[87] *Cargo Lately Laden on Board the Fehmarn (Owners) v Fehmarn (Owners)* [1958] 1 WLR 159 (CA).

[88] *The Fehmarn (CA)* (n 87) 163 (Hodson LJ) 164 (Morris LJ).

[89] ibid, 162.

III. THE ELEFTHERIA

Shortly after *The Fehmarn*, and perhaps because of it, in 1961, Brandon took silk himself and then was appointed in 1966 at the age of 46 as a High Court Judge in the Probate, Divorce and Admiralty Division. He quickly established himself as a judge interested not just in justice but also in the law:[90]

> What had counted in the Admiralty court up to then was a knowledge of good seamanship – preferably from personal experience – and dexterity with the dividers and parallel rule. It was almost considered bad form to take a point of law. Now there came a judge who over the next twelve years scrutinized, spring-cleaned, and put in order every corner of the complex Admiralty jurisdiction. 'What is the authority for that?', he would ask with almost monotonous regularity – not, as counsel sometimes suspected, in order to tease them or be difficult for its own sake – but because he genuinely wanted to know and insisted on knowing before making up his mind.

The dispute in *The Eleftheria* gave Brandon J an early opportunity to make his mark on private international law, and, better still, on a point which he had argued up to the Court of Appeal whilst still at the bar. *The Eleftheria*, like *The Fehmarn*, involved a claim commenced as of right in England where a bill of lading contained a jurisdiction clause in favour of another jurisdiction, albeit this time a more palatable jurisdiction: Greece not the USSR. The claim was for breach of the contracts of carriage in the bills of lading, following the delivery of cargo in Rotterdam not in London and Hull, as had been promised. The defendant ship owners were Greek; Greek law governed the bills of lading; the contract was in English, on standard international terms; and, while it was envisaged that English and Greek witnesses would be called at trial, there would be more of the former than the latter. Having heard argument over two days in January 1969, Brandon J reached the opposite conclusion to that reached in *The Fehmarn* and granted the stay.

The famous numbered propositions from *The Eleftheria*, recited in so many subsequent judgments, have already been set out.[91] It is also worth noting what does not appear in Brandon J's judgment: the arbitration fiction – which had dominated the previous case law – is not even mentioned, consigned to the history books after *The Fehmarn*. The central point in Brandon J's judgment in *The Eleftheria* is the renewed weight given to the usual rule of holding parties to their agreement: 'the court must be careful not just to pay lip service to the principle involved, and then fail to give effect to it because of a mere balance of convenience'.[92] Brandon J made it clear that this was the basis on which stay was ordered. Without that presumption, the factors for and against a stay on

[90] P Coleridge, 'Brandon, Henry Vivian, Baron Brandon of Oakbrook (1920–1999)' in *Oxford Dictionary of National Biography* (Oxford, OUP, 2004).

[91] Text to n 6.

[92] *The Eleftheria* (n 5) 103.

the facts 'more or less balance each other'.[93] On the one hand, the bulk of the factual evidence was in England and proceedings in England were likely to be cheaper and more convenient (to the plaintiffs, at least); on the other hand, the defendants had a real connection to Greece, and the claim was governed by Greek law, which could be materially different from English law.[94] Unlike *The Fehmarn*, security was not an issue because the defendants had proposed terms for the stay which provided it;[95] nor was there any concern that plaintiffs would not get a fair trial.[96] Thus it was the presumption *itself* that carried the day; the plaintiffs had not discharged the burden to show 'strong cause' for not following the jurisdiction agreement.

This emphasis on the strength of the presumption in favour of a derogation agreement was a direct challenge to Lord Denning's approach in *The Fehmarn*, where the Master of the Rolls appeared to adopt a balance of convenience approach; Brandon J's numbered propositions, and his application of them, instead clearly followed Willmer J's approach at first instance in *The Fehmarn*. Brandon J appeared to acknowledge the potential controversy of his approach when granting permission to appeal (although, in the event, that appeal was not pursued): 'I think it is at least arguable that certain observations of Lord Denning MR in *The Fehmarn* … if correct, would indicate a test somewhat different from that which I have thought fit to apply.'[97] This made clear that, although Brandon J had been the successful counsel on the appeal, he did not agree with the way that the Court of Appeal had found for his client in that case. On first blush, this was a bold approach for a first instance judge to take, still more for a relatively fresh Admiralty judge to take against the Master of the Rolls, especially one of Lord Denning's stature.

The reason for Brandon J's apparent boldness lay in two recent cases of the Court of Appeal, post-dating *The Fehmarn*, and decided in the context of an application under Order XI rather than proceedings commenced as of right.[98] Brandon J explained the relevance of these cases thus: 'the governing factor … was the principle that a party should be bound by a jurisdiction clause to which he has agreed, unless there is strong reason to the contrary'.[99] Brandon J considered this approach should apply equally to proceedings commenced as of right. This point about consistency between service in and service out cases in respect of jurisdiction agreements has shades of what Lord Goff would achieve more generally in the law of jurisdiction almost 20 years later,[100] as discussed

[93] ibid, 105.
[94] ibid, 104–05.
[95] ibid, 100 and 104.
[96] ibid, 100.
[97] ibid, 106.
[98] ibid, 103–04.
[99] ibid, 104.
[100] *Spiliada* (n 48) 480.

elsewhere in this collection.[101] However, unlike Lord Goff, here Brandon J was not the originator of that idea, merely its distiller; the point about a consistent approach between prorogation and derogation agreements had already been made in the Order XI cases themselves.

The first case Brandon J cited was *Mackender v Feldia AG*.[102] There, leave was refused to serve out of the jurisdiction even though the claim was properly arguable and a gateway had been established; the existence of a foreign jurisdiction clause meant that the claim was not a 'proper one' for service out. Lord Denning himself said that a jurisdiction clause in favour of the Belgian courts was a 'strong ground' for not giving leave, concluding:[103]

> It all comes to this: the English courts have discretion whether or not to give leave to serve this writ out of the jurisdiction. Seeing that the underwriters have agreed to a foreign jurisdiction clause which gives exclusive jurisdiction to the Belgian courts, I think we should allow these disputes to be decided in the courts of Belgium. We should not give leave to serve this writ out of the jurisdiction.

Lord Denning repeated this point four years later in another Order XI case, *YTC Universal*:[104]

> … if the parties have agreed to give exclusive jurisdiction to a particular forum, effect should usually be given to their agreement, though there may be exceptional cases where a case may be allowed to proceed in these Courts despite such agreement.

Lord Denning added that *The Fehmarn* was one such 'exceptional' case.[105] That was undoubtedly a gloss in his judgment given a decade earlier which, as we have seen, was not at all in those terms.[106] But importantly, for present purposes, the point is that Lord Denning was now drawing a connection between the principles which applied on a stay application in proceedings commenced within the territorial jurisdiction of the Court and those which applied in the exercise of discretion in respect of extra-territorial jurisdiction.

In *The Eleftheria* Brandon J did not cite *YTC*; he probably was not aware of it,[107] because the law report of that case was only published in 1973. However, he did identify a second (earlier) judgment from 1968, *Unterweser Reederei GmbH v Zapata Offshore Co*,[108] given by Willmer LJ (as he had become since

[101] See ch 11 in this volume.
[102] *Mackender v Feldia AG* [1967] 2 QB 590 (CA).
[103] ibid, 598–99. See also 604 (Diplock LJ): given the existence of the jurisdiction agreement meant that 'very strong reasons' needed to be given by the plaintiff to permit him to 'go back on his word'.
[104] *YTC Universal Ltd (in liquidation) v Trans Europa Compania de Aviacion SA* [1973] 1 Lloyd's Rep 480 (Note) (CA) 481. See also 481 (Widgery LJ): 'The general burden of bringing oneself within Rule 11 is on the plaintiff; but the burden of proof that there is an exclusive jurisdiction clause is on the defendant if he relies upon it and that burden is not satisfied.'
[105] ibid, 481.
[106] Text to n 89.
[107] See also text to n 115.
[108] *Unterweser Reederei GmbH v Zapata Offshore Co* [1968] 2 Lloyd's Rep 158 (CA).

The Fehmarn). In that case, concerning a dispute under a towage contract for a ship called the Bremen, leave to serve out was sought under the jurisdiction agreement exception to the gateways:[109] there was a jurisdiction clause in favour of the 'London Court', but the defendant wanted the dispute to be heard in the US. Transplanting his own approach in *The Fehmarn* into the Order XI context, Willmer LJ said:[110]

> *Prima facie* it is the policy of the Court to hold parties to the bargain into which they have entered. *Prima facie* it is to be presumed, therefore, that the plaintiffs should have leave to prosecute their proceedings in this country, and in pursuance of that to serve their writ out of the jurisdiction. But that is not an inflexible rule ... the Court has a discretion, but it is a discretion which, in the ordinary way and in the absence of strong reason to the contrary, will be exercised in favour of holding parties to their bargain. The question is whether sufficient circumstances have been shown to exist in this case to make it desirable, on the grounds of balance of convenience, that proceedings should not take place in this country, the stipulated forum ....

So, for Willmer LJ, the same approach should be taken to jurisdiction agreements no matter whether the proceedings had originated as of right or leave was being sought under Order XI or (putting it another way) the agreement was one of prorogation or derogation. Diplock LJ made the same consistency point in his concurring judgment in *Unterweser*: 'We should, I think, apply the same principle whether the forum of contractual choice is England or of some other country.'[111] The US Supreme Court was to echo the same point a few years later, in 1972, when the jurisdiction dispute between the parties in *Unterweser* reached it on the other side of the Atlantic (the defendant in the English proceedings having commenced proceedings in the US, in breach of the jurisdiction agreement). Chief Justice Burger pointed out that a derogation agreement was simply 'the other side of the proposition' of a prorogation agreement to which US courts already gave effect.[112] A difference in approach could not be justified: what was a derogation agreement from the perspective of the US courts was a prorogation agreement from the English perspective.

IV. AFTER THE ELEFTHERIA

Despite the apparent challenge in *The Eleftheria* to the analysis of Lord Denning MR's approach in *The Fehmarn*, Brandon J's propositions were rapidly adopted as authoritative, albeit with encouragement from Brandon J himself.[113]

[109] Text to n 64.
[110] *Unterweser* (n 108) 162–63. See also 163–64 (Diplock LJ) and 164 (Widgery LJ).
[111] ibid, 164.
[112] *Bremen* (n 10) 1914 (Burger CJ).
[113] The earliest reported example of it being applied by a judge other than Brandon J is probably *Bulk Oil (Zug) AG v Trans-Asiatic Oil Ltd* [1973] 1 Lloyd's Rep 129 (KB) 135–36 (Kerr J). However,

For example, in *The Makefjell*, Brandon J applied *The Eleftheria* principles to stay another action brought in breach of a jurisdiction clause in favour of Oslo.[114] Permission was sought to appeal:[115]

> Mr. Longmore: My Lord, I would ask for leave to appeal. I think I need leave to appeal, and your Lordship gave leave to appeal in *The Eleftheria* ... but it was not pursued. Your Lordship stated in the judgment in *The Eleftheria* ... I think, the grounds on which your Lordship was prepared to give leave in that case.
>
> Mr. Justice Brandon: Yes.
>
> Mr. Longmore: One of which was that it might be argued that the test that your Lordship had applied in *The Eleftheria* – and therefore to some extent in this case – might be considered by some to be slightly different from that applied by the Court dealing with *The Fehmarn*.
>
> Mr. Justice Brandon: Mr. Longmore, I am inclined to think that that point has rather gone, having regard to what the Master of the Rolls said in the *YTC* case ... It seemed to me that in *The Fehmarn* ... he was saying to some extent "The test is with which country has this case the greatest connection", but in the *YTC* case he was posing a test rather more adverse to you; that it was an exceptional case, which, with respect to the Master of the Rolls, I should have thought accorded more closely with the other authorities.
>
> Mr. Longmore: Yes. I have always thought that in fact the Master of the Rolls, likewise, was not entirely clear in the *YTC* case.
>
> Mr. Justice Brandon: Well, there it is Mr. Longmore. I think that point has rather gone. Some of the others may remain ....

Brandon J reluctantly gave permission to appeal, persuaded by other points. In the Court of Appeal, no challenge was made to *The Eleftheria*; it was common ground that the burden was on the claimant to show 'strong cause', and the appeal was dismissed on the basis that there was no obvious error that would entitle the Court of Appeal to interfere in Brandon J's evaluation that no strong cause had been shown.[116]

The next significant milestone was the appeal in *The El Amria*.[117] By then elevated to the Court of Appeal, Brandon LJ was on the panel and (unsurprisingly) gave the leading judgment. The case concerned proceedings brought in England in breach of an Egyptian jurisdiction agreement. Directing himself by reference to *The Eleftheria*,[118] and downplaying the continuing relevance of

there may be earlier *ex tempore* judgments which have not been reported: see, eg, *Carvalho v Hull Blyth (Angola) Ltd* [1980] 1 Lloyd's Rep 172 (CA) 174 (Browne LJ).

[114] *Kitchens of Sara Lee (Canada) Ltd v A/S Falkefejell (The Makefjell)* [1975] 1 Lloyd's Rep 528 (Ad). There are other examples of Brandon J promoting *The Eleftheria* in later judgments at first instance: see, eg, *The Christos* [1976] 1 Lloyd's Rep 109 (Ad) 111.

[115] *The Makefjell (Ad)* (n 114) 536.

[116] *Kitchens of Sara Lee (Canada) Ltd v A/S Falkefejell (The Makefjell)* [1976] 2 Lloyd's Rep 29 (CA) esp 38–39 (Sir Gordon Willmer). See also *The Adolf Warski* [1976] 2 Lloyd's Rep 241 (CA).

[117] *Aratra Potato Co Ltd v Egyptian Navigation Co (The El Amria)* [1981] 2 Lloyd's Rep 119 (CA).

[118] ibid, 123–24 and 127.

Lord Denning's judgment in *The Fehmarn*,[119] Brandon LJ allowed the proceedings to continue in England. The first instance judge, Sheen J, was found to have made three errors in the exercise of his discretion – in respect of the likely evidence at trial, on the parties' respective connections with England and Egypt, and in placing weight on the 'supposed inferiority' of the Egyptian courts – that justified the Court of Appeal 'exercis[ing] its own discretion anew with regard to the defendants' application for a stay'.[120] Of all the considerations, the most significant was that related proceedings would be continuing in England even if the proceedings against the defendant were stayed. Brandon LJ considered this to be 'a potential disaster from a legal point of view', given the overlapping issues.[121] That was decisive in making what was otherwise a 'borderline' case into one that demonstrated 'strong cause' to continue in breach of the jurisdiction agreement.[122]

Briggs has argued that *The El Amria* in fact adopted 'a different approach to the problem' to the *Eleftheria*.[123] With respect, that is not a credible reading of the reasoning in the judgment itself, *a fortiori* when one has regard to the fact that it was the same judge (Brandon J, Brandon LJ) in both cases. Indeed, *The El Amria* is seen as a landmark because it confirmed the imprimatur of the Court of Appeal to the approach taken at first instance in *The Eleftheria*.[124] Certainly, subsequent cases took the two authorities together on that basis.[125] If imprimatur is what mattered, then Brandon LJ's elevation again to the House of Lords consolidated the position. In *The Sennar (No 2)*, where proceedings were brought in England in breach of a jurisdiction agreement in favour of the Sudan, Lord Brandon briefly referred to the 'guidelines' in the *El Amria* and noted that it had been accepted at the bar by the appellant that those were 'correct in law' and merely misapplied on the facts of those proceedings.[126] Lord Brandon considered there was no merit in that complaint, either on the basis that the jurisdiction agreement was allegedly obtained by fraud or the concern about limitation periods in the Sudan. The appeal was dismissed.

[119] ibid, 124: '… it is possible that, if the learned Judge in the present case, which differs radically on its facts from *The Fehmarn*, had directed himself solely by reference to Lord Denning's test in the latter case, he could have been criticized as erring in law in that respect'.

[120] ibid, 127.

[121] ibid, 128.

[122] ibid, 128–29. Weight was also placed on expert evidence being available in England and in English: see text to n 172.

[123] A Briggs, 'The Staying of Actions on the Ground of "Forum non Conveniens" in England Today' [1984] *Lloyd's Maritime and Commercial Law Quarterly* 227, 243. See also Briggs (n 8) 474.

[124] See, eg, R Fentiman, *International Commercial Litigation*, 2nd edn (Oxford, OUP, 2015) 106.

[125] See, eg, *RA Lister & Co Ltd v EG Thompson (Shipping) Ltd* [1985] QB 325 (CA) 343 (Ackner LJ) 349 (Dunn LJ); *Standard Chartered Bank v Pakistan National Shipping Corp* [1995] 2 Lloyd's Rep 365 (Com Ct) 372 (Clarke J); *Citi-march Ltd v Neptune Orient Lines Ltd* [1996] 1 WLR 1367 (Com Ct) 1370 (Colman J); *Mahavir Minterals Ltd v Cho Yang Shipping Co Ltd* [1997] 1 Lloyd's Rep 566 (Ad) 571 (Rix J).

[126] *DSV Silo und Verwaltungsgesellschaft mbH v Owners of the Sennar (The Sennar) (No 2)* [1985] 1 WLR 490 (HL) 500.

The modern law is widely seen as having arrived after Lord Brandon retired from the House of Lords, with the decision in *Donohue v Armco*.[127] In some senses, this is odd because, as Lord Hobhouse recognised in the case itself, the 'appeal has not involved any disputed questions of principle but has turned upon the application of established principles to the factual complexities of international multi-party disputes'.[128] The principles had already been established in the quartet of cases involving Henry Brandon as counsel, Admiralty Judge, Lord Justice of Appeal and Lord of Appeal in Ordinary. Further, the case also concerned not the effect of a jurisdiction agreement on the exercise of jurisdiction by the English court but rather using it as a basis for an anti-suit injunction.[129]

Proceedings were begun in New York by the Armco conglomerate alleging fraud against former Armco executives, Mr Donohue included. The claim centred on a transaction whereby Armco had sold the British National Insurance Group to those executives. The transaction documents provided for the exclusive jurisdiction of the English courts. Mr Donohue applied for an anti-suit injunction in London to enforce that agreement. Lord Bingham gave the leading judgment. He accepted that 'the principles governing the grant of injunctions and stays are not the same', but they were not different on this particular point:[130]

> If contracting parties agree to give a particular court exclusive jurisdiction to rule on claims between those parties, and a claim falling within the scope of the agreement is made in proceedings in a forum other than that which the parties have agreed, the English court will ordinarily exercise its discretion … to secure compliance with the contractual bargain, unless the party suing in the non-contractual forum (the burden being on him) can show strong reasons for suing in that forum. I use the word 'ordinarily' to recognise that where an exercise of discretion is called for there can be no absolute or inflexible rule governing that exercise, and also that a party may lose his claim to equitable relief by dilatoriness or other unconscionable conduct. But the general rule is clear: where parties have bound themselves by an exclusive jurisdiction clause effect should ordinarily be given to that obligation in the absence of strong reasons for departing from it. Whether a party can show strong reasons, sufficient to displace the other party's prima facie entitlement to enforce the contractual bargain, will depend on all the facts and circumstances of the particular case. In the course of his judgment in *The Eleftheria* … Brandon J helpfully listed some of the matters which might properly be regarded by the court when exercising its discretion, and his judgment has been repeatedly cited and applied. Brandon J did not intend his list to be comprehensive, but mentioned a number of matters, including the law governing the contract, which may in some cases be material.

[127] *Donohue* (n 9). See, eg, Briggs (n 8) 474; Fentiman (n 124) 106.
[128] *Donohue* (n 9) [42].
[129] Anti-suit injunctions are discussed further in ch 12 in this volume.
[130] *Donohue* (n 9) [24].

On the facts, however, Lord Bingham declined to order the injunction despite Mr Donohue's 'strong prima facie right'.[131] Proceedings would continue in New York against Mr Donohue's associates regardless of any anti-suit injunction; other, related claims against Mr Donohue also fell outside of the jurisdiction agreement.[132] It would be 'directly counter to the interest of justice' to have the same alleged fraudulent conspiracy or plot tried in parallel proceedings on either side of the Atlantic.[133] Thus, subject to an undertaking from Armco not to enforce any award for multiple or punitive damages available under US law, 'the ends of justice would be best served by a single composite trial in the only forum in which a single composite trial can be procured, which is New York'.[134]

A review of various editions of *Dicey* over the period from *The Eleftheria* to *Donohue* shows the increasing centrality of prorogation and derogation agreements the law of jurisdiction. A team of editors under Dr Morris assumed the editorship from the sixth edition in 1949 to the tenth edition in 1980. Very little text was given over to jurisdiction agreements in the edition immediately preceding *The Eleftheria* (the eighth, in 1967), much of it materially the same as Dicey's original text, and scattered around the book with little coherence.[135] The ninth edition, in 1973, included a new chapter 'Jurisdiction to Stay Actions – Lis Alibi Pendens and Foreign Jurisdiction Clauses', in which Brandon J's numbered propositions were replicated almost unaltered in the text[136] – and remain so to this day.[137] That chapter, insofar as it concerned jurisdiction agreements, was focused on derogation agreements, but was then reworked again to cover prorogation and derogation agreement together in a rational scheme in the first edition under the general editorship of Lawrence Collins (as he then was) in 1987,[138] two years after Lord Brandon's speech in *The Sennar (No 2)*.

V. PREVAILING PRACTICE

The approach articulated by Brandon J's numbered propositions is still treated as good law, but the prominence of the case itself now has receded; the modern

[131] ibid, [29].
[132] ibid, [30]–[31].
[133] ibid, [34]–[35].
[134] ibid, [36] and [39].
[135] JHC Morris (ed), *Dicey and Morris on the Conflict of Laws*, 8th edn (London, Stevens & Sons, 1967) 179–82, 210 and 1087–88.
[136] JHC Morris (ed), *Dicey and Morris on the Conflict of Laws*, 9th edn (London, Stevens & Sons, 1973) 223, but see also 167–70 and 198.
[137] L Collins (ed), *Dicey, Morris & Collins on the Conflict of Laws*, 15th edn (London, Sweet & Maxwell, 2012) 632.
[138] L Collins (ed), *Dicey and Morris on the Conflict of Laws*, 11th edn (London, Stevens & Sons, 1987) 402–417; it may be that this unification was prompted by the need, for the first time, to take account of Art 17 of the Brussels Convention 1968 as brought into English law by the Civil Jurisdiction and Judgments Act 1982.

landmark is *Donohue*, not *The Eleftheria*; and, while *The Eleftheria* is still regularly cited,[139] the particular factors identified by Brandon J in proposition (5)[140] are no longer a particularly helpful checklist. It is suggested that the factors likely to constitute 'strong cause' to depart from a jurisdiction agreement are now better re-arranged into a threefold hierarchy of objections to enforcing that agreement.[141] In descending order of strength, these are:

(a) Where to give effect to the jurisdiction agreement would risk an unjust determination of the dispute.
(b) Where to give effect to the jurisdiction agreement would lead to injustice arising from parallel proceedings and a risk of irreconcilable judgments.
(c) Factors as to convenience, governing law and connection to the jurisdiction.

Each of these can be explored in a little more detail.

A. Real Risk of an Unjust Determination of the Dispute

An English court will not enforce a jurisdiction agreement if there is a risk of an unjust determination of the dispute in the chosen forum, although the evidence supporting such a submission must be 'compelling'[142] or 'cogent'.[143] As Brandon J recognised in proposition (5)(e)(iv) of *The Eleftheria*, this may be because of 'political, racial, religious or other reasons'.[144] In some cases the parties choose a forum which later undergoes political change: so, for example, an exclusive jurisdiction agreement in favour of Germany agreed in 1927 was not enforced against a Jewish claimant in 1939;[145] and, more recently, an agreement in favour of the courts of Portuguese Angola was not enforced after its independence revolution occurred there.[146] But this principle should not just be limited to cases where the relevant risk only arises after the jurisdiction agreement has been agreed, and not foreseeable.[147] It would still have offended public

[139] See, eg, *KMG International NV v Melanie Anne Chipper Management Ltd* [2018] EWHC 1078 (Comm) [30] (Moulder J); *Lyle & Scott Ltd v American Eagle Outfitters Inc* [2021] EWHC 90 (Ch) [79] (Miles J). But often *The Eleftheria* is in fact cited as part of the wider quotation from *Donohue* (n 9) [24]: see, eg, *Impala Warehousing and Logistics (Shanghai) Co Ltd v Wanxiang Resources (Singapore) Pte Ltd* [2015] EWHC 811 (Comm) [108] (Blair J); *Team Y&R Holdings Hong Kong Ltd v Ghossoub* [2017] EWHC 2401 (Comm) [42] (Laurence Rabinowitz QC sitting as a Deputy High Court Judge).

[140] Text to n 6.

[141] For slightly different explanations of the current law, see, eg, *Dicey, Morris & Collins*, 15th edn (n 137) 632–633; Briggs (n 8) 473–76; Fentiman (n 124) 105–10; Joseph (n 7) paras 10.03–10.34; Mills (n 15) 141–49; E Peel, 'Exclusive Jurisdiction Agreements: Purity and Pragmatism in the Conflict of Laws' [1998] *Lloyd's Maritime and Commercial Law Quarterly* 182.

[142] Joseph (n 7) para 10.29.

[143] Peel (n 141) 199.

[144] *The Eleftheria* (n 5) 100.

[145] *Ellinger* (n 50) 23–24 (Morton J).

[146] *Carvalho* (n 113) 1236–38 (Browne LJ) and 1240–41 (Geoffrey Lane LJ).

[147] Fentiman (n 124) 109.

policy to have required a Jewish claimant to sue in Nazi Germany in 1939 *even if* the jurisdiction agreement had been agreed in 1938 and so the risk of injustice entirely foreseeable.

On the other hand, criticisms of the chosen forum which fall short of attacking its integrity should not be enough to outweigh the jurisdiction agreement. Differences of procedure or expertise between the chosen forum and the English court do not engage public policy concerns. The leading case, again, is *The El Amria*. At first instance, Sheen J placed weight on the fact that 'if this matter were to be heard in Egypt the parties would not obtain the full and thorough investigation into the merits of the case, which they both want'.[148] In the Court of Appeal, Brandon LJ deprecated this line of reasoning: 'for an English Court to investigate such a matter and pronounce a judgment on it is not consistent with the mutual respect which the Courts of friendly states, each of which has a well developed system for the administration of justice, owe, or should owe, to each other'.[149]

This is consistent with the approach taken in the second stage of a *forum non conveniens* analysis, when the court asks whether it would be 'unjust that the claimant be deprived to the right to trial in England'.[150] In *Cherney v Deripaska*,[151] for example, the Court of Appeal allowed proceedings to continue in England despite Russia being the natural forum for the dispute, on the basis of there was cogent evidence of a significant risk that there would be no fair trial in Russia given the concerns about assassination attempts and trumped up criminal charges against Mr Cherney, evidence of state pressure on the Russian judiciary in such cases of strategic importance, and the substantial links between Mr Deripaska and the Russian state. As Lord Collins explained in a later case, the party seeking to displace the result that would otherwise follow from identifying the natural forum:[152]

> ... can be satisfied by showing that there is a real risk that justice will not be obtained in the foreign court by reason of incompetence or lack of independence or corruption. Of course, if it can be shown that justice "will not" be obtained that will weigh more heavily in the exercise of the discretion in the light of all other circumstances. ... Comity requires that the court be extremely cautious before deciding that there is a risk that justice will not be done in the foreign country by the foreign court, and that is why cogent evidence is required. But ... even in what they describe as endemic corruption cases (ie where the court system itself is criticised) there is no principle that the court may not rule.

[148] *Aratra Potato Co Ltd v Egyptian Navigation Co (The El Amria)* [1981] 2 Lloyd's Rep 119 (Ad) 392.
[149] *The El Amria* (n 117) 126, approved in *Amin Rasheed Shipping Corp v Kuwait Insurance Co* [1984] AC 50 (HL) 72 (Lord Wilberforce).
[150] *Spiliada* (n 48) 478 (Lord Goff); *Dicey, Morris & Collins*, 15th edn (n 137) 534, r 38(2)(b).
[151] *Cherney v Deripaska* [2009] EWCA Civ 849, [2010] 2 All ER (Comm) 456.
[152] *AK Investment CJSC v Kyrgyz Mobil Tel Ltd* [2011] UKPC 7, [2012] 1 WLR 1804 [95] and [97].

Cherney and *AK Investments* were cases where no reliance was placed on any jurisdiction agreement. However, had there been a jurisdiction agreement in either case, it should have made no difference: it would be contrary to justice to force the parties to litigate in a forum where there was a real risk of no fair trial,[153] and the parties' private interests at the time of contracting in selecting that forum must yield to those overriding considerations of justice.

B. Parallel Proceedings and Risk of Irreconcilable Judgments

The next weightiest factor when considering whether to enforce a jurisdiction agreement at common law is one not mentioned at all in proposition (5) of *The Eleftheria*, namely whether its enforcement would lead to parallel proceedings and a risk of inconsistent judgments. As already explained,[154] that was the determinative feature of both *The El Amria* and *Donohue v Armco*. Another example is *Citi-March Ltd v Neptune Orient Lines Ltd*, where English proceedings against one (of a number) of defendants continued in the face of an exclusive jurisdiction agreement in favour of Singapore because otherwise there would be proceedings in both jurisdictions Colman J considered that to be not only 'inconvenient' but also 'potentially unjust', given the asymmetry of evidence likely to be adduced in each forum and also the risk of inconsistent decisions, to which he gave 'considerable weight'.[155]

The current edition of *Dicey, Morris & Collins* confirms that the court invariably will prefer a dispute to be resolved justly in a single forum, and endorses this approach as 'sound'.[156] Richard Fentiman describes this is a '"convenience" factor' and so argues that normally the claimant 'bears the risk of such parallel proceedings', unless unforeseeable at the time of contracting.[157] While this has some support in the authorities,[158] the better view is that the court seeks to avoid parallel proceedings not merely because of convenience issues (such

[153] If not contrary to Art 6 of the European Convention on Human Rights: for the potential implications of this, see further A Arzandeh, 'Should the *Spiliada* Test be Revised?' (2014) 10 *Journal of Private International Law* 89.

[154] Text to n 117 and n 127.

[155] *Citi-March* (n 125) 1375–77. See also in a different context *889457 Alberta Inc v Katanga Mining Ltd* [2008] EWHC 2679 (Comm) [25] (Tomlinson J): '… the desirability of concentrating proceedings in one jurisdiction so as to avoid the possibility of inconsistent decisions would ordinarily tell in favour of retaining jurisdiction …'.

[156] *Dicey, Morris & Collins*, 15th edn (n 137) 632.

[157] Fentiman (n 124) 109, also 110.

[158] *Konkola Copper Mines plc v Coromin Ltd (No 2)* [2006] EWHC 1093, [2006] 2 All ER (Comm) 400 [32] and [42] (Colman J); *Astrazeneca UK Ltd v Albermale International Corp* [2010] EWHC 1028 (Comm), [2010] 1 CLC 715 [112] (Hamblen J); *Euromark Ltd v Smash Enterprises Pty Ltd* [2013] EWHC EHWC 1627 (QB) [29] (Coulson J); *CH Offshore Ltd v PDV Marina SA* [2015] EWHC 595 (Comm) [63] and [89] (Carr J).

as the likely duplication of resources) but also because of the 'strong public policy in preventing conflicting judgments from coming into existence'.[159] There are obvious issues of justice if the parties obtain, and are meant to be bound by, two judgments which pull in different directions, not least when it comes to recognition and enforcement in third countries. As Brandon LJ put it in *The El Amria*, the courts view this not as an inconvenience but as a 'potential disaster'.[160] The UK Supreme Court recently emphasised in *Vedanta Resources Plc v Lungowe* that this is a 'very important factor', albeit not determinative in every case.[161] But, as a public policy issue, it ought not be limited by considerations of foreseeability.

On the other hand, even when unforeseeable at the time of contracting, this factor will *not* always be decisive. That is why this is a less weighty factor than real risk of an unjust determination of the dispute. The English court is alive to the risk of parties abusing this second factor to create a 'trump card'.[162] A party seeking to invoke it on the basis that it has, or will, breach the jurisdiction agreement by suing elsewhere should not meet the strong cause threshold unless it can show a good reason for breaching the jurisdiction agreement. Assuming that there is no real risk of an unfair trial, the only compelling reason appears to be where there are other parties in the dispute who can only to be sued in the non-chosen forum: that was the factor at play in *The El Amria*, *Donohue* and *Citi-March*.[163] In other cases, the rhetorical question which Lord Briggs recently asked in *Vedanta* (with minimal adaptation) is apt:[164]

> Why (it may be asked) should that risk be a decisive factor in the identification of the proper place, when it is a factor which the [party seeking to show strong cause], having a choice, have brought upon themselves?

A case in point is *Akai Pty Ltd v People's Insurance Co Ltd*,[165] which is considered later in this collection,[166] and so not addressed further here, save to note that neither good reason identified above was suggested in that case. It will depend on the particular facts of the case (and perhaps judicial temperament) as to whether the desire to stop the contract-breaker from benefitting from their own breach of contract outweighs the potential injustice of irreconcilable judgments.

[159] Briggs (n 8) 475. See also Joseph (n 7) para 10.17.
[160] *The El Amria* (n 117) 128.
[161] *Vedanta Resources Plc v Lungowe* [2019] UKSC 20, [2020] AC 1045 [69] (Lord Briggs). See also *ED&F Man Capital Markets Ltd v Straits (Singapore) Pte Ltd* [2019] EWCA Civ 2073, [2020] 2 All ER (Comm) 551 [49] (Flaux LJ).
[162] *Vedanta* (n 161) [92] (Lord Briggs). See also Peel (n 141) 200.
[163] See also Fentiman (n 124) 109–10.
[164] *Vedanta* (n 161) [75].
[165] *Akai Pty Ltd v People's Insurance Co Ltd* [1998] 1 Lloyd's Rep 90 (Com Ct).
[166] See ch 14 in this volume.

C. Other Factors

In contrast to the first two factors, which raise fundamental issues of public policy and justice, it is suggested that other factors, including those identified by Brandon J in *The Eleftheria* at propositions (5)(a)–(d) and (e)(i)–(iii) carry less force and are rightly limited by a reasonable foreseeability requirement. These factors – location of evidence, practicalities and expense of trial, applicable law, connections of the parties to the jurisdiction, motivations for pursuing proceedings in the chosen forum, and so on – can fairly all be characterised as issues of convenience, or at least as risks associated with the chosen forum that were assumed by the parties by agreeing to that forum. These factors should *only* be capable of constituting strong cause (if at all) when not reasonably foreseeable at the time of contracting. As Gloster J put it in *Antec International Ltd v Biosafety USA Inc*:[167]

> … overwhelming or very strong reasons do not include factors of convenience that were foreseeable at the time that the contract was entered into (save in exceptional circumstances involving the interests of justice) … The defendant has to point to some factor which it could not have foreseen at the time the contract was concluded.

Reasonable foreseeability is not, of course, the same as asking whether the parties actually foresaw the factor, and 'the courts will impute considerable foresight to commercial parties'.[168] It has been suggested that:[169]

> … there is a spectrum of cases from the case where the parties have negotiated the jurisdiction clause at one end to the case of a one-off standard term contract at the other and that the Court is perhaps less likely to find the necessary strong cause established in the former case than in the latter.

However, for the purposes of foreseeability it should not matter if the jurisdiction agreement is not specifically negotiated or forms boilerplate in one side's standard terms; unless the validity of the jurisdiction agreement can be challenged in some way, on orthodox contractual principles the parties should be held to reasonable foreseeability at the time of contracting.[170]

Further, even when not reasonably foreseeable, it should be an unusual case where any of the factors in propositions (5)(a)–(d) and (e)(i)–(iii) of

[167] *Antec International Ltd v Biosafety USA Inc* [2006] EWHC 47 (Comm) [7]. This approach to enforcing exclusive jurisdiction agreements can be tracked back to *Mercury Communications Ltd v Communication Telesystems International* [1999] 2 All ER (Comm) 33 (Com Ct) 41 (Moore-Bick J), although in that case the court accepted that there may be 'rare' cases where foreseeable factors amounted to strong cause. Once the two public policy considerations noted above are stripped out, it is difficult to see what else there might be.

[168] Fentiman (n 124) 108.

[169] *The Bergen (No 2)* [1997] 2 Lloyd's Rep 710 (Ad) 715 (Clarke J).

[170] *Mercury Communications* (n 167) 41 (Moore-Bick J); *Import Export Metro Ltd v Compania Sud Americana de Vapores SA* [2003] EWHC 11 (Comm), [2004] 2 CLC 757 [14(iii)]–[15] (Gross J); *Vinmar* (n 14) [36]–[37]. Fentiman (n 124) 109; *cf* Joseph (n 7) para 10.13.

The Eleftheria should have much force, still less constitute strong cause. Addressing them briefly in turn:

> (5)(a) In what country the evidence on the issues of fact is situated, or more readily available, and the effect of that on the relative convenience and expense of trial as between the English and foreign courts.

Despite the fact that Brandon J took account of this factor in *The Eleftheria*,[171] and Brandon LJ gave even greater weight to it in *The El Amria*,[172] this is now something that should rarely (if ever) amount to strong cause.[173] In *Akai*, Thomas J described this as having 'little relevance'.[174] More recently, judges have disclaimed interested in such 'minute evaluation of the witnesses [and] documents' when evaluating whether there is strong cause,[175] especially when it is nearly always foreseeable that witnesses and documents relevant to a dispute may be in a different place to the chosen forum.[176] Peel has suggested that there may be a difference of approach for witnesses of fact, compared to experts who can expect to travel or be replaced.[177] With the courts' recent embrace of remote and hybrid hearings, where witnesses regularly give evidence by video-link, this is unlikely to still be a distinction with force in most cases.

> (5)(b) Whether the law of the foreign court applies and, if so, whether it differs from English law in any material respects.

Usually the governing law will be reasonably foreseeable at the time of contracting, and so it will also be reasonably foreseeable if there is likely to be a disjuncture between the chosen law and the chosen forum. The fact that the chosen court may not apply its own law is simply a product of the parties' bargain. Even when unforeseeable, that is true. Further, the English courts are well-used to applying foreign law,[178] so the prospect of applying foreign law is unlikely ever to persuade an English court to give up jurisdiction conferred by party agreement; the English courts will also usually assume that the foreign court is equally well used to applying a law that is not its own, and an argument to the contrary (short of attacking the integrity of that court) is unlikely

[171] *The Eleftheria* (n 5) 104.

[172] *The El Amria* (n 117) 128–29. See n 122.

[173] Joseph (n 7) para 10.12.

[174] *Akai* (n 165) 105 citing *Attock Cement Co Ltd v Romanian Bank for Foreign Trade* [1989] 1 WLR 1147 (CA) 1161 (Staughton LJ).

[175] *JP Morgan Securities Asia Private Ltd v Malaysian Newsprint Industries Sdn Bhd* [2002] ILPr 17 (Com Ct) [52] (HHJ Chambers QC).

[176] *Middle Eastern Oil LLC v National Bank of Abu Dhabi* [2008] EWHC 2895 (Comm), [2008] 2 CLC 1026 [12] (Teare J).

[177] Peel (n 141) 192.

[178] The most recent Commercial Court Guide, 11th edn (2022) states at para H3.1: 'Expert evidence of foreign law features in a significant proportion of Commercial Court trials', before going on to list ways in which foreign law can be proved even without expert evidence.

to succeed.[179] As Gross J recognised in *Import Export Metro Ltd v Compania Sud Americana de Vapores SA*, this is only likely to amount to strong cause in rare cases where it impacts 'the interests of justice' rather merely constituting 'considerations of convenience'.[180]

> (5)(c) With what country either party is connected, and how closely.

Like proposition (5)(a), the lack of a link to the chosen jurisdiction should rarely amount to strong cause. Indeed, the absence of such a connection may, itself, be a further reason to uphold the jurisdiction agreement as a 'neutral venue'.[181] And even if not intended to be a neutral venue at the time of contracting, it is difficult to see how this could amount to strong cause short of showing that the venue lacks integrity such that there is a real risk of injustice, rather than being simply being a (foreseeable) risk of practical inconvenience. David Joseph KC goes further in his well-known book on jurisdiction agreements, and suggests that proposition (5)(c) could *never* be used in support an application for not giving effect to a jurisdiction agreement.[182] While attractive, that may go too far: combined with other factors, proposition (5)(c) might amount to strong cause if the venue was intended to be neutral at the time of contracting but unforeseeably has since become the home turf for one side.

> (5)(d) Whether the defendants genuinely desire trial in the foreign country, or are only seeking procedural advantages.

There is a tension between this proposition and the principle, expressed by Brandon LJ in *The El Amria*, that the court should not engage in a comparative exercise between the procedural advantages of the rival fora.[183] Further, it is counter-intuitive to hold against the party seeking to enforce the jurisdiction agreement any procedural advantage that had been bargained for.[184] To the extent to which this proposition has any remaining force, it should be only applicable where it can be inferred that the party seeking to enforce the jurisdiction agreement is pursuing an 'illegitimate delaying tactic'.[185] An example is *The Vishva Prabha*, where Sheen J was able to infer that

> the defendants are only seeking the advantage of delay and are not really anxious that the matter should be heard in the Courts of Bombay for any other reason. It seems to me that, trite as the observation may be, justice delayed is justice denied, and justice delayed five years would be justice denied to the plaintiffs in this case.[186]

[179] See, eg, *Middle Eastern Oil* (n 176) [21] (Teare J).
[180] *Import Export* (n 170) [17].
[181] *Attock Cement* (n 174) 1161 (Staughton LJ); Peel (n 141) 195.
[182] Joseph (n 7) para 10.12.
[183] *The El Amria* (n 117) 126. See text to n 149.
[184] Peel (n 141) 195–96.
[185] ibid 196; Joseph (n 7) para 10.31.
[186] *The Vishva Prabha* [1979] 2 Lloyd's Rep 286 (Ad) 288.

As the Singapore Court of Appeal has recently put it, the question here is whether 'the applicant is acting abusively in applying for a stay of proceedings', the threshold for which will be 'very high'.[187] The true question is whether delay has become relevant not as a matter of party convenience but instead as an issue of whether justice will be done in the chosen forum.[188]

> (5)(e) Whether the plaintiffs would be prejudiced by having to sue in the foreign court because they would … (i) be deprived of security for their claim; (ii) be unable to enforce any judgment obtained; (iii) be faced with a time-bar not applicable in England.

These final set of considerations similarly lack the cogency to make a case for strong cause. Security tends to be an issue specific to admiralty proceedings, and the arrest of ships.[189] But, as Peel has pointed out, it is somewhat odd to give legitimacy to this advantage when it has been 'effectively conceded' by the foreign jurisdiction agreement.[190] Judgment enforcement has never really featured in the case law.[191] As for time bars, although the Privy Council confirmed that this remains a factor,[192] in practice this is 'more apparent than real' given the claimant must show it is not at fault in failing to save limitation in the chosen jurisdiction and 'it will be hard to see why it is not culpable to fail to save limitation in the court which has been agreed to by contract'.[193]

VI. IS THIS FORUM NON CONVENIENS?

One outstanding issue is the relationship between the modern principles as to the effect of jurisdiction agreements and the modern law of *forum non conveniens*. There are shared historical roots in the 'balance of convenience' developed under Order XI.[194] The former reached maturity before the latter: what Henry Brandon did for jurisdiction agreements, Robert Goff was later to do for *forum conveniens*.[195] The case law is not consistent on this point. While as counsel in *The Atlantic Star*, Robert Goff QC cited *The Eleftheria* as 'an English case where the court adopted the principle of forum conveniens',[196] and he noted

[187] *Vinmar* (n 14) [130]–[131].
[188] *Cf* Joseph (n 7) para 10.31, which discusses a trend in Singapore whereby illegitimate delaying tactics have been inferred from the fact that there appears to be no real defence to the claim. As Joseph points out, this is potentially problematic as there is a limit to which the court can assess the merits on a jurisdiction challenge. That trend is no longer good law: see *Vinmar* (n 14) [113].
[189] It featured as an issue both *The Fehmarn (Ad)* (n 83 and n 87) and *The Eleftheria* (n 5).
[190] Peel (n 141) 197.
[191] ibid 197–98.
[192] *The Pioneer Container* [1994] 2 AC 324 (PC) 348–49 (Lord Goff).
[193] Briggs (n 8) 475; *cf* Joseph (n 7) para 10.16.
[194] See text to n 50.
[195] See ch 13 in this volume.
[196] *The Atlantic Star* [1974] AC 436 (HL) 445.

the similarities as a first instance judge,[197] his speech in *Spiliada* was silent on this point. In a short concurring judgment in *The El Amria* (which pre-dated *Spiliada*) Stephenson LJ agreed with Brandon LJ's judgment but added that he 'would go no further towards assimilating' the two doctrines.[198] Post-*Spiliada*, in *The Nile Rhapsody*,[199] Hirst J appeared to conflate the two, suggesting the principal difference between them was merely the burden of proof.

The argument typically made in favour of assimilation starts with the 'obvious similarities' between the factors identified by Brandon J in *The Eleftheria* and Lord Goff's formulation in *Spiliada*.[200] The objection that the burden of proof is different in the two exercises is not convincing,[201] given the burden of proof already switches within the *forum non conveniens* exercise between service in and service out cases.[202] The stronger objection, voiced by a range of commentators, is that subsuming the exercise for jurisdiction agreements within *forum non conveniens* risks weakening the strength of the presumption that effect be given to a jurisdiction agreement. As Peel puts it, 'only a quite separate approach … will ensure that … the parties' agreement is given effect in all but exceptional circumstances'.[203] On the other hand:[204]

> If the imperative policy of ensuring compliance with the contractual agreement could somehow be accommodated within a modified *forum non conveniens* approach, then the existence of a separate approach for exclusive jurisdiction clause might be argued to be superfluous.

It is tempting to characterise this as an arid debate which, as Mills puts it, is 'not very significant in practice, as it does not appear to affect what factors are relevant to the discretion or how much weight is attached to them'.[205] It was most recently considered by the Supreme Court of Canada in *Douez v Facebook Inc*. This was a jurisdiction challenge by Facebook to a consumer class action led by Ms Douez in Canada for breach of British Columbian privacy law, relying on a jurisdiction clause in favour of the Californian courts in its terms of use. Giving the majority judgment, Karakatsanis, Wagner and Gascon JJ agreed that the importance of holding parties to jurisdiction agreements, absent exceptional

[197] *Trendtex Trading Corp v Credit Suisse* [1980] 3 All ER 721 (QB) 733–34.

[198] *The El Amria* (n 117) 129.

[199] *Hamed El Chiaty & Co v The Thomas Cook Group Ltd (The Nile Rhapsody)* [1992] 2 Lloyd's Rep 399 (Com Ct).

[200] See, eg, A Arzandeh, *Forum (Non) Conveiens in England: Past, Present and Future* (Oxford, Hart, 2019) 96; P Torremans et al, *Cheshire, North & Fawcett: Private International Law*, 15th ed (Oxford, OUP, 2017) 413.

[201] *Cheshire, North & Fawcett* (n 200) 413–14.

[202] *Spiliada* (n 48) 480 (Lord Goff).

[203] Peel (n 141) 190. See also A Briggs 'Jurisdiction Clauses and Judicial Attitudes' (1993) 109 *Law Quarterly Review* 382 (*cf* Briggs (n 123) 245) and Fentiman (n 124) 106–07.

[204] TK Sing 'Stay of Actions Based on Exclusive Jurisdiction Clauses under English and Singapore Law (Part II' [1991] *Singapore Journal of Legal Studies* 410, 419.

[205] Mills (n 15) 147.

circumstances, justified keeping it separate to the *forum non conveniens* framework.[206]

Despite the conclusion reached in *Douez*, the better view is that *The Eleftheria*'s principles are not conceptually distinct from a *forum non conveniens* exercise but represent a modified application of them. Recent cases which emphasise the difference between the *Spiliada* and *Eleftheria* exercises support this characterisation: the existence of a jurisdiction agreement 'must severely limit the normal diet of *Spiliada* circumstance that is to be served to the judge'.[207] In non-gastronomical terms, this means that the jurisdiction agreement should be given near decisive effect, subject to any unforeseeable factors at the first stage of the *Spiliada* analysis,[208] and any issues of injustice which arise at the second stage. Put another way, within the threefold hierarchy of objections to enforcing a jurisdiction agreement, the third form of objection is part of the first stage of the *Spiliada* analysis whereas the first two objections fall within the second stage of the *Spiliada* analysis. As Hobhouse J explained in *S&W Berisford plc v New Hampshire Insurance Co*, the chosen forum 'should in principle be a jurisdiction to which neither party to the contract can object as inappropriate; they have both implicitly agreed that it is appropriate'.[209] It follows that the rare cases where strong cause is made out will nearly always be cases turning on the second stage of the *Spiliada* test, where the court is considering what injustice may arise from enforcing the jurisdiction agreement. Indeed, *Douez* itself was such a case, where there were 'strong public policy considerations which favour a finding of strong cause'.[210]

VII. CONCLUSION

Commenting on *The Eleftheria* when it was first decided, Lawrence Collins (as he then was) said its importance was as the 'first case to set out in a comprehensive and logical manner the principles on which the court will act' when faced with a choice of court agreement in favour of a foreign court.[211] This chapter has reached substantially the same conclusion: the genius of Brandon J's judgment in *The Eleftheria* was not in its innovation – much of it appears in

[206] *Douez* (n 13) [20]. See also [130]–[131] (McLachlin CJ and Côté J). This followed the earlier decision of the Supreme Court of Canada in *Pompey* (n 13) [21]: 'In my view, a separate approach to applications for a stay of proceedings involving forum selection clauses ... ensures that these considerations are properly taken into account and that the parties' agreement is given effect in all but exceptional circumstances' (Bastarache J).

[207] *JP Morgan* (n 175) [52] (HHJ Chambers QC).

[208] As Sing (n 204) puts it, at 'the first stage of the *Spiliada* approach ... the primary ascertainment of the appropriate forum is left to the parties'.

[209] *S&W Berisford plc v New Hampshire Insurance Co* [1990] 2 All ER 321 (Com Ct) 333.

[210] *Douez* (n 13) [51] (Karakatsanis, Wagner and Gascon JJ).

[211] L Collins, 'Arbitration Clauses and Forum Selecting Clauses in the Conflict of Laws: Some Recent Developments in England' (1971) 2 *Journal of Maritime Law and Commerce* 363, 370.

Willmer J's earlier judgment in *The Fehmarn* – but rather in communicating a clear consolidation of the principles that had been developed over the previous century. Some judges today disparage the use of numbered principles,[212] but the deserved landmark status of *The Eleftheria* lies in the workable framework its numbered propositions provided for dealing at common law with foreign jurisdiction agreements. On the other hand, many of *The Eleftheria*'s propositions no longer reflect the modern common law as to the factors to be considered when giving weight to jurisdiction agreements where the Hague Convention on Choice of Court Agreements 2005 does not apply. It is time for a refresh. The following revised propositions are suggested to summarise the effect which the common law now gives to exclusive jurisdiction agreements:

(1) Where a claimant sues in England, if the claim is otherwise within the scope of an exclusive jurisdiction agreement between the claimant and the defendant, that agreement is a very strong pointer towards the proper place in which to bring the claim.
(2) In particular, where the agreement refers disputes to the English court, the English court is not bound to exercise jurisdiction but should do so unless strong cause is shown by the defendant.[213]
(3) Conversely, where the agreement refers disputes to a foreign court, the English court is not bound to refuse to exercise jurisdiction but should only do so where strong cause is shown by the claimant.
(4) In exercising its discretion, the court should take into account all the circumstances of the particular case. However, save in exceptional cases, only the following factors may (on appropriate facts) amount to strong cause:
    (a) Where to give effect to the jurisdiction agreement would risk an unjust determination of the dispute.
    (b) Where to give effect to the jurisdiction agreement would lead to injustice arising from parallel proceedings and a risk of irreconcilable judgments (but this factor cannot be relied upon by the party seeking to show strong cause where they have created that risk themselves for no good reason).
    (c) Factors as to convenience, governing law and connection to the jurisdiction, but only where not reasonably foreseeable to the parties at the time of contracting.
(5) Propositions (1) to (4) do not apply where the jurisdiction agreement falls within the scope of a particular regime (such as the Hague Convention on Choice of Court Agreements 2005) or where the subject matter is inadmissible (such as if the dispute seeks a determination of title to foreign land).

[212] 'I am not convinced that it is helpful to try to summarise wide-ranging areas of law in numbered principles. That is not really how the common law operates': *Warner Music UK Ltd v TuneIn Inc* [2021] EWCA Civ 441, [2021] Bus LR 1119 [192] (Sir Geoffrey Vos MR).

[213] In practice, the Hague Convention will normally apply here.

11

Spiliada Maritime Corporation v Cansulex Ltd (1986)

EDWIN PEEL

THERE IS NO doubt that *Spiliada Maritime Corporation v Cansulex Ltd*[1] is a landmark case in the conflict of laws. It is perhaps most accurate to describe it as the last of a series of landmark cases which significantly changed English law in so far as it relates to the circumstances in which the English courts will decline to exercise their jurisdiction when there is another available forum. This essay examines the development of the principles still applied today, with particular focus on *Spiliada* itself, before a brief assessment of whether, in practice, it has turned out to be, as some have said, a 'treasure-house'.[2]

In assessing the state of the law prior to the decision of the House of Lords in *The Atlantic Star*, Lord Wilberforce opined that it could only be understood 'against an evolutionary background'.[3] A similar approach assists with our understanding of the law as laid down in *Spiliada* because, while it is Lord Goff's speech in *Spiliada* which has proved to be seminal, a lot of the heavy lifting was done by a number of earlier decisions of the House of Lords.[4] Lord Goff's speech is also notable for a gracious postscript, in the following terms:[5]

> I feel that I cannot conclude without paying tribute to the writings of jurists which have assisted me in the preparation of this opinion. Although it may be invidious to do so, I wish to single out for special mention articles by Mr. Adrian Briggs in (1983) 3 Legal Studies 74 and in [1984] LMCLQ 227, and the article by Miss Rhona Schuz in (1986) 35 ICLQ 374. They will observe that I have not agreed with them on all points; but even when I have disagreed with them, I have found their work to be of assistance.

[1] *Spiliada Maritime Corporation v Cansulex Ltd* [1987] 1 AC 460 (HL).

[2] A Briggs, 'Foreign Judgments: More Surprises' (1992) 108 *Law Quarterly Review* 549, 553.

[3] *Owners of the Atlantic Star v Owners of the Bona Spes (The Atlantic Star)* [1974] AC 436 (HL) 464.

[4] See further A Arzandeh, *Forum (Non) Conveniens in England: Past, Present and Future* (Oxford, Hart Publishing, 2018) ch 3; D Robertson, 'Forum Non Conveniens in America and England: A Rather Fantastic Fiction' (1987) 103 *Law Quarterly Review* 398.

[5] *Spiliada* (n 1) 488.

> For jurists are pilgrims with us on the endless road to unattainable perfection; and we have it on the excellent authority of Geoffrey Chaucer that conversations among pilgrims can be most rewarding.

We start with the cases, before turning to the 'pilgrims'.

I. CASES

In tracing the evolution of the law in *The Atlantic Star*, Lord Wilberforce observed that it was 'not necessary to go back much more than 100 years'.[6] We need only concern ourselves with a much shorter period when it comes to the development of the law from the decision in *The Atlantic Star* in 1973 to the decision in *Spiliada* in 1986.[7] That in itself indicates that this was a period of rapid evolution.[8] It is best described as the erosion (rapid on this occasion, and not gradual[9]) of claimant bias in the selection of venue, and of judicial chauvinism. The leading cases are *The Atlantic Star* itself, *MacShannon v Rockware Glass Ltd*,[10] and *The Abidin Daver*.[11] It is submitted that the most significant of them is *The Atlantic Star*, if only because it set in motion a force which proved impossible to resist.[12]

A. *The Atlantic Star*

In *The Atlantic Star*,[13] a collision occurred in Belgian waters between the *Atlantic Star*, a Dutch container vessel, and two barges, one Dutch-owned and the other Belgian. As one would expect, the barges came off worst and were lost, along with two men who drowned. The owners of the Belgian barge began an action against the owners of the *Atlantic Star* in the Antwerp court, but the owners of the Dutch barge began an action in rem in the Admiralty Court in England,

[6] *The Atlantic Star* (n 3) 464.

[7] A decision which is not directly addressed as part of this evolutionary study is *Amin Rasheed Shipping Corporation v Kuwait Insurance* [1984] AC 50 (HL). This is on the basis that it does not add a great deal to the evolutionary stage covered by *The Abidin Daver*, and the particular context of *Amin Rasheed* (service out of the jurisdiction) is dealt with in *Spiliada* itself. It is however noted that one of the judges in the Court of Appeal in *Amin Rasheed* was Robert Goff LJ. See text at n 38.

[8] As reflected in the title of one of the articles by Adrian Briggs, referred to by Lord Goff: 'Forum Non Conveniens – Now We Are Ten?' (1983) 3 *Legal Studies* 74.

[9] *Cf MacShannon v Rockware Glass Ltd* [1978] AC 795 (HL) 811 (Lord Diplock: 'The progress of the common law is gradual').

[10] ibid.

[11] *Owners of the Las Mercedes v Owners of the Abidin Daver (The Abidin Daver)* [1984] AC 398 (HL).

[12] Given the title of this collection, it may be noted that *The Atlantic Star* was described as a 'landmark' case by Lord Diplock in *The Abidin Daver* (n 11) 407.

[13] *The Atlantic Star* (n 3).

when the *Atlantic Star* was due in Liverpool (arrest being avoided when the owners accepted service and arranged security). There is little doubt that one of the reasons for commencing an action in England was publication of the report of a court appointed surveyor in Antwerp which indicated that the collision was caused by sudden fog, rather than any fault on the part of the *Atlantic Star*. The owners of the *Atlantic Star* applied for a stay. The owners of the Dutch barge then initiated proceedings in Antwerp solely to avoid being out of time, if the English action was stayed, but gave an undertaking to discontinue the Belgian action if the English action was allowed to proceed. Brandon J refused the stay,[14] and his decision was affirmed by the Court of Appeal.[15] By a narrow majority, an appeal was allowed and a stay ordered by the House of Lords.[16]

In terms which have become familiar since the decision in *Spiliada* Brandon J held that the court in Antwerp was 'by far the more appropriate forum', based on the following reasons, as summarised by Lord Reid in the House of Lords: the place of collision; the case was governed by Belgian law and local regulations;[17] five other claims arising out of the collision were pending in Antwerp; the appellants had ensured that full security was available there.[18] For good measure, Brandon J observed that 'the case has absolutely no connection with England, except that, because the defendants' ship trades from time to time to an English port, she is liable to arrest here'. Nonetheless, a stay had been declined in the lower courts because the conduct of the Dutch barge owners in commencing an action in England could not be regarded as 'vexatious' and 'oppressive'.

The language of 'vexation' and 'oppression' is most closely associated with the test formulated in the following terms by Scott LJ in *St Pierre v South American Stores (Gath & Chaves) Ltd*:[19]

> In order to justify a stay two conditions must be satisfied, one positive and the other negative: (a) the defendant must satisfy the court that the continuance of the action would work an injustice because it would be oppressive or vexatious to him or would be an abuse of the process of the court in some other way; and (b) the stay must not cause an injustice to the plaintiff. On both the burden of proof is on the defendant.

This test was applied by the minority in the House of Lords in accordance with the more natural and ordinary meaning of the terms employed, in dismissing

[14] *Owners of the Atlantic Star v Owners of the Bona Spes (The Atlantic Star)* [1972] 1 Lloyd's Rep 534 (Ad).

[15] *Owners of the Atlantic Star v Owners of the Bona Spes (The Atlantic Star)* [1973] QB 364 (CA).

[16] It may be noted that successful counsel for the appellants was Robert Goff QC.

[17] Brandon J referred only to the fact that 'navigation' was governed by Belgian law and local regulations. At the time, the *lex causae* would have been determined by the double actionability rule applicable to torts committed abroad.

[18] *The Atlantic Star* (n 14) 539.

[19] *St Pierre v South American Stores (Gath & Chaves) Ltd* [1936] 1 KB 382 (CA) 398.

the appeal on the basis that the owners of the Dutch barge had not acted 'in bad faith', or with an 'improper motive', so as to 'harass the defendant'.[20] For those who have only known the law as laid down in *Spiliada*, it is worth reminding that the best evidence of the claimant's 'good faith' appears to have been his assessment that an action in England offered better prospects of success than in Belgium,[21] ie the very epitome of forum shopping. The whole point of the '*St. Pierre* test' is that there was nothing wrong with forum shopping; particularly if one was shopping in the English courts.[22] One was only required not to abuse the privilege.

When one turns to the majority, it is tempting to say that it is with the benefit of hindsight that one can see that their speeches entailed a radical change in the law, or at least the first step on the way to such radical change. But one suspects that Lords Reid, Wilberforce and Kilbrandon were only too well aware, even at the time, that they had set the law on a very different path, even if the speeches of all three are a masterclass in the subterfuge that is sometimes practised to avoid the accusation of judicial activism.[23] Thus, the Scottish plea of *forum non conveniens* was not adopted. Rather, any change should be sought 'within the existing framework of English law';[24] and the language of 'vexation' and 'oppression' was still serviceable, but should be interpreted 'more liberally',[25] or in a 'morally neutral' way,[26] and applied as 'pointers rather than boundary marks'.[27] But the substance of the change was all too evident. In particular, it was not enough for the claimant to point to 'any' advantage of suing in England,[28] and certainly not an 'advantage' based on 'nothing more than a hope that in an English court he might stand a better chance of winning'.[29] Since that was all the owner of the Dutch barge could point to, it was not sufficient to outweigh the factors identified by Brandon J in favour of a stay. In his most expansive comment, Lord Wilberforce stated that, in deciding whether to grant a stay, 'the court must take into account (i) any advantage to the plaintiff; (ii) any disadvantage to the defendant: this is the critical equation, and in some cases it will be a difficult one to establish'. 'Critical' and 'difficult' proved to be prescient observations.

[20] *The Atlantic Star* (n 3) 459 (Lord Morris).

[21] ibid.

[22] 'The right of access to the King's court must not be lightly refused': *St. Pierre* (n 19) 398 (Scott LJ).

[23] The principal concern of the majority appears to have been to avoid too radical a departure from the settled view of the law (at least in one step), rather than to avoid accusations of 'judicial legislation'. Parliament has eschewed any opportunity it might have had to develop the law in this area: Briggs (n 8) 74 ('the legislature has declined to get involved in quite remarkable fashion').

[24] *The Atlantic Star* (n 3) 454 (Lord Reid).

[25] ibid, 454 (Lord Reid) 468 (Lord Wilberforce).

[26] ibid, 454 (Lord Kilbrandon)

[27] ibid, 468 (Lord Wilberforce).

[28] ibid.

[29] *The Atlantic Star* (n 3) 471 (Lord Wilberforce).

B. *MacShannon v Rockware Glass Ltd*

In *MacShannon v Rockware Glass Ltd*,[30] the House of Lords heard appeals in four cases,[31] in all of which the claimants were Scotsmen suing English registered companies for injuries sustained in industrial accidents in Scotland. Below the level of the House of Lords, the defendants' applications for a stay were refused. In the House of Lords, they were allowed. On this occasion, the decision was a unanimous one. The speeches of their Lordships are notable for a number of features. First, the language of 'vexation' and 'oppression' only served to confuse and should be abandoned.[32] Second, this allowed the 'gist' of the speeches of the majority in *The Atlantic Star* to be reflected in a restatement of Scott LJ's two stage approach, by Lord Diplock, in the following terms:

> In order to justify a stay two conditions must be satisfied, one positive and the other negative: (a) the defendant must satisfy the court that there is another forum to whose jurisdiction he is amenable in which justice can be done between the parties at substantially less inconvenience or expense, and (b) the stay must not deprive the plaintiff of a legitimate personal or juridical advantage which would be available to him if he invoked the jurisdiction of the English court.[33]

Third, any 'legitimate personal or juridical advantage' must be a 'real one', ie, not just the subjective belief of the claimant or his legal observers, but shown 'objectively and on the balance of probability to exist'.[34]

Since the only connection that any of the actions had with England was the registered office of the defendants, it was clear that Scotland was, and England was not, the 'natural forum'. The claimants could point to no personal advantage. As for juridical advantages, Robert Goff J, at first instance in two of the cases, had condensed them into the following, as alleged by the claimants: higher damages in England; a lengthier and more costly legal process in Scotland; and the reduced likelihood of the recovery of costs. What may be noticed about this condensed list is that questions of cost seem more obviously to be relevant to the first stage of Lord Diplock's restated test, suggesting that more work needed to be done to refine it, but, even if treated as juridical advantages, the claimants failed to prove that any advantage lay with England over Scotland.

A point to be noted for later reference is the extent to which their Lordships thought it relevant to take account of wider questions of 'public policy', or 'public interest'. It was said that the practice of bringing 'Scottish' industrial injury actions in the English courts was widespread. Lord Diplock did not think that this was

[30] *MacShannon v Rockware Glass Ltd* (n 9).

[31] In two of the cases the judge at first instance was Robert Goff J. He had refused to stay the actions.

[32] *MacShannon v Rockware Glass Ltd* (n 9) 811 (Lord Diplock) 819 (Lord Salmon); *cf* 827 (Lord Keith, 'endorsing' a broad and liberal interpretation).

[33] ibid, 812.

[34] ibid, 812 (Lord Diplock); *cf* 829 (Lord Keith).

irrelevant, if it meant that time and effort was wasted on litigation 'which would otherwise be spent on activities that are more directly productive of national wealth or well-being',[35] but he conceded that 'the sole consideration which should influence the judge in exercising his discretion in each individual case was to do justice as between that plaintiff and that defendant'.[36] Their other Lordships thought that matters of public policy should play no part in the decision.[37]

C. *The Abidin Daver*

The particular focus in *The Abidin Daver* was the effect of a *lis alibi pendens* between the parties, in circumstances where the defendant in foreign proceedings already underway (in Turkey in that case, following a collision in the Bosphorus) commences proceedings in England, in the same action, as the claimant. That focus is of no real concern in this study of the evolution of the law. The speeches of their Lordships are perhaps most notable for the acknowledgement by Lord Diplock, based on the decisions in *The Atlantic Star, MacShannon* and *Amin Rasheed Shipping Corporation v Kuwait Insurance*,[38] that English law was now 'indistinguishable from the Scottish legal doctrine of *forum non conveniens*'.[39] Although addressed in the context of *lis alibi pendens*, Lord Diplock also added an important gloss to the question of any personal or juridical advantage to the claimant of suing England: not only did it have to be established 'objectively by cogent evidence', it had to be 'of such importance that it would cause injustice to deprive him of it'.[40] An important terminological marker was also laid down by Lord Keith when he referred to the 'natural forum' as 'that with which the action had the most real and substantial connection'.[41]

As for the decision in *The Abidin Daver* itself, it is a good example of the last vestiges of the 'judicial chauvinism [which] has been replaced by judicial comity'.[42] The Court of Appeal had overturned Sheen J and refused a stay. In doing so, Donaldson LJ had indulged in the very comparison between the relative merits of the English and Turkish courts which he said should not play a part, leading to the memorable observation from Lord Brandon that his 'heart was not really in what he felt obliged to concede'.[43] Turkey was clearly the natural forum and the claimant could point to no personal or juridical advantage of which it would be unjust to deprive him and Sheen J's order was restored.

[35] ibid, 813–14.
[36] ibid, 813.
[37] ibid, 822 (Lord Salmon) 823 (Lord Russell) 833 (Lord Keith).
[38] See comment at n 7 above.
[39] *The Abidin Daver* (n 11) 412.
[40] ibid. This was not a new gloss: see Lord Salmon in *MacShannon* (n 9) 818: 'the real test of a stay depends on what the court in its discretion considers that justice demands'.
[41] *The Abidin Daver* (n 11) 415.
[42] ibid, 411 (Lord Diplock).
[43] ibid, 424.

II. PILGRIMS

Lord Goff did not elaborate on how he had been assisted by the articles by Adrian Briggs and Rhona Schuz. Having revisited them, one suspects that they helped to identify the issues that still needed to be resolved. This brief summary of the issues identified by the pilgrims and dealt with by Lord Goff does scant justice to the analysis in all three articles, but will have to suffice for present purposes. The first of Adrian Briggs' articles referred to by Lord Goff was written before *The Abidin Daver*.[44] The focus of this summary is therefore on his second article[45] and that of Rhona Schuz.[46]

The key issue raised by both was the weight to be given to any legitimate personal or juridical advantage and how to balance what may be advantage to the claimant, but disadvantage to the defendant. As Lord Wilberforce had observed in *The Atlantic Star* (above), this is the 'critical equation'. Both preferred a solution which turned on the 'balance of justice'. As Adrian Briggs put it: 'To attempt to "balance" in these circumstances is difficult … it is submitted that it is better to ask the question in the terms … stated by Lord Diplock [in *The Abidin Daver*[47]] …: is the advantage of such importance that it would be unjust to deprive the plaintiff of it?'[48] Other important, but less central, issues raised were as follows: since all three of the evolutionary cases were concerned with a stay, the need to clarify the position regarding service out of the jurisdiction, including the question of the burden of proof in both contexts;[49] which factors are relevant to the identification of the 'natural forum' and how to weigh, or balance them;[50] and whether, if English law was now 'indistinguishable' from the Scottish doctrine, the Scottish authorities were of assistance in an English application for a stay.[51]

Given the terms in which the law was subsequently stated in *Spiliada*, the proposed formulation by Rhona Schuz of the test to be applied is particularly worthy of note:[52]

> Any action brought in the English courts shall be stayed if the defendant shows that … the courts of another country have a closer and more real connection with the action and that the foreign court has jurisdiction to hear the dispute unless the plaintiff proves that in all the circumstances of the case it would be unjust for the action to be tried in that foreign court.

[44] Briggs (n 8).

[45] A Briggs, 'The Staying of Actions on the Ground of "Forum Non Conveniens" in England Today' [1984] *Lloyd's Maritime and Commercial Law Quarterly* 227.

[46] R Schuz, 'Controlling Forum-Shopping: The Impact of *MacShannon v Rockware Glass Ltd*' [1986] *International & Commercial Law Quarterly* 374.

[47] Text to n 40.

[48] Briggs (n 45) 240; *cf* Schuz (n 46) 395, invoking the dictum of Lord Salmon at (n 40) above.

[49] Briggs (n 45) 240–41; *cf* Schuz (n 46) 399 and 407.

[50] Briggs (n 45) 231.

[51] ibid, 249.

[52] Schuz (n 46). The full version of this included two provisos: 'Provided always that (i) no action shall be stayed if the judgment of the foreign court would not be entitled to be recognised in

III. SPILIADA

When mixed with water, sulphur can cause significant damage to steel. Loading wet sulphur on a ship is not, therefore, a good idea. In 1980 this was the fate of the *Spiliada* when it was chartered to carry a cargo of bulk sulphur from Vancouver to India. The owners of the vessel obtained leave to serve out of the jurisdiction on the shippers on the ground of an action to recover damages for breach of a contract governed by English law.[53] The shippers applied to set aside the order on the ground that the case had not been shown to be 'a proper one' for service out of the jurisdiction.[54] Staughton J dismissed the application, but was overturned by the Court of Appeal. An appeal by the shipowners to the House of Lords was allowed.[55] Having been at the forefront of the development of the law in this area, as counsel,[56] as High Court Judge[57] and as Lord Justice of Appeal,[58] it seems fitting that it should fall to Lord Goff to add the final imprimatur in *Spiliada*. It is helpful to begin with his statement of the law, before turning to its application in the case.

In terms of the issues identified by the 'pilgrims' above, two can be dealt with quite briefly. First, Lord Goff concluded that English law had adopted the Scottish doctrine of *forum non conveniens* and it was necessary 'now to have regard to the Scottish authorities';[59] in particular, the decision of the House of Lords in *Société du Gaz de Paris SA v SA Navigation 'Les Armateurs français'*[60] and the 'classic statement'[61] of Lord Kinnear in *Sim v Robinow*:[62] 'the plea can never be sustained unless the court is satisfied that there is some other tribunal, having competent jurisdiction, in which the case may be tried more suitably for the interests of all the parties and for the ends of justice'. Second, subject to three provisos, the doctrine, in the form stated by Lord Kinnear, applied to both

England; and (ii) no action shall be stayed where to do so would be contrary to express statutory provision.' Proviso (ii) calls for no further comment. For an example of a decision based, in part, on the *relative* enforceability of English and foreign judgment, see *International Credit & Investment Co (Overseas) Ltd v Adham* [1999] ILPr 302 (CA).

[53] RSC Ord 11, r 1(1)(f)(iii) (see now CPR PD 6B para 3.1(6)(c)).

[54] RSC Ord 11, r 4(2) (see now CPR r 6.37(3)). For the view that the courts have not always paid too much attention to what statutory language there is which impinges on this area, as for example in the change from 'the *case* is a proper one for service out' to 'England … is the proper *place* for the *claim* to be brought' (CPR r 6.37(3)), see M Davies, '*Forum Non Conveniens*: Now We Are Much More Than Ten' in A Dickinson and E Peel (eds), *A Conflict of Laws Companion* (Oxford, OUP, 2021) 34–35.

[55] Thus, in the three cases which had developed the law, a *stay* was ordered, whereas in the case which put the final imprimatur on such development, an application to *set aside* jurisdiction was refused.

[56] See n 16.

[57] Text to n 31.

[58] Text to n 6.

[59] *Spiliada* (n 1) 475.

[60] *Société du Gaz de Paris SA v SA Navigation 'Les Armateurs français'* 1926 SC (HL) 13.

[61] *Spiliada* (n 1) 474.

[62] *Sim v Robinow* (1892) 19 R 665, 668.

applications for a stay and applications to set aside service out of the jurisdiction.[63] The main proviso was the burden of proof, which was on the defendant in an application for a stay and on the claimant in an application for leave to serve out of the jurisdiction. This is considered further below. It is debatable whether the two other provisos are regarded as that significant in the present day (if they were at the time),[64] namely that an application for leave to serve out of the jurisdiction invites the court to invoke a 'discretionary power' and permits the exercise of an 'exorbitant' jurisdiction.[65] More recently, it has been said that '[i]t should no longer be necessary to resort to the kind of muscular presumptions against service out which are implicit in adjectives like "exorbitant". The decision is generally a pragmatic one in the interests of the efficient conduct of litigation in an appropriate forum.'[66] That said, there has been no departure from the principal practical effect of these two provisos, namely that the burden on the claimant in an application for leave to serve out is to prove that England is 'clearly' the more appropriate forum, this being the obverse of the burden on the defendant in an application for a stay to prove that there is another forum which 'is clearly or distinctly more appropriate than the English forum'.[67]

The remaining issues identified by the pilgrims are dealt with herein, as they were by Lord Goff in *Spiliada*, as part of his review of how the principle of *forum non conveniens*, now fully acknowledged, applied in cases of stay of proceedings. He formulated the now familiar two-stage test.[68] First, the burden is on the defendant to identify that there is another forum which is the 'natural forum', endorsing in this regard the expression of Lord Keith in *The Abidin Daver*, above, that this is the forum 'with which the action had the most real and substantial connection'. The 'connecting factors' to take account of at this stage are those of 'convenience' and 'expense', such as the availability of witnesses (to which may be added evidence more generally), but also include the governing law and the places where the parties respectively reside or carry on business. If there is no such alternative forum, no stay will be ordered, or it is at least difficult to imagine the circumstances in which a stay would be granted. Second, if the 'natural forum' lies elsewhere, a stay will ordinarily be granted 'unless there are circumstances by reason of which justice requires that a stay should nevertheless not be granted'. The burden of proof at this stage, shifts to the claimant.

[63] *Spiliada* (n 1) 480.

[64] Lord Goff himself counselled caution in the description of jurisdiction in such cases as 'exorbitant': 'an old-fashioned word which perhaps carries unfortunate overtones': ibid, 481.

[65] ibid, 480–81.

[66] *Abela v Baadarani* [2013] UKSC 44, [2013] 1 WLR 2043 [53] (Lord Sumption). For a vigorous debate as to the significance to be attached to this comment, see A Briggs, 'Service Out in a Shrinking World' [2013] *Lloyd's Maritime and Commercial Law Quarterly* 415 and the response of Lord Sumption in *Four Seasons Holdings Inc v Brownlie* [2017] UKSC 80, [2018] 1 WLR 192 [31]. See also L Merrett, 'Forum Conveniens', in W Day and S Worthington (eds), *Challenging Private Law: Lord Sumption on the Supreme Court* (Oxford, Hart Publishing, 2020).

[67] *Spiliada* (n 1) 477.

[68] The points made in the rest of this paragraph are all set out ibid, 477–78.

It is also at this stage that questions of personal or juridical advantage fall to be assessed, which brings us to the 'critical equation' identified above.

It is notable that Lord Goff first singled out one particular factor which might be relevant at the second stage, but chose to deal with the treatment of a 'legitimate personal or juridical advantage' as a quite separate issue later in his speech. The factor singled out is 'the fact, if established objectively by cogent evidence, that the plaintiff will not obtain justice in the foreign jurisdiction'.[69] It seems clear that what Lord Goff is referring to here, as was Lord Diplock in *The Abidin Daver*[70] in a passage to which Lord Goff referred, is the fact that the claimant will not obtain 'even-handed justice' on grounds of corruption, bias or discrimination. The real difficulty with such a factor is setting the standard for 'cogent evidence', and meeting it,[71] but it cannot seriously be disputed that it is a factor which would tip the 'balance of justice' in favour of the claimant and prevent a stay. However, beyond that rather obvious example of an 'injustice factor', it becomes more difficult, as was acknowledged by Lord Goff in the treatment of personal and juridical advantages.

One thing made clear by Lord Goff was the need for a *balanced* approach: 'the mere fact that the plaintiff has such an advantage in proceedings in England cannot be decisive'.[72] That might have sufficed at the second stage of Lord Diplock's two-stage test in *MacShannon*, but no more. Further, a test based on the balance of *justice* would, as a general rule, rule out reliance on certain types of 'advantage', even if objectively proven. The examples given by Lord Goff are: damages awarded on a higher scale; a more complete procedure of discovery; a power to award interest; and a more generous limitation period.[73] Beyond the obvious example of an unfair hearing referred to above, it is necessary for the claimant to prove that the circumstances are such that a stay would not only result in a loss of advantage, but prevent the court from doing 'substantial' or 'practical' justice. The point at which a loss of advantage elides into injustice was always going to be one of the more difficult aspects of the principles formulated by Lord Goff and he deals with an example which arose on the facts of *Spiliada*.

The claimant's claim was time barred in the alternative forum of British Columbia,[74] but not in England. The effect of this factor in deciding the case itself is dealt with below. So far as time bars in general are concerned, Lord Goff conceded that there was 'a strong theoretical argument' that, if there is another

[69] ibid, 478.
[70] *Abidin Daver* (n 11) 411.
[71] See n 103.
[72] *Spiliada* (n 1) 482.
[73] ibid.
[74] The fact that the courts of British Columbia may have had a discretionary power to waive the time bar was regarded by Lord Goff as irrelevant, as was the fact that a claim might still be brought in the Federal Court of another province on the basis that 'it cannot be in the interests of justice that the action should effectively be remitted to a forum which cannot be described as appropriate for the trial of the action': ibid, 487.

clearly more appropriate forum, a stay should generally be granted even though the claimant's action would be time barred there. However, since the ultimate aim was to do practical justice, a stay would be refused if the claimant had not acted unreasonably in failing to commence proceedings in the natural forum.

The facts in *Spiliada* occurred before the Foreign Limitation Periods Act 1984 came into force. The effect of the 1984 Act is to require the English courts to apply the limitation period of the *lex causae*,[75] whereas previously limitation was usually characterised as a question of procedure and governed by the *lex fori*. The 1984 Act will have reduced the circumstances in which a claim may be time barred in the natural forum but not in England, but has not eliminated them (eg, where limitation is characterised as procedural in the natural forum and governed by the *lex fori*, but the *lex causae* is a different law). To ask whether the claimant has behaved 'unreasonably' might be thought to set the bar a little too low if the overriding concern is to do practical justice. In this regard, it may be noted that, under the 1984 Act, the *lex causae* is not applied to the extent to which it would conflict with public policy and this will be the case if its application would cause 'undue hardship'.[76] Perhaps mindful that the bar was set a little low, Lord Goff did comment that, as the principles set out in *Spiliada* should become more clearly established and better known, it would be increasingly difficult for claimants to prove lack of negligence in this respect. A feature of the time bar factor is that, in some circumstances, it is one which can be neutralised by the defendant, eg, where it takes the form of a defence which the defendant has to assert, or can waive. As a consequence, it may not necessarily form the basis for refusing a stay, but rather a condition upon which the court will order the stay, eg, on the basis of an undertaking from the defendant that the time bar in the natural forum will be waived. A similar point can be made about the provision of security.

The time bar proved not to be decisive to the outcome in *Spiliada*. Lord Goff did not, as such, apply the principles he had formulated to the facts as a whole, in order to identify whether British Columbia was the 'natural forum' and, if it was, whether 'substantial' or 'practical' justice nonetheless pointed against setting aside service. Rather, he confined himself to the question of whether the Court of Appeal had been entitled to interfere with Staughton J's exercise of his discretion in refusing the application to set aside. He held that they had not and that it was 'a classic example of a case where the appellate court has simply formed a different view of the weight to be given to the various factors'.[77] To the extent that his decision on the appeal turned on one factor above any

[75] See also Regulation (EC) No 593/3008 (Rome I) (as amended by the Law Applicable to Contractual Obligations and Non-Contractual Obligations (Amendment etc) (EU Exit) Regulations 2019 reg 10), Art 12(d) and Regulation (EC) No 864/2007 (Rome II), (as amended by the Law Applicable to Contractual Obligations and Non-Contractual Obligations (Amendment etc) (EU Exit) Regulations 2019 reg 11), Art 15(h).

[76] Foreign Limitation Periods Act 1984, s 2(1)–(2).

[77] *Spiliada* (n 1) 486.

other, it has proved to be almost unique to *Spiliada* and was referred to as the '*Cambridgeshire* factor'.[78] Staughton J heard the application to set aside while there was proceeding before him a very similar action involving the same defendants in relation to a ship called the *Cambridgeshire*.[79] In that action no fewer than 15 counsel had been engaged and the estimate for the length of the trial was six months. According to Staughton J:

> ... if all other things were equal, I should be inclined to hold that even-handed justice *would* be served best if one action [the *Cambridgeshire* action] were tried here and the other [the *Spiliada* action] in Canada. But all other things are far from equal. The plaintiff's solicitors have made all the dispositions and incurred all the expense for the trial of one action in England; they have engaged English counsel and educated them in the various topics upon which expert evidence will be called; they have engaged English expert witnesses; and they have assembled vast numbers of documents. They have also, no doubt, educated themselves upon the issues in the action. All that has been done on behalf of [the defendants] as well, save that one of their expert witnesses is Canadian. If they now wish to start the process again in Canada, that is their choice. But it seems to me that the additional inconvenience and expense which would be thrust upon the plaintiffs if this action were tried in Canada far outweighs the burden which would fall upon [the defendants] if they had to bring their witnesses and senior executives here a second time.

Not only did Lord Goff agree with Staughton J, he also embellished the point on the basis that, although the shipowners in the two cases were different, their solicitors were in both cases instructed by the same insurers, who were managed in England. He said that it was 'shutting one's eyes to reality to ignore the fact that it is the insurers who are financing the litigation and are dominus litis'.[80] To the extent that it turned on this factor, one might harbour doubts about the decision itself in *Spiliada*, notwithstanding Lord Goff's characterisation of it as a matter which went beyond 'financial advantage' to the shipowners[81] to a matter which should be taken into account 'in the objective interests of justice'.[82] Those doubts are not dispelled if one includes the effect of the time bar which Lord Goff dealt with only briefly because he did not consider it strictly necessary. The shipowners' solicitors were said to have 'stumbled across' the time bar when investigating the availability of suitable lawyers in Vancouver. Their failure to have commenced proceedings there, as a precaution, is excused by Lord Goff

[78] The Court of Appeal held that Staughton J had placed too much weight on this factor and the prospect of the charterers being joined to the proceedings against the shippers, and that he had erred in his findings as to the availability of expert witnesses. Lord Goff did not think that the judge had placed too much weight on the 'multiplicity of proceedings'. Any error in relation to the witnesses had been drawn to Staughton J's attention at the end of his judgment and was a factor which he was better placed to assess than the Court of Appeal.

[79] There had been an application to stay the proceedings in the *Cambridgeshire* action which Staughton J had refused and from which there was no appeal.

[80] *Spiliada* (n 1) 486; *cf Société du Gaz* (n 60) 20 (Lord Sumner).

[81] This was the characterisation of Oliver LJ in the Court of Appeal.

[82] *Spiliada* (n 1) 486. The question of when 'advantage' becomes a 'justice factor' is returned to below.

largely on the basis that, until the decision of the House of Lords in *The Amin Rasheed* case,[83] it was reasonable still to expect that an unexpired limitation period in England would be taken into account as a legitimate personal and juridical advantage. That looks generous against the backdrop of the evolution of the law which started with *The Atlantic Star* and in which, it may be recalled, the owners of the Dutch barge did issue a protective writ in the alternative forum. Perhaps Lord Goff himself shared some of these doubts when he pointed to one further factor which he said Staughton J could have taken into account. The putative governing law of the contract between the shipowners and the shippers was English law and this was 'by no means an insignificant factor' since there was not only a dispute as to the effect of the bill of lading contract, but also as to the nature of the obligations thereunder in respect of 'dangerous cargo'.

One final point to note is the short speech of Lord Templeman which was as equally prescient as that of Lord Wilberforce in *The Atlantic Star*. He offered this well-known, and salutary, warning:[84]

> I hope that in future the judge will be allowed to study the evidence and refresh his memory of the speech of my noble and learned friend Lord Goff of Chieveley in this case in the quiet of his room without expense to the parties; that he will not be referred to other decisions on other facts; and that submissions will be measured in hours and not days. An appeal should be rare and the appellate court should be slow to interfere.

IV. AFTER SPILIADA

While the speech of Lord Goff in *Spiliada* undoubtedly marked the end of the transition from a test of vexation and oppression to one of even-handed discretion aimed at balancing the interests of the parties and the ends of justice, it was perhaps inevitable that it would raise as many questions, or issues, as it resolved.[85] In this final part, three issues fall for brief consideration.

A. Theoretical Basis

In the first of the articles referred to by Lord Goff in *Spiliada*, Adrian Briggs noted that, in some of the 'evolutionary' cases, there was a 'failure to state clearly the theoretical basis upon which the rules for the granting of a stay now rest'.[86] Was that still the case after *Spiliada*? Is it still the case now? One possible

[83] *Amin Rasheed* (n 6).
[84] *Spiliada* (n 1) 465.
[85] For a hostile reception, see AG Slater, 'Forum Non Conveniens: A View From the Shop Floor' (1988) 104 *Law Quarterly Review* 554. For glowing endorsement, see A Briggs, 'Forum Non Conveniens – The Last Word?' [1987] *Lloyd's Maritime and Commercial Law Quarterly* 1.
[86] Briggs (n 8) 77.

candidate is judicial comity. The difficulty with any discussion of 'comity' is to decide exactly what is meant by the term. This is not the place for an extended definitional debate,[87] but it seems reasonably clear that when, in the evolutionary cases, and in *Spiliada*, the courts spoke in terms of 'comity', they meant what has been described as follows: '[a] greater tolerance and respect for other countries' legal systems and their claims … to be able to provide parties with substantial justice in their courts'.[88] That is most evident in the move away from an innate sense of the superiority of the English judicial process[89] and is taken to be what Lord Diplock was referring to in *The Abidin Daver*, when he spoke of the extent to which 'judicial chauvinism has been replaced by judicial comity'.[90] It may also be seen in the requirement that any loss of 'advantage' must be objectively proved.[91] But does it take us much further than that? It is noticeable that 'comity' is referred to only twice in Lord Goff's speech in *Spiliada*. First, in the form of a general acknowledgement that was 'of importance', when he observed that the English approach to the burden of proof was broadly in line with other common law jurisdictions;[92] and, second, only when he cited from the speech of Lord Diplock in the *Amin Rasheed* case.[93]

On one view, while *jurisdiction* can be explained by comity, in the sense at least in which it turns on the recognition of territorial sovereignty, a decision *not to exercise jurisdiction* on the grounds of *forum non conveniens* has been described as follows: 'it has the effect that a case which is, *ex hypothesi*, properly before the English court, should be transferred to some other judge, almost whether he likes it or not. The way in which that supports the principle of comity is … hard to grasp.'[94] It is perhaps not necessary to go that far (and it would, once again, open up debate about what one means by comity) in order to make the point that, while comity may explain some features of the law as stated in *Spiliada*, and the way it developed, it does not provide the theoretical basis for the principles of *forum non conveniens* laid down therein. That lies rather in the concept of doing 'substantial justice', in the sense that it is this which will prevail above and beyond any considerations of comity.[95]

[87] For a flavour of which, see A Briggs, 'The Principle of Comity in Private International Law' (2012) 354 *Recueil des Cours* 65.

[88] A Bell, 'The Natural Forum Revisited' in A Dickinson and E Peel (eds), *A Conflict of Laws Companion* (Oxford, OUP, 2021) 10. This is not offered as a definition of comity as such, but it fits the bill.

[89] In addition to the example provided by Donaldson LJ in *The Abidin Daver* (n 43), see also Lord Denning in *The Atlantic Star* (n 15) 382: 'You may call this 'forum shopping' if you please, but if the forum is England, it is a good place to shop in, both for the quality of the goods and the speed of service.'

[90] Text to n 42.

[91] Text to n 40.

[92] *Spiliada* (n 1) 477.

[93] ibid, 478.

[94] Briggs (n 87) 121. See also the reference, at 119, to 'a form of dumping, possibly of toxic waste' (should that be 'forum dumping'?).

[95] This is not a new idea: A Briggs, 'Crossing the River by Feeling the Stones: Rethinking the Law on Foreign Judgments' (2004) 8 *Singapore Yearbook of International Law* 1, 1 ('judicial comity should not be allowed to become the enemy of justice'.)

This is one possible answer to recent criticism that the principles to emerge from *Spiliada* have, if anything, increased the circumstances in which the English courts are required to adjudicate in a way which is an affront to comity.[96] In a superb essay which revisits the law as it developed in England and Australia,[97] Andrew Bell argues that the 'hard cases' were always destined to be those at the 'second stage' of the *Spiliada* enquiry, ie, where the natural forum lies elsewhere, but 'there are circumstances by reason of which justice requires that a stay should nevertheless not be granted'.[98] How 'hard' such cases are, and the extent to which they might be regarded as an affront to comity, depends to some extent on what it is about proceedings in the natural forum which would be 'unjust', as opposed simply to reflecting the 'advantages' and 'disadvantages' of the two legal systems. This is addressed in the next part of this chapter. For now, one might start with a circumstance which, *if proven*, would undoubtedly be regarded as conducive to injustice. This is the 'one factor' singled out by Lord Goff in *Spiliada*, ie, where it is said that the claimant will not get a fair hearing in the natural forum. Leading examples since *Spiliada* are *Cherney v Deripaska*[99] and *AK Investment CJSC v Kyrgyz Mobil Tel Ltd.*[100] In the former, Russia was the natural forum, but England was held to be the 'proper place' for permission to serve out of the jurisdiction on the basis that there was cogent evidence either that no trial would take place there, or any such trial would not be fair because of the risk for the claimant of assassination, or arrest on trumped up charges, or state interference in the judicial process. In the latter, Kyrgyzstan was the natural forum, but there was held to be 'substantial evidence of specific irregularities, breach of principles of natural justice, and irrational conclusions, sufficient to justify a conclusion that there was considerably more than a risk of injustice'.[101]

The requirement for 'cogent evidence' is derived from the speech of Lord Diplock in *The Abidin Daver* and is clearly intended to ensure that a finding as to the risk of injustice is not lightly reached. That is, of course, an accommodation of the principle of comity,[102] but as the decisions in *Cherney* and *Altimo* indicate, *if* it is met, the aim of doing substantial justice will prevail over any remaining concerns about comity. This is not the place to assess whether the threshold of cogent evidence has been set at the right level, or applied correctly in cases like *Cherney* and *Altimo*.[103] The more general question to be asked is

[96] In addition to the cases discussed in this part, see also the 'funding' cases of *Lubbe v Cape plc* [2000] UKHL 41, [2000] 1 WLR 1545 and *Connelly v RTZ Corporation* [1997] UKHL 30, [1998] AC 854 discussed below.

[97] Bell (n 88). For earlier thoughts, see A Bell, *Forum Shopping and Venue in Transnational Litigation* (Oxford, OUP, 2003).

[98] *Spiliada* (n 1) 478 (Lord Goff).

[99] *Cherney v Deripaska* [2009] EWCA Civ 849, [2009] 2 CLC 408.

[100] *AK Investment CJSC v Kyrgyz Mobil Tel Ltd* [2011] UKPC 7, [2012] 1 WLR 1804.

[101] ibid, [143] (Lord Collins).

[102] ibid, [97] (Lord Collins: 'comity … is why cogent evidence is required').

[103] For expressions of doubt, see A Briggs, 'Decisions of the British Courts 2009' (2010) 80 *British Yearbook of International Law* 575, 577; *cf* A Briggs 'Forum Non Satis: *Spiliada* and an Inconvenient Truth' [2011] *Lloyd's Maritime and Commercial Law Quarterly* 330.

whether the occurrence of such 'hard' cases means that the post-*Spiliada* world is, or is not, an improvement on what went before. It is, surely, an improvement. A test of vexation and oppression based only on the subjective belief of the claimant as to the advantages of English proceedings no doubt had the beneficial side effect that all foreign courts were to a large extent treated alike,[104] but only at the expense of hearing cases that had little or no connection with England. In his essay, Andrew Bell makes the point about the English courts finding themselves faced with 'invidious inquiries as to the quality and integrity of foreign legal systems'[105] in support of the position adopted by the Australian courts, which is not to identify the 'natural forum', but to ask whether the Australian court is a 'clearly inappropriate forum'.[106] As he puts it:

> A refusal to grant a stay of proceedings because the local forum is not clearly inappropriate does not require the same focus to be fixed on the procedures and experience of foreign courts, still less the more problematic charge that the courts of particular countries are creatures of government or beset with endemic corruption or administered with gross incompetence.

He may be right, but two questions arise which will have to be pursued on another occasion. First, is it not better to confront a problem than to avoid it? Second, how effective is the avoidance in a case, say, where Australia is regarded as inappropriate,[107] but allegations of the type made in *Cherney* are presented to the court?

B. From Advantage to Injustice

Another example of 'hard cases' said to be the product of *Spiliada*[108] is provided by cases like *Connelly v RTZ Corporation*,[109] *Lubbe v Cape plc*,[110] and *Vedanta Resources Plc v Lungowe*.[111] They are 'hard' because they raise two key issues

[104] There are echoes here of the approach of the English courts to the recognition of a foreign judgment. The judgment debtor is always afforded the opportunity to deny recognition on the ground that the judgment was obtained by fraud and no fresh evidence is needed; nor does it matter whether a plea of fraud has already been heard in the foreign court. All foreign judgments are treated alike in this regard, though one suspects the 'quality' of adjudication in the foreign court is reflected in other ways, eg, when deciding if the defence of fraud amounts to an abuse of process. For general discussion, see A Briggs, *Civil Jurisdiction and Judgments,* 7th edn (London, Routledge, 2021) [38.30] and also ch 6.

[105] Bell (n 88) 29.

[106] See *Voth v Manildra Flour Mills Pty Ltd* (1990) 171 CLR 538 (HCA); A Briggs, 'Forum Non Conveniens in Australia' (1989) 105 *Law Quarterly Review* 200; A Bell, 'Transnational Litigation and the Current State of Australian Law', in K Lindgren, *International Commercial Litigation and Dispute Resolution* (Sydney, Sydney University Press, 2010).

[107] It does happen. It happened in *Voth* (n 106).

[108] See Bell (n 88) 24.

[109] (n 96).

[110] (n 96).

[111] [2019] UKSC 20, [2020] AC 1045.

about the application of *Spiliada* in practice. The first, and the primary concern of this part, is how to determine when the loss of an advantage to the claimant from proceedings in England is of such importance that it would cause injustice to deprive him of it. We have seen that the requirement of 'injustice' is intended to avoid a comparative assessment of the 'merits' and 'demerits' of the competing legal systems in relation to the level of damages, the scope of discovery etc, but that still leaves the question of when the deprivation of what is otherwise a juridical advantage is unjust. The second issue is that, to the extent that the first issue is concerned with the interests of the parties, is there also room to take account of 'public interest'?

All three cases presented the same basic features[112] which may be summarised by reference to the *Lubbe* case in the first instance. Some 3,000 claimants commenced proceedings in England as of right against Cape plc, the parent company of certain subsidiary South African companies, for injury or disease caused by their exposure to the asbestos produced by mines operated in South Africa by the subsidiaries. Cape plc applied to stay the proceedings. South Africa was clearly the natural forum, but a stay was declined on the basis that a trial was only possible in England. This was the result of a combination of two factors: the complexity of the group litigation involved and the lack of means to fund it in South Africa, either via legal aid, or a conditional fee arrangement, both of which were available in England. At one level, the claimants were seeking to avoid a stay on the basis that they would lose a juridical advantage from suing in England, ie, the availability of legal aid, or conditional fee arrangements. As Lord Bingham acknowledged: 'generally speaking, the plaintiff must take a foreign forum as he finds it, even if it is in some respects less advantageous to him than the English forum'.[113] If the case had depended solely on the absence of established procedures in South Africa for handling group actions, it would have involved 'the kind of procedural comparison which the English court should be careful to eschew',[114] but in combination with the funding issue it became a question of 'substantial justice', ie, of whether the claimants would get their day in court.[115]

Put in such terms, it is hard to argue with the outcome in *Lubbe* but, as Andrew Bell has commented, the 'forum of necessity' recognised in cases like *Lubbe* and, for different reasons, in cases like *Cherney* is 'far removed from both

[112] All three involved claims by individuals for personal injury at the hands of a corporate defendant. For a suggestion that the nature of the formative cases before the English and Australian courts may have had some bearing on how the law developed (eg, *Oceanic Sun Line Special Shipping Company Inc v Fay* (1988) 165 CLR 197 (HCA) (personal injury); *cf The Atlantic Star* (n 7), *The Abidin Daver* (n 11), *Spiliada* (n 1) (all commercial)), see A Briggs, 'The Death of *Harrods*: Forum Non Conveniens and the European Court' (2005) 121 *Law Quarterly Review* 535, 536.

[113] *Lubbe v Cape* (n 96) 1554.

[114] ibid, 1559.

[115] The human rights dimension was perhaps all too evident (ECHR, Art 6), but Lord Bingham did 'not think that article 6 supports any conclusion which is not already reached on application of *Spiliada* principles': *Lubbe v Cape* (n 96) 1559.

the natural forum championed in *The Atlantic Star* and *Spiliada* and the centrality of the concept of comity in those decisions'.[116] It has been suggested above that the answer to this is that substantial justice trumps comity, but that still brings one back to the difficulty that, in *Lubbe*, any injustice was the product of being able to commence proceedings against Cape plc because it was an English registered company, and the fact that the English legal system had advantages for the claimant which were not available in South Africa.

To this one might add the question of 'public interest'.[117] It did not arise at all in *Spiliada* and only indirectly in one of the evolutionary cases. It will be recalled that, in *MacShannon*, Lord Diplock stated that 'the sole consideration which should influence the judge in exercising his discretion in each individual case was to do justice as between [the] plaintiff and [the] defendant'.[118] That too was the approach of Lord Hope in *Lubbe* in response to any concern about the expense and inconvenience to the administration of justice of litigating the actions in England. As he put it: 'the principles on which the doctrine of *forum non conveniens* rest leave no room for considerations of public interest or public policy which cannot be related to the private interests of any of the parties or the ends of justice in the case which is before the court'.[119] It would seem therefore that when Lord Kinnear spoke about the forum which was most suitable 'for the interests of all the parties *and* for the ends of justice',[120] the 'and' is to be read conjunctively and not disjunctively, ie, justice *as between the parties*.[121]

In both respects, ie, in determining when a loss of advantage becomes a question of injustice and when there may be room to allow considerations of public interest which can be related to the private interests of the parties, the dissenting judgment of Lord Hoffmann in *Connelly* might be seen by some[122] as a missed opportunity. In that case, the claimant developed cancer as a result of working in a uranium mine in Namibia operated by the Namibian subsidiary of the defendant, an English registered company. He sued the defendant in England as of right. The defendant applied for a stay. This was ultimately refused by the House of Lords on essentially the same basis as in *Lubbe*. While Namibia was clearly the natural forum, the combination of the nature and complexity of the case and the claimant's lack of funding, other than via legal aid or a conditional fee arrangement in England, meant that this was not just a case where the natural forum was in some respects less advantageous to the claimant than England,

[116] Bell (n 88) 29.

[117] For an extended analysis of the case for taking account of 'public interest', particularly in light of the effect of modern technology on the trial process, see Davies (n 54).

[118] *MacShannon v Rockware Glass Ltd* (n 9) 813.

[119] *Lubbe v Cape* (n 110) 1566. See also Lord Bingham (at 1561): 'in applying [Lord Kinnear's principle] questions of judicial amour propre and political interest or responsibility have no part to play'.

[120] Text to n 62.

[121] And also that CPR 1.1(2)(e) is largely to be ignored when it states that the overriding objective of dealing with cases justly (CPR 1.1(1)) includes 'allotting to [the case] an appropriate share of the court's resources, while taking into account the need to allot resources to other cases'.

[122] But not all: A Briggs, *Civil Jurisdiction and Judgments*, 6th edn (London, Informa, 2015) 415, n 231.

but that substantial justice could not be done in Namibia. Lord Hoffmann noted that 'any multinational with its parent company in England will be liable to be sued here in respect of its activities anywhere in the world' and '... the more speculative and difficult the action, the more likely it is to be allowed to proceed in this country with the support of public funds'.[123] If the primary concern was the deployment of public funds, the subsequent withdrawal of legal aid for any personal injury actions has largely taken care of that. What also seems to have concerned Lord Hoffmann was the risk of the process of turning an advantage into a question of substantial justice becoming an exercise of pulling oneself up by one's own bootstraps, or rewarding the very forum shopping which the doctrine of *forum non conveniens* is supposed to control. This is evident from his endorsement of the following statement of principle by Sopinka J in *Amchem Products Inc v (British Columbia) Workers' Compensation Board*:[124]

> The weight to be given to juridical advantage is very much a function of the parties' connection to the particular jurisdiction in question. If a party seeks out a jurisdiction simply to gain a juridical advantage rather than by reason of a real and substantial connection of the case to the jurisdiction, that is ordinarily condemned as 'forum shopping.' On the other hand, a party whose case has a real and substantial connection with a forum has a legitimate claim to the advantages that that forum provides. The legitimacy of this claim is based on a reasonable expectation that in the event of litigation arising out of the transaction in question, those advantages will be available.

The 'legitimate expectation' referred to by Sopinka J cannot be confined to the advantages available from the forum with the *most* real and substantial connection since that would collapse the *Spiliada* test into the first stage of identifying the natural forum. Lord Hoffmann's assessment that the claimant had no such expectation in *Connelly* has always looked a little harsh. Mr Connelly had returned to Scotland from Namibia in 1983 and did not discover that he had contracted the cancer which formed the basis of his claim until 1986. In *Lubbe*, Lord Hoffmann simply agreed with the speech of Lord Bingham even though it is hard to see how the claimants in that case could meet the test of 'legitimate expectation'. Presumably, he did not press the point because he had failed to take the rest of their Lordships with him in *Connelly* and the concept of 'legitimate expectation' is nowhere to be seen in the latest decision of the Supreme Court in this context, in *Vedanta*. The English courts may have declined to act as 'international policeman' when it comes to the scope of their power to award an anti-suit injunction,[125] but the submission that, in some contexts at least, *Spiliada* has turned them into a 'forum of necessity' is perhaps well founded. Should that be too surprising if the ultimate aim is to ensure 'substantial justice'?

[123] *Connelly v RTZ Corporation* (n 109) 876.

[124] *Amchem Products Inc v (British Columbia) Workers' Compensation Board* (1993) 102 DLR (4th) 96, 110–111.

[125] *Airbus Industrie GIE v Patel* [1998] UKHL 12, [1999] 1 AC 119; E Peel, 'Anti-suit injunctions – The House of Lords declines to act as International Policeman' (1998) 114 *Law Quarterly Review* 543.

C. Cost

It is self-evident that Lord Templeman's prescient warning in *Spiliada* has fallen on deaf ears. There are numerous instances of judges bemoaning the time and resources spent on contested applications for a stay, or to set aside service, but one of the most recent will suffice to give a flavour of the frustration felt in some quarters. In *Vedanta* Lord Briggs observed that 'unless condign costs consequences are made to fall upon litigants, and even their professional advisers, who ignore these requirements [ie, those set out by Lord Templeman], this court will find itself in the unenviable position of beating its head against a brick wall'.[126] One is bound to ask why the courts have not so acted. In his recent essay, Andrew Bell identifies seven reasons why, *if* one endorses the doctrine of *forum non conveniens* as articulated in *Spiliada*, the time and costs involved almost inevitably follow.[127] To them, one might also add that a jurisdictional battle is rarely just about jurisdiction, with the parties moving on, after the question of jurisdiction has been resolved, to the expenditure of yet more time and resource on the merits. Often the jurisdictional battle is *the* battle. When I studied for the BCL, Adrian Briggs made this point by inviting my tutorial colleagues and I to find the reports of the hearing of the merits in the cases on jurisdiction which we had studied. It is anecdotal, of course, and I am not sure how hard we looked, but it is nonetheless an effective methodology and one I still use on my own students today. It may be that one is left simply to ask whether the inevitable cost associated with *Spiliada* is a price worth paying.[128]

V. CONCLUSION

There is no doubt that Lord Goff chose his words carefully in the postscript to his speech in *Spiliada* when he referred to the road to 'unattainable perfection'. The principles he set out are not perfect,[129] but it was always likely that a search for the natural forum, tempered only by a concern to do substantial justice, was bound to have wide appeal and so it has proved, as other common law countries have broadly adopted them.[130] By that measure, as stated at the outset, there can be no doubt that it is a landmark case in the conflict of laws.

[126] *Vedanta* (n 111) [14].

[127] Bell (n 88) 15–17.

[128] There is perhaps a parallel to be drawn with the costs involved in the operation of claims for personal injury and death. For a robust defence that the price is worth paying, but that one should always be looking to reduce cost where possible (and the same point can be made in the present context), see A Burrows, *Understanding the Law of Obligations* (Oxford, Hart Publishing, 1998) ch 6; *cf* P Atiyah, *The Damages Lottery* (Oxford, Hart Publishing, 1997).

[129] See, eg, L Merrett, 'Uncertainties in the First Limb of the *Spiliada* Test' (2005) 54 *International & Comparative Law Quarterly* 211

[130] See, eg, *Club Mediterranee NZ v Wendell* [1989] 1 NZLR 216 (NZ); *Amchem Products Inc v (British Columbia) Workers' Compensation Board* (1993) 102 DLR (4th) 96 (Can); *Rickshaw Investments Ltd v Nicolai Baron von Uexkull* [2007] 1 SLR 377 (Sing); *The Adhiguna Meranti* [1988] 1 Lloyd's Rep 384 (HK).

12

Société Nationale Industrielle Aérospatiale v Lee Kui Jak (1987)

TREVOR HARTLEY*

I. INTRODUCTION

FORUM SHOPPING OCCURS when a claimant deliberately brings proceedings in a court with little or no connection with the case simply because that court provides some special advantage. It is generally regarded as a bad thing. The problem is: what should be done about it; or rather *which* court should do something about it? Should it be the court before which the case is brought – the forum where the claimant chooses to shop – or should it be another court, perhaps the one in which the claimant *should* have brought the claim? This was an underlying issue in *Société Nationale Industrielle Aérospatiale v Lee Kui Jak*,[1] a landmark case in the development of the modern anti-suit injunction.

II. HISTORICAL DEVELOPMENT OF ANTI-SUIT INJUNCTIONS

Anti-suit injunctions have a long history in England. In fact, they were invented in England, where, in the fifteenth century and under a different name, they played a role in the jurisdictional battle of the courts of equity against the courts of common law. These restrained litigants from obtaining judgments from common-law courts that would be contrary to the principles of equity. This relief followed from the successful assertion by the Lord Chancellor of equity's superiority within the English legal system, most famously in the *Earl of Oxford's Case* in 1615.[2]

* I would like to acknowledge the valuable assistance I have received from William Day in the preparation of this chapter.

[1] *Société Nationale Industrielle Aérospatiale v Lee Kui Jak* [1987] AC 871 (PC).

[2] *Earl of Oxford's Case* (1615) Chan Rep 1, 21 ER 485. See further D Ibbetson 'The Earl of Oxford's Case (1615)' in C Mitchell and P Mitchell (eds), *Landmark Cases in Equity* (Oxford, Hart Publishing, 2012).

Later, anti-suit injunctions were used against courts outside England, first in Scotland, Ireland and British colonies, then in foreign countries. An early case was *Love v Baker*[3] in 1665 where the applicant asked the Lord Chancellor to restrain proceedings in Leghorn (now Livorno) in Italy for possession of goods. Lord Clarendon considered this to be 'dangerous' and, after consulting his judicial brethren, dissolved the injunction. But the law report notes that:[4]

> … all the Bar was of another Opinion. It was said, The Injunction did not lie for Foreign Jurisdictions, nor out of the King's Dominions. But to that it was answered, The Injunction was not to the Court, but to the Party.

The justification offered by the bar that equity acts *in personam* for anti-suit injunctions is, of course, very familiar some 350 years later, but is clearly nonsense: the foreign court cannot hear the case unless the claimant brings it. Preventing the claimant from bringing it prevents the court from hearing it.

The basis on which the injunction was sought in *Love v Baker* is not clear from the report. Thomas Raphael suggests that it was on the basis that the foreign court 'might also grant judgments which contravened English principles of equity'.[5] There were obvious difficulties with that argument if that was the basis on which the injunction was sought. It is one thing to argue that equity prevails over the common law in disputes adjudicated within England, but quite another to say that equity can prevail over the law being applied in a foreign court.

Despite the judicial reservations in *Love v Baker*, anti-suit injunctions (although still not under that name) began to be granted by the early nineteenth century. Prominent early examples were *Bushby v Munday* and *The Earl of Portarlington v Soulby*, in 1821 and 1834 respectively.[6] The former restrained proceedings in Scotland, and the latter proceedings in Ireland. One might wonder whether the fact that these were proceedings in countries ruled by the King, albeit not as King of England, made the English court more comfortable about injuncting the other proceedings. However, in *Bushby*, Sir John Leach VC disclaimed any such suggestion:[7]

> Over the Court of Session in Scotland this Court has not, nor can pretend to have, any authority whatsoever. The Court of Session is an independent Court … and the question in this Court is the same, and must depend upon the same principles, as if the foreign Court thus exercising its independent jurisdiction were sitting, not at Edinburgh, but at Paris or Vienna.

In *Bushby*, the Vice-Chancellor considered the case for the injunction made out: the parties were within the jurisdiction of the English court; the 'ends of justice'

[3] *Love v Baker* (1665) 1 Ch Cas 67, 22 ER 698.
[4] ibid, 698.
[5] T Raphael, *The Anti-Suit Injunction*, 2nd edn (Oxford, OUP, 2019) 38.
[6] *Bushby v Munday* (1821) 5 Madd 297, 56 ER 908 and *The Earl of Portarlington v Soulby* (1834) 3 My & K 104, 40 ER 40.
[7] *Bushby v Munday* (n 6) 913. See also 914, dismissing an argument based on the Act of Union.

were the 'only present consideration'; and the court was not 'pretend[ing] to any interference with the other Court' but was acting *in personam*.

The Lord Chancellor, Lord Brougham, adopted a similar analysis in *Portarlington*, disavowing *Love v Baker*, and instead relying on precedents such as *Penn v Lord Baltimore*,[8] discussed elsewhere in this collection,[9] to justify equity's extra-territorial reach. In ordering the injunction, the Lord Chancellor (like the Vice Chancellor in *Bushby*) explained that it was not his claim that the courts in England could reverse judgments of the courts in Ireland: 'This pretension, however, has long ago been abandoned, and has indeed been discontinued by Parliamentary interposition.'[10]

Despite the ambition of the reasoning in *Bushby* and *Portarlington*, which was not limited to coordinate jurisdictions under the Crown, the first reported case of an anti-suit injunction being issued outside the British Empire to interfere with proceedings in a court not administering the King's justice was not until 1866, in *Hope v Carnegie*.[11] Adrian Hope was a British subject who died with property in England and the Netherlands. Proceedings were opened in the Court of Chancery to execute the trusts in Mr Hope's will; but after the decree was obtained, one of his daughters began proceedings in the Netherlands in respect of the property situated there and disputing the validity of the will. The Vice-Chancellor issued an injunction in protection of the English proceedings; on appeal, it was upheld save insofar as it concerned Mr Hope's real estate interests in the Netherlands.

III. THE LAKER AIRWAYS CASES

The use of anti-suit injunctions in international litigation gradually became more prevalent after World War II, when US courts led the way. The term 'anti-suit injunction' is of US origin. Initially, English courts refused to use it, preferring a cumbersome circumlocution. Whatever the label, by this time the English courts had moved away from simply asking whether the anti-suit injunction would meet the 'ends of justice', and began asking whether there would be vexation or oppression (such as where the proceedings were brought in bad faith or unconscionably) if the injunction was not granted, apparently importing that requirement from the then prevailing law on jurisdictional stays. This change to the test contributed to anti-suit injunctions remaining relatively rare, at least until the 1980s,[12] and had the benefit of bringing greater certainty to the law.

[8] *Penn v Lord Baltimore* (1750) 1 Ves Sen 444, 27 ER 1132.
[9] See ch 1 in this volume.
[10] *Portarlington v Soulby* (n 6) 42.
[11] *Hope v Carnegie* (1866) 1 Ch App 320 (CA).
[12] Raphael (n 5) 43–45.

Today, the power to grant anti-suit injunctions is generally accepted in the common-law world. However, injunctions are not often granted in practice except in two countries: the US and the UK. When English and American courts grant injunctions against each other, sparks may fly. By the time *Aérospatiale* was decided in 1987, the English courts were well acquainted with anti-suit injunctions, having fought a bruising battle of injunctions with the US courts in 1984 in the *British Airways v Laker Airways* litigation.[13]

Laker Airways was probably the original economy airline. It did not join the cartel which fixed fares, operated through the International Air Transport Association (IATA). Instead, it offered fares between London and New York which were a long way below those offered by the other airlines. Soon it had built up a significant market-share. Then the established airlines struck back. They lowered their fares on Laker's routes to significantly below what Laker was charging. This meant that they were losing money on every flight, but this did not discourage them. Laker went bankrupt. Then the other airlines raised their fares to the previous level and carried on as before.

The activities of the established airlines constituted predatory pricing, something that was contrary to US antitrust law. So Laker's liquidator brought a civil claim under the Sherman and Clayton Acts in the US against the airlines that had cut their fares. Two of these airlines were British: British Airways and the now-defunct British Caledonian. They immediately brought proceedings in England for an anti-suit injunction. They claimed that Laker's action in the US was an infringement of British sovereignty. The English court of first instance granted the injunction on an interim basis. Laker then brought proceedings in the US for a counter-anti-suit injunction against all the other airlines involved in the action.[14] This was an order by the American court precluding them from obtaining anti-suit injunctions in the UK. It was granted.

The result was something akin to a stalemate. The US court considered whether it should appoint a *curator ad litem* to continue the proceedings against the two British airlines, but it dropped the idea because it was not clear who would pay him. Meanwhile, back in England, the Court of Appeal dismissed Laker's appeal against the injunction. Laker then appealed to the House of Lords.[15] That broke the stalemate. Lord Diplock accepted that Laker's conduct in pursuing proceedings in the US needed (at the very least) to be shown to be unconscionable,[16] but rejected the idea that the American proceedings could be

[13] For a full discussion, see TC Hartley, 'Comity and the Use of Antisuit Injunctions in International Litigation' (1987) 35 *American Journal of Comparative Law* 487.

[14] The various US proceedings were: *Laker Airways v Sabena, Belgian World Airlines* 731 F 2d 909 (1984) (DC Cir); *Laker Airways v Pan American World Airways* 596 F Supp 202 (1984) (DDC); *Laker Airways v Pan American World Airways* 577 F Supp 348 (1983) (DDC); *Laker Airways v Pan American World Airways* 568 F Supp 811 (1983) (DDC); *Laker Airways v. Pan American World Airways*, 559 F Supp 1124 (1983) (DDC) affirmed 731 F 2d 909 (1984) (DC Cir).

[15] *British Airways Board v Laker Airways* [1985] AC 58 (HL).

[16] ibid, 81. See also text to n 44.

characterised in that way. Since the parties flew into the US, they could be taken to have submitted themselves to the US regime, and so the Americans had a right to apply their law to its activities.[17] As a result, the injunction was lifted, and the action went ahead in the US.

IV. AÉROSPATIALE

A. The *Castanho* Controversy

The immediate context to *Aérospatiale* was the shift in the rules on jurisdiction culminating in *Spiliada Maritime Corporation v Cansulex*,[18] which Edwin Peel discusses in chapter eleven. Given that the discretion to grant anti-suit injunctions had previously been tempered by analogy with the restrictive principles on stays in favour of foreign forums, after the liberation of the jurisdiction rules in the *Spiliada* line of cases, the question was whether the discretion to grant anti-suit injunctions ought similarly to be relaxed. In *Castanho v Brown & Root*, Lord Scarman held that it ought to do so. Citing the reformulation of the principles for a jurisdictional stay in *MacShannon v Rockware Glass Ltd*,[19] he continued:[20]

> Transposed into the context of the present case, this formulation means that to justify the grant of an injunction the defendants must show: (a) that the English court is a forum to whose jurisdiction they are amenable in which justice can be done at substantially less inconvenience and expense, and (b) the injunction must not deprive the plaintiff of a legitimate personal or juridical advantage which would be available to him if he invoked the American jurisdiction.
>
> The formula is not, however, to be construed as a statute. No time should be spent in speculating as to what is meant by 'legitimate'. It, like the whole of the context, is but a guide to solving in the particular circumstances of the case the 'critical equation' between advantage to the plaintiff and disadvantage to the defendants.

This judgment was not well received, and rightly so, given the expansive jurisdiction it would create for anti-suit injunctions. Giving judgment in the Court of Appeal in *Bank of Tokyo v Karoon* a few years later, Goff LJ said that jurisdictional stays were 'founded on different principles' to anti-suit injunctions, and diplomatically suggested that the step taken by the House of Lords in *Castanho* was flawed:[21]

> Lord Scarman has taken the principle of *forum non conveniens* as developed in relation to a stay of English proceedings where it was expressly developed in order to

[17] ibid, 82–85.
[18] *Spiliada Maritime Corporation v Cansulex Ltd* [1987] 1 AC 460 (HL).
[19] *MacShannon v Rockware Glass Ltd* [1978] AC 795 (HL) 812 (Lord Diplock).
[20] *Castanho v Brown & Root (UK) Ltd* [1981] AC 557 (HL) 575.
[21] *Bank of Tokyo Ltd v Karoon* [1987] AC 45 (CA) 62 (original emphasis).

> adopt a less nationalistic approach, ie to render the English courts *less* tenacious of proceedings started within its jurisdiction, and has applied it *inversely* in cases of restraint by the English courts of foreign proceedings. The effect would appear to be, not only that in cases of restraint of foreign proceedings the very restrictive principle of protection of the English jurisdiction has been abandoned, but also that the English court will now be more free to grant injunctions restraining foreign proceedings.

On his elevation to the House of Lords, Lord Goff wasted no time in suggesting that Lord Scarman's speech in *Castanho* was not 'the last word on the subject'.[22] The litigation in *Aérospatiale* was Lord Goff's first opportunity to turn the page on Lord Scarman's test for anti-suit injunctions.

B. The Decision in *Aérospatiale*

The facts of the case were relatively straightforward. In 1980, a wealthy Brunei businessman was killed in a helicopter crash in Brunei. The helicopter was manufactured by a French firm, Aérospatiale. It was owned by an English company and operated by a Malaysian company under contract with a Sarawak company. Claims by the widow against these three latter defendants were settled for US$430,000. She then turned her attention to Aérospatiale, bringing proceedings against them in Texas, a state in which Aérospatiale did business. As the law stood at the time, Aérospatiale's contracts with Texas were sufficient to give the courts of that state general jurisdiction over Aérospatiale, that is, jurisdiction even though the facts of the claim did not relate to Texas.[23] Moreover, under Texas law as it stood at the time, dismissal of a claim on the ground of *forum non conveniens* was not possible in wrongful-death cases.[24] The combined effect of these two rules was that Aérospatiale could not ask the Texas courts to stay the proceedings.

Texas was an extremely favourable place to bring the claim. Wide-ranging pre-trial discovery was possible, under which the defendant would have to reveal any evidence of a defect in its product; and the claim would be heard by a jury, Texas juries being well known for their generosity in cases of this kind. A further advantage was that the widow would almost certainly have been able to retain a first-class law firm on a contingency-fee basis: no win, no fee. One can understand why she chose the Lone Star State. Aérospatiale, on the other hand, was not happy. It would have preferred to have been sued in France, where evidence of defects in the helicopter would have been hard to unearth. Since there was no way in which Aérospatiale could get the Texas courts to relinquish the case,

[22] *South Carolina Insurance v Assurantie Maatschappij 'De Zeven Provincien'* [1987] AC 24 (HL) 44.

[23] US law regarding general jurisdiction has since been made more restrictive by the US Supreme Court: *Daimler AG v Bauman* 134 S Ct 746 (2014).

[24] This was subsequently changed by legislation after a battle between the Texas bar (who were against change) and Texas manufacturers (who were in favour of it).

it turned to the courts of Brunei, asking for an anti-suit injunction against the widow. Applying Lord Scarman's test from *Castanho*, and also making reference to *Spiliada*, the Brunei courts refused to grant it. Aérospatiale then appealed to the Privy Council.

When the appeal came before the Privy Council, it granted the injunction, with Lord Goff giving the advice. The main reason for granting the injunction arose from the fact that the cause of the crash might have been faulty maintenance of the helicopter. If this were established, Aérospatiale would want to claim a contribution from the operators of the helicopter. It was, however, uncertain whether the operators would be subject to the jurisdiction of the Texas courts: the issue was still being contested at the time. If they were not, Aérospatiale would have to bring separate proceedings in Brunei, something which would lead to various difficulties. For this reason, the Privy Council considered that the continuance of the Texas action would be unjust to Aérospatiale.[25] It is a little strange that the Privy Council based such an important decision on a factor that was still subject to dispute, rather than waiting until it had been decided.

The injunction was therefore granted. However, the Privy Council made it conditional on Aérospatiale making significant concessions to the widow. Aérospatiale had to provide security to ensure that any judgment given against it would be satisfied; it had to provide various documents; the Texas proceedings were to continue until pre-trial discovery was complete; the costs of the Texas proceedings were to be treated as costs in the Brunei proceedings; Aérospatiale was to co-operate in the temporary admission to the Brunei bar of the Texas attorneys; and it was to do everything possible to ensure that the documents obtained in the Texas proceedings were admitted in the Brunei proceedings. This shows a desire on the part of the Privy Council to give due weight to the interests of both parties.

C. Four Governing Principles after *Aérospatiale*

In *Aérospatiale*, Lord Goff rejected Lord Scarman's test for anti-suit injunctions (even when reformulated to reflect the refinement of the stay principles in *Spiliada*),[26] and instead laid down four principles which continue to apply to this day. These principles do not provide very much guidance to judges. Nor, for that matter, do they provide much guidance to parties trying to predict what a court will do.

The first principle is that there are no clear rules: everything depends on what 'the ends of justice' require.[27] The law on granting an anti-suit injunction based on vexation and oppression was confined by Lord Goff as being important, but

[25] It could not be argued that the application of Texas law on strict liability, punitive damages or jury trial would be unjust to the defendant, since the claimant had undertaken to waive these rights.

[26] *Aérospatiale* (n 1) 895.

[27] ibid, 892 94.

'should not be regarded as the only ground upon which the jurisdiction may be exercised', and 'should be restricted by definition'.[28] Put another way, the existence of vexation and oppression is only one way of answering the question of what the ends of justice require. This revived the approach seen in the mid-nineteenth century in cases such as *Bushby*.[29] It means that the court has a wide discretion, useful in dealing with unforeseen situations, but unhelpful to a party trying to predict what the court will decide. This of course parallels the wide discretion enjoyed by the court in an application for a stay on grounds of *forum non conveniens*. However, in the context of anti-suit injunctions it would have been preferable for the court to retain the threshold of asking whether the suit targeted by the injunction was vexatious or oppressive.

The second principle is that the court cannot grant an injunction unless it has jurisdiction over the defendant.[30] In *Aérospatiale*, this requirement was clearly satisfied, since the widow was resident, and presumably domiciled, in Brunei. In addition, the Privy Council stressed that the injunction was granted against the party bringing the foreign proceedings, not against the foreign court hearing them. The justification can be traced back to the earliest cases, as we have seen, and it is sometimes thought that this somehow absolves the English courts from the charge of interfering with the operation of the foreign court.[31] As I have already said, this fails to recognise the reality of the effect of an anti-suit injunction.[32] Third, the Privy Council said that the power to grant an anti-suit injunction must be exercised with caution, something which is almost always said in this context.[33]

A few years later, in *Airbus Industrie v Patel*, the House of Lords clarified a fourth principle implicit in *Aérospatiale*. This is that a court should not grant an anti-suit injunction unless it is itself the natural forum for the case. In the words of Lord Goff, the English courts should not 'take it on themselves to act as policeman of the world'.[34] He explained that as a matter of comity:[35]

> As a general rule, before an anti-suit injunction can properly be granted by an English court to restrain a person from pursuing proceedings in a foreign jurisdiction in cases of the kind under consideration in the present case, comity requires that the English forum should have a sufficient interest in, or connection with, the matter in question to justify the indirect interference with the foreign court which an anti-suit injunction entails. In an alternative forum case, this will involve consideration of the question whether the English court is the natural forum for the resolution of the dispute.

Airbus Industrie v Patel concerned claims arising out of the crash of an Airbus aircraft in India. Proceedings were brought in Texas against the French manufacturer of the aircraft. One of the claimants, Patel, was resident in England and

[28] ibid, 893.
[29] *Bushby v Munday* (n 6).
[30] *Aérospatiale* (n 1) 892.
[31] See, eg, *Bushby v Munday* (n 5) 913, quoted in *Aérospatiale* (n 1) 892.
[32] Text to n 4.
[33] *Aérospatiale* (n 1) 892.
[34] *Airbus Industrie GIE v Patel* [1999] 1 AC 119 (HL) 121.
[35] ibid, 138.

was therefore subject to the jurisdiction of the English courts. However, since England was clearly not itself an appropriate forum for the claim, the House of Lords held that an injunction would not be granted. In *Aérospatiale*, of course, Brunei clearly was the natural forum for the widow's claim. The conclusion reached by the Privy Council in *Aérospatiale* was that the fact that the court where the injunction is sought is the natural forum for the claim is not in itself a *sufficient* condition for the granting of an injunction. *Airbus Industrie v Patel* clarifies that, although not sufficient, it is still *necessary* for the court granting the injunction to be the natural forum.

D. Whither *Castanho*?

In *Aérospatiale*, when Lord Goff rejected Lord Scarman's approach in *Castanho*, he purported to be determining the law as it stood in England as well as Brunei.[36] But *Castanho* was a decision of the House of Lords. *Aérospatiale* was a decision of the Privy Council and did not (and could not at that time) apply the 1966 Practice Statement to overrule *Castanho*.[37] However, later cases have treated *Aérospatiale* as in substance having replaced *Castanho* as the leading authority in English law. In *Airbus Industrie v Patel*, the House of Lords (albeit led by Lord Goff) treated *Aérospatiale* as correctly stating the law.[38] So too did the House of Lords (with Lord Hobhouse giving the leading speech) in *Turner v Grovit*.[39] In *Donohue v Armco Inc*, Lord Bingham referred to both *Castanho* and *Aérospatiale* and noted euphemistically that the 'decisions reveal some development of principle', before going on to apply the principles from the latter rather than the former.[40] The landmark status of *Aérospatiale*, and its triumph over *Castanho*, was confirmed by Lord Sumption and Lord Toulson in the recent Privy Council case of *Stichting Shell Pensioenfonds v Krys*, where *Aérospatiale* was characterised as the 'leading modern case on the jurisdiction to restrain foreign proceedings'.[41]

V. DIFFICULT CASES

A. Where Courts Take a Different View as to the Natural Forum

In many ways, *Aérospatiale* was an easy case. From almost any perspective, Texas was not the natural forum; Brunei almost certainly was. Things get more difficult, however, when the natural forum is a matter of dispute, particularly

[36] *Aérospatiale* (n 1) 891.
[37] The position is now different: *Willers v Joyce (No 2)* [2016] UKSC 44, [2018] AC 843.
[38] *Airbus Industrie v Patel* (n 34) 133.
[39] *Turner v Grovit* [2001] UKHL 65, [2002] 1 WLR 107 [24]–[25].
[40] *Donohue v Armco Inc* [2001] UKHL 64 [2002] CLC 440 [19].
[41] *Stichting Shell Pensioenfonds v Krys* [2014] UKPC 41, [2015] AC 616 [23].

when that dispute turns on whose law should be applied to determine the matter. In such a case, for one of the possible forums to take it upon itself to decide, and to impose its view on the other forum by means of an injunction against the claimant, is a clear breach of the *nemo judex in causa sua* rule. The well-known case of *Allianz v West Tankers* is an example.[42]

This concerned a contract (a charterparty) between a cargo receiver and a shipping company. The contract contained an English choice-of-law clause and an English arbitration clause. Under the contract, the shipping company was required to deliver a cargo of oil to the receiver's terminal in Italy. When doing so, the ship collided with the receiver's jetty and caused extensive damage. Under English law, the receiver's right to claim damages against the shipping company for the damage to the jetty was subject to arbitration whether the claim was brought in contract or in tort. The jetty was insured under a contract of insurance governed by Italian law. When the jetty was damaged, the receiver claimed against the insurer up to the maximum under the policy. The insurer paid out. Under Italian law (and under English law), this meant that the insurer was subrogated to the receiver's right to sue the shipping company in tort. It brought a claim in tort against the shipping company in the Italian court for the place where the damage occurred. The shipping company then sued in England for an anti-suit injunction against the insurer: it said that the claim in tort was covered by the arbitration agreement even after it passed to the insurer.

In this situation, England was the natural forum for the insurer's claim only if one accepts that the arbitration agreement was attached to the claim, so to speak, and came with it when it passed to the insurer. However, this was the very issue in contention. Under English law, it was attached to the claim, even though the insurer was not a party to the contract in which the arbitration clause was contained and even though its claim was not derived from that contract. Under Italian law, however, the arbitration agreement did *not* apply to the insurer. From the Italian point of view, Italy was the natural forum. Despite this, the English courts would have granted the injunction if the Court of Justice of the European Union (CJEU) had not stopped it.

Even apart from this, it is doubtful whether it is ever proper for one court to sit in judgment on another court and to decide – however reasonably – that the latter court should not hear a case. Most civil law jurisdictions feel that it is never proper. Indeed, many European courts regard it as contrary to international law. This was the reason why the CJEU decided to outlaw anti-suit injunctions in the European Union when they are directed against proceedings in the courts of Member States which come within the scope of the Brussels Regulation.[43] If it is a principle of EU law that all Member States and their institutions are to be regarded as equal, it necessarily follows that each court should be able to

[42] *Allianz SpA v West Tankers Inc* Case C-185/07, ECLI:EU:C:2009:69, [2009] ECR I-663.

[43] *Turner v Grovit* Case C-159/02, ECLI:EU:C:2004:228, [2004] ECR I-3565 and *Allianz v West Tankers* (n 42).

decide for itself, without interference from the courts of another Member State, whether it has jurisdiction under EU law to hear a case. Only the CJEU itself can correct a Member State court if it makes a mistake.

B. Single-forum Cases

One interesting point that arose in the *Laker* case was the distinction between single-forum cases and multi-forum cases. A single-forum case is one in which the claim can, in the nature of things, be brought in only one forum. If an anti-suit injunction prevents it from being brought there, it cannot be brought *at all*. An example is the civil claim in tort under the US Clayton and Sherman Acts that arose in *Laker*. In the eyes of the English courts, such a claim is not justiciable in England. So, if Laker had been precluded from bringing it in the US, it could not have brought it anywhere. As Lord Diplock explained:[44]

> … your Lordships are confronted in the civil actions with a case in which there is a single forum only that is of competent jurisdiction to determine the merits of the claim; and the single forum is a foreign court. For an English court to enjoin the claimant from having access to that foreign court is, in effect, to take upon itself a one-sided jurisdiction to determine the claim upon the merits against the claimant but also to prevent its being decided upon the merits *in his favour*. This poses a novel problem, different in kind from that involved where there are alternative fora in which a particular civil claim can be pursued.

In such a case, an anti-suit injunction deprives the person against whom it is granted of the right to obtain a remedy. For this reason, it is generally thought that, in a single-forum case, an anti-suit injunction should be granted only in exceptional circumstances. In the main *Laker* case, the House of Lords refused to grant an injunction on the basis that Laker's conduct was not unconscionable because the parties had voluntarily submitted themselves to the US regime.

However, an injunction was granted in a later case in the *Laker* saga when Laker sought to sue Midland Bank.[45] In this case, Laker's liquidator claimed that Midland and another bank had joined a conspiracy to deprive it of a financial rescue package. Laker sued the banks in the US under US antitrust law. The English Court of Appeal granted an anti-suit injunction on the ground that the relationship between Laker and the banks was located in England, and it was unjust for Laker to sue the banks in the US simply on the basis of an extraterritorial application of US antitrust law. They were also clearly unimpressed with the thin evidential basis for Laker's case. Lawton LJ said:

> It still remains to consider whether the threatened antitrust suit if instituted would be unconscionable conduct on the part of the liquidator. What he is trying to do

[44] *BA v Laker* (n 15) 80 (original emphasis).
[45] *Midland Bank plc v Laker Airways Ltd* [1986] QB 689 (CA).

> is to make the plaintiff banks liable to the heavy financial penalties which can be awarded in a United States antitrust suit for acts done in England and intended to be governed by English law and in respect of which he has no claim at all in England. In my judgment, this would be unjust and, in consequence, unconscionable; and the more so when, so far as can be seen from an English Bench, the liquidator has not, by English standards, got the beginnings of a case to justify a charge of combination or conspiracy against the plaintiff banks. In my judgment, the weakness of the evidence is a factor which can be taken into account, together with the other more weighty factors, in deciding whether conduct is unconscionable.

Putting aside the point about the strength of the evidence, the difference with the main *Laker* case is that the banks had not voluntarily submitted themselves to the regime of US antitrust law. This may seem like quite a low threshold for characterising the case as involving exceptional circumstances, although at the time it was British policy to prevent the extraterritorial application of US antitrust law to activities in the UK.[46]

C. Choice of Court Agreements and Arbitration Agreements

Another situation in which special considerations apply is where the parties have entered into an exclusive choice of court agreement (or an arbitration agreement). An exclusive choice of court agreement can be regarded as containing an undertaking not to sue except in the designated court. An arbitration agreement could be interpreted in a similar way. The other party could, therefore, be said to have a legal right not to be sued contrary to the agreement. If the first party nevertheless brings legal proceedings contrary to the agreement, an anti-suit injunction might be regarded as the appropriate remedy. The leading case is *Donohue v Armco*, where Lord Bingham said that the discretion to order an anti-suit injunction was based not on the *Aérospatiale* principles but rather those which also arise when a jurisdictional stay is sought on the basis of a choice of court agreement:[47]

> If contracting parties agree to give a particular court exclusive jurisdiction to rule on claims between those parties, and a claim falling within the scope of the agreement is made in proceedings in a forum other than that which the parties have agreed, the English court will ordinarily exercise its discretion … to secure compliance with the contractual bargain, unless the party suing in the non-contractual forum (the burden being on him) can show strong reasons for suing in that forum. I use the word 'ordinarily' to recognise that where an exercise of discretion is called for there can be no absolute or inflexible rule governing that exercise, and also that a party may lose his claim to equitable relief by dilatoriness or other unconscionable conduct. But the

[46] See, eg, *British Nylon Spinners Ltd v Imperial Chemical Industries Ltd* [1953] Ch 19 (CA); *Rio Tinto Zinc Corp v Westinghouse Electric Corp* [1978] AC 547 (HL); also the Protection of Trading Interests Act 1980.

[47] *Donohue v Armco* (n 40) [24].

> general rule is clear: where parties have bound themselves by an exclusive jurisdiction clause effect should ordinarily be given to that obligation in the absence of strong reasons for departing from it.

These principles are discussed further by William Day in chapter ten.[48] One problem with arguments about injunctions based on choice of court agreements is that, in situations of this kind, there is usually a difference of opinion as to whether the agreement is valid or, if so, whether its scope extends to the proceedings which have been begun. The question then arises who should decide this question. In practice, the English courts usually consider that they should decide it.

OT Africa Line v Magic Sportswear Corporation is an example.[49] This case concerned a choice of court clause in a bill of lading. Many countries regard choice of court clauses in bills of lading as objectionable because the shipowner usually has greatly superior bargaining power. Such clauses were excluded from the Hague Choice of Court Convention for this reason.[50] The *Africa Line* case concerned a bill of lading issued in Toronto for a shipment of cargo by an English shipping company from Toronto to Liberia. The choice of court clause gave exclusive jurisdiction to the English courts. Under Canadian law, choice of court agreements in bills of lading were invalid by reason of the Hamburg Rules; so the shipper sued the carrier in Canada. The carrier asked the English courts for an anti-suit injunction. It was granted. Longmore LJ concluded his judgment with an embarrassed plea to *pacta sunt servanda*:[51]

> It is to be hoped that the Canadian courts will not see this decision as an interference of any kind even if the cargo-insurers or their lawyers were to choose to categorise it that way. Freedom of contract is usually much valued in all common law systems; of course if England were to enact the Hamburg Rules or the equivalent of their jurisdictional provisions, there would be no problem. But until that time comes, the maintenance of the principle that parties should be free to choose the courts where their disputes are to be resolved must be of paramount importance and cannot be reduced to a mere legal aspiration.

In the reverse situation, English courts also grant injunctions. This occurred in *Samengo-Turner v March & McLennan*,[52] in which the choice of court agreement was valid under the law of the designated court, but invalid in England. The case concerned a contract of employment in which the employees worked in England. The employer was American. The contract contained a choice of court agreement giving exclusive jurisdiction to the courts of New York. This was valid under New York law. However, at the time, the UK was a Member State

[48] See also chs 14 and 16 in this volume.
[49] *OT Africa Line Ltd v Magic Sportswear Corp* [2005] EWCA Civ 710, [2005] 2 Lloyd's Rep 170.
[50] Article 2(2)(f) of the 2005 Hague Convention.
[51] *OT Africa* (n 49) [43].
[52] *Samengo-Turner v J&H March & McLennan (Services) Ltd* [2007] EWCA Civ 723, [2007] 2 All ER (Comm) 813 (CA)

of the EU and, under EU law, choice of court clauses in contracts of employment were invalid. So, when the employer sued the employees in New York, the English court issued an anti-suit injunction. This is controversial because it assumes (wrongly) that the EU jurisdictional system is a source of substantive civil obligations between parties as opposed to a system of procedural rules to allocate jurisdiction between Member States.

VI. BREXIT

Since Brexit, the EU rule against anti-suit injunctions no longer applies to British courts. However, it might be unwise to think that in future anti-suit injunctions will once more be freely available with regard to proceedings in EU Member States. Already, courts in France and Germany have started granting counter-anti-suit injunctions.[53] A counter-anti-suit injunction is a court order that the party who obtained the anti-suit injunction must have it lifted. Such orders are normally enforced by a penalty of a given sum per day until the injunction is lifted.

Contrary to what might be thought, such a penalty would be enforceable in other EU Member States under Brussels I, provided that the substantive claim to which the anti-suit injunction applies comes within the scope of Brussels I. This would apply even if the penalty was payable to, and enforceable by, the state or some other public authority. This follows from the rule of EU law that in deciding whether an ancillary order falls within the scope of the Regulation, one must consider, not the nature of the order itself, but the nature of the rights it is intended to protect.

The CJEU judgment in *Realchemie Nederland v Bayer CropScience* is an example.[54] This did not concern a counter-anti-suit injunction, but an order given by a German court in a patent-infringement action under which the defendant, a Dutch company, was required to refrain from importing certain products into Germany, or possessing or marketing them there. It was also ordered to provide details of its commercial transactions involving the products and to transfer its stock into the custody of the courts. The fine was imposed when it failed to obey the order. The CJEU held, applying the principle set out above, that the fine had to be enforced in the Netherlands under the Regulation, even though it was payable to the German state, not to the claimant. The final ruling of the CJEU stated that the Regulation applies to 'the recognition and enforcement of a decision of a court or tribunal that contains an order to pay a fine in order to ensure compliance with a judgment given in a civil and commercial matter'. In view of

[53] Munich Court of Appeal (Oberlandesgericht München) 12 December 2019; Paris Court of Appeal (Cour d'appel de Paris), 3 March 2020.

[54] *Realchemie Nederland BV v Bayer CropScience AG* Case C-406/09 [40].

this, a party who obtained an anti-suit injunction in England might find that his assets throughout the EU were in jeopardy.[55]

VII. CONCLUSION

Société Nationale Industrielle Aérospatiale v Lee Kui Jak is undoubtedly a (or the) landmark case in the development of the modern anti-suit injunction. Although it corrected English law from the expansive approach to anti-suit injunctions envisaged by Lord Scarman in *Castanho*, it nonetheless broadened the jurisdiction for such injunctions by replacing a test requiring the proposed injuncted proceedings to be vexatious or oppressive with the principle that everything depends on what the ends of justice require. That is still too broad an approach and has led to undesirable uncertainty. Further, the law has taken too seriously the myth that an anti-suit injunction does not interfere with the jurisdiction of other courts. It is suggested that the considerations raised in this chapter identify serious questions concerning the legitimacy of anti-suit injunctions except, perhaps, where the party against whom they are granted has acted abusively and in bad faith.

[55] One way to prevent this might be for the English court to grant *two* injunctions, one being an ordinary anti-suit injunction and one being an injunction precluding the party bringing the foreign proceedings from obtaining a counter-anti-suit injunction. However, in this case a public official might step in to obtain the counter-anti-suit injunction in order to protect the jurisdiction of the country's courts.

13

Morguard Investments Ltd v De Savoye (1990)

STEPHEN GA PITEL*

I. INTRODUCTION

THERE IS MUCH scope to debate what makes a decision a landmark case. The volume of judicial citations, the extent of academic discussion and the pervasiveness of the analysis across the field could each hold sway as a key criterion. On any reasonable basis of assessment, *Morguard Investments Ltd v De Savoye* is the leading case in Canadian private international law.[1] In a Canadian book about landmark private international law cases, *Morguard* probably deserves three or four chapters. It is that important.

However, this is not a Canadian book. The cases in this collection are almost all from the UK. But the notion of landmark cases in private international law should not be limited to British cases. The field has developed in several similar directions across various common law jurisdictions and many of the key developments have been through landmark cases. Accordingly, whether a case is a landmark should be assessed across those jurisdictions as a whole rather than solely as a matter of British law.

Given its source, readers might be less familiar with or even unaware of *Morguard*. This chapter will accordingly review the decision in more detail than might be typical for other cases in this book. It will then work toward two objectives. The first is to make the case for including it as a landmark case. This is complicated by the fact that several British judges and scholars consider that the core legal principle that *Morguard* establishes is incorrect. The second objective, then, is to continue to make the case that the common law across multiple

* I am grateful to Herschel Chaiet for his research assistance and to Vaughan Black and Joost Blom for their comments.

[1] *Morguard Investments Ltd v De Savoye* [1990] 3 SCR 1077 (SCC), affg (1988) 27 BCLR (2d) 155 (CA), affg (1987) 18 BCLR (2d) 262 (SC). All subsequent references are to the Supreme Court of Canada's decision unless otherwise indicated. All Canadian decisions cited in this chapter are available at www.canlii.org.

jurisdictions must broaden its traditionally narrow approach to the recognition and enforcement of foreign judgments and that *Morguard* is a critical milestone on the path toward that change.

II. THE DECISION

A. The Facts and Proceedings

Douglas De Savoye was the mortgagor of land in Alberta. Morguard Investments Limited and another entity were the mortgagees. De Savoye had lived in Alberta but moved to British Columbia. He defaulted under the mortgages and Morguard sued him in Alberta. He was served with the Alberta process by mail in British Columbia.[2] He did not defend and Morguard obtained default judgment. The land was sold by judicial sale but the proceeds were insufficient to pay off the mortgage. As a result, judgment was granted in Alberta for the amount still owing under the mortgage.

Morguard brought an application against De Savoye in British Columbia to enforce the Alberta judgment. Boyd J granted the application. The reasons for this decision seem to miss the central issue. They state that De Savoye argued that the Alberta court did not 'properly assume jurisdiction'.[3] In response, Boyd J held that Alberta did have jurisdiction to grant the judgment. But the central issue should not have been whether Alberta had jurisdiction under its own rules. Rather, it was whether Alberta took jurisdiction on a basis that met British Columbia's test for the recognition and enforcement of foreign judgments.

The Court of Appeal's analysis was more pointed. It started by noting that British Columbia would have taken jurisdiction in a similar case.[4] It then moved to a focus on reciprocity, a position it expressed thusly: 'we will enforce judgments of courts of another province exercising a jurisdiction that a British Columbia court exercises'.[5] Yet it immediately noted '[t]hat view has not prevailed for judgments *in personam*, and the judgments we are concerned with are judgments *in personam*'.[6] Oddly, the court did not set out an established test for recognition and enforcement of a foreign judgment. It merely noted that the most frequently followed case was *Emanuel v Symon*.[7] Under that decision, the foreign court's jurisdiction must have been based on either the defendant's service with the process of the court within the territory or the defendant's submission or attornment.

[2] Pursuant to an order for substitute service: *Morguard (SC)* (n 1) 264.
[3] ibid, 263.
[4] *Morguard (CA)* (n 1) [7].
[5] ibid, [9] (CA). The court cited *Travers v Holley* [1953] P 246 (CA), a case about recognition of foreign divorce judgments.
[6] *Morguard (CA)* (n 1) [9].
[7] *Emanuel v Symon* [1908] 1 KB 302 (CA).

The appeal court rejected *Emanuel* for several reasons. It was decided at a time when travel to distant countries to litigate was difficult. It reflected a sense of the superiority of the justice available in the forum rather than abroad.[8] It focused on international situations rather than recognition and enforcement within a federation. Of note, the court favoured 'recognizing a difference between interprovincial judgments and foreign judgments'.[9] The court's conclusion – 'that we should recognize and enforce the judgment of a Canadian court exercising a jurisdiction we would exercise' – is rooted in both the concept of a single country and in reciprocity.[10]

The Supreme Court of Canada granted leave to appeal. Seven of the nine judges heard the appeal, which was not unusual, and La Forest J wrote the Court's unanimous decision. Unlike the courts below, he started his analysis by acknowledging the longstanding approach in *Emanuel*, confirmed in many English and Canadian cases over the years.[11] The issue was whether this approach should continue. La Forest J signalled the overall tenor of the decision early on when he referred to Canadian courts having 'unthinkingly' adopted that approach.[12] He also acknowledged having found the work of three Canadian scholars – Robert Sharpe, John Swan and Vaughan Black – to have been 'very helpful' to his analysis, summarising their central point as moving away from reciprocity and instead calling for a correlativity between the law on taking jurisdiction and the law on recognition and enforcement.[13] He distilled their position to be that '[i]f it is fair and reasonable for the courts of one province to exercise jurisdiction over a subject-matter, it should as a general principle be reasonable for the courts of another province to enforce the resultant judgment'.[14]

La Forest J offered several reasons for expanding the scope of recognisable judgments, particularly those from other provinces. One was economic: the need to accommodate 'the flow of wealth, skills and people across state lines'. Another was structural: 'the obvious intention of the Constitution to create a single country'. The lives of Canadians are not confined to a single province. People, trade and commerce flow freely across borders. Accordingly, despite the lack in the Constitution of a 'full faith and credit' clause as found in the American and Australian Constitutions, 'a regime of mutual recognition of judgments across the country is inherent in a federation'.[15]

[8] *Morguard (CA)* (n 1) [13].
[9] ibid, [15].
[10] ibid, [28]. Without stating so expressly, the court extended the approach in *Travers* (n 5) to money judgments.
[11] See in particular *In re Trepca Mines Ltd* [1960] 1 WLR 1273 (CA); *Batavia Times Publishing Co v Davis* (1977) 82 DLR (3d) 247 (Ont HC), affd (1979) 105 DLR (3d) 192 (Ont CA).
[12] *Morguard* (n 1) 1095.
[13] See in particular V Black, 'Enforcement of Judgments and Judicial Jurisdiction in Canada' (1989) 9 *Oxford Journal of Legal Studies* 547 which makes the case for much of the approach the Court adopted.
[14] *Morguard* (n 1) 1094.
[15] ibid, 1100.

In its analysis, the Court also noted that 'the informing principle of private international law' was comity. In La Forest J's view, the approach in *Emanuel* was based on a misunderstanding of comity, treating it as 'respect for the dictates of a foreign sovereign'.[16] He preferred the 'more complete formulation' of comity from *Hilton v Guyot*:[17]

> 'Comity' in the legal sense, is neither a matter of absolute obligation, on the one hand, nor of mere courtesy and good will, upon the other. But it is the recognition which one nation allows within its territory to the legislative, executive or judicial acts of another nation, having due regard both to international duty and convenience, and to the rights of its own citizens or of other persons who are under the protection of its laws ….

This was a different approach than the courts below had adopted, as neither of them emphasised comity as an important consideration.

Based on these considerations, La Forest J concluded that the courts in one province should recognise the judgments of a court in another province, so long as that court properly exercised jurisdiction in reaching its decision. This in turn raised the crucial question of what amounted to the proper exercise of jurisdiction. The Court's answer was that jurisdiction is properly exercised on the basis of the defendant's presence in the forum when the proceedings are commenced and on the basis of the defendant's consent. But that was not the entire answer. Jurisdiction is also properly exercised on the basis of a 'real and substantial connection' between the forum and the dispute.[18]

Accordingly, the Court dismissed the appeal and upheld the conclusion that the Alberta judgment was enforceable in British Columbia. Indeed, on this test, the case was remarkably easy. The Court observed that 'it is difficult to imagine a more reasonable place for the action for the deficiencies to take place than Alberta'.[19] The land in question was in Alberta and the mortgages were made in Alberta between two parties in Alberta.

B. The Context

Morguard reflects the context in which it was decided in several ways. It was decided at a time when Canadian law was moving away from following earlier English law principles and was increasingly looking to American law as a leading comparative source. Canada had, less than a decade earlier, adopted the Canadian Charter of Rights and Freedoms[20] and finalised a lengthy process of

[16] ibid, 1096.
[17] *Hilton v Guyot* 159 US 113 (1895), 163–64.
[18] *Morguard* (n 1) 1104–08, drawing on *Moran v Pyle National (Canada) Ltd* [1975] 1 SCR 393, 408–09.
[19] *Morguard* (n 1) 1108.
[20] Part I of the Constitution Act 1982, being Sch B of the Canada Act 1982 (UK).

patriating its Constitution so that changes to it no longer required approval of the UK. The Supreme Court of Canada had, in *Aetna Financial Services Ltd v Feigelman*, recently noted that rules developed in England should not be applied in the Canadian context without careful consideration.[21] In *Morguard* La Forest J's analysis drew heavily on the American ideas of full faith and credit under its constitutional order.

In addition, for several years in the late 1980s Canada and the US had been negotiating a broad free trade agreement, a significant move away from the protectionist policies of some previous eras. The Canada-United States Free Trade Agreement came into force at the start of 1989.[22] In his decision La Forest J expressly refers to the importance of cross-border economic activity. Subsequently in *Hunt v T&N plc* he noted that

> the old common law rules relating to recognition and enforcement were rooted in an outmoded conception of the world that emphasized sovereignty and independence, often at the cost of unfairness. Greater comity is required in our modern era when international transactions involve a constant flow of products, wealth and people across the globe.[23]

In an analysis of *Morguard*, Pepa argues that Canada's constitutional order and structure from 1867 is rooted in classical free trade theory.[24] Under such a theory, direct or indirect barriers to free trade within Canada, whether legislatively or judicially imposed through artificial regulations or conflict of laws, are unacceptable. These barriers prevent market efficiency and increase transactional costs. Pepa contends that the court in *Morguard* applied this economic analysis to reform a traditional conflict of laws rule.

In a similar vein, Finkle and Labrecque argue the decision was an important step toward the creation of a more unified and efficient national market, something that was a core reason for the creation of Canada as a nation over a century earlier.[25] To be a unified market, a federation must make private legal rights easily transferable throughout the nation. Finkle and Labrecque note that at the time *Morguard* was litigated and decided, the federal government was particularly concerned about 'competitiveness and efficiency in the national marketplace'.[26] Economic concerns of 'considerable urgency' needed to be addressed by the court. Allowing Canadians to vindicate their economic rights

[21] *Aetna Financial Services Ltd v Feigelman* [1985] 1 SCR 2 (SCC) 35.

[22] Five years later with the addition of Mexico this became the North American Free Trade Agreement. This was superseded in 2020 by the Canada-United States-Mexico Agreement.

[23] *Hunt v T&N plc* [1993] 4 SCR 289 (SCC) 321–22. See also *Tolofson v Jensen* [1994] 3 SCR 1022 (SCC) 1047: 'to accommodate the movement of people, wealth and skills across state lines, a byproduct of modern civilization, [states] will in great measure recognize the determination of legal issues in other states'.

[24] SM Pepa, 'Extraterritoriality and the Supreme Court's Assertion of the Economic Constitution' (2001) 34 *Canadian Business Law Journal* 231, 235, 241–42.

[25] P Finkle and C Labrecque, 'Low-Cost Legal Remedies and Market Efficiency: Looking Beyond *Morguard*' (1993) 22 *Canadian Business Law Journal* 58, 58–59.

[26] ibid 64–65.

against defendants resident anywhere in the country achieved, in their view, not only increased national integration but also 'enhanced equality and fairness'.[27]

The court's 'avowedly instrumentalist and economic perspective' was also noted by Black, who considered *Morguard*, ten years after the decision, to be the court's clearest direction as to how the common law should be modified to address the new global economic order.[28] In his view, *Morguard* embraced the promotion of free trade as a single over-riding economic goal.[29] While he agrees with others as to the key contextual factors at work, he has concerns about the court's lack of critical engagement with that context. The decision followed the victory by Prime Minister Brian Mulroney in an election dominated by free trade, yet as Black notes a majority of voters supported candidates and parties opposed to the Canada-United States Free Trade Agreement. The court could have offered some support for, or at least acknowledgement of, values that run counter to free trade. In his view, '[h]ad *Morguard* acknowledged that consumer protection concerns can sometimes operate to justify laws that have the effect of creating limits to free trade, … [a]t the very least, its reasoning would more comprehensively have dealt with the difficult value choices that the internationalization of market activity presents'.[30]

III. LEGACIES OF THE DECISION

A. Within Canada

As a matter of jurisprudence, the core legacy of *Morguard* is the change to the common law test for recognition and enforcement of a foreign judgment.[31] The breadth of this change, in itself, goes a long way to establishing *Morguard* as a landmark private international law case. However, this is only the beginning of what came to be called 'the *Morguard* revolution' in Canadian conflict of laws. The decision has had so much influence in so many areas.

[27] ibid 85–86.

[28] V Black, 'Commodifying Justice for Global Free Trade: The Proposed Hague Judgments Convention' (2000) 38 *Osgoode Hall Law Journal* 237, 248–49.

[29] V Black, J Blom and J Walker, 'Current Jurisdictional and Recognitional Issues in the Conflict of Laws' (2011) 50 *Canadian Business Law Journal* 499. The article is written as a trialogue between its authors.

[30] ibid 506. See also Black (n 28) 249–50. For other criticisms of the court's vision of the international economic order see N Hume, 'Four Flaws: Reflections on the Canadian Approach to Private International Law' (2006) 44 *Canadian Yearbook of International Law* 161; R Wai, 'In the Name of the International: The Supreme Court of Canada and the Internationalist Transformation of Canadian Private International Law' (2001) 39 *Canadian Year Book of International Law* 117.

[31] The focus of this chapter is on the common law of Canada. The law in Quebec is different in several respects, though *Morguard* has been influential there also. The private international law of Quebec is found in the *Civil Code of Quebec*, CCQ-1991, Book 10. Title 4, starting at Art 3155, deals with recognition and enforcement of foreign judgments.

First, *Morguard* was an interprovincial case. However, in its wake Canadian courts were virtually unanimous in holding that the new test applied to international judgments as well as interprovincial ones.[32] One of the factors driving the analysis in *Morguard*, the federal nature of Canada, had no relevance to truly foreign judgments. However, courts were strongly persuaded by the other factor, economic globalisation.

There was a possible fork in this road after about a decade, when in the course of hearing argument in *Beals v Saldanha*,[33] the Supreme Court of Canada seemed open to reconsider the law. At issue in *Beals* was whether a default judgment obtained by plaintiffs in Florida could be enforced against defendants in Ontario. The plaintiffs' claim in the Florida litigation related to flaws in a 1984 purchase of Florida land worth US$8,000. When the defendants chose not to defend, in 1991 a Florida jury awarded damages of US$260,000, which included US$50,000 in punitive damages. By 1998, when the trial judge heard the Ontario action for enforcement, post-judgment interest and the exchange rate meant that the defendants owed roughly $800,000 on the judgment. Given the strength of the connections between Florida and the dispute, *Beals* was an unlikely case in which to reconsider *Morguard*. In any case, having thought the matter through, the majority confirmed what was by then the orthodox approach, holding that the real and substantial connection test should be extended to international judgments. Major J stated that 'while there are compelling reasons to expand the test's application, there does not appear to be any principled reason not to do so'.[34] He noted that accommodating the flow of wealth, skills and people in a world economy was 'as much an imperative internationally as it is interprovincially'.[35]

While not at issue in *Morguard*, it is also worth noting that the decision, rooted as it was in comity and a willingness to modernise the law, paved the way for the Supreme Court of Canada subsequently to expand the recognition and enforcement of foreign judgments to include non-monetary decisions such as injunctions. In *Pro Swing Inc v Elta Golf Inc*, Deschamps J for the majority observed that 'frontiers remain relevant to national identity and jurisdiction, but ... the globalization of commerce and mobility of both people and assets make them less so'.[36] The influence of globalisation applies equally to non-monetary judgments.

[32] See *Moses v Shore Boat Builders Ltd* (1993) 83 BCLR (2d) 177 (CA). This development is explained in J Blom, 'The Enforcement of Foreign Judgments: *Morguard* Goes Forth into the World' (1997) 28 *Canadian Business Law Journal* 373, 379–84.

[33] *Beals v Saldanha* 2003 SCC 72. The appeal was argued in February 2003 and additional written submissions were filed during the next two months. For an analysis see SGA Pitel, 'Enforcement of Foreign Judgments: Where *Morguard* Stands After *Beals*' (2004) 40 *Canadian Business Law Journal* 189; SGA Pitel, 'A Modern Approach to Enforcing Judgments: *Beals v Saldanha*' [2004] *Lloyd's Maritime and Commercial Law Quarterly* 288.

[34] *Beals* (n 33) [19].

[35] ibid, [26].

[36] *Pro Swing Inc v Elta Golf Inc* [2006] 2 SCR 612, [1]. For an analysis see SGA Pitel, 'Enforcement of Foreign Non-Monetary Judgments in Canada (and Beyond)' (2007) 3 *Journal of Private International Law* 241.

Second, *Morguard* was a common law decision. However, its reliance on Canada's federal nature led many to question whether there was a constitutional dimension to the decision. This has major practical significance, because a provincial legislature can pass legislation to override the common law but cannot act unconstitutionally. So, in the wake of *Morguard*, could a province have enacted legislation to codify *Emanuel* as the test for interprovincial recognition and enforcement? In *Hunt* the Supreme Court of Canada answered in the negative.[37] La Forest J held that:[38]

> *Morguard* was not argued in constitutional terms, so it was sufficient there to infuse the constitutional considerations into the rules that might otherwise have governed issues of enforcement and recognition of judgment. But the issue was very clearly raised in this case and in fact a constitutional question was framed. Now ... the constitutional considerations raised are just that. They are constitutional imperatives, and as such apply to the provincial legislatures as well as to the courts.

This constitutional aspect of *Morguard* is arguably as important a legacy as its change to the scope of recognition and enforcement. It has become so well accepted, despite the lack of explicit language in the Canadian Constitution on such issues, that in *Club Resorts Ltd v Van Breda*, LeBel J could say for the Supreme Court of Canada that '[g]iven the nature of private international law, its application inevitably raises constitutional issues'.[39] He also noted that '[i]n developing the real and substantial connection test, the Court crafted a constitutional principle rather than a simple conflicts rule'.[40]

Third, while *Morguard* was a case about enforcing a foreign judgment, arguably its biggest influence in Canada has been on the law relating to the taking of jurisdiction, most notably on what is known as assumed jurisdiction.[41] This refers to jurisdiction that is not based either on the defendant's presence or residence in the forum at the time of the litigation or on the defendant's submission or attornment to the forum. Recall that in *Morguard* the court held that the proper exercise of jurisdiction, for a Canadian province, included assuming jurisdiction on the basis of a real and substantial connection between the forum and the dispute. It set this out as part of the test for assessing the jurisdiction of the rendering court for recognition purposes, but Canadian courts came to use this same notion as the test for assuming jurisdiction. Indeed, and crucially,

[37] *Hunt* (n 23).

[38] ibid, 324.

[39] *Club Resorts Ltd v Van Breda* 2012 SCC 17 [21].

[40] ibid, [22]. Several commentators have expressed concern about the constitutional elements of the analysis. See, eg, P Finkle and S Coakley, '*Morguard Investments Limited*: Reforming Federalism from the Top' (1991) 14:2 *Dalhousie Law Journal* 340; JA Woods, 'Recognition and Enforcement of Judgments between Provinces: The Constitutional Dimensions of *Morguard Investments Ltd*.' (1993) 22 *Canadian Business Law Journal* 104; E Edinger, 'The Constitutionalization of the Conflict of Laws' (1995) 25 *Canadian Business Law Journal* 38.

[41] See V Black, 'The Other Side of *Morguard*: New Limits on Judicial Jurisdiction' (1993) 22 *Canadian Business Law Journal* 4.

the real and substantial connection test operated as a limitation on the court's ability to take jurisdiction, since in the absence of such a connection assumed jurisdiction would not be proper.[42]

In *Club Resorts* the Supreme Court of Canada observed that 'the framework established for the purpose of determining whether a court has jurisdiction may have an impact on the choice of law and on the recognition of judgments, and vice versa'.[43] It noted that the real and substantial connection requirement in *Morguard* 'was designed to ensure that claims are not prosecuted in a jurisdiction that has little or no connection with either the transactions or the parties'.[44] While in *Club Resorts* the Court claimed to separate the constitutional requirement for the proper taking of jurisdiction from the common law test for assumed jurisdiction, it remained clear that the latter was subject to the limitations in the former.[45] The Court went on to develop a specific methodology for assessing the proper assumption of jurisdiction, holding that a court could not assume jurisdiction in the absence of a 'presumptive connecting factor' linking the forum and the dispute.[46]

Consistent with *Hunt*, the limitations on assumed jurisdiction were constitutional ones, so that a province could not by legislation assert a greater jurisdiction. However, because the Court conceived of these limits as not only found in implied principles of federalism but also in the territorial limits of provincial courts, they applied equally to both international and interprovincial cases.[47]

Fourth, and related to some of the points above, *Morguard* has had a significant impact on the formulation of uniform conflict of laws legislation in Canada. The Uniform Court Jurisdiction and Proceedings Transfer Act (CJPTA) replaces the common law rules on the taking of jurisdiction with a statutory framework.[48] One of the explicit aims of the CJPTA is to embody the substantive principles of jurisdiction articulated in *Morguard*. Section 3 provides that a court has 'territorial competence' in a proceeding brought against a person

[42] See *Tolofson* (n 23) 1049: 'a court may exercise jurisdiction only if it has a "real and substantial connection" (a term not yet fully defined) with the subject matter of the litigation'. To clarify, this is a reference to assumed jurisdiction. It does not change the law on jurisdiction based on presence or residence or on submission.

[43] *Club Resorts* (n 39) [16].

[44] ibid, [26].

[45] ibid, [33]–[34].

[46] ibid, [78], [82], [93]; *Lapointe Rosenstein Marchand Melançon LLP v Cassels Brock & Blackwell LLP* 2016 SCC 30 [25]–[26]. See V Black, 'Simplifying Court Jurisdiction in Canada' (2012) 8 *Journal of Private International Law* 411; TJ Monestier, '(Still) a Real and Substantial Mess: The Law of Jurisdiction in Canada' (2013) 36 *Fordham International Law Journal* 396.

[47] *Club Resorts* (n 39) [31]–[32]. See J Blom, 'Constitutionalizing Canadian private international law – 25 years since *Morguard*' (2017) 13 *Journal of Private International Law* 259, 268–69.

[48] The original statute was adopted by the Uniform Law Conference of Canada in 1994. It was recently updated in 2021. For the current version see www.ulcc-chlc.ca/ULCC/media/EN-Uniform-Acts/Uniform-Court-Jurisdiction-and-Proceedings-Transfer-Act-(2021).pdf (accessed 8 May 2022).

only in six specific situations, one of which is that 'there is a real and substantial connection between [enacting province or territory] and the facts on which the proceeding against that person is based'. Section 10 sets out a non-exclusive list of types of proceedings in which a real and substantial connection is presumed to exist, such as a proceeding concerning a tort committed in the forum. There are strong parallels between this framework and the insistence on presumptive connecting factors at common law in *Club Resorts*. Three provinces and one territory have adopted the CJPTA and so use it rather than the common law for taking jurisdiction.[49]

Morguard has also influenced the development of uniform legislation allowing for the registration of judgments and decrees. A leading example is the Uniform Enforcement of Canadian Judgments and Decrees Act (ECJDA).[50] Notably, the statute goes beyond the idea of allowing registration of Canadian judgments and decrees in which there was a real and substantial connection between the dispute and the rendering court. In section 6(3)(a) it precludes the defendant, in opposing the registration, from arguing that the rendering court lacked jurisdiction. The scheme proceeds on the basis that a court in another part of Canada has properly exercised its jurisdiction and that accordingly 'full faith and credit' must be given to the decision. As a practical matter, this requires a defendant to raise any objections to jurisdiction in the court in which the defendant is sued. This approach is based not on *Morguard*'s change to the test for recognising judgments but on the constitutional limitations on taking jurisdiction operating on all provinces. Several provinces have adopted the ECJDA or a similar statute.[51]

Fifth, *Morguard* has also influenced some thinking about choice of law. It may be questioned whether the notion of 'full faith and credit' implied as an aspect of federalism means that the orthodox notion that choice of law is voluntary, in the sense that it must be raised by one of the parties, is open to challenge. Perhaps the courts of a province are obliged, on their own, to consider whether a legal issue is governed by the law of another province, since otherwise those courts would not be giving full faith and credit to the substantive law of that province. A similar argument has been suggested in the context of the Australian federation.[52] To date, however, there is very little support for this notion in the jurisprudence. Canadian courts have continued to treat choice of law as a matter for the parties to raise, even as it concerns other parts of Canada.[53]

[49] See, eg, Court Jurisdiction and Proceedings Transfer Act SBC 2003 c 28. For detailed analysis of the statute prior to the 2021 update see V Black, SGA Pitel and M Sobkin, *Statutory Jurisdiction: An Analysis of the Court Jurisdiction and Proceedings Transfer Act* (Toronto, Carswell, 2012).

[50] Adopted by the Uniform Law Conference of Canada in 1998. See www.ulcc-chlc.ca/ULCC/media/EN-Uniform-Acts/Uniform-Enforcement-of-Canadian-Judgments-and-Decrees-Act_3.pdf (accessed 8 May 2022). It has been amended since and was itself based on a 1992 model statute dealing only with money judgments.

[51] See, eg, Enforcement of Canadian Judgments and Decrees Act SBC 2003 c 29.

[52] See EI Sykes and MC Pryles, *Australian Private International Law*, 3rd edn (Sydney, Law Book Company, 1991) 275–76.

[53] See the approach in *Boulanger v Johnson & Johnson Corp* (2003) 64 OR (3d) 208 (Div Ct).

B. Outside Canada

Given the influence described above, it should be clear why *Morguard* is a landmark case within Canada. Beyond this, one measure of its significance is the extent to which courts in other countries have engaged with its principles and reasoning. In particular, courts in several other common law countries have considered whether to adopt its approach to recognition of foreign judgments. In doing so, they have had to take account of similar contextual factors. As in Canada, the courts of other common law countries have similarly had to question the extent to which they should evolve the law beyond earlier English principles. They have also had to consider how best to take account of a massive increase in cross-border economic activity.

In *Rubin v Eurofinance SA*, the United Kingdom Supreme Court considered whether a judgment of a foreign court in proceedings to adjust or set aside prior transactions, such as preferences or transactions at an undervalue, will be recognised and enforced in England.[54] This led it to examine the scope of judgment recognition at common law more generally.[55] In doing so, it noted the expansion in Canada beginning in *Morguard*. Referring to the Canadian position, the Court held that '[t]here is no support in England for such an approach except in the field of family law'.[56] Returning to the narrower issue of insolvency proceedings, the Court refused to expand the scope of recognisable foreign judgments beyond the traditional position.[57] It offered several reasons for this refusal. First, the proposed expansion was too radical: '[t]his would not be an incremental development of existing principles, but a radical departure from substantially settled law'.[58] This made it the purview of legislation, not 'judicial innovation'.[59] Second, such a change would only be detrimental to defendants from the UK, who would have to submit to foreign jurisdictions to which they only have a 'sufficient connection' for worry of later enforcement at home.[60] Third, no serious injustice would likely result if the Court upheld the traditional rules.[61] The Court based this view in part on the possibility that the claimants in the foreign proceedings might have been able to advance similar claims in the UK.

The Supreme Court of Ireland considered *Morguard* in *Re Flightlease (Irl) Ltd*.[62] The Court was asked to recognise a Swiss *in personam* decision for the

[54] *Rubin v Eurofinance SA* [2012] UKSC 46, [2013] 1 AC 236.

[55] The Court referred to *Adams v Cape Industries Plc* [1990] Ch 433 (CA), 512–25 as the key authority on the issue.

[56] *Rubin* (n 54) [109]–[110]. The family law precedent in question was *Indyka v Indyka* [1969] 1 AC 33 (HL) where the court held that a foreign divorce would be recognised if there was a 'real and substantial connection' between the petitioner and the country where the divorce was obtained.

[57] *Rubin* (n 54) [115]–[117].

[58] ibid, [128].

[59] ibid, [129]. See also *Owens Bank Ltd v Bracco* [1992] 2 AC 443 (HL) in which the House of Lords held that significant development of the law on recognition and enforcement should be left to Parliament.

[60] *Rubin* (n 54) [130].

[61] ibid, [131].

[62] *Re Flightlease (Irl) Ltd* [2012] 1 IR 722, affg [2006] IEHC 193.

payment of money on the basis of there having been a real and substantial connection between Switzerland and the dispute. For a majority of the Court, Finnegan J refused to follow the approach in *Morguard* and retained the traditional test for assessing the foreign court's taking of jurisdiction. He set out six reasons, identified by the trial judge, with which he agreed. First, no other common law jurisdiction has made such a change. Second, some academic commentary has been critical of the Canadian approach. Third, people rely on the law as it exists and so it should not be changed 'lightly'. Fourth, a 'radical' change in the law, applied retrospectively, could amount to an injustice. Fifth, the common law should not be changed in such a way that would 'amount to legislation'. Sixth, there is no consensus on the need for a change to the Canadian approach.[63] Drawing these points together, Finnegan J concluded 'the change contended for … is of such significance that it would in my opinion exceed the judicial function to re-state the common law in such a way. Such a change should be by legislation'.[64]

In a separate concurring decision, O'Donnell J placed more emphasis on concerns that the real and substantial connection basis for jurisdiction is inherently uncertain. Defendants would accordingly have trouble applying the *Morguard* test at the outset of a foreign proceeding and thus face considerable uncertainty as to whether to submit to that proceeding. Like the other judges, he concluded that it would be best for a legislature to innovate in this area of the law, preferably in cooperation with other countries.[65]

In Singapore, the law on recognition of foreign judgments continues to follow *Emanuel*. However, the Court of Appeal has recently indicated some support for the *Morguard* approach. In *Merck Sharp & Dohme Corp v Merck KGaA* the court considered the principles of issue estoppel arising from a prior foreign decision.[66] In doing so it addressed what it understood to be the possible reasons why a defendant could legitimately be bound by the foreign decision: obligation, comity and finality of litigation. On behalf of the court, Sundaresh Menon CJ noted that there had been criticisms of the obligation rationale and expressed the view that 'considerations of transnational comity and reciprocal respect among courts of independent jurisdictions have come to undergird the recognition of foreign judgments at common law and, by extension, the doctrine of transnational issue estoppel'.[67] The court noted that in *Beals* these were the considerations that had led to the extension of the bases for recognition of a foreign judgment. Without deciding the issue, the court indicated a willingness to extend the scope of recognisable judgments in an appropriate future case.[68]

[63] ibid, 753–54.
[64] ibid, 754.
[65] ibid, 763–64.
[66] *Merck Sharp & Dohme Corp v Merck KGaA* [2021] SGCA 14.
[67] ibid, [33].
[68] ibid, [39]. See also JC Junhao, 'Problems in the Recognition and Enforcement of US Class Action Judgments in Singapore' (2013) 25 *Singapore Academy Law Journal* 51.

The reasons in *Rubin* and *Re Flightlease* trigger some significant debate.[69] While there may not be a consensus in favour of the Canadian approach, there is a significant amount of concern that the common law approach from *Emanuel* is outdated and badly in need of reform. This point was made by O'Donnell J in *Re Flightlease*. Further, the overall degree of judicial timidity in both decisions is regrettable. This is a common law rule, developed by judges, and so amenable to further reform by the courts. It is hyperbolic to claim that the kind of evolution seen in *Morguard* exceeds the judicial function. This reasoning suggests that the common law should never be changed if doing so would negatively impact a party that had relied on the law as previously understood.[70] It also ignores the possibility, available to courts in the more extreme of cases, to render an explicitly prospective decision. As Hutchinson contends in his analysis of leading cases, 'it is the relentless critic who most closely grasps and continues the common law tradition than the complacent apologist who insists on a timid acceptance of what has already been decided'.[71] Further, the court does not engage with any sense of the likelihood that the UK or Irish Parliament would choose to reform the law in this area. Those bodies might well consider this a proper matter for the courts. When it comes to determining which judgments to enforce, the courts and the legislature share responsibility for the ongoing development of the law. It was the courts that initially took the lead by being prepared to accept, as authoritative, foreign judgments. Their role has surely not ended.

The suggestion in *Rubin* that an expansion of the scope of the rule would only be detrimental to defendants based in the UK unfortunately reflects the judicial protectionism evident in *Emanuel* itself. It lacks balance and a broader understanding of the modern global economy.[72] In a given case, parties in the UK might well have an economic interest in broader recognition of foreign judgments, so that the interests of more than just local judgment debtors should be

[69] On the latter see D Kenny, '*Re Flightlease*: The Real and Substantial Connection Test for Recognition and Enforcement of Foreign Judgements Fails to Take Flight in Ireland' (2014) 63 *International & Comparative Law Quarterly* 197. See also J Swan, 'How Should a Court Approach the Recognition and Enforcement of a Foreign Judgment?' (2007) 29 *Dublin University Law Journal* 443.

[70] This concern is also at odds with the traditional view that judges reveal what the common law is and so there is, in a technical sense, no retroactive application of a change in that law. Any reliance would have been based on an incorrect understanding of what the common law rule actually was.

[71] AC Hutchinson, 'The Importance of Leading Cases' in E O'Dell (ed), *Leading Cases of the Twentieth Century* (Dublin, Round Hall Sweet & Maxwell, 2000).

[72] For a related economic argument as to why Ireland would benefit from expanding the scope of enforceable judgments, advanced prior to *Re Flightlease*, see J Newman, 'Enforcement of Foreign Judgments in Non-Convention Cases' (2000) 5 *The Bar Review* 354: 'Ireland's civil and commercial interests are better served by enhancing the level of confidence that can be placed in dealings as between Irish residents and US and other foreign residents, and not by undermining that confidence by facilitating the evasion by Irish residents of the enforcement of obligations arising out of those dealings' (354). This is because 'orderly and fair Irish enforcement rules encourage dealing with parties linked to Ireland by enhancing certainty and confidence in commercial arrangements' (at 358).

considered. Moreover, a fairer approach to recognition benefits the international exchange in which the UK is engaged at a much more general level. In addition, there are reputational costs when a legal system insists on a particular position primarily for reasons of domestic self-interest. Such a position, in this and other contexts, could undercut many of the central objectives of private international law.

IV. ASSESSING THE DECISION

Landmark cases generate significant debate. Already in this chapter many of the arguments for and against expanding the scope of recognition of foreign judgments have been identified. Several of these can be developed further. Some are of a more theoretical nature and others are more practical.

One way to analyse the issue of judgment enforcement is to identify the reasons why the defendant should, in the enforcing jurisdiction, be treated as bound by the decision of the foreign court. Briggs has explained this as based on a doctrine of obligation. As he has expressed it,

> the foreign judgment, if it is recognised, imposes an obligation on the party against whose interest it is to be asserted. Where the recognition proceeds from the private agreement of the parties, the obligation is one arising by agreement. Where the recognition is a consequence of the rule that the exercise of sovereign authority within the territory of the sovereign is to be accepted without question, the obligation is one arising otherwise than by agreement.[73]

As set out, these appear to be two distinct obligations and they each appear capable of being understood in different ways. Does the defendant owe an obligation to the rendering court, to the plaintiff or to both? Are both obligations based on the defendant's consent to them? In the absence of agreement, why is the only relevant action inside the territory of the sovereign the service of process? Could not an exercise of sovereign authority sufficient to create a similar obligation be based on a defendant's other actions within that territory, even though the service is *ex juris*? In *Rubin* Lord Collins stated that

> [t]he theoretical basis for the enforcement of foreign judgments at common law is that they are enforced on the basis of a principle that where a court of competent jurisdiction has adjudicated a certain sum to be due from one person to another, a legal obligation arises to pay that sum, on which an action of debt to enforce the judgment may be maintained.[74]

This statement uses the notion of obligation in a different, broader sense. And he continued by noting that 'this is a purely theoretical and historical basis for the enforcement of foreign judgments at common law', suggesting that the

[73] A Briggs, 'Recognition of Foreign Judgments: A Matter of Obligation' (2013) 129 *Law Quarterly Review* 87, 93 (footnote omitted).

[74] *Rubin* (n 54) [9].

modern approach could be quite different. Enforcement could instead be justified based on comity, fairness, justice and the demands of modern international commerce.[75]

Briggs has argued that the expansion in *Morguard* cannot be explained under the doctrine of obligation.[76] Admittedly a real and substantial connection, on the facts, is not consent in the same way as is participation in the litigation itself. But in many cases the defendant will have voluntarily engaged in the actions involving the foreign jurisdiction and be aware of the prospect of possible litigation there. Some element of consent is present in these cases.[77] In addition, a willingness to respect a foreign sovereign's assertion of authority need not be limited to cases where the form of that assertion is service within the forum. A defendant's actions may have a sufficient effect within that forum that the sovereign is justified in asserting the ability to resolve disputes relating to those actions.

It would be remarkable, in the modern age, if our theory could not justify enforcement of the decision of a court 'which of all courts has the closest connection to the facts of and the dispute, or which may be regarded as the natural forum for the resolution of the dispute'.[78] Such a forum is likely to be the place where the interests of justice can best be served, such that the defendant should have elected to defend there on the merits. Indeed, it has been noted that English law, rather than having started with a narrow scope for enforcement and refused to develop it further, once was more open to enforcing foreign judgments than it is now.[79] On this view, the court in *Schibsby v Westenholz*,[80] and other decisions, improperly 'denuded the law of flexibility' by introducing rigid criteria for the recognition and enforcement of foreign judgments.[81]

The dominant practical consideration in debates about *Morguard* has been whether the test is too vague and so does not allow the defendant a fair ability to assess whether a foreign judgment, if they choose not to defend on the merits, will be enforced where they have assets. The certainty of the *Emanuel* rule has been praised as its best feature. In contrast, the idea of a real and substantial connection is seen by many as too open-ended and unpredictable. In Canada, debates about the meaning of a real and substantial connection[82] have tended to

[75] See A Briggs, *The Conflict of Laws*, 2nd edn (Oxford, OUP, 2008) 137–39.

[76] Briggs (n 73) 94, 100.

[77] See J Blom 'Conflict of Laws – Enforcement of Extraprovincial Default Judgment – Real and Substantial Connection: *Morguard Investments Ltd v De Savoye*' (1991) 70 *Canada Bar Review* 724, 741.

[78] A Briggs, 'Crossing the River by Feeling the Stones: Rethinking the Law on Foreign Judgments' (2004) 8 *Singapore Yearbook of International Law* 1, 12.

[79] A Dickinson, '*Schibsby v Westenholz* and the Recognition and Enforcement of Judgments in England' (2018) 134 *Law Quarterly Review* 426. See also A Dickinson, 'Keeping Up Appearances: The Development of Adjudicatory Jurisdiction in the English Courts' (2016) 86 *British Yearbook of International Law* 6.

[80] *Schibsby v Westenholz* (1879–71) LR 6 QB 155 (QB).

[81] Dickinson (n 79) 448. See also ch 4 in this volume.

[82] Scholarship about the meaning of the test started very shortly after the decision and has maintained a brisk pace. Leading examples include Blom (n 77); J-G Castel, 'The Uncertainty Factor in Canadian Private International Law' (2007) 52 *McGill Law Journal* 555.

arise in the context of taking jurisdiction rather than the enforcement context, *Club Resorts* being a leading example. In that case the Supreme Court of Canada made a considerable effort to provide a more concrete explanation of a real and substantial connection, requiring that it be established by the identification of a presumptive connecting factor. While there is no closed list of such factors, the courts are beginning to establish consensus around several of these factors.[83] And while there is not yet definitive appellate guidance as to whether these factors are also part of the analysis of the foreign court's jurisdiction in the test for enforcement, the law seems likely to move in that direction.[84] Having created a more specific analytical framework to assess a real and substantial connection in one context, it might seem unusual not to use that same framework in a related context. Moreover, in many cases it is clear, on the facts, that the connection to the foreign forum is quite strong, leaving little ambiguity as to whether the domestic court would find the real and substantial connection requirement to be met. In practice, then, a defendant is frequently able, at the outset of foreign litigation, to recognise that one of the presumptive connecting factors is present to link the dispute to that forum, such that the enforcing court will find that the jurisdiction was proper. This goes a long way to reducing the uncertainty said to impair the real and substantial connection approach.[85]

It has also been argued that while the approach in *Emanuel* is too narrow, the approach in *Morguard* and *Beals* is too broad. Blom, for one, has expressed concern that the Canadian approach to enforcing foreign judgments is too liberal.[86] Yet little concern has been expressed, in the jurisprudence or elsewhere, that Canadians are being treated unfairly by their own law and that foreign judgments are being enforced against them inappropriately. As noted above, the extension in *Beals* to judgments from outside Canada does not have a constitutional foundation, and accordingly any province could enact legislation scaling back the law, either to the position in *Emanuel* or some intermediate position. The only province with legislation limiting enforcement in this way is New Brunswick,[87] and this legislation is not a response to *Beals* but rather dates

[83] See SGA Pitel and V Black, 'Assumed Jurisdiction in Canada: Identifying and Interpreting Presumptive Connecting Factors' (2018) 14 *Journal of Private International Law* 193; SGA Pitel, 'Checking in to *Club Resorts*: How Courts are Applying the New Test for Jurisdiction' (2013) 42 *Advocates' Quarterly* 190.

[84] See *Sincies Chiementin SpA v King* 2012 ONCA 653, [11]–[13]; Blom (n 47) 283. For an argument that the approach in *Club Resorts* should not apply in the recognition context see TJ Monestier, 'Jurisdiction and the Enforcement of Foreign Judgments' (2013) 42 *Advocates' Quarterly* 107. See also J Blom and E Edinger, 'The Chimera of the Real and Substantial Connection Test' (2005) 38 *University of British Columbia Law Review* 373.

[85] The use of presumptive connecting factors in this way is similar to the argument in A Arzandeh, 'Reformulating the Common Law Rules on Recognition and Enforcement of Foreign Judgments' (2019) 39 *Legal Studies* 56 that the court should accept as proper jurisdiction based on the equivalent of the enumerated English 'gateways' for service *ex juris*.

[86] Blom (n 47) 282–83.

[87] Foreign Judgments Act RSNB 2011 c 162.

back to at least the 1970s.[88] It chose to codify the common law test and then, in the wake of *Morguard*, limited that codification to judgments from outside Canada.[89] No province has, since *Morguard*, enacted legislation to protect its residents against enforcement of the judgments covered by that decision. *Beals* itself, heralded by some as a prime example of inappropriate enforcement, is not an unreasonable decision. Florida was, on the facts, the jurisdiction with the best connection to the dispute. The Ontario defendants, served with process, consulted counsel and on incorrect advice chose not to defend. On correct advice they would have defended, and the results of the litigation would have been quite different.[90]

Canadian defendants sued abroad have, in the main, adapted to the new rule and responded appropriately to those proceedings. Of course, their ability to challenge those proceedings by contesting jurisdiction or seeking a stay remains available. And if that fails, modern technology makes it easier than it ever has been – certainly easier than it was three decades ago when *Morguard* was first extended to judgments from outside Canada – to arrange a defence on the merits in a foreign forum.

Another way of thinking about the approach in *Morguard* is that, while correct in its expansion of the scope of enforcement, this is contingent on further development of the defences.[91] The expansion makes it essential to consider the possible defences carefully. But the jurisdiction test and the defences address different considerations and serve different purposes. The former addresses the basis on which the court rendered its decision while the latter addresses the way in which it did so. The jurisdiction element insists on some minimum degree of connection between that court and the dispute. Views on how strong or weak that connection should be should impact on the test for jurisdiction. On the other hand, the defences focus on the fairness of the foreign proceedings. Views of how much protection should be provided to defendants sued abroad should impact on the nature and scope of the defences. While related, these are not the same considerations.[92]

The development of the defences was expressly addressed by the Supreme Court of Canada in *Beals*. For the majority, Major J acknowledged that 'unusual' situations might arise which would justify the creation of a new defence to the

[88] Foreign Judgments Act RSNB 1973 c F-19.

[89] See A Warner La Forest, 'New Brunswick's Continuing Policy of Splendid Isolation in the Recognition and Enforcement of Judgments' (2016) 58 *Canada Business Law Journal* 57.

[90] Pitel (n 33) 196, 217. For a contrary view of the merits of the decision see J Goodman and JA Talpis, '*Beals v Saldanha* and the Enforcement of Foreign Judgments in Canada' (2004) 40 *Canadian Business Law Journal* 227; J Ziegel, 'Enforcement of Foreign Judgments in Canada, Unlevel Playing Fields, and *Beals v Saldanha*, A Consumer Perspective' (2003) 38 *Canadian Business Law Journal* 294.

[91] See Briggs (n 78) 22.

[92] See HL Ho, 'Policies Underlying the Enforcement of Foreign Commercial Judgments' (1997) 46 *International & Comparative Law Quarterly* 443, 459.

enforcement of an international judgment. Such a defence would have to be narrow, like the existing defences. In any case, the facts of *Beals* did not, according to both the majority and Binnie J, require the creation of a new defence.[93] The majority held that none of the existing defences assisted the defendants, while Binnie J held that the defendants came within the traditional scope of the defence of natural justice.

In *Beals* only LeBel J was prepared to reformulate the defences of fraud and natural justice to afford increased protection to defendants. He also urged that 'serious consideration' be given to refusing to enforce judgments whose enforcement 'would shock the conscience of Canadians'.[94] The latter notion gives individual judges remarkable latitude to refuse to enforce foreign judgments. It is difficult to see that it is a workable test, capable of sustained consistent application. On the other defences, an aspect of accepting the enforcement of the decision of a foreign court under the real and substantial connection test arguably involves concluding that when the test is satisfied it is reasonable to expect the defendant to engage appropriately with the foreign court's process. This same expectation operates in cases of presence and submission. It is therefore difficult to see why and how the fraud or natural justice defence would require expansion.[95]

V. CONCLUSION

In *Morguard*, the Supreme Court of Canada broke new ground for the common law's recognition and enforcement of judgments. Its approach has stood the test of time in Canada and remains a clarion call for reform of the common law approach in other jurisdictions. The decision is notable for its explicit focus on social and economic considerations as they affect the legal rules under consideration. Another important aspect of the decision is its appreciation of the inter-relationship between various areas of the law, grappling with the way enforcement relates to jurisdiction and to the nature of the country's constitutional order. This is a better way to approach these areas than to treat them as separate, walled off from each other. Two decades ago, I described the Canadian law on judgment enforcement as follows:[96]

> [T]he argument that the Canadian position is out of step may be overstated. The United States, the source of the large majority of foreign judgments sought to be

[93] *Beals* (n 33) [41]–[42], [86].
[94] ibid, [216]–[218].
[95] On the scope of the fraud defence see ch 6 in this volume.
[96] Pitel (n 33) 226 (footnotes omitted). While detailed analysis is beyond the scope of this chapter, for an introduction to the position in the US see the Uniform Foreign-Country Money Judgments Recognition Act (2005), online www.uniformlaws.org/committees/community-home?CommunityKey=ae280c30-094a-4d8f-b722-8dcd614a8f3e (accessed 8 May 2022). This legislation has been enacted in 28 states.

> enforced in Canada, has a relatively liberal test for the enforcement of foreign judgments. While England retains the common law test based on presence or submission, it has very liberal enforcement of judgments from other European Union countries. Further, having analyzed the *Morguard* test, several English academics have concluded that '[t]here is much to be said for adopting the real and substantial connection test, or something similar, in England'. So even to the extent Canada might be out of step, it might equally be leading a reform of the common law which will spread to other countries.

That broader reform has not happened. It is now overdue.

14

Akai v The People's Insurance Company (1996)

MARY KEYES

I. INTRODUCTION

THIS CHAPTER CONSIDERS *Akai Pty Ltd v The People's Insurance Company*,[1] a landmark case in Australia which is the leading authority for several fundamental issues in international commercial litigation. Decided in 1996, it is the most recent authority of the High Court of Australia, the apex Australian appellate court, concerning exclusive jurisdiction clauses, including their interaction with forum public policy, as well as contract choice of law. Some of the principles established by this case are uncontroversial, but the majority's approach to the impact of forum public policy is contentious. This case is of particular interest because, following the decision of the Australian court on jurisdiction, the defendant to Australian proceedings sought relief in the Singaporean and the English courts. While this chapter focuses on the Australian decision, the decisions of the Singaporean and English courts are also considered.

II. AKAI v THE PEOPLE'S INSURANCE COMPANY

A. The Background to *Akai*

Before considering the litigation in *Akai* in detail, it is necessary to provide some context for the decision of the High Court of Australia. Australian private international law is principally derived from case law,[2] much of which

[1] *Akai Pty Ltd v The People's Insurance Company* [1996] HCA 39, (1996) 188 CLR 418.

[2] There are three major exceptions. The first is that most of the principles of jurisdictional competence are, as in England, found in the rules of court. These were heavily influenced by the English rules in force from time to time, and the rules of the superior courts continue closely to resemble the English legislation enabling service ex juris. The second is that Australia is a contracting state to 11 Hague Conventions, each of which is given effect in legislation. The third is that Australia

is strongly influenced by English case law, although there are some differences in the relevant English and Australian principles. There have been several bursts of concentrated activity focusing on specific issues in the history of the High Court's development of Australian private international law. Three such bursts are relevant to the issues that arose in *Akai*: two decisions on jurisdiction clauses in the 1950s,[3] two decisions on *forum non conveniens* in 1987 and 1990,[4] and four decisions on contract choice of law in the 1930s.[5] Over a longer period, the High Court has wrestled several times with the vexed question of the application of forum legislation in contract choice of law cases.[6]

Akai was a jurisdictional dispute about the effect to be given to a foreign exclusive jurisdiction clause. The Australian principle determining the effect of foreign exclusive jurisdiction clauses was set down by the High Court in two cases decided in the 1950s: *Huddart Parker Ltd v The Ship 'Mill Hill'*,[7] and *Compagnie des Messageries Maritimes v Wilson*.[8] These cases established, following English authority, and by analogy to the treatment of arbitration clauses, that exclusive foreign jurisdiction clauses should ordinarily be enforced by staying proceedings. A passage from the judgment of Dixon J in *The Ship 'Mill Hill'* is often quoted: 'the Court begins with the fact that there is a special contract between the parties to refer, and therefore in the language of Lord Moulton in *Bristol Corporation v John Aird & Co*, consider the circumstances of a case with a strong bias in favour of maintaining the special bargain'.[9]

While these two decisions both gave significant emphasis to expressed choices of court, the High Court did not enforce the foreign jurisdiction clause in either case. In *The Ship 'Mill Hill'*, this was because all of the evidence was located in Australia, and the jurisdiction clause did not bind all parties to the dispute.[10] In *Compagnie Messageries Maritime v Wilson*, the court did not enforce the foreign jurisdiction clause because the Australian Carriage of Goods by Sea Act 1924 rendered void any agreement 'purporting to oust or lessen the jurisdiction of the Court of the Commonwealth or of a State [of Australia] in respect of any bill of lading or document relating to the carriage of goods from any place

concluded a treaty regulating jurisdiction and judgment recognition with New Zealand in 2008, which establishes a separate regime that is quite distinct from the regime applicable in other international cases. That treaty is given effect in legislation, called the Trans-Tasman Proceedings Act 2010 (Cth). See n 17.

[3] *Huddart Parker v The Ship 'Mill Hill'* [1950] HCA 43, (1950) 81 CLR 502; *Compagnie des Messageries Maritime v Wilson* [1954] HCA 62, (1954) 94 CLR 577.

[4] *Oceanic Sun Line Special Shipping Co Inc v Fay* [1988] HCA 32, (1988) 165 CLR 197; *Voth v Manildra Flour Mills Pty Ltd* [1990] HCA 55, (1990) 171 CLR 538.

[5] *Barcelo Electrolytic Zinc Co of Australasia Ltd* (1932) 48 CLR 391; *Merwin Pastoral Co Pty Ltd v Moolpa Pastoral Co Pty Ltd* (1933) 48 CLR 565; *Wanganui-Rangitikei Electric Power Board v Australian Mutual Provident Society* (1934) 50 CLR 581; *Mynott v Barnard* (1939) 62 CLR 68.

[6] *Mynott v Barnard* (1939) 62 CLR 68; *Kay's Leasing Corporation Pty Ltd v Fletcher* (1964) 116 CLR 124.

[7] *The Ship Mill Hill* (n 3).

[8] *Compagnie Messageries* (n 3).

[9] *The Ship Mill Hill* (n 3) 508–09.

[10] ibid, 509, 510–11.

outside Australia to any place in Australia'.[11] This clearly invalidated the French jurisdiction clause in issue.

Before the High Court appeal in *Akai*, the authority of *Huddart Parker v The Ship 'Mill Hill'* and *Compagnie des Messageries Maritimes v Wilson* had not been challenged. However, there was some confusion as to their continuing application following two decisions in 1987 and 1990 in which the High Court developed the current Australian version of the principle of *forum non conveniens*. In particular, some lower courts expressed uncertainty as to whether this revised principle of *forum non conveniens* applied in cases in which the defendant relied on a foreign exclusive jurisdiction clause.[12] *Oceanic Sun Line Shipping Co Inc v Fay* and *Voth v Manildra Flour Mills* established the peculiar Australian version of *forum non conveniens*, according to which the court may stay proceedings if the defendant establishes that the forum is 'clearly inappropriate'.[13] This version remains founded on the court's responsibility to prevent abuse of its processes, and in particular to prevent vexation or oppression of the defendant. While there are a few defenders of the Australian *forum non conveniens* principle,[14] most academics are critical of its propensities for chauvinism and parochialism, and for giving plaintiffs an unfair advantage.[15] I suggest that *Akai* also demonstrates anti-internationalist and inequitable tendencies.

Oceanic was similar to *Akai* in two respects relevant to the discussion in this chapter: first, the defendant relied on an exclusive foreign jurisdiction clause in its application for a stay of Australian proceedings; second, the plaintiff invoked forum legislation. In *Oceanic*, all five members of the court held that the jurisdiction clause had not been agreed,[16] and decided the dispute on the basis of

[11] Sea-Carriage of Goods Act 1924 (Cth).

[12] This was notwithstanding that in *Oceanic Sun Line Special Shipping Co Inc v Fay*, Brennan J stated that 'cases of a stay to enforce an exclusive foreign jurisdiction clause should not be assimilated to cases where, in England, a stay is sought on the principle forum non conveniens [sic]': (1988) 165 CLR 197, 230. See likewise at 259–61 (Gaudron J). In *Leigh-Mardon Pty Ltd v PRC International Pty Ltd*, Beazley J held that the question was open, but expressed her view that what she referred to as 'the traditional rule that the court should give primacy to a foreign jurisdiction clause' was correct: [1993] FCA 324, [20], [44]; (1993) 44 FCR 88. The majority in the New South Wales Court of Appeal, in the first appeal in *Akai*, agreed with Beazley J's reasoning that the traditional rule was correct, but also stated that until the earlier cases were overruled, they remained binding on lower courts: *Akai Pty Ltd v The People's Insurance Co Ltd* (1995) 126 FLR 204, 227.

[13] *Oceanic* (n 4) 248, 251–52; *Voth* (n 4) 564–65.

[14] P Prince, 'Bhopal, Bougainville and Ok Tedi: Why Australia's Forum non Conveniens Approach is Better' (1998) 47 *International & Commercial Law Quarterly* 573. Arzandeh argues that 'the accounts pointing to differences between *Voth* and *Spiliada* are overstated': 'Reconsidering the Australian Forum (Non) Conveniens Doctrine' (2016) 65 *International & Commercial Law Quarterly* 475, 476.

[15] See, eg, L Collins, 'The High Court of Australia and Forum Conveniens: The Last Word?' (1991) 107 *Law Quarterly Review* 182; R Garnett, 'A Stay of Proceedings in Australia: A 'Clearly Inappropriate' Test?' (1999) 23 *Melbourne University Law Review* 30; PE Nygh and M Davies, *Conflict of Laws in Australia,* 7th edn (Melbourne, LexisNexis Butterworths, 2002) 129–30.

[16] *Oceanic* (n 4) 229 (Brennan J). Deane J agreed with Wilson and Toohey JJ (256). Gaudron J agreed with Brennan J's conclusion that the jurisdiction clause was not incorporated into the contract (261).

forum non conveniens. However, two members of the majority, Brennan and Gaudron JJ, in separate judgments, discussed the effect in principle of exclusive foreign jurisdiction clauses. These discussions are regularly cited in later cases, including *Akai*.

An important point of distinction between *Oceanic* and *Akai* is that the plaintiff in *Oceanic*, Dr Fay, was a consumer whereas the plaintiff in *Akai* was a corporation. Australian private international law in general does not explicitly distinguish commercial from non-commercial cases, and there are no general principles of private international law that are tailored to consumer cases.[17] Nonetheless, Australian courts almost invariably do not enforce exclusive foreign jurisdiction clauses against consumers,[18] applying a number of different principles. The most common of these is to apply forum law as to contract formation to conclude that the jurisdiction clause was not agreed. Without explicitly characterising Dr Fay as a consumer, this is how the High Court effectively protected him from the exclusive jurisdiction clause in *Oceanic*.[19] Applying forum law to determine whether a jurisdiction clause was agreed is controversial in principle, but this is now well-established in Australian case law, both in consumer and commercial cases.[20]

[17] However, under the Trans-Tasman Proceedings Act 2010 (Cth), which regulates the allocation of jurisdiction in international litigation between Australia and New Zealand, the specific provisions which apply to exclusive choice of court agreements (which are based on but not identical to the Hague Choice of Court Convention) explicitly do not apply to agreements 'the parties to which are or include an individual acting primarily for personal, family, or household purposes' (a definition commonly used in Australian legislation to define consumer transactions): Trans-Tasman Proceedings Act 2010 (Cth), s 20(3)(b). The consequence is that the normal *forum non conveniens* rule, which in that legislation enables the Australian court to stay proceedings if it concludes that the New Zealand court is 'the more appropriate court', assuming that the New Zealand court has jurisdiction to determine the matters in issues, applies: s 17(1). In that determination, the Australian court is directed to take into account a list of factors, amongst which is any choice of court agreement other than an agreement to which s 20 applies. That means that an exclusive choice of court agreement, in a trans-Tasman *consumer* case, is reduced to the status of a non-exclusive jurisdiction clause.

Some substantive Australian legislative provisions only apply to consumer transactions. The most important of these are the consumer guarantees which are imported into all consumer transactions by the Australian Consumer Law: Australian Consumer Law 2010, Part 3-2, Div 1. On the other hand, the statutory prohibitions of misleading or deceptive conduct, and of unconscionable conduct, which are commonly invoked in international commercial disputes, apply equally to commercial and consumer disputes: ibid, ss 18(1), 21(1).

[18] There is a rapidly growing number of private international law cases in Australia involving consumers; many of which concern the effect to be given to foreign exclusive jurisdiction clauses. In most, the court either finds that, applying forum law, the jurisdiction clause was not validly incorporated in the contract, or that there are strong grounds for refusing to enforce the jurisdiction clause. The outstanding exception to this is *Gonzalez v Agoda Company Pte Ltd*, in which the court found that the jurisdiction clause was validly incorporated in the contract: [2017] NSWSC 1133, [122]–[125].

[19] Brennan and Gaudron JJ expressly justified applying the law of the forum: *Oceanic* (n 4) 225, 260–61. Wilson and Toohey JJ applied forum law without justifying doing so, and Deane J agreed with them on this point: 202, 256.

[20] *Venter v Ilona MY* [2012] NSWSC 1029; *Hargood v OHTL Public Company Ltd* [2015] NSWSC 446; *Central Petroleum Ltd v Geoscience Recovery LLC* [2017] QSC 223.

The lack of distinction between consumer and commercial cases is evident in that, in discussing the effect of jurisdiction clauses in general in *Oceanic*, neither Brennan nor Gaudron JJ suggested that different considerations were relevant in consumer transactions. Both assumed that the principle articulated by the High Court in the two commercial cases from the 1950s would have been applicable if the jurisdiction clause had been agreed in *Oceanic*.[21] Both affirmed the principle that the court should ordinarily enforce a foreign jurisdiction clause unless there were 'countervailing reasons',[22] 'substantial grounds',[23] or 'strong reasons',[24] implying that the approach developed in the commercial context was relevant in what was obviously a consumer case.[25] Brennan J stated that if the jurisdiction clause had been binding, 'there would have been no reason why the relief to which the plaintiff was entitled should not have been determined by the Athenian courts'.[26]

The second similarity between *Oceanic* and *Akai* relevant to the present discussion is that in both cases, the plaintiff relied on forum legislation as a reason for non-enforcement of the foreign jurisdiction clause. In *Oceanic*, this was the New South Wales Contracts Review Act. For different reasons, Wilson and Toohey JJ, in their joint judgment, and Brennan J held that the Act was inapplicable.[27] But Brennan J went on to suggest that 'if the exclusive foreign jurisdiction clause had been part of the contract of carriage, Greek law would probably have been held to be the proper law of the contract and the contract would thus have been outside the reach of the Contracts Review Act'.[28] This was because section 17(3)(a) of the Contracts Review Act provides that the Act applies to contracts of which New South Wales law is the proper law. Brennan J did not refer to section 17(3)(b), which states that the Act applies if 'the proper law of the contract would, but for a term that it should be the law of some other place or a term to the like effect, be the law of the State [of New South Wales]'.

[21] *The Ship Mill Hill* (n 3).

[22] *Oceanic* (n 4) 224 (Brennan J).

[23] ibid, 231 (Brennan J).

[24] ibid, 259 (Gaudron J).

[25] In the New South Wales Court of Appeal, Kirby P similarly referred to earlier commercial cases which took the view that 'the prima facie rule is that the parties should be held to their bargain', and made no allowance for the fact that Dr Fay was a consumer: *Oceanic Sunline Special Shipping Co Inc v Fay* (1987) 8 NSWLR 242, 257. This starkly contrasts with the view he took in the New South Wales Court of Appeal in *Akai*, in which he insisted on the court's responsibility to enforce the Australian legislation, which he described as 'reforming' and 'beneficial': *Akai Pty Ltd v The People's Insurance Co Ltd* (1995) 8 ANZ Ins Cas 61-254, 75-839.

[26] *Oceanic* (n 4) 231. Gaudron J did not express a view as to whether there would have been strong reasons not to enforce the jurisdiction clause, if the clause had been agreed.

[27] Wilson and Toohey JJ stated that the claim under the legislation was out of time: ibid, 214; see Contracts Review Act 1980 (NSW), s 16. Brennan J held that because the jurisdiction clause was not agreed, it was not necessary to rely on the Contracts Review Act to exclude its effect: *Oceanic* (n 4) 230. Deane and Gaudron JJ, in their separate judgments, did not mention the legislation.

[28] ibid, 231.

While *Akai* was a jurisdictional dispute, the High Court of Australia also addressed aspects of contract choice of law.[29] In a series of cases decided between 1932 and 1939, the High Court established that the governing law of the contract is the law which the parties intended to apply, expressly or by implication; if no shared intention can be established, the applicable law is that with the closest connection to the contract.[30] These authorities had not been questioned before the decision in *Akai*. In *Oceanic*, Brennan and Gaudron JJ both stated that an exclusive jurisdiction clause was an indication of the parties' intentions as to the subjective proper law.[31]

Several cases decided by the High Court of Australia before *Akai* raised the question of the interaction between contract choice of law and the application of forum legislation. The parties' freedom to choose the applicable law, accepted in Australia in the early 1930s, is not unconstrained. In 1939, Latham CJ stated that 'Parties cannot by agreeing that their contract should be governed by the law of a foreign country exclude the operation of a "peremptory rule" otherwise applicable to their transaction.'[32] It is unusual for Australian legislation expressly to stipulate its intended scope of application, and so the court has on several occasions had to decide whether a generally worded statutory provision applies in a cross-border case. In some cases, the High Court relied on a presumption that the application of forum legislation was subject to the contract choice of law rule,[33] but more often, it has interpreted the legislation to determine the circumstances in which it was intended to apply, without reference to a choice of law analysis.[34] In *Kay's Leasing Corporation v Fletcher*, the latter approach was taken. In a famous passage, Kitto J emphatically rejected the former approach. He stated that:[35]

> Where a provision renders an agreement void for non-compliance by the parties or one of them with statutory requirements, especially where the requirements can be seen to embody a specific policy directed against practices which the legislature has deemed oppressive or unjust, a presumption that the agreements in contemplation are only those of which the law of the country is the proper law according to the rules

[29] This was because the governing law of the contract is the criterion of application of the Australian Insurance Contracts Act, and the plaintiff's claim relied on the application of that Act, as discussed further below.

[30] *Barcelo Electrolytic Zinc Co of Australasia Ltd* (1932) 48 CLR 391; *Merwin Pastoral Co Pty Ltd v Moolpa Pastoral Co Pty Ltd* (1933) 48 CLR 565; *Wanganui-Rangitikei Electric Power Board v Australian Mutual Provident Society* (1934) 50 CLR 581; *Mynott v Barnard* (1939) 62 CLR 68.

[31] *Oceanic* (n 4) 224–25 (Brennan J, describing this as a 'significant indicium' of the parties' intentions), 260 (Gaudron J, stating that 'A foreign jurisdiction clause may, but does not necessarily, indicate an intention that the contractual rights and obligations of the parties should be governed by the law of the agreed jurisdiction').

[32] *Mynott v Barnard* (1939) 62 CLR 68, 80.

[33] *Wanganui-Rangitikei Electric Power Board v Australian Mutual Provident Society* (1934) 50 CLR 581, 601; *Barcelo v Electrolytic Zinc Co of Australasia Ltd* (1932) 48 CLR 391, 423–25.

[34] *Kay's Leasing Corporation Pty Ltd v Fletcher* (1964) 116 CLR 124; *Freehold Land Investments Ltd v Queensland Estates Pty Ltd* (1970) 123 CLR 418.

[35] *Kay's Leasing* (n 34) 143.

of private international law has no apparent appropriateness to recommend it, and indeed, for a reason of special relevance here, it would produce a result which the legislature is not in the least likely to have intended. It would mean that provisions enacted as salutary reforms might be set at nought by the simple expedient adopted in the present case of inserting in an agreement a stipulation that validity should be the matter for the law of some other country.

Each of these four issues arose in *Akai v The People's Insurance Company*. *Akai* is a landmark Australian case in that it is the authority for a number of fundamental principles that arise in international commercial litigation. In particular, it clarified principles relevant to the effect of exclusive jurisdiction clauses and the contract choice of law rule. It also addressed the interaction of forum legislation and common law private international law principles.

B. The Facts

The plaintiff, Akai Pty Ltd, was incorporated in New South Wales. It was a wholly owned subsidiary of a Japanese company. In 1991, Akai took out a credit insurance policy with the defendant, the People's Insurance Company (PIC), which was incorporated in Singapore. PIC's standard form policy designated the Singaporean courts and Singaporean law, to which Akai objected. Akai counter-proposed Australian courts and Australian law, which PIC rejected. PIC then suggested English courts and English law. Akai, after taking legal advice, assented to that proposal and the policy was amended accordingly. Following that amendment, clause 9 of the policy provided, under the heading 'Governing Law', that 'This policy shall be governed by the laws of England. Any disputes arising from this policy shall be referred to the Courts of England.' This negotiation confirms intuitions that parties (or their advisors) will each prefer to designate their home courts and laws, will reject the designation of the counterparty's home courts and laws, and, in the event of such a stalemate, will agree to the courts and laws of an unconnected legal system as a neutral alternative. *Akai* is unusual in Australian cases in that the jurisdiction and choice of law provision was negotiated.

In 1992, Akai claimed indemnity under the policy of insurance. PIC rejected the claim, on the basis of several breaches by Akai. *Akai* is an especially interesting case because it was litigated in three jurisdictions: Australia, Singapore, and England. On 5 March 1993, Akai commenced proceedings both in Australia and England: first, in the Supreme Court of New South Wales seeking a declaration that PIC was liable to indemnify it under the policy; later on the same day, Akai commenced proceedings in the English High Court seeking similar relief but did not pursue those proceedings. The Australian proceedings were stayed in December 1993. An appeal to the New South Wales Court of Appeal was dismissed in April 1995; and the final appeal to the High Court of Australia was allowed in December 1996. That decision was not the end of the jurisdictional dispute. In March 1997, the High Court of Singapore issued an anti-suit injunction, which it discharged in June 1997.[36] Finally, in July 1997, the English High Court granted an anti-suit injunction restraining the continuation of the substantive Australian proceedings.[37]

The decision of the High Court of Australia is the focus of discussion in this chapter, but the decisions of the Singapore and English High Courts are considered, particularly in order to demonstrate the overall impact of the Australian decision.

C. The Australian Proceedings

This case involved a conflict of laws. Under English law, PIC would not have been liable to indemnify because of Akai's breaches of the insurance contract, whereas under Australian law, it would have been liable. This was because section 54 of the Australian Insurance Contracts Act modifies the common law by apportioning liability if the insured is in breach of its obligations, unless the breach did not cause or contribute to the loss, in which case the insurer may not refuse to indemnify. Akai's breaches had neither caused nor contributed to the loss.

While most Australian statutes do not explicitly stipulate their intended scope of application in international cases, the Insurance Contracts Act does. Subsection 8(1) relevantly states that 'the application of this Act extends to contracts of insurance and proposed contracts of insurance the proper law of which is or would be the law of' an Australian State or Territory. Subsection 8(2) elaborates that:

> For the purposes of subsection (1), where the proper law of a contract or proposed contract would, but for an express provision to the contrary included or to be included in the contract or in some other contract, be the law of a State or a Territory in which this Act applies or to which this Act extends, then, notwithstanding that provision, the proper law of the contract is the law of that State or Territory.

The Insurance Contracts Act also explicitly prohibits 'contracting out'. Subsection 52(1) provides that 'Where a provision of a contract of insurance … purports to exclude, restrict or modify, or would, but for this subsection, have the effect of excluding, restricting or modifying, to the prejudice of a person other than the insurer, the operation of this Act, the provision is void.' These three provisions were at the heart of the High Court's decision. The Act did not explicitly refer to jurisdiction clauses.

The appeal to the High Court was heard by a bench of five. On the central question of whether the jurisdiction clause should be enforced, Toohey,

[36] *People's Insurance Co Ltd v Akai Pty Ltd* [1998] 1 SLR 206.
[37] *Akai Pty Ltd v People's Insurance Co Ltd* [1998] 1 Lloyd's Rep 90 (Com Ct).

Gaudron and Gummow JJ, in the majority, insisted that ensuring the application of what they characterised as 'remedial' Australian legislation,[38] where it seemed probable that the English court would not apply it, required that the Australian proceedings should not be stayed. Dawson and McHugh JJ, in the minority, were firmly in favour of upholding the parties' agreement by ordering a stay. While they differed in the result, the majority and minority agreed on two important issues. First, both judgments endorsed the principle established by the High Court in the 1950s, that an exclusive foreign jurisdiction clause should be enforced absent strong grounds for non-enforcement.[39] This was an important clarification of the Australian law following *Oceanic* and *Voth*. As the minority said, cases in which there was an exclusive foreign jurisdiction clause 'should not be assimilated to a case in which a stay is sought on the basis of *forum non conveniens*'.[40] The minority also articulated the general test for whether a jurisdiction clause is exclusive, namely 'whether on its true construction the clause obliges the parties to resort to the relevant jurisdiction irrespective of whether the word exclusive is used'.[41]

The second issue on which the majority and minority agreed is that an exclusive jurisdiction clause is highly relevant in determining the parties' unexpressed intention as to the governing law of their contract.[42] The minority characterised such a clause as 'a strong indication' of the parties' intention.[43] The majority said that the jurisdiction clause 'would be significant in deciding whether the parties had selected a proper law which was not the law of [an Australian] State or Territory',[44] for the purposes of ascertaining the application of the Insurance Contracts Act. Whether they would necessarily regard a jurisdiction clause as always being such a significant indication of the parties' intention is unclear.

While the majority and minority agreed on those two issues, they strongly disagreed on three other issues: the relevance of the application of the Insurance Contracts Act to the jurisdictional dispute; whether there were strong grounds for non-enforcement of the jurisdiction clause; and whether the jurisdiction clause was void under section 52(1) as an attempt to 'contract out' of the Insurance Contracts Act.

In relation to the first issue on which the majority and minority disagreed, the majority took the view that the potential application of that Insurance Contracts Act was relevant to the jurisdictional dispute. They held that the Act applied, because they found that the governing law of the insurance contract was the law of New South Wales. Citing the passage from *Kay's Leasing Corporation v Fletcher* referred to above,[45] the majority held that the Act was intended to

[38] *Akai* (n 1) 431.
[39] ibid, 427–29, 444–45.
[40] ibid, 428.
[41] ibid, 425.
[42] ibid, 441–442.
[43] ibid, 425.
[44] ibid, 437.
[45] *Kay's Leasing* (n 34) 116, 124, 143 (Kitto J). The passage is quoted above at text to n 35.

apply to contracts the objective proper law of which is that of an Australian State or Territory.[46] The express choice of law term clearly had to be discounted, but they also found that the jurisdiction clause was 'an express provision to the contrary' within the meaning of subsection 8(2), and so like the choice of law clause, the jurisdiction clause should be excluded in determining the governing law of the insurance contract. Given that the contract had its closest connection to New South Wales, the Act applied.

The minority disagreed that the potential application of the Act was relevant, stating that:[47]

> it was unnecessary and premature to determine the proper law of the contract, whether applying or not applying s 8 of the Act. The application for a stay of the New South Wales proceedings could and should have been determined by reference to the choice of courts provision alone.

They insisted that the Act was not intended to prevent the parties to insurance contracts from agreeing to the exclusive jurisdiction of foreign courts. They stated that 'It would be a serious and far-reaching interference with the freedom of the parties to [international] contracts to prevent them from making provision to that effect. If that were the intention of the legislature one would expect, at least, express words.'[48]

Second, the majority and minority disagreed as to whether there were strong reasons not to enforce the jurisdiction clause. As already noted, the majority decided that the Insurance Contracts Act was applicable and that its applicability was relevant to the jurisdictional question. They stated that the question of the stay was 'to be determined on the footing that the Policy is a contract of insurance to which the Act' does apply.[49] Given their earlier observation that:[50]

> ss 52 and 8 manifest a legislative intent not only that there should be no power to contract out of the provisions of the Act, but also that the regime established by the Act should be respected as regards contracts the proper law of which is, or but for selection of another law would be, that of [an Australian] State or Territory,

and their view that this 'defeats evasion' of the Act,[51] it is no surprise that the majority found that there were strong reasons not to enforce the jurisdiction clause. There was no evidence as to whether the English court would apply section 54 of the Insurance Contract Act. Filling this 'evidentiary hiatus' by applying the 'common law rules of choice of law as they are understood in this

[46] *Akai* (n 1) 435–36. The majority did not refer to Brennan J's discussion in *Oceanic* concerning the application of the Contracts Review Act 1980 (NSW), s 17(3), which is in similar terms to s 8 of the Insurance Contracts Act. Brennan J took the view that, had the jurisdiction clause been agreed, it would have meant that the applicable law of the contract was Greek law, and hence that the Contracts Review Act would have been inapplicable: above, text to n 28.

[47] *Akai* (n 1) 424.

[48] ibid, 426.

[49] ibid, 444.

[50] ibid, 433.

[51] ibid.

country', the majority assumed that the English courts would not apply the Australian legislation.[52]

The majority declared that 'A stay may be refused where the foreign jurisdiction clause offends the public policy of the forum.'[53] In support, they cited subsection 9(2) of the Sea Carriage of Goods Act 1924 (Cth), which was in issue in *Compagnie des Messageries Maritimes v Wilson*.[54] As noted above, subsection 9(2) expressly invalidated contractual provisions which attempted to exclude the jurisdiction of Australian courts, whereas the Insurance Contracts Act did not explicitly invalidate jurisdiction clauses. The majority also cited *The 'Hollandia'*,[55] and a Canadian case, *Agro Co of Canada Ltd v The 'Regal Scout'*,[56] in both of which the court did not enforce a foreign jurisdiction clause where the foreign court would have imposed a lesser liability on the carrier than the forum court, contrary to the Hague-Visby and Hague Rules, in force in the UK and Canada respectively at the relevant times.

In determining the relevant public policy of the forum, the majority stated that 'considerations of public policy present in an Australian court may flow from, even if not expressly mandated by the terms of, the Constitution or statute in force in the Australian forum',[57] and that such public policy should be 'discerned from a consideration of the scope and purpose of the particular statute'.[58] The majority held that in this case, the policy of the Insurance Contracts Act was 'against the use of private engagements to circumvent its remedial provisions', and that upholding this policy was a strong reason for not enforcing the jurisdiction clause.[59]

The minority vehemently disagreed, holding that neither the contract's relatively close connection to New South Wales, nor that the fact that the English court would not apply the Insurance Contracts Act, were strong reasons for not enforcing the jurisdiction clause.[60]

The third difference between the majority and minority positions relates to whether the jurisdiction clause was void as an attempt to 'contract out' of the operation of the Insurance Contracts Act.[61] The majority held that it was not necessary to resolve the stay application solely on the basis that there was a strong reason for not enforcing the jurisdiction clause, and that the stay application could be determined directly by subsection 52(1). As explained above, this renders void any provision of an insurance policy which 'would have the effect of excluding, restricting or modifying, to the prejudice of a person other

[52] ibid, 444–45.
[53] ibid, 445.
[54] *Compagnie des Messageries Maritime v Wilson* [1954] HCA 62; (1954) 94 CLR 577. See text to n 11.
[55] *The Hollandia* [1983] AC 565.
[56] *Agro Co of Canada Ltd v The 'Regal Scout'* (1983) 148 DLR (3d) 412.
[57] *Akai* (n 1) 447.
[58] ibid.
[59] ibid.
[60] ibid, 429.
[61] Insurance Contracts Act 1984 (Cth), s 52(1).

than the insurer, the operation of this Act'. The majority held that Akai would be prejudiced if the Australian proceedings were stayed because it would be deprived of the benefit of section 54 of the Act if the proceedings were litigated in the English courts, and therefore that the jurisdiction clause was void.[62]

The minority disagreed, relying on their conclusion that the Insurance Contracts Act did not apply. They stated that 'the Act has no operation where the parties have agreed to have their disputes determined by the courts of another jurisdiction in circumstances where effect should be given to their intention by an Australian court'.[63]

Akai is also an important authority in Australia because, while it was a jurisdictional dispute, it addressed three important points of contract choice of law, which arose because the Insurance Contracts Act uses the criterion of the governing law of the contract to determine its scope of application. First, the majority corrected 'a classification stated in some texts and decisions to supply the methodology employed in ascertaining choice of law', referring in particular to 'a tripartite hierarchy of express, inferred and objective choice of law'.[64] The majority rejected criticisms that 'inferred choice is really no choice at all',[65] and held that 'the better view is that the first and second categories are but species of the one genus, that concerned with giving effect to the intention of the parties'.[66] The majority explained that 'It is not a question of implying a term as to choice of law. Rather it is one of whether, upon the construction of the contract …, the court properly may infer that the parties intended their contract to be governed by reference to a particular system of law.'[67]

The second, related, more controversial point of principle relating to contract choice of law which arises from the majority judgment in *Akai* concerns the application of the law of the forum to the issue of interpreting the contract to discern the parties' intention as to the governing law. In discussing the construction of the contract to ascertain the parties' inferred intention as to the applicable law, which the majority held required the court to consider 'the terms and nature of the contract and "the general circumstances of the case"', they cited a domestic Australian case on contractual construction,[68] implying that forum law should be applied to this question, without explaining why.

[62] *Akai* (n 1) 447–48.

[63] ibid, 427.

[64] ibid, 440, citing L Collins (ed), *Dicey & Morris on the Conflict of Laws,* 11th edn (London, Stevens & Sons, 1987) 1161–62; PM North, *Cheshire & North's Private International Law,* 11th edn (London, Butterworths, 1987) 457–461; EI Sykes and MC Pryles, *Australian Private International Law,* 3rd edn (Sydney, Law Book Co, 1991) 600–11; *US Surgical Corporation v Hospital Products* [1983] 2 NSWLR 157, 189–90.

[65] In this context, they cited PM North, *Private International Law Problems in Common Law Jurisdictions* (Dordrecht, Martinus Nijhoff, 1993) 105–06.

[66] *Akai* (n 1) 440.

[67] ibid, 441.

[68] Namely *Codelfa Construction Pty Ltd v State Rail Authority of NSW* (1982) 149 CLR 337, which, at the time *Akai* was decided, was the leading High Court authority on the construction of contracts.

Third, as already noted, both majority and minority stated that an exclusive jurisdiction clause is an indicator of the parties' intention that the law of the country of the courts designated in the jurisdiction clause is the governing law of the contract.[69] The minority suggested that an exclusive jurisdiction clause is a 'strong' indicator of such intention, while for the majority, the exclusive jurisdiction clause was decisive in indicating the parties' intention, in that they treated it as 'an express provision to the contrary', for the purposes of subsection 8(2) – in other words, as having the same effect as the express choice of law clause. The view of the minority should be preferred; an exclusive jurisdiction clause alone surely cannot always be a decisive indicator. The majority's view about the weight to be given to the jurisdiction clause should be confined to the context of interpreting subsection 8(2) of the Insurance Contracts Act.

While some aspects of the decision of the High Court of Australia are uncontroversial clarifications of principle, the majority's approach to enforcing negotiated jurisdiction clauses in commercial agreements is problematic. While the Australian courts clearly have a constitutional obligation to enforce forum legislation which directly invalidates foreign jurisdiction clauses, the nature of the public policy exception to enforcing exclusive foreign jurisdiction clauses articulated by the majority is not only difficult to justify in principle, but also difficult to apply in practice.[70] Peter Nygh suggested that *Akai* 'smack[s] strongly of judicial chauvinism', and pointed out that:[71]

> A policy whereby the forum discovers local unenunciated directions in legislation and applies them to bargains reached in ostensibly international commercial transactions does not assist certainty in international commerce, nor does it really assist the weaker party. It assists the relatively strong who want to escape their obligations.

In fact, the outcome of the jurisdictional dispute in the High Court of Australia ultimately did not actually assist Akai, because the People's Insurance Company subsequently applied to both the Singaporean and the English courts for injunctive relief to restrain Akai from continuing with the Australian proceedings. The decisions of those courts are briefly considered next.

D. The Singaporean Proceedings

In March 1997, three months after the decision of the High Court of Australia was handed down, the People's Insurance Company applied ex parte to the Singapore High Court for an anti-suit injunction restraining the continuance of the Australian proceedings. That injunction was initially granted but was discharged in June 1997. In discharging the injunction, Choo Han Teck JC

[69] *Akai* (n 1) 425, 441–42, see above, text to nn 42–44.

[70] R Garnett, 'The Enforcement of Jurisdiction Clauses in Australia' (1998) 21 *University of New South Wales Law Journal* 1, 21.

[71] P Nygh, *Autonomy in International Contracts* (Oxford, OUP, 1999) 170.

noted that neither party intended to litigate in Singapore (although the People's Insurance Company expected that any judgment against it would have to be enforced there),[72] and that Akai was not amenable to the jurisdiction of the Singaporean court.[73] He stated that 'the Singapore court should not assume the role of an international busybody and direct that the parties litigate in England when the English court may well decline to assume jurisdiction on the ground of *forum non conveniens*'.[74] The application for an anti-suit injunction in Singapore was, like the Australian proceedings, brought in breach of the parties' agreement to litigate exclusively in England, but this appears not to have been raised before the Singaporean court.[75]

E. The English Proceedings

Finally, in 1997, the People's Insurance Company applied to the English court, in which Akai had commenced proceedings on the same day in 1993 that it commenced proceedings in Australia. PIC counter-claimed against Akai for a declaration that Akai's claim was time-barred and sought summary judgment. PIC also sought anti-suit and anti-enforcement injunctions. In response, Akai applied to have PIC's counterclaim struck out or stayed. Thomas J held that the Australian decision was not binding on PIC, which he held had not submitted to the jurisdiction of the Australian courts.[76] The English court would give effect to the jurisdiction clause, which Thomas J emphasised was 'freely chosen'[77] after Akai had taken legal advice.[78] The English court would not, as a matter of comity, give effect to the High Court of Australia's decision, based as it was on upholding Australian public policy, even taking into account the insurance policy's 'very close connection with Australia'.[79] Thomas J refused to stay the English proceedings, and granted an anti-suit injunction to restrain Akai from continuing the Australian proceedings,[80] although he refused to grant an anti-enforcement injunction because there was no indication that Akai would breach

[72] *People's Insurance Co Ltd v Akai Pty Ltd* [1998] 1 SLR 206, 208.
[73] ibid, 209.
[74] ibid.
[75] TM Yeo, 'The Contractual Basis of the Enforcement of Exclusive and Non-exclusive Choice of Court Agreements' (2005) 17 *Singapore Academy of Law Journal* 306, 335. In the English proceedings, Thomas J held that PIC's application to the Singaporean court was 'unjustifiable', but that it did not disentitle PIC from the grant of an anti-suit injunction by the English court: *Akai* (n 37) 108. He held that Akai should be compensated 'by an indemnity against all the expense to which they have been wrongly put in Singapore': ibid.
[76] *Akai* (n 37) 98.
[77] ibid, 100.
[78] ibid, 93.
[79] ibid, 100.
[80] ibid, 108. This was granted on terms that PIC indemnify Akai against the costs of the Singaporean proceedings, and discontinue the Singaporean proceedings.

the anti-suit injunction.[81] He stated that 'there are very powerful arguments that it is more consistent with comity to leave it to the Courts in Singapore to decide what course to take in the light of their own law', in terms of the effect of any eventual judgment that might be awarded against PIC.[82]

F. The Australian, Singaporean and English Proceedings Taken Together

This trilogy of cases demonstrates, in case there was any doubt of it, the futility of the High Court of Australia's insistence on retaining jurisdiction, in an attempt to preserve and ensure the application of Australian legislation. As important as a particular policy might be to Australian legislators and judges, attempting to ensure the application of such a policy in litigation involving foreign defendants, where legally advised commercial parties had agreed in advance to litigate exclusively in another court, is likely to present challenges, particularly when any judgment will require enforcement in a foreign jurisdiction.[83] For the reasons stressed by Thomas J in the English proceedings (ie that the choice of court and choice of law clause was specifically negotiated and agreed, and that Akai was legally advised in the negotiation), protecting a commercial party like Akai was a questionable use of scarce judicial resources.[84] Admittedly, difficulty in enforcing a judgment is an ever-present risk in international litigation, and this risk cannot be controlled by the courts of any country. Although there may sometimes be compelling reasons for a court to retain jurisdiction, even though the recognition of its eventual orders might seem doubtful,[85] it is suggested that *Akai* was clearly not such a case.

III. THE IMPACT OF AKAI

Akai is the most recent authority of the High Court in terms of the effect of exclusive foreign jurisdiction clauses, the role of public policy as a strong reason for non-enforcement of a foreign jurisdiction clause, and the basic contract choice of law rule. The first and third of these are uncontroversial. But the majority's

[81] ibid, 108.

[82] ibid.

[83] FMB Reynolds, 'Overriding Policy of the Forum: The Other Side of the Coin' [1998] *Lloyd's Maritime and Commercial Law Quarterly* 1, 3.

[84] Garnett preferred the view of the minority 'especially since, in this case, there was no evidence of any inequality in bargaining power between the parties which may have justified legislative intervention': Garnett (n 70) 22.

[85] The most obvious example is where the litigation involves public interests: see *Humane Society International Inc v Kyodo Senpaku Kaisha Ltd* [2006] FCAFC 116. But 'public interests' is an imprecise category, and it has been recently successfully been asserted in a commercial case to ensure that a foreign jurisdiction clause was not enforced: *Epic Games, Inc v Apple Inc* [2021] FCAFC 122, discussed below at text to nn 96–98.

endorsement, and its specific formulation, of public policy as a strong reason for not enforcing foreign jurisdiction clauses remains problematic in commercial cases and obscure in consumer cases.

The protective attitude adopted by the majority in *Akai* might be justified in the consumer setting, in which jurisdiction clauses are not negotiated, are unlikely to have been comprehended by consumers, and impose disproportionate burdens of cost and inconvenience on consumers. As already explained, Australian private international law does not clearly differentiate commercial from consumer transactions, although some Australian judges have remarked that these types of transactions require different responses.[86] In most consumer cases, exclusive jurisdiction clauses are held not to have been agreed.[87] If the clause is held to have been agreed, the courts are likely to find that there are strong reasons not to enforce the foreign jurisdiction clause if the consumer relies on protective Australian legislation.[88] As a result, Australian courts rarely enforce jurisdiction clauses in consumer cases. This is not objectionable.

On the other hand, the Australian courts' record in enforcing exclusive jurisdiction clauses in commercial cases is mixed.[89] In some cases, Australian courts have insisted on strictly enforcing exclusive jurisdiction clauses, even where the plaintiff has invoked forum legislation,[90] and occasionally, even where there are third parties to the jurisdiction clause.[91] *Global Partners Fund Ltd v Babcock & Brown Ltd (in liq)*,[92] a 2010 decision of the New South Wales Court of Appeal, is an influential example. Spigelman CJ stated that:[93]

> the case law with respect to exclusive jurisdiction clauses is clear and unequivocal. The cases reflect important policy considerations, relevantly, that parties should be held to their contractual bargains and that resolution of disputes arising from contractual arrangements should occur in a coherent and consistent manner and as expeditiously and efficaciously as possible.

While noting that the Australian courts' record in upholding exclusive jurisdiction clauses was inconsistent, Richard Garnett suggested in 2013 that Australian

[86] *Quinlan v Safe International Försäkrings AB* [2005] FCA 1362 [46].

[87] *Knight v Adventure Associates Pty Ltd* [1999] NSWSC 861; *Hargood v OHTL Public Company Ltd* [2015] NSWSC 446. An exception is *Gonzalez* (n 18).

[88] *Quinlan* (n 86) [50]; *Karpik v Carnival plc (The 'Ruby Princess') (Stay Application)* [2021] FCA 1082.

[89] Garnett (n 70); R Garnett, 'Jurisdiction Clauses Since Akai' (2013) 87 *Australian Law Journal* 134.

[90] See, eg, *Nicola v Ideal Image Development Corporation Inc* [2009] FCA 1177.

[91] *Global Partners Fund v Babcock & Brown* [2010] NSWCA 196 [71]–[80]; *Yperion Technology SAS v Luminex Pty Ltd* [2012] FCA 554. More recent cases have taken a stricter approach to the 'party scope' of exclusive jurisdiction clauses: *Babcock & Brown DIF III Global Co-Investment Fund, LP v Babcock & Brown International Pty Ltd* [2016] VSC 623; *Australian Health & Nutrition Association Ltd v Hive Marketing Group Pty Ltd* [2019] NSWCA 61 [90] and *Urban Moto Imports Pty Ltd v KTM AG* [2021] VSC 616 [63].

[92] *Global Partners Fund Ltd v Babcock & Brown Ltd (in liq)* [2010] NSWCA 196.

[93] ibid, [84].

courts had, since *Akai* was decided, become 'more supportive of jurisdiction clauses'.[94]

Notwithstanding Spigelman CJ's suggestion in 2010 that the case law was 'clear and unequivocal', and Garnett's observation of an improvement in the Australian courts' record in enforcing jurisdiction clauses in commercial disputes, a trend has recently emerged in which Australian courts seem inclined to accept arguments that the availability in Australian proceedings of claims under Australian legislation is a strong reason justifying non-enforcement of a foreign jurisdiction clause.[95] *Epic Games, Inc v Apple Inc* is a recent example in which the Full Court of the Federal Court of Australia refused to enforce a foreign jurisdiction clause because it offended 'the public policy of the forum'.[96] According to the Full Court, the plaintiffs' claims under Australian competition law raised important issues of Australian public policy which should be heard by Australian courts, requiring the plaintiff to litigate in the designated US forum would deprive it of 'legitimate forensic advantages',[97] and in addition, the jurisdiction clause did not bind a legitimate third party to the Australian proceedings.[98] While protecting consumers from foreign jurisdiction clauses, which are likely effectively to exclude foreign suppliers' liability, is laudable, the justifications for protecting commercial parties are far more debatable. One is left wondering about the overall purpose of doing so unless the case involves unusually significant issues of forum policy, given the likely futility of any Australian orders, and the distinct possibility that the designated foreign court will enjoin the continuation of Australian proceedings. As Raphael suggested, 'There may be cases where naked national self-interest dictates a particular rule, but they are likely to be a regrettable breach of comity, and will find little sympathy elsewhere.'[99]

While *Akai* is a landmark case in Australia, it has had a muted response internationally. It has attracted little attention in Canada[100] and New Zealand,[101] and

[94] Garnett (n 89) 134.

[95] *Commonwealth Bank of Australia v White* [1999] VSC 262, [89]; *Lew Footwear Holdings v Madden International* [2014] VSC 320, [235].

[96] *Epic Games* (n 85) [90], citing the majority in *Akai* (n 1) 445.

[97] *Epic Games* (n 85) [84], [122].

[98] ibid, [76].

[99] T Raphael, 'Do As You Would be Done By? System-transcendent Justification and Anti-suit Injunctions' [2016] *Lloyd's Maritime and Commercial Law Quarterly* 256, 256–57.

[100] CanLII lists only two references to it, both of which are to the judgment of the minority of the Supreme Court of Canada in *Douez v Facebook, Inc* 2017 SCC 33, [2017] 1 SCR 751 [148] (in which the minority also cites UK, US and New Zealand case law in support of its statement that 'Forum selection clauses are well-established and routinely enforced around the world').

[101] Hook and Wass include only two references to *Akai: The Conflict of Laws in New Zealand* (Auckland, LexisNexis, 2020) 160 (fn 975) (citing the Australian decision in *Akai* in the context of a brief discussion of *The Hollandia* [1983] AC 565 (HL)) and 177 (fn 1097) (citing the decisions of both the Australian and English courts in *Akai* in the context of whether it is appropriate to issue an anti-suit injunction to prevent the breach of an exclusive jurisdiction clause, suggesting that the New Zealand court, designated in an exclusive jurisdiction clause, should take an internationalist approach and 'simply trust the foreign court to do the right thing'). NZLII lists no references to *Akai*, which is notable given that the New Zealand and Australian legal systems are generally close.

while it is noted in English works,[102] the decision of Thomas J in the English High Court, reacting negatively to the decision of the High Court of Australia by granting an anti-suit injunction, has been more influential.

IV. CONCLUSION

Like other cases included in this collection,[103] *Akai* demonstrates that landmark cases are not necessarily without controversy. The decision of the High Court of Australia manifests a parochial tendency, also evident in other aspects of Australian private international law,[104] albeit that this is not a consistent feature.[105] Parochialism lends itself to forum shopping, and in the context of exclusive jurisdiction clauses, to manipulation by well-resourced commercial parties seeking to avoid their contractual obligations. This anti-internationalist characteristic of some aspects of Australian private international law is unfortunate, and it is regrettable that at the time of writing in April 2022, it appears to be enjoying a resurgence.

[102] See, eg, Lord Collins (ed), *Dicey, Morris & Collins on the Conflict of Laws,* 15th edn (London, Sweet & Maxwell 2012) paras 1-058, 12R-098, 12-117, 12-151, 32-007, 32-085, 32-092, 33-171, 33-085 and 32-092; A Briggs, *Agreements on Jurisdiction and Choice of Law* (Oxford, OUP, 2008) paras 6.49, 11.23, 11.26, 11.62, 11.81 and 11.83.

[103] See, eg, ch 9 in this volume.

[104] These include the Australian version of *forum non conveniens* (see text to n 13), the application of forum law to determine whether a jurisdiction clause was agreed (see text to nn 19–20), and the application of forum law to determine, as a matter of contractual construction, whether it is possible to ascertain the parties' unexpressed intention as to the applicable law of the contract (see text to n 68).

[105] For example, as noted above, Australia is a contracting state to 11 Hague Conventions (n 2), some of which materially altered the pre-existing principles, such as the 1996 Hague Convention on Jurisdiction, Applicable Law, Recognition, Enforcement and Co-operation in Respect of Parental Responsibility and Measures for the Protection of Children.

15

Canada Trust Co v Stolzenberg (No 2) (2002)

PIPPA ROGERSON

I. INTRODUCTION

LORD STEYN IN *Canada Trust Co v Stolzenberg (No 2)*[1] approved Waller LJ's articulation of the concept of the 'good arguable case' as the standard of proof necessary to justify a claimant's use of a ground under RSC Ord 11 (now a gateway under CPR PD 6B) such that the English court can exercise jurisdiction over a dispute with a defendant not present within the territorial jurisdiction to be served with the claim form. Known as the '*Canada Trust* gloss', Waller LJ explained the good arguable case is a standard 'which reflects that the plaintiff must properly satisfy the court that it is right for the court to take jurisdiction'.[2] It is also a concept that has to take into account the context of an interlocutory determination in which evidence is not tested by examination and the decision should be speedy. There is a tension between those objectives. No wonder that it is a concept 'not capable of very precise definition'.[3] Waller LJ settled on the claimant having 'much the better of the argument'.[4]

The good arguable case test is not limited to the gateways in CPR PD 6B. It is also used for other interlocutory determinations in matters of jurisdiction such as deciding the validity and scope of a jurisdiction agreement.[5] The test is used to decide the availability of a freezing injunction,[6] and there is statutory

[1] *Canada Trust Co v Stolzenberg (No 2)* [1998] 1 WLR 547 (CA) and [2002] AC 1 (HL).
[2] *Canada Trust (n 1) (CA)* 555.
[3] ibid.
[4] ibid.
[5] Jurisdiction agreements conferring jurisdiction on the English courts will fall under the Hague Convention on Choice of Court Agreements 2005, unless expressly non-exclusive. There is no role for a discretionary stay of English proceedings. Nonetheless, a challenge to the validity or scope of a jurisdiction agreement covering the dispute will have to be determined at an interlocutory decision to the standard of a good arguable case as was the case at before the Convention came into force.
[6] *Kazakhstan Kagazy Plc v Arip* [2014] EWCA Civ 381, [2014] 1 CLC 451.

reference to 'good arguable case' in some legislative provisions.[7] It is probably correct, but not articulated, that the good arguable case applies to the exercise of discretion in *forum conveniens* in which matters of fact are in issue. That is for the same reasons that the good arguable case is appropriate for the determination of the gateway. Any factual issue necessary for decision at an interlocutory stage should not be subject to the standard appropriate at trial. It has also been cited in much litigation.[8] At few recent cases in the Supreme Court have revisited the concept, seeking a clearer exposition than the *Canada Trust* gloss. Lady Hale disliked glosses,[9] and Lord Sumption preferring a three-part test based on 'plausible evidence'.[10] However, clarity remains illusive.

Canada Trust is not at first blush an obvious contender for a landmark case in private international law. It was a case decided under the Brussels Regulation.[11] Therefore the particular basis of jurisdiction relied upon, domicile of the defendant, is no longer of such force after Brexit. Nevertheless, the facts of the case and its reasoning are all the more salient now that jurisdiction of the English courts is solely within the common law rules. It is perhaps a case deciding a 'boring' matter of procedure. But the question of the standard of evidence which a claimant has to prove at the earliest stage of the case in order to justify the jurisdiction of the English court is a problematic one. First, the standard is a bulwark to counter the tendency to privilege the English court at the expense of the defendant. It requires the claimant to provide enough evidence to justify the exercise of jurisdiction. Second, the standard balances the practicalities of deciding jurisdictional matters with dispatch and efficiency with the countervailing pressure of the parties to contest jurisdiction to the utmost. Third, the standard becomes fraught when the issues contested go both to the matter of jurisdiction but also could be critical to resolution of the dispute at trial.

Although finally determined by the House of Lords, the issue of the good arguable case test discussed in this chapter was actually decided in the Court of Appeal. It is a rather incremental decision. It does not signal some sharp change of direction on a substantive rule. Nevertheless, in practice questions of jurisdiction are critical. Whether a claimant can bring their dispute to be determined as a matter of substance in the English court should be reasonably predictable. Not just for the claimant but also the defendant. Both sides deserve clear indication of whether the English court has and will exercise jurisdiction over their dispute. Being party to proceedings in England is not for the faint-hearted nor for those

[7] See, eg, Proceeds of Crime Act 2002, ss 254A, 246 and 255A; Serious Organised Crime and Police Act 2005, s 98. On the 2002 Act, see *The Director of the Assets Recovery Agency v Szeplietowski* [2007] EWCA Civ 766.

[8] Since 2000, it has been referred to in 234 reported decisions of the High Court, of which 45 were in the Court of Appeal and has been discussed in 3 decisions of the Supreme Court or Privy Council (as at 23 February 2022).

[9] *Brownlie v Four Seasons Holdings Inc* [2017] UKSC 80, [2018] 1 WLR 192 [33].

[10] ibid, [7].

[11] Regulation (EC) No 44/2001.

short of ready cash. Expending a great deal of time and more expense in making that determination has been rightly criticised with a plea for a proportionate approach to matters of jurisdiction.[12] The good arguable case has a pivotal role to play not merely deciding the matter of jurisdiction by the court, but also as importantly, in facilitating lawyers giving predictable advice on the likelihood of success in an argument on jurisdiction before the dispute ever reaches court. Every case in private international law therefore requires a consideration of whether a good arguable case has been made out such that the case should be heard in England. The *Canada Trust* decision itself has been referred to in some 234 reported cases since 2000 and recently been reviewed afresh by the Supreme Court. It has been extensively discussed in the secondary literature.[13]

II. THE DECISION IN CANADA TRUST

In *Canada Trust* the claimants were Canadian trustees of a Canadian pension fund which had lost Can$240 million (£120 million) after fraudulent misrepresentations made by the first defendant induced loans to a company which became bankrupt owing Can$1.8 billion. The claimants alleged that the other defendants were aware of and were party to the fraudulent misrepresentations. In 1996 the claimants issued the claim in the English court for damages, knowing receipt of the funds, and dishonest assistance, basing jurisdiction on the first defendant's domicile in England. At the time, the Brussels Regulation required the courts of the Member State of the defendant's domicile to take jurisdiction. Domicile is defined in section 41 of the Civil Jurisdiction and Judgments Act 1982. A person is domiciled in England if they are resident in England and the nature and circumstances of their residence indicate a substantial connection with England. Domicile under this provision therefore required determination of facts (identification of a place of residence), and of intention (a quality of

[12] See, eg, *VTB Capital plc v Nutritek International Corp* [2013] UKSC 5, [2013] 2 AC 337 [81]; *Vedanta Resources plc v Lungowe* [2019] UKSC 20, [2020] AC 1045 [6]; *Okpabi v Royal Dutch Shell plc* [2021] UKSC 3, [2021] 1 WLR 1294 [20]. The latter two cases were questioning whether there was a serious issue to be tried on the merits rather than a good arguable case on jurisdiction. Even on that lower test, both were only finally decided by the Supreme Court. See further ch 19 in this volume for criticism.

[13] In addition to L Collins (ed), *Dicey, Morris & Collins on The Conflict of Laws*, 15th edn (London, Sweet & Maxwell, 2012) paras 11–145–11-147, see, eg, E Crawford 'The Uses of Putativity and Negativity in the Conflict of Laws' (2005) 54 *International & Comparative Law Quarterly* 829; J Weale 'A Good Arguable Case for Restricting the Canada Trust Gloss' [2010] *Journal of Business Law* 36; I Bergson, 'Service out in the Supreme Court' (2018) 134 *Law Quarterly Review* 344; W Day, 'Jurisdictional Gateways in the CPR' (2018) 77 *Cambridge Law Journal* 36; A Dickinson 'Faulty Powers: One-Star Service in the English Courts' [2018] *Lloyd's Maritime and Commercial Law Quarterly* 189; A Dickinson 'Lax Standards' (2019) 135 *Law Quarterly Review* 369; L Gillies 'Appropriate Adjustments post Brexit: Residual Jurisdiction and Forum non Conveniens in the UK Courts' [2020] *Journal of Business Law* 161; D Foxton, 'The Jurisdictional Gateways – Some (very) Modest Proposals' [2022] *Lloyd's Maritime and Commercial Law Quarterly* 71.

residence as a place of 'settled abode'). In complex cases, the latter is especially contentious, as the plentiful cases on the common law of domicile and those for the purposes of section 41 indicate.[14]

The 36 other defendants[15] were not within the jurisdiction to be served with the claims in knowing receipt and dishonest assistance. The claimants sought to join those defendants either as 'necessary and proper parties' under RSC Ord 11 r 1(1)(f)[16] or the equivalent provision under the Brussels Regulation (or the Lugano Convention). The only issue we are concerned with here is the standard of proof for the basis of jurisdiction of the first defendant's domicile. The claimants had asserted the first defendant's domicile was in England. The first defendant was known to have a house in which he resided in London until some time in 1997. However, as that defendant was not before the court this assertion of domicile was not challenged by him, but by the other defendants. Without the presence of the first defendant before the court the decision on his domicile was clearly only impressionistic. He also had residences in Canada and Frankfurt.

How could his intention to make England his 'settled abode' be proven to any degree of satisfaction? This was a crucial part of the English court's jurisdiction, on which everything else turned. The extensive case against the other defendants could *only* be heard in England if the first defendant's domicile was established. The other defendants had insufficient connection with England to justify a separate ground of jurisdiction. Inspecting the case from their perspective,[17] those defendants could not have reasonably expected to have to defend themselves in England against a case founded in fraudulent misrepresentations made by an international businessman by which a Canadian pension fund made loans to a Canadian company.

A. The Decisions at First Instance, in the Court of Appeal and in the House of Lords

Rattee J at first instance had applied the test of the 'good arguable case' to determine the defendant's domicile and refused to accept the alternative test of 'on the balance of probabilities'.[18] The latter is the standard at which a judge must be satisfied at the trial of the substantive issues before a court. Where all the evidence can be tested by testimony and examination after proper disclosure.

[14] See, eg, cases cited in *Mark v Mark* [2005] UKHL 42, [2006] 1 AC 98 and in *OJSC Oil Company Yugraneft (in liquidation) v Abramovich* [2008] EWHC 2613 (Comm) in which Mr Abramovich's domicile for the purposes of s 41 CJJA 1982 took extensive judicial determination at [440]–[487].

[15] Later increased to at least 54 defendants.

[16] Now a gateway under CPR PD 6B.

[17] And fast forward to *Brownlie* (n 9) and *FS Cairo (Nile Plaza) LLC v Brownlie* [2021] UKSC 45, [2021] 3 WLR 1011 the same argument can be made for those defendants. See further ch 18 in this volume.

[18] *Canada Trust Co v Stolzenberg (No 2)* [1997] 5 WLUK 639.

In comparison, the 'good arguable case' is a test which applies at an interlocutory stage. That is before disclosure has been given by each side of documentary evidence relevant to the substance of the dispute. Interlocutory hearings are necessarily imperfect, where evidence is solely documentary, and without challenge of the evidence by oral examination. At first instance therefore, the question was whether good arguable case captured the standard or whether a higher standard, appropriate to determine issues at trial was preferable.

In the Court of Appeal,[19] Waller LJ held that the correct standard of proof had been articulated by Lord Goff in the House of Lords in *Seaconsar (Far East) Ltd v Bank Markazi Jomhouri Islami Iran*.[20] That case, building on earlier authorities, had established that the words 'No such leave shall be granted unless it shall be made sufficiently to appear' in RSC Ord 11[21] directed the court to be *properly satisfied* that the claimant has made out the case of the court's jurisdiction. That case also drew a distinction between the lower standard of 'a serious issue to be tried' in relation to the merits of the claim and the higher standard of 'a good arguable case' as to matters of jurisdiction. Waller LJ clarified the difference between what standard was necessary at trial of the substance of the dispute (the balance of probabilities), and what was practicable at the interlocutory stage. For the latter, where jurisdiction is in issue, he was content to use a 'good arguable case' as reflecting 'the context that one side has a much better argument on the material available'.[22] Nonetheless, Waller LJ was frank that 'what the court is endeavouring to do is find a concept not capable of very precise definition'.[23] He concluded that the good arguable case has to be contextualised:[24]

> It is the concept which the phrase reflects on which is important to concentrate, ie of the court being satisfied or as satisfied as it can be having regard to the limitations which an interlocutory process imposes that factors exist which allow the court to take jurisdiction.

Nourse LJ noted that there had been confusion over the meaning of good arguable case and serious issue to be tried as 'these expressions can mean different things to different minds' but that there was no doubt that the balance of probabilities was not appropriate to a question as to jurisdiction.[25]

The House of Lords did not call upon the plaintiffs to deal with the issue of the standard of proof but agreed that it was the good arguable case rather than

[19] *Canada Trust (CA)* (n 1) 553.

[20] *Seaconsar (Far East) Ltd v Bank Markazi Jomhouri Islami Iran* [1994] 1 AC 438 (HL).

[21] Now expressed in CPR r 6.36 as 'The court will not give permission unless *satisfied* that England and Wales is the proper place in which to bring the claim' (emphasis added).

[22] *Canada Trust (CA)* (n 1) 555.

[23] ibid.

[24] ibid.

[25] ibid, 572–73.

the balance of probabilities. There was no explicit reference to the meaning of the concept other than approval of that part of Waller LJ's judgment.[26]

B. Critique

Canada Trust was on its facts a hard case, in which objective justification for the exercise of jurisdiction by the English court is not readily found. In an earlier judgment in the litigation, Millett LJ considered that there was no natural forum 'other than perhaps Canada'.[27] Plainly, Canada was much more obviously the natural forum than England. The defrauded claimants were Canadian, the defrauded money came from Canadian pension funds, the first defendant had a house in Canada as well as London, most of the events giving rise to the fraud had occurred in Canada, and the loss to the pension fund had been felt in Canada. The post-fraud events were connected to parties around the world who were not themselves subject to the English court's jurisdiction. The only explicit connection with England was that the first defendant had a house there (where he lived after his companies became insolvent), and an allegation that some of the transactions occurred there. It might be thought that money passed through accounts in London, though that point was not made by Waller LJ. In total it appears clear that there was less significant connection with England than with Canada.

In the event, the Canadian courts dealt with the insolvency of the Canadian companies and charged Stolzenberg with fraud. As there was no extradition treaty with Germany, Stolzenberg remained at liberty. The following cases in Canada against the accountants Coopers & Lybrand resulting in the longest trial there, at over 23 years. Canada was the court better placed to determine all the issues, including those against the other defendants.

At the time of the case, jurisdiction against the first and other major defendants fell within the Brussels regime, in which natural forum plays no part. The first defendant's domicile was critical as a general ground of jurisdiction. Nonetheless, the gateway of jurisdiction was based on the defendant's domicile in England, even if that defendant is not present within the jurisdiction to be served, remains in CPR PD 6B. A similar case would be decided in the same way. All that is needed to ground jurisdiction is a good arguable case that the anchor defendant is domiciled in England, and bring in other defendants as 'necessary and proper parties'. A requirement that England is the *forum conveniens* remains the backstop against excessive resort to the jurisdiction of the English court.

We know that 'fraud unravels all' as a defence to recognition of foreign judgments.[28] The facts of this case were entirely couched in a huge international

[26] *Canada Trust (HL)* (n 1) 13 (Lord Steyn).
[27] *Canada Trust Co v Stolzenberg* [1997] 1 WLR 1582 (CA) 1585.
[28] See ch 6 in this volume.

fraud. The initial application was not for the substance of the dispute to be heard in England but for protective relief: worldwide freezing orders to freeze the assets in dispute and ancillary disclosure orders. In practice those were probably the critical matters for the claimants. In order to be able to obtain that protective relief, the claimants also had to be able to commence proceedings on the substance of the dispute. As matters turned out, the main case against Stolzenberg appears to have been dropped in favour of pursuing the other defendants Gambazzi (a Swiss Attorney), other individuals, and two companies Mora and Chascona. That action resulted in default judgments of the English court of Can$480 million plus US$269 million.[29] In effect, there was never a trial of the facts of the dispute. The enormity of the sums at issue, and the recalcitrant behaviour of the defendants (both at the time of the events and during the dispute) must have skewed the outcome towards determination in England of a case which had no prior connection with England at all. All because there was apparently a 'good arguable case' that one man was domiciled in England. It is remarkable that neither the substantive nor the jurisdictional case against the first defendant was ever made out in England.

III. CASES AFTER CANADA TRUST

The *Canada Trust* test of a much better argument on the material available was approved specifically by Lord Rodger in *Bols Distilleries BV v Superior Yacht Services Ltd*,[30] and by Lord Collins in *AK Investment CJSC v Kyrgyz Mobil Tel Ltd*.[31] However, later cases have understood that Waller LJ's test for the good arguable case in *Canada Trust* resulted in a gloss. The gloss is particularly in point when the claimant is seeking the permission of the court to serve the claim form out of the jurisdiction without notice to the defendant. At this stage judges should be most alert to allegations which have not been tested. Once the defendant has been served and returns to challenge the permission given, the judge can decide between arguments made by each party. The gloss at that point may do no more than reiterate that it is the claimant that bears the burden of satisfying the judge that England is the best place for trial. At the earlier stage, however, it focusses attention on ensuring that the defendant is not drawn into spending time, trouble and expense to challenge an unwarranted exercise of jurisdiction. At either stage the standard to be applied in determining whether there is a good arguable case on jurisdiction is not as high as the balance of probabilities. That is for two reasons. There is at this point of proceedings no disclosure nor trial of the evidence and the court should not be drawn into pre-judging issues which

[29] *CIBC Mellon Trust Company v Stolzenberg* [2003] EWHC 13 (Ch).
[30] *Bols Distilleries BV v Superior Yacht Services Ltd* [2006] UKPC 45, [2007] 1 WLR 12 [26]–[28].
[31] *AK Investment CJSC v Kyrgyz Mobil Tel Ltd* [2011] UKPC 7 [71].

might arise at trial for final determination.[32] Also, jurisdictional disputes should not be permitted to consume vast quantities of time and expense. However, mere allegations by the claimant have to be tested in the defendant's favour before committing the defendant to the inconvenience and expense of defence in England.[33]

Cases after *Canada Trust* continued to dissect whether a good arguable case needed 'much' or just 'a better' argument. In *JSC 'Aeroflot Russian Airlines' v Berezovksy*,[34] Aikens LJ disliked 'much' as running the risk of imposing too high a standard of proof at the interlocutory stage. However, most cases up to *Brownlie*[35] adopted the 'much better argument' as the test that the claimant had to show to satisfy a good arguable case. In *Cherney v Deripaska*,[36] Christopher Clarke J said that avoiding a concluded view of the merits when applying the good arguable case test can be achieved by treating the decision as an assessment of the arguments which he distinguished from a determination of fact. Others, such as Beatson LJ in *Trust Risk Group SpA v AmTrust Europe Ltd*[37] drew a distinction between a jurisdictional issue which raises a question of law – which should be decided at the interlocutory stage[38] – and one which raises a matter of fact, which only needs to be arguable. The former can include the interpretation of a gateway, such as was in issue in the *Brownlie* cases. As has been already noted, the test of a good arguable case laid out in *Canada Trust* has been used for many jurisdictional and similar issues. Although the same test is apparently used – the relevant party has to show a much better argument – the outcome is context driven. For example, showing a much better argument is the standard to determine if the parties are the same for the purposes of Article 27 of the Brussels Regulation.[39] Where proceedings between the same parties and on the same cause of action are already continuing in another Member State, the proceedings in the court not first seised have to be stayed. Here, the good arguable case is part of a challenge to jurisdiction otherwise properly established. The defendant must show the good arguable case.

In *Bols Distilleries BV v Superior Yacht Services Ltd*,[40] the claimant failed to show much the better argument that a Gibraltarian jurisdiction agreement

[32] *Erste Group Bank AG v JSC 'VMZ Red October'* [2013] EWHC 2926 (Comm) [8]–[15] (Flaux J).

[33] *Trust Risk Group SpA v AmTrust Europe Ltd* [2015] EWCA Civ 437, [2016] 1 All ER (Comm) 325 [41] (Beatson LJ) and [74] (Christopher Clarke LJ). Both Beatson LJ and Christopher Clarke LJ used the protection of the defendant as a justification both for a 'much the better of' argument and for being less circumspect in overturning the first instance judge's decision.

[34] *JSC 'Aeroflot Russian Airlines' v Berezovksy* [2013] EWCA Civ 784, [2013] 2 Lloyd's Rep 242.

[35] *Brownlie* (n 9).

[36] *Cherney v Deripaska* [2008] EWHC 1530 (Comm) [19]–[44].

[37] *Trust Risk* (n 33) [35].

[38] See too *VTB Capital Plc v Nutritek International Corp* [2012] EWCA Civ 808, [2012] 2 Lloyd's Rep 313 [99] (Lloyd LJ) and *Chellaram v Chellaram (No 2)* [2002] EWHC 632 (Ch), [2002] 3 All ER 17 [136] (Lawrence Collins J).

[39] *Kolden Holdings Ltd v Rodette Commerce Ltd* [2008] EWCA Civ 1468. Now Regulation (EU) No 1215/2012, art 29.

[40] *Bols Distillery* (n 30) [28].

was incorporated into a contract for the purposes of Article 23 of the Brussels Regulation.[41] Lord Rodger noted that the good arguable case here performed a role in ensuring that the effectiveness of the Regulation would not be impaired. This was clearly the right result. Jurisdiction under the Brussels Regulation operated within a rule-based (not discretionary) schema. Exceptional jurisdiction, such as that based on agreement in Article 23, required a high degree of certainty in order to remove the defendant from the general jurisdiction of the court of the defendant's domicile. Likewise much the better argument was used to assess the required consent to an agreement on jurisdiction for Brussels I Regulation, Article 23.

In contrast, *Antonio Gramsci Shipping Corp v Recoletos Ltd* raised more complex factual and legal matters at the jurisdictional stage.[42] Was there a good arguable case that the controller of a corporate body was bound by a jurisdiction agreement in a contract which the claimants alleged the controller required the corporate body to enter into? Answering that matter involved serious issues of corporate law in piercing the corporate veil, factual matters as to the relationship between the controller and the company, as well as purely jurisdictional questions on the effect of Article 23. The first two were also likely to be in issue at the trial of the substance of the dispute. Focussing only on the last Beatson LJ, after careful inspection of Teare J's decision at first instance, agreed with that judge that the claimant had not made out the case for Article 23 to apply. It had not had 'the better of the argument'. There was insufficient evidence of piercing the veil to allow the court to take jurisdiction based on the controllers 'deemed consent' to the jurisdiction agreement.

As in *Canada Trust* itself, the claimant in *Young v Anglo American South Africa Ltd* had to show much the better argument to decide if a company had its 'central administration' in England for the purposes of Article 2 of the Brussels Regulation.[43] That conclusion required a close investigation of the company's corporate structure and operations, both of itself and its holding company. After lengthy argument, the Court of Appeal agreed with the first instance judge that the company did not have its central administration in England. The matter would not arise again at trial so extensive discussion of the evidence raised no problem of pre-judging an issue. In this example, the good arguable case was used to decide whether a defendant was subject to the general jurisdiction of the court.

At common law, the good arguable case test decides whether a foreign jurisdiction clause is effective to disturb general jurisdiction founded in domicile in England. Here the burden falls on the defendant to show a good arguable case that the proceedings should be stayed. In *Konkola Copper Mines plc v Coromin Ltd*,[44] that jurisdictional issue was one aspect of what was to be the likely merits of

[41] Now Regulation (EU) No 1215/2012, Art 25.
[42] *Antonio Gramsci Shipping Corp v Recoletos Ltd* [2013] EWCA Civ 730, [2013] 4 All ER 157.
[43] *Young v Anglo American South Africa Ltd* [2014] EWCA Civ 1434, [2014] Bus LR 1434.
[44] *Konkola Copper Mines plc v Coromin Ltd* [2006] EWCA Civ 5, [2006] 1 All ER (Comm) 437.

the case. So, the court was careful it should not decide between the competing arguments on jurisdiction, noting that 'both parties had made out a good arguable case'.[45] Nevertheless, the defendant had failed to make out a 'sufficiently good' case to displace established jurisdiction, and therefore it had not discharged its burden. Rix LJ accepted it was therefore a different case to one where the claimants need to establish a basis of jurisdiction. However, he noted generally in relation to the *Canada Trust* gloss that it ran the risk of prejudicing the merits by determining issues at the interlocutory stage which might be determined differently at trial. He said 'the power to give leave to serve out of the jurisdiction is at the end of the day a discretionary one. However important the proper disposition of a jurisdictional challenge is, it is not something which should be allowed to subvert the merits of a potential trial'.[46] I do not agree with that conclusion in a case where jurisdiction of the English court is not already established. Otherwise a difficult case on the merits could be allowed to circumvent the defendant's ability to be able to predict a court in which the dispute should be heard.

In a similar vein, the good arguable case has been used to determine whether the jurisdiction of the English court has been ousted by a Swiss arbitration agreement. One of the defendants in *Aeroflot* discharged its burden and obtained a stay of English proceedings.[47] The claimants could not satisfy the court that the arbitration agreement was inoperative. However, they did obtain leave to serve out on a different defendant using the 'necessary and proper party' gateway by showing a much better argument on that issue.

The good arguable case has also been argued as the test whether England and Wales is clearly the most appropriate place in which to bring an action in respect of an allegedly defamatory statement under section 9 of the Defamation Act 2013.[48] Although the point was not explained, it would be inconsistent not to use the same test as at common law.

IV. MORE RECENT CASES

A. *Brownlie v Four Seasons Holdings Inc*

The Supreme Court in *Brownlie v Four Seasons Holdings Inc* criticised the *Canada Trust* 'gloss' on the good arguable case. As already noted, Lady Hale explicitly disliked glosses,[49] and Lord Sumption laid out a three-step test for the good arguable case instead.[50]

[45] ibid, [96] (Rix LJ).
[46] ibid, [81] (Rix LJ).
[47] *Aeroflot* (n 34).
[48] *Wright v Ver* [2020] EWCA Civ 672.
[49] *Brownlie* (n 9) [33].
[50] ibid, [7].

The facts of the case are well-known, and also discussed in chapter eighteen by counsel who appeared in that case. Lady Brownlie was suing in damages both in contract and in tort for her personal injuries, for her loss of her husband under the Fatal Accidents Act 1976 and, as executrix, for her husband's damage. The losses resulted from a car accident in Egypt organised by the Four Seasons Hotel. She initially sued the Canadian holding company. A central issue was whether she had satisfied the Court as to its jurisdiction to the level of a good arguable case. This turned on whether a gateway was available: was the contract made in England or governed by English law (for the contract claim) and had the damage been sustained in England (for the tort claim), both at the appropriate standard of a good arguable case. This appeal was solely as to where the damage was sustained. Although the accident had happened in Egypt, the claimant argued that she suffered consequential loss in England. The defendants argued that the gateway was restricted to direct damage.

Arden LJ in the Court of Appeal noted that the English court in deciding its own jurisdiction must 'scrutinise most jealously the factor which gives rise to jurisdiction', citing the inconvenience to a foreign defendant of being brought to England to defend his rights.[51] Therefore her starting point was that the Court should be cautious in the exercise of jurisdiction. She accepted that the *Canada Trust* gloss is not easy to apply in cases where the facts are in dispute and which may need to be decided at trial. The balance is between a fair resolution of a matter of jurisdiction (which requires making a determination) and not pre-judging issues where there has been no proper trial of the evidence. In her words:[52]

> The words used by Waller LJ, namely a 'much better argument', mean more than that, on the material available, the case is arguable. There must be some substance to it: since we are deciding a question of jurisdiction, the evidence must achieve an acceptable level of quality and adequacy. However, the standard to be attained is not that of succeeding on a balance of probabilities because there is no trial.

The Supreme Court held that the defendant parent company could not be liable to the claimants, and so all that was said about the good arguable case was strictly obiter. Lord Sumption, with whom the others agreed on this point (Lady Hale suggesting that Lord Sumption's approach was not a gloss),[53] articulated the same balance as Lady Arden but reformulated the test for the good arguable case:[54]

> (i) that the claimant must supply a plausible evidential basis for the application of a relevant jurisdictional gateway; (ii) that if there is an issue of fact about it, or some other reason for doubting whether it applies, the court must take a view on the

[51] *Brownlie v Four Seasons Holdings Inc* [2015] EWCA Civ 665, [2016] 1 WLR 1814 [17].

[52] ibid, [23].

[53] Although he was in the minority on the question whether the gateway was satisfied, concluding that it was limited to direct damage.

[54] *Brownlie* (n 9) [7].

> material available if it can reliably do so; but (iii) the nature of the issue and the limitations of the material available at the interlocutory stage may be such that no reliable assessment can be made, in which case there is a good arguable case for the application of the gateway if there is a plausible (albeit contested) evidential basis for it.

He continued 'I do not believe that anything is gained by the word 'much', which suggests a superior standard of conviction which is both uncertain and unwarranted in this context.'[55]

In some ways this reformulation says very little. The burden remains with the claimant to produce the evidence which justifies the gateway, and the evidence has to have some persuasive power ('plausibility'). The change seems to me that the defendant has to go the extra mile in contesting the evidence such that it is no longer plausible in order to avoid the jurisdiction. It may have been that Lord Sumption, by focusing on the *with notice* stage, has possibly overlooked the important role played by the good arguable case at the *without notice* permission step.

Lord Sumption reiterated his three stage test of the good arguable case in *Goldman Sachs International v Novo Banco SA*,[56] to determine whether the English court had jurisdiction in the light of decisions of the Portuguese court which the defendants argued should be given effect under Article 3 of the Reorganisation Directive.[57] Initially Lord Sumption declared this was a case in which the dispute as to jurisdiction relied upon an issue of fact: whether the liability had been transferred to Novo Banco and, if so, Novo Banco was bound by the English jurisdiction agreement. On the other hand, the effect of the transfer was as much a matter of law as of fact, which Lord Sumption explicitly recognised towards the end of his judgment.[58] In the event he held that the court did not have jurisdiction. Presumably the claimants had not satisfied the court that their arguments on Article 3 were even plausible.

B. *Kaefer Aislamientos SA de CV v AMS Drilling Mexico SA de CV*

The Court of Appeal in *Kaefer Aislamientos SA de CV v AMS Drilling Mexico SA de CA* returned to the test of the good arguable case after the decisions in *Brownlie v Four Seasons* and *Goldman Sachs International v Novo Banco*.[59] Here the claimant sought the jurisdiction of the English court on the basis of Article 25 Brussels I Regulation against four defendants. It alleged that the third and fourth defendants were bound by the agreement entered into by the first two

[55] ibid.
[56] *Goldman Sachs International v Novo Banco SA* [2018] UKSC 34, [2018] 1 WLR 3685 [9].
[57] Directive (EC) No 2001/24.
[58] *Goldman Sachs* (n 56) [33].
[59] *Kaefer Aislamientos SA de CV v AMS Drilling Mexico SA de CA* [2019] EWCA Civ 10, [2019] 1 WLR Civ 10.

defendants acting as their undisclosed principals. The third and fourth defendants sought a declaration that they were not bound by the jurisdiction agreement. This was not a straightforward challenge to the jurisdiction but was to the same effect. The claimants appealed the decision of the first instance judge. Peter MacDonald Eggers QC (the Deputy Judge at first instance)[60] decided the claimants had failed to show the better of the argument against the third defendant, and that they had failed to establish a good arguable case against the fourth defendant.

In dismissing the claimants' appeal Green LJ gave the majority opinion on this point. It was clear from the first instance judgment that the Deputy Judge had carefully assessed the evidence before him to decide that the claimants had an arguable case but that the defendants' arguments were more plausible, so the defendants had the better of the argument. Green LJ summarised the key conceptual dispute as whether the test of a good arguable case is an absolute test or a relative one. Does the claimant have to surpass a specified threshold without engaging the judge in assessing the relative merits of the competing arguments – which is easier for a claimant. Or does the court have to determine which of the claimants' or defendants' arguments are stronger – which is preferable for a defendant? 'An argument might be arguable but still wrong.'[61]

Green LJ carefully inspected each of the three limbs in Lord Sumption's restatement of *Canada Trust* in *Brownlie* and *Goldman Sachs*.

He argued that the first limb is relative, the claimant must show the better argument.[62] The burden of proof remains on the claimant but the test is not on the balance of probabilities. He reasserted that 'the court must be astute not to express any view on the ultimate merits of the case, even if there is a close overlap between the issues going to jurisdiction and the ultimate substantive merits'. His Lordship clearly banished the word 'much'. If the test is relative, the claimant only has to show the better case and 'a plausible case is not one where the claimant has to show it has 'much' the better of the argument'. I suspect he overlooked the need at the without notice stage – where the defendant's arguments are not made – for the claimant to show a sufficiently strong case. Mere plausibility at that stage is probably insufficient to protect a defendant. At the interlocutory with notice stage, it must be enough that one party has made out the better argument.

The second limb, in Green LJ's view, is 'an instruction to use judicial common sense and pragmatism' and to come to a conclusion if it reliably can.[63] Judicial common sense is needed to come to a decision 'with due despatch and without hearing oral evidence'.[64] This is whistling in the wind. In his next breath Green LJ

[60] *Kaefer Aislamientos SA de CV v AMS Drilling Mexico SA de CA* [2017] EWHC 2698 (Comm).
[61] *Kaefer* (n 59) [61].
[62] ibid, [73]–[77].
[63] ibid, [78].
[64] *Canada Trust (HL)* (n 1) 13 (Lord Steyn).

noted that it was common for claimants to seek 'extensive disclosure' and witnesses for jurisdictional disputes.

Turning to the third limb, Green LJ faced the critical dilemma. What if the court is unable to form a decided conclusion as to which party has the better argument? It would be unfair to cast out the claimant as 'on fuller analysis, it might turn out that the claimant did have the better of the argument'. However, it would not be right to wait to decide jurisdiction until a full trial of the dispute. Green LJ ducked. In his view the third limb moved away from the relative test and towards one 'combining the good arguable case and plausibility of evidence'.[65] He recognised that that leaves 'room for debate'.[66] This debate will only continue.

Davis LJ also confessed to being:[67]

> in something of a fog as to the difference between an 'explication' and a 'gloss'. But whatever the niceties of language involved, it is sufficiently clear that the ultimate test is one of good arguable case. For that purpose, however, a court may perfectly properly apply the yardstick of 'having the better of the argument' (the additional word 'much' can now safely be taken as consigned to the outer darkness). That, overall, confers, in my opinion, a desirable degree of flexibility in the evaluation of the court: desirable, just because the standard is, for the purposes of the evidential analysis in each case, between proof on the balance of probabilities (which is not the test) and the mere raising of an issue (which is not the test either).

He too agreed in the end that there was no sufficiently arguable case that the third and fourth defendants were undisclosed principals. The English court therefore would not hear the dispute. It is a terrible waste of resources that the claim was permitted to get as far as it did before that apparently obvious state of affairs was given full effect. However much his Lordship found it 'very regrettable that applications of this kind seem … to be generating so much complexity of debate',[68] it remains the case that the courts have not found a way to define a good arguable case to avoid the complexity. As Dickinson so aptly says: 'one is struck by the common law's propensity to paper over the cracks of an approach to resolving jurisdictional issues that has not only been a cause of great uncertainty but is also insensitive to the wording and purpose of the particular rule of jurisdiction being applied'.[69]

C. *Brownlie v FS Nile Plaza (Cairo) LLC*

In 2021, the Supreme Court returned to the facts of *Brownlie*. The claimants in *Brownlie v FS Nile Plaza (Cairo) LLC* brought the same actions for damages

[65] *Kaefer* (n 59) [80].
[66] ibid.
[67] ibid, [119].
[68] ibid, [124].
[69] Dickinson (n 13) 371.

as in *Brownlie I* against the defendant Egyptian hotel at which she and her family had been staying.[70] She was granted permission to serve the claim form out of the jurisdiction using the tort gateway. The differing obiter views of the Supreme Court on the same point in *Brownlie I* required further analysis. Lord Lloyd-Jones considered he had no factual disputes to determine, the appeal turned on two questions of law: what was the meaning of 'damage', and was the claim time-barred under Egyptian law as the applicable law. Therefore, he was untroubled by the standard of a good arguable case. Lord Leggatt disagreed with the conclusion on the meaning of 'damage', but equally had no difficulty in assessing the disputed expert evidence on Egyptian law. There had been a mini-trial at the case management stage of the expert evidence. The case is a good example, therefore, of the court being perfectly willing to decide facts in the assessment of the exercise of jurisdiction.

V. TO DECIDE OR NOT TO DECIDE?

Waller LJ in *Canada Trust* made it clear that where an issue to be decided as to jurisdiction also goes to the substantive merits of the claim, the court must not be seen to prematurely judge the merits of those substantive issues: 'The court in such cases must be concerned not even to appear to express some concluded view as to the merits, e g as to whether the contract existed or not.'[71]

That statement brings a great deal of confusion. On the one hand, the court must make a decision on jurisdiction, whether the claimant loses as not having satisfied the court or the defendant loses and the case continues in England. In coming to that determination, not only does the court have to assess that the claimant has a serious issue to be tried here, that the claimant has satisfied the court of a good arguable case that the gateway is available but also that England is the forum conveniens. On the other hand, there is a risk that the court would come to an erroneous conclusion on partial evidence which might be contradicted at trial.

However, often matters of a gateway raise intertwined questions of law and fact which go to jurisdiction and which may arise again at trial. For example, whether a contract is concluded, whether it is breached and where, or whether damage has been suffered in the jurisdiction. Deciding the matter of jurisdiction in such cases necessarily requires expressing an opinion on the merits. Rix LJ articulated this risk in *Konkola Copper Mines*,[72] and sought to limit the use of the *Canada Trust* gloss only to those cases in which jurisdictional questions did not go to the merits. It was not absolutely clear what the alternative test is used in these cases. Arden LJ in *Brownlie* applied something quite close to the good arguable case 'much the better of the argument' test explicitly in order to protect the defendant from the excessive exercise of the jurisdiction of the

[70] *Brownlie* (n 17).
[71] *Canada Trust (CA)* (n 1) 555.
[72] *Konkola* (n 44).

English court. She sought evidence which achieved 'an acceptable level of quality and adequacy'.[73] Plausibility for her was inadequate, something more was necessary. As she also noted:[74]

> In any event, the court is not bound to accept a witness statement which is inherently defective, and certainly should not do so if it conflicts with other incontrovertible evidence or is unreliable for some other tangible reason, or, as Christopher Clarke J put it in *Cherney v Deripaska* … 'wholly implausible'.

No case has explained exactly why there is a problem in the court expressing a decision at this stage on what may be in issue in trial or may never be further decided. It could be thought a waste of time and money to have to go over the material again at trial. It might be considered that the decision would not be worth reassessing once a judge has opined on the evidence, leading to a premature settlement. Perhaps there is a concern for appearance where a judge could be seen publicly in making an error. Or that if a decision is going to be made at this jurisdictional stage, the parties would be tempted into expending money and time in obtaining partial disclosure and requiring extensive examination of the evidence. That would be antithetical to the proposition that jurisdictional disputes should be speedy and cheap.

It is somewhat fanciful to allege that, even at the interlocutory stage, a concluded view of something of the merits is not taken. For example, there appears to be no hesitation in concluding matters of law. The House of Lords in *Amin Rasheed Shipping Corporation v Kuwait Insurance Co* had no difficulty in deciding that the applicable law of the contract was English law (an issue surely in question at trial) in order to establish the gateway for the dispute to be heard in England.[75] It also took for granted that it could decide a range of other, more factual matters, such as the residence of the likely witnesses, in coming to a conclusion that England was not the forum conveniens. More recently in the second *Brownlie* appeal the majority in the Supreme Court also decided that the tort gateway included indirect damage.[76] These hearings can be extensive and subject to lengthy appeals. So that justification of not trying matters of fact at the interlocutory stage is not conclusive.

The third of Lord Sumption's three-limbed further explication in the first *Brownlie* appeal is an attempt to address the problem of the disputed evidence.[77] He noted that:

> (iii) the nature of the issue and the limitations of the material available at the interlocutory stage may be such that no reliable assessment can be made, in which case there is a good arguable case for the application of the gateway if there is a plausible (albeit contested) evidential basis for it.

[73] *Brownlie (CA)* (n 51) [23].
[74] ibid, [24].
[75] *Amin Rasheed Shipping Corporation v Kuwait Insurance Co* [1984] AC 50 (HL).
[76] *Brownlie* (n 17).
[77] *Bronwlie* (n 9) [7].

As we saw in *Kaefer* that formulation of the good arguable case has been described as returning to a more absolute hurdle for the claimant to surpass rather than any relative assessment of the arguments.[78] However, the third limb is no more useful than that of the *Canada Trust* gloss. A judge must be satisfied, given the context of the interlocutory process, the evidence available at the time, and the ground of jurisdiction in dispute, that the English court should take jurisdiction. Without a clearer direction to make an assessment, the risk is that judges are too easily satisfied with (merely) plausible arguments made by a claimant, particularly at the without notice stage. From the reported cases it appears that once cases are commenced in the English court, they tend to have a life of their own. Defendants have an uphill struggle to persuade the court that it should not hear the case. Both *Canada Trust* and the *Brownlie* cases prove that.

VI. CONCLUSION

Canada Trust v Stolzenberg (No 2) was a valiant attempt to define the standard of a good arguable case. In settling on 'much the better of the argument' I consider it found the right balance between the parties. Ensuring that the defendant's position is appropriately borne in mind by the judge particularly at the without notice stage. Once the parties are both before the court to argue as to jurisdiction, the good arguable case should do no more than focus the attention on which party bears the burden of satisfying the judge on jurisdiction. Waller LJ's gloss also has a pleasing simplicity of expression. Twenty-two years after the decision in *Canada Trust* and several appellate court cases later, we do not seem to have arrived at any greater clarity as to the standard to be applied. Green LJ in *Kaefer* lamented:[79]

> A test intended to be straightforward has become befuddled by 'glosses', glosses upon glosses, 'explications' and 'reformulations'. In relation to the standard of proof, that which the claimant must establish to found jurisdiction, the courts have referred to a test of 'good arguable case', who has the 'better argument' or 'much' the better argument, the need for 'reliable' evidence, the need for 'clear and precise' evidence, 'credible' evidence, evidence of real 'substance', 'plausible' evidence, and 'sufficient' evidence. Disputes abound over whether the test is a single test or comprised of two parts and, in any event, as to whether the test is absolutist and/or relative.

Canada Trust v Stolzenberg (No 2) highlighted the practical realities of the interlocutory process. Deciding a complex matter of jurisdiction while at the same time not permitting that decision to become a great burden on the parties and

[78] *Kaefer* (n 59).
[79] ibid, [59].

the court is always challenging. Nevertheless, the decision has to be made. If the decision is a matter of 'pure' law, it can be decided by the court. But it will often require some sort of determination of both fact and law. Where jurisdiction can be established without relying on the outcome of the contested evidence, the way is clear. In other cases, a limited disclosure and mini-trial of the evidence may have to be undertaken. However, excessive reluctance to decide a matter which may be in issue at the trial of the merits could result in an unsatisfactory decision on jurisdiction to the defendant's detriment.

16

Fiona Trust & Holding Corp v Privalov (2007)

SIR MARCUS SMITH

I. INTRODUCTION

Premium Nafta Products Ltd v Fili Shipping Co Ltd, on appeal to the House of Lords from *Fiona Trust & Holding Corp v Privalov*, as it was known in the Court of Appeal, is referred to generally as '*Fiona Trust*'.[1] It is one of the most well-known, and most often cited, cases on jurisdiction and arbitration clauses. Rightly rated by Westlaw as 'significant', that database gives page-after-page of cases citing *Fiona Trust*. Even demanding a list of 'key' cases citing *Fiona Trust* gives the database pause for thought as it compiles its list of references.

Re-reading *Fiona Trust* in the abstract brought back memory of all the old arguments – killed off by Longmore LJ in the Court of Appeal and by the House of Lords in *Fiona Trust* – about the scope of jurisdiction clauses. I well remember making arguments of the sort described by Lord Hoffmann:[2]

> … It may well be a great disappointment to the judges who explained so carefully the effects of the various linguistic nuances if they could learn that the draftsman of so widely a used standard form as Shelltime 4 obviously regarded the expressions "arising under this charter' in clause 41(b) and 'arisen out of this charter' in clause 41(c)(1)(a)(i) as mutually interchangeable. So I applaud the opinion expressed by Longmore LJ in the Court of Appeal … that the time has come to draw a line under the authorities to date and make a fresh start …

Abandoning an approach to the construction of jurisdiction and arbitration clauses that turns more on the significance of such clauses as magical incantations, divorced from meaning, is obviously a good thing. Arguments about whether parallel claims in tort, or whether questions as to formation and validity, fall within or without a clause should not depend upon the deployment of the 'correct' incantation in the clause.

[1] *Premium Nafta Products Ltd v Fili Shipping Co Ltd* [2007] UKHL 40, [2007] 4 All ER 951.
[2] ibid, [12].

It may be that my tribute to the significance of *Fiona Trust* ought to stop here, with a recognition that the House of Lords did us all a considerable favour in sweeping away the 'clanking chains' of formulaic construction, and ushering us into a brave new world where, to mis-quote *The Hitchhiker's Guide to the Galaxy*, 'jurisdiction clauses were real jurisdiction clauses'.[3] Yet there is a reason we struggled so hard over the scope of the different incantations, working out (or trying to work out) what fell within and what fell without such clauses. I do not believe that we entered into these detailed, Jesuitical, arguments out of a perverse desire simply to render complex that which was in fact simple. The question of the proper scope and effect of jurisdiction and arbitration clauses is, I am going to suggest, a really difficult issue. On the one hand, *Fiona Trust* has done us all a favour, in ushering in a simpler rule set, avoiding technical arguments of construction and interpretation. On the other hand, I wonder whether *Fiona Trust* is not guilty of sweeping real difficulties 'under the carpet', where they lurk as obstructions, waiting to trip us up. The bulk of this chapter is going to focus on the workability of the test that Lord Hoffmann and Lord Hope used to replace the old law.

The *Fiona Trust* solution, it will come as no surprise to students of Lord Hoffmann's work to learn, turns on construction:[4]

> In approaching the question of construction, it is therefore necessary to inquire into the purpose of the arbitration clause. As to this, I think there can be no doubt. The parties have entered into a relationship, an agreement or what is alleged to be an agreement or what appears on its face to be an agreement, which may give rise to disputes. They want those disputes decided by a tribunal which they have chosen, commonly on the grounds of such matters as its neutrality, expertise and privacy, the availability of legal services at the seat of the arbitration and the unobtrusive efficiency of its supervisory law. Particularly in the case of international contracts, they want a quick and efficient adjudication and do not want to take the risks of delay and, in too many cases, partiality, in proceedings before a national jurisdiction.
>
> If one accepts that this is the purpose of an arbitration clause, its construction must be influenced by whether the parties, as rational businessmen, were likely to have intended that only some of the questions arising out of their relationship were to be submitted to arbitration and others were to be decided by national courts. Could they have intended that the question of whether the contract was repudiated should be decided by arbitration but the question of whether it was induced by misrepresentation should be decided by a court? If, as appears to be generally accepted, there is no rational basis upon which businessmen would be likely to wish to have questions of the validity or enforceability of the contract decided by one tribunal and questions

[3] 'In those days spirits were brave, the stakes were high, men were real men, women were real women and small furry creatures from Alpha Centauri were real small furry creatures from Alpha Centauri.' Or, as Adrian Briggs put it in A Briggs, *Civil Jurisdiction and Judgments,* 7th edn (London, Routledge, 2021), 'This heroic judgment consigned many troublesome earlier authorities, which are mentioned below only for their appalling curiosity value, to history and semi-oblivion.'

[4] *Fiona Trust* (n 1) [6]–[8].

about its performance decided by another, one would need to find very clear language before deciding that they must have had such an intention.

A proper approach to construction therefore requires the court to give effect, so far as the language used by the parties will permit, to the commercial purpose of the arbitration clause ....

What we have is, effectively, an interpretational presumption that all disputes arising out of the relationship between rational businessmen should be before the same court or tribunal. That is what Lord Hoffmann said a little later his judgment:[5]

In my opinion the construction of an arbitration clause should start from the assumption that the parties, as rational businessmen, are likely to have intended any dispute arising out of the relationship into which they have entered or purported to enter to be decided by the same tribunal. The clause should be construed in accordance with this presumption unless the language makes it clear that certain questions were intended to be excluded from the arbitrator's jurisdiction. As Longmore LJ remarked ... 'if any businessman did want to exclude disputes about the validity of a contract, it would be comparatively easy to say so'.

Lord Hope similarly stressed the desirability of a single tribunal hearing all relevant disputes:[6]

... if the parties wish to have issues as to the validity of their contract decided by one tribunal and issues as to its meaning or performance decided by another, they must say so expressly. Otherwise they will be taken to have agreed on a single tribunal for the resolution of all such disputes.

Often, the desirable outcome described by Lords Hoffmann and Hope is referred to as the 'one-stop-shop', where all disputes arising out of a particular relationship come before a single tribunal.

Can it really be this easy? The main theme of this chapter is that it is not, and that whilst *Fiona Trust* should be lauded for its dismissal of the formulaic in favour of the purposive, *Fiona Trust*'s great failing is that it paid insufficient heed to the very real difficulties that the scope of jurisdiction clauses and arbitration clauses gives rise to in many cases, apart from the paradigm cases, where the answer is obvious. There are two points that can be made about *Fiona Trust*, right at the outset. First, *Fiona Trust* was itself a paradigm, and actually pretty easy, case. I have no issues with the outcome – and I suspect very few of us do. Second, and perhaps more importantly, *Fiona Trust* was itself a creature or case of its time, decided when (largely because of the thinking of Lord Hoffmann) construction was seen as the solution to many problems. It may very well be said that the pendulum has now swung the other way. But that does not diminish

[5] ibid, [13].

[6] ibid, [26]. See, also, [28]: '... one should be slow to attribute to reasonable parties an intention that there should in any foreseeable eventuality be two sets of proceedings ...'.

the significance of the decision, which retains a pervasive influence over English lawyers' approach to clauses like this.

Before I come to this question of 'scope', and the difficulties it engenders, it is a good idea to get a few points out of the way. To 'clear the decks' prior to battle, as it were. Terminologically, I am going to be addressing 'jurisdiction clauses' and 'arbitration clauses'. These, of course, come in all kinds of shapes and sizes, and I am going to have to try to keep things simple, for the sake of ease of exposition. By the former, a 'jurisdiction clause', I intend to refer to an exclusive, symmetric, clause referring all disputes of a particular description to a single jurisdiction. By the latter, an 'arbitration clause', I mean an exclusive, symmetric, clause referring all disputes of a particular description to arbitration. I recognise that non-exclusive and/or asymmetric jurisdiction and arbitration clauses give rise to additional nuances of analysis, but there is no scope to address these. The analysis of such clauses will, however, at least be coloured by the subject-matter of the present discussion.

Thereafter, my 'clearing the decks' points are the following. First, is *Fiona Trust* all about arbitration clauses? Or does it speak, also, and with equal force, to jurisdiction clauses? Second, to what extent is *Fiona Trust* of greater importance now, post the UK's withdrawal from the European Union, than it was when it was decided, when jurisdiction clauses were in large part the subject of what I will call the 'Brussels regime'?[7] That, more widely, leads on to the question of how differently (and, if so, in what way) the common lawyer sees jurisdiction clauses in contrast with their civilian counterpart. Third, the extent to which the *kompetenz kompetenz* question informed the outcome in *Fiona Trust*, and the extent to which this is an important (or unimportant) part of the decision. Thereafter, I shall get on to the main course, which is how, post-*Fiona Trust*, we deal with – or do not deal with – the question of what is 'in' and what is 'out'.

II. ARBITRATION CLAUSES ONLY – OR JURISDICTION CLAUSES MORE GENERALLY?

The opinions of Lord Hoffmann and Lord Hope are infused with references to arbitration clauses, rather than jurisdiction clauses.[8] Yet the clause in question – the Shelltime 4 form charterparty – contained an arbitration clause nested within a jurisdiction clause. Clause 3(b) provided that '[a]ny dispute arising under this

[7] Which I shall use to refer, indifferently, to all versions, starting with the Brussels Convention.

[8] *Fiona Trust* (n 1) [1]: '… this appeal concerns the scope and effect of arbitration clauses …'; at [5]: 'Both of these defences raise the same fundamental question about the attitude of the courts to arbitration. Arbitration is consensual. It depends upon the intention of the parties as expressed in their agreement'; at [7]: 'If one accepts that this is the purpose of an arbitration clause …' (all Lord Hoffmann); and, albeit to a lesser extent, [24] '… in agreeing to an arbitration provision …' (Lord Hope).

charter shall be decided by the English courts to whose jurisdiction the parties hereby agree',[9] whilst clause 3(c) provided that 'either party may, by giving written notice of election to the other party, elect to have any such dispute referred … to arbitration …'.[10] Lord Hoffmann referred to this when he determined that 'I shall for the sake of convenience discuss the clause as if it was a simple arbitration clause.'[11]

This can only be right if the rules regarding jurisdiction clauses are the same as the rules regarding arbitration clauses. Absent differences of approach between cases falling within the Brussels regime and cases falling outside it – to which I shall come – Lord Hoffmann's 'sake of convenience' approach has much to commend it. But eliding a jurisdiction clause into an arbitration clause has the effect of applying the principles of construction that Lord Hoffmann *expressly* applies to arbitration clauses *tacitly* to jurisdiction clauses. Whilst this tacit equation of one with the other is almost certainly right – and is the way *Fiona Trust* has been read in later case law – it would, perhaps, have been better to make this equivalence express, and not tacit. As I will come to describe, even if the approach to *construing* jurisdiction and arbitration clauses is the same in each case, there are differences in the way such clauses operate – *independent* of their wording – which suggest that treating them equivalently misses a trick.

III. POST-BREXIT

Whilst the UK was a member of the European Union, the Brussels regime applied with full rigour. It is no part of this chapter to describe that regime, save to note that in cases falling within its scope, it was the Brussels regime that prevailed, at the expense of the common law. Entirely unsurprisingly, that regime made provision for jurisdiction based upon consent – specifically, where that consent was manifested in advance in the form of a jurisdiction clause.

For the future – there will, obviously, be old cases that must be run-off – the Brussels regime is history. The UK sought to become party to the Lugano Convention,[12] but that application was nixed by the European Union, who regarded the Brussels regime as too much an aspect of the 'internal market' to permit a third country, as the UK now is, to participate.[13] It is no part of this chapter to comment upon the EU Commission's concerns with the internal market, except perhaps to note *first* that international co-operation does not stop at the frontiers of the EU's internal market; and *second* that concerns with

[9] ibid, [3] (Lord Hoffmann).
[10] ibid.
[11] ibid, [4].
[12] Convention on jurisdiction and the recognition and enforcement of judgments in civil and commercial matters.
[13] Even though Art 70 expressly envisages accession by what the EU would term 'third states'.

the internal market have, perhaps, more to do with the assertion of power, and less with forms of international legal order.[14]

Be that as it may, *Fiona Trust* was a case handed down under the Brussels regime, and is now liberated by that regime's non-application. That makes little difference to the analysis, but it does mean that what was once the 'rump end' of common law, applicable only when the Brussels regime did not apply, is now a rule of general principle for the courts of this jurisdiction.

The effect of the application of the Brussels regime on jurisdiction clauses at the time when *Fiona Trust* was decided *may* explain Lord Hoffmann's keenness to categorise the clause as a pure arbitration clause. Let me expand on this thought:

(1) The regime for allocating jurisdiction to a Member State pursuant to a jurisdiction clause under the Brussels regime is much less based on party autonomy and discretion than the common law approach.
(2) The general objective in the drafting of the Brussels regime is to try to eliminate discretion, so that there is a hierarchy of rules that achieves certainty of outcome in every case. That is, of course, naïve: there comes a time when discretion, properly controlled and judicially exercised, is actually more predictable and more consistent with the rule of law than byzantine 'special' rules and regimes, with exceptions within carve-outs within 'special' regimes for particular cases. The hallmark of the Brussels regime is the substantial elimination of judicial discretion at the (for me) high price of legal certainty for parties.[15]
(3) Article 25 of the Brussels Regulation Recast[16] sets out a complete code for the determination of whether a jurisdiction clause in fact confers jurisdiction, to the exclusion of any applicable principles of national law.[17] A jurisdiction clause sought to be relied upon must be in writing or evidenced in writing; in a form which accords with practices which the parties have established between themselves; or in international trade or commerce, in a form which accords with a usage of which the parties are or ought to have been aware and which in such trade or commerce is widely known to, and regularly observed by, parties to contracts of the type involved in the particular trade or commerce concerned.
(4) These points are not particularly unfamiliar to the English lawyer, but the crucial issue – underlying all these requirements – is that a real consent

[14] See A Bradford, *The Brussels Effect* (Oxford, OUP, 2020).

[15] Of course, the rule of law does not favour discretion, but discretion can be defended within system that is rule of law 'compliant': see, eg, T Bingham, *The Rule of Law* (London, Penguin, 2010) ch 4.

[16] Regulation (EU) No 542/2014.

[17] See, eg, *Public Institution for Social Security v Al Rajaan* [2020] EWHC 2979 (Comm) [107] (Henshaw J).

or acceptance is shown.[18] There is, in this, the treatment of a jurisdiction clause as something more akin to the English court's attitude to an exclusion clause. Jurisdiction clauses seem to be regarded as a case where an adverse outcome is imposed by one party on another. This does not sit easily with the view of Lord Hoffmann espoused in *Fiona Trust*, where he regarded arbitration clauses (and, I think, jurisdiction clauses) as a sensible and consensual way *for the parties* to allocate jurisdiction to a particular tribunal. And that, I suppose, is the difference. The Brussels Regime sees jurisdiction clauses as a *derogation* from the ordinary and proper case; the common law sees them as a manifestation of party autonomy. As Briggs puts it, when considering the difference between the common law and the civilian approaches, 'the true nature of agreements on jurisdiction within the Lugano/Brussels scheme is that they are not contract terms at all, but written (or otherwise formal) acceptances of the jurisdiction of a court'.[19] How far this is the true explanation of the difference is not something I am going to debate: but of the fact that there is a difference, there can be no doubt.

(5) A difference is similarly discernible where Article 25 is engaged. In such cases, the jurisdiction clause bites, and serves to allocate jurisdiction, even if that outcome is not particularly sensible in the scheme of things overall.[20] On the other hand, the common lawyer sees the jurisdiction clause as a very strong, but by no means *inevitable*, determinant of jurisdiction.[21]

IV. KOMPETENZ-KOMPETENZ

A. In the Case of Arbitration Clauses

As Lord Hoffmann noted in *Fiona Trust*, 'there was for some time a view that arbitrators could never have jurisdiction to decide whether a contract was valid. If the contract was invalid, so was the arbitration clause'.[22] There was, therefore, a clear distinction between disputes going to questions of performance or

[18] ibid, [110]. It is worth stressing that such 'real consent or acceptance' may not be the same thing as 'contractual consent', and certainly not the same thing as 'contractual consent according to English law'. There is a danger in eliding, or treating as equivalent, what are likely to be rather different concepts. *Cf* A Briggs, 'The Hidden Depths of the Law of Jurisdiction' [2016] *Lloyds Maritime and Commercial Law Quarterly* 236, 247–52.

[19] Briggs (n 3) 452.

[20] Again, rules, rather than discretion, are the order of the day.

[21] See, for instance, the decision of the House of Lords in *Donohue v Armco Inc* [2001] UKHL 64, [2002] 1 All ER 749, where the House of Lords declined to grant an anti-suit injunction in support of an English exclusive jurisdiction clause and to prevent proceedings in the US – brought in partial breach of the English jurisdiction clause – from continuing.

[22] *Fiona Trust* (n 1) [9].

interpretation (where the validity of the contract was not in dispute) and questions going to the essential validity of the contract. The former – depending on its construction – might fall within an arbitration clause; the latter, no matter how widely framed, could not because a dispute as to essential validity undercuts the very clause that accords jurisdiction.

This is the well-known 'chicken-and-egg' problem: how does one adjudicate upon an issue in circumstances where, if the outcome goes one way, there is no jurisdiction, whereas if the outcome goes the other way, there is?[23] It is a common enough problem in interlocutory matters, seen very regularly in 'putative proper law' decisions, where matters are determined by reference to a 'putative' proper law of the contract, where the contract is only valid according to one but not all of several possible applicable laws.[24] The fact is that these questions are impossible to answer logically. The validity question can only be determined at a trial before a court or tribunal whose jurisdiction is ascertainable only if the validity question is resolved. The problem, at heart, is that the answer to any given question *may* be different according to which jurisdiction addresses and resolves that question, which is why jurisdiction clauses can matter so much to the parties litigating about them.

Kompetenz-kompetenz is the term generally given to such questions and, as Lord Hoffmann noted, the matter in the context of arbitration clauses was resolved by the decision of the Court of Appeal in *Harbour Assurance Co (UK) Ltd v Kansa General International Insurance Co Ltd*,[25] and put beyond doubt by section 7 of the Arbitration Act 1996:

> Unless otherwise agreed by the parties, an arbitration agreement which forms or was intended to form part of another agreement (whether or not in writing) shall not be regarded as invalid, non-existent or ineffective because that other agreement is invalid, or did not come into existence or have become ineffective, and it shall for that purpose be treated as a distinct agreement.

This articulates the principle that an arbitration clause is separate from the rest of the agreement of which it may form a physical part. There is, unless the

[23] The point was put in this way in *Harbour Assurance Co (UK) Ltd v Kansa General International Insurance Co Ltd* [1993] 1 QB 701 (CA) 707 (Ralph Gibson LJ): 'The orthodox view in English law has always been, it has been said for the plaintiffs, that if the contract in which the arbitration clause is contained is void *ab initio*, and therefore nothing, so also must be the arbitration clause in the contract. That is the proposition that nothing can come of nothing: *ex nihil nil fit*. It has also been called in this case the argument of logic.'

[24] Dicey squared the circle by defining the proper law of the contract as 'the law or laws by which the parties to a contract intended, or may fairly be presumed to have intended, the contract to be governed …': see AV Dicey, *A Digest of the Law of England with reference to the Conflict of Laws*, 2nd edn (London, Stevens & Sons, 1908) rule 146. The essential validity of the contract would be governed 'indirectly' by that law: rule 151.

[25] *Harbour Assurance Co (UK) Ltd v Kansa General International Insurance Co Ltd* [1993] 1 QB 701 (CA).

contrary is otherwise agreed, a presumed distinction between the arbitration clause and the rest of the agreement between the parties.

As Lord Hoffmann made clear, the principle of separability only means that the invalidity or rescission of the main contract does not *necessarily* entail the invalidity or rescission of the arbitration agreement.[26] The arbitration agreement's status as a *distinct* agreement may protect it or insulate it. But the arbitration agreement can nevertheless be void or voidable on grounds which relate *directly* to the arbitration agreement.[27] As Merkin and Flannery make clear:[28]

> Separability and the right to determine jurisdiction are distinct (but closely related) concepts. The former is concerned with the right of the tribunal to rule on that validity of the main contract, whereas the latter is concerned with the right of the tribunal to determine whether they have any power to sit as arbitrators at all.

The latter question is determined by section 30 of the Arbitration Act 1996, which provides that the arbitral panel may rule on its own substantive jurisdiction, including as to whether there is a valid arbitration agreement. The concept of considering one's own jurisdiction and the separability of the arbitration clause are indeed closely related: for example, the ability to examine one's own competence enables the tribunal to consider whether the validity attack extends from the 'main' agreement to the arbitration clause itself.[29]

B. In the Case of Jurisdiction Clauses

The judgments in *Fiona Trust* again disregarded the 'nested' nature of the arbitration clause in the case. Whilst it may be that the arbitration clause could – notwithstanding its 'nested' nature – be considered sufficiently separate for the purposes of section 7 of the 1996 Act, the point is not an altogether clear-cut one, and should have been dealt with either by explaining why the effect of the validity allegations on the jurisdiction clause was irrelevant or by explaining why the law was the same in relation to jurisdiction clauses.

[26] *Fiona Trust* (n 1) [17]. See also *Enka Insaat ve Sanayi AS v OOO Insurance Company Chubb* [2020] UKSC 38, [2020] 1 WLR 4117 [41], [60] to [64], discussed further in ch 17 in this volume.

[27] *Fiona Trust* (n 1) [17] and [18]. See, further, R Merkin and L Flannery, *Merkin and Flannery on The Arbitration Act 1996*, 6th edn (London, Routledge, 2020) [7.3].

[28] *Merkin and Flannery* (n 27) 151.

[29] Although the borderlines remain intellectually obscure, the presumption is now of a 'one-stop method of adjudication': ibid, 323. One of the questions, to which we will come, is the extent to which such a 'one-stop' approach extends beyond separability and *kompetenz-kompetenz* to the allocation of particular disputes 'within' or 'without' an arbitration (or jurisdiction) clause.

The position as regards jurisdiction clauses is, however, surprisingly unclear. Although there is a great deal of force in asserting that *Fiona Trust* ought to apply by analogy,[30] there is a surprising dearth of authority both on the question of severability *and* on whether a court can rule on its own jurisdiction where the validity of the jurisdiction clause is itself under attack. The better view, on both questions, is that the answer is the same as in the case of an arbitration clause: the jurisdiction clause is to be regarded as a separate agreement[31] and the court able to rule on its own jurisdiction.[32]

C. Importance of the Point

I am going to suggest that these points, interesting though they are, are a bit of a distraction from the primary point that I want to discuss, and to which I am shortly going to come. *Kompetenz-kompetenz* and separability are pretty easy to understand, but impossible to resolve satisfactorily (by which I mean through the operation of inexorable logic). They simply represent an attribution of value to the parties' consent that may not – in a world of perfect knowledge – actually be justified or – perhaps putting the same point differently – a pragmatic compromise that puts workability above theoretical justifiability. Either way, it does seem to follow that we are here talking about a form of consent 'in the international sense',[33] which makes the term less like a contractual term and more like the Brussels regime notion of submission to jurisdiction as an independent rule. But there is nothing intrinsically odd in defining and applying consent widely in this way.

V. EXPECTATIONS OF REASONABLE PARTIES

It is the fundamental premiss of *Fiona Trust* that 'one-stop-shops' are intrinsically desirable, a 'good thing'. The notion that the parties, as rational businessmen, were likely to have intended all of the questions arising out of their relationship to be submitted to the jurisdiction of a single court and single set of proceedings underlies the decision. Yet the premiss, whilst fundamentally sound, has its limits, and these need to be explored.

[30] Briggs (n 3) 452–53.

[31] See, eg, Briggs, *Agreements on Jurisdiction and Choice of Law* (Oxford, OUP, 2008) [3.09] and [3.19].

[32] ibid, [3.38]–[3.40]. See also, eg, *IFR Ltd v Federal Trade SpA* (Commercial Court, Unreported, 19 September 2001) and *Sonatrach Petroleum Corp (BVI) v Ferrell International Ltd* [2002] 1 All ER (Comm) 627 (Com Ct) [31] (Colman J).

[33] Just as an English court will, in a conflicts case, treat questions of characterisation 'in a broad internationalist spirit': *Raiffeisen Zentralbank Österreich AG v Five Star Trading LLC* [2001] QB 825 (CA) [26] (Mance LJ).

A. Limits to the Efficacy of the *Fiona Trust* Premiss

There are two limits – obvious in themselves – which need to be articulated. They are really the flipsides of the same coin, which is that whilst disputes or claims arising out of a contractual relationship between *A* and *B* ought generally to be heard together, for the reasons articulated in *Fiona Trust*, the relationship between *A* and *B* is not the sole driver of why it is sensible to hear certain disputes or claims together.

The two limits to the *Fiona Trust* premiss are these.[34]

First, jurisdiction and arbitration agreements in general bind on the parties to it, and *not* third parties. That can mean that certain disputes that should be heard together, cannot be. The extent to which that is true depends on the degree to which the jurisdiction clause or arbitration clause is rigorously enforced. As we have seen, under English law, a jurisdiction clause may be disregarded, where there is good enough reason.[35] That is not the case where the agreement in question is an arbitration clause. Thus, it is often the case that an insurance dispute, where the insured seeks an indemnity from their insurer, gives rise to two claims: a claim by the insured against the insurer for the indemnity under the policy; and an alternative claim – predicated on the insurer's defence being sound, and the policy not responding – against the broker who arranged the cover. If – as is often the case – the contract of insurance contains an arbitration clause, and the insurer insists upon it, and there is no ad hoc agreement for the broker to join the arbitration (which is, of course, possible), the insured will have no choice but to commence two separate sets of proceedings, one against the insurer, the other against the broker. It is not possible, in such a case, for the court to force the parties into a single set of proceedings, no matter how convenient or efficient this might be.

Second, and relatedly, there are claims or disputes that are efficiently heard together, where that efficiency does *not* arise out of the contractual relationship between the parties, but out of other factors. The example in the preceding paragraph is a case in point: the claim by the insured for an indemnity, and the alternative claim for damages for negligence/breach of contract against the broker, are both informed and linked by the insured's desire to get what was paid for, either from the insurer or the broker. The courts of this jurisdiction are very sensitive to hearing claims that are linked together, where this is legally possible.[36] Should it be necessary to seek to join parties out of the jurisdiction,

[34] This assumes an unproblematic case where the parties have agreed a single (or clearly delimited) jurisdiction or arbitration clause. The 'one-stop-shop' approach becomes rather harder to apply where one has apparently competing jurisdiction/arbitration clauses. See, eg, *BNP Paribas SA v Trattamento Rifiuti Metropolitani SpA* [2019] EWCA Civ 768, [2020] 1 All ER 762. Cases such as this rather reinforce the point that the *Fiona Trust* reasoning really only works without undue difficulty in the 'easy' or 'paradigm' case.

[35] *Donohue v Armco* (n 21). The position is rather different under the Brussels Regulation.

[36] See the rules in CPR 19.

so that service out needs to be sought, there is an appropriate 'gateway' under CPR PD 6B, para 3.1(3), which provides:

> The claimant may serve a claim form out of the jurisdiction with the permission of the court under rule 6.36 where – …
>
> (3) A claim is made against a person ('the defendant') on whom the claim form has been or will be served (otherwise than in reliance on this paragraph) and –
>
> (a) there is between the claimant and the defendant a real issue which it is reasonable for the court to try; and
>
> (b) the claimant wishes to serve the claim form on another person who is a necessary or proper party to that claim ….

There are, of course, similar provisions under the Brussels regime, but given the withdrawal of the UK and the fact that *Fiona Trust* was not a Brussels case, my focus is not on this particular regime, save to the extent that it elucidates the present law in this jurisdiction.

The short point is that whilst, of course, it is sensible to say that disputes and claims arising out of a given relationship should be heard together, and not separately and in different proceedings, this is a truth that is *not* absolute. There are times where the bilateral relationship between *A* and *B* prevents the efficient hearing of related disputes or claims because it enables one of the parties to insist on or at least press for a form of process that is actually inefficient, possibly unjust, and actually contrary to the expectations of reasonable parties. A great deal depends on the ambit and the weight that is given to the jurisdiction clause or arbitration clause in issue. That, of course, leads right back into the issues of interpretation and distinction that *Fiona Trust* was supposed to have consigned to history.

B. The Extent to which Jurisdiction Clauses Arise Out of a Consensual Arrangement

Usually the jurisdiction clause will be in a contract. But it would be dangerous to assume that jurisdiction clauses are always founded on contract or that where jurisdiction clauses are founded on contract, they are treated like ordinary contractual terms. Neither of these assumptions is, in my judgment, true: but they are assumptions that pervade the *Fiona Trust* analysis, and give the decision its impetus towards 'party autonomy' and the 'relationship' between the parties.

This section considers these two – in my view, misplaced – assumptions in the context of jurisdiction clauses. Of course, I am not saying that jurisdiction clauses do not often have a contractual basis. They often do. But, often, they do not. Thus, by way of example:

(1) If *A* seeks to assign their right to *B*, it is trite that such an assignment does not have to be contractual. But, equally, it is quite possible for the assignment to be sufficiently complex to be reduced to writing, and for it

to contain a jurisdiction (and choice of law) clause. The same is true of declarations of trust or settlement of trust property. These instances are sufficiently close to contract not to provoke much alarm, but what they do suggest is that whilst the validity of jurisdiction clauses may very well rest on some form of consent or conditional benefit, the basis is not, in the strict sense, contractual. That, of course, fits very well with the general approach of English law to questions of characterisation. An issue of contract remains – in private international law terms – a contractual issue even if the contract is not, stricta sensu, a contract according to English domestic law (eg, because there is no consideration).

(2) There is, in English law, insufficient analysis of gifts, and promises to make gifts. Where the proprietary transaction (the 'gift') is itself preceded by some kind of expressed intention to make the gift, questions of legal validity immediately arise. Absent contract or trust, these sorts of transaction are not really recognised in English law, but other jurisdictions will be different. A choice of law clause is likely to be very significant here, and a jurisdiction clause important. But in a very real sense, these clauses will have an analytically difficult foundation, probably covered by characterising the issue as relating to a contract in the 'international sense'.

(3) In the law of torts, Stapleton articulates the allocation of risk that can arise in the following terms:[37] '[i]t is long settled that tort law will, subject to any statutory controls, give effect to an indication by one party that he disclaims *or limits* a potential tort liability for a risk to a second party if that second party was given reasonable notice of this before he voluntarily chose to encounter the risk rather than walk away. The law takes that choice as a manifestation of acceptance of the risk allocation on offer.' Stapleton is careful to eschew the language of contract. Indeed, that is her point: she discusses the 'notice' cases in the context of 'co-operative arrangements between parties who are not linked by a contract'.[38] That, indeed, appears to be the analysis in the cases, at least so far as access to land is concerned, as seen in *Ashdown v Samuel Williams & Sons Ltd*.[39] *Bennett v Tugwell* is an interesting variant on a theme.[40] The defendant mistakenly believed that his father's car was only insured to be on the road, and decided to protect his father from any liability by placing a notice in the case informing any

[37] J Stapleton, *Three Essays on Torts* (Oxford, OUP, 2021) 36 (emphasis added).

[38] ibid, 35. That is a distinction that also emerges from the Unfair Contract Terms Act 1977, which also applies to the exclusion of liability by 'a notice given to persons generally or to particular persons' (s 2). Whether that is a distinction noted by the Consumer Rights Act 2015, and whether that Act only applies to contractual obligations, is not a matter that I propose to debate in this chapter.

[39] *Ashdown v Samuel Williams & Sons Ltd* [1957] 1 QB 49 (CA). In this case, a notice was relied upon to exclude liability in negligence for the landowner. The Court of Appeal explicitly proceeded on the basis that there was not contract, and that the plaintiff was a mere licensee: 418 (Singleton LJ), 425 (Jenkins LJ) and 428 (Parker LJ).

[40] *Bennett v Tugwell* [1971] 2 QB 267 (QB).

> passengers that they travelled 'at their own risk'. The plaintiff, knowing of and accepting the terms of the notice, nevertheless attempted to claim against the father's insurers, the insurance in fact being comprehensive. The plaintiff failed, but by reason of the principle of *volenti non fit injuria*. Ackner J held in terms that the plaintiff had assumed the risk of injury.[41] These cases are, of course, very far removed from our present subject-matter: the basis for the bindingness of a jurisdiction clause. But I do not see why a notice of the sort contained in *Ashdown* or in *Bennett v Tugwell* could not contain, instead of or in addition to an exclusion of liability, a clause stating that the jurisdiction for the resolution of any dispute was to be that of Ruritania.

Jurisdiction clauses in civilian systems (like the Brussels Regime) are more to do with a process where an appropriate court is selected by a route that attaches some weight to party choice, but ultimately sees a jurisdiction clause as a *negative* thing, like a clause excluding or limiting liability, taking jurisdiction *away* from the court that would otherwise have it, and to be treated with corresponding caution. Common law systems, by contrast, have been seen as attaching far more weight to party autonomy, and consider party choice to be, if not paramount, then at least more significant than in civilian jurisdictions.

The subject of autonomy in international contracts and disputes lies beyond this chapter.[42] But what is here being discussed is the extent to which the parties to a given relationship may, by agreement, sculpt that relationship. It is the borderline between party autonomy and mandatory rules.[43] Nygh says this about mandatory rules generally:[44]

> According to Savigny, the category of 'exceptional laws' must reflect a public, rather than a private interest. That interest might be declared by the legislature, but that was rare. It was implicit in laws which sought to protect moral values, such as a marriage law which excludes polygamy; or they may 'rest on reasons of public interest, whether these relate to politics, police or political economy'.
>
> This was the genesis of the concept now known as 'mandatory rules', namely an ill-defined category of national laws which override the normal conflictual rules, including the choice made by parties to an international contract. The notion of 'public interest' has expanded since Savigny's time: often the mandatory rules serve to protect the interests of private citizens, such as consumers and employers. Nor are such rules of necessity territorially-based: they may not only affect transactions by foreigners within the jurisdiction, but extend to transactions entered into abroad by nationals of the enacting state.

It will readily be appreciated from this that party autonomy is classed by the writer as the 'norm', with restrictions on party autonomy being regarded as

[41] ibid, 273.
[42] See, generally, P Nygh, *Autonomy in International Contracts* (Oxford, OUP, 1999).
[43] ibid, ch 9.
[44] ibid, 199.

'exceptional' mandatory rules. That is a borderline that might very well be debated, and I suspect that a civilian lawyer would ask *why* primacy ought to be given to party autonomy: why cannot jurisdiction be allocated according to rules that have far less to do with party autonomy?

It is not the point of this chapter to debate these difficult questions, but it *is* important to understand the landscape which English law inhabits, and which underpins *Fiona Trust*. For present purposes, I am quite prepared to accept that party autonomy should be, and is, given primacy in our private international law. Hence our reading of jurisdiction and arbitration clauses. But, if and to the extent that primacy is considered to arise *purely* out of a contractual agreement and as a matter of *right* (if the agreement is construed sufficiently widely), then that is an error. As has been described, the basis for the bindingness of jurisdiction clauses is not always contractual, although it is fair to say that English law would not be attracted to giving binding effect to a jurisdiction clause that was imposed and not (in some way) voluntarily acceded to. Further, it is important to understand the manner in which English law gives force to jurisdiction clauses.

First, leaving – as we must – the Brussels regime to one side, formal jurisdiction is established by either serving in the jurisdiction (ie commencing the proceedings as of right) or obtaining permission to serve out of the jurisdiction (ie deploying the so-called exorbitant jurisdiction). Service of a claim form is – according to the English view of the world – the foundation of jurisdiction.[45] This is in contrast to the civilian view, which is characterised by the view that service is not the foundation of jurisdiction, but grounds for jurisdiction are based on the existence of specific connecting factors:[46]

> In civil law systems jurisdiction is founded on statute. The statutory jurisdiction grounds are based on the existence of particular connections between the litigation and the forum. The mere physical presence of the defendant in the forum is not regarded as a sufficiently connecting factor.

Further, generally speaking – and this is no doubt a consequence of the 'rules-based' civilian approach – there is no discretion as to jurisdiction.[47]

Second, obtaining permission to serve out – and avoiding having service ordered set aside – requires three things: (a) the claimant must satisfy the court that in relation to the foreign defendant there is a serious issue to be tried on the merits; (b) the claimant must satisfy the court that there is a good arguable case that the claim falls within one of the 'gateways' set out in paragraph 3.1 of Practice Direction 6B of the Civil Procedure Rules; and (c) England and Wales must be clearly and distinctly the proper forum for the trial of the claims.[48] Jurisdiction clauses in contracts constitute an exception to this regime of

[45] N McLachlan and P Nygh, *Transnational Tort Litigation: Jurisdictional Principles* (Oxford, OUP, 1996) ch 2.

[46] ibid, 41.

[47] ibid, 46–48.

[48] See, eg, *Microsoft Mobile Oy (Ltd) v Sony Europe Ltd* [2017] EWHC 374 (Ch) [88].

'exorbitant' jurisdiction. By CPR 6.33(2B)(b), a claimant may serve a claim form on a defendant out of the jurisdiction where, 'for each claim made against the defendant to be served and included in the claim form … a contract contains a term to the effect that the contract shall have jurisdiction to determine that claim'. Thus, a jurisdiction clause – provided it is in a contract – requires no permission, and the distinction between ordinary jurisdiction and exorbitant jurisdiction is, to that extent, eroded.[49]

However, the *forum conveniens* or *forum non conveniens* requirement remains. The first edition of Joseph's book on jurisdiction and arbitration agreements puts the point in the following way:[50]

> At common law, notwithstanding the general discretion to stay proceedings or decline jurisdiction, the English courts will uphold a jurisdiction agreement and keep their parties to their bargain unless strong cause or strong reason is shown why this should not be so. This will apply irrespective of whether a party is seeking permission to issue and serve proceedings on a defendant outside the jurisdiction or whether a defendant, having been served as of right in the jurisdiction, seeks the stay of those proceedings pursuant to the inherent jurisdiction of the court. The policy of keeping parties to their bargain will apply equally to jurisdiction agreements in favour of a foreign court and in favour of English courts. The different procedures that apply in cases of a challenge to the jurisdiction and an application for a stay are discussed … below. In an ordinary case, although the pathways differ, the result should be the same irrespective of the procedure involved ….

It would be remiss not to note, at least, that this is a controversial proposition, but one that underlies much of the thinking of this chapter, namely that the court can (through the *forum non conveniens* mechanism) *choose* not to give effect to a contractual term. There is a contrary view – forcefully articulated by many – where this approach is branded 'unique' and inferentially undesirable:[51]

> It is difficult to think of any other contract term which, although part of the contract between the parties and not otherwise unenforceable, may nonetheless be overridden at the discretion of the courts. Is it a wholly convincing answer to say that this uniqueness of approach is justified by the uniqueness of the context in which foreign jurisdiction clauses operate, namely the regulation of jurisdiction.

My answer to this point appears generally through this chapter, but the following brief points need to be made:

(1) As a matter of comity, there should be as little difference as possible between jurisdiction clauses in favour of England and jurisdiction clauses in favour of other countries.

[49] The change is a relatively recent one, brought about by the 127th CPR Practice Direction Update (February 2021): see *Civil Procedure 2021*, 429. Previously, para 3.1(6)(d) constituted this a 'gateway'.

[50] D Joseph, *Jurisdiction and Arbitration Agreements and their Enforcement,* 1st edn (London, Sweet & Maxwell, 2005) [10.03].

[51] See, eg, E Peel, 'Exclusive Jurisdiction Agreements: Purity and Pragmatism in the Conflict of Laws' [1998] *Lloyds Maritime and Commercial Law Quarterly* 182.

(2) At the end of the day, it is the courts, and not the parties, that determine which cases are heard, and which are not.
(3) The *forum conveniens* jurisdiction is extremely helpful where the jurisdiction clause cuts across interests of jurisdiction clause ought to be significantly greater where only *A* and *B*'s interests are implicated.

A number of additional points, following on from this, can and should be made. First, there is an understandable, but perhaps unwarranted, distinction drawn between consensual jurisdiction selections that arise out of contract and those that do not. So far as the former are concerned, there is little distinction between service in the jurisdiction and service out (subject to the inevitable question of mechanics). Both can be achieved without permission but both are subject to a *forum conveniens* test.

Second, that will not be the case if the consensual selection of jurisdiction is *non-contractual*, unless the question of the meaning of 'a contract' is resolved in an extremely wide sense. In such a case, in addition to the *forum conveniens* test, an appropriate 'gateway' will have to be identified if service out is sought.

Third, be that as it may, the reason jurisdiction clauses are enforced is not because they are contractual and contracts should be complied with but because there is a *policy* in English law that such promises should be complied with. That might be seen as a distinction without a difference, but I disagree. For reasons that I shall come to, the difference is extremely significant because it moves the debate away from 'party autonomy' and into the realm of public law control, which accords substantial weight to 'party autonomy'. In short, jurisdiction clauses are certainly not like 'ordinary' contractual terms.[52]

This part of my analysis has not mentioned arbitration clauses. There is a reason for this: whereas jurisdiction clauses have a solid basis in domestic law, and can be informed by (as it were) 'local' policies, arbitration clauses have a far greater basis on party autonomy, which is buttressed by international convention. I will be returning to arbitration clauses in due course, but it is entirely appropriate at this stage just to acknowledge that what has here been said is quite deliberately focussed on jurisdiction clauses, and the extent to which party autonomy plays a role.[53]

VI. CONSENT, PARTY AUTONOMY AND THE PROTECTION OF THIRD PARTIES

It must be a logical consequence of the 'party autonomy' approach to jurisdiction clauses (and, even more so, arbitration clauses) that the interests of third

[52] That, perhaps, will have a number of implications, which cannot all be completely teased out in this chapter. One such implication is the extent to which damages ought to lie for the 'breach' of a jurisdiction clause.
[53] On this, see J Paulsson, *The Idea of Arbitration*, 1st edn (Oxford, OUP, 2013) ch 1. The ubiquity of the New York Convention on the Recognition and Enforcement of Foreign Arbitral Awards is also very significant.

parties – strangers to the relationship – are protected. Really, this is the obverse of the value being attributed to party autonomy: a person who is *not* a party to the relationship ought not to be affected by the other person's choice. That would be to undermine that third party's autonomy. This might be more acceptable in a civilian 'mandatory rules' environment (where party autonomy counts for less) than in a common law environment, where party autonomy (as I have described) counts for a great deal.

So far, the 'relationship' stressed by *Fiona Trust* has been used as the basis for justifying a 'one-stop-shop' for the hearing and determination of all disputes arising out of that relationship, and construing jurisdiction and arbitration clauses accordingly. But the 'relationship' stressed in *Fiona Trust* is – or ought to be – also a critical *limitor* on such clauses: third parties to the relationship should not – save in very limited circumstances – be affected by them. They ought to be entitled to rely on the 'ordinary' jurisdiction of the courts, unaffected by a clause selecting a particular jurisdiction or referring the matter to arbitration. As will be seen, this is, in fact, *not* the way jurisdiction clauses – as opposed to arbitration clauses – are treated by the English courts. In other words, third parties – who ought not to be affected by jurisdiction clauses – *are* affected, in circumstances where they would not be if the clause in question was an arbitration clause and not a jurisdiction clause. I will consider arbitration clauses first, for that reason.

A. Arbitration Clauses

Merkin and Flannery note that:[54]

> One of the thorniest issues in arbitration derives from the notion that the arbitration agreement in general binds only the parties to it, and not third parties. In the common law world, this derives from the nineteenth-century concept, now abrogated in many jurisdictions, of privity of contract. It is really part of arbitration's problem as a process, because it can create a huge difficulty in so many cases.

I have already referenced the inconvenient case of the coverage dispute between insured and insurer being governed by an arbitration clause, but where any contingent claim against the broker cannot (without the consent of all) be introduced into the arbitration. The same is true of guarantors, where (unless the guarantor is a party to the agreement between debtor and creditor) the creditor will arbitrate against the debtor and then seek to enforce the guarantee separately against the guarantor under separate proceedings.[55]

[54] *Merkin and Flannery* (n 27) 70; Briggs (n 31) [6.65].
[55] *Merkin and Flannery* (n 27) [6.1.9.2].

The fact is that this inconvenience – for such it undoubtedly can be, when viewed objectively[56] – is sometimes circumvented by adopting a liberal construction of the relevant agreements, so as to 'stretch' the ambit of the arbitration clause so as to extend to persons who might otherwise be regarded as third parties to it. Thus, in *Stellar Shipping Co LLC v Hudson Shipping Lines*,[57] Hamblen J construed the various – separate – contracts between creditor, debtor and guarantor as incorporating the *same* agreement to arbitrate before a common tribunal.[58] In reaching this conclusion, Hamblen J expressly referred to the one-stop-shop principle in *Fiona Trust*.[59]

B. Jurisdiction Clauses

One might think that what goes for arbitration clauses ought also to go for jurisdiction clauses, but that is not – and ought not to be – the case. There is greater flexibility in the case of jurisdiction clauses, in the sense that they may – in the appropriate case – be overridden. *Donoghue v Armco* is such an instance, albeit a rare one.[60] That was a case where a party was permitted to sue *in breach of* an exclusive jurisdiction clause. One would ordinarily expect that where the nature of a dispute is such that litigating in accordance with the strict terms of the jurisdiction clause would involve third parties in litigation in a jurisdiction to which they would not otherwise be subject, the *Donoghue v Armco* approach would be taken. That, certainly, is the view of Briggs.[61]

But there is very little case law on the point. The Court of Appeal, in *Public Institution for Social Security v Banque Pictet & Cie SA*,[62] appears to have permitted the forum for disputes *not* within a jurisdiction clause to be dictated by the forum for disputes *mandated* by that clause, but this was a Brussels Regime case, and one where the forum mandated by the jurisdiction clause was *also* the domicile of the defendants relying on the jurisdiction clause. So there was a perhaps unhealthy competition between different mandatory rules of jurisdiction, resulting in what is tantamount to an unclear and not fully articulated discretion.

The use of 'anchor' defendants to found jurisdiction against other defendants, who would not otherwise be subject to the jurisdiction of the English courts,

[56] There may very often be a huge tactical advantage in the third party refusing to consent to joining an arbitration, even where both parties to the arbitration agreement wish it. Thus, in many coverage disputes, both insurer and insured will want the broker in, who will not agree to participate.

[57] *Stellar Shipping Co LLC v Hudson Shipping Lines* [2010] EWHC 2985 (Comm).

[58] ibid, [56].

[59] ibid, [55].

[60] *Donohue v Armco* (n 21).

[61] Briggs (n 3) [6.66].

[62] *Public Institution for Social Security v Banque Pictet & Cie SA* [2022] EWCA Civ 29.

using the 'necessary or proper party' gateway of CPR PD 6B, para 3.1(3), is well-established and well-used. But where jurisdiction against the anchor defendant arises because of a jurisdiction clause in favour of England, it is suggested that the joinder of third parties to the jurisdiction clause as necessary and proper parties to the dispute is a matter warranting the most careful consideration. A court ought, equally, to consider whether the proceedings brought against the anchor defendant ought – when considering the totality of the proceedings – to be stayed, notwithstanding the existence of a jurisdiction clause binding the anchor defendant.

These are, I suspect, areas of law that will arise with greater frequency in these post-Brexit times, particularly with the rise of the wide-ranging damages actions arising out of infringements of competition law. But the general approach of the English courts seems to me to be setting course in the right direction. The decision of the Court of Appeal in *Erste Group Bank AG (London Branch) v JSC 'VMZ Red October'*[63] suggests that the 'necessary or proper party' gateway will be patrolled quite carefully. In that case, the gateway was relied upon in circumstances where the jurisdiction against the anchor defendant arose by virtue of a jurisdiction clause in favour of the English courts. The Court of Appeal made clear that when considering this gateway, the Court had to examine the nature of the claim which arose against the anchor defendant in isolation, on the assumption that there would be no additional joinder of any foreign defendants. The Court had to be satisfied not only that there was a real issue between the claimant and the anchor defendant, but also that it was an issue which it was reasonable for the court to try. Only at that second stage would the court go on to consider whether the foreign party was a necessary or proper party to that claim.

Erste does not consider the application of the *forum conveniens* test in such contexts, but it seems to me that the foundations exist for a sensitive application of *Donohue v Armco* in cases where there is a real issue to be tried between the anchor defendant and the claimant *and* where it can be said that *if* that claim is tried in England, the third party *would be* a necessary or proper party. My point is that this should not be the end of the inquiry: the Court ought to go on and ask – should the third party, a necessary or proper party to the litigation, nevertheless be 'sucked in' because of a jurisdiction clause to which it is not a party? The Court should at least consider staying the claims against the anchor defendant in favour of some foreign jurisdiction. My sense is that this is precisely where English law is heading and that although, in some sense, this conclusion might seem to be antipathetic to *Fiona Trust*, it is actually entirely consistent with the spirit of that decision.

[63] *Erste Group Bank AG (London Branch) v JSC 'VMZ Red October'* [2015] EWCA Civ 379, [2015] 1 CLC 706.

VII. WIDENING THE NET – EXTENDING MATTERS TO NON-PARTIES

So far, the discussion has been in relation to *not* extending the effect of a jurisdiction or arbitration clause to third parties, which is (I suggest) a necessary part of the *Fiona Trust* reasoning. That reasoning is underlined by those instances where, even though there might be said to be a good reason for joining a stranger to the clause, that route is not taken. Such cases are briefly considered next. Thereafter, I consider what might be called an exception to this rule – the position of assignees. I will there suggest that in fact assignments are *confirmatory* of the general rule. Finally, I will consider what appears to be a genuine exception.

A. Instances Confirmatory of the Rule

Merkin and Flannery note that in civil law jurisdictions, there is a 'group of companies' doctrine, whereby an arbitration clause signed by one company in a group of companies widens the scope of persons bound by the clause.[64] It may be that such an approach extends also to jurisdiction clauses: I have not examined the doctrine in any detail. What is clear, however, is that such a doctrine has no place in English law, which (as has been described) approaches matters on the basis of the doctrine of privity of contract.[65]

B. Assignments

It is wrong to speak of the assignment of contracts. Since contracts typically involve obligations going both ways, a *contract* cannot be assigned, because an assignment cannot, for obvious reasons, transfer a burden to a third party. Only benefits can be assigned.

Where the benefit that has been assigned is sought to be enforced or vindicated by the assignee against the debtor, the assignee will be constrained in the process by any procedural limitations that were agreed between the assignor and the debtor.[66] Such limitations will include jurisdiction and arbitration clauses. Thus, an assignee of rights under a contract was only entitled to enforce those rights in accordance with the terms of the contract, which included an exclusive jurisdiction clause.[67]

[64] *Merkin and Flannery* (n 27) 70.

[65] In relation to groups of companies, see *Peterson Farms Inc v C&M Farming Ltd* [2004] 1 Lloyd's Rep 603 (Com Ct).

[66] M Smith and N Leslie, *The Law of Assignment*, 3rd edn (Oxford, OUP, 2018) [21.27].

[67] *Glencore International AG v Metro Trading International Inc* [1999] 2 All ER (Comm) 899 (Com Ct) 917 (Moore-Bick J).

The same is true where there is an arbitration clause.[68] Indeed, the Arbitration Act 1996 makes express provision for this. Section 9 of the Act provides for a more-or-less automatic stay in favour of arbitration[69] on the application of a party to an arbitration agreement. Section 82(2) of the Act defines a party to an arbitration agreement as including 'any person claiming under or through a party to the agreement'. This clearly embraces an assignee.[70]

The fact that an assignee is bound by an arbitration or jurisdiction clause is actually confirmatory of the autonomy theory, rather than an exception to it. The fact is an assignee is *not* a third party.

C. Third Parties

Where a right is conferred on a third party, enabling that third party to enforce that right pursuant to the Contracts (Rights of Third Parties) Act 1999, the position is unsurprisingly similar to the position on assignment. Section 1(4) of the 1999 Act provides that 'this section does not confer a right on a third party to enforce a term of a contract otherwise than subject to and in accordance with any other relevant terms of the contract', and section 8 makes specific provision in relation to arbitration clauses.[71]

Of greater interest, for present purposes, are so-called 'Himalaya' clauses, which purport to grant to sub-contractors, servants and/or agents the benefit of the same exclusions granted to the contracting party. Such clauses are designed to prevent the circumvention of contractual exclusion clauses by the bringing of proceedings against sub-contractors in tort. They derive their name from the cruise liner 'Himalaya' in *Adler v Dickson*.[72] The extent to which third parties can in fact benefit from such clauses *independent* of the 1999 Act is a very difficult one, and not a matter that there is time to analyse exhaustively in the chapter.[73] However, the following points can be made, which are relevant to the present discussion:

(1) The common law controversies can be side-stepped by the use of the 1999 Act. As has been noted already, jurisdiction clauses and arbitration clauses

[68] *The Jordan Nicolov* [1990] 2 Lloyd's Rep 11 (Com Ct) 15–16 (Hobhouse J); *Schiffahrtsgesellschaft Detlev von Appen GmbH v Voest Alpine Intertrading GmbH* [1997] 2 Lloyd's Rep 279 (CA) 284–85, 286 (Scott VC); *West Tankers Inc v Ras Riunione Adriatica di Securta* [2005] EWHC 454 (Comm), [2005] 2 All ER 454 (Comm) (Colman J).

[69] See s 9(4): 'On an application under this section the court shall grant a stay unless satisfied that the arbitration agreement is null and void, inoperative, or incapable of being performed'.

[70] *Merkin and Flannery* (n 27) [6.1.9.1] and [9.2.1].

[71] I assume the specific reference to arbitration clauses is to ensure a seamless transition between this Act and the Arbitration Act – but it does seem a little curious that s 8 is limited to arbitration clauses.

[72] *Adler v Dickson* [1955] 1 QB 158 (CA).

[73] The controversies are helpfully set out and considered in H Beale (ed), *Chitty on Contracts*, 34th edn (London, Sweet & Maxwell, 2021) [17-045], [17-049]–[17-052].

will bind the beneficiary of such a contract in much the same way as an assignee would be.

(2) Furthermore, section 1(6) of the 1999 Act provides: 'Where a term of a contract excludes or limits liability in relation to any matter references in this Act to the third party enforcing the term shall be construed as references to his availing himself of the exclusion or limitation.'

(3) Where a person has the benefit of an exclusion or limitation clause, that person is not going to be *initiating* proceedings as a claimant, but *reacting to them* as a defendant. Suppose, as may often be the case, proceedings are initiated against the beneficiary of the exclusion or limitation clause in breach[74] of the jurisdiction or arbitration clause governing the contract. According to the operation of the 1999 Act, the beneficiary of the exclusion/limitation clause ought to be able to deploy the jurisdiction clause or the arbitration clause in support of an application for a stay of proceedings brought in an English court where either a foreign jurisdiction or arbitration has been selected by the parties to the contract.

(4) The operation of the 1999 Act can be excluded if it appears that the parties to the contract did not intend a term to be enforceable by a third party,[75] and my experience is that the Act is often expressly excluded in a contract. However, the Act does not abrogate any other right or remedy of a third party that might exist apart from the Act.[76] But a beneficiary under a 'Himalaya' clause will unlikely be able to contend that English proceedings brought in contravention of a jurisdiction or arbitration clause ought to be stayed.[77]

VIII. RELEVANCE OF THE AMBIT OF THE JURISDICTION OR ARBITRATION CLAUSE

So far, I have been considering the limits and extents of the *Fiona Trust* 'one-stop-shop' approach by reference to the 'relationship' between the parties to the contract. The unsurprising point that emerges is that there is great deal of reluctance to extend the benefit/burden of arbitration clauses to third parties. The perhaps more surprising point is that there is – or at least can be – significantly more flexibility so far as jurisdiction clauses are concerned. One of the points that emerges with insufficient clarity from *Fiona Trust* is the importance and significance of the distinction between jurisdiction and arbitration clauses.

However, I have been silent on the question of *construction* or *interpretation* of jurisdiction and arbitration clauses. That is for the very good reason

[74] There will likely be questions of construction arising. I will be coming to these.

[75] See s 1(2) of the 1999 Act.

[76] See ss 7(1) (generally) and 6(5) (in relation to contracts for the carriage of goods).

[77] *The Mahkutai* [1996] 1 AC 650 (PC); *Bouygues Offshore SA v Caspian Shipping Co (No 2)* [1997] 2 Lloyd's Rep 485 (Ad).

that these questions were all intended by the decision in *Fiona Trust* to be put behind us. But is that really the case? I am going to suggest not. Before I do so, it might be worth having a bit of a refresher course on the sort of distinctions that were drawn before *Fiona Trust* apparently removed them for ever from material consideration.

A. The 'Old' Law

Inevitably, the construction of jurisdiction and arbitration clauses needs to be informed by the canons of construction that apply generally, and even specific and often used forms of words are going to be context sensitive. Nevertheless, parties – particularly parties to commercial and standard form agreements – use word forms that have 'worked in the past', and that is how the 'linguistic nuances' Lord Hoffmann complained of in *Fiona Trust* accrete. The law as it stood in 2005 was described by Joseph (from whose work I draw unashamedly) as follows:

(1) *Disputes or differences as to the construction of the contract.* Joseph says that '[h]is is a narrow form of words and has been held to cover the interpretation of the contract but not a claim for rectification. Tort claims also fall outside this form of wording.'[78]
(2) *Disputes arising under the contract / Disputes in respect of the contract / Disputes arising from the contract.* Joseph says that '[a]s a general rule these wordings cover claims arising from an alleged repudiation or frustration of the contract'.[79]
(3) *Disputes arising out of the contract.* Joseph says '[t]his is accepted on the balance of authorities as being a wide form of words and wider than 'disputes under'. This form of wording generally evinces an intention to submit a wider category of disputes than simply those matters that arise concerning the rights and obligations created by the contract itself and covers virtually the full range of disputes, except for a dispute as to the existence of the contract itself.'[80]
(4) *Disputes in relation to a contract or concerning the contract.* Joseph says that '[a]n agreement to refer disputes in relation to the contract to a designated forum is generally considered to be a wide form of words that clearly reaches beyond the four corners of the contract itself and, on its face, indicates an intention to refer all disputes that relate to the transaction'.[81]

[78] Joseph (n 50) [4.50].
[79] ibid, [4.51].
[80] ibid, [4.52].
[81] ibid, [4.55].

(5) *Claims arising out of or in connection with*. Joseph says '[t]his is a very wide form of wording and is used in a number of model arbitration clauses. The ambit is even wider than a clause that provides for disputes arising out of the contract to be referred to the chosen forum. The wording is capable of extending not only to claims in contract and tort, but also to pre-contractual misrepresentation, rectification, mistake, avoidance and claims under the Civil Liability Contribution Act 1978.'[82]

(6) *Claims or counterclaims to be submitted to arbitration*. Joseph says '[t]his is again a wide form of words. It has been said by the Court of Appeal in *Woolf v Collis Removal Service* that such a clause is expressed in the widest possible terms as to ambit. Such a clause does not speak of 'claims under the contract' but simply of 'claims'. It is still necessary to establish a relationship between the claim and the transaction covered by the contract, but such a contract will extend to related tort claims.'

B. The 'Old' Law Not Yet Dead?

The last clause is, I would suggest, what Lord Hoffmann and Lord Hope had in mind in *Fiona Trust* as the essential 'default' construction for jurisdiction and arbitration clauses. Where the parties agree on jurisdiction and arbitration, then all disputes arising out of that relationship should come before one forum. There is, of course, nothing wrong with this. Indeed, it is beguiling in its rather delightful simplicity, consigning the distinctions so helpfully articulated by Joseph into the jurisprudential dustbin.

Why, one might ask, did not Lord Hoffmann and Lord Hope go further, and say that where a jurisdiction clause or an arbitration clause is agreed between *A* and *B*, then it extends to *all* claims *A* might have against *B* – and vice versa – whether such claims arise out of the relationship between *A* and *B* or not? So – to take a slightly unreal example – if *A* were negligently to run over *B* in London, why should not *B*'s claim against *A* be resolved in New York, because *A* and *B* have a business relationship for the provision of goods and services which contains a New York arbitration clause?

The example is unreal, because it depends on a huge coincidence. But, accepting the coincidence, I doubt very much that any court would reach this conclusion, absent the clearest of wording (and perhaps not even then). It is worth asking why. It is not that the arbitration clause affects third parties. The only – somewhat unexpected – outcome is that the personal injury claim *B* has against *A* gets determined in New York. I suggest that the outcome is not only unexpected, but undesirable, and for a number of reasons.

[82] ibid, [4.56].

First, we, as common lawyers brought up in the *forum conveniens* tradition – albeit attenuated now by many years of service under the Brussels Regime – have an acute sense of the appropriateness of jurisdiction. And in this case, all our instincts are telling us that New York is the wrong place to litigate.

Second, and relatedly, even if no third party is involved, *B*'s claims against *A* are *generic* in the sense that it does not matter who the defendant is: the outcome of the case ought to be the same. It should not matter by whom *B* was run down – whether it was *X* or whether it was *A* ought not to make a difference, even as to jurisdiction.

Third, and only as a potentiality, we are conscious that *A*'s bad driving, resulting in *B*'s injury, could easily involve other people: *A* might hit *C*, as well as *B*, in the same accident. In such a case, it would be both odd and undesirable for *B* to be compelled to sue in a New York arbitration, in which *C* could not (as of right) join. *C*, of course, would claim in England – but *B* would not be able to participate absent *A*'s consent.

The fact is that a provision that refers certain disputes to resolution in a particular forum that would not otherwise be the forum for the resolution of the dispute inevitably arises out of some kind of relationship between the parties, and it would be perverse not to allow that relationship to colour the ambit of the clause. In a sense, that is exactly what *Fiona Trust* is saying: there is a relationship between *A* and *B*, in the shape of their agreement, and the implication of that relationship/agreement is the 'one-stop-shop' for the resolution of disputes between *A* and *B*.

These factors – and particularly the point that disputes arising out of a relationship between *A* and *B* may well affect *C*, *D* and *E* – are factors that simply do not appear on the *Fiona Trust* radar, and I think they should have done. The point is perhaps best illustrated by my decision in *Microsoft Mobile OY (Ltd) v Sony Europe Ltd*,[83] a case that I have a great deal of affection for, because it was the first case I decided as a judge on the High Court bench. This was a wide-ranging jurisdiction dispute concerning a cartel regarding mobile phone batteries. One of the issues that I needed to determine was an application for a stay in favour of an arbitration clause pursuant to section 9 of the Arbitration Act 1996. The significance of this application in the context of the wider dispute concerning jurisdiction over the (tortious) competition infringement claims was that – if successful – it removed from the fray a party who had been deployed in the litigation as an 'anchor' defendant.

I construed the arbitration clause in light of *Fiona Trust*.[84] The submissions before me, however, stressed that generally speaking, tortious competition claims had been held to be outwith jurisdiction clauses, relying in particular on *Ryanair Ltd v Esso Italiana Srl*.[85] I distinguished *Ryanair* because of the very

[83] *Microsoft Mobile* (n 48).
[84] ibid, [42]–[46].
[85] *Ryanair Ltd v Esso Italiana Srl* [2013] EWCA Civ 1450, [2015] 1 All ER (Comm) 152.

interesting terms that subsisted in the contract containing the arbitration clause in this case. Specifically, the contract contained a 'good faith' provision in the following terms:[86]

> The Price(s) are stated in Appendix 2 and shall include all SELLER's obligations in accordance with this Agreement. Changes in Price(s) shall be mutually agreed in writing *and negotiated in good faith*....

The contract effectively provided an umbrella containing general terms that would inform the more specific terms for agreements for the supply of multiple goods over time. I concluded that:[87]

> It is very difficult to see how a party to the [agreement] ... could knowlingly engage in cartelist behaviour of the sort alleged by Microsoft Mobile without at the same time breaching Article 10.1 and triggering the obligation to inform under Article 21.1.

In these circumstances, I concluded that the tortious (competition) claims actually being advanced in this litigation were sufficiently closely related to a (potential) breach of contract claim based upon Article 10.1 (the 'good faith' provision) so as to be covered by the (widely-drawn) arbitration clause in the agreement.[88] In short, the combination of the relations between the parties and the arbitration clause compelled this particular outcome.

Yet there can be little doubt as to the inconvenience of this result. I leave on one side the jockeying for jurisdictional position, and the significance of the first defendant as 'anchor' defendant. The fact is that cartel claims sound in tort, and involve (by definition) multiple parties, who are jointly and severally liable for their involvement in what is a common scheme, the cartel. Trying one of these claims in a different forum does not make particularly good sense.

So, drawing these threads together, I am saying a number of things:

(1) First of all, wording of jurisdiction clauses and arbitration clauses *matters*, and I am not sure that one can, so easily, abandon the 'clanking chains' of prior case law, in the manner suggested by *Fiona Trust*. So far as I can see, in jurisdiction disputes where there is a jurisdiction or arbitration clause in play, issues of interpretation loom as large as they ever did.

(2) Second, an important question arises as to how one should construe jurisdiction and arbitration clauses. Should the approach be based simply on construing the clause as it was objectively understood by the parties to the relationship that it governs at the time of contracting without reference to effects on third parties? Perhaps, in the case of these clauses, a broader interpretational approach should be taken.

[86] *Microsoft Mobile* (n 48) [59]. Emphasis added.
[87] ibid, [70].
[88] ibid, [72]–[73].

(3) Third, although it would be difficult to defend a *different* approach to construing arbitration clauses and jurisdiction clauses, the fact is that there is much more ability (or, at least, potentiality) in a court overriding a jurisdiction clause than in a court overriding an arbitration clause.

IX. SOME CONCLUSIONS

This is a commentary on what is, undoubtedly, a landmark case, and detailed conclusions would be inappropriate. However, this chapter can, very profitably, be read with William Day's chapter on Brandon J's decision in *The Eleftheria*.[89] Brandon J helpfully stated – and Day helpfully explores – the various propositions that Brandon J held to be the law regarding the right to continue proceedings in England in the face of a foreign jurisdiction clause. The general consensus is that jurisdiction clauses ought to be treated in the same way, whether they are in favour of an English jurisdiction or a foreign, non-English, jurisdiction.

If that is right, then *Fiona Trust* and *The Eleftheria* ought to be regarded as twin pillars, supporting the same roof and leading to consistent outcomes. In terms of *outcome*, I strongly suspect that this is indeed the case, but the approach – in terms of reasoning – is very different. As I have described, the reasoning in *Fiona Trust* is very much based on the importance of interpreting consensual provisions as to jurisdiction, and it is the *party consent* that is paramount in the reasoning. Much less so, in the case of *The Eleftheria*, where the public nature and importance of jurisdiction clauses is much more evident.

Without in any way seeking to minimise the importance of construing that which has been agreed, and the importance of party autonomy – a value clearly recognised by this jurisdiction – it may be that the pendulum has begun to swing again, away from the 'contract' reasoning of *Fiona Trust* (and, to be fair, the cases that preceded it), and back toward a more nuanced view of allocation of jurisdiction, that takes fuller account of the public importance of allocating the correct case to the correct jurisdiction.

If that is the case, then there are a number of implications that will need to be worked out. I said[90] that it would not be possible to consider damages claims for the breach of jurisdiction clauses in this chapter, and that remains true. But it is self-evident that the nature of such claims will be affected by what is understood to be as the juridical basis for the jurisdiction and the arbitration clause.

[89] *Owners of Cargo Lately Laden on Board the Eleftheria v Owners of the Eleftheria* [1970] P 94 (Ad). See ch 10 in this volume.

[90] See n 52 above.

17

Enka Insaat ve Sanayi AS v OOO Insurance Company Chubb (2020)

DAVID JOSEPH KC*

I. INTRODUCTION

FOR MORE THAN a century in the post-industrial era, business has looked increasingly to resolve disputes otherwise than by trial in a local or national court. This trend has been given greater push and emphasis in the recent decades which has witnessed the very considerable internationalisation of capital and ever wider deployment of investment. In turn this has led to an explosion in the popularity of international arbitration as the go to means of alternative dispute resolution. It is of course arguable that this wave may have already reached its peak and will be challenged by smarter technological means of resolving disputes which may not even require lawyers, let alone collections of this nature to explore but that would be the subject of another chapter and another forum. For now, international arbitration appears still to reign supreme and boasts considerably more than an 80 per cent market share in terms of the resolution of commercial contractual disputes between parties of more than one nationality.

International arbitration is nothing if not an interesting construct. It is the creature of the parties' agreement sitting side by side with statutory control, where the legislation itself looks to international treaty and rules for content and inspiration. So once the initial excitement of the possibilities created by this form of dispute resolution subsided, it turned out that there was quite a lot for the parties to agree upon and in the absence of express agreement, a wide canvas on which national courts started to impose private international law solutions. This included questions of: (a) the law governing the substance of the parties' dispute; (b) the law governing court supervision of the arbitration reference and its process; (c) the governing law of the agreement to arbitrate; and (d) the relevant laws governing questions of enforcement.

* In memory of Robin Dicker QC, 1961–2021.

There have been attempts to codify the rules specifically governing the choice of law of contractual obligations, most notably under the Rome I Convention then the Rome I Regulation,[1] which post Brexit was converted into domestic law applied across the UK, albeit with some relatively minor consequential and non-substantive amendment post Brexit,[2] as further amended by Jurisdiction, Judgments and Applicable Law Amendment Regulations.[3] In this chapter, reference throughout will be made to Rome I by way of shorthand. Nevertheless, these rules do not apply to the law governing an agreement to arbitrate.[4]

So, in the area of the law governing the arbitration agreement itself, we are thrown back to the test at common law, albeit in the wider context of the rules of Rome I, given that an arbitration agreement is, at least in the great majority of cases, found as a provision within a wider matrix contract, which will itself be subject to the provisions of Rome I. Under the common law, the debate has principally focussed upon whether, in the absence of an express choice of the law to govern the arbitration agreement, the governing law should, on the one hand, follow the parties' chosen seat or place of arbitration or, on the other, follow the law governing the matrix contract in which the arbitration agreement is found, albeit constituting a separable agreement.

Before turning to this in greater detail, it is important to ask why does the governing law of the arbitration agreement matter at all? The answer to this is straightforward. The governing law of the arbitration agreement will itself determine amongst other things questions of the scope or the breadth of the clause (in other words what disputes fall to be arbitrated and not litigated), its validity, who is party to or bound by the agreement to arbitrate, whether the agreement to arbitrate has been waived, repudiated or otherwise brought to an end, or whether it has been novated so as to bind new parties. All in all, the governing law of the arbitration agreement is likely to be of some fundamental importance. The answer to these questions will in turn very likely dictate whether two or more persons who find themselves in dispute are obliged to arbitrate and not litigate, will be compulsorily referred to arbitration, or indeed whether they should be restrained by means of anti-suit injunction from bringing proceedings in foreign courts in breach of the agreement to arbitrate and not litigate. It will also have a bearing, as we will see, on whether parties are bound by an award made against one of them.

In *Enka Insaat ve Sanayi AS v OOO Insurance Company Chubb*,[5] although the first question put to the Supreme Court related to the governing law of the

[1] Regulation (EC) No 593/3008 (Rome I).

[2] Law Applicable to Contractual Obligations and Non-Contractual Obligations (Amendment etc.) (EU Exit) Regulations 2019.

[3] Jurisdiction, Judgments and Applicable Law (Amendment) (EU Exit) Regulations.

[4] Rome I, Art 1(2)(e).

[5] *Enka Insaat ve Sanayi AS v OOO Insurance Company Chubb* [2020] UKSC 38, [2020] 1 WLR 4117.

agreement to arbitrate, what was ultimately at stake was the validity and scope of the arbitration agreement and whether or not Chubb was free to pursue delictual (non-contractual claims) in their preferred courts; namely the courts of the Russian Federation and not in arbitration in London. The decision of the majority of the Supreme Court on this question resolved what the minority referred to as 'an intriguing'[6] debate in private international law that had raged with quiet dignity for over 100 years amongst commentators and in our law reports with decisions falling either side and, because it settled the matter (at least for now), merits its place as a landmark decision. There were three speeches in the Supreme Court first that of the majority (Lords Leggatt, Hamblen and Kerr) and two given by the dissenting minority (Lords Burrows and Sales). In addition to this first question, the Supreme Court also made some observations of the proper approach governing the grant of anti-suit injunctions in cases where the arbitration agreement was governed by a foreign and not English law. This additional aspect of the decision, whilst perhaps not at the 'landmark' level of importance is nonetheless of considerable practical significance to practitioners.

This chapter will examine: the case in question and the Supreme Court decision in relation to governing law (the first question), the impact of the decision on the first question and whether the reasoning is open to criticism, the Supreme Court's observations on anti-suit injunctions (the second question), and whether the Law Commission's review of the Arbitration Act 1996 provides a suitable opportunity for reform in relation to the first question and if not then what should parties otherwise do to address the first question.

II. THE FACTS IN ENKA v CHUBB

The facts of *Enka v Chubb* are in the majority's judgment and can be stated very shortly.[7] Enka, a global engineering firm based in Turkey, was engaged as one of a number of sub-contractors for the construction of a power plant at Bersezovskaya in Russia under the terms of a contract dated 27 June 2012 which was of substantial length with extensive attachments. The document was executed in parallel Russian and English versions with the Russian version said to prevail. Article 50 of the contract made provision for multi-tier dispute resolution with an obligation to escalate disputes through a hierarchy of layers and in the absence of resolution in this manner for disputes to be referred to arbitration in London under the ICC Rules. The original employer, Energoproekt, transferred its rights and obligations under the contract to Unipro, and Unipro and Enka expressly agreed that disputes between them would be resolved in London by arbitration under the ICC Rules in accordance with the contract.

[6] ibid, [187] (Lord Burrows).
[7] ibid, [7]–[24] (Lord Hamblen and Lord Leggatt).

On 1 February 2016, there was a substantial fire at the plant. Chubb Russia the insurers paid out approximately US$400 million and became subrogated to the rights of Unipro including against Enka. On 25 May 2019, Chubb Russia filed a claim in the Russian courts seeking damages against Enka and ten other defendants whom they said were also liable in delict for the fire damage. On 17 September 2019, Enka sought to have the claim against them dismissed or referred to arbitration pursuant to the mandatory obligations contained in the Russian legislation implementing Article II(3) of the New York Convention. The Russian First Instance Court dismissed Enka's motion to refer to arbitration and at the same time dismissed Chubb's case on the merits. Both sides appealed the respective decisions.

In the meantime, and at a time before the outcome of the appeal could be known, on 16 September 2019, Enka sought an anti-suit injunction in the Commercial Court asserting that the Russian proceedings were brought in breach of the arbitration agreement to which Chubb was bound, in the sense that if Chubb sought to advance claims against Enka then it was bound to do so in accordance with the arbitration clause for the resolution of both contractual and delictual disputes in relation to the contract. An important plank of Enka's argument was that this flowed from the governing law of the arbitration agreement being English law. Chubb's response was that if the arbitration agreement was governed by English law then it was accepted that the Russian delictual claims would be caught by the arbitration clause, as the rights it had acquired through subrogation were themselves subject to the arbitration clause (and the conditional benefit analysis of Hobhouse LJ, as he was then, in *The Jay Bola*).[8] Nevertheless, Chubb's starting point was that the construction contract was governed by Russian law, so was the arbitration agreement and that under Russian law there was no obligation or indeed right to arbitrate these multi-party delictual claims.

Baker J refused the anti-suit injunction.[9] He did not decide the governing law or scope of the arbitration agreement issue, but held that the Russian courts was best placed to decide this. In other words, it was disposed of on a *forum non conveniens* analysis. A very strong commercial bench in the Court of Appeal consisting of Flaux, Males and Popplewell LJJ, reversed Baker J, and held that it was for the courts of the seat or place of arbitration to determine the question of governing law and scope and whether or not the arbitration agreement would be protected by an anti-suit injunction. The Court of Appeal overturned Baker J's *forum non conveniens* analysis. Further, the Court of Appeal decided the substantive question in favour of Enka; namely that the governing law of

[8] *Schiffahrtsgesellschaft Detlev von Appen GmbH v Voest Alpine Intertrading GmbH (The Jay Bola)* [1997] 2 Lloyd's Rep 279 (CA) 286.

[9] *Enka Insaat ve Sanayi AS v OOO Insurance Company Chubb* [2019] EWHC 3568 (Comm), [2020] 1 Lloyd's Rep 71.

the London arbitration agreement was English law and granted the anti-suit restraining Chubb's pursuit of the Russian appeal.[10]

Chubb appealed to the Supreme Court. In relation to the governing law question, Chubb argued that the arbitration agreement was governed by Russian law as it would ordinarily follow the law chosen by the parties to govern the matrix contract. In relation to the *forum non conveniens* question, Chubb argued that it would not be appropriate for the English courts to determine questions of scope of the arbitration agreement governed by foreign law and so the anti-suit should be discharged and in essence Chubb be allowed to pursue its appeal in Russia.

The short facts as set out above make clear that the determination of the governing law of the arbitration agreement was key. It should also be observed that only ten months passed between the decision at first instance and that of the Supreme Court, once more emphasising how the courts in this jurisdiction are able to deliver answers to complex problems in a very short time span. It is hard to think of another tiered jurisdiction where this could be achieved. For the more procedurally minded practitioners amongst us, there is at least something of an argument for landmark status on this ground alone.

III. THE DECISION IN ENKA v CHUBB

The governing law of the arbitration agreement had to be determined in accordance with test at common law. This requires first to examine whether parties have expressly or impliedly chosen a law to govern the arbitration agreement; and in the absence of any such choice the law with which it is most closely connected.[11] In the course of argument before the Supreme Court and indeed in the Court of Appeal below, three principal propositions or solutions were identified:

(a) First, that save in cases where the parties have made an express choice of law to govern the arbitration agreement (which would include a sufficiently clearly worded express choice of law clause in the main contract), the presumption should be that the law governing the arbitration agreement is the curial law, or law of the seat, on the basis that the choice of seat is an implied choice of the law to govern the arbitration agreement. This was the view of the Court of Appeal.[12] Lord Burrows referred to this as the 'seat approach'.[13]
(b) Second, that where any choice of law is found to have been made (express or implied) to govern the main contract that should generally extend and

[10] *Enka Insaat ve Sanayi AS v OOO Insurance Company Chubb* [2020] EWCA Civ 574, [2020] 2 Lloyd's Rep 389.
[11] L Collins (ed), *Dicey, Morris & Collins on the Conflict of Laws,* 15th edn (London, Sweet & Maxwell, 2012) rule 64 (1). *Enka* (n 5) [27] (Lord Hamblen and Lord Leggatt).
[12] *Enka* (n 10) [90]–[91] (Popplewell LJ).
[13] *Enka* (n 5) [236], [239], [253] and [260] (Lord Burrows).

apply (with some limitation and exception) so as to constitute a choice of law to govern the arbitration agreement as well. This is referred to by the majority as the general rule. Further, in the absence of such a choice (express or implied) the default rule should be that the governing law of the arbitration follows that of the seat, as this will be the system of law with the closest connection to the arbitration agreement.

(c) Third, that where no choice, express or implied is made with respect to the law governing the main contract, then the law governing the arbitration agreement should still generally be the law of the main contract determined by reference to the closest connection test such that the main contract and arbitration agreement will be governed by the same law. Lord Burrows referred to this as the 'main contract approach'.[14]

The Court of Appeal in *Enka* proceeded on the first proposition stated above. The Supreme Court upheld the decision of the Court of Appeal but did so preferring the second solution stated above. The majority in the Supreme Court went on then to find that there was no express or implied choice of Russian law (as contended for by Chubb); that the juridical seat or place of arbitration was London and that English law was as a result the system of laws which the arbitration agreement was most closely connected. Nevertheless, before this can be examined further, the Supreme Court found it necessary to clear the decks of some sundry preliminary points. The first preliminary question then is what system of laws is applied to ascertain whether or not a choice has been made. The view of the majority was that this should be the law of the forum – here English rules and not the putative proper law, as that could lead to uncertainty and circularity.[15] It was also said by the majority to be consistent with previous decision of the House of Lords.[16] The second preliminary question that the majority addressed is whether there is for this purpose any material distinction between an express and an implied choice of governing law. The majority made it clear that there is not. An implied choice is still just as effective choice of law.[17] Having cleared away these points the majority then came to examine in more detail what it described as the general and default rules.

A. The General Rule

The key starting point of the majority was to express the view that whilst it is possible for parties to agree or for courts to conclude that different parts of or

[14] ibid, [239] (Lord Burrows).

[15] ibid, [33] (Lord Hamblen and Lord Leggatt).

[16] *Whitworth Street Estates v James Miller & Partners* [1970] AC 583 (HL) and *Compagnie d'Armement Maritime SA v Compagnie Tunisienne de Navigation SA* [1971] AC 572 (HL) 603 and the view in *Dicey, Morris & Collins*, 15th edn (n 11) para 32-036.

[17] *Enka* (n 5) [35] (Lord Hamblen and Lord Leggatt).

issues in a contract would be governed by different laws (sometimes referred to as *dépeçage*), in the ordinary case, unless there was good reason, a clause in a contract expressing that all terms were governed by a stated law, would apply as well to the arbitration agreement.

The arbitration agreement is said to be a separable or distinct agreement, and the arbitration agreement is not to be regarded as invalid because the main contract is invalid or terminated.[18] Nevertheless, the arbitration is mostly found as a clause within a wider matrix or main contract, and, applying the dictum of Mustill J (as he then was) in *Black Clawson* who expressed the matter as follows, '[i]n the ordinary way, the law governing the arbitration would be likely to follow the law of the substantive contract'.[19] This approach was said by the majority to be consistent with a number of the leading commentators on both arbitration law and conflicts of law, and likewise prior decisions both in the courts of this jurisdiction and in Singapore.[20] The Supreme Court recognised, however, that a different view was expressed in *XL Insurance v Owens Corning*,[21] and a number of other first instance authorities.[22]

There were, the Supreme Court concluded, powerful reasons to support the general rule and so without more, align a choice of law to govern the main contract as generally extending to a choice of law to govern the arbitration agreement.[23] Fundamentally, the majority considered that the general rule promoted certainty; achieved consistency; avoided complexity and artificiality.[24] It might be observed however, that irrespective of whether the Supreme Court adopted the Court of Appeal's reasoning or its own general rule, there would be certainty and consistency. That is the function of a general rule and indeed formed a strong foundational reason for the Court of Appeal's own decision namely to introduce 'certainty and clarity'.

Before reaching its conclusion with regard to the general rule, the majority in the Supreme Court did have to address certain specific arguments advanced by Enka in support of the Court of Appeal's own version of the general rule. These were broadly: (i) that agreeing to arbitrate in England was itself an express choice of a law, albeit a procedural law; (ii) the importance of the overlap between procedural and governing laws; and (iii) separability of the arbitration agreement from the main contract. The Supreme Court was not persuaded by any of

[18] Arbitration Act 1996, s 7.

[19] *Black Clawson International Ltd v Papierwerke Waldhof-Aschaffenburg AG* [1981] 2 Lloyd's Rep 446 (Com Ct) 456.

[20] *Sonatrach Petroleum Corp (BVI) v Ferrell International Ltd* [2002] 1 All ER (Comm) 627 (Com Ct) [32] (Colman J). See also the further case references in *Enka* (n 5) [46] (Lord Hamblen and Lord Leggatt) and more recently in Singapore in *BCY v BCZ* [2016] 2 Lloyd's Rep 583 (Sing HC) and *BNA v BNB* [2020] 1 Lloyd's Rep 55 (Sing CA) [44] (Steven Chong J).

[21] [2001] 1 All ER (Comm) 530 (Com Ct).

[22] *Enka* (n 5) [47]–[51] (Lord Hamblen and Lord Leggatt).

[23] ibid, [54] (Lord Hamblen and Lord Leggatt).

[24] ibid, [53] (Lord Hamblen and Lord Leggatt).

these arguments. The majority concluded agreeing to arbitrate in England was not a choice of law but an agreement of a juridical seat which carried with it a consequence that certain laws and limitations would apply as to the conduct of the arbitration and the supervision of the arbitration by the courts.[25]

The Supreme Court did accept that there was something of an interplay between the governing law of the arbitration agreement and the procedural law but was not persuaded that this militated in favour of a single unity between the governing law of the arbitration and the procedural law; noting that section 4(5) of the Arbitration Act 1996 made provision to cater for this with respect to so called non mandatory provisions of the Arbitration Act, such that the parties' choice of foreign law would also govern the non-mandatory provisions of the Act.[26]

The Supreme Court was also unpersuaded of the strength of the separability argument noting that separability was something of an artificial construct itself and that section 7 of the Arbitration Act 1996 made it clear that it applied not for all purposes but in a specific stated context.[27]

B. The Validation Principle

Nevertheless, the majority did make some observations as to an important carve out to the general rule by reference to what has in certain other cases – notably the House of Lords in *Hamlyn v Talisker*,[28] and the Court of Appeal in *Sul America*[29] – been referred to as a principle of construction or interpretation to uphold and not invalidate a bargain. This was given the shorthand by the majority of the validation principle. In each of these cases, if the arbitration agreement in question had been held to have been governed by Scottish law (*Hamlyn*) or Brazilian law (*Sul America*) then the parties' apparent agreement would have been void or at least at a serious risk of invalidity.

The majority accepted that to the extent the putative governing law failed to recognise the validity of the parties' choice of arbitration as a one stop method of commercial dispute resolution, then it is inherently unlikely that the parties would have intended that law to govern the validity and scope of the agreement to arbitrate.[30] The majority accepted that there would be argument in future cases as to what level of impairment of risk would be sufficient to override the general rule, but concluded that they could not improve on the formulation of Moore Bick LJ in *Sul America*; that commercial parties are generally unlikely to have intended a choice of governing law for the contract to apply to an arbitration 'if there is at least a serious risk that a choice of that law would significantly

[25] ibid, [67] (Lord Hamblen and Lord Leggatt).
[26] ibid, [75] (Lord Hamblen and Lord Leggatt).
[27] ibid, [60]–[64] (Lord Hamblen and Lord Leggatt).
[28] *Hamlyn & Co v Talisker Distillery* [1894] AC 202 (HL).
[29] *Sulamerica Cia Nacional de Seguros SA v Enesa Engenharia SA* [2013] 1 WLR 102 (CA).
[30] *Enka* (n 5) [109] (Lord Hamblen and Lord Leggatt).

undermine that agreement'.[31] It should also be noted that this has been examined once more by the Supreme Court in *Kabab Ji SAL v Kout Food Group*, and it was re-emphasised that the validation principle is fundamentally a principle of contractual interpretation, such that contractual provisions including choice of law provisions should be interpreted so as to give effect to and not undermine the presumed intention of efficacy and validity. Nevertheless, the Supreme Court underscored that this did not permit the principle to be invoked to create a contract that would not otherwise exist.[32]

C. The Default Rule

The Supreme Court then proceeded to examine the position in the absence of a choice of law (express or implied) for the main or matrix contract. In such circumstances, the majority concluded that the law most closely connected with the arbitration would in general be the law of the seat,[33] and this was underpinned by a number of factors: the fact the place of performance would be that of the seat;[34] it accords with the scheme of the New York Convention and in particular Article V.1.a which appears to equate the law of the seat as being the default governing law in the absence of choice;[35] it would also accord with the parties' presumed intentions;[36] and it give rise to increased certainty.[37]

This analysis would appear to be unimpeachable but, as is further considered below, appears to some material extent to argue against the conclusion reached by the Supreme Court with respect to the general rule. Further, it should be noted that the majority also alluded to a potential exception to the default rule so as to uphold the validity of the arbitration agreement by way of parallel reasoning to that already considered.[38]

D. Application

Applying these principles, the majority concluded that there was no express or implied choice of law governing the main contract (the detail of that argument was extremely involved but of only indirect relevance to the argument pursued in this chapter), therefore no express or implied choice of law to govern the

[31] ibid, [109] (Lord Hamblen and Lord Leggatt).
[32] *Kabab-Ji SAL (Lebanon) v Kout Food Group (Kuwait)* [2021] UKSC 48, [2022] 2 All ER 911 [49]–[51] (Lord Hamblen and Lord Leggatt).
[33] ibid, [145] (Lord Hamblen and Lord Leggatt).
[34] ibid, [121]–[124] (Lord Hamblen and Lord Leggatt).
[35] ibid, [126]–[141] (Lord Hamblen and Lord Leggatt). This analysis was reinforced in *Kabab Ji* (n 32) [26], [35]–[36] (Lord Hamblen and Lord Leggatt).
[36] *Enka* (n 5) [142]–[143] (Lord Hamblen and Lord Leggatt).
[37] ibid, [144] (Lord Hamblen and Lord Leggatt).
[38] ibid, [146] (Lord Hamblen and Lord Leggatt).

arbitration agreement, that the default rule therefore applied, and that the closest connection was that of England, the seat of the arbitration, so that the arbitration agreement was governed by English law. Given this conclusion it was not necessary to express any view on whether, if governed by Russian law, the validation principle would have had any application, given the apparent reluctance of the Russian courts to force claims expressed in delict to be arbitrated even where the words of the arbitration agreements itself are widely expressed.

E. Reasoning of the Minority

Lords Burrows and Sales agreed with the majority with respect to the general rule and provided a measure of expansion as regards the reasons that would favour this approach. In other words, if the parties have either expressly or impliedly chosen a law to govern the main contract then generally that choice ought to extend to govern the arbitration clauses contained in the main agreement. Lord Burrows, however, did not agree with the default rule in the absence of choice, expressing the view that the answer to the closest connection test with respect to the main contract should generally apply to the arbitration agreement as well.[39] Lord Burrows concluded that the reasons which led to application of the main contract approach applied equally to the closest connection test.[40] Lord Burrows and Lord Sales each concluded that there is a thin distinction between the first stage of express or implied choice and closest connection and often the same factors are relevant to implied choice as to closest connection.[41] The minority also expressed the view that in essence having one rule; namely that the law of the arbitration agreement should follow that of the main contract whether found by choice of closest connection would achieve the certainty and clarity that the Court of Appeal rightly sought, albeit in the opposite direction.[42] Finally, Lords Burrows and Sales did not address in any detail the validation principle referred to above, save to say that it did not arise in a case which only concerned the scope of the agreement as opposed to its validity.[43]

IV. CRITIQUE

It may seem churlish in the extreme to engage in any criticism of such a recent Supreme Court decision, especially one which this chapter seeks to champion as

[39] ibid, [256] and [231]–[255] (Lord Burrows).
[40] ibid, [231]–[255] (Lord Burrows).
[41] ibid, [281] (Lord Sales).
[42] ibid, [256]–[257] (Lord Burrows) and [284]–[288] (Lord Sales).
[43] ibid, [199] and [210] (Lord Burrows) and [277] (Lord Sales).

being 'landmark', and yet further being a case in which the author appeared in as co-counsel, and even more so having defended the outcome of the Court of Appeal and prevailed in obtaining the anti-suit injunction sought. So, it should be stated at the outset that the Supreme Court has resolved a long-standing debate and it has to be recognised that this makes it a good deal easier for lawyers to advise their clients and to take appropriate action in support of the enforcement of the obligation to arbitrate. That should be recognised and welcomed. What follows seeks further to analyse whether the general rule as expressed in the Supreme Court best achieves the certainty for users of London arbitration and if not, what other solutions are available.

As explained below, there is a serious argument that the general rule proposed by the Court of Appeal is the more satisfactory one for commercial practice. Likewise, there is a serious argument that it is for the reasons explained more consistent with the original development of the common law choice of law rules and its later manifestation in international convention and regulation.

Each of the Court of Appeal, and the majority and minority in the Supreme Court invoked the desirability of simplicity and of certainty. Ultimately, each solution proffered respectively by the Court of Appeal and the Supreme Court provides a measure of certainty. As far as certainty is concerned, as the minority commented, it is really akin to which end of the telescope instinctively you prefer to grasp. The case for grabbing the 'seat end' of the telescope is not without serious merit. A number of points are examined in this section.

A. Arbitration as a Package

First, and perhaps above all, the context of this particular debate is extremely important. Parties from all corners of the globe agree to arbitrate on these shores with disputes arising out of a great variety of contracts from the dizzyingly complex to the run of the mill. On very few occasions will the parties express an identified law to govern the arbitration clause itself. This was noted by the majority. This is not of course because such commercial parties have been avid students of conflicts of laws and are content with the general rule, but rather because objectively the only clear concept that is being expressed by providing for arbitration in England or in London is for a package of alternative dispute resolution to be supervised and enforced under a reliable legal system and perhaps also an identified set of arbitral institution rules. It might be thought to be somewhat self-serving to pose the question in terms of the mythological traveller on the Clapham omnibus, but the point can be well grasped. Such businessmen objectively should not be taken readily to accept that providing for London arbitration will give rise to an intricate mixture of governing laws, both procedural and substantive. Arbitration is generally thought of as a single unified package, albeit for differing reasons: efficiency; relative simplicity and in some particular areas such as maritime and trade arbitration a well-developed specialist cadre of arbitrators.[44]

Underpinning each of these factors as regard this jurisdiction is an extremely favourable regime for enforcement of the obligation to arbitrate, if appropriate backed up by an anti-suit injunction, as was noted in the decision of the Court of Appeal.[45] Lord Mance made this very point in extra judicial remarks[46] with respect to the reasons underpinning the choice of seat being directed at a package of rights both procedural and substantive in nature. The choice of England or London for this package is not simply a choice of geographical convenience but should be understood in commercial terms to be the critical choice to govern and feed through into all aspects of the arbitration. Indeed, no other choice is likely to be made in the great majority of arbitration agreements other than that single indication. The importance of the selection of the seat as a deliberate and conscious decision is not simply a London centric obsession: it was also emphasised in extra judicial remarks of Chief Justice Sundaresh Menon of Singapore in a speech given in February 2018.[47] The Chief Justice noted that, since arbitration was anxious at each turn to uphold party autonomy, the selection of the seat should be understood to form a key part of that autonomy. If in reality parties are choosing a unified or integrated package to aid their resolution of disputes should they arise, it is only a short step to see that choice of English arbitration as a presumed or implied choice of a governing law for the arbitration agreement as well as a choice of procedural law.

There is perhaps some analogy in terms of the package with the reasoning of Willes J in *Lloyd v Guibert*,[48] which has been analysed with great eloquence and precision in Professor Briggs' parallel paper.[49] In *Lloyd v Guibert*, Willes J was reaching for some principled basis for arriving at the governing law of the contract in the absence of express choice and found that the place where the contract was concluded to be a weak connection. On the other hand, the law of the flag of the vessel seemed more closely to be aligned with the parties' presumed intentions as regards disputes arising out of a contract of affreightment. Willes J developed his ideas by first making references to the usages of a market and expressing the old adage that, 'for those whose go to Rome must do as those at Rome do'.[50] When arriving at his conclusion in favour of the law of the flag as the presumed intention for the governing law of the contract

[44] K Fan, 'The Social & Psychological Underpinning of Commercial Arbitration in Europe' (23 March 2022) www.commercialarbitrationineurope.wordpress.com (accessed 30 August 2022).

[45] *Enka v Chubb* (n 10) [48] (Popplewell LJ).

[46] Giving the 30th Annual Freshfields Lecture in November 2015. See now Lord Mance, 'Arbitration: A Law unto itself?' (2016) 32 *Arbitration International* 223.

[47] Referenced in *Enka v Chubb* (n 10) [49] (Popplewell LJ).

[48] *Lloyd v Guibert* (1865) LR 1 QB 115.

[49] At the Cambridge symposium, this chapter was discussed alongside that of Professor Briggs. See now ch 2 in this volume.

[50] *Lloyd v Guibert* (n 48) 121.

affreightment, Willes J referred to the vessel at sea as a floating island of French sovereignty.[51] Of course no analogy fits perfectly, but it can readily be seen that parties who choose to arbitrate in a particular place might to borrow Willes J's phrase be presumed to intend to do as they do in Rome. It is suggested it would be stretching the refinement of their presumed intentions to divide that intention into procedural and substantive law issues governing the arbitration agreement. There is a serious argument that presumed intention is best viewed in this commercial context as a package of rights and obligations.

B. Simplicity

Second, parties who choose arbitration are to be taken to choose a simple, efficient and speedy method of dispute resolution. This is reinforced in section 1 of the Arbitration Act 1996 and likewise in the UNCITRAL Model Law and is rightly considered to form the foundational pillars of the process. Simplicity once more would point towards there being a unity between governing law of the arbitration agreement and the relevant governing procedural law (ie the law of the seat) unless the parties have expressly chosen otherwise. The Supreme Court in *Enka* tried to play down the consequences introduced by the twin law approach by reference to section 4(5) of the Arbitration Act 1996 which, frankly speaking, gives little comfort and to the contrary introduces further complexity that few parties can be aware of. The Supreme Court concluded that if parties have chosen a law to govern their arbitration through the application of the general rule (either expressly or impliedly) then, on a true construction of section 4(5) of the Arbitration Act 1996, that choice would be sufficient to disapply any non-mandatory provision of the 1996 Act in so far as it would otherwise affect a matter governed by the law applicable to the arbitration agreement.[52] If therefore the Supreme Court had held that the contract in question had indeed been governed by Russian law, that choice would have also fed into the arbitration agreement (the general rule). The consequence would be that, pursuant to section 4(5) of the Act, Russian law would also apply to questions of separability (section 7 of the Act).[53] This in turn would mean that if a question arose as whether the contract had been repudiated, the effect of such repudiation on the agreement to arbitrate would not be determined in accordance with section 7 of the Act (ie without more, no effect) but rather under principles of Russian law. This hardly seems credible in terms of the parties' presumed intentions. Those who arbitrate their disputes in a well-known centre for arbitration can hardly be presumed to intend this kind of quagmire. Quite the opposite. It is simplicity

[51] ibid, 127.
[52] *Enka* (n 5) [75] (Lord Hamblen and Lord Leggatt).
[53] ibid, [87] and [90]–[93] (Lord Hamblen and Lord Leggatt).

and certainty that is intended in each case. Even the Supreme Court accepted that section 4(5) gave rise to complex questions on its analysis.

C. The International Plane

Third, there is serious argument that the alignment between the choice of place for resolution of disputes and determination of substantive validity of dispute resolution clause is further embedded now in international convention and European regulation and should be considered as the governing or overriding principle on the international plane. In this context it should not be ignored that Article 25 of the Brussels Regulation provides that the court chosen by the parties 'shall have jurisdiction unless the agreement is null and void as to its substantive validity under the law of that [ie the chosen] Member State'.[54] That principle is likewise reflected in the wording of Article 5(1) of the Hague Convention on Exclusive Choice of Court Agreements 2005. Article V.1.a of the New York Convention is addressed below.

D. The Validation Principle

Fourth, as already discussed, the Supreme Court correctly recognised need for the validation principle to assist the upholding of an apparent bargain in certain circumstances. The majority recognised that there is a well-established principle of interpretation dating back to Sir Edward Coke in 1624 that an interpretation which upholds the validity of a transaction is to be preferred to one which would render it invalid or ineffective (or if you prefer *ut res magis valeat quam pereat*). This principle would apply if in determining whether the parties agreed on a choice of governing law, a putative governing law would render all or part of the contract ineffective.[55] The Supreme Court recognised that at the edges this principle may well be hard to police and define,[56] and the further need for refinement of the principle in *Kabab Ji* as explained above demonstrates that this debate is perhaps far from over. Moreover, it should be noted that it would most likely only ever apply when parties had gone to the expense of having to instruct foreign law experts to argue out what the effect might be of applying a putative foreign law to the arbitration agreement. Nevertheless, underlying all this is perhaps a more profound point. By agreeing to London arbitration, the parties are taken objectively to have agreed a one stop method of dispute resolution.[57] There is a serious argument that the route by which this conclusion

[54] Regulation (EU) No 542/2014.
[55] *Enka* (n 5) [96] (Lord Hamblen and Lord Leggatt).
[56] ibid, [106] (Lord Hamblen and Lord Leggatt).
[57] ibid, [108] (Lord Hamblen and Lord Leggatt).

is best supported is perhaps not through the application of the validation principle but rather the conclusion that by choosing London arbitration parties have impliedly agreed English law which, as discussed by Sir Marcus Smith in chapter sixteen, upholds the 'one stop' approach.[58]

E. Institutional Rules

Fifth, it cannot be ignored in this context that consideration has already been given to the question of whether the so-called seat or main contract approach is to be preferred by the leading international arbitration institution in this jurisdiction; namely the London Court of International Arbitration (the 'LCIA'). Its rules make clear that the law applicable to the arbitration agreement and the arbitration itself shall be the law applicable at the seat of the arbitration unless the parties have agreed in writing on the application of other laws or rules and that such agreement is not prohibited by the law at the arbitral seat.[59] This would therefore require an express choice of a law to govern the arbitration agreement other than that of the seat. The Court of Appeal's decision therefore does appear to be following in the mainstream view, adopting the same solution expressed by the LCIA. Many parties who arbitrate in England would be familiar with the LCIA rules. It is therefore somewhat counter-intuitive for a conflicts solution to be adopted which departs from that position.

F. Multi-Tier Resolution Clauses

Sixth, the Supreme Court considered that the general rule was supported by the increased prevalence of what is often referred to as multi-tier resolution clauses which provide for a number of steps to be exhausted before arbitration is to be resorted to.[60] This sometimes involves 'good faith' discussion between executives and sometimes a more formal mediation process. The majority considered that this leant in favour of the general rule so as to align the main contract with the arbitration agreement's governing law. By way of example only, the obligation to mediate and arbitrate related to disputes as defined in the contract and there ought to be a single applicable law and definition of what is encompassed by that concept. On proper analysis, however, this is very doubtful and in fact logic dictates that it leans in the opposite direction.

For some time the prevailing view under a series of cases governed by English law, was that a properly worded multi-tier clause could give rise to an enforceable

[58] *Fiona Trust & Holding Corp v Privalov* [2007] UKHL 40, [2007] 4 All ER 951.
[59] LCIA 2020 Rules, Art 16.4.
[60] *Enka* (n 5) [53(iii)] and [168] (Lord Hamblen and Lord Leggatt).

obligation by way of contractual condition precedent not to commence arbitration until certain steps had been undertaken and that if the party in question acted in breach by commencing arbitration without taking those steps then the arbitral tribunal would be without jurisdiction and that the subsequent award could be challenged. These cases were analysed by Teare J in *Emirates Trading Agency LLC v Prime Mineral Exports Private Ltd* who endorsed that view, albeit in that case he found no breach had taken place and upheld the award.[61] The logic of this approach is that a multi-tier clause ought to be looked at as single multi-tiered obligation. Therefore, if the parties are taken to have impliedly chosen the law of the seat to govern the arbitration agreement (the Court of Appeal's proposed solution) then that implied choice ought to extend to any pre-conditions to the invocation of that right.

More recently, however, a different and more nuanced view has been expressed in the Commercial Court of the correct approach to challenges to the invocation of arbitration in alleged breach of a multi-tier clause. Sir Michael Burton (sitting as a High Court Judge) in *Republic of Sierra Leone v SL Mining Ltd* expressed what is, with respect, the better view. The question of whether or not an arbitration has been brought prematurely before the supposed exhaustion of the multi-tier steps (which is never an exact science in the author's experience) is not a question of contractual condition precedent going to jurisdiction in accordance with the governing law of the arbitration agreement. Rather it is a question of procedural admissibility, which falls within the discretion of the tribunal as to whether it is appropriate for them to hear the case at the time in question and not whether they have any power to hear a case.[62] Sir Michael concluded that the tribunal will be best armed with the facts to determine whether it is appropriate for them to hear or admit the case at that time and their decision does not go to jurisdiction. This is certainly consistent with the position adopted in investment treaty tribunals, a consistent body of academic literature as well as the highest courts in the US and Singapore. The logic of this analysis, however, leans heavily towards the desirability of a unity between the applicable law to govern the arbitration agreement (and its multi-tier provisions) and the procedural law of the seat and is a further demonstration of the overlap between issues which relate to governing law and procedural law.

G. Section 9

Seventh, the Court of Appeal's solution resolves a number of potential difficulties that might otherwise be encountered in the operation of the compulsory stay provision in section 9 of the Arbitration Act 1996. As is well understood, in

[61] *Emirates Trading Agency LLC v Prime Mineral Exports Private Ltd* [2014] EWHC 2104 (Comm), [2015] 1 WLR 1145.

[62] *Republic of Sierra Leone v SL Mining Ltd* [2021] EWHC 286 (Comm), [2021] Bus LR 704.

line with the provisions of the UNCITRAL Model Law and Article II.3 of the New York Convention, the English Arbitration Act 1996 requires a court before whom substantive proceedings have been brought, to stay those proceedings, and refer the parties to arbitration if the proceedings brought are in respect of a matter which the parties have agreed to refer to arbitration. An application has to be made in accordance with the procedure of section 9 of the Act but an order for stay will be made if these conditions are met and the court is not satisfied that the arbitration is null, void, inoperative or incapable of being performed. This is a mandatory provision of the Act and hence would not be displaced under section 4(5) of the Act by any choice of a foreign governing law even if that were made.

It is beyond the scope of this chapter to explore the principles that apply under section 9 of the Arbitration Act 1996. It is sufficient to say that it is well covered by authority. Nevertheless, one short example will suffice in order to illustrate the potential overlap between questions of procedure, the governing law of the arbitration agreement, the policy of the court of the seat and the operation of the statutory provisions with regard to stay of court proceedings. This is not to suggest that it is not possible for parties expressly to choose a foreign governing law to apply to their arbitration agreement but rather that the Court of Appeal's solution focussing on the law of the seat by way of implied choice to govern both questions of procedure and the law of the arbitration agreement itself unless there was a clear indication to the contrary is the more satisfactory and to be preferred.

The potential difficulties can be illustrated by reference to questions of arbitrability. Parties sometimes seek to resist a stay on the grounds that it is not possible to arbitrate the claims in question but rather that such claim must be brought in the courts. As a matter of English law, this argument is most often raised when the claims it referred to arbitration would affect or determine third party rights or establish rights *in rem* or would otherwise offend public policy of the forum. It is often said that such claims are inarbitrable. Inarbitrability, if established, would fall with the recognised exceptions to enforcement of an arbitration agreement in section 9(4) of the Arbitration Act 1996. This is mirrored in the language of Article II.I of the New York Convention which requires national courts of the contracting states to recognise and enforce agreements to arbitrate differences that 'are capable of settlement by arbitration'. The difficultly is that neither the New York Convention nor the Arbitration Act expressly prescribe what law should be applied in order to determine arbitrability. It is suggested that where parties have agreed to arbitrate their disputes at a particular place or seat then there ought to be a strong presumption that the subject matter or reach of the kinds of matters that are capable of being arbitrated would be determined in accordance with the law or policy of the forum in question, the seat. The way this conclusion is best applied in practice is through the Court of Appeal's decision since there would be a strong presumption of alignment between the governing law of the arbitration (which will dictate scope) and the law of the seat (which will either dictate or influence the answer to the closely allied question of what matters can and cannot be arbitrated). Looked at another way, assume English law did not allow a claim of a particular type to be arbitrated; namely a claim expressly said on its face to be between two highwaymen but that the law governing the main contract (Russian law) did. It would be surprising that by agreeing to arbitrate in London, the parties would be required to arbitrate a subject matter that under the law of the seat was inarbitrable.

H. The New York Convention

Finally, a word should be said of the architecture of the New York Convention and specifically Article V.1.a. Much was said of this by the majority in *Enka* as supporting the default rule; namely that in the absence of a chosen law to govern the arbitration agreement then its validity would be determined in accordance with the law of the place the award was made – ie the law of the seat.

It is suggested, however, that Article V.1.a of the New York Convention is ultimately neutral as to whether the solution adopted by the Court of Appeal or the Supreme Court majority is to be preferred. It can provide support for either approach. It does, however, firmly stand in the way of the view of the minority in *Enka*. Article V.1.a. will apply to all contracting states of the New York Convention and is designed to reinforce the connection between questions of validity of the arbitration agreement and the law of the seat which was the Court of Appeal's conclusion. The New York Convention (indeed as did the Court of Appeal) allows for the possibility of parties subjecting their arbitration agreement to another choice of law but in the absence of any such indication, the law of the seat should apply to resolve questions of the validity of the arbitration agreement. It should be emphasised that the New York Convention is focussed on a choice of law to govern the arbitration agreement and not a choice of law for the main contract.

I. Conclusion

The critique set out above does of course have a core weakness as was carefully explained and set by the majority in *Enka*; namely that it is over-reliant upon some call on the supposed exceptionalism of arbitration, when in truth an arbitration agreement is at the end of the day a contract – albeit most often contained as a term of a wider agreement and is concluded in a very specialised context. The words of Mustill J in *Black Clawson* cited above are and have proved to be very influential.[63] It may well be that ultimately the real point being made here is that parties would be wise, for all the reasons set out in this section,

[63] See text to n 19.

expressly to choose a governing law of the arbitration agreement which aligns to the seat. Subject to what is said below with respect to law reform, this does seem altogether the most simple and effective response. Furthermore, it should also be borne in mind that irrespective of what conflicts rule(s) is adopted one of the features of international arbitration is that it cannot remove all uncertainty or risk of conflicting decisions. This is illustrated by the underlying facts in *Kabab Ji SAL v Kout Food Group* where the English and French courts and tribunals took differing views.[64] All this only serves to underscore that certainty can really only be achieved by express agreement.

V. ANTI SUIT INJUNCTION

Before leaving the Supreme Court decision in *Enka*, it is desirable to say a word about its reasoning on the second question; namely the right approach to the availability of an anti-suit injunction to restrain breach of an arbitration agreement. The Supreme Court's treatment of this issue was strictly obiter, because the majority concluded that the arbitration agreement was governed by English law.

Fundamentally, the Supreme Court considered that the principles governing the grant of an anti-suit injunction in support of an arbitration agreement with an English seat did not differ according to whether or not the arbitration agreement was governed by English or a foreign law,[65] and that comity had little if any ground to play where anti-suit injunctive relief is sought on the grounds of breach of contract.[66] This is welcome and principled. Accordingly, the Supreme Court (unanimously) concluded that if they had determined the arbitration agreement was governed by Russian law, a trial would have to take place in the English courts to determine whether or not the Russian claims fell within its scope and if it did then an anti-suit injunction would be granted on the same basis as an arbitration agreement governed by English law.[67] The Supreme Court also indicated that it would have imposed interim relief (through the provision of undertakings) to protect Enka's position pending the determination of the scope under Russian law.

This clarification has some significance for practitioners in the field. The reason being that the Supreme Court indicated that it would have protected Enka's position pending the determination of the issue under Russian law. Up until *Enka*, a series of decisions at first instance and Court of Appeal has set the bar for the grant of interim relief in this particular context at a very high threshold; namely a high degree of probability that the applicant/claimant is right that there is a breach of the arbitration agreement, or a clear case of breach.[68]

[64] *Kabab Ji SAL v Kout Food Group* (n 32).
[65] *Enka* (n 5) [181]–[184] (Lord Hamblen and Lord Leggatt).
[66] ibid, [180] (Lord Hamblen and Lord Leggatt).
[67] ibid, [185] (Lord Hamblen and Lord Leggatt), [261] (Lord Burrows) and [293] (Lord Sales).
[68] *American International Specialty Lines Insurance Co v Abbott Laboratories* [2002] EWHC 2714 (Comm), [2003] 1 Lloyd's Rep 267 and *Continental Bank v Aeakos* [1994] 1 WLR 588 (CA).

It would seem, without having expressly decided this issue, that the Supreme Court has moved towards a more pragmatic solution that it may be necessary in the interests of justice to protect a party's position by way of interim anti suit pending the determination of whether there has been a breach of contract. Prior to the trial of the issue, it would be hard to say that there was a clear case of breach, that being the very issue to be determined at trial. Nevertheless, in the interests of justice it would be necessary to protect the applicant party's position pending trial. It is suggested that this is a welcome development.

VI. THE FUTURE

On 30 November 2021, the Law Commission announced that it would conduct a review of the Arbitration Act 1996 with the aim of ensuring that the UK remained at the forefront of international dispute resolution.[69] It has invited the views of numerous stakeholders. The Law Commission is due to issue an interim report in the autumn of 2022. It is not clear at this stage whether the Law Commission will make any recommendations with respect to governing law or indeed to section 4(5) of the Arbitration Act.

The case for addressing the potential uncertainties created has been set out above and is not repeated here. One ready-made solution would be to recommend that England and Wales adopt the text of section 6 of the Arbitration Act of Scotland 2010 which provides that:

> Where (a) the parties to an arbitration agreement agree that an arbitration is to be seated in Scotland, but ((b) the arbitration agreement does not specify the law which is to govern it, then unless the parties otherwise agree, the arbitration agreement is to be governed by Scots law.

This would bring English law in line with Scotland and the proposed solution of the Court of Appeal. In case the Law Commission is not brave enough itself to tackle the subject by way of statutory provision, or it is considered to be too soon after *Enka* to take stock of its effect in practice, the only remaining solution is for the parties' legal advisers to take much greater care in the drafting of arbitration agreements and to make provision expressly to align provision for an English seat with English governing law or for provision of arbitration rules such as the LCIA that achieve the same objective or in the absence of either potentially face the increased prospect of complex litigation in multiple fora. What is clear, however, is that in the field of conflicts of laws, even landmark decisions tend to be waypoints on a journey rather than final destinations. Maybe we should rejoice in this and not complain as it one of the greatest aspects of our common law tradition.

[69] Law Commission, 'Law Commission to review the Arbitration Act 1996' (30 November 2021) www.lawcom.gov.uk/law-commission-to-review-the-arbitration-act-1996/ (accessed 30 August 2022).

18

Brownlie v Four Seasons Holdings Inc (2017) and *Brownlie v FS Cairo (Nile Plaza) LLC* (2021)

BENJAMIN PHELPS

I. INTRODUCTION

THIS CHAPTER CONSIDERS two Supreme Court decisions on jurisdiction in the long-running Brownlie litigation: *Four Seasons Holdings Inc v Brownlie* ('*Brownlie I*') and *FS Cairo (Nile Plaza) LLC v Brownlie* ('*Brownlie II*').[1] The litigation arose out of the tragic death of Professor Sir Ian Brownlie QC, a distinguished academic and practitioner, who died in a road traffic accident in Egypt. His widow Lady Christine Brownlie, who was injured in the accident, brought proceedings in the English court seeking compensation arising from her husband's death and for her own personal injury.

The decisions in *Brownlie I* and *II* address a number of points of central importance concerning the approach of the English courts to jurisdiction over foreign defendants.[2] Although the litigation was commenced at a time when the Brussels Regulation still applied in the English courts, jurisdiction in the *Brownlie* cases was governed by the CPR rules on jurisdiction pursuant to which the court's permission to serve out is required. In respect of each defendant Lady Brownlie required permission to serve out and, in respect of each claim had to show: (i) a good arguable case that the claim falls within a

[1] *Four Seasons Holdings Inc v Brownlie* [2017] UKSC 80, [2018] 1 WLR 192, and *FS Cairo (Nile Plaza) LLC v Brownlie* [2021] UKSC 45, [2021] 3 WLR 1011.

[2] Both judgments have been the subject of extensive commentary, see for instance: A Dickinson 'Faulty Powers: One-Star Service in the English Courts' [2018] *Lloyd's Maritime and Commercial Law Quarterly* 189; A Briggs, 'Holiday Torts and Damage Within the Jurisdiction' [2018] *Lloyd's Maritime and Commercial Law Quarterly* 196; W Day, 'Jurisdiction Gateways in the CPR' (2018) 77 *Cambridge Law Journal* 36; J Crampin, 'Fog in the Gateway: Brownlie v Four Seasons Holdings Inc' (2019) 82 *Modern Law Review* 376; I Bergson, 'Service out in the Supreme Court (again)' (2022) 138 *Law Quarterly Review* 138; W Day, 'Pleading and Proving Foreign Law' (2022) 81 *Cambridge Law Journal* 24; A Arzandeh, '*Brownlie II* and the Service-out Jurisdiction under English Law' (2022) 71 *International & Comparative Law Quarterly* 727.

jurisdictional gateway; (ii) that the claim has reasonable prospects of success – the merits threshold; and (iii) that England is the proper place in which to bring the claim – the *forum conveniens*.

Issues were raised in *Brownlie I* and *II* on all three elements. *Brownlie II* qualifies as a landmark case because it settled the ambit of the tort gateway for jurisdiction, an issue fiercely debated in the case law for over 30 years. The decision on this issue increases the number of cases that might pass through the gateway and, as discussed further below, likely requires a re-calibration of the role of *forum conveniens*. *Brownlie II* also addressed the approach to foreign law and the role of the presumption in the merits threshold for permission to serve out – Lord Leggatt's judgment on this point arguably represents the genesis of a new line of case law which will test the limits of the rationale underpinning the existence of the presumption. Both aspects of the decision have far-reaching consequences. Further, in *Brownlie I*, Lord Sumption revisited the standard of proof for jurisdictional facts. His judgment on this point has already been extensively applied.

Those three issues – the evidential standard, the tort gateway, and the presumption – will be discussed in this chapter.

II. RELEVANT BACKGROUND

In January 2010, the claimant, Lady Brownlie, and her husband Sir Ian Brownlie QC, were on holiday in Egypt staying at the Four Seasons Hotel Cairo. Prior to travelling to Egypt, Lady Brownlie telephoned the hotel and booked an excursion in a hired chauffeur-driven car. The excursion took place on 3 January 2010. The car left the road and crashed. Sir Ian died, as did his daughter, Rebecca, and Rebecca's two children. Sir Ian's widow, Lady Brownlie was seriously injured. Lady Brownlie brought claims arising out of the accident seeking damages in respect of her own injury, damages as executrix of Sir Ian's estate on behalf of the estate and its heirs, and in respect of her dependency.

Lady Brownlie issued a claim form in December 2012 which she served out of the jurisdiction – permission being granted *ex parte* by Master Yoxall. The named defendant at this stage was Four Seasons Holdings Inc ('Holdings'), the holding company of the Four Seasons hotel group which is incorporated in British Columbia.[3] It was alleged that the contract in respect of the excursion had been made with Holdings and that Holdings was vicariously liable for the acts of the driver of the car.

Holdings' challenge to the jurisdiction was first heard by Master Cook, who, by order dated 31 July 2013, set aside Master Yoxall's order and declared the

[3] The claim form also included as second defendant, Nova Park SAE, an Egyptian company who were said to be the owner of the hotel building, however the Claim Form was never served on Nova Park SAE and they took no part in the claim.

Court had no jurisdiction to hear the claims. The claimant's appeal was allowed by Tugendhat J on 27 February 2014,[4] and the Court of Appeal dismissed Holdings' appeal.[5] Holdings appealed again to the Supreme Court who unanimously allowed the appeal (*Brownlie I)* and held that the claimant had sued the wrong defendant – so there was no prospect of the claimant succeeding against Holdings and, necessarily, permission to serve out should not have been granted.[6]

The Supreme Court at the close of *Brownlie I* remitted the matter to the High Court, where Lady Brownlie applied to substitute Holdings for FS Cairo (Nile Plaza) LLC ('FS Cairo'), to serve the claim form on FS Cairo out of the jurisdiction in Egypt, and to amend her pleadings. Nicol J acquiesced to the claimant's applications.[7] That decision was upheld by a majority in the Court of Appeal,[8] and FS Cairo's appeal against the order was dismissed by the Supreme Court, again by a majority.[9]

III. REVISED STANDARD OF PROOF FOR JURISDICTIONAL FACTS

The gateways frequently require factual inquiries to determine whether they are engaged. An example is where a claimant, as Lady Brownlie did, seeks to fall within CPR PD6B 6(a), ie a claim is made in respect of a contract which was 'made within the jurisdiction'. A claimant has the burden of showing that the gateway relied upon is satisfied to the standard of 'good arguable case'.

Lady Brownlie adduced evidence of her recollection of the conversation with the concierge of the Hotel in which the contract for the excursion was formed. Neither Holdings, nor latterly FS Cairo adduced evidence from the concierge in reply. Lady Brownlie, owing to the limitations of the jurisdiction stage was not cross examined. It was therefore a question of whether Lady Brownlie's evidence was sufficient to demonstrate that the contract was 'made' with the jurisdiction. The Court of Appeal in *Brownlie I* (when Holdings was alleged to be the relevant defendant) held that the contract was made within the jurisdiction. Nicol J for similar reasons in *Brownlie II* (with respect to FS Cairo) agreed.

As explored further by Pippa Rogerson in chapter fifteen, the application of 'good arguable case' has been far from straightforward. There has been a

[4] *Brownlie v Four Seasons Holdings Inc* [2014] EWHC 273 (QB).

[5] *Four Seasons Holdings Inc v Brownlie* [2015] EWCA Civ 665, [2016] 1 WLR 1814.

[6] *Brownlie I* (n 1). The Supreme Court took the unusual step of directing mid-appeal that Holdings produce a witness statement on the corporate structure which demonstrated that Holdings was a non-trading holding company which did not own or operate the Hotel; rather, at the material time the Hotel was operated by an Egyptian subsidiary of Holdings, FS Cairo. Lord Sumption considered that this evidence substantially corresponded to that before Master Cook at first instance: [15].

[7] *Brownlie v Four Seasons Holdings Inc* [2019] EWHC 2533 (QB).

[8] *FS Cairo (Nile Plaza) LLC v Brownlie* [2020] EWCA Civ 996, [2021] 2 All ER 605.

[9] *Brownlie II* (n 1).

plethora of case law where the test and its application has been directly in issue. In *Canada Trust Co v Stolzenberg (No 2)* the test was explained with reference to new terminology by Waller LJ:[10]

> 'Good arguable case' reflects … that one side has a *much better argument on the material available*. It is the concept which the phrase reflects on which it is important to concentrate, ie of the court being satisfied or as satisfied as it can be having regard to the limitations which an interlocutory process imposes that factors exist which allow the court to take jurisdiction.

Lord Sumption in *Brownlie I* took the opportunity to consider the test and outlined that in his view it was a 'serviceable test'. Lord Sumption then offered the following further explanation of what the test meant in practice:[11]

> (i) that the claimant must supply a plausible evidential basis for the application of a relevant jurisdictional gateway; (ii) that if there is an issue of fact about it, or some other reason for doubting whether it applies, the Court must take a view on the material available if it can reliably do so; but (iii) the nature of the issue and the limitations of the material available at the interlocutory stage may be such that no reliable assessment can be made, in which case there is a good arguable case for the application of the gateway if there is a plausible (albeit contested) evidential basis for it. I do not believe that anything is gained by the word 'much', which suggests a superior standard of conviction that is both uncertain and unwarranted in this context.[12]

The Supreme Court ultimately held in *Brownlie I* that on analysis of the evidence there was no realistic prospect that the claimant would establish that she had contracted with Holdings, or that Holdings would be held vicariously liable for the negligence of the driver. As a result, the claimant's claim did not satisfy the factual requirements of the gateways.[13]

Lord Sumption's test was subsequently endorsed by a unanimous Supreme Court in *Goldman Sachs International v Novo Banco SA*,[14] and followed by the Court of Appeal in *Kaefer Aislamentios SA de CV v AMS Drilling Mexico SA de CV*,[15] in the context of facts going to the application of the Brussels Recast Regulation.[16] In *Kaefer*, Green LJ set out further detail on how to apply Lord Sumption's test in practice.[17] The importance of Lord Sumption's revised

[10] *Canada Trust Co v Stolzenberg (No 2)* [1998] 1 WLR 547 (CA) 555. Emphasis added. Waller LJ's analysis was approved in general terms by Lord Steyn, with whom Lord Cooke and Lord Hope agreed, but without full argument: *Canada Trust Co v Stolzenberg (No 2)* [2002] AC 1 (HL) 13.

[11] *Brownlie I* (n 1) [7].

[12] Lady Hale agreed that the test was one of 'good arguable case' and considered that glosses on the test should be avoided, but did not consider Lord Sumption's 'explication' to be a gloss: *Brownlie I* (n 1) [33].

[13] *Brownlie I* (n 1) [15]. Moreover, the claimant did not satisfy the merits test.

[14] *Goldman Sachs International v Novo Banco SA* [2018] UKSC 34, [2018] 1 WLR 3685 [9].

[15] *Kaefer Aislamientos SA de CV v AMS Drilling Mexico SA de CA* [2019] EWCA Civ 10, [2019] 1 WLR Civ 10.

[16] Regulation (EU) No 1215/2012.

[17] *Kaefer* (n 15) [72]–[86].

approach is illustrated by the fact that it has been applied in numerous cases in the relatively short period following judgment.[18] Lord Sumption's revised approach is a useful contribution to the jurisprudence in this area: it translates the rather vague adjectives of 'good', 'arguable' and 'much better' into a distinctly practical, structured analysis which poses simpler questions.

The approach to proving jurisdictional facts can highlight substantive issues with the rule itself. The inquiry into where the contract was made imports the common law rules on contract formation and the well-known rule in *Entores v Miles Far East Corpn*,[19] which holds that the contract was made when, and where, the acceptance of an offer was received. This has been criticised as being somewhat arbitrary. The evidential limitations of the jurisdiction context throw the artificiality of the *Entores* test into sharp relief. At the jurisdiction stage in litigation, parties are often in the early stage of their investigation of the facts. The judge will not have the benefit of oral evidence and, therefore, a party's recollection of an oral conversation often some years prior will go untested. The unsatisfactory nature of the evidence must be contrasted with the significance of holding that a contract was indeed made within the jurisdiction such that a foreign defendant may be required to attend the courts of England and Wales to defend the same. Lord Sumption and Lady Hale both considered that this issue could be reviewed by the Rules Committee.[20]

IV. THE AMBIT OF THE TORT GATEWAY

To establish jurisdiction in respect of a claim in tort it is necessary for a claimant to show that they have a good arguable case that they fall within CPR PD 6B paragraph 3.1(9), namely, that:[21]

(a) damage was sustained [or will be sustained] within the jurisdiction; or
(b) damage [which has been or will be] sustained results from an act committed [or likely to be committed] within the jurisdiction.

The issue in *Brownlie II* on the tort gateway,[22] and one that has troubled courts for decades, is what does 'damage' mean – ie what damage is jurisdictionally relevant? Does damage refer only to the initial or direct damage suffered by a claimant, or does damage permissibly include any and all damage suffered by

[18] See, eg, *Canara Bank v MCS International Limited* [2022] EWHC 2012 (Comm); *Pal v Damen* [2022] EWHC 4697 (QB); *Chep Equipment Pooling v ITS Limited* [2022] EWHC 741 (Comm); *Abu Dhabi Commercial Bank PJSC v Shetty* [2022] EWHC 529 (Comm). These are just a few recent examples.

[19] *Entores v Miles Far East Corpn* [1955] 2 QB 327 (CA).

[20] *Brownlie I* (n 1) [16] and [34]. See also *Ditto Limited v Drive-Thru Records LLC* [2021] EWHC 2035 (Ch) [48] (Deputy Master Francis).

[21] Square brackets denote words added by amendment with effect from 1 October 2015.

[22] This issue was also subject of detailed consideration, albeit obiter, in *Brownlie I*, in which by a 3:2 majority the Supreme Court favoured a wider interpretation of the gateway.

a claimant? The former interpretation ('the narrow interpretation') is compatible with the purpose of the gateways to delimit those cases which have a sufficiently strong connection with the jurisdiction. The latter ('the wide interpretation') is more compatible with the strict reading of the gateway. The wide interpretation runs the risk of catching disputes without a real connection to the jurisdiction and placing more weight on discretion in the form of *forum conveniens*. The narrow interpretation might cause injustice to individual litigants forcing them to litigate their disputes abroad.

In the context of a road traffic accident causing personal injury, or death resulting from personal injury, the difference in the two interpretations is evident: the initial or direct damage is that sustained by the injured person at the time and place of the accident, ie when the conduct of the tortfeasor physically harms the injured person.

A. The Judgment of the Majority

In the Supreme Court the majority favoured a wide interpretation of the tort gateway. Lord Lloyd-Jones gave a judgment with which Lord Reed, Lord Briggs and Lord Burrows agreed. Lord Lloyd-Jones held that 'damage' in the context of the gateway was not confined 'to the element necessary to complete a cause of action but includes all the detriment, physical, financial and social which the claimant suffers as a result of the tortious conduct of the defendant'.[23] Accordingly, each of the claimant's claims passed through the gateway.

The structure of Lord Lloyd-Jones's judgment was to effectively reject all the arguments which sought to displace the natural and ordinary meaning of 'damage'.

First, it had been argued that the interpretation of 'damage' should match the interpretation in the context of Article 7(2) of the Brussels Recast Regulation,[24] which focused on only the direct and immediate damage as the jurisdictionally relevant damage, rather than extending to consequential damage, as only the former, in the jurisprudence of the European Court of Justice, was deemed to establish a sufficient connection with the jurisdiction. Further the legislative history demonstrated that the domestic rules of jurisdiction had been amended to bring them into line with the EU rules when the Civil Jurisdiction and Judgments Act 1982 came into force.

Lord Lloyd-Jones disagreed. He considered the scope of 'damage' in the EU rules was not relevant to the meaning of damage in the scope of domestic rules. Whilst the domestic gateway had been widened to include cases covered under

[23] *Brownlie II* (n 1) [83].

[24] See also Art 5(3) of the Brussels Convention 1968 and Art 5(3) of the Brussels I Regulation (EC) No 44/2001, and Art 5(3) of the 2007 Lugano Convention, in materially identical terms.

the EU regime, it did not follow that the amendment to the domestic rules had not intended to go wider. It also did not follow that after the amendment to the domestic rules, that the understanding of the scope of 'damage' was then tied to the developing understanding in the EU case law. The fundamental differences between the two systems made such assimilation inappropriate: the Brussels system featured a general rule in Article 4 of the Brussels Recast Regulation[25] that a defendant should be sued in the Court of their domicile and limited derogations which, as exceptions were to be interpreted narrowly, including the equivalent of the tort ground of jurisdiction. Further, the role of *forum conveniens* in the English system was a substantial difference.[26]

Second, there was a split in the case law – there was a body of first instance personal injury decisions which preferred the wide interpretation, and a group of decisions primarily in the economic loss context which preferred the narrow interpretation. Lord Lloyd-Jones considered the former, relied on by the claimant, was an impressive and coherent line of authority.[27] The economic loss cases were to be treated with caution because they largely stemmed from the erroneous understanding of the assumption that the domestic tort gateway should be interpreted in line with the special rule of tort jurisdiction under the EU scheme.[28] Further, wholly economic damage was 'simply not comparable' with that suffered by Lady Brownlie.[29] Lord Lloyd-Jones did agree that the mere fact of economic loss, however remote, felt by a business seat would be an unsatisfactory basis for jurisdiction.[30]

Third, the effect of the wide interpretation, necessarily, was to expand the number of cases which might pass through it. Further, the consequence of permitting remote forms of damage to found jurisdiction in England is that it very often yields some identifiable form of damage in the claimant's domicile: English law has never asserted jurisdiction based on the claimant's connections, whether presence, residence, domicile or nationality. The argument in favour of the narrow interpretation contended that it was not possible, as a matter of principle, to resort to *forum conveniens* to deal with the effect of the wide interpretation. It was argued that the gateways and *forum conveniens* have distinct roles – the former identifies a list of factual connections which demonstrate a sufficient connection with the jurisdiction, the latter, looks primarily to the practicality of the resolution of the litigation in the jurisdiction, and whether the claim could be more appropriately resolved elsewhere. Lord Lloyd-Jones considered, however, that both the gateways and *forum conveniens* were equal parts of the jurisdiction test.

[25] Previously Art 2 in the Brussels I Regulation.
[26] *Brownlie II* (n 1) [54] and [55].
[27] ibid, [64].
[28] ibid, [74].
[29] ibid, [75].
[30] ibid, [76].

For that reason, the fear that the wide construction of the gateway would lead to claimants being able to sue in the courts of their domicile, and in a country with only a limited connection to the dispute was unfounded. If *forum conveniens* was correctly applied, it was a 'robust and effective mechanism'[31] which could be 'trusted to prevent the acceptance of jurisdiction in situations where there is merely a casual or adventitious link between the claim and England'.[32]

B. Lord Leggatt's Dissent on the Tort Gateway

Lord Leggatt delivered a powerful dissent on the tort gateway. He considered that the wide interpretation was 'not so much a gateway … as an open territory with no fence' and the breadth of the construction was without a principled basis.[33] Lord Leggatt considered that the 'main, if not the only, positive argument'[34] in favour of the wide interpretation was that it accorded with 'ordinary and natural meaning', but that was not determinative of what damage meant in the context of the gateway. Rather it was implicit from the context that damage refers only to damage which is in some way connected to the claim in tort that the claimant sought to bring.[35]

Central to Lord Leggatt's preference for the narrow interpretation was the purpose of the jurisdiction gateways. He endorsed Lord Sumption's analysis in *Brownlie I* that all the gateways were in different ways 'concerned to identify some substantial and not merely casual or adventitious link between the cause of action and England'.[36] The crux of Lord Leggatt's judgment is as follows:[37]

> Treating it as sufficient to satisfy the tort jurisdictional gateway that an individual who sustained bodily injuries in an accident abroad returns to England, or visits England, bringing their injuries with them, would be inconsistent with this purpose. As noted earlier, the practical effect of such an interpretation would be that, in any claim in tort for serious injuries sustained in another country, it is treated as a link with England sufficient to satisfy the gateway test that the claimant is ordinarily resident here. That stands the underlying principle on its head since, as Lord Sumption observed in Brownlie I at para 28, personal connections between the parties and England are generally relevant to jurisdiction only in the case of the defendant. Indeed, the claimant would not even need to show residence in England. On the broad interpretation of ground 9(a) for which the claimant contends, the gateway is

[31] ibid, [82].
[32] ibid, [79].
[33] ibid, [171].
[34] ibid, [175].
[35] ibid, [177].
[36] ibid, [192].
[37] ibid, [194].

> portable. If that interpretation is correct, a claimant can create a link with England which satisfies the gateway requirement for suing a foreign defendant in the English courts by travelling to England, for example for medical treatment, after the event giving rise to the damage has occurred. Thus, it would be enough to satisfy the gateway requirement for bringing a claim in tort in the English courts that, for example, an Egyptian claimant badly injured in Egypt in a road traffic collision with a vehicle driven by another Egyptian driver afterwards comes to England while still suffering pain or disability. An interpretation which has this consequence is not in my opinion a rational or defensible interpretation of the rules of court.

In Lord Leggatt's view, it was not sufficient to have recourse to *forum conveniens* to cater for the wide interpretation of the tort gateway as they were fundamentally distinct – *forum conveniens* was:[38]

> an inquiry of a different kind and with a different purpose from the question whether there is a sufficient connection between the defendant and the jurisdiction to make it just or legitimate for the courts of England and Wales to assert jurisdiction over the defendant. Whereas the gateways look back to the events which gave rise to the claim, the test of *forum conveniens* looks forward to the nature and shape of the dispute at a trial.

C. The Impact of the Decision

The Supreme Court decision has resolved a long-standing debate in English law. It is valuable for legal certainty and protects the interests of injured English claimants in permitting them, in a greater range of circumstances to sue in the courts of their domicile in respect of injuries suffered abroad.

The decision has been followed recently by the Hong Kong Court of Appeal in *Fong Chak Wan v Ascentic Ltd*,[39] in a personal injury case where the claimant suffered an injury at work when he fell four metres into a trench as a metal-plank he was walking on gave way. The accident occurred in Ningbo, China. The claimant then travelled to Hong Kong four days after the accident where he received medical attention and was on sick leave. Lord Collins gave the leading judgment on the issue of jurisdiction and described the reasoning of the majority in *Brownlie II* as 'compelling'.[40] The 'natural and ordinary meaning' of the equivalent jurisdiction provision to paragraph 3.1(9)(a) 'leads to the conclusion that it includes indirect or consequential damage' and there was no good reason to depart from that meaning.[41]

[38] ibid.
[39] *Fong Chak Wan v Ascentic Ltd* [2022] HKCFA 12.
[40] ibid, [104].
[41] ibid, [121].

On the other hand, the Supreme Court's decision on the tort gateway has not passed without criticism. It has been described as 'questionable' and as effectively rewriting gateway 9(a) with the potential consequence of diminishing the importance of the gateways altogether.[42] It is important to understand what the consequences might be for the ambit of the Court's jurisdiction and the practice of challenging jurisdiction.

D. Economic Loss Claims

An area in which the majority decision will have substantial consequences is that of the tortious claims in respect of purely financial loss. Purely financial loss might be felt in multiple places around the world with limited connection to the underlying tort – a company might point to loss suffered at its company seat, in the diminishment of a bank account it holds, or in the money it expended unpicking the consequences of the tort, all of which might be sited in different countries. Lord Lloyd-Jones's judgment that 'damage' 'simply refers to actionable harm, direct or indirect, caused by the wrongful act alleged',[43] is wide enough to catch the most remote financial loss consequences. Lord Lloyd-Jones was live to this issue:[44]

> The nature of pure economic loss creates a need for constraints on the legal consequences of remote effects and can give rise to complex and difficult issues as to where the damage was suffered, calling for a careful analysis of transactions. As a result, the more remote economic repercussions of the causative event will not found jurisdiction …
>
> … I would certainly not disagree with the proposition, supported by the economic loss cases, that to hold that the mere fact of any economic loss, however remote, felt by a claimant where he or she lives or, if a corporation, where it has its business seat would be an unsatisfactory basis for the exercise of jurisdiction.

It does not follow, however, that the narrow interpretation to the gateway would have been more straightforward in the pure financial loss context. In the choice of law context, under Article 4 Rome II, the courts have grappled with the difficulty of identifying a principled approach to determining the place in which the damage occurs. For instance, if the effect of a fraud is to procure the payment of money out from the victim in respect of goods that the victim wanted that in fact did not exist – is the relevant damage the loss of the money, or the fact that the goods did not exist as the victim hoped?[45]

[42] Arzandeh (n 2) 729.
[43] *Brownlie II* (n 1) [81].
[44] ibid, [75] and [76].
[45] See on this point the EC Study on the Rome II Regulation (EC) 864/2007 on the law applicable to non-contractual obligations (2021) and in particular the UK's submission on Art 4 at 689.

Lord Lloyd-Jones is right to observe that 'the more remote economic repercussions of the causative event will not found jurisdiction'. It accords with the need to identify a sufficient connection to the jurisdiction. It is not clear from the passages above whether Lord Lloyd-Jones intends that the scope of the gateway is narrower for economic loss claims, or whether the work in restricting the economic loss cases that may be brought in England will be done by *forum conveniens*. If it is the former, it is likely undesirable as a matter of principle for a gateway to bear two meanings. If it is the latter, for the reasons which follow, it may prove difficult to ensure consistency and predictability.

E. A Greater Role for *Forum Conveniens*?

It is perhaps trite to say but the most immediate consequence of the Supreme Court's decision is it greatly expands the situations in which the courts of England and Wales may accept jurisdiction over tort claims, including cases which at first glance have only a tangential connection to the jurisdiction. The majority's answer to this scenario is that *forum conveniens* is a suitably robust tool to ensure sufficient connection. There are questions over the ability of *forum conveniens* to fulfil this role.

First, it requires judges to grapple with nebulous concepts, for instance weigh the damage suffered in different locations. This is an inherently unpredictable task. Further, the sufficiency of damage must also be weighed against harder edged *forum conveniens* factors such as the location of witnesses, making a difficult evaluative balancing exercise, even more testing.

Second, whilst the decision on the tort gateway promotes certainty after a long period of debate, an increased role for *forum conveniens* arguably has the opposite effect – *forum conveniens* is by design discretionary and when coupled with the nebulous exercise undertaken will make the situations in which the court will exercise jurisdiction less predictable.

Third, there is also some doubt whether *forum conveniens* has demonstrated itself to be a sufficiently robust mechanism of determining the appropriate place for trial in personal injury claims. As Lord Leggatt considered:[46]

> A further concern about an approach which leaves almost everything to *forum conveniens* is that, if invited to exercise a largely unfettered discretion, judges cannot be relied on to require a real and substantial connection between the defendant's conduct and England and Wales to be shown before permitting a claimant to sue a foreign defendant. That at least is the lesson I draw from the series of first instance decisions which I have cited … holding that pain or financial loss felt in England in consequence of personal injuries sustained in an accident abroad was enough to

[46] *Brownlie II* (n 1) [203] and [206].

> get through the tort gateway. In each of those cases the judge went on to consider whether England was 'the proper place in which to bring the claim'. In every case the judge felt able to conclude that it was. …
>
> I have no doubt that the judges who decided that England was the appropriate forum in these cases were doing their best to be impartial. But it is human nature to wish, if possible, to allow a person who is before the court and who has suffered what may have been catastrophic injuries apparently as a result of another's wrongdoing to proceed with a claim for compensation rather than sending him or her away to try to bring proceedings in a foreign country. It is also human nature for a judge who has spent his or her professional career working in a particular legal system to attach more weight to its perceived advantages than those of the legal system of a faraway country of which the judge may know little or nothing. Such factors are likely, on the evidence of these cases, to incline a judge who is afforded a discretion to exercise it in favour of permitting service outside the jurisdiction, even if the claimant's injuries were sustained abroad and there is no real or substantial connection between the proposed defendant and the conduct which gave rise to the claim and England and Wales.

Over time *forum conveniens* may develop to be an effective mechanism of determining jurisdiction. Regardless, the Supreme Court's judgment will lead to a proliferation of challenges to jurisdiction in tort claims based on *forum conveniens*. There is a danger that this may increase the time and cost associated with the issue of jurisdiction.

V. THE MERITS TEST IN CLAIMS GOVERNED BY FOREIGN LAW

A. Lord Leggatt's Judgment

The context for the argument on the presumption was unusual and specific. In *Brownlie II*, it was common ground that Egyptian law applied to the claimant's claims in both contract and tort. However, the claimant's pleadings by the time of *Brownlie II* asserted only that the claimant's claims were brought pursuant to Egyptian law but did not plead the content or sources of the Egyptian law relied upon. The parties adduced expert evidence on the content of Egyptian law. The claimant's evidence however had significant gaps in it.

FS Cairo argued that in respect of those claims not covered by expert evidence Lady Brownlie could not satisfy the merits threshold, and further that the failure to plead the content or sources of Egyptian law was fatal to the claimant's ability to demonstrate that her claims brought pursuant to Egyptian law had reasonable prospects of success. In respect of both issues, the claimant sought to rely on the presumption that in the absence of evidence to the contrary foreign law is presumed to be the same as English law.

The argument that the presumption cannot apply in these circumstances had two pillars to it. First, the fact that foreign law applies pursuant to mandatory choice of law rules.[47] To permit reliance on the presumption in such a case subverts the choice of law rules by applying English law in place of the foreign law. Second, the claimant seeking to serve a claim out of the jurisdiction bears the burden of establishing reasonable prospects of success, but to permit reliance on the presumption in effect reverses the burden of proof: the defendant must prove that recourse to the presumption is inappropriate. The purpose of the merits test is to ensure that a foreign defendant is not brought to the jurisdiction to answer an unmeritorious claim. That has to be assessed on a real basis, ie in light of the law that actually applies.

The argument that the presumption can fill the gaps portrays the rule as one of mere evidence and procedure, long established by case law, designed to make litigation more cost effective and efficient. The existence of the rule was rooted in pragmatism. It allows the court to proceed in a manner which is proportionate and keeps evidence focussed on areas of material difference between the parties. It avoids significant unnecessary expense, delay, and complication.

The Supreme Court unanimously dismissed FS Cairo's appeal on the issue of the presumption. Lord Leggatt gave the leading judgment with which Lord Reed, Lord Lloyd-Jones, Lord Briggs and Lord Burrows agreed.

Lord Leggatt noted that the presumption had been criticised by commentators, referring to the following passage from Professor Fentiman's *Foreign Law in English Courts: Pleading, Proof and Choice of Law* (1998):[48]

> It is intuitively unacceptable for a party to seek the application of foreign law and at the same time, with luminous inconsistency, to invite the court to apply English law by declining to offer evidence of any other. It is also potentially unfair that one party should (in effect) be made to prove (or disprove) a matter which another has introduced .... Such arguments suggest that a party who relies upon foreign law must normally offer evidence as to its content or face dismissal of its claim or defence.

That criticism however was misplaced in Lord Leggatt's view, as the presumption was rather more flexible and realistic in its application. The existence of the presumption was justified by three factors:[49]

(1) The often substantial similarities between English law and the laws of other states: 'In *Muduroglu Ltd v TC Ziraat Bankasi* ... Mustill LJ observed that 'in so many practical respects there is insufficient difference between the commercial laws of one trading nation and another to make it worth while asserting and proving a difference'.'

[47] The relevant choice of law rules are those in Rome I and II. The provisions defining the scope of application in Art 1 of both Regulations provide that '*This Regulation* shall *apply*' (emphasis added) and the wording of the individual choice of law rules is framed in mandatory terms.

[48] *Brownlie II* (n 1) [121] citing R Fentiman, *Foreign Law in English Courts: Pleading, Proof and Choice of Law* (Oxford, OUP, 1998) 152–53.

[49] *Brownlie II* (n 1) [122] to [125].

(2) The requirement of 'materiality': 'Unless there is a real likelihood that any differences between the applicable foreign law and English law on a particular issue may lead to a different outcome, there is no good reason to put a party to the trouble and expense of adducing evidence of foreign law. The object of adjudication is not to achieve a goal of abstract legal purity but to do practical justice between the parties.'
(3) The presumption does not determine any legal issue or alter the burden of proof; it merely places the burden of adducing evidence on the party who wishes to displace the presumption.

The justifications for the presumption also inform its limits. Lord Leggatt considered:[50]

> There is no warrant for applying the presumption of similarity unless it is a fair and reasonable assumption to make in the particular case. The question is one of fact: in the circumstances is it reasonable to expect that the applicable foreign law is likely to be materially similar to English law on the matter in issue (meaning that any differences between the two systems are unlikely to lead to a different substantive outcome)?

There was no hard and fast rule that it was impermissible to resort to the presumption in circumstances where evidence of foreign law had been served, but there were gaps in the same. It narrowed the circumstances in which the presumption could be relied on, but whether the presumption was open at all depended on the circumstances.[51] In Lord Leggatt's view there were justifiable reasons why a party's evidence might be incomplete. The expert relied upon might not have considered the point would arise, or it might have been disproportionate to address the same.

Lord Leggatt assessed the evidence of the party's respective Egyptian lawyers and considered that the claims were reasonably arguable for the purposes of establishing the Court's jurisdiction. Lord Leggatt did consider however that the claimant should be required 'to serve revised particulars of claim giving proper particulars of how she intends to put her case under Egyptian law going forward'. At the point the claimant had amended her Particulars of Claim to expressly claim damages pursuant to Egyptian law it was 'incumbent on the claimant to specify in her statement of case any rules or provisions of Egyptian law on which she intends to rely so that the defendant knows in outline the case it has to meet'.[52]

[50] ibid, [126].
[51] ibid, [151].
[52] ibid, [160].

B. The Impact of the Decision

Lord Leggatt's judgment in articulating the rationale for the presumption represents a valuable contribution to the jurisprudence in this area. It has been described as 'pragmatic and uncontroversial'.[53] Much of the debate which follows will be on the limits of the rule. Perhaps the immediate issue is that the test formulated by Lord Leggatt (whether it is 'reasonable to expect that the applicable foreign law is likely to be materially similar to English law on the matter in issue') is uncertain and difficult to apply. There is a risk therefore, initially at least, of cases arguing over the reasonableness of a claimant's assumption.

Lord Leggatt was perhaps live to this very point and offered some guidance:[54]

(1) The presumption is more likely to be appropriate where the applicable law is a common law system rather than one founded on Roman law, but there are 'great and broad' principles which are likely to impose an obligation in any developed legal system.
(2) It is less likely to be appropriate where the relevant domestic law is contained in a statute subject to the nature of the statute in question – there is a difference between a statute which codifies general principles and one which introduces a local scheme of regulation.
(3) Given the inherent uncertainties of the test, it is always open to either party to adduce evidence of the foreign law.
(4) There is more scope to rely on the presumption at an early stage in proceedings – to run a case to trial relying solely on the presumption may be a 'much more precarious course'.

This represents useful guidance but considering the nature of the test uncertainties still remain, and in the near future, it may mean that it is difficult for litigants to predict what circumstances will attract the application of the presumption.

Lord Leggatt's judgment may also prove to have an impact in the form in which evidence of foreign law is presented. He considered that the practice that foreign law could only be proved with evidence from an expert in the foreign system of law may be 'outdated':[55]

> I would add that it should not be assumed that the only alternative to relying on the presumption of similarity is necessarily to tender evidence from an expert in the foreign system of law. The old notion that foreign legal materials can only ever be brought before the court as part of the evidence of an expert witness is outdated. Whether the court will require evidence from an expert witness should depend on the nature of the issue and of the relevant foreign law. In an age when so much

[53] Arzandeh (n 2) 729.
[54] *Brownlie II* (n 1) [143]–[147].
[55] ibid, [148].

> information is readily available through the internet, there may be no need to consult a foreign lawyer in order to find the text of a relevant foreign law. On some occasions the text may require skilled exegesis of a kind which only a lawyer expert in the foreign system of law can provide. But in other cases it may be sufficient to know what the text says. If, for example, the question is whether a spouse has a right to claim damages for bereavement under the applicable foreign law, producing a copy of the relevant foreign legislation (with, if necessary, an English translation) is a much more secure basis for a finding than presuming that the foreign law is the same as the English law. Of course, a judge needs to be alert to whether the text relied on is current. But even if that cannot be guaranteed, the presumption of continuity may be a more reliable foundation in the absence of contrary evidence than the presumption of similarity.

There are certainly situations where evidence of foreign law may be adequately dealt with by a translated copy of the provision alone. However, as Lord Leggatt notes, this is a question of the nature of the issue and the relevant foreign law. Those with experience of foreign law in practice will be aware that a copy of the relevant foreign provision rarely tells the whole story. There are frequently points of construction, foreign law principles of interpretation,[56] case law, and local practice of a foreign jurisdiction which complicate matters. This is likely another area, where there will be future arguments on the form and adequacy of evidence.

Lord Leggatt's guidance was applied in *Suppipat v Narongdej*,[57] where Calver J held at the pre-trial review that the judge could be supplied with provisions of Singapore law (and, if necessary, any legal principles as to the interpretation and status of those sources) and that there was no need for oral expert evidence at trial on the issue. Calver J noted: (i) that Singapore was a common law system; (ii) English judges were used to reading, analysing and applying Singaporean law; and (iii) there was only one issue of Singaporean law in the extensive list of issues.

Lastly, it should not be overlooked that, whilst the Supreme Court's decision does not formally change the burden of proof on the claimant to show that their claim has reasonable prospects of success to permit service out of the jurisdiction, it does in practice place the onus of the issue of foreign law on the foreign defendant. The foreign defendant must now adduce evidence of the content of foreign law to displace any reliance by the claimant on the presumption. This approach may be open to question – the foreign defendant is not under the jurisdiction of the court yet is required to spend increased time and costs to demonstrate the claim against it is legally defective.

[56] See, eg, *Deane v Barker* [2022] EWHC 1523 (QB) at [33]–[39] (Richard Hermer QC sitting as a Deputy High Court Judge).

[57] *Suppipat v Narongdej* [2022] EWHC 1806 (Comm).

VI. JURISDICTION REFORM

The *Brownlie* litigation raised significant and important issues which developed our domestic scheme of jurisdiction. When such developments occur, there is some merit in standing back to ask whether the scheme of jurisdiction itself can be reviewed or altered. There have been two recent suggestions of reform following *Brownlie II* (albeit not necessarily prompted by *Brownlie II*). First, the Rules Committee are considering various changes to the gateways to expand and reformulate the grounds of jurisdiction. This topic was addressed by Sir David Foxton in his article 'The jurisdiction gateways – some (very) modest proposals'.[58] Second, more radically, Professors Briggs and Dickinson have proposed a new statutory scheme of jurisdiction.[59] Their new scheme suggests entirely removing the merits from jurisdiction leaving deficiencies in the claimants' case to be addressed by summary judgment and strike out applications by foreign defendants. It also proposes re-drawing the grounds of jurisdiction into three categories – first, are grounds of jurisdiction which are established merely by falling within the terms of a rule; second, are those for which establishing that the rule is engaged is not enough, rather it is necessary that a claimant additionally show a real and substantial connection between the claim and England and; third, a free-standing ground for jurisdiction where access to justice or the right to a fair trial requires. This chapter is not the correct place to address the merits of these proposals beyond noting that there is value in keeping the scheme of jurisdiction under continuous review. It is important, however, to keep in mind the overarching aim of the jurisdiction scheme – ensuring that a dispute is sufficiently connected to the jurisdiction to make the exercise of jurisdiction logically coherent and practical.

[58] D Foxton, 'The Jurisdictional Gateways – Some (very) Modest Proposals' [2022] *Lloyd's Maritime and Commercial Law Quarterly* 70.

[59] A Briggs and A Dickinson, 'Reframing Jurisdiction: A New Scheme', presented at British Institute of International and Comparative Law (11 May 2022) www.blackstonechambers.com/news/reframing-jurisdiction-a-new-scheme (accessed 12 September 2022). See also ch 19 in this volume.

19

Future Landmarks: Scanning the Horizon

ANDREW DICKINSON

I. INTRODUCTION

THE MANDATE WHICH this chapter seeks to fulfil is to consider what the next landmarks in English private international law might be. With scarcely concealed scorn, Cicero observed that:[1]

> There is an ancient belief, handed down to us even from mythical times and firmly established by the general agreement of the Roman people and of all nations, that divination of some kind exists among men; this the Greeks call μαντική – that is, the foresight and knowledge of future events. A really splendid and helpful thing it is – if only such a faculty exists – since by its means men may approach very near to the power of gods.

In Cicero's view, 'there is no such thing as divination', with conjecture being a matter of educated guesswork.[2] Nonetheless, even an experienced lawyer may approach the task of predicting future private international law landmarks with a measure of trepidation. Whereas the authors of the contributions in the preceding chapters of this collection have charted the known landscape, the present task involves a venture into the unknown, relying on knowledge gained from the study of past events to speculate as to the subject's future topology.

To look forwards, we must first travel back in time.

II. THE PAST WAS ONCE THE FUTURE

The third edition of Dicey's *Conflict of Laws* was published a century ago, shortly before the death of its title author.[3] The fifth edition, edited by Arthur

[1] *De Divinatione*, I.I, trans WA Falconer (Harvard, Harvard University Press, 1923).

[2] ibid, II.V. As Cicero put it: 'Can any soothsayer, augur, prophet, or dreamer conjecture better than a physician, a pilot, or a general that an invalid will come safely out of his sickness, or that a ship will escape from danger, or that an army will avoid an ambuscade?'

[3] AV Dicey and A Berriedale Keith (eds), *A Digest of the Law of England with Reference to the Conflict of Laws*, 3rd edn (London, Stevens & Sons, 1922). Dicey died on 7 April 1922, a few days after publication.

Berridale Keith was completed a decade later, in 1932.[4] Writing in 1949, in the preface to the sixth edition of that work (and the first under his general editorship), Dr John Morris observed:[5]

> Since that date [1932] an enormous development has taken place in the Conflict of Laws. In England, the courts have been busy with problems arising out of the Russian Revolution,[6] the Italo-Abyssinian war, the Spanish civil war, and the second world war and the world-wide movement of populations associated with these events. Important new statutes have been enacted by the legislature. The literature of the subject has shown a sudden and remarkable tendency to expand. … Refugee scholars have enriched the literature of the subject both in England and the United States. Increasing attention is being paid to the Conflict of Laws by the periodical legal journals.

In his preface to the seventh edition, published in 1958, Morris referred to 'rapid developments in this branch of the law', necessitating 'very considerable rewriting'.[7] More explicitly, in the ninth edition, published in 1973, he asserted that:[8]

> Since the last edition of this book was published in the summer of 1967, more important changes have taken place in the English conflict of laws than during any comparable period in the history of the subject. Not only have the courts been busy in elaborating and refining the rules of the conflict of laws, but several statutes have radically altered some of these rules, especially in the field of family law.

Writing again in 1980, in the last edition under his editorship, Morris wrote:[9]

> Dramatic changes have taken place in the English rules of the conflict of law since the last edition of this work was published seven years ago. Perhaps the most significant of these changes is the increasing tendency for statutes to replace the common law.

Following Morris' death in 1984, the baton passed to his successor as general editor, Lawrence Collins. There was no dimming of the fervour. As Mr Collins (as he then was) put it:[10]

> The dramatic changes in this area of the law have continued, and involve at least one change which is revolutionary. It is not easy to exaggerate the importance of the changes effected by the Civil Jurisdiction and Judgments Act 1982, which brings into

[4] A Berridale Keith (ed), *A Digest of the Law of England with Reference to the Conflict of Laws*, 5th edn (London, Stevens & Sons, 1932).

[5] JHC Morris (ed), *Dicey's Conflict of Laws*, 6th edn (London, Stevens & Sons, 1949) xiii.

[6] See ch 7 in this volume.

[7] JHC Morris (ed), *Dicey's Conflict of Laws*, 7th edn (London, Stevens & Sons, 1958) viii.

[8] JHC Morris (ed), *Dicey and Morris on the Conflict of Laws*, 9th edn (London, Stevens & Sons, 1973) ix.

[9] JHC Morris (ed), *Dicey and Morris on the Conflict of Laws*, 10th edn (London, Stevens & Sons, 1980) ix.

[10] L Collins (ed), *Dicey and Morris on the Conflict of Laws*, 11th edn (London, Stevens & Sons, 1987) ix.

effect the Brussels Convention on jurisdiction and the enforcement of judgments in civil and commercial matters.

In following the four editions, Dr, then Sir, and finally Lord, Collins continued to observe the growing influence of the body of law created by the institutions of what would become the European Union.[11] Tellingly, in the fourteenth edition, Sir Lawrence noted that 'Professor Dicey, and even Dr Morris, could not of course have foreseen the huge impact which a supranational body of law, namely European law, would have on the subject of the conflict of laws',[12] adding that 'the impact of European law is not by any means entirely for the good',[13] judging by the adverse reaction to the trio of decisions in *Erich Gasser Gmbh v MISAT srl*,[14] *Turner v Grovit*,[15] and *Owusu v Jackson*.[16] In the penultimate edition of *Dicey*, published almost a decade ago,[17] Lord Collins reported that since 'the last edition was published in 2006, the EU has demonstrated its intention to legislate for virtually the whole area, and four extremely important Regulations[18] have come into force'.[19]

In the twelfth edition (1993), Mr Collins also emphasised what he saw as an important structural change in the subject:[20]

> the most significant developments have been in the law of jurisdiction and the enforcement of judgments. … the overwhelming preponderance of new cases in this edition is in [these] fields …. These topics have become of enormous practical importance as Europe has grown smaller, and as transnational litigation in general has increased. But they have not been matched by an increase in developments in choice of law.

In the preface to the fourteenth edition, published at the turn of the millennium, Dr Collins reported that:[21]

> The number of reported decisions continues to reflect the great practical importance of conflicts over jurisdiction. Questions of jurisdiction and foreign judgments now take up more than three times the space devoted to them by Professor Dicey in the first edition, and more than twice the amount which Dr Morris first devoted to them in 1949.

[11] See, in addition to the following references, L Collins (ed), *Dicey and Morris on the Conflict of Laws*, 12th edn (London, Sweet & Maxwell, 1993) xv and L Collins (ed), *Dicey, Morris & Collins on the Conflict of Laws*, 13th edn (London, Sweet & Maxwell, 2000) xv.

[12] L Collins (ed), *Dicey, Morris & Collins on the Conflict of Laws*, 14th edn (London, Sweet & Maxwell, 2006) xv.

[13] ibid.

[14] Case C-116/02 *Erich Gasser Gmbh v MISAT srl* [2003] ECR I-14693, [2005] QB 1.

[15] Case C-159/02 *Turner v Grovit* [2004] ECR I-3565, [2005] 1 AC 101.

[16] Case C-281/02 *Owusu v Jackson* [2005] ECR I-1383, [2005] QB 801. See P de Vareilles-Sommières (ed), *Forum Shopping in the European Judicial Area* (Oxford, Hart Publishing, 2007).

[17] The principal reason for the delay, greater than that for any edition since 1949, will be obvious.

[18] The 16th edition (2022) (n 51) has been published only very recently. Regulation (EC) No 864/2007 (Rome II); Regulation (EC) No 593/2008 (Rome I); Regulation (EC) No 1393/2007; and Regulation (EC) No 4/2009.

[19] L Collins (ed), *Dicey, Morris & Collins on the Conflict of Laws*, 15th edn (London, Sweet & Maxwell, 2012) xvii.

[20] *Dicey and Morris*, 12th edn (n 11) xvi.

[21] *Dicey, Morris & Collins*, 13th edn (n 11) xv.

Finally, on the same occasion, Dr Collins also drew his readers' attention to: 'the enormous increase in the use of the internet, both for electronic mail and electronic commerce (if, which is doubtful, a sharp distinction can be made between them)'.[22] He continued:

> It is plain that in the next few years electronic commerce will revolutionise cross-border trade. A very distinguished former Law Lord recently expressed in a public lecture the view that the internet meant the end of private international law. That is certainly an exaggeration, but it is true that rules previously based on a 'place' such as the place of a contract … are difficult, and perhaps impossible to apply where websites have no, or no identifiable, location. There is no doubt that, by the time of the next edition, the internet will have had a major impact on some areas of the conflict of laws.

III. THE PAST SPEAKS TO THE FUTURE

Are there any lessons to be learned from this brief (and, admittedly, limited) retrospective? Four potentially valuable points emerge. First, no feature of the landscape, however deeply embedded its roots may seem to be, is immune from rapid and catastrophic change. This fact loomed large in the minds of the current editors of *Dicey, Morris & Collins*,[23] as they worked to bring the sixteenth edition into a world in which the UK is no longer a member of the European Union. The trio of decisions of the European Court,[24] which seemed so significant and generated so much heat at the time of their delivery, now languish.

Second, there is a tendency to over-state, or over-predict, the significance of more recent events as engines of legal development.[25] Conflict and political upheaval in Europe were, for good reason, at the forefront of Dr Morris' mind in 1949, but those events have not had a significant long-lasting impact on the rules applied by the English courts today. Similarly, not only has private international law survived the technological revolution brought about by the internet, the latter's impact on the rulebook and on the contours of the subject more generally has been limited.[26]

[22] ibid, xv.

[23] Including the present author.

[24] Text to nn 13–16.

[25] This may be a product of 'recency bias': see A Tversky and D Kahneman, 'Judgment under Uncertainty: Heuristics and Biases' (1974) 185 *Science* 1124, 1127.

[26] See, eg, *Berezovsky v Forbes Inc* [2000] UKHL 25, [2000] 1 WLR 1004; *Dow Jones & Co Inc v Gutnick* [2002] HCA 56, (2003) 210 CLR 575; *Lucasfilm Ltd v Ainsworth* [2009] EWCA Civ 1328, [2010] 1 Ch 503, [193], affirmed [2011] UKSC 39, [2012] 1 AC 208 without reference to this point. For a balanced and informative assessment, see T Lutzi, *Private International Law Online* (Oxford, OUP, 2020).

Third, we must appreciate the more subtle forces at play in the law's development. Arguably, the most important effects of war in Europe and the more recent technological revolution have been to change the way in which legal systems interact with one another, whether through an influx of refugee scholars or the ready availability of online materials, allowing greater comparative insight.

Fourth, the development of the conflict of laws in the twentieth and early twenty-first centuries has been principally characterised not by landmarks, whether cases or statutes, but by more pervasive changes in the landscape: from common law to statute, and from a subject dominated by choice of law to one dominated by questions of jurisdiction and cross-border civil procedure. The European 'revolution' in private international law took almost half a century to define the contours of this landscape. Its overthrow, by popular vote, has washed away many (but not all)[27] of its architectural features. It has left, however, ways of thinking about and engaging with the subject that will surely endure.

This is not to deny that there have been, and may continue to be, cases which are landmarks in the sense that they represent 'an object in the landscape, which, by its conspicuousness, serves as a direction of one's course'.[28] However, we should not seek to invest those cases with a spiritual and totemic significance that places them apart from the landscape which they serve. *Spiliada Maritime Corporation v Cansulex*,[29] and *Société Nationale Industrielle Aérospatiale v Lee Kui Jak*,[30] may be cases in point. Delivered within a few months of each other,[31] each represents, no doubt, an important milestone in the development, respectively, of the framework governing the discretion possessed by courts of common law jurisdictions in the exercise of jurisdiction and their equitable powers to restrain the prosecution of civil claims before foreign courts. However, a tendency[32] to read the pronouncements of Lord Goff as if they were the words of a statute, or to treat them as *res sanctae*,[33] immune from criticism or renovation has (at least in the view of the present author)[34] hindered the development of the conflict of laws in England in the past 35 years.

[27] The Rome I and Rome II Regulations (n 18) survive in slightly modified form: see Law Applicable to Contractual Obligations and Non-Contractual Obligations (Amendment etc.) (EU Exit) Regulations.

[28] See discussion of the Oxford English Dictionary definition in the preface.

[29] *Spiliada Maritime Corporation v Cansulex* [1987] AC 460. See ch 11 in this volume.

[30] *Société Nationale Industrielle Aérospatiale v Lee Kui Jak* [1987] AC 871. See ch 12 in this volume.

[31] The two decisions were briefly mentioned in the preface to *Dicey and Morris*, 12th edn (n 11) xvii.

[32] See, eg, *Soriano v Forensic News LLC* [2021] EWCA Civ 1952, [2022] 2 WLR 807, [11] and [43]; *SAS Institute v World Programming Ltd* [2020] EWCA Civ 599, [2020] 1 CLC 816 [90].

[33] *Spiliada* has been described as the '*locus classicus* in relation to issues of appropriate forum at common law': *VTB Capital plc v Nutritek International Corp* [2013] UKSC 5, [2013] 2 AC 337 [12] (Lord Mance).

[34] See, in particular, A Dickinson, 'Taming Anti-Suit Injunctions' in A Dickinson and E Peel (eds), *A Conflict of Laws Companion: Essays in Honour of Adrian Briggs* (Oxford, OUP, 2021).

To put this last point more briefly: landmarks may stand out in the landscape, and guide travellers within it. But the landscape of the law is characterised by much more than the landmarks within it.

IV. A NEW, NEW THING?

For the internet in the early twenty-first century, it may well be possible to substitute 'smart contracts' and 'digital assets' today.

Smart contracts consist of '[c]omputer code that, upon the occurrence of a specified condition or conditions, is capable of running automatically according to pre-specified functions'.[35] The label is inapt: the programmes are not inherently smart and, in many cases, they will not be a source of contractual obligations.[36] The quality of computer code, like any traditional contract, depends on the combined intelligence and skill of the draftsperson (coder) and those giving instructions (parties). Insofar as the code not only defines what is to be done but executes steps in the performance of the 'smart contract', it operates as a high-end vending machine.[37] Equally, from a legal perspective, there seems little new under the sun, as the Law Commission concluded in its recent 'Advice to Government':[38]

> Current legal principles can apply to smart legal contracts in much the same way as they do to traditional contracts, albeit with an incremental and principled development of the common law in specific contexts. In general, difficulties associated with applying the existing law to smart legal contracts are not unique to them, and could equally arise in the context of traditional contracts. In addition, even though some types of smart legal contract may give rise to novel legal issues and factual scenarios, existing legal principles can accommodate them.

This comment extends to the sphere of the conflict of laws.[39] In particular, the central question – whether a smart contract is a source of legal obligations

[35] Law Commission, *Advice to Government on Smart Legal Contracts* (Law Com No 401, 2021) vii. See also UK Jurisdiction Taskforce, *Legal statement on cryptoassets and smart contracts* (November 2019) [135].

[36] A Litan, 'Smart Contracts are Neither Smart nor are they Contracts' (3 March 2020) www.blogs.gartner.com/avivah-litan/2020/03/03/smart-contracts-neither-smart-contracts (accessed 12 September 2022).

[37] See M Durovic and A Janssen, 'The Formation of Blockchain-based Smart Contracts in the Light of Contract Law (2019) 6 *European Review of Private Law* 753, [6]; also C Nicoll, 'Can Computers Make Contracts?' (1998) *Journal of Business Law* 35, 37–42; G Klass, 'How to Interpret a Vending Machine: Smart Contracts and Contract Law' (2022) 7 *Georgetown Law Technology Review* (forthcoming). The automation of processes for the conclusion and performance of contracts is, of course, not a recent phenomenon: see Hero, *Pneumatics*, 1.21, trans in JW Humphrey, JP Oleson and AN Sherwood, *Greek and Roman Technology: A Source Book* (London, Routledge, 1998) 66–7. Almost two millennia later, Lord Denning MR delivered his well-known judgment in *Thornton v Shoe Lane Parking* [1978] 2 QB 163 (CA), applying established principles of contract law to a contract concluded automatically.

[38] Law Commission Advice to Government (n 35) [1.26].

[39] ibid, ch 7.

(ie is it 'a smart legal contract') – can be answered by reference to the general rules governing the formation of contractual obligations, contained in the Rome I Regulation (as carried forward into the body of retained EU law).[40]

There are, of course, certain complicating factors resulting from the intermediation of the code, operating on a number of devices which may not have a fixed location, and in some cases from the pseudonymity of the parties.[41] This does not detract, however, from the fact that the putative parties to a smart legal contract are human beings who, with technological aids, must take the steps necessary to commit themselves to legal obligations. They may, in accordance with the rules set out in the Rome I Regulation,[42] validly choose the law of England or another country. If the indicator of choice appears in the code itself, whether in natural language or in encoded form,[43] this raises not only a question as to the existence of consent (similar to that arising when a choice is contained in terms and conditions to which the contractual instrument refers) but also, in the case of a choice within the coding, the threshold question whether such a choice (particularly in encoded form) is 'made expressly or clearly demonstrated by the terms of the contract or the circumstances of the case'.[44] If there is no valid choice of law, the law applicable to the putative smart legal contract will need to be determined by reference to the rules contained in Article 4 or, in the case of a consumer contract, Article 6 of the Rome I Regulation.[45] In such cases, the phenomenon of pseudonymity may obscure not only the identity of the parties but also their habitual residences, which provide the principal indicator of the applicable law under those rules.[46] This is not, in itself, a reason to disregard that connecting factor. In particular, in the case of a consumer contract, the application of the law of the consumer's country of habitual residence is subject to the condition that the trader has pursued or directed activities in or to that country, which establishes the requisite link.[47] It may, however, bear upon the weight to be attributed to that factor in applying the Article 4(3) 'escape clause'.[48]

As the Law Commission has recognised in its recent Call for Evidence, Interim Update, and Consultation Paper on the subject,[49] the term 'digital assets'

[40] ibid, [7.51].

[41] See ibid, [7.13]–[7.46], with respect to questions of jurisdiction.

[42] In particular, Arts 3(1), 3(5) and 10.

[43] See Law Commission Advice to Government (n 35) [7.71]–[7.80].

[44] Rome I, Art 3(1).

[45] Art 6(2) of the Regulation provides additional protection for the consumer even if there is a choice of law. Arts 5, 7 and 8 of the Regulation contain rules governing, respectively, contracts of carriage, insurance contracts and employment contracts, but these appear to be of limited significance here.

[46] Rome I, Arts 4(1)–(2) and 6(1).

[47] ibid, Art 6(1). It is doubtful whether a causal link must be established between the targeted activity and the contract: see *Khalifeh v Blom Bank SAL* [2021] EWHC 3399 (QB) [79]–[85] (Foxton J).

[48] See Law Commission Advice to Government (n 35) [7.85]–[7.93].

[49] Law Commission, *Digital Assets: Call for Evidence* (April 2021); Law Commission, *Digital Assets: Interim Update* (November 2021); and Law Commission: *Digital Assets: Consultation Paper* (Law Com CP No 256, 2022).

broadly covers 'assets that are represented digitally or electronically, including cryptoassets'.[50] The latter term includes, but is by no means limited to, cryptocurrencies and cryptosecurities.[51] From a domestic law perspective, digital assets are difficult to fit within traditional concepts in the law of property.[52] In analysing their treatment in the conflict of laws, however, it is important to take a step back, recognising the need for flexibility to accommodate differences in treatment between legal systems. A number of key points emerge.

First, although digital assets are represented digitally or electronically, the 'asset' is neither the code (as a body of information) nor the physical manifestations of that code on a hard drive or other storage medium. It is, rather, an intangible thing of value, the precise nature of which will vary according to the exact characteristics of the digital asset.[53]

Second, in general, digital assets gain their value by reason of the legal and/or factual relationships between the participants in the underlying network or system.[54]

Third, in assessing their significance for the conflict of laws, those relationships have both an internal and external aspect.[55] The legal consequences of those relationships (if any) as between the participants themselves are governed by the law applicable to the network or system.[56] This includes, most importantly, the question whether those participants owe each other legal obligations or are bound only non-legal (including technological) forces. Beyond this, when the entitlements of third parties are in issue, it is necessary to engage with the 'proprietary dimension' of the digital asset.[57] This dimension has its own choice of law rules, which will need to be developed by analogy with those

[50] Law Commission, *Call for Evidence* (n 49) [1.5]. See also UK Jurisdiction Taskforce (n 35) [24]–[34].

[51] Law Commission, *Call for Evidence* (n 49) [1.20]. With respect to conflict of laws issues, see generally A Dickinson, 'Cryptocurrencies and the Conflict of Laws' in D Fox and S Green (eds), *Cryptocurrencies in Public and Private Law* (Oxford, OUP, 2019); M Ng, 'Choice of Law for Property Issues Regarding Bitcoin under English Law' (2019) 15 *Journal of Private International Law* 315; M Ooi, 'Choice of Law in the Shifting Sands of Securities Trading', in A Dickinson and E Peel (eds), *A Conflict of Laws Companion: Essays in Honour of Adrian Briggs* (Oxford, OUP, 2021); L Collins and J Harris (eds), *Dicey, Morris & Collins on the Conflict of Laws*, 16th edn (London, Sweet & Maxwell, 2022) paras 23-050, 25-080, 37-014–37-015, 37-087.

[52] Law Commission, *Call for Evidence* (n 49) ch 2; Law Commission, *Consultation Paper* (n 49) chs 2–4. For the evolving case law in England, see in particular *AA v Persons Unknown* [2019] EWHC 3356 (Comm), [2020] 4 WLR 35; *Ion Science v Persons Unknown* (Commercial Court, Unreported, 21 December 2020); *Fetch.AI v Persons Unknown* [2021] EWHC 2254 (Comm); *Tulip Trading Ltd v Bitcoin Association for BSV* [2022] EWHC 667 (Ch).

[53] See, with respect to cryptocurrencies, Dickinson (n 51) [5.96]–[5.98].

[54] ibid, [5.100]–[5.101].

[55] ibid, [5.93]–[5.95]; Ooi (n 51) 232; *Dicey, Morris & Collins*, 16th edn (n 51) para 25–080.

[56] Dickinson (n 51) section II.

[57] The same boundary line has been drawn with respect to contractual, and other claims: see Case C-548/18 *BGL BNP Paribas SA v TeamBank AG Nürnberg* [2019] ECLI:EU:C:2019:848. Proprietary questions fall outside the rules for voluntary assignments contained in Rome I, Art 14.

governing other species of intangible property, including claims, securities and goodwill.[58]

Fourth, in the case of 'tokenised' assets, which represent another thing, tangible or intangible,[59] a preliminary question arises as to whether the entitlement to a token within a network or system also entitles the holder to an interest in the underlying thing. As a matter of principle, that question is to be answered by reference to the law governing the proprietary dimension of the tokenised asset, by analogy with the treatment of negotiable or bearer instruments.[60] For example, if the tokenised asset is land, first, the issue whether entitlement to a token carries with it an entitlement to an interest in land must be answered by reference to the *lex situs* of the land, and, second, in addressing questions of 'entitlement' to a token, it is necessary to distinguish between the legal and non-legal ties existing between the participants in the tokenised system (the internal aspect) and the legal effects of transactions which take place outside that system but which relate to the entitlements existing within it (the external aspect).

V. REPAIRING THE FABRIC

In December 2012, following the death of her husband in Egypt in 2010, Lady Christine Brownlie issued a claim form in the English High Court seeking damages, on her own behalf and as executor of her husband's estate. In May 2013, the named defendant, Four Seasons Holdings Inc, challenged jurisdiction. In December 2017, after four tiers of judgments addressing a number of issues of interpretation of the rules governing service out of the jurisdiction,[61] the Supreme Court held that Lady Brownlie had sued the wrong defendant, that her claim had no reasonable prospect of success and that, as a result, the English court had no jurisdiction.[62] In August 2018, Lady Brownlie sought to amend her claim to substitute a different entity within the same group, FS Cairo LLC, as defendant.[63] For three more years, the new defendant opposed the application, unsuccessfully at every stage.[64] In October 2021, the Supreme Court rejected the defendant's remaining legal and evidential arguments, bringing the jurisdictional phase of the proceedings to an end.

[58] Dickinson (n 51) [5.106]–[5.120]; Ooi (n 51) 211–23; *Dicey, Morris & Collins*, 16th edn (n 51) paras 23-050 and 25-080.

[59] Law Commission, *Call for Evidence* (n 49) [2.53].

[60] ibid [2.55]. See *Dicey, Morris & Collins*, 16th edn (n 51) paras 33-407–33-410.

[61] *Brownlie v Four Seasons Holdings Inc* [2014] EWHC 273 (QB); [2015] EWCA Civ 665, [2016] 1 WLR 1814; [2017] UKSC 80, [2018] 1 WLR 192.

[62] CPR r 6.37(1)(b).

[63] *Brownlie v Four Seasons Holdings Inc* [2019] EWHC 2533 (QB).

[64] ibid; *FS Cairo (Nile Plaza) LLC v Brownlie* [2020] EWCA Civ 996, [2021] 2 All ER 605; [2021] UKSC 45, [2021] 3 WLR 1011.

In 2015, two sets of proceedings, involving almost 45,000 claimants, were issued in the English High Court against Royal Dutch Shell plc and its Nigerian subsidiary. The claims related to oil pollution in the Niger Delta. The defendants challenged jurisdiction. Although that application raised several issues, the central question was whether a claim brought in negligence against the parent company in respect of damage caused by its subsidiary's activities was viable. In January 2017, Fraser J held that it was not.[65] In reaching that decision, after a hearing lasting three days, he considered over 300 pages of written legal submissions, 39 witness statements and five expert reports.[66] That decision was upheld by the Court of Appeal, in February 2018,[67] after three further days of argument and further lengthy written submissions.[68] In February 2021,[69] the Supreme Court reached a different conclusion. Although this did not resolve the challenge to jurisdiction, the defendants soon gave up their objection, allowing the claims to proceed.[70]

In 2019, a Kuwaiti institution operating the country's national social security system brought proceedings in the English High Court against 37 defendants for sums totalling almost US$850 million, alleging their involvement in corruption. Several of those defendants challenged jurisdiction. In November 2020, Henshaw J upheld that challenge,[71] after a hearing lasting four days, involving voluminous evidence of foreign law and running up costs exceeding £13.5 million.[72] In January 2022, the Court of Appeal dismissed an appeal against that decision.[73] The costs of the three-day appeal, as advised to the Court, exceeded £5 million.[74] Carr LJ did not hide her disquiet. While noting that the challenge raised some novel legal issues, and involved serious allegations and substantial sums, she pointedly remarked that 'these features did not create a licence to turn a jurisdictional dispute into an extensive and essentially self-standing piece of litigation'.[75]

Although the legal and procedural issues involved in these three cases were very different, they evidence structural and cultural weaknesses in the current legal framework for determining questions of jurisdiction, resulting in increased delay, cost and complexity. The judicial reflex to blame the parties and their advisors for this state of affairs seems over-active.[76] After all, as Lord Leggatt

[65] *Okpabi v Royal Dutch Shell plc* [2017] EWHC 89 (TCC), [2017] Bus LR 1335.
[66] *Okpabi v Royal Dutch Shell plc* [2021] EWCA Civ 191, [2018] Bus LR 1022 [17].
[67] ibid.
[68] ibid, [18].
[69] *Okpabi v Royal Dutch Shell plc* [2021] UKSC 3, [2021] 1 WLR 1294.
[70] 'Shell Drops Jurisdictional Arguments' (2021) 7941 *New Law Journal* 5.
[71] *Public Institution for Social Security v Al Rajaan* [2020] EWHC 2979 (Comm).
[72] *Public Institution for Social Security v Al Rajaan* [2022] EWCA Civ 29 [10].
[73] ibid, [144].
[74] ibid, [151].
[75] ibid, [13].
[76] *VTB Capital plc v Nutritek International Corp* [2013] UKSC 5, [2013] 2 AC 337 [82]–[83] (Lord Neuberger); *Vedanta Resources plc v Lungowe* [2019] UKSC 20, [2020] AC 1045 [14] (Lord Briggs).

pointed out on the second occasion that *Brownlie* reached the Supreme Court,[77] it is unsurprising that they seek to exploit an imperfect system in their efforts to gain a litigation advantage.

Even if a major overhaul of the rules may be a distant prospect,[78] there is much that could be done at the coalface both by individual judges, in the exercise of their case management powers,[79] and by the Civil Procedure Rules Committee, in the exercise of its rule making powers.[80] For example:

(a) As the CPR already accommodate circumstances in which a claim form can be served outside England without permission,[81] the cumbersome requirement for a claimant to obtain permission to serve a claim form outside the jurisdiction should be replaced with a system in which the claimant certifies[82] the existence of circumstances which justify such service, such circumstances being drawn from the grounds that are currently exiled in Practice Direction 6B. This practice operated for many years in cases to which the black-letter rules in the Brussels-Lugano regime applied,[83] and it would be advantageous to build upon this experience.[84]
(b) The requirement, currently set out in rule 6.37(1)(b), that the claimant establish a claim that has a reasonable prospect of success as a pre-condition to establishing jurisdiction should be removed, so as to distance jurisdictional issues from the merits of the claim.[85] Instead, a defendant who considers that the claim brought against it is hopeless should be required to pursue a separate application (for strike out or summary judgment), while at the same time being protected from an argument that it has thereby submitted to the jurisdiction.[86]
(c) Appellate courts should not merely grumble about cost and delay, but should instead provide detailed guidance to judges handing jurisdiction applications as to the exercise of their case management powers to further the overriding objective, in particular, by controlling the number of hearings, the length of written submissions and the number of permitted witness statements and expert reports.[87] Applications for permission to appeal should also be carefully scrutinised.

[77] *Brownlie (SC No 2)* (n 64) [201].
[78] For a detailed proposal, see A Briggs and A Dickinson, 'Reframing Jurisdiction: A New Scheme?' (2022) 41 Civil Justice Quarterly 317.
[79] *VTB* (n 76) [89].
[80] Civil Procedure Act 1997.
[81] CPR rr 6.32–6.33.
[82] Reinforced by a statement of truth.
[83] CPR r 6.34.
[84] See Briggs and Dickinson (n 78) 319–320, 330–331, suggesting that the statement could be incorporated within the main body of the claim form, rather than in a separate certificate.
[85] ibid, 334–335.
[86] CPR, Part 11 could be tweaked to achieve this result: see r 11(3).
[87] Alternatively, such guidance could be provided by means of a Practice Direction.

VI. A CHOICE OF LAW REVIVAL?

The adoption of measures of the kind countenanced in the preceding section may also serve as a counterweight to the shift in the centre of the gravity of the subject towards questions of jurisdiction. In particular, isolating the jurisdictional enquiry from the merits of the dispute may be thought likely to bring choice of law issues into sharper focus. At present, such issues tend to arise for determination incidentally in the course of 'litigation about where to litigate', and in that context the lower bar set by the 'reasonable prospect' and 'good arguable case'[88] standards means that they do not need to be fully ventilated and are often addressed tentatively based on relatively brief submissions, in the absence of properly pleaded statements of case or detailed expert evidence.[89] The claimant may rely on the default rule, by not pleading that a foreign law applies, or the presumption of similarity, by not pleading any specific rules of foreign law, so taking the choice of law question out of play unless the defendant advances a contrary case.[90] By contrast, choice of law issues are less frequently argued at trial and both substantive and theoretical aspects of the choice of law process are underdeveloped.[91] There is, for example, no modern English decision that authoritatively settles the choice of law rule governing the proprietary dimension of assignments and transfers of debts and other claims[92] or which resolves the question whether the doctrine of *renvoi* applies in determining questions of title to tangible moveables.[93]

The UK's withdrawal from the European Union may bring a further factor into play in encouraging a revival of interest in questions of choice of law. Although the Rome I and Rome II Regulations have been maintained in slightly modified form, the provisions of section 6(4) of the European Union (Withdrawal) Act 2018 (as extended by regulations made under section 6(5A))[94] open up the prospect of an autonomous UK approach to conflict of laws

[88] See ch 15 in this volume.

[89] See, eg, *Fortress Value Recovery Fund I LLP v Blue Skye Special Opportunities Fund LP* [2013] EWHC 14 (Comm), [2013] 1 All ER (Comm) 973 [56]–[62].

[90] See, eg, *Qatar Airways Group QCSC v Middle East News FZ LLC* [2020] EWHC 2975 (QB) [171]–[180]; *Brownlie (SC No 2)* (n 64) [113]–[125] and [142].

[91] *Macmillan Inc v Bishopsgate Investment Trust plc* [1996] 1 WLR 387 (CA) remains the leading case on structural and theoretical aspects of the choice of law enquiry more than a quarter of a century after it was decided. In the intervening period, the highest UK court has only occasionally decided cases with choice of law issues at their heart: see, eg, *Harding v Wealands* [2005] UKHL 67, [2006] 2 AC 1, *Cox v Ergo Versicherung AG* [2014] UKSC 22, [2014] AC 1379 and *Soldiers, Sailors, Airmen and Families Association v Allgemeines Krankenhaus Viersen GmbH* [2022] UKSC 29, [2022] 3 WLR 1111.

[92] *Dicey, Morris & Collins*, 16th edn (n 51) para 25-059; A Dickinson, 'Assigning Priorities in the Conflict of Laws' [2020] *Lloyd's Maritime and Commercial Law Quarterly* 198. Rome I does not address the proprietary dimension.

[93] *Dicey, Morris & Collins*, 16th edn (n 51) paras 2-121–2-124 and 25-008.

[94] European Union (Withdrawal) Act 2018 (Relevant Court) (Retained EU Case Law) Regulations extending the Supreme Court's power (s 6(4)) to depart from retained EU law to other appellate courts. See also the Retained EU Law (Revocation and Reform) Bill, currently before Parliament.

issues emerging in the sphere of contractual and non-contractual obligations, developing the limited body of retained EU case law[95] in a way that eventually distinguishes the retained Rome Regulations from their progenitors. For example,[96] there may in the future be a growing judicial willingness to apply the 'escape clauses' in Article 4(3) of each Regulation, bringing the rule based structure of the Regulations a step closer to the 'proper law' approach of the common law that (with distinguished advocates)[97] had grown in influence prior to the legislative reforms of the late twentieth century,[98] and the common law's traditionally broad view of the class of procedural matters governed by the law of the forum[99] may, over time, shape the way in which the courts approach the (autonomous) scope of the category of matters of 'evidence and procedure' that fall outside the Rome Regulations.[100]

VII. NEW HORIZONS?

If the loss of ties to its former European partners may bring about a future in which the conflict of law rules applied UK's legal systems gain (or regain) a distinct identity, we are also frequently reminded that it is necessary to look for new opportunities. Now that the UK's application to re-join the Lugano Convention has been kicked over the top of the grandstand,[101] the Hague Convention on the Recognition and Enforcement of Foreign Judgments in Civil or Commercial Matters 2019 may prove a tempting and viable option, especially as the EU has itself recently taken the decision to accede. Section 2 of the Private International Law (Implementation of Agreements) Act 2020 would facilitate this.

There may, however, be reasons to hesitate. First, accession by the UK to the Hague Convention would validate the Commission's reasons for not supporting Lugano re-accession, and would likely further distance the latter prospect.[102] Second, the prospect of a significant broadening of the criteria governing the competence of the foreign court (see Article 5) may generate objections that UK

[95] At a European level, cases concerning jurisdictional rules also significantly outnumber those concerning Rome I and Rome II.

[96] These examples are offered to illustrate the point made in the text, and not in support of the direction of travel that they would involve.

[97] See *Dicey, Morris & Collins*, 16th edn (n 51) paras 32-006–32-008, 35-004 and 35-007.

[98] The sentiment of Cranston J in *Pickard v Marshall* [2017] EWCA Civ 17 [16] that the status of Art 4(3) of the Rome II Regulation as an 'escape clause … does not mean that its ambit should be unduly narrowed' may provide a foothold for arguments of this kind.

[99] *Dicey, Morris & Collins*, 16th edn (n 51) ch 4.

[100] Rome I, Art 1(3); Rome II, art 1(3). See *Actavis UK Ltd v Eli Lilly & Co* [2015] EWCA Civ 555, [2016] 4 All ER 666 [133] (Floyd LJ).

[101] Commission Assessment on the application of the United Kingdom of Great Britain and Northern Ireland to accede to the 2007 Lugano Convention, COM(2021) 222 final, 4 May 2021; Communication from the European Commission to the Swiss Federal Council as the Depositary of the 2007 Lugano Convention, Ares(2021)4053632, 22 June 2021.

[102] Commission Assessment (n 101) 3–4.

residents and businesses (and others with substantial assets in England) would be exposed to excessive liabilities, or put in an unacceptable state of jeopardy or to the risk of being exposed to legal proceedings before foreign courts that do not uphold the common law's standards of natural justice.[103]

Nevertheless, the arguments in favour of speedy accession seem compelling. First, it may be doubted whether accession to the Lugano Convention was ever a realistic option given the nature of the trading relationship with the EU that the UK wanted to pursue.[104] Second, by becoming an early participant in the Hague Judgments Convention and continuing to participate in ongoing discussions at the Hague Conference,[105] the UK will emphasise its commitment to international co-operation in the field of civil justice, thereby fulfilling one of the objectives underlying the 2020 Act.[106] Third, the mechanism in Article 29(2) of the Convention would enable the UK to investigate the credentials of newly acceding states with a view to determining whether it wished to establish relations with them with a view to mutual recognition and enforcement of judgments. The grounds for opposing recognition in Article 8(1)(a)-(c) of the Convention would protect defendants against the risk of injustice in individual cases, and Article 10 would offer a means of protection against disproportionate monetary awards. Fourth, and perhaps most significantly, the recognition in Article 5(1)(m) of jurisdiction based on an agreement that is not an 'exclusive choice of court agreement', as defined, would support recognition of judgment given by UK courts acting on the basis of non-exclusive, or asymmetric, choice of court agreements, falling outside the 2005 Hague Choice of Court Convention.[107] Coupled with the EU's own accession to the Hague Judgments Convention (effective from 1 September 2023), this would remedy at least some of the uncertainty for commercial parties resulting from the UK's withdrawal from the Brussels-Lugano regime.

VIII. REACH FOR THE STARS

If Dr Morris was writing, in 1949,[108] at a time when the world was moving from a period of conflict and destruction to one of relative order and prosperity,

[103] See, in relation to proposals to extend the common law grounds for recognition, A Briggs, 'Recognition of Foreign Judgments: A Matter of Obligation' (2013) 129 *Law Quarterly Review* 87, 94–95; A Briggs, *Private International Law in English Courts* (Oxford, OUP, 2014) [6.175]. See ch 4 in this volume.

[104] Commission Assessment (n 101) 2–3.

[105] 'Jurisdiction Project' www.hcch.net/en/projects/legislative-projects/jurisdiction-project (accessed 12 September 2022). It is more doubtful whether this project will have a valuable end product, but that is not a reason for the UK to distance itself at the negotiating stage.

[106] Private International Law (Implementation of Agreements) Bill Deb 2 September 2020, col 216 (Robert Buckland MP, Lord Chancellor).

[107] See *Etihad Airways PJSC v Flother* [2020] EWCA Civ 1707, [2022] QB 303 [85]–[86]; *Dicey, Morris & Collins*, 16th edn (n 51) ch 4 and paras 12–089–12-091; B Marshall, *Asymmetric Jurisdiction Clauses* (Oxford, OUP, 2022) ch 4.

[108] Text to n 5.

the reverse seems true today. War, internal conflict, disease, hunger and alarming climatic change have been brought about by increasing demands upon the earth's scarce resources. In this new, troubling era, cross-border disputes about those scarce resources will increase, and (when legal mechanisms are used to resolve those disputes) the boundary between private law and private law is likely to become increasingly blurred.

Two cases from the Supreme Court's recent schedule may serve as illustrations of this trend.[109] The first, *Maduro Board of the Central Bank of Venezuela v Guaidó Board of the Central Bank of Venezuela*, an appeal decided in December 2021,[110] results from an internal political conflict in Venezuela, with two factions wrestling for control of that country's abundant natural and financial resources. Although the Supreme Court has unpicked some of the issues, the case has some way to run.[111] The second, *Law Debenture Trust Corporation plc v Ukraine*,[112] may represent the thorniest case on the Supreme Court's docket. Argued in November 2021, but not yet decided, it concerns the effect upon ostensibly private law transactions (falling within the scope of the Rome I Regulation) of alleged coercion by one state (Russia) against another (Ukraine), pre-dating the current conflict.

The UK's accession to what was then the European Economic Community in 1973 was undoubtedly a landmark in English private international law. It took, however, almost four decades for the significance of that landmark moment to unfold. Its unravelling, from 2016 onwards, was both unexpected and rather hurried. However, if it is true that 'one must still have chaos within, in order to give birth to a dancing star'[113] then perhaps the events of recent years may generate a new constellation within the conflict of laws in England. That process is likely to be one of evolution rather than revolution, but we should be prepared to look beyond the horizon. There is much work to be done if this area of the law is to play its part in addressing the terrestrial challenges that we now face.

[109] In the new edition of *Dicey, Morris & Collins* (n 51) a new Part (chs 7–9), entitled 'Foreign Affairs and the Conflict of Laws', concerns itself with the interface between the conflict of laws and public international law, but this part is as much concerned with the boundary between private and public law in cross-border cases. What was 'rule 3' (enforcement of foreign, penal or public laws and acts of state) is now rule 20. See A Dickinson, 'Acts of State and the Frontiers of Private (International) Law' (2018) 14 *Journal of Private International Law* 1.

[110] *Maduro Board of the Central Bank of Venezuela v Guaidó Board of the Central Bank of Venezuela* [2021] UKSC 57, [2022] 2 WLR 167.

[111] See A Dickinson 'Foreign Acts of State and the Conflict of Laws' (2022) 138 *Law Quarterly Review* 519 and, subsequently, *Deutsche Bank AG v Central Bank of Venezuela* [2022] EWHC 2040 (Comm) and [2022] EWHC 2702 (Comm).

[112] On appeal from *Law Debenture Trust Corporation plc v Ukraine* [2018] EWCA Civ 2026, [2019] QB 1121.

[113] F Nietsche, *Thus Spoke Zarathrustra*, first part, section 5 trans G Parks (Oxford, OUP, 2005) 15.

Index

www.ingramcontent.com/pod-product-compliance
Ingram Content Group UK Ltd.
Pitfield, Milton Keynes, MK11 3LW, UK
UKHW020257051026
15470UKWH00020B/393